.NET Programming with Visual C++

Tutorial, Reference, and Immediate Solutions

MAX I. FOMITCHEV Ph.D.

San Francisco and New York

Published by CMP Books
An imprint of CMP Media LLC
Main office: CMP Books, 600 Harrison St., San Francisco, CA 94107 USA
Phone: 415-947-6615; Fax: 415-947-6015
Sales office: 12 W. 21st St., New York, NY 10010 USA
www.cmpbooks.com
Email: books@cmp.com

ISBN: 1-57820-129-2

For individual orders, and for information on special discounts for quantity
orders, please contact:
CMP Books Distribution Center, 6600 Silacci Way, Gilroy, CA 95020
Tel: 1-800-500-6875 or 408-848-3854; Fax: 408-848-5784
Email: cmp@rushorder.com; Web: www.cmpbooks.com

Distributed to the book trade in the U.S. by:
Publishers Group West, 1700 Fourth Street, Berkeley, California 94710

Distributed in Canada by:
Jaguar Book Group, 100 Armstrong Avenue, Georgetown, Ontario M6K 3E7
Canada

Cover design by Greene Design

Printed in the United States of America

CONTENTS SUMMARY

Primary Audience
The book is intended for current intermediate to advanced Visual C++ 6.0 users migrating to Visual C++ .NET. The book can be used as a reference for .NET developers.

Secondary Audience
Novice C++ developers who want to learn C++ programming for the .NET Framework.

Structure of the Book

Chapter 1 provides overview of the .NET Framework. The material is intended mostly for novice users.

Chapter 2 is a tutorial into Managed Extensions to C++. Prior knowledge of C++ is assumed. Fifteen complete code samples.*

Chapter 3 provides a complete reference of the basic types (Array, String, Delegate) contained in .NET Framework System namespace. Fifteen complete code samples.*

Chapter 4 provides a complete reference of the advanced types (Attribute, GC, etc.) contained in .NET Framework System namespace. Twelve complete code samples.*

Chapter 5 provides a complete reference of the System::Threading namespace and teaches how to use multithreading, interlocking and thread synchronization in .NET. Thirteen complete code samples.*

Chapter 6 provides a complete reference of the System::Collections namespace and teaches how to use .NET collections. Fifteen complete code samples.*

Chapter 7 provides a complete reference of the System::IO namespace and teaches how to work with the .NET file and stream I/O, including isolated storage. Sixteen complete code samples.*

Chapter 8 is an introduction into ADO.NET. The chapter provides a complete reference of the System::Data namespace focusing on DataSet and DataTable classes, reading/writing structured data from XML, and in-memory representations of arbitrary heterogeneous data sets. Eleven complete code samples.*

Chapter 9 teaches how to use ADO.NET OLEDB and SQL Server data providers to add, modify, navigate database data and how to perform transactions. The chapter provides a complete reference of the System::Data::Common, System::Data::OleDb, and System::Data::SqlClient namespaces. Thirteen complete code samples.*

Chapter 10 is an introduction into ASP.NET web services. The chapter focuses on ASP.NET web service architecture and basic web service development issues. Prior experience with ASP/web services is not required.

Chapter 11 introduces web service protocols such as HTTP-GET, HTTP-POST and SOAP and tailoring web services and web service consumers to use a particular protocol.

Chapter 12 covers Web Services Definition Language (WSDL), web service discovery, configuration and security.

Chapter 13 discusses .NET interoperability with unmanaged code and teaches how to access .NET types from COM components and vice versa. Five complete code samples.* For intermediate/advanced users.

Chapter 14 covers "other" (i.e., nonmanaged) Microsoft extensions to C++ language focusing on new compiler intrinsics (MMX/SSE/SSE2/3DNow!), support for 64-bit data types and data alignment, native C++/COM event handling, new keywords and other language enhancements. Five complete code samples.* For advanced users.

Chapter 15 covers C Runtime Library enhancements focusing on runtime error checking. Nine complete code samples.* For advanced users.

Chapter 16* discusses enhancements and changes to MFC 7.0 focusing on new features related to DHTML (editing, DHTML dialogs), Windows XP support, resource localization (satellite DLLs) and 64-bit portability. Prior knowledge of MFC is required. Six complete code examples.*

Chapter 17* introduces unmanaged attributed programming, focuses on compiler and ATL COM attributes and teaches how to declare COM coclasses/interfaces using attributes, how to handle COM events. Provides a reference of COM attributes. For advanced users. Three complete code examples.*

Chapter 18* introduces attributed ATL OLEDB programming and provides a complete reference of ATL OLEDB attributes. The Chapter teaches how to retrieve, update, navigate database data using OLE DB, issue database commands and perform transactions. For intermediate/advanced users. Familiarity with OLE DB is helpful, but not required. Seven complete code examples.*

Appendix A summarizes new features of the Visual C++ .NET Integrated Development Environment (IDE), including the coverage of basic editing, building, and debugging steps.

Appendix B MFC Application Wizard Reference.

Appendix C Visual C++ .NET Project Property Pages Reference.

Appendix D .NET Framework System Namespace Hierarchy.

Appendix E .NET Framework System::Data Namespace Hierarchy.

Appendix F .NET Framework System::Data::Common, System::Data::OleDb and System::Data::SqlClient Namespaces Hierarchy.

*Downloads: Code examples in the form of small programs corresponding to each chapter, as well as PDF files for chapters 16-18, can be found at: http://www.cmpbooks.com/dotnet/

CONTENTS IN DETAIL

CHAPTER 3

.NET System Namespace: Arrays, Strings, Delegates And Other Essential Classes **79**

CHAPTER 4

.NET System Namespace: Attributes, Garbage Collector, and Other Advanced NET **139**

CHAPTER 5

Multithreaded Programming with .NET **173**

CHAPTER 6

Using .NET Collections 227

CHAPTER 7

.NET File and Stream I/O **290**

CHAPTER 8

ADO.NET:
DataSets, DataTables, and XML . . . 362

CHAPTER 9

ADO.NET: OLE DB and
SQL Server Data Providers 436

CHAPTER 10
Creating ASP.NET Web Services . . 502

CHAPTER 11

Consuming Web Services Made with HTTP-GET, HTTP-POST, and SOAP **531**

CHAPTER 12

Web Services: Definition Language (WSDL), Discovery, Security, and Configuration **569**

CHAPTER 13

.NET Interoperability with Unmanaged Code and COM **604**

CHAPTER 14

Microsoft Extensions to C++ Language **627**

APPENDIX B

MFC Application Wizard Reference **683**

APPENDIX C

Visual C++ .NET Project Property Pages Reference **691**

APPENDIX D

.NET Framework System Namespace Hierarchy **705**

APPENDIX E

.NET Framework System::Data Namespace Hierarchy **708**

APPENDIX F

.NET Framework System::Data:: Common, System::Data::OleDb and System::Data::SqlClient Namespace Hierarchy **709**

Additional Material Online

Download PDF files of Chapters 16 to 18, plus code samples for many of the chapters, from http://www.cmpbooks.com/dotnet/

INTRODUCTION

Thanks for buying .NET Programming with Visual C++. This book will be your reference and a jump-start programming guide to the Microsoft .NET Framework using the Visual C++ .NET.

If you have been programming with the Visual C++ 6.0, this book will help you to learn new features of Visual C++ .NET programming language, including:

*   Managed Extensions to C++;

*   .NET Framework Class Library – System namespace, .NET collections, multithreaded programming, file and stream I/O, ADO.NET;

*   Attributed programming using .NET, compiler ATL COM, and ATL OLEDB attributes;

*   ASP.NET Web Service development, debugging, securing and deployment;

*   Interoperability with other .NET languages such as C# or VB.NET, interoperability between managed and unmanaged code, COM and .NET;

*   New Microsoft extensions to standard C++ language, CRT and MFC 7.0 libraries.

If you are familiar with C++ programming but new to Visual C++, you can use this book to master Managed C++ and .NET Framework programming, for which no prior knowledge of Visual C++ or other Microsoft technologies is required.

Is This Book for You?

.NET Programming with Visual C++ was written with the intermediate or advanced user in mind. Although the book can be effectively used by novice C++ programmers wanting to master Managed C++ and .NET Framework programming.

Among the topics that are covered, are:

*   Introduction into .NET Framework and Managed C++ Programming;

*   Overview of the .NET Framework Class Library;

*   In-depth coverage of .NET programming including multithreading, using collections, file and stream I/O, database access (via ADO.NET using OLE DB and SQL Server providers), and interoperability with COM and unmanaged code;

*   Overview of ASP.NET XML Web Service development, WSDL and SOAP;

*   COM and OLE DB programming using ATL attributes.

How to Use This Book

.NET Programming with Visual C++ serves two main purposes: to be a guide into .NET Framework and Managed C++ programming for novice programmers, and serve as reference for intermediate/advanced developers.

In general, the material in the book is organized in such a way that subsequent chapters rely on material presented in preceding chapters with no forward references and very little presumption of prior knowledge of related technologies.

.NET Framework Class Library/Namespace Reference

The lions share of this book—Chapters 2 through 13—covers various aspects of .NET programming such as multithreading, collections, I/O, etc., with each chapter corresponding to a .NET Framework Class Library namespace (or namespaces) related to the programming topic being discussed. These chapters have similar structure. First a general problem pertaining to the topic in hand is posed. Then the corresponding .NET Framework Class Library namespace is introduced with the following information supplied on each namespace:

* Summary of all namespace classes, attributes, exceptions, value types, interfaces, enumerations, and delegates (except for the classes designated by Microsoft as "supporting the .NET Framework infrastructure"—such classes are not intended to be used by application developers and therefore not discussed in this book);

* Namespace class hierarchy (if the diagram is too big, it is given in appendix);

* Namespace interface hierarchy (if applicable);

* Overview of the base interfaces defined in the namespace including summary of the interface properties and methods;

* Overview of the key namespace classes including the class inheritance diagram, detailed summary of class constructors, properties, methods, delegates, and events;

* Immediate solutions—short code samples illustrating the most important programming scenarios involving the discussed namespace classes.

Comments on Book Chapters

Chapter 1 gives an overview of the .NET Framework. You can safely skip this chapter if you are already familiar with the .NET Framework

Chapter 2 contains the coverage of Managed Extensions to C++. This chapter will be your guide to Managed C++ programming. If you are not familiar with Managed C++ programming already, you must read this chapter in order to be able to comprehend subsequent chapters on .NET programming.

Chapters 3 and 4 provide in-depth overviews of the .NET Framework Class Library System namespace. The System namespace contains fundamental classes such as **Object**, **String**, **Delegate**, **Array**, etc. that represent the backbone of the .NET Framework and are essential for Managed C++ programming. It is highly recommended that you read (or at least browse through) these chapters before reading any other chapters on .NET programming.

Chapter 5 discusses multithreaded programming. For the most part, you may skip this chapter if you are going to write single-threaded code.

Chapter 6 focuses on .NET collections. Collection classes are ubiquitous in the .NET Framework class library, thus, it is a good idea to at least browse through the chapter to get an idea on what are the collections classes in the .NET Framework

Chapter 7 covers file and stream I/O. This chapter may be of particular interest to C++ programmers because .NET stream I/O is very different from the standard C++ stream I/O in the sense that .NET Framework classes do not support >> and << serialization operators.

Chapters 8 and 9 introduce ADO.NET programming and provide tips and techniques for accessing database data using OLE DB and SQL Server ADO.NET providers. Since virtually all applications nowadays use some kind of database connectivity, reading this chapter is a must.

Chapter 10 talks about ASP.NET web services—the cornerstone of the .NET Framework. The chapter introduces ASP.NET web service architecture and teaches developing and consuming simple web services, including declaration of web service proxy classes and declaration of web service classes using **WebService** and **WebMethod** attributes.

Chapter 11 focuses on web service protocols: HTTP-GET, HTTP-POST and SOAP and related .NET Framework classes. The chapter gives an overview of SOAP, including SOAP messages, encodings, and headers. The chapter teaches declaring web services and web service proxy classes using a particular protocol, and communication using SOAP headers.

Chapter 12 discusses important aspects of web service development such as Web Services Definition Language (WSDL), web service discovery, security, and configuration. The chapter teaches how to programmatically discover web services, retrieve web service definition, and secure web services using SSL and Windows authentication.

Chapter 13 is about .NET interoperability with COM and unmanaged code. Unless you are planning on using your .NET components with unmanaged code, or tapping into COM components from .NET classes, you can safely skip this chapter.

Chapter 14 covers unmanaged extensions to the C++ language introduced by Microsoft in the Visual C++ .NET. The extensions include C++ language changes, SIMD instruction set support, new keywords, data types, and compiler-intrinsic functions. This chapter is for die-hard C++ programmers.

Chapter 15 discusses C Runtime Library enhancements—advanced error handling, security threat detection, etc.—that can be considered "black belt programming." This chapter will be of interest to experienced C++ developers.

Chapter 16* briefly goes through to incremental enhancements to MFC 7.0 from MFC 4.2. The chapter discusses new MFC classes such as **CHtmlView**, **CHtmlEditView**, **CDHtmlDialog**, **CMultiPageDHtmlDialog**, **CLinkCtrl**, etc., and new methods/functionality added to existing MFC classes such as **CDC**, **CWnd**, **CListCtrl**, and others. This chapter requires prior knowledge of MFC. Chapters 16-18 can be downloaded

Chapter 17* introduces ATL attributed programming and focuses on COM component development using Active Template Library (ATL). Knowledge of COM/ATL and experience in COM development is helpful for reading this chapter, although not required—Most COM-component related issues and terms are explained along the way.

Chapter 18* unleashes new attributes intended to simplify OLE DB programming using ATL classes. Prior experience with ATL and OLE DB programming is helpful, albeit not required.

Appendix A introduces the new features of the Visual Studio .NET development environment. This chapter is intended to help Visual C++ 6.0 developers and novice programmers get comfortable with Visual C++ .NET and use the development environment efficiently. You can forgo reading this chapter if you are already familiar with the Visual Studio .NET development environment.

---

* Chapters 16-18 can be downloaded, along with code samples for many of the chapters, from http://www.cmpbooks.com/dotnet

Appendix B provides a reference on the MFC Application Wizard.

Appendix C provides a reference on the Visual C++ .NET Project Property Pages, summarizes and explains Visual C++ project configuration options, compiler and linker command line switches.

Appendices D, E, and F represent class hierarchy diagrams for System, System::Data, System::Data::Common, System::Data::Common::OleDb and System::Data::Common::SqlServer .NET Framework Class Library namespaces.

Namespace Hierarchy Diagrams

The following rules apply when reading the namespace hierarchy diagrams in this book:

* Namespace class names are given without the namespace prefix;

* Base classes originating outside the namespace are listed with the full namespace prefix;

* Interfaces implemented by a class are listed to the right from the class name following the arrow symbol;

* With the exception of the System namespace class hierarchy diagram (which is given in Appendix C), value types are not listed;

* Enumerations are never listed.

Class Information

For each discussed namespace class, the following information is provided:

* Class hierarchy diagram;

* The list of attributes applied to the class definition;

* The list of interfaces implemented by the class;

* An indication whether the class is abstract or sealed.

Base class members (including virtual properties and methods) as well as members defined by the interfaces implemented by the class are almost never listed in the tables summarizing the class properties, methods, events, and delegates. The only situation when overloaded base class members may appear in the class summary is when the overloaded member behaves differently from the base class and such behavior is worthy of comment.

Class properties and methods implied by interfaces implemented by the class are generally not listed: The class must provide implementations of all properties and methods defined by the interface, which are summarized elsewhere in the book (usually in the "In Depth" sections at the start of the book chapters).

Most of the code samples* discussed in the immediate solution section of the book correspond to small yet complete programs focusing on a specific task isolated from everything else. Usually, an immediate solution project for each chapter contains individual files for each immediate solution: Simply add a desired file to the project, compile it, and run the code to see the theory in action.

I welcome your feedback on this book. You can either email Dr. Dobb's Journal at **editors@ddj.com** or email me directly at **fomitchev@cox.net**.

---

* Code samples can be downloaded from http://www.cmpbooks.com/dotnet

.NET Programming with Visual C++

CHAPTER 1

Introducing the Microsoft .NET Framework

In this chapter, I will describe the new Microsoft .NET Framework and explain the terminology and concepts you'll need to understand to develop applications with this powerful platform. This chapter will provide the basic groundwork you'll need in order to begin working with .NET, helping you to make the transition to .NET development. I'll also set the stage to make it easier for you to use tools such as the Visual Studio .NET development environment. In the next chapter will dive right in and learn about the Managed Extensions with Visual C++.NET. If you are already familiar with .NET development, you can skip this chapter, but if this is your first introduction, you'll find that the material presented here will help you jumpstart your .NET programming experience.

What Is .NET?

The release of Visual C++ .NET introduces a big shift in development languages and platforms. Let's face it, the .NET platform represents a revolutionary change in software development, as you are about to learn. And mastering this new technology involves learning a number of new concepts and programming techniques. Don't be fooled into thinking that Visual C++ .NET is only an incremental update to Visual C++ 6.0.

So, what is .NET anyway? Until recently, .NET was thought of as a platform for developing XML Web Services, allowing applications to communicate and share data over the Internet, regardless of the operating system or programming language used. Microsoft's more recent official definition (found at **www.microsoft.com/net/whatis.asp**) offers a much more general description:

> Microsoft .NET is a set of Microsoft software technologies for connecting your world of information, people, systems, and devices.

Although the .NET Framework was mainly created to be a platform for developing web services .NET offers many other development advantages. It is a platform for rapid application development that provides developers with simplified programming, improved code robustness, and cross-language interoperability. It also contains three major components:

* Common Language Runtime
* .NET Framework Class Library
* ASP.NET

We'll take a closer look at each of these components later in this chapter, but first I'll provide you with some of my expertise on when and how you should upgrade to Visual C++ .NET.

When to Upgrade to Visual C++ .NET

Upgrading to Visual C++ .NET is a big step, so to help you master the transition, here are four key reasons why you should consider upgrading:

* You do not rely on any code or third party components generated with Visual C++ 6.

* You want to build .NET Framework applications and XML Web Services.

* You are looking for an opportunity to boost your productivity and improve the quality of your code by using Managed Extensions to C++. These topics will be covered in detail in Chapters 2 through 13.

* You are going to collaborate intensively with Visual Basic.NET or ASP.NET, or you plan on working with C# developers.

The first two reasons are fairly straightforward, especially if you are anxious to get in and develop web services. The managed extensions feature, on the other hand, is one that some programmers overlook. I'm bullish on this feature because managed extensions may indeed boost your productivity by eliminating most, if not all, memory management hassles. In fact, porting to managed extensions can improve existing applications by eliminating those hard-to-find memory leaks and making further memory management a no-brainer. Also, you'll find that attributed programming and enhanced COM support simplify component development and provide an additional incentive for upgrading to Visual C++ .NET.

When Not to Upgrade

You definitely should not upgrade to Visual C++ .NET if you fall into one of the following situations:

* If You Are Not Running Windows 2000 or Windows XP.
In this case, you can't upgrade to Visual C++ .NET because the Visual Studio .NET integrated development environment (IDE) requires the Windows 2000 or Windows XP operating system.

* If You Rely on Third-Party Object Modules.
If you are using third-party object modules that you statically link to your project, you are facing a purely technical obstacle. Object modules (.obj files) produced by previous versions of Visual C++ are incompatible with Visual C++ .NET, and an attempt to link them with object modules produced by Visual C++ .NET will result in link errors.

* If You Rely on Third-Party Static Libraries that Statically Link to MFC.
If you are using third-party static libraries that export function calls or classes that are dependent on previous versions of MFC, you may get unresolved externals when compiling your code in Visual C++ .NET. For one thing, Microsoft has changed the definition of the common **CString** class, effectively turning it into a template class. Therefore, if a third-party library that you use exports a function similar to void **foo(CString** *S*), it exposes a reference to MFC 4.2 **CString** object, and the new **CString** object defined in Visual C++ .NET MFC 7.0 header files will not match the old definition.

As an act of desperation, you may attempt to link with both MFC 7.0 and MFC 4.2 libraries. Unfortunately, some of the MFC 7.0 classes may match older MFC 4.2 definitions and you may get multiple symbol definitions linker errors.

Tip: There is a workaround to the linking problem discussed above. Using Visual C++ 6.0, you can convert a third-party static library into a DLL that exports only standard C/C++ definitions and does not depend on MFC at all. If the overhead of such a conversion is not too big and you are ready to go the extra mile for the extra features of Visual C++ .NET, then you should try this approach.

NOTE: Of course, it is far better just to recompile a third-party library using Visual C++ .NET. Yet, in most cases, third-party libraries and components come without source code and with little or no documentation, rendering such recompilation impossible. In my opinion, such situations make a strong vote for open-source distribution. Source code availability eases, if not eliminates, software portability issues, ultimately improving software quality by means of a peer review process.

Web Services

Since .NET is all about web services, it is important to understand what a web service is. Let's once again consider the official Microsoft definition (http://www.microsoft.com/net/defined/whatis.asp):

> An XML Web Service is a small, reusable application written in XML, a universal language for data exchange.

Sounds fairly general, right? Reading between the lines what this says is that a web service is Microsoft's vision of a new universal building block for developing *distributed Internet applications*. Web services are black-box components that, unlike current technologies, do not rely on object-model-specific protocols, such as Microsoft's Distributed Component Object Model (DCOM) or Sun's Remote Method Invocation (RMI). Instead, web services are accessible using the most common Hypertext Transfer Protocol (HTTP) and Extensible Markup Language (XML). But why HTTP and XML, you're probably wondering? Because HTTP is the least common denominator for the Internet and the only protocol that can penetrate the tightest firewalls, while XML, on the other hand, provides a very convenient machine- and OS-independent, human-readable data representation.

As long as both a client and a server can send and receive HTTP requests, any server can host a web service and any client can access a web service, regardless of the operating system and programming language used. Hosting web services on Internet servers opens new opportunities for software developers and service providers. Microsoft's vision is that the Internet is not just a distributed information system but also a platform for distributed computing. Along with regular text information and digital media, Internet servers may contain little pieces of software—web services—that anybody can harness to perform specific tasks, such as data access, authentication, data mining, financial analysis, secure shopping—you name it.

Another useful application of web services comes from the notion that a web service can be used as a wrapper around a legacy application to expose its functionality for other web services and other Internet applications. Thus, web services can be used as glue for integrating legacy applications into a new system.

Web Service Architecture

Web services are essentially objects. As with any object, a web service contains methods for performing useful operations. Figure 1.1 depicts the most generic web service architecture.

In general, a web service contains 5 layers:

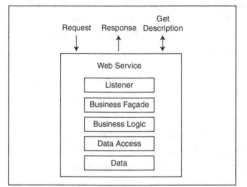

Figure 1.1 Web Service Architecture.

* Data: Databases, data files, and so on.

* Data access: A logical representation of the physical data that isolates the rest of the object from possible changes in the location or structure of the underlying physical data.

* Business logic: The core code performing some useful business functions (e.g., managing user account information, credit-card transaction processing, and so on).

* Business façade: A simple interface that maps business logic into a functionality exposed by the web service.

* Listener: Receives incoming requests, parses them, and dispatches them to the appropriate business façade method. If the service also sends a response, the listener is responsible for packaging data returned by the business façade into a message and sending it back to the client.

The architecture of a web service is very similar to the three-tier architecture commonly found in middleware. The only difference is that the data/data access and the business façade/business logic each forms a single layer in the three-tier model.

SOAP and WSDL

Typically web services exchange data by means of a *Simple Object Access Protocol* (SOAP). SOAP is a lightweight protocol that specifies rules on how to form requests and how to use XML to pass and return data. Although SOAP can use any network transport in principle, at the moment of this writing, only one defined SOAP binding exists—to the HTTP protocol.

Whenever you access a web service by calling one of its methods, you must generate a SOAP request, which is mapped into an HTTP request. If you pass data to the web service, SOAP converts it to XML. Similarly, when you receive a response from the web service, it must be a SOAP response encoded in an HTTP header. If such a response returns data, once again, SOAP will use XML to represent it.

Web Service Discovery

With web services, a mechanism must be provided to expose them to the rest of the Internet in order to describe and document their capabilities. Microsoft, working jointly with IBM, has developed an XML-based Web Service Description Language (WSDL) that documents web service features by describing the kinds of requests the web service accepts. WSDL describes a web service as an object, declares publicly accessible methods—including their parameters—and returns a value, if any. By examining a WSDL description file of a web service, you can find out everything that the web service can do for you.

Also, potential web service consumers should have means for locating (or discovering) web services on the web. For that reason, Microsoft developed an XML-based Discovery Protocol (Disco) that allows developers to retrieve web service descriptions from specific URLs. However, in most cases, you will not know a URL that contains a web service you want to consume. For that matter a Universal Description, Discovery, and Integration (UDDI) mechanism enables service providers to advertise their web services and facilitates location of a specific service by a web service consumer.

Web Service Requirements

Since web services are going to participate in distributed computing as integral parts of third-party applications, extreme care and attention should be exercised when developing them. Web services must be completely dependable, handle all incoming requests without being in danger of losing any, not crash or fail, and handle malformed requests gracefully. In summary, they must ensure uninterrupted service.

Fortunately, if you are going to use the Microsoft .NET Framework to write your own web services, most of these requirements will be satisfied automatically by the .NET Framework itself or by the common language runtime.

> **NOTE:** XML and web services are huge topics in themselves. To successfully develop and deploy web services using Visual C++ .NET, you do not have to understand the web service and underlying protocols, such as SOAP and UDDI, in all technical details. The .NET Framework hides all technicalities from you so you can focus on the business logic programming instead.

Development Challenges

The major IT problem and software development challenge of the decade is to integrate disparate applications, making them interoperate and use each other's data. This challenge has also been further complicated by the variety of software tools, languages, protocols, and operating systems used to develop, run, and maintain software. It's like using mismatched parts to build an automobile. On top of that, you have a crew of "mismatched" developers that are proficient in different programming tools, languages, and methodologies. In some cases, it is just as hard to reconcile different programming languages and methodologies as it is to develop software.

To summarize, the most common development challenges include:

*   Integrating incompatible pieces of software

*   Meeting deadlines

*   Maintaining a high quality of code

The solution to some of these challenges is simple. To reduce incompatibilities, one must rely on standards (e.g., XML, HTTP, ANSI C++). To meet the deadlines, developers must use rapid application development (RAD) tools, reuse the code, and rely on a comprehensive set of high-level libraries and components.

But maintaining high quality code is much more difficult. Lack of proper training or technical knowledge, poorly written or incomplete design specifications, and coding errors can all negatively impact software quality. Since it is extremely hard (if even possible) to make everyone smarter and more educated in a very short period of time, the least we can do is to devise a programming language or development framework that in some way simplifies programming, and automatically improves the quality of the code.

Introducing Microsoft's Solution: .NET

Microsoft's solution to the three problems just outlined can be answered with the .NET Framework, which includes:

* *A comprehensive set of development tools*—the Microsoft .NET SDK.

* *RAD tools*—the Visual Studio.NET Integrated Development Environment (IDE).

* *A comprehensive class library for all (or almost all) of your programming needs*—the .NET Framework Class Library.

* *Extensions to existing Microsoft languages*—Visual C++.NET, VB.NET, JScript.NET, and ASP.NET. The language extensions simplify common programming tasks, such as memory allocation, and provide seamless cross-language interoperability. Source code written using .NET languages is compiled into a CPU-independent set of instructions—Microsoft Intermediate Language (MSIL).

* *A new programming language*—C#.

* *The Common Language Runtime (CLR)*. This manages execution of code produced by .NET languages.

Sun's Solution Java

Sun Microsystems introduced Java in an attempt to address the development challenges outlined above long before Microsoft ever came up with .NET. The Java platform is similar to the .NET Framework in that it includes:

* *A comprehensive set of development tools*—Java SDK.

* *RAD tools provided by Sun and third parties*—Sun Forte, IBM VisualAge for Java, WebGain VisualCafé, and so on.

* *A comprehensive class library for all of your programming needs*—Java Class Library.

* *The Java language*—The language simplifies common programming tasks, such as memory allocation, and ensures type safety. Java is considered cross-platform because Java source code is compiled into a CPU-independent set of instructions—Java byte code—that can run on any platform that has a JVM.

* *Java Virtual Machine (JVM)*—The tool that interprets or just in time compiles (JIT) Java byte code and manages Java code execution.

In my opinion, competition by Sun and others in the server and middleware markets forced Microsoft to produce a competing platform that could measure up to Java. Obviously, previous Microsoft battle gear, comprised of Component Object Model (COM), Active Server Pages (ASP), and Internet Information Server (IIS), did not hold well and lost some ground to various application servers running Enterprise JavaBeans (EJB).

.NET vs. Java

Will .NET crush Java? Probably not because the main goal of the .NET Framework is to simplify development for the Windows platform, whereas Java is not platform specific. However, the .NET platform could become less platform specific over time. Efforts are now underway to port .NET to other operating systems. The most notable is the Mono project (www.go-mono.com) by Ximian (www.ximian.com), which represents an effort to create an open-source implementation of the .NET Development Framework. After all, Microsoft, Intel, and Hewlett-Packard—the driving force behind .NET, submitted the .NET to the ECMA committee for standardization. Once standardized, the .NET will no longer belong to Microsoft, but will live on its own. It may crash-land on Java, or on Microsoft itself. Time will tell. But for now, the .NET Framework will remain Microsoft's child with MS Windows as the only supported platform.

Table 1.1 contains a comparison of key features of .NET and Java.

Table 1.1 .NET and Java feature comparison.

Feature	.NET	Java
Platform	Windows	Any
Language	Any	Java
Class Library	Yes	Yes

Both platforms are complimentary in a way. The Java platform supports one language (Java) running on multiple platforms, and the .NET Framework supports multiple languages running on one platform (Windows). Sun's slogan is that people should not be tied to a single *operating system*, while Microsoft's comeback to this is that people should be tied to a single *language*. Also, Sun says Java is a *platform* whereas Microsoft says Java is a *language* and that .NET is a platform. Will Sun then say that .NET is just a set of *languages*?

My advice is that if you are looking into cross-platform portability and want your application to run on a variety of hardware and operating systems from different manufacturers, stick with Java. But if you already have much invested in Windows, .NET gives you an incentive *not* to switch to Java. After all, this would mean that you wouldn't have to learn a whole new language and could simply continue programming in VB or Visual C++, choosing to upgrade your knowledge incrementally by mastering extensions that the .NET Framework provides for those languages. Otherwise, when it really comes down to it, both Java and .NET provide somewhat equal amount of features and development ease. Also, because .NET appeared much later than Java, it learned from past mistakes. In a way .NET borrowed and learned from Java, and went further by supplying much more feature-rich and mature class library. .The immense NET Framework Class Library contains considerably more standard features, especially in the field of data/database access and XML parsing than Java Class Library. These features allow reducing XML/data access development time even further and firmly set .NET Framework apart of Java platform.

Is .NET Strictly About Web Services?

Visual Studio.NET, and Visual C++.NET, in particular provides a means for developing a full spectrum of .NET applications. For instance, Visual C++ .NET offers built-in support for creating .NET web services, .NET console applications, and .NET class libraries. Visual C# offers developers visual tools for creating Windows Forms applications, while ASP.NET is geared towards WebForms and web service application development. In other words, Visual Studio .NET offers you an opportunity to select the best language for a task at hand while the .NET Framework provides common APIs for rapid application development.

You can use the Common Language Runtime (CLR) and .NET Framework Class Library to develop a variety of client GUI applications, reusable components, server components, database applications, as well as web services. I'll explain more about the benefits of CLR in the next section.

Inside .NET

The .NET Framework offers developers a wide range of tools and a very rich API. But .NET is more than a software development kit. The .NET Framework is more like a platform that breaks conventional Windows development stereotypes and defines its own rules that ultimately make the software development process faster, easier, and better.

Cross-Language Interoperability

The two most important tasks of the .NET Framework are to simplify application development in multiple languages and enhance cross-language interoperability. From the early days, the issue of cross-language interoperability was addressed by Microsoft in incremental steps. Initially, DLLs provided means of language interoperability. You could write a DLL in Visual Basic or C# and call it from a C++ program and vice versa. Unfortunately, numerous problems with passing complex data types, handling exceptions, and accessing classes emerged. In fact, it was impossible to access a C++ class exported by Win32 DLL from a VB program directly. Nor was it possible to handle exceptions thrown by C++ code in VB program and vice versa.

The next attempt to solve the problem of cross-language interoperability comes from the Component Object Model (COM). Because of COM, developers can build components in C++ and access them in a VB application or in ASP pages. But COM has its drawbacks, too. For one thing, COM programming in C++ is no picnic. And COM still does not allow the handling of exceptions across the language border nor the manipulation of COM components in the same way you can manipulate C++ classes by deriving your own classes and overriding functions.

.NET solves the problem of cross-language interoperability and, by introducing common language specification and common language runtime, provides a means to the seamless integration of code written in different languages.

Common Language Specification

Complete cross-language interoperability requires that different languages have something in common, namely, that they should be able to work with objects/classes in the same way. This also requires not only that exceptions be handled in a uniform manner but also that there should be a common type system so that there is no more confusion or necessary conversion to pass parameters from one language to another. To achieve this goal, Microsoft has developed a Common Language Specification (CLS) that dictates the rules that languages and language compilers should follow to ensure cross-language interoperability within the .NET Framework.

To implement the new cross-language operability, Microsoft developed Common Language Runtime (CLR) extended existing languages, such as VB.NET, C++ .NET, ASP.NET, and JScript.NET, and created new languages (C#) and compilers that adhere to CLS. On top of that, CLS is intended to be a public specification, so that developers can go ahead and build their own CLS-compliant languages that could just as easily interoperate with your code as if it were written in the same language.

At first it seemed that CLS would make all languages the same, except for syntactic differences. But this was not so, since different CLS-compliant languages can contain features that are not CLS-compliant. You can use non-CLS-compliant features to write code that is intended for cross-language interoperability as long as you do not expose those features from outside the code. Only exported public classes, public properties, and public methods that are going to be used outside the code that defines and implement them have to be CLS-compliant.

C++ .NET fits nicely into this picture. In Chapter 2, "Managed Extensions to C++," I'll discuss the CLS-compliance necessary for building .NET applications. But as you'll learn, you can still program in C++ and use MFC to develop ordinary Win32 applications. Remember that only the features that you expose need to be CLS-compliant, and nobody cares that you used inline assembler and MFC classes in places nobody would have access to.

> **NOTE:** The MFC class **CString** is not CLS-compliant. If you were to define a class member, **foo**, that you wished to expose and use a local **CString** variable in the implementation of **foo**, **foo** would still be CLS compliant because your local **CString** variable would be inaccessible from outside the body of **foo**. Yet, if you decided to add a parameter of type **CString** to **foo**, turning **foo** into **foo(CString)**, the **foo** function would become non-CLS-compliant because the **CString** parameter would be visible and accessible from outside the body of **foo**.

In order to write CLS-compliant code, you must expose only CLS-compliant functionality in the following places:

* Definitions of your public classes.

* Definitions of public members of public classes and of members accessible to derived classes (family access).

* Parameters and return types of public methods of public classes and of methods accessible to derived classes.

Common Type System

The common type system defines how types are declared, used, and managed at runtime. It supports two general categories:

* value types
* reference types

Instances of value types are stored and represented by their values, whereas instances of reference types merely point to a location in memory where the actual type data is stored (i.e., like C++ pointers and references).

Both value and reference types can be built-in or user-defined. Figure 1.2 illustrates common type system-type classification.

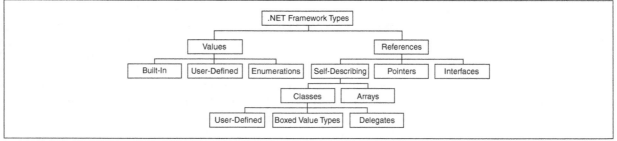

Figure 1.2 Common type system-type classification.

Value Types

Value types are stored as efficiently as primitive types, such as integers or character strings. Yet, you can call methods on value types and define virtual functions. Value types do not have to have constructors (e.g., similar to C++ **struct**), although virtual functions defined for value types are pretty much useless because you cannot derive your own classes from value types. In other words, value types are *sealed*.

To create a reference equivalent of a value type, you must *box* the value type. To create a value type again based off boxed value type, you must *unbox* the reference. Both boxing and unboxing is presented in Chapter 2, "Managed Extensions to C++."

Table 1.2 contains some of the built-in value types that the .NET Framework supplies, along with the equivalent managed extensions to C++ data types.

Table 1.2 Built-in value types of the .NET framework. Note that most unsigned integer types are not CLS-compliant.

Class name	Description	Managed Extensions for C++ Data Type
Byte	8-bit unsigned integer	**char**
SByte	8-bit signed integer (not CLS compliant)	**signed char**
Int16	16-bit signed integer	**short**
Int32	32-bit signed integer	**int** or **long**
Int64	64-bit signed integer	**__int64**
UInt16	16-bit unsigned integer (not CLS compliant)	**unsigned short**
UInt32	32-bit unsigned integer (not CLS compliant)	**unsigned int** or **unsigned long**
UInt64	64-bit unsigned integer (not CLS compliant)	**unsigned __int64**
Single	Single-precision (32-bit) floating-point number	**float**
Double	Double-precision (64-bit) floating-point number	**double**
Boolean	Boolean value (**true** or **false**)	**bool**
Char	Unicode (16-bit) character	**wchar_t**
Decimal	96-bit decimal value	**Decimal**
IntPtr	Signed integer whose size depends on the underlying platform (a 32-bit value on a 32-bit platform and a 64-bit value on a 64-bit platform)	**IntPtr**
UIntPtr	Unsigned integer whose size depends on the underlying platform (a 32-bit value on a 32-bit platform and a 64-bit value on a 64-bit platform) (not CLS compliant)	**UIntPtr**
Object	The root of the object hierarchy	**Object***
String	Immutable, fixed-length string of Unicode characters	**String***

WARNING! char data type in managed extension to C++ is unsigned by default. This is contrary to the ANSI C++ standard.

Enumerations
Enumerations are almost identical to C++ **enum**s.

Classes
Classes are the most generic data types. Just like C++ classes, CLS classes can contain members, properties (fields), and events.

Similar to standard C++ classes, .NET classes can be sealed (i.e., marked to disallow you to derive your own classes from the sealed base class) and abstract (i.e., contain pure virtual functions). They can also implement multiple interfaces (see below) or inherit from a single base class.

Unlike standard C++, which allows multiple inheritance, CLS restricts inheritance to one base class. When writing CLS-compliant code, you should use interfaces instead of multiple inheritance.

> **NOTE:** Standard C++ does not support interfaces.

Interfaces

If you are familiar with COM or Java, then you probably understand the concept of an interface. An *interface* is a kind of stripped-down class, which provides functionality that is intended to be shared among one or more classes. And just like classes, interfaces can have static members, nested types, abstract and virtual methods, properties, and events. Any non-abstract class implementing an interface must supply definitions for all abstract members declared in the interface.

Delegates

A *delegate* is a .NET equivalent of a C++ function pointer. Unlike C++ function pointes, delegates are always type-safe and can reference static and virtual class members. They are frequently used as event handlers and callbacks in the .NET Framework. For a more detailed discussion on delegates, see Chapter 3.

Pointers

CLS pointers are always type-safe. Although a common type system supports arithmetic operations, such as adding or subtracting integer values to or from pointer values on certain pointer types, such operations are not CLS-compliant.

Microsoft Intermediate Language

Adherence to CLS on a language level is, by itself, not enough to ensure cross-language operability. Because software written in different languages must interoperate after it has been compiled and deployed, the interoperability must also occur on a binary level. Microsoft's solution to this is to compile CLS-compliant code into Microsoft Intermediate Language (MSIL) that is interpreted or just-in-time (JIT) compiled and executed by the CLR virtual machine.

MSIL is very similar to Java byte code. It contains a CPU-independent set of instructions for loading, storing, accessing, and initializing classes, class members, virtual functions, arithmetic and logical operations, control flow, memory access, and exception handling. In order to be executed by a CPU, MSIL must be interpreted or compiled using a JIT compiler. And CPU-independent architecture of MSIL opens the possibility for porting the code to other platforms that implement the interpreter. The code compiled into MSIL is referred to as *managed code*.

Managed Execution

Execution of MSIL code is called *managed execution*. There is a good reason why it is called *managed*. Execution of MSIL code involves not only JIT compilation, but also includes runtime type checking, security checking, exception handling, and garbage collection.

It's been a common perception that most programming errors arise from the fact that software developers cannot always manage pointers and allocate or deallocate memory properly. Looking at Microsoft applications, I tend to agree (but I certainly would not imply that *all* developers have difficulties managing memory). Common pointer and memory allocation errors include attempts to access invalid or uninitialized pointers, unsafe type conversion and memory leaks resulting from the fact that not all of allocated memory is freed when it is no longer needed.

Managed execution takes care of all these problems. The "necessary evil" of manual memory management is therefore replaced with garbage collection. As with Java, the .NET Framework will run a garbage collector process, the process that will kick in every once in a while by temporarily suspending all managed code threads and releasing heap memory no longer referenced by any managed objects.

Metadata

Type safety and correct pointer or reference access is maintained by means of *metadata*—comprehensive information about managed code. Metadata is generated by a compiler along with MSIL code. Metadata contains a complete class description, including class member definitions (properties, methods, events), security, and access permissions. In addition, metadata contains garbage collection, version, and possibly debugging information.

Common Language RunTime

Common Language RunTime is a centerpiece of the .NET Framework. CLR is similar to the Java Virtual Machine (JVM) and provides runtime environment for executing managed code. It is responsible for loading managed code, examining embedded metadata, handling JIT-compilation of MSIL, and taking care of garbage collection.

CLR truly manages the code that it executes. It is also responsible for resolving code dependencies, including version dependencies and runtime checking. CLR is the engine that makes .NET run.

Assemblies

The .NET Framework defines a new application building block, which is called an *assembly*. An assembly is a package that groups together application code with application resources. It forms a unit of application deployment, version control, reference scope, type scope, and security permissions.

The .NET Framework supports two kinds of assemblies: static and dynamic. Static assemblies exist on disk as a set of files united by an assembly manifest. Dynamic assemblies are created programmatically as they are needed and usually are not saved to disk.

Assemblies can be a single DLL or .EXE file or can contain multiple DLLs, .NET modules (.netmodule files), text files, HTML files, JPEG images, or other documents (see Figure 1.3).

> **NOTE:** An assembly can contain one and only one file that has **DllMain**, **WinMain** or **Main** entry point. It means that any assembly can contain a single executable file (.EXE) or a single DLL for the exception of resource-only DLLs, because resource-only DLLs do not export any functions or classes that have an entry point. Additional .NET classes can be included into an assembly as .NET module (.netmodule) files. All files that comprise an assembly must reside in the same folder.

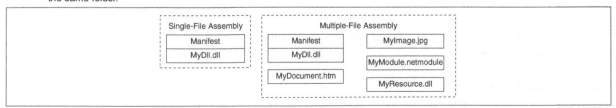

Figure 1.3 Single and multiple file assembly.

Assembly Manifest

Every assembly must contain a *manifest* metadata that describes the content of the assembly. An assembly manifest contains the following information:

*   simple assembly name

*   version number

*   culture, meaning language and locale-specific information (optional)

*   strong name public key (optional)

*   list of files that make up the assembly

*   type reference information used by the runtime to map classes exported by the assembly into modules that declare and implement them (optional)

*   static dependency information—a list of other assemblies that are statically referenced by this assembly (optional)

In a single-file assembly, the manifest is stored alongside with another metadata contained in the file. In a multifile assembly, the manifest can either be stored in any of the portable executable (PE) files that comprise the assembly or it can reside in a separate PE file that contains only the assembly manifest metadata.

Assembly Functions

Assemblies form the fundamental unit of deployment, version control, type scope, and security permissions in addition to grouping together related files, such as executable code and resources. Here is a summary of the most important properties of an assembly:

*   It is the unit at which permissions are requested and granted.

*   Types that have the same name but which reside in different assemblies are considered different types and must be referred by the assembly name and the type name from outside the assemblies that define them.

*   It is the smallest versionable unit in the common language runtime.

An assembly can specify in its manifest metadata that it requires a specific version of another assembly. In this event, the assembly will not load unless the desired version of the referenced assembly is present in the system. Earlier or later versions of the referenced assembly will not satisfy the reference unless the system policy or the application configuration data permits such substitution.

Different versions of the same assembly can be referenced by different applications and run side by side without any collisions or side effects. Thus, assembly-level version control is intended to solve the well-known "DLL Hell" problem—a problem that is known to occur when DLLs referenced by an application are overwritten with different versions of the same DLLs that are either not fully compatible with the replaced version or were not tested with the application.

Simplified deployment, version control, and side by side execution of different versions of the same DLL are the main advantages of assemblies.

Global Assembly Cache

Assemblies are meant to be private so that an application can minimize dependencies. However, you may need to share assemblies among applications in some cases. To make an assembly shared, the assembly must be given a strong name and it must be deployed into the global assembly cache (GAC). You can use the .NET Framework SDK gacutil.exe tool to deploy an assembly to the global assembly cache.

If your application deploys one or more assemblies to the global assembly cache, you can no longer deploy your application by simply copying the application folder from one machine to another. You would also need to deploy the necessary assemblies to the target machine's global assembly cache.

NOTE: To deploy assemblies to the global assembly cache, you must have administrator privileges on the target machine.

Although it is sufficient to drag and drop shared assemblies onto the GAC folder on the target system, it is better to use the Windows Installer because it maintains proper reference counting and provides means for automated uninstallation of assemblies.

.NET applications do not rely on Windows Registry for storing configuration information. Instead, .NET applications use application configuration files. Registry-less operations greatly simplify application and assembly deployment by reducing it to a simple file copy operation.

To inspect the contents of your system's global assembly cache, open your GAC folder (e.g., c:\windows\assembly) in Windows Explorer. A sample of GAC folder content is also shown in Figure 1.4, with the version numbers listed alongside each assembly, as well as culture information and public key tokens.

Strong Names

A *strong name* consists of the simple assembly name, version number, culture information (if specified), a public key, and a digital signature. A strong name contains assembly manifest information (including names and hashes of the files to combine the assembly) encrypted with a private key of the software publisher. Since the private key is unique and secret, you can be sure that nobody else will be able to produce a subsequent version of the assembly or alter the contents of the assembly and forge a new strong name that matches the changes done to the assembly. Uniqueness of the private key ensures the uniqueness of the strong name and the assembly signed with the strong name. For that reason, assemblies with equivalent strong names are considered to be equivalent.

TIP: Use the .NET Framework SN.exe utility to assign a strong name to your assembly.

Another purpose of strong names is to provide a means for assembly versioning. When developing assemblies that are going to be shared by several applications, you should keep track of changes by assigning a new version number to each subsequent release of the assembly. When you install a new version of the assembly, the old version of the assembly will not be removed. Both the old and the new versions will be accessible to applications and can be executed side by side. Such behavior ensures that existing applications, which worked perfectly with the old version of the assembly, will continue operating properly and not be adversely affected by the changes that you implemented in the new version. At the same time, you can direct new applications to use the new version of the assembly. Also, you can direct an existing application to start using the new version of the assembly either by modifying the application manifests or by updating the application configuration files. If the existing application begins malfunctioning when configured to use the new assembly, you can always reset the application manifest or configuration to use the old version of the assembly.

Strong names are required only for shared assemblies deployed in the global assembly cache. Because private assemblies are never shared, they need not have strong names and be versioned. Private assemblies are always installed by the application that references them and must reside in the application directory. Thus, there is no need to worry about version conflicts.

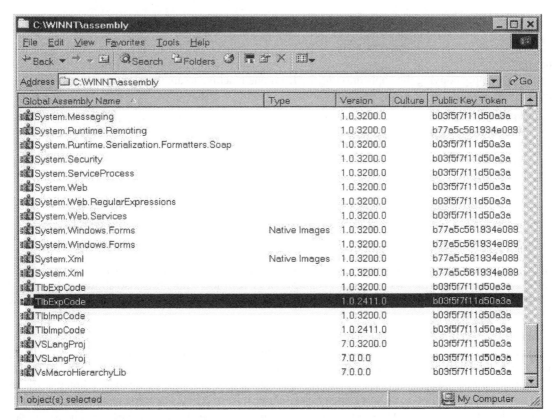

Figure 1.4 The global assembly cache view through Windows Explorer.

Assembly Version Resolution

When runtime is looking for a specific version of an assembly, it first checks the configuration files, such as application policy, publisher policy, and machine policy to obtain the correct version of the assembly. The configuration files can direct the runtime to load a different version of the referenced assembly than specified in the referencing assembly manifest. Once the correct version is determined, the runtime checks whether the desired version of the referenced assembly is already loaded. If the desired version of the referenced assembly is not loaded, the runtime searches the global assembly cache, the application directory, and all subdirectories in the application directory for the assembly.

Assembly Security

Security policy set on the computer where the assembly will run may limit the operations the assembly can perform. If your assembly attempts an operation restricted by the security policy, a security exception occurs.

To provide maximum functionality and reliability, you should handle the security exceptions in your code. However, if your code requires all-or-none security permissions, you can explicitly insert necessary security requests in the assembly startup code and handle the load-time failure when the desired security permissions are not granted.

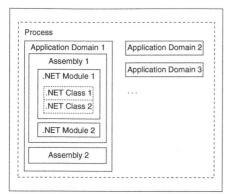

Figure 1.5 The .NET Framework execution hierarchy.

Application Domains

Application domains sit at the top of the .NET Framework execution hierarchy (see Figure 1.5). Application domains provide a level of isolation between individual applications. Although you can run multiple application domains within the same process, application domains are just as well isolated from each other as Win32 applications running in different processes. Grouping multiple application domains in the same process improves performance by saving memory and CPU time otherwise wasted on managing multiple processes.

Assemblies are loaded into application domains in a manner that's similar to the loading of DLLs with the **LoadLibrary** Win32 API call. Most assemblies are loaded as domain-specific and are accessible only by the application that loaded them. Alternatively, you can load assemblies as domain-neutral. You would normally load shared assemblies from the global assembly cache as domain-neutral so you could share the code among multiple application domains and save system memory.

When deciding whether to load an assembly as domain-specific or domain-neutral, you must consider the memory vs. performance trade-off. You will encounter a performance hit when accessing static data or invoking static methods of a domain-neutral assembly because extra code is required to ensure proper application domain isolation.

> **NOTE:** You can unload individual application domains but you can't unload individual assemblies or .NET Framework types/classes.

The .NET Framework Class Library

The .NET Framework supplies a CLS-compliant class library for all your programming needs. The .NET Framework Class Library can be used in any CLS-compliant language, such as Visual C++ .NET, C#, VB.NET, etc. The .NET Framework types contained in the library form the foundation on which .NET applications, components, and controls are built. The .NET Class Library contains:

* base data types and exceptions

* common data structures

* runtime type information classes

* security classes

* I/O classes

* data-access classes

* client-side GUI glasses (i.e., Windows Forms)

* server-controlled, client-side GU classes (i.e., WebForms)

System Namespace

System namespace is the root namespace for .NET Framework classes. It contains base data types, such as **Object** (the root of the inheritance hierarchy), **Byte**, **Char**, **Array**, **Int32**, and **String**. Besides the base data types, the System namespace contains about 100 additional classes that encapsulate a wide range of tasks, including exception handling, core runtime functionality, application domains management, and garbage collection. System namespace is discussed in depth in Chapters 3 and 4.

The System namespace is divided into many second-level namespaces. Table 1.3 shows the categories and the functionality covered by the System namespace and the underlying second-level namespaces.

Table 1.3 System namespace and the underlying second-level namespaces functionality groups.

Category	Namespace	Functionality
Component model	System.CodeDom	Source-code document representation, source-code compilation support.
Component model	System.ComponentModel	Implementation of components, including licensing and design-time adaptation.
Configuration	System.Configuration	Retrieval of application configuration data.
Data management	System.Data	Data and database access, data source management.
Data management	System.Xml	XML data access.
Data management	System.Xml.Serialization	Support for object storing to/retrieving from XML.
Framework services	System.Diagnostics	Application instrumentation and diagnostics.
Framework services	System.DirectoryServices	Active Directory of an Active Directory service provider access.
Framework services	System.Management	Support for Web-Based Enterprise Management (WBEM) standards.
Framework services	System.Messaging	Microsoft Message Queue (MSMQ) access and management, sending and receiving of messages.
Framework services	System.ServiceProcess	Windows-based service applications (e.g. NT Service) support.
Framework services	System.Timers	Programmable timer event support.
Globalization and localization	System.Globalization	Internationalization and globalization of the application support.
Globalization and localization	System.Resources	Resource management and access, including support for localization.
Network services	System.Net	Network communication and network protocols.
Common tasks	System.Collections	Collections of objects, lists, queues, arrays, hash tables, and dictionaries.
Common tasks	System.IO	Basic data stream access, file I/O, memory I/O, and isolated storage.
Common tasks	System.Text	Character encoding, character conversion, and string manipulation.
Common tasks	System.Text.RegularExpressions	Regular expression support.
Multithreading	System.Threading	Multithreaded programming, locking and synchronization.
Reflection	System.Reflection	Access to type metadata and dynamic creation and invocation of types.
Client-side GUI	System.Drawing	2-D graphics, GDI+.
Client-side GUI	System.Windows.Forms	User interface features for Windows-based applications.

<Continued on Next Page>

<Table 1.3 Continued>

Category	Namespace	Functionality
Runtime infrastructure services	System.Runtime.CompilerServices	Support for compilers that target the runtime.
Runtime infrastructure services	System.Runtime.InteropServices	Interoperability with COM and other unmanaged code.
Runtime infrastructure services	System.Runtime.Remoting	Support for creating tightly or loosely coupled distributed applications.
Runtime infrastructure services	System.Runtime.Serialization	Object serialization and deserialization, including binary and SOAP encoding support.
Security	System.Security	.NET Framework security system, including policy resolution, stack walks, and permissions management.
Security	System.Security.Cryptography	Cryptographic services, hashing, random number generation, message authentication, and digital signature formation.
Web Services	System.Web	Web server and client management, communication, and design. Core infrastructure for ASP.NET, including Web Forms.
Web Services	System.Web.Services	Client- and server-side support for SOAP-based web services.

In Summary

Microsoft's .NET Framework is an environment for rapid application development and seamless cross-language interoperability geared towards the development of XML Web Services.

The benefits of .NET Framework for C++ users include:

* Increased productivity and improved code robustness when using Managed Extensions to C++ and Common Language Runtime.

* Rapid application development with .NET Framework Class Library.

* Simplified web service development when using .NET Framework Class Library.

* Ability to share code with developers who use other languages, such as C# or VB.NET, as easily as with other C++ developers.

CHAPTER 2

Managed Extensions to C++

QUICK JUMPS

CHAPTER 2
Managed Extensions to C++

In Depth

In this chapter, I'll introduce the key new feature of the Visual C++ .NET—Managed Extensions to C++. You'll learn how to create managed applications and managed classes and how to program in Managed C++. Before starting this chapter, you should read Chapter 1 to familiarize yourself with the basic concepts of the .NET Framework.

Introducing Managed Extensions

The Managed Extensions to Visual C++ is a new set of Microsoft extensions intended to facilitate programming for the .NET Framework. Managed Extensions include new keywords, attributes, compiler options, and runtime behavior that actually defines a new language—Managed C++. Managed C++ borrows many features from Java and C# but it represents a flavor of the standard C++ language rather than a totally new language.

So, why didn't Microsoft just create a new language instead of supercharging Visual C++? Well, actually they did—C#. Managed Extensions to C++, on the other hand, offers something for the C++ developer that no other language does: C++ and Managed C++ code can seamlessly be blended together to create powerful and flexible applications.

Benefits of Managed Extensions

The Microsoft .NET Framework offers developers exciting new features intended to simplify and improve the software development process without compromising code quality. Managed Extensions to C++ encompass the new features of .NET and bring them to C++ developers as you'll learn next.

Simple Memory Management

Managed C++ supports a garbage collection memory-management scheme. Garbage collection is a classical memory management technique that relieves you of the burden of deallocating memory manually. You only need to allocate memory for your needs and you do not have to worry about releasing the memory when it's no longer needed. Thus, you don't have to worry about running out of memory due to hard-to-find memory leaks.

When you instantiate a *managed class*, the system will allocate a memory block for the class on a *managed heap*. The managed heap exists independently of a standard C++ unmanaged heap. To keep track of the allocated memory blocks, the common language runtime traces object references to identify objects that can no longer be referenced by running code. Tracing of object references successfully identifies circular references undetectable when using reference counting.

To remove unused memory blocks, the CLR runs a *garbage collector* process, which kicks in every once in a while by temporarily stopping all managed threads to free unused memory blocks and to compact the heap by grouping allocated blocks together. Then, the garbage collector resumes the threads it suspended and sleeps for a while before resuming the garbage collection process.

In addition to allocating managed classes, the managed heap is used to dynamically allocate managed arrays.

> **NOTE:** To keep the allocated memory from being garbage collected, you must ensure that the reference to the allocated memory does not disappear by going out of scope or being initialized with null.

Safer, More Robust Code

Code written in Managed C++ compiles in MSIL. When executed, MSIL is JIT-compiled by CLR into native code that is processed by the CPU. In addition to being CPU–independent, MSIL offers improved run-time error checking, run-time type checking, and enhanced security in comparison with native CPU-dependent code produced by the standard C++ compiler. Thus, managed code is safer and potentially more reliable than native code. You can restrict what a particular managed component or application can do by setting appropriate security permissions. Also, you can catch and possibly recover from runtime errors (e.g., unsafe type conversions) that would normally result in a native-application crash.

Seamless Interoperability

Using Managed C++, you can seamlessly interoperate with developers using other .NET languages such as C# or Visual Basic .NET. You can work with classes written in VB .NET as if they were written in C++, including calling methods and deriving your own classes. Here's an example:

```
#using <mscorlib.dll>
// Import MyVBClass class
#using <MyVBClass.dll>

// Override MyVBClass written in VB
class MyCppClass: public MyVBClass {
public:
    // Override method
    virtual void MyTestMethod()
    {
        // New method body
    }
};

void main()
{
    MyCppClass* CppClass = new MyCppClass();
    CppClass->MyTestMethod();
}
```

Similarly, developers who use other CLS-compliant languages can work with your code as if it was written in their language without any overhead of manual data marshalling or interfacing.

Wealth of the .NET Framework Class Library
CLS-compliant languages including Managed C++ gain full access to the .NET Framework Class Library. The .NET Framework Class Library dwarfs MFC in power and size. The .NET Framework Class Library is fairly complete and covers most, if not all, everyday programming needs.

Tradeoffs and Limitations of Managed Extensions
The convenience and benefits of .NET introduced by Managed C++ come at a price, however. You should know the tradeoffs and limitations of the Managed Extensions before you use them to avoid potential problems with your software.

Nondeterministic Destruction
The biggest limitation of the garbage collection memory-management scheme is *nondeterministic destruction*. This refers to the fact that you cannot predict with absolute certainty when the destructor for a deleted managed class is going to be called. Nondeterministic destruction can present a problem when working with managed C++ classes that acquire important system resources that must be released when an object is destroyed such as file handles, network or database connections, and so on. Since the garbage collection usually happens frequently, chances are good that your program and other concurrently running applications won't starve on system resources that are delay-released unless the system resources involved are very scarce and you wrote some unusual code that can quickly utilize most of them.

To get around the limitations of nondeterministic destruction, you may have to release the resources explicitly when you no longer need them to ensure correct operation of your program. The limitation is further emphasized by the established C++ programming practice of using stack-allocated classes that typically release the acquired resources in the destructor. The destructor for a stack-allocated object is called immediately when the object goes out of scope. Many existing programs are written with this behavior in mind and do not release the acquired resources explicitly. Furthermore, if an exception occurs, stack-allocated objects will go out of scope during the stack unwind process caused by the exception handling mechanism, and the resources will be freed automatically as the destructors for stack-allocated classes are called.

Since you can't allocate managed classes on the stack, you can't rely on automatic and immediate object destruction when a managed object goes out of scope or when an exception is thrown. To ensure predictable and immediate release of the important resources when using managed classes, you must enclose your code in a **try-catch-__finally** block and put code in the **__finally** section to free the resources when an exception occurs.

Since some developers don't always remember to release the resources explicitly and are too lazy to include a **try-catch-__finally** block in every function, there is a good chance that the acquired resources will be released when the garbage collector kicks in. While this may be okay in *most* cases, in *some* situations it could result in a bad program crash. To make matters worse, such a crash or malfunction will be unpredictable and sporadic—just the kind of bug you *love* to track down.

Let me illustrate my point using the following two examples. Consider a situation where you are writing a Managed C++ program to quickly open HTTP connections:

```
bool TryConnection(char* SomeURL)
{
    try {
        MyInternetConnection* pConn = new MyInternetConnection(SomeURL);
        pConn->Open();
        // Do something that may throw an exception
        return true;
    }
    catch(...) {
        return true;
    }
    __finally {
    }
    return false;
}
void GenerateURL(char* SomeURL)
{
    // Function for generating URLs
}
void main()
{
    char SomeURL[128];
    for ( int i = 0; i < 100000; i++ )
    {
        GenerateURL(SomeURL);
        if ( TryConnection(SomeURL[i]) )
        {
            // Hooray! We did it!
        }
    }
}
```

This code misses the **pConn->Close()** statement prior to the function **return** statement, thus, the program will quickly run out of HTTP connection handles and crash. Since the program crashes on the first run, you will quickly remember to put the **pConn->Close()** statement in the **try** block but may overlook the need to insert the statement in the **__finally** block. On the second run, the program performs flawlessly so you hand it your client. The next day, you receive a surprise phone call that your program crashes. You try it on your system and it works perfectly, so you travel across town to your client's site to observe the program crashing. After pulling some hairs out, you realize that your client's network is messed up, and routes to some URLs are convoluted and unstable. The HTTP connection requests in your code occasionally time out and your connection object throws an exception. Since you did not release the connection handle in the **__finally** block, your program occasionally runs out of Internet connection handles. The adverse behavior is sporadic and unpredictable because the network conditions constantly change. None of these problems would have occurred had you used standard C++ and stack-allocated classes with deterministic destruction. Thus, the nondeterministic destruction and the lack of stack allocation support for managed classes may cause unexpected errors in programs that you port to Managed C++ as well as in the new programs that you write under the influence of your established automatic-out-of-scope-destruction habits.

Reduced Performance

Managed Code takes more time to load and execute than C++ code, thus, any program written in Managed C++ will be slower than a similar program written in standard C++. This can be a significant limitation for mission critical tasks. Consider a situation where your Internet storefront is implemented as an ATL Server component that, besides supporting shopping-cart and credit-card transactions, performs data mining to better serve returning customers and your marketing department. Data mining typically requires extensive database I/O as well as sophisticated statistical computations. Chances are that if you port such software to Managed C++, you will reduce the request handling capacity of your storefront component and degrade the user experience by the diminished server responsiveness. Of course, you can install more servers and some load-balancing gear. Unfortunately, you'll spend more money maintaining additional servers than you saved by using Managed C++. Thus, you must give careful consideration to the performance requirements of your application and decide which portions of code to write in Managed C++ and which to write in good old standard C++.

Reduced performance of a JIT-compiled MSIL code results from three factors:

1. The JIT-compiler does not have the luxury of time to optimize the code at runtime the way a stand-alone compiler can optimize it. Furthermore, the JIT compiler has a very narrow view of the code typically limited to the section of code being JIT compiled, thus, it is very difficult for a JIT compiler to perform global optimizations.

2. Runtime error and type and security checking require extra code. The extra code makes your program slower.

3. Garbage collection also reduces application performance because the garbage collector periodically suspends all managed threads to perform garbage collection and managed heap compacting.

Application Deployment Issues

Managed code relies on CLR and will not run if the .NET Framework is not installed. Because of this, you must make sure that you install and configure CLR and the .NET Framework Class Library if they are missing on the target machine. You can address the problem in two ways: You can require your users to have .NET Framework installed making it a prerequisite for your software, or you can bundle the framework CLR components with your installation. The first approach may discourage users from trying your software if they do not have the .NET Framework installed.

The bundling approach may cost you a pretty penny because the size of your installation will grow considerably. In the era of network software distribution, the increased installation package size may quickly exhaust your network capacity. You would then have to spend money upgrading your network connection and installing additional file and web servers to handle download requests, or you could loose potential customers frustrated with slow download speeds.

When to Use Managed Extensions?

Since you now have learned the pros and cons of Managed C++, the proper question to ask is "when should Managed Extensions be used?" The buzz is that the .NET Framework and Managed C++ are the tools for rapid application development (RAD). The implication here is that you should *always* use managed C++/.NET if you want to develop your applications *faster*. The truth is that if you are used to native C++/COM programming, switching technologies involves a learning curve. Plus, given the disadvantages of managed code such as porting issues and reduced performance, choosing Managed Extensions for every project may not be such a good idea.

The most compelling reason for a C++ programmer to use Managed C++ is to expose the power of C++ to other .NET developers by wrapping native C++ code inside of a managed class. Another reason for using Managed C++ is when you are implementing complicated memory management schemes. The Managed Extensions eliminates memory management headaches altogether.

Finally, you should use managed extensions if you want to exploit the wealth of the .NET Framework Class Library.

Managed Code vs. Native Code

Programming in Managed C++ is similar to native C++ programming, except that additional rules and restrictions apply when working with managed code:

* *Class programming*. Managed C++ supports both *managed* and *unmanaged* (i.e., native) classes. Managed classes are *always* allocated on the managed heap, while unmanaged classes can be allocated on the stack, C++ heap, or the managed heap.

* *Class data members*. In managed C++, class data members are referred to as *fields*. In managed C++, classes fields are less common than in standard C++ classes.

* *Properties*. Managed C++ classes allow you to define properties that are largely similar to standard C++ data members. Unlike standard C++ data members, Managed C++ properties can be get-only or set-only.

* *Function pointers*. In managed C++, function pointers are referred to as *delegates*. Unlike in standard C++, where function pointers are loosely types and always point to global functions, delegates in Managed C++ are strictly typed and always point to class methods.

* *Class description*. Managed C++ relies on *metadata* to describe classes. Metadata is stored with the code and can be accessed both in compile and runtime. Standard C++, in comparison, describes classes by means of C++ header files (.h-files), and the class description is usually available only at compile time.

* *Class libraries*. Managed C++ supports organizing managed class in libraries corresponding to .NET modules (.netmodule-files) or assemblies (.dll-files). Both .NET modules and assemblies correspond to dynamic libraries that are self-described by means of metadata. On the other hand, standard C++ supports both static (.lib-files) and dynamic (.dll-files) libraries that are described by means of C++ header files.

    NOTE: Managed C++ executables (.EXE files) are assemblies and, therefore, can be used by other applications and dynamic libraries.

* *Importing metadata*. Managed C++ uses the **#using** keyword to import metadata (i.e., class descriptions) from a specified .NET module or assembly. Standard C++ relies on header files (that are included using the **#include** keyword) to provide class and function definitions contained in a particular static or dynamic library.

* *Memory management*. Managed C++ supports automatic memory deallocation, while in standard C++ you must manually delete classes/free unused memory.

NOTE: When programming in Managed C++, you can mix both native C++ code with managed code. If you want to use a single feature of Managed C++, however, your entire code must be compiled as managed (i.e., with the /CLR switch).

Managed C++ Project Types

The Visual C++ .NET Application Wizard supports four Managed C++ project types:

* *Managed C++ Application*–allows you to create console or Windows executables:

* *Console subsystem.* Used to target the console subsystem. The code must define the **main** or **_tmain** program entry point;

* *Windows subsystem.* Used to target the Windows subsystem. The code must define the **WinMain** program entry point.

* *Managed C++ Class Library.* This project allows you to create .NET module (.netmodule) files or assemblies (.dll-files).

* *Managed C++ Empty Project.* Used for creating an empty project configured to target CLR.

* *Managed C++ Web Service.* Used for creating a managed web service DLL (see Chapters 10 through 12).

Hello World in Managed C++

The tradition of introducing new languages in programming books involves writing a "Hello World" program, so here's mine in Managed C++:

```
// Must be compiled with the /CLR option
#using <mscorlib.dll>
using namespace System;

int main(int argc, char* argv[])
{
    Console::WriteLine("Hello World");
    return 0;
}
```

The code example above corresponds to a simple console program that outputs a single line of text. The **main** function is defined in the same way as in unmanaged code: Even managed code has to use the same signature for **main**, **_tmain** or **WinMain** program entry point as good-old unmanaged C++ code.

The **#using <mscorlib.dll>** and the **using namespace System** statements comprise the first two lines of code of virtually all Managed C++ applications. The **#using <mscorlib.dll>** statement can not be omitted under any circumstances as it creates a reference to the **mscorlib.dll** core .NET Framework assembly, which is necessary for compiling and running any managed application. The **using namespace System** statement, on the other hand, is inserted for convenience and allows avoiding having to prefix base .NET classes such as **Object** or **Delegate** with the 'System::' namespace prefix.

> **WARNING!** Unlike Java, Managed C++ does not require or enforce object-oriented or class-based programming, thus, there is nothing in the language to stop you from continuing to write C-style procedural code.

Immediate Solutions

Compiling Managed C++ Code

Whether you create a Managed C++ project using the Application Wizard or create a project manually, the managed code must be compiled using the /CLR compiler command line switch. Specifying the /CLR compiler switch is equivalent to setting the "Use Managed Extensions" option on the General page on the Project Property Pages dialog to "Yes."

When you specify the /CLR compiler switch, the compiler generates MSIL code and metadata rather than native CPU instructions. Compiling into MSIL and emitting metadata is essential for .NET programming.

If you attempt to compile a Managed C++ program without the /CLR option a compile error is generated.

Initializing Character Strings

Character strings are represented in Managed C++ by means of the **System::String** class, which is discussed in detail in Chapter 3. Character strings in Managed C++ are implicitly converted to the **System::String** type. Thus a **String** pointer can be initialized using an ordinary C++ string literal as shown here:

```
String* str1 = "abc";
String* str2 = L"abc"; // Wide string literal
```

Managed C++ also provides new string literals with the 'S'-prefix:

```
String* str = S"abc";
```

Using the 'S'-prefix with string literals results in more efficient code because the **String** object associated with the 'S'-prefixed string literal is allocated once and used everywhere the literal is referenced. All instances of the 'S'-prefixed string literal point to the same **String** object.

Declaring Namespaces (**using namespace** Keyword)

Namespaces are widely used throughout the .NET Framework Class Library. The original intent of namespaces was to provide means for grouping related classes. You can also use namespaces for resolving otherwise ambiguous names. To define your own namespace you should use the **namespace** keyword as shown here:

```
namespace NamespaceName {
    Definitions
}
```

The namespace keyword defines a scope where you can insert your own class, structure, enumeration, constant, function, and whatever else definitions. To reference the namespace definitions later in your code, you must either use the **using namespace** *NamespaceName* statement or prefix the definition names with the namespace name. You can also use the **namespace** keyword to define nested namespaces. Here's an example:

```
namespace NamespaceName1 {
    NamespaceName1 Definitions
    namespace NamespaceName2 {
        NamespaceName2 Definitions
    }
}
```

The **namespace** keyword in Managed C++ is equivalent to the **namespace** keyword in Standard C++. In order to refer to a class (or any other entity) defined in a particular namespace, the class name must be prefixed with the namespace name, e.g., *MyNamespace::MyClass*. Just like Standard C++ namespaces, managed namespaces can contain same-named entities, which nevertheless will be treated as totally different entities when prefixed with the proper namespace name. Thus, you can have two namespaces *X* and *Y* that define class *Z*, and in order to reference the class *Z* outside the scope of either namespace you must specify the namespace prefix-*X::Z* or *Y::Z*-in order to indicate which class you are referring to.

The following code example illustrates the usage of namespaces by defining the **MyNamespace** namespace and referencing **MyClass** class defined within the **MyNamespace** scope:

```
#using <mscorlib.dll>
using namespace System;

// 1. Declare namespace
namespace MyNamespace {
    __gc class MyClass {
    };
};

void main()
{
    // 2. Refer to the MyClass (prefix is required)
    MyNamespace::MyClass* pMyClass;
    pMyClass = new MyNamespace::MyClass();
}
```

Referencing Namespaces (**using namespace** Keyword)
When you develop large applications that contain many namespace and references classes imported from other assemblies, it becomes tedious to prefix classes with fully qualified namespace names every time you declare a

class variable. To avoid the necessity of writing class names prefixed with long namespace names the **using namespace** statement should be used. The **using namespace** statement has the following syntax:

using namespace *Namespace***::***NestedNamespace1***::**...

There is no limit on how many nested namespace levels you can specify as long as you use the double-colon (::) separator to separate namespace names, while in the simplest case it is sufficient to specify just the namespace name with no nested namespaces.

The following code example illustrates the usage of the **using namespace** statement by defining the **MyNamespace** namespace containing a single **MyClass** class and referencing the **MyNamespace** by means of the **using namespace MyNamespace** statement to avoid the necessity of specifying the '**MyNamespace::**' prefix when referring to the **MyClass** class:

```
#using <mscorlib.dll>
using namespace System;

// 1. Declare namespace
namespace MyNamespace {
    __gc class MyClass {
    };
};

// 2. Reference MyNamespace
using namespace MyNamespace;

void main()
{
    // 3. Refer to the MyClass (no prefix required)
    MyClass* pMyClass;
    pMyClass = new MyClass();
}
```

Importing Classes and Other Metadata from External Assemblies (**#using** Precompiler Directive)

If you want to use classes or other metadata defined in an external assembly in your code you must import the assembly metadata in your program. This task, if importing external metadata, is typically achieved using the **#using** precompiler directive.

The **#using** directive is similar to the **#include** directive in the sense that the imported metadata becomes accessible to your code. You can instantiate objects and derive your own classes from public classes declared in the assembly, which you are importing metadata from.

The following code example illustrates importing .NET Framework Class Library core metadata from the mscorlib.dll assembly and importing the **Uri** class from the sstem.dll assembly:

```
// 1. Import metadata from mscorlib.dll
#using <mscorlib.dll>
// 2. Import metadata from system.dll
#using <system.dll>
using namespace System;

void main()
{
    // 3. Instantiate Uri class defined in system.dll
    Uri* MyUri;
    MyUri = new Uri("http://www.UltraMax-Music.com");
}
```

> **Tip:** As an alternative to using the **#using** precompiler directive in your code, you can specify the /FU*FileName* compiler option (same as specifying the Force #using option on the Advance page in the C/C++ folder on the Project Property Pages dialog), which is equivalent to inserting the **#using** <*FileName*> statement in every source C++ file in your Managed C++ project.

Declaring Managed Classes (__gc Keyword)

The most interesting part of programming in Managed C++ pertains to managed classes that are also referred to as *managed types*. To define a managed class, simply add the __gc keyword to a standard C++ class definition as shown here:

```
__gc class GCClass {
public:
    GCClass() {}
};
```

The __gc keyword indicates that the class is *garbage-collected*, and its lifetime will be managed by the CLR. You can allocate garbage collected classes only on the managed heap, and you can't allocate them on the stack. Given the **GCClass** definition above, the following construct will cause a compile error:

```
void main()
{
    GCClass GCObj; // C3149: illegal use of managed type 'GCClass'
}
```

The correct instantiation of a **GCClass** object is on managed heap using the managed __gc **new** operator:

```
void main()
{
    GCClass* GCObj = __gc new GCClass();
}
```

You do not have to explicitly qualify the **new** operator with the __gc keyword. The compiler will automatically select the managed **new** operator (__gc new) when allocating the managed class.

Managed classes are automatically deleted by the garbage collector when they can no longer be referenced by running code. You do not have to explicitly dispose of managed classes using the **delete** operator. In fact, you can delete a managed type with the **delete** operator *only* if the managed type provides the destructor. Unlike the unmanaged **delete** operator, the managed **delete** simply calls the object's destructor without freeing the object memory. Here's an example:

```
__gc class GCClass {
public:
    GCClass() {}
    ~GCClass() {}
};
void main()
{
    GCClass* GCObj = new GCClass();
    delete GCObj; // Calls the destructor, but does not release memory
}
```

__gc classes are more constrained than standard C++ classes. The __gc keyword imposes the following restrictions on a managed class:

* Inheritance from unmanaged classes is not allowed

* Multiple inheritance is not allowed

* Unmanaged classes cannot be derived from managed classes

* User-defined copy constructors are not allowed

* Friend classes and friend functions are not allowed

* Overloading of **new, delete,** and **&** operators is not allowed

* **const** and **volatile** modifiers are not allowed

* __gc unions cannot be declared (only __gc classes and structures are allowed)

The **System::Object** base class is assumed if no base class is specified.

> NOTE: All managed classes are directly or indirectly derive from the **System::Object** class, which represents the root of the managed class hierarchy.

Additional limitations include that you have to pass managed objects in parameters or return values by reference or as pointers, and the **offsetof** and the **sizeof** operators can not be used with managed classes.

Defining Managed Constructors

The semantics of __gc class constructors are slightly different than that of standard C++ classes. Let's consider an example where we have two classes, **BaseClass** and **DerivedClass**. In this case, the **DerivedClass** will be derived from the **BaseClass**:

```
__gc class BaseClass {
public:
   BaseClass() { Count = 10; ShowCount(); }
   virtual void ShowCount()
   {
      Console::WriteLine("BASE");
      Console::WriteLine(Count);
   }
   int Count;
};

__gc class DerivedClass: public BaseClass {
public:
   DerivedClass(int Count) : DerivedCount(Count)
   {
       Console::WriteLine(DerivedCount);
   }
   virtual void ShowCount()
   {
      Console::WriteLine("DERIVED");
      Console::WriteLine(DerivedCount);
   }
   int DerivedCount;
};

void main()
{
   DerivedClass* MyDerived = new DerivedClass(10);
}
```

The program will output:

```
DERIVED
0
10
```

> **NOTE:** The program outputs 0 because when a managed C++ is allocated all class members are automatically initialized with zeros.

The **BaseClass** calls overloaded **DerivedClass::ShowCount** from its constructor. Thus, the **DerivedClass::ShowCount** displays the **Count** value *before* it's set by the **DerivedClass** constructor. This behavior is different from standard C++. You must exercise care when overloading methods called from the base class constructor, and make sure that they do not rely on the derived class member variables not yet initialized by the derived class constructor.

Defining Static Constructors

Managed C++ classes can have static constructors, which are similar to the static constructors for standard C++ classes:

```
__gc class GCClass {
public:
    // Defines static constructor
    static GCClass() { }
};
```

Static constructors cannot accept parameters and are invoked to initialize the class before a class is used for the first time or before any static methods are called on the class. You cannot predict when a static constructor for your class is going to be called.

Defining Managed Destructors

Destructors of managed classes are always assumed to be virtual with the destructor of a derived class automatically calling the destructor of the base class. Destructors are called only when you explicitly delete your object with the **delete** operator.

When a managed class is compiled, the compiler automatically renames the destructor into the **Finalize** method and injects new destructor code. Thus the following class declaration:

```
__gc class GCClass {
public:
    ~GCClass()
    {
        Console::WriteLine("~GCClass()");
    }
};
```

Will be transformed by the compiler into:

```
__gc class GCClass {
public:
    // Renamed ~GCClass()
    void Finalize()
    {
        Console::WriteLine("~GCClass()");
    }
    // New destructor
    virtual ~GCClass()
    {
        GC::SuppressFinalize(this);
        GCClass::Finalize();
    }
};
```

The **Finalize** method is called by the garbage collector to finalize the class. You can neither overload the **Finalize** method nor access it from outside the class (the **Finalize** is a **protected** method). Instead you should overload your class destructor and rely on the compiler to generate the **Finalize** method for you.

In the code example above, the **GC::SuppressFinalize(this)** method suppresses the finalization for the class that's already been finalized; see Chapter 4.

Declaring Abstract Classes (__abstract Keyword)

To define an abstract managed class you should use the __**abstract** keyword in the class definition. Unlike standard C++ abstract classes, abstract managed classes do not have to contain a pure virtual method. In fact, abstract managed classes can supply bodies for all their methods. The __**abstract** keyword means that you cannot instantiate the abstract class directly, but rather should derive your own classes from it. The following code example demonstrates how to define an abstract class called **AbstractClass** and derive the concrete **DerivedClass** from it:

```
#using <mscorlib.dll>
// Abstract class
__abstract __gc class AbstractClass {
public:
    void MyAbstractMethod() { /* do something */ }
};

// Derived class (not abstract)
__gc class DerivedClass: public AbstractClass { };

void main()
{
    AbstractClass* MyAbstract =
        new AbstractClass();// Error C3622: cannot instantiate __abstract class
    DerivedClass* MyDerived = new DerivedClass();   // OK
    MyDerived->MyAbstractMethod(); // OK
}
```

Declaring Sealed Classes and Sealed Class Members (__sealed Keyword)

Class designers often want to restrict developers from overriding certain classes or particular class methods. Classes or class methods that cannot be overridden are called *sealed*. Managed C++ supports class sealing via the new **__sealed** keyword. If you define a class with the **__sealed** keyword nobody will be able to derive from the class. If you declare a virtual function with the **__sealed** keyword nobody will be able to override the function in a derived class. In the case of a virtual function you can have a base class where a particular function is not sealed but you can seal it in the derived class.

The following code demonstrates how you declare a sealed class virtual function:

```
#using <mscorlib.dll>
// Sealed class
__gc __sealed class MySealed {
};
// A class attempting to derive from the sealed class
__gc class MyDerived: public MySealed {   // C3246: can't derive from a sealed
                                           // class
};
// A class with sealed virtual function
__gc class BaseClass {
public:
    __sealed virtual void MyFunc() { }
};
// A derived class attempting to override the sealed function
__gc class DerivedClass: public BaseClass {
    void MyFunc() { }    // C3248: can't override a sealed function
};
```

> **NOTE:** The __**sealed** keyword is applicable only for virtual functions and it canot be used in interface definitions. The __**sealed** keyword is ignored when applied to nonvirtual members.

Declaring Identifiers Matching C++ Keywords (__**identifier** Keyword)

Cross-language interoperability of Managed C++ implies that occasionally you may use classes written in other CLS-compliant languages. Since other CLS-compliant languages may have a different set of keywords, it is possible that an external class name that you are going to use in your C++ code coincides with one of C++ keywords.

Managed C++ provides a new __**identifier** keyword that allows resolving class names matching C++ keywords. The __**identifier** keyword has the following syntax:

__**identifier**(*identifier*)

where the *identifier* corresponds to a name matching a C++ keyword, which should be treated as an identifier and not as the keyword.

Anywhere you want to use an identifier that matches a C++ keyword you must enclose it within the __**identifier** scope. You can also create classes in Managed C++ with names matching C++ keywords.

The following code example demonstrates how you define a managed class named "class" and how to reference the class in the code using the __identifier C++ keyword:

```
#using <mscorlib.dll>
// Declare a class named "class"
__gc class __identifier(class) {
};

void main()
{
    // Create an instance of the "class"
    __identifier(class)* pClass = new __identifier(class)();
}
```

Declaring Properties (__property Keyword)

Common language specification dictates that alongside with member variables and member functions a class can have one or more *properties*. From outside the class a property appears as an ordinary data member, but internally a property must be implemented using get and set methods.

Managed C++ supports properties by means of the __property keyword. To declare a property X you must declare two class member functions get_X and set_X using the __property keyword.

The following code example defines the MyClass, which declares the Data property supporting both get and set methods:

```
#using <mscorlib.dll>
__gc class MyClass {
public:
    __property int get_Data() {   return PropData; }
    __property void set_Data(int Value) { PropData = Value; }
private:
    int PropData;
};

void main()
{
    MyClass* obj = new MyClass();
    // Set property value: set_Data method is called
    obj->Data = 10;
    // Get property value: get_Data method is called
    System::Console::WriteLine(obj->Data);
}
```

When you set the property value the property set method is called. Similarly, when you get the property value the property get-method is called. You can implement get/set methods any way you want and do however complex processing necessary. Although, you do not have to declare both get and set methods for a property: You can define a *get-only* property if you declare only the get method, or you can define a *set-only* property if you declare only the set method.

The property defined in the example above is called *scalar* and it can not be overloaded (although property get/set methods can be declared as **virtual**). Pure virtual get/set methods are also allowed.

Declaring Indexed Properties

Besides scalar properties you can define *indexed* properties. Indexed properties behave like member arrays and can be accessed using one ore more indices. Unlike member arrays, indexed property indices are not limited to integer values and can be of any type.

Declaring indexed properties is similar to declaring scalar properties: To define an indexed property you must supply more parameter indexes to both set and get methods. To get/set the indexed property value you must specify the index values in square brackets.

The following code example defines the **MyClass**, which declares the **Data** property that accepts two integer indices in both get and set methods:

```
#using <mscorlib.dll>
__gc class MyClass {
public:
    // Get-method
    __property int get_Data(int Index1, int Index2) {
        return PropData[Index1][Index2];
    }
    // Set-method
    __property void set_Data(int Index1, int Index2, int Value) {
        PropData[Index1][Index2] = Value;
    }
private:
    int PropData __nogc[10] __nogc[10];
};

void main()
{
    MyClass* obj = new MyClass();
    // Set property value: set_Data method is called
    obj->Data[1][2] = 10;
    // Get property value: get_Data method is called
    System::Console::WriteLine(obj->Data[1][2]);
}
```

Indexes of an indexed property need not be of the same type. For instance you can declare an indexed property corresponding to a database lookup query with individual indexes serving as parameters to the query.

Declaring Interfaces (__interface Keyword)

Multiple inheritance is now out of fashion. After all, Java does not allow multiple inheritance, nor does Common Language Specification. In both Java and .NET multiple inheritance is superceded by *interfaces*. An interface is similar to a pure abstract class: It defines common functionality that can be used by a number of different classes implementing the interface.

Visual C++ .NET provides support for declaring interfaces by introducing the new __**interface** keyword. Interfaces declarations are similar to class declarations, and the following rules apply:

* Interfaces can inherit from zero or more base interfaces.

* Interfaces cannot inherit from a base class.

* Interfaces can only contain public pure virtual methods.

* Interfaces cannot contain constructors, destructors, or operators.

* Interfaces cannot contain static methods.

* Interfaces cannot contain data members.

The following code example illustrates how to define an interface and how to define a class implementing the interface:

```
__interface MyInterface {
    void MyMethod1();
    int MyMethod2(char*);
};
class MyClass: public MyInterface {
    void MyMethod1() {}
    int MyMethod2(char*) { return 0; }
};
```

> **NOTE:** You do not have to explicitly mark interface members as pure virtual by adding = 0 . All interface methods are pure virtual by definition.

When a class implements an interface it must provide bodies for all methods defined by the interface. If the class does not provide implementations for all interface members, the class is considered abstract and cannot be instantiated.

Declaring Value Types (__value Keyword)

Allocating Managed C++ classes on the managed heap is convenient and easy but it comes at a price of decreased performance due to garbage collection. When performance is critical, or when you are dealing with large numbers of small data types you may want to resort to good old stack allocation with the deterministic destruction and efficient memory management scheme.

Because managed classes defined using the __gc keyword cannot be allocated on stack, Visual C++ .NET provides a new __**value** keyword that allows declaring managed *value types* that unlike __gc-classes support stack allocation. Value types are meant to represent small data items with short life times. Value types can be used in declarations of local or global variables, in function parameters and return value, or even in data members in __gc classes.

To declare a value type you must prefix a C++ class or structure definition with the **__value** keyword. Rules for declaring value types are similar to the rules for declaring **__gc** classes, except:

*   Value types cannot server as base classes for any other types (i.e. value types are implicitly sealed);

*   Value types cannot define any virtual methods (because you are denied an opportunity to derive your own class from a value type and override virtual methods);

*   Value types implicitly inherit from **System::ValueType**;

*   Value types can override virtual methods of the **System::ValueType** class;

*   Value types cannot contain managed pointer members.

Besides being allocated on stack, value types can be allocated on unmanaged C++ heap using the **__nogc new** operator, but cannot be allocated on managed heap using the **__gc new** operator unless you define a managed pointer to value type.

The following code example demonstrates the definition of a value type and allocation of a value type object on stack and unmanaged C++ heap:

```
#using <mscorlib.dll>
__value struct MyValueType {
};

void main()
{
   MyValueType Data;                                  // Allocate on stack
   MyValueType* pData = __nogc new MyValueType;  // Allocate on unmanaged heap
   MyValueType* pData2 = new MyValueType;        // C2716 error: can't allocate
                                                      // value type on managed heap
}
```

> **NOTE:** If a value type does not supply a constructor, the CLR automatically initializes all its members with zeros upon creation.

Boxing Value Types (__box Keyword)

All **__gc** classes have common root and inherit from the **System::Object** class. Although value types inherit from the **System::ValueType**, which in turn inherits from the **System::Object**, due to the different memory allocation schemes, value types cannot be directly converted to **Object** pointers. Thus, it is impossible to reference both **__gc**-classes and value types with a generic **Object** class pointer. The lack of a common base between **__gc** classes and value types complicates development of generic classes/routines such as collections and sort functions that could operate on both value types and garbage collected classes.

Managed C++ provides a solution to the problem through value type *boxing*. Boxing is a mechanism for converting value types into **__gc** classes. Boxing of a value type means wrapping it in a **__gc** class. A boxed value type, just like any **__gc** class, inherits from **System::Object** and can be passed to a function expecting an **Object*** parameter.

Unlike in C#, in Managed C++ value types are not boxed automatically. You must box value types explicitly using the __**box** keyword, which has the following syntax:

BoxedValueType* __box(ValueType)

where the *BoxedValueType* is an **Object**-derived type of type __**box** *ValueType**. Thus, the second usage of the __**box** keyword is to declare boxed value types:

__**box** *ValueType* VarName*

> **NOTE:** A boxed value type is represented by a __**gc** pointer and implicitly inherits from the **System::ValueType** class. Thus, you can call the **System::ValueType** methods on the boxed object, but until the value type is boxed, attempts to invoke the **System::ValueType** methods on the object will result in compilation errors.

Boxing of a value type actually creates a copy of the original object. Thus modifications to the boxed value type object will not reflect on the unboxed original. The __**box** keyword creates a new object every time it is used. For improved performance you may want to declare a boxed equivalent of your value type object and use it throughout your code, rather than resort to frequent boxing.

The following code example demonstrates value type boxing and performs the following actions:

1. Declares and instantiates a sample **MyData** value type.
2. Declares a pointer to the boxed **MyData** value type using the __**box** keyword and initializes the pointer by boxing the **ValueData** value type instance using the __**box** keyword.
3. Modifies the boxed value type data.
4. Initializes an **Object** pointer by boxing the **ValueData** variable.

```
#using <mscorlib.dll>
using namespace System;

__value struct MyData {
   int MyInt;
};

void main()
{
   // 1. Instantiate a value type
   MyData ValueData;
   ValueData.MyInt = 10;
   // 2. Declare boxed value type
   MyData __box* BoxedData = __box(ValueData);
   // 3. Modify boxed value type data
   BoxedData->MyInt = 20;
   // 4. Box again
   Object* Obj = __box(ValueData);
}
```

Unboxing Value Types

To unbox a boxed value type you can use direct assignment of a boxed value type instance to an unboxed value type instance:

ValueType VarName = *BoxedValueType

To unbox a value type from an arbitrary __gc pointer you should use the **dynamic_cast** operator:

*ValueType VarName = ****dynamic_cast<__box** ValueType*>*(Pointer)***;**

Similarly to boxing, unboxing creates a copy of the boxed value type.

The following code example illustrates value type unboxing. The code performs the following steps:

1.   Declares and instantiates a sample **MyData** value type.
2.   Declares a pointer to the boxed **MyData** value type using the **__box** keyword and initializes the pointer by boxing the **ValueData** value type instance using the **__box** keyword.
3.   Unboxes the value type using direct assignment.
4.   Boxes the value type into an **Object** pointer and unboxes the value type using the **dynamic_cast** operator.

```
#using <mscorlib.dll>
using namespace System;

__value struct MyData {
   int MyInt;
};

void main()
{
   // 1. Instantiate a value type
   MyData ValueData;
   ValueData.MyInt = 10;
   // 2. Declare boxed value type
   MyData __box* BoxedData = __box(ValueData);
   // 3. Unbox through direct assignment
   MyData ValueData2 = *BoxedData;
   // 4. Unbox through dynamic casting
   Object* Obj = __box(ValueData);
   ValueData2 = *dynamic_cast<__box MyData*>(Obj);
}
```

Using Primitive Types

The C++ language supports a number of primitive types such as **int**, **char**, **float**, and so on. The .NET Framework defines a corresponding value type for each C++ primitive type as shown in Table 2.1.

Table 2.1 C++ primitive types and the corresponding .NET Framework types.

C++ Primitive Type	.NET Framework Type
char	SByte
signed char	SByte
short	Int16
int	Int32
long	Int32
__int64	Int64
unsigned char	Byte
unsigned short	UInt16
unsigned int	UInt32
unsigned long	UInt32
unsigned __int64	UInt64
float	Single
double	Double
void	Void

WARNING! Contrary to standard C++ specification Common Language Specification requires **char** to be an unsigned 8-bit integer (i.e., byte). To make the **char** type to default to **unsigned char** you must compile your code with /J option (same as setting the Default Char Unsigned option to "Yes" on the Language Page in the C/C++ folder on the project Property Pages dialog).

When you use primitive types in Managed C++ code you are in fact using the corresponding value types. Thus you can declare an **int** variable and access the methods of the underlying **Int32** value type:

```
#using <mscorlib.dll>
using namespace System;

void main()
{
   // Same as declaring Int32 a = 10;
   int a = 10;
   // Call the Int32::ToString method
   Console::WriteLine(a.ToString());
}
```

Declaring Managed Pointers

Managed C++ supports two types of pointers: managed and unmanaged. To declare a managed pointer you must prefix the star ('*') in the pointer declaration with the __gc keyword. To declare an unmanaged pointer, on the other hand, you must prefix the star in the pointer declaration with the __nogc keyword:

```
Type __gc* PointerName;      // Managed pointer
Type __nogc* PointerName;    // Unmanaged pointer
```

When declaring pointers, __gc and __nogc keywords are almost never required because of the following rules:

*   Pointers to managed classes are *always* managed and it is impossible to declare an unmanaged pointer to a managed class;
*   Pointers to unmanaged classes and primitive types are unmanaged by default;
*   Pointers to value types are managed by default;
*   Multilevel pointers to managed classes, i.e., **ManagedClass*** ...*** default to **ManagedClass __gc* __gc* __nogc*... __nogc***;
*   Multilevel pointers to value types, i.e. **ValueType*** ...*** default to **ValueType __gc* __nogc* __nogc*... __nogc***.

Managed pointer is the most commonly used data type in Managed C++ because in order to instantiate a managed class you must declare a managed pointer, plus all of the .NET Framework Class Library classes accept managed pointers as parameters to their methods.

Using Interior and Whole Pointers

Managed C++ distinguishes two types of __gc pointers: *whole* and *interior*. Although both types of pointers point to managed heap their behavior is different. The whole pointers point to *whole* objects, while the interior pointers can point to sub-objects contained in a managed class or to value types. Just like ordinary C++ pointers, the interior pointers permit increment/decrement operators.

> **NOTE:** Any __gc pointer to a __value class is an interior pointer.

The following code example illustrates the declaration of an interior pointer to the array of characters, and an interior pointer to a managed class data member:

```
#using <mscorlib.dll>

__gc struct MyManagedClass {
    MyManagedClass* pNext;
};

void main()
{
    // Interior pointer to the array of characters
    char __gc* pChar = new char[1024];
    pChar++;        // OK, interior pointer

    MyManagedClass* pClass = new MyManagedClass();
    pClass++;       // Error, whole pointer

    // Interior pointer to a managed class member
    MyManagedClass** pNextPtr = &pClass->pNext;
    pNextPtr++;     // OK, interior pointer
}
```

You do not have to do anything to declare interior or whole pointers. Compiler and CLR differentiate pointers for you. There are a few things to remember, however. Since it is much harder for CLR to keep track of interior pointers, the interior pointers are not allowed as class members. Therefore, the following construct will result in a compilation error:

```
__gc struct MyManagedClass {
    MyManagedClass* pNext;  // OK, whole pointer
    int __gc* pInt;   // C3160: can not declare interior pointer as a member
};
```

Also, you cannot declare global __gc pointers of any kind, nor can you declare managed pointers as members of unmanaged (__nogc) classes.

Pinning Pointers (__pin Keyword)

Occasionally you may want to pass managed data, including managed classes and managed value pointers, as parameters to unmanaged (i.e., native C++) functions. But the compiler prohibits direct conversion from a __gc pointer to a __nogc pointer because the garbage collector may move the __gc pointer in the managed heap rendering its address stored in a __nogc pointer invalid.

To restrict the managed object dislocation and to allow implicit conversion between __gc and __nogc pointers, you should declare a *pinning pointer* to a managed object using the __pin keyword:

```
Type __pin* PointerName;  // Pinning pointer
```

When you initialize a pinning pointer with a pointer to a managed object, the managed object becomes fixed (i.e., pinned) in managed heap until the pinning pointer is initialized with another value or NULL reference, or goes out of scope. Thus, when a managed object is pinned you can safely convert the pinning pointer to a **__nogc** pointer without worrying that the object may be moved by the garbage collector.

Also, it is possible to convert unmanaged (**__nogc**) pointers back to pinning pointers when the pinning pointer is an interior pointer.

The following code snippet illustrates how to pin convert a managed pointer to unmanaged pointer by pinning:

```
// Create managed array
char __gc* ManagedArray = new char[1024];
// Pin the managed array
char __pin* PinnedPtr = ManagedArray;
// Obtain the unmanaged pointer to the managed array
char* NativeArray = PinnedPtr;
```

> **NOTE:** Pinning a sub-object of a managed class pins the entire managed class.

Using Address-Of Operator

Since value types can be allocated either on the managed or on the C++ heap, the address-of operator (**&**) applied to a value type pointer can return either a **__gc** pointer or a **__nogc** pointer. Fortunately, the implicit conversion between **__nogc** and **__gc** pointers is allowed. Here's an example:

```
char __nogc* pUnanagedPtr = new char[1024];
char __gc* pManagedPtr = pUnanagedPtr;   // OK, implicitly converted
```

The garbage collector detects that a **__gc** pointer actually points to the C++ heap and does not perform garbage collection on the object.

Reverse conversion from **__gc** to **__nogc** is not possible to accomplish directly. Instead, you must use pinning pointers for **__gc** to **__nogc** pointer conversion (see the "Pinning Pointers" section above).

The address of a static class member for both **__gc** and **__nogc** classes returns an unmanaged **__nogc** pointer if the static member is of a primitive type. The address of a static class member of managed type is always a **__gc** pointer.

Dynamic Pointer Casting (**dynamic_cast** Operator)

.NET Framework Class Library extensively uses **Object*** parameters in class methods and employs pointer casting to convert the **Object*** pointers to a desired type.

The most common type of casting is *dynamic*. Dynamic casting allows converting a base class pointer to a pointer to a derived class and performs necessary runtime checks to ensure that such conversion is valid. Dynamic casting is effected by means of the **dynamic_cast** operator, which has the following syntax:

*TargetType*** dynamic_cast<*TargetType***>(*Pointer*)

where *Pointer* is the source pointer, and the *TargetType* is the desired type.

The **dynamic_cast** operator returns a pointer to the *TargetType* if the conversion is successful or returns **NULL** otherwise.

> NOTE: The **dynamic_cast** can be used to convert both **__gc** and **__nogc** pointers. Also, the **dynamic_cast** can not be used to convert value type pointers.

The following code example demonstrates dynamic pointer casting and performs the following actions:

1.   Dynamically casts an **Object**-pointer to a **MyClass**-pointer using the **dynamic_cast** operator.
2.   Checks the resulting pointer value for NULL to determine if the pointer casting was successful.
3.   Dynamically casts the **Object**-pointer to a **MyClass**-pointer using the **__try_cast** operator inside of a try-catch block and catches the **InvalidCastException** exception in case the try-cast fails.

```
#using <mscorlib.dll>
using namespace System;

__gc class MyClass: public Object {};

void main()
{
   Object* Obj = new MyClass();
   // 1. Dynamic-cast
   MyClass* MyPtr = dynamic_cast<MyClass*>(Obj);
   // 2. Was casting successful?
   if ( MyPtr )
   {
      // Casting successful
   }
   else
   {
      // Casting failed
   }

   try {
      // 3. Try-cast
      MyClass* MyPtr2 = __try_cast<MyClass*>(Obj);
      // Cast successful
   }
   catch(InvalidCastException*) {
      // Try-cast failed
   }
}
```

Try-Casting (__try_cast Operator)

Frequent casting of unknown types with the **dynamic_cast** operator may result in spaghetti code since you should check the return value for zero to determine a successful cast. For a cleaner code you may want to use a throwing version of the dynamic casting operator-**__try_cast**, which has the following syntax:

TargetType* **__try_cast**<*TargetType**>(*Pointer*)

where *Pointer* is the source pointer, and the *TargetType* is the desired type.

The **__try_cast** operator returns a pointer to the target type if the conversion is successful or throws a **System::InvalidCastException,** otherwise.

Static Pointer Casting (**static_cast** Operator)

Dynamic pointer casting is made absolutely safe at the expense of extra computations necessary to perform type checking at runtime. When writing performance-critical code, or when you are absolutely sure about the compatibility of the types being cast, you can use the C++ **static_cast** operator that bypasses the run-time type checking and converts pointers directly. The **static_cast** operator has the following syntax:

TargetType* **static_cast**<*TargetType**>(*Pointer*)

where *Pointer* is the source pointer, and the *TargetType* is the desired type.

The **static_cast** operator *always* returns a pointer to the target type.

> **WARNING! static_cast**-ing of incompatible types may result in corrupt **__gc** pointers and garbage collection failure.

The **static_cast** operator should be used to convert a base type pointer to a derived type pointer. Also, the **static_cast** operator cannot convert value type pointers except for converting from the type **Void***.

Converting Between Unrelated Types (**reinterpret_cast** Operator)

Occasionally you may want to convert between unrelated types, i.e., between classes and integral types. For this purpose you should use the C++ **reinterpret_cast** operator:

TargetType* **reinterpret_cast**<*TargetType**>(*Pointer*)

Although the **reinterpret_cast** operator can be used to convert **__gc** pointers, such practice is not recommended. The **reinterpret_cast** operator poses a threat to the managed memory integrity by allowing you gaining direct access to the managed heap.

The main purpose of the **reinterpret_cast** operator is to convert between pointers and value types other than **Void***.

Constant Casting (**const_cast** Operator)

Just like in standard C++ you can use the **const_cast** operator to remove the **const** attribute from a class. The **const_cast** operator has the following syntax:

TargetType* **const_cast**<*TargetType**>(*Pointer*)

where *Pointer* is the source pointer of type **const** *TargetType**, and the *TargetType* is the desired type.

C-Style Pointer Casting

Despite the wealth of pointer casting operators many C++ programmers continue using C-style pointer casting, which is characterized by the following syntax:

(TargetType*)Pointer

In most cases the C-style pointer casting is equivalent to static casting, considered obsolete and is generally discouraged. C-style pointer casting generates a C4303 compiler warning when converting a base type pointer to a derived type pointer. For based-to-derived type pointer conversion the compiler automatically replaces C-type casting with the **__try_cast** operator to detect unsafe type conversion at runtime.

Declaring Managed References

References in Managed C++ are almost identical to the standard C++ references. You can declare a **__nogc** references for **__nogc** classes or **__gc** references for managed classes:

```
#using <mscorlib.dll>
__gc class MyClass {};
void main()
{
    MyClass& Obj = *new MyClass;
}
```

On one hand, using references yields safer and cleaner code because unlike pointers you cannot modify reference values or set them to zero. Therefore, you can always be sure that an object represented by the reference is valid and not null. On the hand, the .NET Framework Class Library accepts pointers as class method parameters. If you choose to use user references to represent managed types you would have to explicitly convert them to pointers when calling the .NET Framework Class Library method.

Declaring Managed Arrays

No programming language is complete without arrays, and Managed C++ is not an exception. Managed C++ supports both managed (**__gc**) and unmanaged (**__nogc**) arrays. Managed arrays are significantly different from unmanaged arrays both syntactically and semantically. To declare a **__gc** array you must use the **__gc** keyword followed by empty square brackets:

```
Type ArrayName __gc[];
```

> **WARNING!** Unlike in standard C++ you cannot specify the size of the managed array as part of the array declaration.

In standard C++ you can use pointers to represent arrays. The same can not be done in Managed C++ because managed pointers cannot be used with indexes to access array elements.

Managed C++ imposes strict limitations on elements of a managed array: Managed arrays can contain either **__value** types or **__gc** pointers to **__gc** classes. You cannot create a managed array of unmanaged classes or any type of pointers to unmanaged classes. Managed arrays of primitive types are allowed, but managed arrays of pointers to primitive types are not.

Managed arrays are allocated on a managed heap using the **new** operator. The following code snipped illustrate how to declare and allocate an array of managed pointers to **MyBase __gc** class, an array of **int** primitive types, and an array of **Int32** value types:

```
MyBase* ArrayOfPointers[] = new MyBase*[32];      // Array of __gc pointers
int ManagedArray __gc[] = new int __gc[32];       // Array of primitive types
DateTime ManagedArray2[] = new DateTime[32];      // Array of value types
```

When declaring an array of managed types you do not have to specify the **__gc** keyword explicitly. Thus an array of **DateTime** and **MyBase*** is declared without the **__gc** keyword. But you must specify the **__gc** keyword when declaring a managed array of primitive types.

In Managed C++ any **__gc** array implicitly inherits from the **System::Array** class, which is discussed in detail in Chapter 3.

When you allocate a managed array, the array elements are automatically initialized:

*   If a managed array holds pointers or primitive types then the array elements are zero-initialized;

*   If a managed array holds value types and the value type provides the default constructor, CLR uses the default constructor to initialize each array element. Otherwise, data members of each value type element are zero-initialized.

Exploiting Array Covariance

Manage C++ supports *array covariance*. The array covariance is best explained by example. Suppose that you have two managed classes: **BaseType** and **DerivedType**, where the **DerivedType** is derived from the **BaseType**. If you define two arrays of **BaseType** and **DerivedType** pointers, the array covariance allows assigning the array of the **DerivedType** pointers to the array of **BaseType** pointers:

```
BaseType* BaseArray[] = new DerivedType*[16];
```

Array covariance should be exploited carefully. Once you have assigned an array of derived classes to the array of base classes you must treat array elements as pointers to the derived class. Thus, the following code will throw a run-time exception:

```
BaseType* BaseArray[];
DerivedType* DerivedArray[] = new DerivedType*[16];
// OK because of the array covariance
BaseArray = DerivedArray;
// Will throw an TypeMismatchException because
// BaseArray[0] is now of type DerivedType*
BaseArray[0] = new BaseType();
```

Declaring Arrays as Function Return Values

To declare a function that returns a managed array use the following syntax:

```
Type FunctionName()[];
```

If the *Type* in the declaration above is not a pointer to a **__gc** class, you may have to explicitly designate the array as managed by adding the **__gc** keyword in front of the square brackets:

```
Type FunctionName() __gc[];
```

Declaring Multidimensional Arrays

Managed Extensions to C++ supports managed multidimensional arrays. The syntax of a multidimensional managed array declaration is different from the standard C++ syntax: You must use commas to separate array dimensions:

```
Type ArrayName[,];   // 2-dimensional array
Type ArrayName[,,];  // 3-dimensional array
```

To allocate a multidimensional array you must specify array dimensions in the **new** operator:

```
Type ArrayName[,] = new Type[Dimension1, Dimension2];   // 2-D array
Type ArrayName[,,] = new Type[Dimension1, Dimension2, Dimension3];   // 3-D
```

Similarly you must use commas to access array elements:

```
ArrayName[Index1, Index2] = Value;         // 2-dimensional array
Value = ArrayName[Index1, Index2, Index3]; // 3-dimensional array
```

Using Aggregate Array Initialization

Managed C++ supports aggregate initialization of managed arrays by listing the array elements in curly braces:

```
Type ArrayName[] = {value0, value1, …};
```

When you use aggregate initialization, the managed array is automatically allocated on managed heap.

> **WARNING!** Unlike standard C++, Managed C++ does not allow aggregate initialization of a multidimensional __gc arrays.

When using aggregate initialization, you can use the **new** operator and functions to initialize individual array elements. For instance, the following code constructs a three-element array of **Object** pointers and initializes the new **Object** instance, "abc" text string and the string representation of the integer value of 123:

```
Object* MyArray[] = {new Object, new String("abc"), Int32(123).ToString()};
```

Declaring Unmanaged Arrays

You can declare a stack-allocated unmanaged array by preceding the square brackets in the array declaration with the **__nogc** keyword:

```
UnmanagedType ArrayName __nogc[Size];
```

Except for the **__nogc** keyword in the array declaration, the unmanaged array syntax is equivalent to the standard C++ array syntax. When declaring unmanaged arrays you *must* specify the size of the array. Also, multidimensional unmanaged arrays are declared as multidimensional standard C++ arrays where each dimension is enclosed in a separate pair of square brackets as shown here:

```
UnmanagedType ArrayName __nogc[Size1][Size2];  // 2-D array
```

An unmanaged array can hold three types of elements: primitive types, value types, **__nogc** classes, or pointers to **__nogc** classes. Unmanaged arrays of pointers to managed types are not allowed.

You can also use the standard C++ pointer declaration to declare an unmanaged array and later allocate the unmanaged array on unmanaged C++ heap using the **new** operator:

```
UnmanagedType* ArrayName;
ArrayName = new UnmanagedType[NumberOfElements];
```

Declaring Unmanaged (**__nogc**) Classes

If you do not specify the **__gc** keyword in the class definition, the compiler assumes that you are defining an unmanaged class. You can also explicitly declare a class as "unmanaged" using the **__nogc** keyword as shown here:

```
__nogc class UnmanagedClass {
    // ...
};
```

You can use unmanaged classes in your Managed C++ program the same way you work with them in standard C++. Instances of unmanaged classes, as well as pointers and references to unmanaged classes, are treated as unmanaged. You can also create managed pointers to an unmanaged class by adding the **__gc** keyword to a pointer declaration:

```
UnmanagedClass* pUnmanagedPtr;      // Unmanaged pointer
UnmanagedClass __gc* pManagedPtr;   // Managed pointer
```

Managed pointers will be allocated on the managed heap, while unmanaged pointers will be allocated on the unmanaged C++ heap. The **new** operator automatically chooses the proper heap type based on the type of the pointer involved.

Declaring Nested Classes

Managed C++ allows you to declare nested classes. Nested classes can access private and protected members of the surrounding class and have the visibility defined by the preceding **public:**, **private:**, or **protected:** keyword. To define a nested class, simply insert a new class definition inside of an existing class definition, e.g.,

```
#using <mscorlib.dll>
__gc class OuterClass {
public:
    // Nested class declaration
    __gc class NestedClass {};
};
void main()
{
    // Nested class instantiation
    OuterClass::NestedClass* MyNestedClass = new OuterClass::NestedClass();
}
```

You can define **__gc**, **__nogc**, and **__value** classes nested in a **__gc** class. But you cannot declare **__gc** or **__value** classes nested in an unmanaged class.

> **NOTE:** To refer to a nested public class outside the surrounding class, you must precede the nested class name with the surrounding class name in the same way you use namespace prefixes.

Declaring Managed Enumerations

Enumerations are handled in Managed C++ pretty much like in standard C++. To declare an enumeration, you should use the C++ **enum** keyword. If you want to declare an **enum** as a member of a **__gc** or **__value** class you must precede the enumeration definition with the **__value** keyword:

```
__gc class ClassName {
    __value enum EnumName {Value1, Vaslue2, …};
};
```

Managed enumerations implicitly derive from the **System::Enum** class, which in turn derives from the **System::ValueType** class, thus, all managed enumerations are value types.

To refer to an **enum** value, you can simply specify its name if there are no other symbols in your code with the same name. If there are name conflicts, you can refer to an **enum** value by using its fully qualified name prefixed with the **enum** name, e.g., *EnumName::ValueName*.

Managed C++ allows specifying the type of the numeration values by specifying the type name following the enumeration name in the **enum** declaration:

```
__value enum EnumName:ElementType {Value1, Value2, …};
```

The list of allowed enumeration element types includes primitive integral data types (i.e., **int**, **char**, etc.) or the corresponding .NET Framework Class Library value types.

Declaring Function Pointers (__**delegate** keyword)

In Managed C++ callback functions are implemented by means of *delegates*. Delegates are essentially method pointers. Unlike standard C++ function pointers that are loosely typed and can point to only global functions, managed delegates are strictly typed and can point to instance or static methods of a class. To declare a delegate you must declare a function prototype and prefix it with the __**delegate** keyword:

```
__delegate ReturmValueType DelegateName(parameters);
```

The name of the function prototype corresponds to the name of the delegate.

Delegates are managed classes that implicitly derive from the **System::Delegate** class, which is discussed in more detail in Chapter 3. You must use the **new** operator to instantiate a delegate object:

```
DelegateType* DelegateName = new DelegateType(ClassPtr, ClassName::MethodName);
```

The first parameter (*ClassPtr*) to a delegate constructor is a pointer to an instance of a class, and the second parameter is the name of the class method associated with the delegate. If you want to associate a static class method with a delegate, you must specify NULL for the class pointer parameter. In both cases the signature of the class method that you want to associate with a delegate *must* match the delegate definition.

Once you initialize a delegate you can invoke the associated method by calling the delegate **Invoke** method and supplying parameters required by the delegated function.

The following code example illustrates the usage of a delegate type and performs the following actions:

1.   Declares a **MyFunctionDelegate** delegate type using __**delegate** keyword.
2.   Instantiates a **MyDelegate** delegate variable using the **new** operator and the delegate constructor. The **MyDelegate** delegate is associated with the **MyClass::MyFunction** instance method of the **Obj** object.
3.   Invokes the delegate using the **Delegate::Invoke** method.

```
#using <mscorlib.dll>

// 1. Declare a delegate
__delegate void MyFunctionDelegate(int Param);

__gc class MyClass {
public:
   void MyFunction(int Param) {
       System::Console::WriteLine("MyClass:MyFunction()");
   }
};

void main()
{
   MyClass* Obj = new MyClass();
   // 2. Instantiate delegate
   MyFunctionDelegate* MyDelegate = new MyFunctionDelegate(Obj,
       &MyClass:: MyFunction);
   // 3. Invoke delegate
   MyDelegate->Invoke(10);
}
```

> **NOTE:** The delegate name and the class method names need not match. Only function signatures (i.e., return type and parameter types) must match.

Specifying Class Visibility

When developing a class library you may want to specify which classes are to be visible from outside of the assembly and which classes are hidden (i.e., for internal assembly use only). You can do this by typing **public** or **private** global visibility specifiers in front of a class definition:

```
// Public class is accessible from outside the assembly
public __gc class PublicClass {
};
// Private class is inaccessible from outside the assembly
private __gc class PrivateClass {
};
```

All classes are **private** by default. You can apply **public/private** global visibility specifiers to any class definition in your class library, including structure, enumeration, or delegate definitions.

Specifying Class Member Visibility

Managed C++ allows specifying two types of visibility for class members: internal and external. *Internal* visibility is the same as standard C++ visibility, which is defined with respect to other classes within the assembly. *External* visibility is defined with respect to other assemblies. By combining internal and external visibility you can declare a **public** class with internally **public** members that will appear as **private** members externally when you import the class in another assembly.

To specify an external visibility of a class member you must precede member definition with *two* visibility specifiers:

InternalVisibility ExternalVisibility: MemberDefitnition;

For instance the following code snippet defines an externally public **TestClass** with the internally public and externally private field **MyData**:

```
public __gc class TestClass {
public private:
    Int32 MyData;
};
```

> **NOTE:** It makes no sense specifying external member visibility for private classes because you cannot access them from another assembly anyway.

Using a combination of internal and external visibility specifiers may easily create confusion and result in errors since not all combinations of visibility specifiers are legal. There is a rule to remember, however: External visibility cannot be greater than internal. For your convenience all possible combinations of internal and external visibility specifiers are listed in Table 2.2.

> **NOTE:** By default, external member visibility is the same as internal visibility.

Table 2.2 Legal combinations of internal and external member visibility specifiers.

Internal visibility	External visibility	Comment
public	public	Externally and internally public.
public	private	Externally private, internally public.
public	protected	Externally protected, internally public.
private	public	Externally private, internally public.
private	private	Externally and internally private.
private	protected	Externally private, internally protected.
protected	public	Externally protected, internally public.
protected	private	Externally private, internally protected.
protected	protected	Externally and internally protected.

Declaring Managed Operators

Operators are frequently used by C++ programmers for math and data type conversion. Managed C++ classes can declare operators, although the operator declaration syntax is different from standard C++.

To declare an operator you must declare a **static** class member function using the following syntax:

static *ReturnType OperatorName(Parameters)*

where *OperatorName* is the literal operator name.

Unlike standard C++, Managed C++ does not support the **operator** keyword and does not allow operator symbols in the operator declaration. Tables 2.3 and 2.4 list names of all unary and binary operators supported by Managed C++.

Unary operators accept a single parameter, while binary operators accept two parameters. In all cases the first parameter must be of the type as the class declaring the operator. The second parameter can be of any type. All operators, except for the comparison operators, should return a value of the same type as the class declaring the operator. Comparison operators, such as **op_Equality**, **op_Inequality**, **op_GreaterThan**, etc. should return a Boolean value.

Table 2.3 Unary operators.

Literal name	Symbol
op_Decrement	
op_Increment	++
op_Negation	!
op_UnaryNegation	-
op_UnaryPlus	+

Table 2.4 Binary operators.

Literal name	Symbol
op_Addition	+
op_Assign	=
op_BitwiseAnd	&
op_BitwiseOr	|
op_Division	/
op_Equality	==
op_ExclusiveOr	^
op_GreaterThan	>

<Continued on Next Page>

<Table 2.4 Continued>

Literal name	Symbol
op_GreaterThanOrEqual	>=
op_Inequality	!=
op_LeftShift	<<
op_LessThan	<
op_LessThanOrEqual	<=
op_LogicalAnd	&&
op_LogicalOr	||
op_Modulus	%
op_Multiply	*
op_RightShift	>>
op_Subtraction	-

There is a difference in defining operators for __gc-classes and value types: Value type operators can accept parameters passed both by value and by reference, while __gc-class operators can accept only parameters passed by reference. Thus, when you use a __gc-class operator in your code you must convert the operator input parameters to references.

Unfortunately, it is impossible to use operators with pointers to managed classes: Operators executed on pointers are considered by the compiler applicable to the pointer type itself, and the managed class operators can not overload pointer operators.

Still, you can define an operator that accepts pointer parameters. Then in order to use the operator you would have to invoke it as a method using the full operator name and method invocation syntax.

Implementing Operators in Value Types

Follow these steps to define an operator for a value type:

1. In the value type definition declare a static method with the name corresponding to the desired operator literal name.

2. The operator method should accept an instance/instances of the source value type or references to the source __gc-type and return a Boolean value if the operator is a comparison operator or a new instance of the target value type or a reference to a new instance of the target __gc-type (if the operator is a math operator).

    NOTE: Unary operators such as +, -, !, ++, should always accept an instance of the source value type and return a new instance of the source value type. Binary operators should always accept an instance of the source value type in the first parameter and can specify a return value different from the source type.

The code sample shown next demonstrates how to define an equality (==) operator for the **Complex** value type and how to use it to compare instances of the **Complex** class:

```
#using <mscorlib.dll>

// Value type
__value struct Complex {
   Complex(float r, float i) {
      Re = r; Im = i;
   }
   // Equality operator
   static bool op_Equality(const Complex& a, const Complex& b)
   {
      return a.Re == b.Re && a.Im == b.Im;
   }
   float Re, Im;
};

void main()
{
   // Instantiate objects
   Complex a(1, 2);
   Complex b(1, 2);

   // Compare using the op_Equality operator
   if ( a == b )
      System::Console::WriteLine("a equals to b");
   else
      System::Console::WriteLine("a not equals to b");
}
```

Implementing Operators in __gc Classes

Follow these steps to define an operator for a __gc class:

1.   In the __gc class definition, declare a static method with the name corresponding to the desired operator literal name.

2.   The operator method should accept an instance/instances of the source value type or references to the source __gc type and return a Boolean value if the operator is a comparison operator or a new instance of the target value type or a reference to a new instance of the target __gc type if the operator is a math operator.

> **NOTE:** Unary operators such as +, -, !, ++, should always accept a reference to the source __gc type and return a reference to a new instance of the source __gc type. Binary operators should always accept a reference to the source __gc type in the first parameter and can specify a return value different from the source type.

The code sample shown next demonstrates how to define an equality (==) operator for the **Complex __gc** class and how to use it to compare instances of the **Complex** class:

```
#using <mscorlib.dll>

// Managed type
__gc struct Complex {
   Complex(float r, float i) {
      Re = r; Im = i;
   }
   // Equality operators
   static bool op_Equality(const Complex* a, const Complex* b)
   {
      return a->Re == b->Re && a->Im == b->Im;
   }
   static bool op_Equality(const Complex& a, const Complex& b)
   {
      return a.Re == b.Re && a.Im == b.Im;
   }
   float Re, Im;
};

void main()
{
   // Instantiate objects
   Complex* a = new Complex(1, 2);
   Complex* b = new Complex(1, 2);
   // 1. Compare using the operator literal name
   if ( Complex::op_Equality(a, b) )
      System::Console::WriteLine("a equals to b");
   else
      System::Console::WriteLine("a not equals to b");

   // 3. Compare using references
   if ( *a == *b )
      System::Console::WriteLine("a equals to b");
   else
      System::Console::WriteLine("a not equals to b");
}
```

The **Complex** class supplies two versions of the equality operator: one accepting pointers to **Complex** objects and another accepting references to the **Complex** objects. The first version of the operator can be used only if the operator is invoked as an ordinary class method, while the second version of the operator can be invoked using the operator symbol (==) when the pointer operands are converted to references.

Declaring Managed Conversion Operators

C++ programming often involves conversion between different data types. Thus, when programming in Managed C++ it may be helpful to be able to convert from one value or __gc type to another. To facilitate such conversion Managed C++ allows defining *conversion* operators. There are two types of conversion operators:

* *implicit* for lossless conversion;
* *explicit* potentially involves the loss of data and, therefore, should be specified explicitly.

Also, you can define implicit or explicit conversion operators that convert other types to the type of your class (*convert-from* operators), or convert your type to another type (*convert-to* operators).

> **NOTE:** Standard C++ does not directly support convert-from operators.

Declaring Convert-To Operators

To define an implicit/explicit convert-to operator, you must declare an **op_Implicit/op_Explicit** static class member that accepts a parameter of the same type as the class defining the operator and returns an instance of the target class:

static *AnyType* **op_Implicit(***ClassType***)**

static *AnyType* **op_Explicit(***ClassType***)**

Implicit convert-to operator methods are automatically invoked when you are converting the *ClassType* to the target *AnyType* without explicitly casting to the target *AnyType*:

```
ClassType a;
AnyType b;
b = a; // Calls the static AnyType op_Implicit(ClassType) operator method
```

Implicit convert-to operator methods are invoked when you are converting the *ClassType* to the target *AnyType* and explicitly cast to the target *AnyType*:

```
ClassType a;
AnyType b;
b = (AnyType)a; // Calls the static AnyType op_Explicit(ClassType) operator
```

Implementing Convert-To Operators in Value Types

Follow these steps to implement an implicit/explicit convert-to operator in a value type:

1. In the value type definition, declare a static **op_Implicit** method for an implicit convert-to operator or a static **op_Explicit** method for an explicit convert-to operator.
2. The **op_Implicit/op_Explicit** method operator should accept an instance of the source type (i.e., the value type where the operator is defined) and return a reference to a new instance of the target __gc-type or new instance of the target value type.
3. To use the defined implicit convert-to operator in the code you must assign an instance of the source value type to a reference to the target __gc-type or the target value type instance.

4.   To use the defined explicit convert-to operator in the code, you must use explicit C-style casting when assigning an instance of the source value type to a reference to the target __**gc**-type or the target value type instance.

The code sample shown next demonstrates how to define an implicit convert-to-**int** operator and an explicit convert-to-**String** operator for the value type **MyIntClass**:

```
#using <mscorlib.dll>
using namespace System;

// Value type
__value class MyIntClass {
public:
    MyIntClass(int Value) { IntValue = Value; }
    // Implicit conversion operator
    static int op_Implicit(MyIntClass v)
    {
        return v.IntValue;
    }
    // Explicit conversion operator
    static String* op_Explicit(MyIntClass v)
    {
        return v.IntValue.ToString();
    }
private:
    int IntValue;
};

void main()
{
    MyIntClass Obj(100);
    // 1. Convert to int using op_Implicit operator
    int myInt = Obj;
    // 2. Convert to String using op_Explicit operator
    String* myString = (String*)Obj;
}
```

This code example defines an implicit convert-to-**int** operator and an explicit convert-to-**String*** operator. Note that when using the operators you do not have to explicitly cast to **int** and must explicitly cast to **String***.

Implementing Convert-To Operators in __gc-Classes

Follow these steps to implement an implicit/explicit convert-to operator in a __gc-class:

1. In the __gc-class definition declare a static **op_Implicit** method for implicit convert-to operator or static **op_Explicit** method for explicit convert-to operator.

2. The **op_Implicit/op_Explicit** method operator should accept a reference of the source type (i.e., the __gc-class where the operator is defined) and return a reference to a new instance of the target __gc-type or new instance of the target value type.

    NOTE: If you define the **op_Implicit/op_Explicit** operators that accept a pointer to the source type rather than a reference, the only way of using the operators will be to invoke them as ordinary class members.

3. To use the defined implicit convert-to operator in your code, you must assign a reference of the source __gc-type to a reference to the target __gc-type or the target value type instance.

4. To use the defined explicit convert-to operator in your code, you must use explicit C-style casting when assigning a reference of the source __gc-type to a reference to the target __gc-type or the target value type instance.

The code sample shown next demonstrates how to define an implicit convert-to-**int** operator and an explicit convert-to-**String** operator for managed class **MyIntClass**.

```
#using <mscorlib.dll>
using namespace System;

// Managed type
__gc class MyIntClass {
public:
    MyIntClass(int Value) { IntValue = Value; }
    // Implicit conversion operator
    static int op_Implicit(MyIntClass& v)
    {
        return v.IntValue;
    }
    // Explicit conversion operator
    static String* op_Explicit(MyIntClass& v)
    {
        return v.IntValue.ToString();
    }
private:
    int IntValue;
};

void main()
{
    MyIntClass* Obj = new MyIntClass(100);
    // 1. Convert to int using op_Implicit operator
    int myInt = *Obj;
    // 2. Convert to String using op_Explicit operator
    String* myString = (String*)*Obj;
}
```

When declaring a convert-to operators for **__gc** classes you should supply a reference to the class as an operator parameter. Thus, if in your code you declare a pointer to the managed class you must convert it to a reference using the * operator before you can invoke an implicit/explicit conversion operator though the variable assignment.

Declaring Convert-From Operators

To define an implicit/explicit convert-from operator you must declare an **op_Implicit/op_Explicit** static class member that accepts a parameter of the type you are converting from and returns an instance of your class:

static *ClassType* **op_Implicit**(*AnyType*)

static *ClassType* **op_Explicit**(*AnyType*)

Unfortunately, convert-from operators are never invoked automatically and must be used as ordinary class members.

Declaring "Initialize-From" Constructors

Using explicitly qualified convert-from operators results in rather clumsy looking code. If you are working with value types and looking for a more elegant solution, you should use *initialize-from* constructors rather than convert-from operators.

To define an "initialize-from" constructor, it is sufficient to declare a constructor accepting a single value of the source type. Such "initialize-from" constructor is called implicitly when you initialize a value type variable using an instance of the source type class.

The following code illustrates implicit "initialize-from" constructor usage. The code defines the **MyIntClass** that provides an "initialize-from" constructor for the **int** source type. The constructor is implicitly called when an instance of **MyIntClass** is initialized with an integer value.

```
#using <mscorlib.dll>

__value class MyIntClass {
public:
    // "Initialize-from" constructor
    MyIntClass(int IntValue)
    {
        MyIntValue = IntValue;
    }
private:
    int MyIntValue;
};

void main()
{
    int IntValue = 100;
    MyIntClass MyInt = IntValue;   // Invokes MyIntClass(int)
}
```

You can define as many initialize-from constructors as you want to initialize an instance of your value type from whatever source type you want.

Using Attributes

Managed C++ introduces a new concept into the C++ language *attributes*. Attributes allow extending class metadata with custom properties that can be examined at runtime both by CLR and by application code itself by means of the .NET *reflection* mechanism. The goal of managed attributes is to specify additional information about code elements such as classes, class members, member parameters, etc. This additional information is examined at runtime by the CLR and used to control the behavior of the element to which the attributes apply: for instance, you can mark the class definition with the **Serializable** attribute to indicate that the class can be serialized in a stream.

Syntactically attributes correspond to keywords enclosed in square brackets:

```
[attribute] AttributeTarget
```

The square brackets define the attribute block, and the *AttributeTarget* specifies the target source code element to which the attribute applies. Attribute blocks can contain multiple attributes separated by a coma, e.g.:

```
[Serializable, CLSCompliant(FALSE)]
__gc class MyClass { … };
```

More complex attributes can accept one or more parameters enclosed in parentheses:

```
[attribute(ParamName1="param value", param2=ParamValue2, ParamValue3)]
```

Attribute parameters can accept values of various types: text strings, integers, enumeration values, and can be optional or required. There are two ways for specifying attribute parameter values:

*   *By name* by specifying *ParamName=ParamValue* pairs;
*   *By position* by specifying comma-separated parameter values.

With the first approach you can put parameters in arbitrary order. The second approach requires specifying parameter values in the order they appear in the attribute definition. You can mix both named and positional attribute initialization syntax by initializing positional parameters first and initializing named parameters second (positional parameters cannot follow named parameters).

Managed attributes correspond to managed classes derived from the **System::Attribute** class. The attribute name is the same as the **System::Attribute**-derived class name. If the attribute class name ends with the "Attribute" suffix, you can omit the latter from the attribute name when applying the attribute. For instance if there is an attribute class called **MyAttribute** the following constructs are legal:

```
[MyAttribute]  // Full name
[My]  // Short name
```

The positional attribute initialization syntax corresponds to the attribute class constructors, while the name/value syntax corresponds to initializing public properties of the attribute class. For instance, if you have an attribute class **MyAttribute** that provides a default constructor, a constructor accepting a single text value, and a public integer property **Value** that you can initialize the attribute in the following ways:

```
[MyAttribute]  // Default constructor
[MyAttribute("text")] // Second constructor
[MyAttribute("text", Value=123)] // Second constructor + property
[MyAttribute(Value=123)] // Default constructor + property initialization
```

You can define your own attribute classes and use them to extend your code metadata. For details on using custom attributes to extend your code metadata see Chapter 4.

Specifying Global Attribute Context

Most attributes can be applied only to certain code elements: For instance some attributes can be applied only to class definitions, others only to class member parameters. Thus, attributes can be used only in a particular *attribute context* specified in the attribute class definition.

Some attributes are *global* and do not apply to a particular code element. Global attributes can be inserted anywhere in the code, and the attribute block that hosts the global attributes must be terminated with a semicolon (;):

```
[GlobalAttribute];
```

Specifying Global Assembly Attributes

Global attributes can be applied to the current .NET module or to the current assembly. The global assembly attributes allow specifying metadata to be stored in the assembly manifest and have the following syntax:

```
[assembly:attribute];
```

The most commonly used global assembly attributes are defined in **System::Reflection** namespace. These are:

* **AssemblyTitleAttribute**–specifies user-friendly assembly name;

* **AssemblyDescriptionAttribute**–specifies textual assembly description;

* **AssemblyConfigurationAttribute**–specifies assembly configuration: "retail", "debug", "beta", "pre-release", etc;

* **AssemblyCompanyAttribute**–specifies a company name, which created the assembly;

* **AssemblyProductAttribute**–specifies a product name, which the assembly is a part of;

* **AssemblyCopyrightAttribute**–specifies copyright information;

* **AssemblyTrademarkAttribute**–specifies trademark information;

* **AssemblyCultureAttribute**–specifies culture information. Specify empty string ("") to designate the main assembly containing executable code, or specify culture information (i.e. "en", "de", "es", etc.) to indicate a satellite (i.e. resource-only) assembly containing locale-specific resources;

* **AssemblyVersionAttribute**–specifies assembly version information in the format "*major.minor.build.revision*". You do not have to specify the build and revision numbers and can use '*' for default build and revision values, e.g., "1.2.*";

* **AssemblyDelaySignAttribute**–specify "yes" to reserve a space in the assembly manifest for a signature when you do not have the private key and somebody else is going to sign the assembly later using the SN.exe or similar utility;

* **AssemblyKeyFileAttribute**–specifies a key file name for the assembly (i.e., "myKey.snk". You should specify the key file name when you want to assign your assembly a strong name. The key file path must be relative your project's path;

* **AssemblyKeyNameAttribute**–specifies the name of a cryptographic key (e.g., "myKey") that is already installed in the Crypto Service Provider. If the key is not installed and you specified a key file name using the **AssemblyKeyFileAttribute** attribute, the key from the key file will be installed.

  NOTE: You can add **using namespace System::Reflection** statement to the source file where you define global assembly attributes to avoid explicit qualifications of the attribute names with the namespace prefix.

Global assembly attributes can be inserted anywhere in the code. For convenience, projects, generated using the Visual C++ .NET Application Wizard, contain a separate AssemblyInfo.cpp file that represents a placeholder for the global assembly attributes. You do not have to modify any of the wizard-generated attributes, but you are welcome to do so to specify additional information about your managed application/assembly.

Declaring Functions with Variable Number of Arguments

Managed C++ does not support class member functions with a variable number of arguments; Therefore, the following declaration will not compile:

```
__gc struct Test {
   void MyFunc(...) { }   // C3269 error
};
```

Yet other .NET languages such as C# support functions with variable number of arguments. Managed C++ provides a workaround that involves using **ParamArray** attribute. Simply declare a class method that accepts an array of **Object** pointers and apply the **ParamArray** attribute to the array parameter:

```
ReturnType FunctionName([ParamArray] Object* Args[]);
```

Since Managed C++ does not support member functions with variable number of arguments, in Managed C++ code you would have to initialize the array parameter manually. When used in C#, however, the member function will support variable number of arguments thanks to the **ParamArray** attribute.

Mixing Managed and Unmanaged Code

The true power of Managed C++ comes from the fact that you can freely combine and mix managed C++ code with unmanaged code. There are important rules to remember, however.

Using Unmanaged Classes as Members of Managed Types

You can declare an unmanaged class nested in a managed class. To declare an unmanaged nested class you must prefix its declaration with the **__nogc** keyword:

```
__gc class ManagedClass {
    ...
    __nogc class UnmanagedClass { ... };
};
```

Also, you can declare unmanaged classes as members of a managed class:

```
__nogc class UnmanagedClass { ... };

__gc class ManagedClass {
    ...
    UnmanagedClass MemberName;
};
```

To access an unmanaged member of a managed class, you must pin the managed class first, or the code will not compile (without pinning the unmanaged class you can't safely use the **this** pointer).

The following code example demonstrates how to use an unmanaged class as a member of a managed type and performs the following actions:

1.   Define an unmanaged class **UnmanagedClass**.

2.   Define a managed type **ManagedClass** that contains the **Unmanaged** field of type **UnmanagedClass**.

3.   In the main program code, instantiates a **ManagedClass** object, declare a pinning pointer to the **ManagedClass** using the **__pin** keyword, and initialize the pointer with the **__gc** pointer to the **ManagedClass**.

4.   Access the unmanaged class in the **Unmanaged** field of the **ManagedClass** by invoking the **UnmanagedClass::UnmanagedMethod** method on the pinned pointer.

```
#using <mscorlib.dll>

// Unmanaged class
__nogc class UnmanagedClass {
public:
    void UnmanagedMethod() {}
};

// Managed type
__gc class ManagedClass {
public:
    // Member of unmanaged type
    UnmanagedClass Unmanaged;
};

void main()
{
    // Create __gc pointer to managed class
    ManagedClass* Obj = new ManagedClass();
    // Create pinned pointer to managed class
    ManagedClass __pin* PinnedClass = Obj;
    // Access unmanaged member
    PinnedClass->Unmanaged.UnmanagedMethod();
}
```

Declaring Managed Pointers as Members of Unmanaged Classes

While you can create an unmanaged class as member of a managed type, you can not declare a managed type (i.e., pointers or references to the managed type) as member of an unmanaged class directly. Instead, Visual C++ .NET provides a workaround that allows declaring *virtual* __gc pointers as unmanaged class members.

To declare a __gc pointer as a member of an unmanaged class, you must include the vcclr.h header file in your Managed C++ source and use the **gcroot** template class to wrap the managed pointer in the unmanaged class:

```
__nogc class UnmanagedClass {
    ...
    gcroot<ManagedClass*> MemberName;
};
```

Once you wrap the managed pointer using the **gcroot** template, you can use the wrapped managed class pointer just like any other __gc pointer.

The code example shown next demonstrates declaration of the __gc pointer to the managed type **ManagedClass** as the **Managed** data member of the unmanaged class **UnmanagedClass**. In the main program code the **Managed** data member is allocated as an ordinary __gc pointer using the **new** operator, and the method

ManagedClass::ManagedMethod is invoked.

```
#using <mscorlib.dll>
#include <vcclr.h>

// Managed type
__gc class ManagedClass {
public:
    void ManagedMethod()
    {
        System::Console::WriteLine("In managed code");
    }
};

// Unmanaged class
__nogc class UnmanagedClass {
public:
    // Managed member
    gcroot<ManagedClass*> Managed;
};

void main()
{
    UnmanagedClass Obj;
    // 1. Instantiate managed member of unmanaged class
    Obj.Managed = new ManagedClass();
    // 2. Call managed method
    Obj.Managed->ManagedMethod();
```

Passing Managed Pointers to Unmanaged Code

To pass managed pointers as parameters to unmanaged functions, you must undertake the following actions:

1. Declare a pinning pointer to the managed type using the **__pin** keyword.
2. Assign the value of the managed pointer to the pinning pointer.
3. Call the unmanaged code function/method supplying the pinning pointer instead of the managed pointer.

The following code example demonstrates how to declare and initialize a pinning pointer to a managed type, and how to use it to invoke an unmanaged function supplying the pinned object class member as parameter:

```
#using <mscorlib.dll>

// Unmanaged function
void UnmanagedFunc(int* pValue)
{
    *pValue = 10;
}

// Managed type
__gc struct ManagedClass {
    int SomeValue;
};

void main()
{
    ManagedClass* Obj = new ManagedClass();
    // 1. Declare and initialize pinning pointer to Obj
    ManagedClass __pin* PinObj = Obj;
    // 2. Call unmanaged function
    UnmanagedFunc(&PinObj->SomeValue);
    // This statement will not compile
    //UnmanagedFunc(&Obj->SomeValue);
}
```

Creating Managed Applications

Follow these steps to create a new Managed C++ application using the Visual C++ .NET Application Wizard:

1.   Select File | New | Project menu item.
2.   Pick Managed C++ Application from the list of templates, type project name *ProjectName*, and click OK to generate the code.

Visual C++ .NET will automatically generate a sample "Hello World" application project containing *ProjectName*.cpp and AssemblyInfo.cpp files. The *ProjectName*.cpp contains your program entry point: **main** routine for ASCII character set console applications, **_tmain** for multibyte character set console applications, or **WinMain** for Windows applications.

You can also create a Managed C++ application manually by following these steps:

1.   Select File | New | Project menu item.
2.   Pick Managed C++ Empty Project from the list of templates, type project name *ProjectName*, and click OK to generate the code.
3.   Create a new C++ file named *ProjectName*.cpp and type the following code required to support a managed executable:

```
#using <mscorlib.dll>
using namespace System;

int main(int argc, char* argv[])
{
    return 0;
}
```

Creating Managed Class Libraries

Follow these steps to create a managed class library (i.e., a managed assembly DLL) using the Visual C++ .NET Application Wizard:

1. Select File | New | Project menu item.

2. Pick Managed C++ Library from the list of templates, type in the project name *ProjectName,* and click OK to generate the code.

3. Open the *ProjectName*.h header file and insert the definitions of your classes, delegates, enumerations, and so on within the *ProjectName* **namespace** scope (public classes and externally public class members should be prefixed with the **public** visibility specifiers):

```
#using <mscorlib.dll>
using namespace System;

// Class library namespace
namespace ProjectName {
    // Public class definition
    public __gc class ClassName {
        // Public method definition
        public: ReturnType MethodName(Parameters);
        ...
    };
    ...
}
```

4. Open the *ProjectName*.cpp source file and provide implementations for the class methods defined in the header file (you should include the **using namespace *ProjectName*** statement at the top of the file to reference classes defined within the *ProjectName* namespace scope without the namespace prefix):

```
#include "ProjectName.h";
using namespace ProjectName;

// Class member implementation
ReturnType ClassName::MethodName(Parameters)
{
    ...
}
```

You can also create a Managed C++ application manually by following these steps:

1. Select File | New | Project menu item.

2. Pick Managed C++ Empty Project from the list of templates, type project name *ProjectName,* and click OK to generate the code.

3. Open the Project Property Pages dialog and on the General page set the Configuration Type option to the "Dynamic Library (.dll)."

4. Create new C++ file named *ProjectName*.h header file, declare the *ProjectName* **namespace,** and within the namespace scope insert definitions of public classes, delegates, enumerations, and so on (public classes and externally public class members should be prefixed with the **public** visibility specifiers).

    Create new C++ file named *ProjectName*.cpp and provide bodies for the class members defines in the header file (you should include the **using namespace *ProjectName*** statement at the top of the file to reference classes defined within the *ProjectName* namespace scope without the namespace prefix).

Creating Multimodule Assemblies

If you want to share common classes among different assemblies, you can create a shared assembly (which would have to be strong-named). Alternatively, you can compile the common code into a .NET module (.netmodule-file). Then, when building another assembly, you can specify the .NET module as a part of the assembly.

To create a .NET module file you must follow these steps:

1. Create a new Managed C++ Class Library project using the Visual C++ .NET project wizard.

2. Add definitions of the common classes to the class library header file and provide implementations of the class members to the class library C++ source file.

3. Remove AssemblyInfo.cpp file from the project if there is one.

4. Open the Project Property Pages dialog and change the Output File extension from .dll to .netmodule on the General page in the Linker folder.

5. Turn off assembly generation by setting the Turn Off Assembly Generation option to Yes (same as /NOASSEMBLY linker option) on the Advanced page in the Linker folder on the project Property Pages dialog.

Build the module project to generate a .netmodule-file.

> **NOTE:** It is OK for different .NET module files in an assembly to define their own namespaces.

To add the generated .NET module to another assembly open the assembly project and specify the module file name in the Add Module to Assembly edit box (same as /ASSEMBLYMODULE:*FileName* linker option) on the Input page in the Linker folder on the project Property Pages dialog. Then build the assembly project.

> **WARNING!** When distributing the multimodule assembly do not forget to distribute the .netmodule files included in the assembly.

Creating Shared/Strong-Named Assemblies

To create a shared assembly that can be deployed to global assembly cache and accessed by any .NET applications, the assembly must be signed with a strong name. Follow these steps to create a strong-named assembly:

1. If you do not have an assembly already, create a new assembly using the Visual C++ .NET Application wizard.

2. Generate a key pair using the SN.exe utility by running the following command:

    ```
    SN.exe -k KeyFile.snk
    ```

    NOTE: If you used the default installation directories for Visual Studio .NET then the SN.exe utility can be found in the \Program Files\Microsoft Visual Studio .NET\FrameworkSDK\Bin directory.

3. Copy the generated *KeyFile*.snk key pair file into the assembly project folder.

4. Specify the signature attributes in the AssemblyInfo.cpp file or where you reserved place for global assembly attributes:

    ```
    [assembly:AssemblyDelaySignAttribute(false)];
    [assembly:AssemblyKeyFileAttribute("KeyFile.snk")];
    ```

5. Build the assembly.

Delay-Signing Assemblies

When developing .NET application/shared assemblies you may not have access to the private key at all times: the private key is usually a closely guarded commodity. Thus, you may have to partially sign your assembly with the public key and rely on somebody else to fully sign the assembly with the private key at a later time (i.e., *delay-sign* the assembly).

To delay-sign an assembly you must have a *PubKeyFile*.snk key file containing the public key at compile time. You can extract the public key from a public/private key pair by executing the following command:

```
SN.exe -p KeyPairFile.snk PubKeyFile.snk
```

NOTE: If you used the default installation directories for Visual Studio .NET then the SN.exe utility can be found in the \Program Files\Microsoft Visual Studio .NET\FrameworkSDK\Bin directory.

Then follow these steps to delay-sign an assembly:

1. Specify the signature attributes in the AssemblyInfo.cpp file or where you reserved place for global assembly attributes:

    ```
    [assembly:AssemblyDelaySignAttribute(true)];
    [assembly:AssemblyKeyFileAttribute("KeyFile.snk")];
    ```

2.   Build the assembly. For debugging and testing purposes register the assembly for verification skipping by executing the following command:

```
SN.exe -Vr AssemblyName
```

NOTE: If you enable verification skipping for an assembly you can deploy the assembly into the global assembly cache on your local system despite the fact that the assembly is only partially signed. Thus enabling of the verification skipping allows debugging and testing of a partially signed shared assembly deployed into GAC.

3.   At a later time fully sign the assembly using the SN.exe utility:

```
SN.exe -R AssemblyName KeyPairFile.snk
```

NOTE: You can unregister the fully signed assembly from verification skipping by executing the following command: SN.exe—Vu *AssemblyName*.

.NET System Namespace: Arrays, Strings, Delegates, and Other Essential Classes

QUICK JUMPS

CHAPTER 3

.NET System Namespace: Arrays, Strings, Delegates, and Other Essential Classes

In Depth

The System namespace represents the foundation of the .NET Framework Class Library. The namespace contains base classes and interfaces from which all other types in the framework derive. Some of these classes defined in the System namespace, such as **Object**, **Array**, and **Enum,** serve as implicit base classes for managed classes, arrays, and enumerations. In this chapter, you will learn about the System namespace classes including **Object**, **Array**, **String**, **DateTime**, and **Console** and how to use them. Be prepared to see lots of tables summarizing class constructors, properties, and methods.

System Namespace Class Hierarchy

Table 1.3 in Chapter 1 illustrated that the .NET Framework is equipped with an immense class library that is intended to address the full spectrum of programming needs. The .NET Framework Class Library is organized as a hierarchy of *namespaces* where each namespace groups together types optimized for a specific task. In the root of the .NET Framework namespace hierarchy lies the System namespace that defines fundamental types from which all other .NET classes are derived. Therefore, any .NET programming project requires types from the System namespace, and virtually all managed C++ programs include the following two lines as the first two statements of the code:

```
#using <mscorlib.dll>
using namespace System;
```

The majority of the System namespace classes are defined in the mscorlib.dll assembly; therefore, you must reference the assembly in your code using the **#using** statement. The System namespace is quite large and this book dedicates two chapters (this chapter and Chapter 4) to covering it. All System namespace types can be divided in five categories:

* *classes*: ordinary managed types defined using the __**gc class** keyword.

* *structures*: managed types defined using the __**gc struct** keyword.

> **NOTE:** All System namespace structures are in fact *value types* and derived from the **ValueType** class.

* *attributes*: managed classes derived from the **System::Attribute** class.

* *exceptions*: managed classes derived from the **System::Exception** class.

* *enumerations*: managed enumerations defined using the **enum** keyword.

NOTE: All managed enumerations are implicitly derived from the **System::Enum** class.

The complete System namespace class hierarchy is presented in Appendix D. The System namespace's general classes, attributes, exceptions, structures, and their descriptions are listed in Tables 3.1 through 3.4.

Table 3.1 System namespace general classes.

Class	Description
Activator	Allows creating objects locally or remotely and obtaining references to existing remote objects.
AppDomain	Represents an application domain, an isolated environment for running .NET executables.
AppDomainSetup	Represents an application-domain setup information.
Array	Base class for all managed arrays.
AssemblyLoadEventArgs	Represents data for the **AssemblyLoad** event.
Attribute	Base class for custom attributes.
BitConverter	Allows converting primitive types such as **int**, **double**, and so on into managed arrays of bytes and vice versa.
Buffer	Allows copying, reading, and writing managed arrays on byte level.
CharEnumerator	Allows read-only access to **String** object characters.
Console	Implements console I/O.
ContextBoundObject	Base class for all context-bound classes.
Convert	Allows conversion among primitive types, **String***, **Object***, and **DateTime** types.
DBNull	Represents a database Null value.
Delegate	Base class for delegates.
Enum	Base class for enumerations.
Environment	Allows querying environment variables and other information including the OS version, computer and user name, system directory path, program exit code, logical drives, command-line arguments, current directory, and so on.
EventArgs	Base class for event data.
Exception	Base exception class.
GC	Allows controlling the garbage collection.
LocalDataStoreSlot	Implements thread-local and context-local data storage.
MarshalByRefObject	Base class for objects capable of communicating across application-domain boundaries by exchanging messages via proxy.
Math	Contains math constants such as *e* and *pi*, as well as trigonometric, logarithmic, and other math functions.
MulticastDelegate	Multicast delegate a delegate capable of containing multiple method pointers in its invocation list.

<Continued on Next Page>

<Table 3.1 Continued>

Class	Description
Object	The root of the .NET Framework Class hierarchy.
OperatingSystem	Allows obtaining OS platform and version information.
Random	Pseudorandom number generator.
ResolveEventArgs	Represents data for the **TypeResolve**, **ResourceResolve**, and **AssemblyResolve** events.
String	Immutable character string.
SystemException	Base class for all .NET Framework Class Library exceptions. The class differentiates between system and user-defined exceptions.
TimeZone	Time zone.
Type	The root of all reflection operations, also represents class, interface, array, value, and enumeration type information.
UnhandledExceptionEventArgs	Represents data for the event that is raised when an unhandled exception occurs.
Uri	Represents a Uniform Resource Identifier URI (URLs are a subset of URIs).
UriBuilder	Provides constructors for common URIs and useful operations for modifying URI parameters.
ValueType	Base class for value types.
Version	Represents a version number.
WeakReference	Represents a weak reference to an object. The weak reference allows you to access the object while it won t keep the object from being garbage collected if no strong references to the object exists.

Table 3.2 System namespace attributes.

Attribute constructor	Description
AttributeUsage	Attribute for specifying attribute usage rules and requirements when defining custom attributes.
CLSCompliant	Attribute for indicating CLS-compliant or incompliant assemblies, classes, or class members.
ContextStatic	Attribute for indicating static members unique for a particular context.
Flags	Attribute for indicating **enum** values as bit fields.
LoaderOptimization	Attribute for instructing the assembly loader to optimize an assembly for usage in a single or multiple application domains. The attribute is applicable only to the assembly entry point function or method.
MTAThread	Attribute for specifying the multithreaded apartment (MTA) threading model for a COM interoperability application.
NonSerialized	Attribute for indicating nonserializable fields of a serializable class.

<Continued on Next Page>

<Table 3.2 Continued>

Class	Description
Obsolete(*msg, error*)	Attribute for marking classes as obsolete or deprecated. The *msg* message will be printed at compile time. Set the *error* parameter to **true** to prevent compilation of classes marked as obsolete from succeeding.
ParamArray	Attribute for indicating an array parameter in a function accepting a variable number of arguments.
Serializable	Attribute for indicating serializable classes.
STAThread	Attribute for specifying the single-threaded apartment (STA) threading model for a COM interoperability application.

Table 3.3 System namespace exception classes.

Exception	Description
AppDomainUnloadedException	Represents an exception thrown when one attempts accessing an unloaded application domain.
ApplicationException	Represents an exception thrown when a recoverable application error occurs.
ArgumentException	Represents an exception thrown when one invokes a method and passes an incorrect parameter to it.
ArgumentNullException	Represents an exception thrown when one invokes a method and passes a Null reference parameter to it while the method requires a valid reference.
ArgumentOutOfRangeException	Represents an exception thrown when one invokes a method and passes a parameter to it with value outside the allowable range.
ArithmeticException	Represents an exception thrown when an arithmetic, casting, or conversion error occurs.
ArrayTypeMismatchException	Represents an exception thrown when one attempts to store an element of the wrong type in an array.
BadImageFormatException	Represents an exception thrown when one attempts loading an invalid DLL or an executable.
CannotUnloadAppDomainException	Represents an exception thrown when one attempts to unload the default application domain, an application domain, an application domain that is still executing and cannot be stopped immediately, or an application domain that is already unloaded.
ContextMarshalException	Represents an exception thrown when an attempt to marshal an object across a context boundary fails.
DivideByZeroException	Represents an exception thrown when one attempts to divide by zero.
DllNotFoundException	Represents an exception thrown when a DLL specified in a DLL import is not found.
DuplicateWaitObjectException	Represents an exception thrown when an object appears more than once in an array of synchronization objects supplied to the **WaitHandle::WaitAll** method.

<Continued on Next Page>

<Table 3.3 Continued>

Class	Description
EntryPointNotFoundException	Represents an exception thrown when one attempts to load an assembly missing an entry point.
ExecutionEngineException	Represents an exception thrown when a CLR internal error occurs.
FieldAccessException	Represents an exception thrown when one attempts accessing private or protected class data members. The exception can occur only when one changes the class member access specification without recompiling the assemblies referencing the class members formerly declared as public.
FormatException	Represents an exception thrown when one invokes a function and supplies an incorrectly formatted parameter to it (i.e., if a function expects a four-character **String*** and you supply a three-character string, the exception is thrown).
IndexOutOfRangeException	Represents an exception thrown when one attempts accessing an array element with index exceeding the array bounds.
InvalidCastException	Represents an exception thrown when the **try_cast** or an explicit conversion operator fails due to incompatible data types being converted.
InvalidOperationException	Represents an exception thrown when one calls a method inappropriate for the object's current state (i.e., reading a file after it's been closed).
InvalidProgramException	Represents an exception thrown when an MSIL code being executed or program metadata is corrupt.
MemberAccessException	Represents an exception thrown when one attempts accessing private or protected class members using **MethodBase::Invoke** or **Delegate::DynamicInvoke**. Also a base class for all missing member or member-access exceptions.
MethodAccessException	Represents an exception thrown when one attempts accessing private or protected class methods. The exception can occur only when one changes a class method-access specification without recompiling the assemblies referencing the class methods formerly declared as public.
MissingFieldException	Represents an exception thrown when one attempts accessing a nonexisting class data member. The exception can occur only when one removes or renames a class member without recompiling the assemblies that reference it.
MissingMemberException	Base class for **MissingFieldException** and **MissingMethodException**.
MissingMethodException	Represents an exception thrown when one attempts accessing nonexisting class method. The exception can occur only when one removes or renames a class method without recompiling the assemblies that reference it.
MulticastNotSupportedException	Represents an exception thrown when one attempts to combine two noncombinable delegates.
NotFiniteNumberException	Represents an exception thrown when a math operation produces a floating-point value that is an infinity, or Not-a-Number (NaN).

<Continued on Next Page>

<Table 3.3 Continued>

Class	Description
NotImplementedException	Represents an exception thrown when one requests a method or operation that is not implemented.
NotSupportedException	Represents an exception throw by derived classes to indicate unsupported base class methods.
NullReferenceException	Represents an exception thrown when one attempts dereferencing (i.e., calling methods or accessing data members) a Null object reference.
ObjectDisposedException	Represents an exception thrown when one attempts accessing a disposed object.
OutOfMemoryException	Represents an exception thrown when there is not enough memory for allocating an object or array or for boxing a value type.
OverflowException	Represents an exception thrown when an arithmetic, conversion, or casting operation results in an overflow.
PlatformNotSupportedException	Represents an exception thrown when one attempts using a CLR feature not supported on a particular platform.
RankException	Represents an exception thrown when one passes as a function or method parameter an array containing the wrong number of dimensions.
StackOverflowException	Represents an exception thrown when a stack overflow occurs.
TypeInitializationException	Represents an exception thrown when a class initializer fails to initialize a class.
TypeLoadException	Represents an exception thrown when one references a particular class in the code and the CLR cannot find an assembly that implements the class or cannot locate the class in the assembly.
TypeUnloadedException	Represents an exception thrown when one attempts accessing an unloaded class.
UnauthorizedAccessException	Represents an exception thrown by the OS to indicate I/O restrictions or security access limitations.
UnhandledExceptionEventArgs	Represents data for the event that is raised when is an unhandled exception occurs.
UriFormatException	Represents an exception thrown when one attempts to use an invalid URI.

Table 3.4 System namespace value types.

Structure	Description
ArgIterator	Variable-length argument list (only useful for writing compilers).
Boolean	Boolean value.
Byte	8-bit unsigned integer.
Char	Unicode character.
DateTime	Date / time value.
Decimal	Decimal number.
Double	Double-precision floating-point number.
Guid	Globally unique identifier (GUID).
Int16	16-bit signed integer.
Int32	32-bit signed integer.
Int64	64-bit signed integer.
IntPtr	A platform-specific integer, i.e., 32-bit integer on 32-bit platforms, 64-bit integer on 64-bit platforms. Also represents a pointer or a handle.
RuntimeArgumentHandle	Variable-length argument list class that exists only to support C/C++ functions accepting a variable number of arguments. Can be used only with **ArgIterator**.
RuntimeFieldHandle	Represents a class field metadata. The value of an instance of this class is a reference to the field represented by the instance.
RuntimeMethodHandle	Represents a class method metadata.
RuntimeTypeHandle	Represents a type metadata.
SByte	8-bit signed integer.
Single	Single-precision floating-point number.
TimeSpan	Time interval.
TypedReference	Represents a type / value combination for use with **varargs**. **TypedReference**s cannot be used in arrays.
UInt16	16-bit unsigned integer.
UInt32	32-bit unsigned integer.
UInt64	64-bit unsigned integer.
UIntPtr	A platform-specific unsigned integer, i.e., 32-bit integer on 32-bit platforms, 64-bit integer on 64-bit platforms. Also represents a pointer or a handle.
Void	Equivalent of **void**.

.NET Framework Class Library classes, in general, and System namespace classes, in particular, provide numerous overloaded methods that differ only by the number of parameters. The numerous overloads are needed because the CLS does not support optional arguments. Thus, classes typically provide additional overloaded methods accepting extra parameters to simulate the C++ optional argument syntax.

> **NOTE:** Class members listed in the tables in this chapter and in subsequent chapters are presumed to be declared as **public** unless the member definition explicitly specifies another modifier such as **private** or **protected**.

Base Interfaces

Along with a multitude of classes, the System namespace defines 11 interfaces representing fundamental operations such as object cloning, object comparison, type conversion, custom formatting, and so on. The System namespace interfaces are summarized in Table 3.5.

Table 3.5 System namespace interfaces.

Interface	Description
IAppDomainSetup	Supplies properties for the **AppDomain** class representing assembly setup information.
IAsyncResult	Used by classes implementing asynchronous methods to represent the status of an asynchronous operation.
ICloneable	Supplies the **Object* Clone()** method for object cloning.
IComparable	Supplies the **int CompareTo(Object*** *obj***)** method for object comparison. The method must return <0 if the current object is lesser than *obj*, = 0 if two objects are equal, or >0 if the current object is greater than *obj*.
IConvertible	This not CLS-compliant interface defines the **TypeCode GetTypeCode()** method and the plurality of *TYPE* **To***TYPE***(IFormatProvider*** *provider***)** methods for converting the class into a specified value type *TYPE*. Supported conversion *TYPE*s include **Boolean**, **SByte**, **Byte**, **Int16**, **UInt16**, **Int32**, **UInt32**, **Int64**, **UInt64**, **Single**, **Double**, **Decimal**, **DateTime**, **Char**, and **String**. If a class implementing **IConvertible** cannot provide a meaningful conversion to one of the value types listed above, the method should throw an **InvalidCastException**.
ICustomFormatter	Supplies the **String* Format(String*** *format***, Object*** *arg***, IFormatProvider*** *formatProvider***)** method for converting a class into a **String** representation.
IDisposable	Supplies the **void Dispose()** method to allow releasing allocated unmanaged resources.
IFormatProvider	Supplies the **Object* GetFormat(Type*** *formatType***)** method for retrieving an instance of the object providing formatting services for the class implementing the interface.
IFormattable	Supplies the **String* ToString(String*** *format***, IFormatProvider*** *formatProvider***)** method for formatting the object using the specified format provider interface.
IServiceProvider	Supplies the **Object* GetService(Type*** *serviceType***)** method for retrieving a service object (i.e., an object that provides custom support to other objects) for the class.
_AppDomain	Interface for the **AppDomain** class.

System Namespace Enumerations

System namespace enumerations serve as parameters to various System namespace class constructors and methods. The System namespace enumerations are listed in Table 3.6.

Table 3.6 System namespace enumerations.

Enumeration	Description
AttributeTargets	Specifies an application element on which one can apply attributes: **All** (i.e., any application element), **Assembly**, **Class**, **Constructor**, **Delegate**, **Enum**, **Event**, **Field**, **Interface**, **Method**, **Module**, **Parameter**, **Property**, **ReturnValue**, and **Struct**.
DayOfWeek	Specifies a day of the week: **Monday**, **Tuesday**, **Wednesday**, **Thursday**, **Friday**, **Saturday**, and **Sunday**.
Environment.SpecialFolder	Specifies constants identifying system folders: **ApplicationData**, **CommonApplicationData**, **CommonProgramFiles**, **Cookies**, **DesktopDirectory**, **Favorites**, **History**, **InternetCache**, **LocalApplicationData**, **Personal**, **ProgramFiles**, **Programs**, **Recent**, **SendTo**, **StartMenu**, **Startup**, **System**, and **Templates**.
LoaderOptimization	Specifies application-domain internal resource-sharing constants for the **LoaderOptimizationAttribute** class: **MultiDomain** (share resources across application domains)**, MultiDomainHost** (share resources across application domains only for strong-named assemblies), **NotSpecified, SingleDomain** (do not share resources).
PlatformID	Specifies platform ID values supported by an assembly: **Win32NT**, **Win32S**, and **Win32Windows** (i.e., Windows 9x family).
TypeCode	Specifies object type: **Boolean**, **Byte**, **Char**, **DateTime**, **DBNull**, **Decimal**, **Double**, **Empty** (i.e., Null reference), **Int16**, **Int32**. **Int64**, **Object**, **SByte**, **Single**, **String**, **UInt16**, **UInt32**, and **UInt64**.
UriHostNameType	Specifies host name types for the **Uri::CheckHostName** method: **Basic**, **Dns**, **IPv4**, and **IPv6**.
UriPartial	Specifies parts of a URI for the **Uri::GetLeftPart** method: **Unknown**, **Authority**, **Path**, and **Scheme**.

System Namespace Delegates

The System namespace provides six delegate types supporting system event notifications and asynchronous operations. The delegates are summarized in Table 3.7. All delegates in the System namespace are defined as **public __gc __delegate**; therefore, these keywords are omitted from the delegate definition in the table.

Table 3.7 System namespace delegates.

Delegate	Description
void AssemblyLoadEventHandler(Object* *sender*, **AssemblyLoadEventArgs*** *args***)**	Represents a delegate for handling **AppDomain::AssemblyLoad** events.
void AsyncCallback(IAsyncResult* *result***)**	Represents a callback that is called on completion of an asynchronous operation.
void CrossAppDomainDelegate()	Represents a delegate that can be called across the application domains (used by the **AppDomain::DoCallBack**).
void EventHandler(Object* *sender*, **EventArgs*** *e***)**	Represents a delegate for handling events that do not rely on custom event data.
Assembly* ResolveEventHandler(Object* *sender*, **ResolveEventArgs*** *args***)**	Represents a delegate for handling **TypeResolve**, **ResourceResolve**, and **AssemblyResolve** events of the **AppDomain** class.
void UnhandledExceptionEventHandler(Object* *sender*, **UnhandledExceptionEventArgs*** *e***)**	Represents a delegate for handling events caused by unhandled application-domain exceptions.

Object Class: The Root of the Hierarchy

All managed types are implicitly derived from the System namespace **Object** class, which represents the root of the .NET Framework class hierarchy. All classes defined using the **__gc** keyword are implicitly derived from the **Object**. Even primitive data type, such as **char**, **int**, **float**, are directly related to the **Object** class as they are represented by the managed value types such as **Char**, **Int32**, and **Float** that derive from the **Object** class. The **Object** class has the following inheritance diagram:

```
Object

Attributes: Serializable, ClassInterface(ClassInterfaceType.AutoDual)
Abstract: No
Sealed: No
Implemented Interfaces: None
```

The **Object** class is defined using the **ClassInterface** attribute. The **ClassInterface** attribute is required to ensure seamless interoperability between managed types and COM. Since all managed types derive from the **Object** class, they inherit the COM interoperability qualities of the **Object** class and can be exposed to unmanaged code as COM objects. COM interoperability is discussed in depth in Chapter 13.

The **Object** class has no constructors and provides just a handful of methods, which are summarized in Table 3.8.

Table 3.8 **Object** class members.

Member	Description
Object()	Default Constructor.
virtual bool Equals(Object* *object***)**	Returns **true** if the two specified objects are equal.
static bool Equals(Object* *obj1***, Object*** *obj2***)**	Returns **true** if the two specified objects are equal.
virtual int GetHashCode()	Calculates the object's hash value. When designing a hash function keep in mind that two objects of the same type representing the same value must yield equivalent hash values. Also, the object's hash value should be based on the immutable class data members and should not change as you modify the object's fields.
Type* GetType()	Returns the **Type** of the object.
static bool ReferenceEquals(Object* *obj1***, Object*** *obj2***)**	Returns **true** if the specified **Object** pointers are pointing to the same object.
virtual String* ToString()	Returns a **String** representation of the object.
protected: void Finalize()	Performs object destruction. You cannot override the **Finalize** method directly. You must override the destructor instead. The compiler automatically renames the destructor into the **Finalize** method and creates a new destructor that calls the **Finalize** method.
protected: Object* MemberwiseClone()	Returns a *shallow* copy of the object by creating a new instance of the **Object** and copying nonstatic data members of the original object.

The most important methods of the **Object** class are **GetType**, which returns the type of the object, and the **ToString**, which converts the object value into the string representation.

Array Class

All **__gc** arrays implicitly derive from the System namespace **Array** class. Thus, a managed array is actually an object and has much more functionality to offer than an unmanaged array. The **Array** class inheritance diagram is shown here:

```
Object
|- Array
```

Attributes: **Serializable**
Abstract: Yes
Sealed: No
Implemented Interfaces: **ICloneable, IList, ICollection, IEnumerable**

The **Array** object provides numerous methods for searching arrays for a particular element (**BinarySearch** methods), copying arrays (**Copy** methods), setting array elements (**SetValue** methods), and sorting (**Sort** methods).

Although the **Array** is a collection class and implements the **ICollection** and **IList** interfaces (see Chapter 6), managed arrays correspond to the fixed-length collections and do not support adding or removing elements. If you call the **IList::Add/IList::Remove** or similar methods, the **Array** class throws the **NotSupportedException**. Also, the **Array** class provides the **Length** and **Rank** properties to indicate the number of elements in the array and the array rank.

The **Array** class constructors, properties and methods are summarized in Tables 3.9 through 3.11.

Table 3.9 **Array** class constructors.

Constructor	Description
protected: Array()	Default constructor.

Table 3.10 **Array** class properties.

Get/Set	Type	Property	Virtual	Description
Get	**bool**	**IsFixedSize**	Yes	Contains **true** if the array has a fixed size. Arrays are fixed-size by default.
Get	**bool**	**IsReadOnly**	Yes	Contains **true** if the array is read-only. Arrays are not read-only by default.
Get	**bool**	**IsSynchronized**	Yes	Contains **true** if the array is thread-save. Arrays are not thread-safe by default.
Get	**int**	**Length**	No	Contains the total number of elements in all the dimensions of the array.
Get	**int**	**Rank**	No	Contains the number of dimensions of the array.
Get	**Object***	**SyncRoot**	Yes	Contains the array synchronization object that can be used for implementing a thread-safe multithreaded array access.

Table 3.11 **Array** class methods.

Member	Description
static int BinarySearch(Array* *array*, **Object*** *value***)**	
static int BinarySearch(Array* *array*, **Object*** *value*, **IComparer*** *comparer***)**	Searches a one-dimensional sorted *array* for a *value* element. The optional *comparer* argument allows specifying a custom comparer interface.
static int BinarySearch(Array* *array*, **int** *index*, **int** *length*, **Object*** *value***)**	
static int BinarySearch(Array* *array*, **int** *index*, **int** *length*, **Object*** *value*, **IComparer*)**	Searches a section (from *index* to *index* + *length*) of a one-dimensional sorted *array* for a *value*. The optional *comparer* argument allows specifying a custom comparer interface.
static void Clear(Array* *array*, **int** *index*, **int** *length***)**	Sets a range of *array* elements (from *index* to *index* + *length* - 1) to zero.
static void Copy(Array* *src*, **Array*** *dest*, **int** *length***)**	Copies a range of elements (from 0 to *length* - 1) from *src* array to *dest*.
static void Copy(Array* *src*, **int** *srcIndex*, **Array*** *dest*, **int** *destIndex*, **int** *length***)**	Copies *length* elements starting at *srcIndex* from *src* array to *dest* starting at *destIndex*.
virtual void CopyTo(Array* *dest*, **int** *destIndex***)**	Copies all elements of the current one-dimensional array to the one-dimensional array *dest* starting at the destination index *destIndex*.
static Array* CreateInstance(Type* *elementType*, **int** *length1***)**	
static Array* CreateInstance(Type* *elementType*, **int** *length1*, **int** *length2***)**	
static Array* CreateInstance(Type* *elementType*, **int** *length1*, **int** *length2*, **int** *length3***)**	Creates one-, two- or three-dimensional array of the specified type.
static Array* CreateInstance(Type* *elementType*, **int** __gc[] *lengths***)**	
static Array* CreateInstance(Type* *elementType*, **int** __gc[] *lengths*, **int** __gc[] *lowerBounds***)**	Creates a multidimensional array of the specified type. The *length* array argument specifies sizes of each array dimension. The optional *lowerBounds* argument specifies starting index for each array dimension.

<Continued on Next Page>

<Table 3.11 Continued>

Member	Description
virtual IEnumerator* GetEnumerator()	Returns an **IEnumerator** for the array. **IEnumerator** allows reading array elements into a collection.
int GetLength(int *dimension*)	Returns the number of elements in the specified dimension.
int GetLowerBound(int *dimension*)	Returns the starting index of the specified dimension.
int GetUpperBound(int *dimension*)	Returns the upper bound of the specified dimension.
Object* GetValue(int *index1*)	
Object* GetValue(int *index1*, **int** *index2*)	
Object* GetValue(int *index1*, **int** *index2*, **int** *index3*)	Returns the one-, two-, or three-dimensional-array element identified by the specified index or indices.
Object* GetValue(int __gc[] *indices*)	Returns the multidimensional-array element specified by the *indices* array.
int IList::Add(Object* *value*)	Throws **NotSupportedException**.
void IList::Clear()	Sets all elements in the **Array** to zero, to **false**, or to a Null reference, depending on the element type.
bool IList::Contains(Object* *value*)	Returns **true** if the *value* is found in the array.
int IList::IndexOf(Object* *value*)	Returns the index of the first occurrence of the *value* element in the one-dimensional array or -1 if the *value* is not found.
void IList::Insert(int index, Object* value)	Throws **NotSupportedException**.
void IList::Remove(Object* value)	Throws **NotSupportedException**.
void IList::RemoveAt(int index)	Throws **NotSupportedException**.
static int IndexOf(Array* *array*, **Object*** *value*)	
static int IndexOf(Array* *array*, **Object*** *value*, **int** *index*)	

<Continued on Next Page>

<Table 3.11 Continued>

Member	Description
static int IndexOf(Array* *array*, **Object*** *value*, **int** *index*, **int** *count***)**	Searches the array for the *first* occurrence of the specified **value**. Optional *index* argument specifies the starting index for the search, while optional *count* argument specified the number of array elements to search among.
void Initialize()	Initializes elements of the value-type array by calling the default constructor of the value type.
static int LastIndexOf(Array* *array*, **Object*** *value***)**	
static int LastIndexOf(Array* *array*, **Object*** *value*, **int** *index***)**	
static int LastIndexOf(Array* *array*, **Object*** *value*, **int** *index*, **int** *count***)**	Searches the array for the *last* occurrence of the specified **value**. Optional *index* argument specifies the starting index for the search, while the optional *count* argument specified the number of array elements to search among.
static void Reverse(Array* *array***)**	
static void Reverse(Array* *array*, **int** *index*, **int** *length***)**	Reverses the sequence of the one-dimensional array elements. Optional *index* and *length* arguments identify the section of the array to reverse.
void SetValue(Object* *value*, **int** *index1***)**	
void SetValue(Object* *value*, **int** *index1*, **int** *index2***)**	
void SetValue(Object* *value*, **int** *index1*, **int** *index1*, **int** *index3***)**	Sets the one-, two-, or three-dimensional array element value identified by the specified index or indices.
void SetValue(Object* *value*, **int __gc[]** *indices***)**	Sets the multidimensional array element value. The *indices* array specifies the indices of a multidimensional array element.

<Continued on Next Page>

<Table 3.11 Continued>

Member	Description
static void Sort(Array* *array*)	
static void Sort(Array* *array*, IComparer* *comparer*)	Sorts a one-dimensional array. Optional ***comparer*** argument allows specifying a custom comparer interface.
static void Sort(Array* *array*, int *index*, int *length*)	
static void Sort(Array* *array*, int *index*, int *length*, IComparer* *comparer*)	Sorts a section (from ***index*** to ***index*** + ***length*** - 1) of a one-dimensional array. Optional ***comparer*** argument allows specifying a custom comparer interface.
static void Sort(Array* *keys*, Array* *items*)	
static void Sort(Array* *keys*, Array*items, IComparer* *comparer*)	Sorts a pair of one-dimensional arrays (one contains the keys and the other contains the corresponding items) based on the keys in the ***keys*** array. The optional ***comparer*** argument allows specifying a custom comparer interface.
static void Sort(Array* *keys*, Array* *items*, int *index*, int *length*)	
static void Sort(Array* *keys*, Array* *items*, int *index*, int *length*, IComparer* *comparer*)	Sorts a section (from ***index*** to ***index*** + ***length*** - 1) of a pair of one-dimensional arrays (one contains the keys and the other contains the corresponding items) based on the keys in the ***keys*** array. The optional ***comparer*** argument allows specifying a custom comparer interface.

NOTE: *In order to be able to sort the array using the **Sort** method, the array elements must implement the **IComparable** interface.*

String Object

Character strings in the .NET Framework Class Library are represented by the **String** class. **String** objects correspond to immutable strings of Unicode characters. Therefore, all text and character manipulation operations on **String** objects return a new pointer to a **String** object representing the result of the operation. In-place modification of **String** objects is not permitted. Mutable character strings are represented by the **StringBuilder** class defined in System::Text namespace, which is discussed later in this chapter.

The **String** class inheritance diagram is shown here:

```
Object
|- String
```

Attributes: **Serializable**
Abstract: No
Sealed: Yes
Implemented Interfaces: **IComparable, ICloneable, IConvertible, IEnumerable**

The **String** class supports the following major operation on character strings:

*   *comparison*: **Compare** method
*   *concatenation*: **Concat** and **Join** methods
*   *formatting:* **Format** method
*   *substring search*: **EndsWith, IndexOf,** and **LastIndexOf** methods
*   *character/string replacement*: **Replace** method
*   *case conversion*: **ToUpper** and **ToLower** methods
*   *padding*: **PadLeft** and **PadRight** methods
*   *trimming*: **Trim**, **TrimStart,** and **TrimEnd** methods
*   *delimited string splitting*: **Split** method

Unlike the MFC **CString** class, the **String** type does not support the [] operator to access string characters. Instead, the **String** class provides the **Chars** property to get string characters. Unfortunately, **String** characters cannot be set because strings are immutable.

Similar to the MFC **CString** class, the **String** class supports == and != operators, but the <, >, <=, and >= operators are not supported because strings in Managed C++ are represented by **String** pointers and such operations are interpreted as operations on pointers, not on string values.

The complete summary of the **String** class constructors, fields, properties, methods, and operators is provided in Tables 3.12 through 3.16.

Table 3.12 **String** class constructors.

Constructor	Description
String(__wchar_t* *str*)	
String(__wchar_t* *str*, int *index*, int *length*)	Initializes the **String** from the Unicode string. Optional *index* and *length* arguments identify a section of the source string to copy into the **String** object (not CLS compliant).

<Continued on Next Page>

<Table 3.12 Continued>

Constructor	Description
String(__wchar_t __gc[] *str***)**	
String(__wchar_t __gc[] *str***, int** *index***, int** *length***)**	Initializes the **String** from the managed Unicode character array. Optional *index* and *length* arguments identify a section of the source string to copy into the **String** object.
String(__wchar_t *chr***, int** *count***)**	Initializes the **String** by repeating the Unicode character *chr count* times.
String(char* *str***)**	
String(char* *str***, int** *index***, int** *length***)**	
String(char* *str***, int** *index***, int** *length***, Encoding*** *enc***)**	Initializes the **String** from the ASCII string. Optional *index* and *length* arguments identify a section of the source string to copy into the **String** object. Optional *enc* parameter specifies the source string encoding, e.g., **ASCIIEncoding**, **UnicodeEncoding**, **UTF7Encoding**, or **UTF8Encoding** such that the source ASCII string is properly decoded (not CLS compliant).

Table 3.13 **String** class fields.

Field	Description
static String* Empty	Empty string.

Table 3.14 **String** class properties.

Get/Set	Type	Property	Description
Get	**__wchar_t**	**Chars(int** *index***)**	Returns a character at a specified index.
Get	**int**	**Length**	Returns the number of characters in the string.

Table 3.15 **String** class methods.

Member	Description
static int Compare(String* *str1***, String*** *str2***)**	
static int Compare(String* *str1***, String*** *str2***, bool** *ignoreCase***)**	
static int Compare(String* *str1***, String*** *str2***, bool** *ignoreCase***, CultureInfo*** *culture***)**	Compares the *str1* with the *str2* and returns < 0 if *str1* < *str2*, 0 if *str1* == *str2* and > 0 if *str1* > *str2*. Optional *ignoreCase* argument specifies case-sensitive or case-insensitive comparison, while the optional *culture* argument allows specifying the language locale for comparison.

<Continued on Next Page>

<Table 3.15 Continued>

Member	Description
static int Compare(String* *str1*, int *index1*, String* *str2*, int *index2*, int *length*)	
static int Compare(String* *str1*, int *index1*, String* *str2*, int *index2*, int *length*, bool *ignoreCase*)	
static int Compare(String* *str1*, int *index1*, String* *str2*, int *index2*, int *length*, bool *ignoreCase*, CultureInfo* *culture*)	Compares the *length* characters in the *str1* starting at the *index1* with the *length* characters in the *str2* starting at the *index2*. Optional *ignoreCase* argument specifies case-sensitive or case-insensitive comparison, while the optional *culture* argument allows specifying the language locale for comparison.
static int CompareOrdinal(String* *str1*, String* *str2*)	Compares the *str1* with the *str2* ignoring the local national language or culture.
static int CompareOrdinal(String* *str1*, int *index1*, String* *str2*, int *index2*, int *length*)	Compares the *length* characters in the *str1* starting at the index *index1* with the *length* characters in the *str2* starting at the index *index2* ignoring the local national language or culture.
static String* Concat(Object* *obj*)	Converts the *obj* object to **String**.
static String* Concat(Object*[] *array*)	Returns concatenated string representations of the *array* element values.
static String* Concat(String*[] *array*)	Returns concatenated elements of a specified **String** array.
static String* Concat(Object* *obj1*, Object* *obj1*)	
static String* Concat(Object* *obj1*, Object* *obj2*, Object* *obj3*)	
static String* Concat(Object** *obj1*, Object** *obj2*, Object** *obj3*, Object** *obj4*, ...)	Returns concatenated string representations of two or more objects. The overload variable-length argument list is not CLS compliant.
static String* Concat(String* *str1*, String* *str2*)	
static String* Concat(String* *str1*, String* *str2*, String* *str3*)	
static String* Concat(String* *str1*, String* *str2*, String* *str3*, String* *str4*)	Returns concatenated two or more strings.
static String* Copy(String* *str*)	Creates a copy of the specified string.
void CopyTo(int *srcIndex*, __wchar_t *dest* __gc[], int *destIndex*, int *count*)	Copies the *count* **String** characters starting at the *srcIndex* into a managed Unicode character array *dest* starting at the *destIndex*.

<Continued on Next Page>

<Table 3.15 Continued>

Member	Description
bool EndsWith(String* *str***)**	Returns **true** if the current string ends with the *str*.
bool Equals(String* *str***)**	Returns **true** if the current string is the same as the *str*.
static bool Equals(String* *str1***, String*** *str2***)**	Returns **true** if the *str1* is the same as the *str2*.
static String* Format(String* *format***, Object*** *arg***)**	
static String* Format(String* *format***, Object*** *arg1***, Object*** *arg2***)**	
static String* Format(String* *format***, Object*** *arg1***, Object*** *arg2***, Object*** *arg3***)**	Formats the string (similar to **printf**).
static String* Format(String* *format***, Object[]** *args***)**	Formats the string.
static String* Format(IFormatProvider* *provider***, String*** *format***, Object[]** *args***)**	Formats the string using the specified culture-specific format provider interface.
CharEnumerator* GetEnumerator()	Returns an **IEnumerator** for the string. **IEnumerator** allows iterating through the string characters.
int IndexOf(__wchar_t *chr***)**	
int IndexOf(__wchar_t *chr***, int** *index***)**	
int IndexOf(__wchar_t *chr***, int** *index***, int** *count***)**	Returns the index of the *first* occurrence of the specified Unicode character in the string, or -1 if the character is not found. Optional *index* and *count* arguments specify the section of the **String** to search in.
int IndexOf(String* *str***)**	
int IndexOf(String* *str***, int** *index***)**	
int IndexOf(String* *str***, int** *index***, int** *count***)**	Returns the index of the *first* occurrence of the specified substring *str* in the string, or -1 if the substring is not found. Optional *index* and *count* arguments specify the section of the **String** to search in.
int IndexOfAny(__wchar_t __gc[] *chars***)**	
int IndexOfAny(__wchar_t __gc[] *chars***, int** *index***)**	
int IndexOfAny(__wchar_t __gc[] *chars***, int** *index***, int** *count***)**	Returns the index of the *first* occurrence of any of the Unicode characters in the *chars* array in the string, or -1 if the character is not found. Optional *index* and *count* arguments identify the section of the **String** to search in.

<Continued on Next Page>

<Table 3.15 Continued>

Member	Description
String* Insert(int *index*, String* *str*)	Inserts a specified string into the current string starting at the position ***index***.
static String* Intern(String* *str*)	Returns from or creates an instance of the specified string in the CLR string pool.
static String* IsInterned(String* *str*)	Returns a reference to the specified string from the CLR string pool or Null if the string is not found in the pool.
static String* Join(String* *separator*, String*[] *array*)	
static String* Join(String* *separator*, String*[] *array*, int *index*, int *count*)	Concatenates strings in the ***array***, using the specified ***separator*** to delimit the individual elements. Optional ***index*** and ***count*** arguments specify the starting index and the number of the ***array*** strings to concatenate.
int LastIndexOf(__wchar_t *chr*)	
int LastIndexOf(__wchar_t *chr*, int *index*)	
int LastIndexOf(__wchar_t *chr*, int *index*, int *count*)	Returns the index of the *last* occurrence of the specified character or - 1 if the character is not found. Optional ***index*** and ***count*** arguments specify the section of the **String** to search in.
int LastIndexOf(String* *str*)	
int LastIndexOf(String* *str*, int *index*)	
int LastIndexOf(String* *str*, int *index*, int *count*)	Returns the index of the *last* occurrence of the specified substring ***str*** or - 1 if the substring is not found. Optional ***index*** and ***count*** arguments specify the section of the **String** to search in.
int LastIndexOfAny(__wchar_t __gc[] *chars*)	
int LastIndexOfAny(__wchar_t __gc[] *chars*, int *index*)	
int LastIndexOfAny(__wchar_t __gc[] *chars*, int *index*, int *count*)	Returns the index of the *last* occurrence of any of the Unicode characters in the ***chars*** array in the string, or -1 if the character is not found. Optional ***index*** and ***count*** arguments identify the section of the **String** to search in.

<Continued on Next Page>

<Table 3.15 Continued>

Member	Description
String* PadLeft(int *length*)	
String* PadLeft(int *length*, __wchar_t *padChr*)	Left-pads the string until the desired length is reached. Optional ***padChr*** specifies the desired padding character (blank is used by default).
String* PadRight(int *length*)	
String* PadRight(int *length*, __wchar_t *padChr*)	Right-pads the string until the desired length is reached. Optional ***padChr*** specifies the desired padding character (blank is used by default).
String* Remove(int *index*, int *count*)	Deletes the ***count*** characters from the current string starting at the index ***index***.
String* Replace(__wchar_t *oldChr*, __wchar_t *newChr*)	Replaces all occurrences of the ***oldChr*** with the ***newChr*** in the current string.
String* Replace(String* *oldStr*, String* *newStr*)	Replaces all occurrences of the ***oldStr*** string with the ***newStr*** string in the current string.
String* Split(__wchar_t *separator* __gc[]) __gc[]	
String* Split(__wchar_t *separator* __gc[], int *count*) __gc[]	Returns an array of substrings extracted from the current string delimited by the characters specified in the ***separator*** array. Optional ***count*** argument specifies the maximum number of substrings to extract.
bool StartsWith(String* *str*)	Returns **true** if the current string starts with the ***str***.
String* Substring(int *index*)	
String* Substring(int *index*, int *length*)	Returns a substring starting at the specified ***index***. Optional ***length*** argument specifies the length of the substring.
__wchar_t ToCharArray() __gc[]	
__wchar_t ToCharArray(int *index*, int *length*) __gc[]	Copies the characters in the string to a Unicode character array. Optional ***index*** and ***length*** arguments identify a section of the **String** to copy.
String* ToLower()	
String* ToLower(CultureInfo* *culture*)	Converts the string to the lower case. Optional ***culture*** argument allows specifying the language locale for conversion.

<Continued on Next Page>

<Table 3.15 Continued>

Member	Description
String* ToUpper()	
String* ToUpper(CultureInfo* *culture*)	Converts the string to the upper case. Optional*culture* argument allows specifying the language locale for conversion.
String* Trim()	Removes leading and trailing white space characters from the string.
String* TrimEnd(__wchar_t *trimChars* __gc[])	Removes trailing characters specified by the *trimChars* from the string.
String* TrimStart(__wchar_t *trimChars* __gc[])	Removes leading characters specified by the *trimChars* from the string.

Table 3.14 **String** class operators.

Operator	Return Type	Operands	Description
==	**bool**	**String*, String**	Returns **true** if the strings are equal.
!=	**bool**	**String*, String**	Returns **true** if the strings are not equal.

NOTE: *The **String** equality/inequality operators do not compare text stored in strings, but rather compare **String** pointers. Thus, two distinct instances of the **String** object will never be equal even though they may contain equivalent text.*

String Formatting

You can use the **String::Format** method to format a string. The **Format** method is somewhat similar to the C++ **sprintf** method except that the format of the .NET Framework employs different syntax for format specifiers. The .NET Framework format specifiers have the following syntax:

```
{N[,M] [:formatString] }
```

where *N* is a zero-based number of the argument to format, *M* is the optional width in characters of the formatted value (if *M* is negative, the value will be right-padded with blanks rather than left-padded with blanks). The *formatString* specifies what type of data is being formatted and how it should be formatted. The most common format specifiers for numeric and date/time data types are listed in Tables 3.16 and 3.17.

Numeric format specifiers can be followed by the optional integer value corresponding to the precision parameter. The precision parameter normally specifies the desired number of decimal places and significant digits.

Table 3.16 Number format specifiers.

Specifier	Description	Example
C, c	Currency	$2,000.34
D, d	Decimal (applies to integers only)	2034
E	Exponential representation	2.000340E+003
e	Exponential representation	2.000340e+003
F, f	Fixed-point representation	2000.34
G, g	General	2000.34
N, n	Number	2,000.34
P, p	Percent	2000,034.00 %
R, r	Round-trip (ensures lossless reverse conversion from string to floating-point number)	200.34
X	Hexadecimal uppercase (applies to integers only)	80FF
x	Hexadecimal lowercase (applies to integers only)	80ff

Table 3.17 Date/Time Format specifiers.

Specifier	Description	Example
d	Short date	11/07/2001
D	Long date	Wednesday, November 7, 2001
t	Short Time	4:56 PM
T	Long Time	4:56:56 PM
f	Long date and short time	Wednesday, November 07, 2001 4:56 PM
F	Long date and long time	Wednesday, November 07, 2001 4:56:56 PM
g	Short date and short time	11/7/2001 4:56 PM
G	Short date and long time	11/7/2001 4:56:56 PM
M, m	Month and day	November 07
R, r	RFC1123 format	Wed, 07 Nov 2001 16:56:56 GMT
s	Sortable date/time (ISO 8601)	2001-11-07T16:56:56
u	Universal sortable date/time	2001-11-07 16:56:56Z
U	Universal sortable date/time	Wednesday, November 07, 2001 10:56:56 PM
Y, y	Year and month	November, 2001

If no *formatString* is specified, the **ToString** method will be used to obtain string representation of the object being formatted.

StringBuilder Class

Immutability of the **String** class can be very annoying. The **String** immutability means that all text string operations must be performed out-of-place and a new instance of the **String** object is constructed each time a modified string is returned by a **String** class method. Besides being annoying, **String** immutability can result in reduced performance due to excessive memory allocation to hold the results of string operations.

If you feel that the **String** class is not very well suited for a particular kind of text processing, you can use a *mutable* equivalent of the **String** object—**StringBuilder** class, which is defined in the System::Text namespace:

```
Object
|- System::Text::StringBuilder
```

```
Attributes: Serializable
Abstract: No
Sealed: Yes
Implemented Interfaces: none
```

The **StringBuilder** class supports the following operations:

appending values: **Append** methods

formatting and appending text: **AppendFormat** methods

inserting text/characters: **Insert** methods

replacing text/characters: **Replace** methods

Unlike the **String** class, all operations on the **StringBuilder** are in place. For consistency reasons the **StringBuilder** class methods return a pointer to the original **StringBuilder** object.

Also, the **StringBuilder** class supports the **Chars** property, which unlike the **String::Chars** property allows modifying the **StringBuilder** characters.

The **StringBuilder** can be converted to **String** using the **ToString** method. The complete summary of the **StringBuilder** class constructors, fields, properties, methods, and operators is given in Tables 3.18 through 3.20.

Table 3.18 **StringBuilder** class constructors.

Constructor	Description
StringBuilder()	Default constructor.
StringBuilder(int *capacity*)	
StringBuilder(int *capacity*, int *maxCapacity*)	Constructs a **StringBuilder** with the specified initial capacity. Optional *maxCapacity* argument specifies maximum number of characters the **StringBuilder** can contain.
StringBuilder(String* *str*)	
StringBuilder(String* *str*, int *capacity*)	Initializes a **StringBuilder** with the specified string. Optional *capacity* argument specifies the suggested initial capacity of the **StringBuilder**.
StringBuilder(String* *str*, int *index*, int *length*, int *capacity*)	Constructs a **StringBuilder** with the specified initial capacity and initializes it with the specified string by copying the *length* characters starting at the index *index*.

Table 3.19 **StringBuilder** class properties.

Get/Set	Type	Property	Description
Get/set	**int**	**Capacity**	Gets/sets the capacity of the **StringBuilder**.
Get/set	**__wchar_t**	**Chars(int *index*)**	Gets/sets a character at the specified index.
Get/set	**int**	**Length**	Gets/sets the number of characters in the **StringBuilder**.
Get	**int**	**MaxCapacity**	Contains the maximum number of characters the **StringBuilder** can hold.

Table 3.20 **StringBuilder** class methods.

Member	Description
StringBuilder* Append(*TYPE value***)**	Appends the string representation of the specified value to the **StringBuilder**.

NOTE: Possible values of TYPE are: bool, unsigned char, __wchar_t, __wchar_t[], Decimal, double, short, int, __int64, Object*, char, float, String, unsigned short, unsigned int, unsigned __int64.

StringBuilder* Append(__wchar_t *value*, int *repeatCount*)	Appends the specified character repeated the *repeatCount* times to the **StringBuilder**.
StringBuilder* Append(String* *value*, int *startIndex*, int *count*)	Appends the *count* characters from the specified string starting at the *startIndex* to the **StringBuilder**.

<Continued on Next Page>

<Table 3.20 Continued>

Member	Description
StringBuilder* Append(__wchar_t *value[]*, int *startIndex*, int *count*)	Appends the *count* characters from the specified character array starting at the *startIndex* to the **StringBuilder**.
StringBuilder* AppendFormat(String* *format*, Object* a*rg*)	
StringBuilder* AppendFormat(String* *format*, Object* a*rg1*, Object* a*rg2*)	
StringBuilder* AppendFormat(String* *format*, Object* arg1, Object* arg2, Object* arg3)	Formats and appends the specified string to the **StringBuilder**.
StringBuilder* AppendFormat(String* *format*, Object* a*rgs[]*)	
StringBuilder* AppendFormat(IFormatProvider* *provider*, String* *format*, Object* a*rgs[]*)	Formats the specified string and appends the result to the **StringBuilder.** Optional *provider* argument specifies custom **IFormatProvider** interface for formatting.
int EnsureCapacity(int *capacity*)	Increases the capacity of the **StringBuilder** to the specified capacity.
StringBuilder* Insert(int *index*, *TYPE value*)	Inserts the string representation of the specified value into the **StringBuilder** starting at the specified index.

NOTE: *Possible values of TYPE are:* **bool, unsigned char, __wchar_t, __wchar_t[], Decimal, double, short, int, __int64, Object*, char, float, String, unsigned short, unsigned int, unsigned __int64.**

Member	Description
StringBuilder* Insert(int *index*, String* *value*, int *count*)	Inserts the *count* characters from the specified string into the **StringBuilder** starting at the specified index.
StringBuilder* Insert(int *index*, __wchar_t *value[]*, int *startIndex*, int *count*)	Inserts the *count* characters from the specified array of characters starting at the *startIndex* into the **StringBuilder** starting at the index *index*.
StringBuilder* Remove(int *index*, int *length*)	Removes the *length* characters starting at the specified index.
StringBuilder* Replace(__wchar_t *oldChar*, __wchar_t *newChar*)	
StringBuilder* Replace(__wchar_t *oldChar*, __wchar_t *newChar*, int *index*, int *count*)	Replaces all occurrences of the specified old character with the new character. Optional *index* and *count* arguments specify the section of the string to conduct the replacement within.

<Continued on Next Page>

<Table 3.20 Continued>

Member	Description
StringBuilder* Replace(String* *oldStr*, **String*** *newStr***)**	
StringBuilder* Replace(String* *oldStr*, **String*** *newStr*, **int** *index*, **int** *count***)**	Replaces all occurrences of the specified old string with the new string. Optional *index* and *count* arguments specify the section of the string to conduct the replacement within.
String* ToString(int i*ndex*, **int** *length***)**	Converts a section of the **StringBuilder** identified by the *index* and *length* arguments into the **String**.

Console I/O

Console I/O is a must have feature of any language. Managed C++ implements console I/O by means of the **Console** class. The **Console** class has no constructors and is entirely comprised of static members for reading/writing data to/from standard input/output and error streams. The **Console** class has the following inheritance diagram:

```
Object
|- Console

Attributes: none
Abstract: No
Sealed: Yes
Implemented Interfaces: none
```

The **Console** class provides four main methods with numerous overloads for reading/writing console input/output:

* **Read**—For reading a single character from the standard input stream.
* **ReadLine**—For reading a CR/LF-terminated line of characters from the standard input stream.
  NOTE: The **Read/ReadLine** methods block program execution until the data is read from the input stream.
* **Write**-for writing a value to the standard output stream.
* **WriteLine**-for writing a CR/LF-terminated value to the standard output stream.

Also, the **Console** class allows specifying user streams in place of the standard input, output, and error streams using the **SetIn**, **SetOut,** and **SerError** methods. The complete reference of the **Console** class properties and methods is given in Tables 3.21 and 3.22.

Table 3.21 **Console** class properties (all static).

Get/Set	Type	Property	Description
Get	**TextWriter***	**Error**	Returns the standard error output stream.
Get	**TextReader***	**In**	Returns the standard input stream.
Get	**TextWriter***	**Out**	Returns the standard output stream.

Table 3.22 **Console** class methods.

Method	Description
static Stream* OpenStandardError()	
static Stream* OpenStandardError(int _bufferSize_)	Opens the standard error stream. Optional **_bufferSize_** argument specifies the desired buffer size.
static Stream* OpenStandardInput()	
static Stream* OpenStandardInput(int _bufferSize_)	Opens the standard input stream. Optional **_bufferSize_** argument specifies the desired buffer size.
static Stream* OpenStandardOutput()	
static Stream* OpenStandardOutput(int _bufferSize_)	Opens the standard output stream. Optional **_bufferSize_** argument specifies the desired buffer size.
static int Read()	Reads a character from the standard input stream.
static String* ReadLine()	Reads a line from the standard input stream. A line must be terminated with the CR/LF pair before it can be read.
static void SetError(TextWriter* _stream_)	Specifies the new standard error stream.
static void SetIn(TextReader* _stream_)	Specifies the new standard input stream.
static void SetOut(TextWriter* _stream_)	Specifies the new standard output stream.
static void Write(bool _value_)	
static void Write(__wchar_t _value_)	
static void Write(Decimal _value_)	
static void Write(double _value_)	
static void Write(int _value_)	
static void Write(__int64 _value_)	
static void Write(Object* _value_)	
static void Write(float _value_)	
static void Write(String* _value_)	
static void Write(unsigned int _value_)	
static void Write(unsigned __int64 _value_)	Writes the specified primitive **_value_** to the output stream.

<Continued on Next Page>

<Table 3.22 Continued>

Method	Description
static void Write(__wchar_t __gc[] *str***)**	
static void Write(__wchar_t __gc[] *str***, int** *index***, int** *length***)**	Writes the Unicode character array to the output stream. Optional *index* and *length* arguments identify the section of the array to output.
static void Write(String* *format***, Object*** *arg1***)**	
static void Write(String* *format***, Object*** *arg1***, Object*** *arg2***)**	
static void Write(String* *format***, Object*** *arg1***, Object*** *arg2***, Object*** *arg3***)**	
static void Write(String* *format***, Object*** *arg1***, Object*** *arg2***, Object*** *arg3***, Object*** *arg4***, ...)**	Formats the string and writes it to the output stream. The overload accepting variable number of format arguments is not CLS compliant.
static void Write(String* *format***, Object[]** *args***)**	Formats and writes the *args* arguments to the output stream.
static void WriteLine()	Writes a CR/LF pair to the output stream.
static void WriteLine(bool *value***)**	
static void WriteLine(__wchar_t *value***)**	
static void WriteLine(Decimal *value***)**	
static void WriteLine(double *value***)**	
static void WriteLine(int *value***)**	
static void WriteLine(__int64 *value***)**	
static void WriteLine(Object* *value***)**	
static void WriteLine(float *value***)**	
static void WriteLine(String* *value***)**	
static void WriteLine(unsigned int *value***)**	
static void WriteLine(unsigned __int64 *value***)**	Writes the specified primitive *value* and a CR/LF pair to the output stream.
static void WriteLine(__wchar_t __gc[]*array***)**	
static void WriteLine(__wchar_t __gc[] *array***, int** *index***, int** *length***)**	Writes the Unicode character array and a CR/LF pair to the output stream. Optional *index* and *length* arguments identify the section of the array to output.

<Continued on Next Page>

<Table 3.22 Continued>

Method	Description
static void WriteLine(String* *format*, **Object* arg1)**	
static void WriteLine(String* *format*, **Object*** *arg1*, **Object*** *arg2*)	
static void WriteLine(String* *format*, **Object*** *arg1*, **Object*** *arg2*, **Object*** *arg3*)	
static void WriteLine(String* *format*, **Object*** *arg1*, **Object*** *arg2*, **Object*** *arg3*, **Object*** *arg4*, ...)	Formats the string and writes it to the output stream terminating with the CR/LF pair. The overload accepting variable number of format arguments is not CLS compliant.
static void WriteLine(String* *format*, **Object[] args)**	Formats and writes the *args* arguments to the output stream including a CR/LF pair.

DateTime Class

The .NET Framework Class Library supports date/time operations by means of the **DateTime** value type. The **DateTime** class can represent dates in the range of 1/01/01 to 12/31/9999. Internally, the **DateTime** class stores date/time information in a 64-bit integer representing the number of 100-ns ticks elapsed since 12:00 AM January 1, 1 AD.

The **DateTime** class has the following inheritance diagram:

```
Object
|- DateTime
```

```
Attributes: Serializable
Abstract: No
Sealed: No
Implemented Interfaces: IComparable, IFormattable, IConvertible
```

Because the **DateTime** is a value type, the class supports comparison operators: ==, !=, >, <, >=, <= for comparing **DateTime** objects and arithmetic operators: + and – for adding/subtracting time spans to/from the **DateTime** and calculating time spans.

The complete reference of the **DateTime** class constructors, fields, properties, methods, and operators is given in Tables 3.23 through 3.27.

Table 3.23 **DateTime** class constructors.

Constructor	Description
DateTime(__int64 *ticks***)**	Constructs a **DateTime** object initialized with a number of 100-ns ticks elapsed since 12:00 AM January 1, 1 AD.
DateTime(int *year***, int** *month***, int** *day***)**	
DateTime(int *year***, int** *month***, int** *day***, Calendar*** *calendar***)**	Constructs a **DateTime** object accurate to the day. The optional *calendar* parameter allows specifying calendar type, e.g., **GregorianCalendar**, **JulianCalendar**, **HebrewCalendar**, etc.
DateTime(int *year***, int** *month***, int** *day***, int** *hour***, int** *minute***, int** *second***)**	
DateTime(int *year***, int** *month***, int** *day***, int** *hour***, int** *minute***, int** *second***, Calendar*** *calendar***)**	Constructs a **DateTime** object accurate to the second. The optional *calendar* parameter allows specifying calendar type, e.g., **GregorianCalendar**, **JulianCalendar**, **HebrewCalendar**, etc.
DateTime(int *year***, int** *month***, int** *day***, int** *hour***, int** *minute***, int** *second***, int** *millisecond***)**	
DateTime(int *year***, int** *month***, int** *day***, int** *hour***, int** *minute***, int** *second***, int** *millisecond***, Calendar*** *calendar***)**	Constructs a **DateTime** object accurate to the millisecond. The optional *calendar* parameter allows specifying calendar type, e.g., **GregorianCalendar**, **JulianCalendar**, **HebrewCalendar**, etc.

Table 3.24 **DateTime** class fields.

Field	Description
static DateTime MaxValue	Max date value: 23:59:59.9999999, 12/31/9999.
static DateTime MinValue	Min date value: 00:00:00.0000000, 1/1/0001

Table 3.25 **DateTime** class properties.

Get/Set	Type	Property	Description
Get	**Date**	**int**	Returns the date portion of the **DateTime** with time set to 12:00 AM.
Get	**Day**	**int**	Returns the day of month portion of the **DateTime** object.
Get	**DayOfWeek**	**DayOfWeek**	Returns the day of week of the **DateTime** object.
Get	**int**	**DayOfYear**	Returns the day of year of the **DateTime** object.
Get	**int**	**Hour**	Returns the hours portion of the **DateTime** object.
Get	**int**	**Millisecond**	Returns the millisecond portion of the **DateTime** object.
Get	**int**	**Minute**	Returns the minutes portion of the **DateTime** object.
Get	**int**	**Month**	Returns the month portion of the **DateTime** object.
Get	**static DateTime**	**Now**	Returns the current date/time.

<Continued on Next Page>

<Table 3.25 Continued>

Get/Set	Type	Property	Description
Get	int	**Second**	Returns the seconds portion of the **DateTime** object.
Get	__int64	**Ticks**	Returns the **DateTime** object representation in 100-ns ticks.
Get	**TimeSpan**	**TimeOfDay**	Returns the time portion of the **DateTime** object.
Get	**static DateTime**	**Today**	Returns the current date with time set to 12:00 AM.
Get	**static DateTime**	**UtcNow**	Returns the current date/time expressed at the Universal Coordinated Time (UTC).
Get	int	**Year**	Returns the year portion of the **DateTime** object.

Table 3.26 **DateTime** class methods.

Method	Description
DateTime Add(TimeSpan *value***)**	Adds the specified **TimeSpan** to the date.
DateTime AddDays(double *value***)**	Adds the specified number of days (fractional OK) to the date.
DateTime AddHours(double *value***)**	Adds the specified number of hours (fractional OK) to the date.
DateTime AddMilliseconds(double *value***)**	Adds the specified number of milliseconds (fractional OK) to the date.
DateTime AddMinutes(double *value***)**	Adds the specified number of minutes (fractional OK) to the date.
DateTime AddMonths(int *value***)**	Adds the specified number of month to the date.
DateTime AddSeconds(double *value***)**	Adds the specified number of seconds (fractional OK) to the date.
DateTime AddTicks(__int64 *value***)**	Adds the specified number of 100-ns ticks to the date.
DateTime AddYears(int *value***)**	Adds the specified number of years to the date.
static int Compare(DateTime *date1***, DateTime** *date2***)**	Compares two dates and returns <0 if *date1*<*date2*, 0 if *date1*=*date2*, >0 if *date1*>*date2*.
__sealed int CompareTo(Object* *value***)**	Compares the date with a **DateTime** object represented by the *value* parameter.
static int DaysInMonth(int *year***, int** *month***)**	Returns the number of days in the specified month of the specified year.
static DateTime FromFileTime(__int64 *fileTime***)**	Creates a **DateTime** equivalent to the specified OS file timestamp.

<Continued on Next Page>

<Table 3.26 Continued>

Method	Description
File Time	OS File Time is calculated in 100-ns ticks elapsed since 1/1/1601 12:00 AM, UTC.
static DateTime FromOADate(double *d*)	Creates a **DateTime** equivalent to the specified OLE Automation Date.
String* GetDateTimeFormats() __gc[]	
String* GetDateTimeFormats(IFormatProvider* *provider*) __gc[]	Returns an array of **String** objects corresponding to all possible **DateTime** format representations supported by the standard **DateTime** format specifier. Optional *provider* argument specifies custom **IFormatProvider** interface for date formatting.
String* GetDateTimeFormats(__wchar_t *format*) __gc[]	
String* GetDateTimeFormats(__wchar_t *format*, IFormatProvider* *provider*) __gc[]	Returns an array of **String** objects corresponding to all possible **DateTime** format representations supported by the specified *format* specifier. Optional *provider* argument specifies custom **IFormatProvider** interface for date formatting.
static bool IsLeapYear(int *year*)	Returns true if the specified year is a leap year.
static DateTime Parse(String* *str*)	
static DateTime Parse(String* *str*, IFormatProvider* *provider*)	
static DateTime Parse(String* *str*, IFormatProvider* *provider*, DateTimeStyles *flags*)	Converts the specified string into a **DateTime**. Optional *provider* and *flags* arguments allow specifying custom **IFormatProvider** interface for date parsing and parsing options.
static DateTime ParseExact(String* *str*, String* *format*, IFormatProvider* *provider*)	
static DateTime ParseExact(String* *str*, String* *format*, IFormatProvider* *provider*, DateTimeStyles *style*)	
static DateTime ParseExact(String* *str*, String* *formats* __gc[], IFormatProvider* *provider*, DateTimeStyles *style*)	Converts the specified string into a **DateTime**. Optional *provider* and *flags* arguments allow specifying custom **IFormatProvider** interface for date parsing and parsing options. The string must match a specified format(s) exactly.
TimeSpan Subtract(DateTime *value*)	Calculates a time span by subtracting two dates.
DateTime Subtract(TimeSpan *value*)	Calculates a new date by subtracting a time span from the date.

<Continued on Next Page>

<Table 3.26 Continued>

Method	Description
__int64 ToFileTime()	Converts the date into an OS file time.
DateTime ToLocalTime()	Converts the UTC date/time into local date/time.
String* ToLongDateString()	Formats the date into a long string representation (e.g., January 18th, 1976).
String* ToLongTimeString()	Formats the time portion of the date into a long string representation.
double ToOADate()	Converts the date into an OLE Automation date.
String* ToShortDateString()	Formats the date into a short string representation (e.g., 01/18/1976).
String* ToShortTimeString()	Formats the time portion of the date into a short string representation.
DateTime ToUniversalTime()	Converts the local date/time into a UTC date/time.

NOTE: *The **DateTime** class **ToShortDateString**, **ToLongDateString**, **ToShortTimeString**, and **ToLongTimeString** methods are very convenient for formatting dates because they do not require the knowledge of the date/time format specifiers used in conjunction with the **Console::WriteLine** and **String::Format** methods.*

Table 3.27 **DateTime** class operators.

Operator	Return Type	Operands	Description
+	DateTime	DateTime, TimeSpan	Adds a time span to a date and returns a new date.
==	bool	DateTime, DateTime	Returns **true** if two dates are equal.
>	bool	DateTime, DateTime	Returns **true** if the first date is greater than the second date.
>=	bool	DateTime, DateTime	Returns **true** if the first date is greater than or equal to the second date.
!=	bool	DateTime, DateTime	Returns **true** if two dates are not equal.
<	bool	DateTime, DateTime	Returns **true** if the first date is less than the second date.
<=	bool	DateTime, DateTime	Returns **true** if the first date is less than or equal to the second date.
-	DateTime	DateTime, TimeSpan	Subtracts a time span from a date and returns a new date.
-	TimeSpan	DateTime, DateTime	Subtracts two dates and returns a time span between the two dates.

Time Intervals

The .NET Framework represents time intervals by means of the **TimeSpan** value type, which has the following inheritance diagram:

```
Object
|- TimeSpan
```

Attributes: **Serializable**
Abstract: No
Sealed: No
Implemented Interfaces: **IComparable**

The **TimeSpan** class is tightly linked to the **DateTime** class and, similarly to the **DateTime,** uses internal interval representation in 100-ns ticks. The default string representation of a time span has the following syntax: *days.hours:minutes:seconds*, i.e., 47.00:00:00.

Because the **TimeSpan** is a value type, the class supports comparison operators: ==, !=, >, <, >=, <= for comparing **TimeSpan** objects and arithmetic operators: + and – for adding/subtracting time spans to/from the **DateTime** and calculating new time spans.

The detailed account of the **TimeSpan** class constructors, fields, properties, methods, and operators is given in Tables 3.28 through 3.32.

Table 3.28 **TimeSpan** class constructors.

Constructor	Description
TimeSpan(__int64 *ticks*)	Constructs a **TimeSpan** class using the specified number of ticks.
TimeSpan(int *hours*, int *minutes*, int *seconds*)	
TimeSpan(int *days*, int *hours*, int *minutes*, int *seconds*)	
TimeSpan(int *days*, int *hours*, int *minutes*, int *seconds*, int *milliseconds*)	Constructs a **TimeSpan** class using the specified number of days, hours, minutes, and seconds and milliseconds.

Table 3.29 **TimeSpan** class fields.

Field	Description
static TimeSpan MaxValue	Maximum **TimeSpan** value.
static TimeSpan MinValue	Minimum **TimeSpan** value.
const __int64 TicksPerDay	Number of ticks in 1 day.
const __int64 TicksPerHour	Number of ticks in 1 hour.
const __int64 TicksPerMillisecond	Number of ticks in 1 millisecond.
const __int64 TicksPerMinute	Number of ticks in 1 minute.
const __int64 TicksPerSecond	Number of ticks in 1 second.
static TimeSpan Zero	Zero time span.

Table 3.30 **TimeSpan** class properties.

Get/Set	Type	Property	Description
Get	int	**Days**	Returns the number of whole days in the time span.
Get	int	**Hours**	Returns the number of whole hours in the time span.
Get	int	**Milliseconds**	Returns the number of whole milliseconds in the time span.
Get	int	**Minutes**	Returns the number of whole minutes in the time span.
Get	int	**Seconds**	Returns the number of whole seconds in the time span.
Get	__int64	**Ticks**	Returns the number of 100-ns ticks in the time span.
Get	double	**TotalDays**	Returns the time span value in days.
Get	double	**TotalHours**	Returns the time span value in hours.
Get	double	**TotalMilliseconds**	Returns the time span value in milliseconds.
Get	double	**TotalMinutes**	Returns the time span value in minutes.
Get	double	**TotalSeconds**	Returns the time span value in seconds.

Table 3.31 **TimeSpan** class methods.

Method	Description
TimeSpan Add(TimeSpan *t*)	Adds the specified **TimeSpan** to the current time span.
static int Compare(TimeSpan *t1*, TimeSpan *t2*)	Compares two **TimeSpan** values and returns = 0 if two intervals are equal, or >0 if *t1* is greater than *t2*, or <0 if *t1* is less than *t2*.
__sealed int CompareTo(Object* *value*)	Compares the current time span with the *value* object.
TimeSpan Duration()	Returns the current time span (negative intervals are made positive).
static TimeSpan FromDays(double *days*)	Creates a **TimeSpan** object from the interval in days.
static TimeSpan FromHours(double *hours*)	Creates a **TimeSpan** object from the interval in hours.
static TimeSpan FromMilliseconds(double *ms*)	Creates a **TimeSpan** object from the interval in milliseconds.
static TimeSpan FromMinutes(double *minutes*)	Creates a **TimeSpan** object from the interval in minutes.
static TimeSpan FromSeconds(double *seconds*)	Creates a **TimeSpan** object from the interval in seconds.
static TimeSpan FromTicks(__int64 *ticks*)	Creates a **TimeSpan** object from the interval in 100-ns ticks.
TimeSpan Negate()	Negates the time interval.
static TimeSpan Parse(String* *str*)	Creates a **TimeSpan** object by parsing the string.
TimeSpan Subtract(TimeSpan *t*)	Subtracts the specified **TimeSpan** from the current time span.

Table 3.32 **TimeSpan** class operators.

Operator	Return Type	Operands	Description
+	**TimeSpan**	**TimeSpan, TimeSpan**	Adds two time intervals.
==	**bool**	**TimeSpan**, **TimeSpan**	Compares two time intervals.
>	**bool**	**TimeSpan, TimeSpan**	Returns **true** if the first time interval is greater than the second.
>=	**bool**	**TimeSpan, TimeSpan**	Returns **true** if the first time interval is greater than or equal to the second.
!=	**bool**	**TimeSpan, TimeSpan**	Returns **true** if the two time intervals are not equal.
<	**bool**	**TimeSpan, TimeSpan**	Returns **true** if the first time interval is less than the second.
<=	**bool**	**TimeSpan, TimeSpan**	Returns **true** if the first time interval is less than or equal to the second.
-	**TimeSpan**	**TimeSpan, TimeSpan**	Subtracts two time intervals
-	**TimeSpan**	**TimeSpan**	Unary negation operator returns the negated current interval.
+	**TimeSpan**	**TimeSpan**	Unary plus operator returns the current interval.

Math Class

The .NET Framework does not utilize global functions. For that reason, the .NET Framework Class Library implements math functions as static methods of the **Math** class:

```
Object
|- Math
```

```
Attributes: None
Abstract: No
Sealed: Yes
Implemented Interfaces: None
```

The set of functions in the **Math** class is similar to the set of functions defined in the math.h standard C++ math header file. The **Math** class defines **E** and **PI** constants as well as **Abs**, trigonometric, hyperbolic, logarithmic (**log**, **log10**), **Min/Max**, square root (**sqrt**), exponent (**exp**), **Sign**, and rounding functions (**Floor**, **Ceil**, **Round**).

The **Math** class fields and methods are summarized in Tables 3.33 through 3.34.

Table 3.33 **Math** class fields.

Field	Description
const double E	The natural logarithm base e = 2.7182818284590452354.
const double PI	π = 3.14159265358979323846.

Table 3.34 **Math** class methods.

Method	Description
static Decimal Abs(Decimal *x*)	
static double Abs(double *x*)	
static short Abs(short *x*)	
static int Abs(int *x*)	
static __int64 Abs(__int64 *x*)	
static char Abs(char *x*)	
static float Abs(float *x*)	Returns the absolute value of a specified number.
static double Acos(double *x*)	Returns the angle whose cosine is the specified number.
static double Asin(double *x*)	Returns the angle whose sine is the specified number.
static double Atan(double *x*)	Returns the angle whose tangent is the specified number.
static double Atan2(double *y*, double *x*)	Returns the angle whose tangent is the quotient of two specified numbers.
static double Ceiling(double *x*)	Returns the smallest whole number greater than or equal to the specified number.
static double Cos(double *x*)	Returns the cosine of the specified angle.
static double Cosh(double *x*)	Returns the hyperbolic cosine of the specified angle.
static double Exp(double *x*)	Returns *e* raised to the specified power.
static double Floor(double *x*)	Returns the largest whole number less than or equal to the specified number.
static double IEEERemainder(double *x*, double *y*)	Returns the remainder resulting from the division of a specified number by another specified number.
static double Log(double *x*)	
static double Log(double *x*, double *base*)	Returns the logarithm of a specified number. If *base* is not specified, natural logarithm is assumed.
static double Log10(double *x*)	Returns the base 10 logarithm of a specified number.

<Continued on Next Page>

<Table 3.34 Continued>

Method	Description
static unsigned char Max(unsigned char *x*, unsigned char *y*)	
static Decimal Max(Decimal *x*, Decimal *y*)	
static double Max(double *x*, double *y*)	
static short Max(short *x*, short *y*)	
static int Max(int *x*, int *y*)	
static __int64 Max(__int64 *x*, __int64 *y*)	
static char Max(char *x*, char *y*)	
static float Max(float *x*, float *y*)	
static unsigned short Max(unsigned short *x*, unsigned short *y*)	
static unsigned int Max(unsigned int *x*, unsigned int *y*)	
static unsigned __int64 Max(unsigned __int64 *x*, unsigned __int64 *y*)	Returns the larger of two specified numbers.
static unsigned char Min(unsigned char *x*, unsigned char *y*)	
static Decimal Min(Decimal *x*, Decimal *y*)	
static double Min(double *x*, double *y*)	
static short Min(short *x*, short *y*)	
static int Min(int *x*, int *y*)	
static __int64 Min(__int64 *x*, __int64 *y*)	
static char Min(char *x*, char *y*)	
static float Min(float *x*, float *y*)	
static unsigned short Min(unsigned short *x*, unsigned short *y*)	
static unsigned int Min(unsigned int *x*, unsigned int *y*)	
static unsigned __int64 Min(unsigned __int64 *x*, unsigned __int64 *y*)	Returns the smaller of two numbers.
static double Pow(double *x*, double *y*)	Returns a specified number raised to the specified power.
static Decimal Round(Decimal *x*)	
static Decimal Round(Decimal *x*, int *digits*)	
static double Round(double *x*)	
static double Round(double *x*, int *digits*)	Returns the number nearest the specified value. Optional ***digits*** argument specifies the number of significant fractional digits in the resulting rounded number.

<Continued on Next Page>

<Table 3.34 Continued>

Method	Description
static int Sign(Decimal *x*)	
static int Sign(double *x*)	
static int Sign(short *x*)	
static int Sign(int *x*)	
static int Sign(__int64 *x*)	
static int Sign(char *x*)	
static int Sign(float *x*)	Returns a value indicating the sign of a number.
static double Sin(double *x*)	Returns the sine of the specified angle.
static double Sinh(double *x*)	Returns the hyperbolic sine of the specified angle.
static double Sqrt(double *x*)	Returns the square root of a specified number.
static double Tan(double *x*)	Returns the tangent of the specified angle.
static double Tanh(double *x*)	Returns the hyperbolic tangent of the specified angle.

Random Number Generator

Generating random (or more precisely pseudorandom) numbers is essential for many applications including statistical computations, games, and cryptography. The .NET Framework Class Library supports random-number generation by means of the **Random** class:

```
Object
|- Random
```

```
Attributes: Serializable
Abstract: No
Sealed: No
Implemented Interfaces: None
```

The **Random** class produces uniform distribution of random numbers. You can implement your own random-number distribution by deriving from the **Random** class and overriding its methods.

The **Random** class constructors and methods are summarized in Tables 3.35 and 3.36.

Table 3.35 **Random** class constructors.

Constructor	Description
Random()	Default constructor.
Random(int *Seed*)	Initialized the random-number generator using the specified seed.

Table 3.36 **Random** class methods.

Method	Description
virtual int Next()	Returns a random number between 0 and **MaxValue** (0x7FFFFFFF).
virtual int Next(int *max*)	Returns a random number between 0 and *max*.
virtual int Next(int *min*, int *max*)	Returns a random number between *min* and *max*.
virtual void NextBytes(unsigned char *array* __gc[])	Initializes the elements of the specified *array* with random numbers.
virtual double NextDouble()	Returns a random number between 0 and 1.
virtual double Sample()	Returns a random number between 0 and 1.

Exceptions

All .NET Framework exceptions derive from the System namespace **Exception** class, which has the following inheritance diagram:

```
Object
|- Exception

Attributes: Serializable
Abstract: No
Sealed: No
Implemented Interfaces: ISerializable
```

Although you can throw any type using the **throw** operator, you should derive your own exception types from the **Exception** class. All system exceptions, however, are derived from the **SystemException** class that directly inherits from the **Exception**.

The **Exception** class provides a few useful properties such as **Message** for error message, **HResult** for the error **HRESULT** code, and **TargetSite** to identify the message that threw the exception. The **Exception** class constructors, properties, and methods are summarized in Tables 3.37 through 3.39.

Table 3.37 **Exception** class constructors.

Constructor	Description
Exception()	Default constructor.
Exception(String* *errorMsg*)	Constructs an **Exception** object with the specified error message.
protected: Exception(SerializationInfo* *info*, StreamingContext *context*)	Constructs an **Exception** object with the specified serialized information about the exception being thrown.
Exception(String* *errorMsg*, Exception* *innerExcept*)	Constructs a new exception with the specified error messages based on the previously thrown exception *innerExcept*.

Table 3.38 **Exception** class properties.

Get/Set	Type	Property	Virtual	Description
Get/Set	**String***	**HelpLink**	No	Gets/sets a URL or URN of the exception help information, e.g., file:///C:/Program Files/Gems 3D/Gems3D.htm#SomeError.
Get/Set	**int**	**HResult**	No	Gets/sets **HRESULT** of an exception.
Get	**Exception***	**InnerException**	Yes	Contains a pointer to the exception that caused the current exception.
Get/Set	**String***	**Message**	Yes	Gets/sets an exception error message.
Get	**String***	**StackTrace**	Yes	Contains a snapshot of the call stack at the moment when an exception occurred.
Get	**MethodBase***	**TargetSite**	Yes	Contains information about the method that threw the exception.

Table 3.39 **Exception** class methods.

Method	Description
virtual Exception* GetBaseException()	Returns the first exception in the chain of exceptions that caused the current exception.

Delegates

All delegates (i.e., function or class method pointers) in Managed C++ are defined using the **__delegate** keyword implicitly derive from the System namespace **Delegate** class:

```
Object
|- Delegate
   |- MultiCastDelegate


Attributes: Serializable
Abstract: Yes
Sealed: No
Implemented Interfaces: IClonable, ISerializable
```

The .NET Framework Class Library supports two types of delegates:

* *singlecast* that invokes exactly one method.

* *multicast* that can invoke more than one method in a chain manner.

The multicast delegates are implemented by means of the **MulticastDelegate** class. Both the **Delegate** and the **MulticastDelegate** classes have essentially the same methods. Thus, only the **Delegate** class constructors, fields, properties, methods, and operators are listed in Tables 3.38 through 3.41.

You only have to use the **Delegate** class methods on extremely rare occasions. In most cases operations involving delegates are focused around declaring delegates using the __**delegate** keyword and constructing delegate pointers using the delegate constructor:

```
__delegate void MyDelegateType(int a);
...
MyDelegateType* MyDelegate = new MyDelegateType(SomeClassPtr,
    SomeClassType::MethodName);
```

Delegates are distinguished by name and the signature of the method or function they represent. Delegates can be hooked to both static and instance class methods. If you construct a delegate using the static method, the target pointer in the delegate constructor must be null (zero):

```
MyDelegateType* MyDelegate = new MyDelegateType(0,
    SomeClassType::StaticMethodName);
```

Table 3.38 **Delegate** class constructors.

Constructor	Description
protected: Delegate(Object* *target*, String* *method*)	Initializes a delegate that invokes the specified instance method on the *target* class instance.
protected: Delegate(Type* *target*, String* *method*)	Initializes a delegate that invokes the specified static method from the specified *target* class.

Table 3.39 **Delegate** class properties.

Get/Set	Type	Property	Description
Get	**MethodInfo***	**Method**	Returns information on the static method represented by the delegate.
Get	**Object***	**Target**	Returns the object on which the current delegate invokes the instance method(s).

Table 3.40 **Delegate** class methods.

Method	*Description*
static Delegate* Combine(Delegate* *delegates***[])**	Creates a new multicast delegate with the invocation list corresponding to the concatenated invocation lists of all *delegates*.
static Delegate* Combine(Delegate* *a***, Delegate*** *b***)**	Creates a new multicast delegate with the invocation list corresponding to the concatenated invocation lists of the *a* and *b* delegates.
protected: virtual Delegate* CombineImpl(Delegate* *d***)**	Creates a new multicast delegate by concatenating the invocation list of the current delegate with the invocation list of the *d* delegate.
static Delegate* CreateDelegate(Type* *type***, MethodInfo*** *method***)**	Creates a delegate of the specified type representing the specified static method.
static Delegate* CreateDelegate(Type* *type***, Object*** *target***, String*** *method***)**	Creates a delegate of the specified type representing the specified instance method of the *target* object.
static Delegate* CreateDelegate(Type* *type***, Type*** *target***, String*** *method***)**	Creates a delegate of the specified type representing the specified method of the *target* type.
static Delegate* CreateDelegate(Type* *type***, Object*** *target***, String*** *method***, bool** *ignoreCase***)**	Creates a delegate of the specified type representing the specified instance method of the *target* object. The *ignoreCase* parameter specifies whether to honor case when resolving the delegate method name.
Object* DynamicInvoke(Object* *args* **__gc[])**	Dynamically invokes the late-bound method represented by the current delegate.
protected: virtual Object* DynamicInvokeImpl(Object* *args* **__gc[])**	Dynamically invokes the late-bound method represented by the current delegate.
virtual Delegate* GetInvocationList() []	Returns the delegate's invocation list.
protected: virtual MethodInfo* GetMethodImpl()	Returns the static method represented by the current delegate.
virtual void GetObjectData(SerializationInfo* *info***, StreamingContext** *context***)**	Implements the **ISerializable** interface and returns the data needed to serialize the delegate.

<Continued on Next Page>

<Table 3.40 Continued>

Method	Description
static Delegate* Remove(Delegate* *a*, Delegate* *b*)	Returns a new delegate with the invocation list equal to the invocation list of the delegate *a* minus the invocation list of the delegate *b*.
protected: virtual Delegate* RemoveImpl(Delegate* *d*)	Returns a new delegate with the invocation list equal to the invocation list of the current delegate minus the invocation list of the delegate *d*.

Table 3.41 **Delegate** class operators.

Operator	Return Type	Operands	Description
==	**bool**	**Delegate***, **Delegate***	Returns **true** if the two delegates are equal.
!=	**bool**	**Delegate***, **Delegate***	Returns **true** if the two delegates are not equal.

Multicast Delegates

Multicast delegates are represented in the .NET Framework by means of the **MultiCastDelegate** class:

```
Object
|- Delegate
   |- MultiCastDelegate
```

```
Attributes: Serializable
Abstract: Yes
Sealed: No
Implemented Interfaces: None
```

Just like the **Delegate** class, the **MulticastDelegate** class is special and you cannot explicitly derive your own classes from it. When you instantiate a delegate object, you always instantiate a singlecast delegate. Then the singlecast delegate is automatically converted to a multicast delegate as soon as you associate more than one method with it.

Multicast delegates internally implement a linked list of single-cast delegates and invoke delegates from the list sequentially. If a multicast delegate must return a value it will return the return value produced by the last delegate in the linked list.

If a multicast delegate accepts parameters that are objects passed by reference and one of the single-cast delegates in the chain modifies the objects, the delegates that appear later in the chain will see the changes done to the objects passed by reference.

Multicast delegates are constructed as single-cast delegates using the **new** operator and the delegate constructor. If you use the **new** operator in conjunction with the assignment operator (=) you will create a single-cast delegate initially. To add additional methods to a single-cast delegate and thus turn a single-cast delegate into a multicast delegate, you should use the += operator:

```
MyDelegateType* MyDelegate += new MyDelegateType(SomeClassPtr,
    SomeClassType::SomeMethod);
```

To remove a method from a multicast delegate invocation list you can use the -= operator:

```
MyDelegateType* MyDelegate -= new MyDelegateType(SomeClassPtr,
    SomeClassType::SomeMethod);
```

Alternatively, you can use the **static Delegate* Remove(Delegate* *a*, Delegate* *b*)** method, which effectively computes and returns a difference of the invocation lists (*a* - *b*) of the specified delegates *a* and *b*.

> **NOTE:** If you remove all methods from a multicast delegate invocation list the delegate object becomes a null reference and you should not attempt invoking the delegate as an exception will be thrown.

Events

Delegates are commonly used to handle events. There is an important difference between invoking events and invoking delegates, however. The compiler automatically injects code in your class that makes event delegates behave differently from ordinary delegates.

First of all, to declare an event delegate, you must use the **__event** keyword:

```
__event StartEvent* OnStart;
```

Then you can use the += and the **new** operators to add methods to an event delegate, or the -= and the **new** operator to remove methods from an event delegate.

The differences between event delegates and ordinary multicast delegate are the following:

* The compiler automatically injects code that makes your event delegate member private. Thus, you cannot initialize it with the = operator as ordinary delegate members;

* The compiler automatically injects **Add_*DelegateName*** and **Remove_*DelegateName*** methods to support += and -= operators for adding/removing delegates to/from the event;

* The compiler automatically injects a protected method with the same name as your event delegate member for raising delegated events. Thus, you cannot raise events from outside of the class and must declare a public method for raising events;

* It is safe to call disassociated event delegates because the compiler automatically injects code for Null-reference checking.

Immediate Solutions

Creating Arrays, Iterating Through Array Elements

Arrays are very easy to work with. When dealing with explicitly defined arrays you can rely on the C++ language syntax to get or set the array elements. When properties of the array are unknown, however (e.g., the array indices are not specified or the array is defined is a generic **Array*** pointer), you can use the **Array** class methods to obtain the array rank and dimension sizes as well as set or get the array elements.

To illustrate how the **Array** class is used, consider the following code example, which performs these actions:

1. Creates a two-dimensional array of ints using C++ syntax.

2. Creates an equivalent two-dimensional array of ints using the static **Array::CreateInstance** method (the returned **Array*** pointer is explicitly casted to the two dimensional array).

3. The **Interate** function is called and the array is passed as an **Array*** parameter.

4. The **Interate** function reports the array rank using the **Rank** property.

5. The function obtains the sizes of the array dimensions using the **GetLength** method and iterates thorough the array elements.

6. The array elements are set using the **SetValue** method.

The array elements are obtained using the **GetValue** method.

> **NOTE:** The **GetValue/SetValue** methods get or set the boxed array elements.

```
#using <mscorlib.dll>
using namespace System;

void Interate(Array* arr)
{
    // 4. Report the array rank
    Console::WriteLine("Array Rank is {0}", __box(arr->Rank));

    // 5. Iterate through the array elements
    for ( int i = 0; i < arr->GetLength(0); i++ )
        for ( int j = 0; j < arr->GetLength(1); j++ )
        {
            // 6. Set the array value
            arr->SetValue(__box(i + j), i, j);
            // 7. Get the array value
            Console::WriteLine("arr[{0}, {1}] = {2}", __box(i), __box(j),
                arr->GetValue(i, j));
        }
}

void main()
{
    // 1. Create two-dimensional array
    int arr __gc[,] = new int __gc [2,4];
    // 2. Same as the above
    arr = (int __gc[,])Array::CreateInstance(__typeof(int), 2, 4);
    // 3. Call the function
    Interate(arr);
}
```

Creating Arrays Dynamically

In most cases you will create an array dynamically using the **new** operator. Here's an example:

```
int SizeA = 2, SizeB = 4;
int arr __gc [,] = new int __gc[SizeA, SizeB];
```

The disadvantage of this approach is that you have to know the array rank beforehand. Also, all arrays created with the **new** operator have their lower bounds set to zero. If you do not know the array rank before hand or if you want the array to have lower bounds other than zero, you can use the **CreateInstance** method to instantiate an array:

```
#using <mscorlib.dll>
using namespace System;

void main()
{
    int Length __gc[] = {2, 4};
    int LowerBounds __gc[] = {1, 1};
    // Create a two-dimensional array with 1-based indices
    Array* arr = Array::CreateInstance(__typeof(int), Length, LowerBounds);
}
```

Sorting and Searching Arrays

You can sort an array using the **Sort** method. Keep in mind that only one-dimensional arrays can be sorted. Similarly, the **Array** class provides **BinarySearch** methods for searching one-dimensional arrays. The following code example illustrates sorting and searching an array of integers:

```
#using <mscorlib.dll>
using namespace System;

void main()
{
    int arr __gc[] = new int __gc[10];
    // Initialize the array
    for ( int i = 0; i < arr->GetLength(0); i++ )
        arr[i] = 10 - i;

    // Sort the array
    Array::Sort(arr);
    // Find element with value 4
    int pos = Array::BinarySearch(arr, __box(4));

    Console::WriteLine("Element with value 4 is at position {0}", __box(pos));
}
```

This program will output:

```
Element with value 4 is at position 3
```

> **NOTE:** If you want to sort an array of user-defined types, make sure that the type implements **IComparable** interface.

Creating and Initializing Strings

The two basic methods for instantiating or initializing **String** objects are shown here:

*   Use the **String** constructor:

```
String* str = new String("ABCD");
```

*   Initialize a **String*** pointer with a string literal:

```
String* s1 = "ABCD";
```

By default, Unicode characters are assumed. If you want to declare an ASCII string constant you use the S-prefix in the string literal as shown here:

```
String* s = S"ABCD"; // ASCII string
```

To explicitly specify a Unicode string you can use the L-prefix:

```
String* s = L"ABCD"; // Unicode string
```

Internally, the **String** class maintains text characters as Unicode, thus specifying the string literal prefix affects only the literal constant representation in the code.

Accessing String Characters

To access **String** characters you can use either the **Chars** indexed property or convert a **String** object into a **__wchar_t** Unicode character array. Here's an example:

```
#using <mscorlib.dll>
using namespace System;

void main()
{
    String* s = "ABCD";

    __wchar_t str __gc[] = s->ToCharArray();
    Console::WriteLine(str[2]);      // Outputs 'C'
    Console::WriteLine(s->Chars[2]); // Outputs 'C'
}
```

Concatenating Strings

Unlike the MFC **CString** class, the .NET Framework **String** class defines no concatenation operators. Therefore, you have no choice but to use the clumsy **Concat** method. To concatenated strings using a specified separator character you should use the **Join** method as shown here:

```
#using <mscorlib.dll>
using namespace System;

void main()
{
    String* a = "a", *b = "b";
    // 1. Concatenate strings
    String* s = String::Concat(a, b, "c", __box(1)->ToString());
    // Prints "abc1"
    Console::WriteLine(s);

    String* Src[] = {"a", "b", "c"};
    // 2. Joins strings using comma separator
    s = String::Join(",", Src);
    // Prints "a,b,c"
    Console::WriteLine(s);
}
```

Formatting Strings

To format a **String** you should use the **String::Format** method:

```
#using <mscorlib.dll>
using namespace System;

void main()
{
    int i = 123;
    // Format string
    String* str = String::Format("{0} {1:E3} {2}",
        __box(i), __box(12345.6789), S"abc");
    Console::WriteLine(str);

    Object* args[] = {__box(i), __box(12345.6789), S"abc"};
    // Format string
    str = String::Format(S"{0} {1} {2}", args);
    Console::WriteLine(str);
}
```

NOTE: Remember to box value types when supplying them as arguments to the **Format** method.

Using Console I/O

To read console input or to write to the console, you should use the static **Console** class members. The following code example illustrates how to use the **Console** class and perform these actions:

1.   Reads from the console text typed by the user using the **ReadLine** method (the text must be CR/LF terminated, in other words, the user must press Enter).

Outputs the inputted text back to the console using the **WriteLine** method.

> **NOTE:** You can use the **Console::Write/WriteLine** methods to output formatted text.

3.   Writes to error stream using the **Error** property.

4.   Reads a single character from the console using the **Read** method.

```
#using <mscorlib.dll>
using namespace System;

void main()
{
    String* s;
    // 1. Read console input
    while ( (s = Console::ReadLine())->CompareTo("exit") != 0 )
    {
        // 2. Write to console
        Console::WriteLine("You have entered: {0}", s);
    }
    // 3. Write to the error stream
    Console::Error->WriteLine("Simulating error output... Press any key");
    // 4. Read single character from console
    int c = Console::Read();
}
```

> **NOTE: Console::Read** and **Console::ReadLine** methods block program execution until user provides console input.

Using **StringBuilder** Objects

If you feel that the performance of your code will benefit from the usage of mutable string objects, you should use the **StringBuilder** class for in-place operations on character strings. To use the **StringBuilder** class you must reference the System::Text namespace in the **using namespace** statement.

The following code example illustrates the usage of the **StringBuilder** class and performs the following actions:

1.   Constructs a **StringBuilder** object and initializes it with the **String** value.

2.   Reports the **StringBuilder** text length using the **Length** property.

3.   Modifies the **StringBuilder** characters using the **Chars** property.

4.   Replaces the **StringBuilder** text using the **Replace** method.

5.   Inserts new text into the **StringBuilder** using the **Insert** method.

6. Appends value to the **StringBuilder** text using the **Append** method.

7. Appends formatted value to the **StringBuilder** text using the **AppendFormat** method.

8. Converts the **StringBuilder** value to **String** using the **ToString** method.

```cpp
#using <mscorlib.dll>
using namespace System;
using namespace System::Text;

void main()
{
    String* str = "Test text";
    // 1. Create a StringBuilder object
    StringBuilder* str2 = new StringBuilder(str);
    // 2. Report the string builder length
    Console::WriteLine("Length={0}", __box(str2->Length));
    // 3. Modify the string builder characters
    str2->Chars[0] = 't';
    // 4. Replace text
    str2->Replace("text", "experimental");
    // 5. Insert Age=26
    str2->Insert(5, "Age=");
    str2->Insert(9, 26);
    // 6. Append value
    str2->Append(" Name=Max");
    // 7. Append formatted value
    str2->AppendFormat(" DOB={0}", DateTime(1975, 5, 1).ToShortDateString());
    // 8. Assign back to String
    str = str2->ToString();
    Console::WriteLine(str2);
}
```

Working with Dates and Time Intervals

To represent date/time you should use the **DateTime** value type, and to represent time intervals you can use the **TimeSpan** value type.

The following code medley showcases the basic operations on the **DateTime/TimeSpan** values, including:

1. Obtaining current date and time using the **DateTime::Now** property.

2. Extracting year, month, date, hour, minute, and second information from a **DateTime** value type using the **Year**, **Month**, **Date**, **Hour**, **Minute**, and **Second** properties.

3. Calculating tomorrow's date by adding one day to the current date using the **AddDays** method.

4. Constructing a date/time corresponding to Christmas 2002 using the **DateTime** constructor.

5. Calculating time until Christmas in the form of **TimeSpan** by subtracting tomorrow's date from the Christmas date.

6. Constructing a one-day time span using the **TimeSpan** constructor and subtracting time span using the '-' operator.

7. Comparing dates using the '>' operator.

8. Converting the **DateTime** to short date representation using the **ToShortDateString** method.

```cpp
#using <mscorlib.dll>
using namespace System;

void main()
{
    // 1. Get current date/time
    DateTime d = DateTime::Now;

    Object* args[] = { __box(d.Year), __box(d.Month), __box(d.Date),
        __box(d.Hour), __box(d.Minute), __box(d.Second) };
    // 2. Report current date/time
    Console::WriteLine("Now: {0}/{1}/{2} {3}:{4}:{5}", args);

    // 3. Get tomorrows date
    d.AddDays(1);

    // 4. This year's Christmas day: 12/25/2002
    DateTime Xmas(2002, 12, 25);
    // 5. Calculate days until Christmas
    TimeSpan t = Xmas - d;
    Console::WriteLine("Days until Christmas {0}", __box(t.Days));
    // 6. Subtract one day to the time interval
    t = t - TimeSpan(1/*Days*/, 0/*hrs*/, 0/*min*/, 0/*sec*/);
    // 7. Compare dates
    if ( Xmas > d )
        // 8. Format date using short date format
        Console::WriteLine("Today {0}", d.ToShortDateString());
}
```

Using Math Functions

To use common math functions such as trigonometric functions, exponent, or square root you should use static methods of the **Math** class:

```cpp
#using <mscorlib.dll>
using namespace System;
void main()
{
    double x = Math::PI/2;
    double y = Math::Cos(x);
}
```

Generating Random Numbers

To generate random numbers you can use the .NET Framework random number generator represented by the **Random** class. To use the random number generator you must create an instance of the **Random** class. If you use the default constructor, the system initializes the random number generator seed using the current system time. Alternatively, you can supply your own seed as a parameter to the **Random** class constructor.

To generate random numbers within a desired integer range you should use the **int Next(int *min*, int *max*)** method. If you need *normalized* random numbers (i.e., floating-point values in the range from 0.0 to 1.0), use the **NextDouble** method.

The following code example instantiates a random number generator, initializes it with a custom seed, generates a random integer in the range of 1..100, and generates normalized random number in the range 0.0-1.0:

```
#using <mscorlib.dll>
using namespace System;

void main()
{
    // 1. Create RNG seeded with the system time
    Random* rnd = new Random();
    // 2. Create RNG seeded manually
    rnd = new Random(123);
    // 3. Get random number in the range 1-100
    int RandomVal = rnd->Next(1, 100);
    // 4. Get normalized random number in the range 0.0-1.0
    double NormalizedRandom = rnd->NextDouble();
}
```

Working with Exceptions

Working with managed exceptions is very similar to working with standard C++ exceptions: You can throw exception using the **throw** operator and catch them using the **catch** operator.

To create a custom exception class, you should derive your own exception type from the **Exception** class. When deriving your own exception class, you should invoke the base **Exception** class constructor to specify custom error message text. Also, it is recommended that you initialize the **HResult** property to indicate the exception **HRESULT** code for interoperability with COM—see Chapter 13.

The following code example demonstrates the definition of the custom **MyException** class. The user-defined **MyException** class accepts the error code as a parameter and formats the custom error message. The main program throws an instance of the **MyException** using the **throw** operator, catches the exception, and reports the stack trace using the **StackTrace** property, the name of the method that threw the exception (**TargetSite->Name** property) and the error message (**Message** property).

```
#using <mscorlib.dll>
using namespace System;

// 1. Define custom exception class
__gc class MyException: public Exception {
public:
    MyException(int errorCode) :
        // Call the Exception constructor
        Exception(String::Format("Error occured, code={0}", __box(errorCode)))
    {
        ErrorCode = errorCode;
    }
private:
    int ErrorCode;
};

void main()
{
    try {
        // 2. Throw
        throw new MyException(12);
    }
    catch(Exception* e) {
        // 3. Print stack trace
        Console::Error->WriteLine(e->StackTrace);
        // 4. Report the name of the method that threw the exception
        Console::Error->WriteLine("Exception happened in method {0}",
            e->TargetSite->Name);
        // 5. Report the exception message
        Console::Error->WriteLine(e->Message);
    }
}
```

Working with Delegates

Delegates correspond to strongly typed function/method pointers. You can declare delegates in your code using the **__delegate** keyword as shown here:

```
__delegate void MyDelegate(int value);
```

Then you can instantiate a delegate object in your code using the **new** operator in conjunction with the delegate constructor:

```
MyDelegateType* MyDelegate = new MyDelegateType(SomeClassPtr,
    SomeClassType::MethodName);
```

In the delegate constructor you must specify a pointer to the class instance and a pointer to the class method to which you want to attach the delegate (for static methods you must specify zero for the class instance pointer). To attach additional methods to the delegate and thus convert the delegate into a multicast delegate, you can use the += operator in conjunction with the **new** operator and the delegate constructor:

```
MyDelegateType* MyDelegate += new MyDelegateType(SomeClassPtr,
    SomeClassType::MethodName);
```

Similarly, to remove methods from the delegate invocation list you can use the -= operator in conjunction with the **new** operator and the delegate constructor:

```
MyDelegateType* MyDelegate -= new MyDelegateType(SomeClassPtr,
    SomeClassType::MethodName);
```

The following code example shows how to use single-cast and multicast delegates by defining the **StartEvent** delegate that is used to invoke the **WorkerClass1::StartWork** and the **WorkerClass2::StartMoreWork** methods. The code performs these actions:

1. Creates a delegate using the delegate constructor and associates the **StartWork** instance method of the **w1** object with the delegate.

2. Converts the delegate to multicast using the += operator, which adds the **StartMoreWork** instance method of the **w2** object to the delegate invocation list.

3. Invokes the delegate (both instance methods are called).

4. Removes the **StartMoreWork** instance method of the **w2** object from the delegate invocation list using the -= operator.

5. Removes the **StartWork** method from the delegate invocation list by computing the invocation list difference using the **Delegate::Remove** method.

6. Attempts to invoke the delegate for the last time. Since the delegate invocation list is now empty, the code checks to see whether the delegate holds a valid (i.e., not Null) reference. Because the delegate with an empt invocation list corresponds to a Null reference, the delegate invocation is bypassed.

```
#using <mscorlib.dll>
using namespace System;
// Delegate declaration
__delegate void StartEvent(int value);

__gc class WorkerClass1 {
public:
    void StartWork(int value) { Console::WriteLine("StartWork({0})",
        __box(value)); }
};
__gc class WorkerClass2 {
public:
```

```
    void StartMoreWork(int value) { Console::WriteLine("StartMoreWork({0})",
        __box(value)); }
};

int main()
{
    WorkerClass1* w1 = new WorkerClass1();
    WorkerClass2* w2 = new WorkerClass2();

    // 1. Create singlecast delegate using = operator
    StartEvent* OnStart = new StartEvent(w1, WorkerClass1::StartWork);
    // 2. Turn the delegate into multicast by attaching another method with +=
    OnStart += new StartEvent(w2, WorkerClass2::StartMoreWork);
    // 3. Invoke delegate
    OnStart(12);
    // 4. Remove a method from the invocation list
    OnStart -= new StartEvent(w2, WorkerClass2::StartMoreWork);
    // Invoke delegate
    OnStart(12);

    StartEvent* OnStart2 = new StartEvent(w1, WorkerClass1::StartWork);
    // 5. Remove another method from the invocation list
    OnStart = dynamic_cast<StartEvent*>(Delegate::Remove(
        OnStart, OnStart2));
    // 6. Must check for null or the invocation may fail!
    if ( OnStart ) OnStart(12);
    return 0;
}
```

Using Delegates to Handle Events

You can use delegates in class members to raise or handle events. Follow these steps to declare an event as a member of the class:

1.   Declare a delegate type using the **__delegate** keyword.

2.   Declare a class member as an event by adding delegate member to the class declared using the **__event** keyword.

3.   Declare a public raise-event method for invoking the event delegate. (The compiler automatically makes the event delegate member inaccessible from outside the class.)

Then, in your code you can use the +=/-= to add or remove event handler methods to the class's event delegate and call the class's raise-event method to handle the events.

The following code example illustrates event handling with delegates. The code defines the **StartEvent** delegate and the **EventClass** that exposes the **OnStart** event of type **StartEvent**. The **EventClass** also defines the public **RaiseEvent** method for raising the **OnStart** event. The main program attaches two event handler methods to the **EventClass::OnStart** event, calls the public **EventClass::RaiseEvent** method to raise the events, detaches the event handlers from the **EventClass::OnStart** event, and raises the events again. When the events are raised for the second time, no action is taken because the event handlers are now detached from the **OnStart** event.

```
#using <mscorlib.dll>
using namespace System;
// Delegate type
__delegate void StartEvent(int value);

__gc class EventClass {
public:
   // Event delegate
   __event StartEvent* OnStart;
   // Public method for raising the OnStart event
   void RaiseEvent()
   {
      OnStart(12);
   }
};
__gc class WorkerClass {
public:
   void StartWork(int value)
   {
      Console::WriteLine("StartWork({0})", __box(value));
   }
};

int main()
{
   EventClass* EventTest = new EventClass();
   WorkerClass* w1 = new WorkerClass();
   WorkerClass* w2 = new WorkerClass();

   // 1. Attach event handling methods to the OnStart delegate
   EventTest->OnStart += new StartEvent(w1, WorkerClass::StartWork);
   EventTest->OnStart += new StartEvent(w2, WorkerClass::StartWork);

   // 2. Raise the event
   EventTest->RaiseEvent();

   // 3. Remove the event handling methods to the OnStart delegate
   EventTest->OnStart -= new StartEvent(w1, WorkerClass::StartWork);
   EventTest->OnStart -= new StartEvent(w2, WorkerClass::StartWork);

   // Raise events
   //EventTest->OnStart(12); // Won't compile because event raising methods
                             // are never public
   // 4. Raise events, but no event handlers are called
   EventTest->RaiseEvent();
   return 0;
}
```

.NET System Namespace: Attributes, Garbage Collector, and Other Advanced Classes

QUICK JUMPS

CHAPTER 4

.NET System Namespace: Attributes, Garbage Collector, and Other Advanced Classes

In Depth

The System namespace supplies advanced classes for attribute support, type conversion, memory management, and garbage collection in addition to providing the foundation for the .NET Framework Class Library. In this chapter, you will learn how to declare custom attributes, access numeric types on the byte level using the **BitConverter** class, convert between managed types using the **Convert** class, use and build URIs using the **Uri/UriBuilder** classes, obtain environment information using the **Environment** class, and control garbage collection using the **GC** class. Throughout the chapter, I'll provide numerous tables summarizing class constructors, properties, and methods to help you use these components.

Custom Attributes

The Common Language Runtime relies on attributes for specifying additional information about classes, fields, parameters, properties, and entire assemblies. Attributes are saved in the application metadata and can be examined at runtime using the *reflection* mechanism.

Reflection

Reflection is a mechanism for discovering type information and examining type metadata at runtime. Reflection allows you to obtain information on types contained in a particular assembly or module, as well as to obtain information on class constructors, properties, and methods. Also, reflection allows you to examine attributes applied to classes and class members. In the .NET Framework Class Library, reflection is implemented by means of the classes defined in the System::Reflection namespace.

You can extend your application metadata by defining and applying your own custom attributes in addition to applying preexisting attributes. To define a custom attribute, you should define your own class based on the System namespace **Attribute** class, which has the following inheritance diagram:

```
Object
|- Attribute

Attributes: Serializable
Abstract: Yes
Sealed: No
Implemented Interfaces: none
```

The **Attribute** class provides numerous **GetCustomAttribute/GetCustomAttributes** and **IsDefined** methods for retrieving attribute information from assembly, module, class member, and class member parameter metadata. The complete reference of the **Attribute** class constructors, fields, properties, and methods is listed in Tables 4.1 through 4.3.

Table 4.1 **Attribute** class constructors.

Constructor	Description
protected: Attribute()	Default constructor.

Table 4.2 **Attribute** class properties.

Get/Set	Type	Property	Virtual	Description
Get	**Object***	**TypeId**	Yes	Returns the attribute type.

Table 4.3 **Attribute** class methods.

Operator	Description
static Attribute* GetCustomAttribute(Assembly* *element*, Type* *attrType*)	Returns a custom attribute of the specified type (if any) applied to the specified assembly.
static Attribute* GetCustomAttribute(Assembly* *element*, Type* *type*, bool *inherited*)	Returns a custom attribute of the specified type (if any) applied to the specified assembly.
static Attribute* GetCustomAttribute(Module* *element*, Type* *attrType*)	Returns a custom attribute of the specified type (if any) applied to the specified module.
static Attribute* GetCustomAttribute(Module* *element*, Type* *attrType*, bool *inherited*)	Returns a custom attribute of the specified type (if any) applied to the specified module.
static Attribute* GetCustomAttribute(MemberInfo* *element*, Type* *attrType*)	Returns a custom attribute of the specified type (if any) applied to the specified class member.
static Attribute* GetCustomAttribute(MemberInfo* *element*, Type* *attrType*, bool *inherited*)	Returns a custom attribute of the specified type (if any) applied to the specified class member.
static Attribute* GetCustomAttribute(ParameterInfo* *element*, Type* *attrType*)	Returns a custom attribute of the specified type (if any) applied to the specified parameter of a class member.
static Attribute* GetCustomAttribute(ParameterInfo* *element*, Type* *attrType*, bool *inherited*)	Returns a custom attribute of the specified type (if any) applied to the specified parameter of a class member.

<Continued on Next Page>

<Table 4.3 Continued>

Operator	Description
static Attribute* GetCustomAttributes(Assembly* *element*) []	Returns an array of all custom attributes applied to the specified assembly.
static Attribute* GetCustomAttributes(Assembly* *element*, Type* *attrType*) []	Returns an array of custom attributes of the specified type applied to the specified assembly.
static Attribute* GetCustomAttributes(Assembly* *element*, bool *inherited*) []	Returns an array of all custom attributes applied to the specified assembly.
static Attribute* GetCustomAttributes(Assembly* *element*, Type* *attrType*, bool *inherited*) []	Returns an array of custom attributes of the specified type applied to the specified assembly.
static Attribute* GetCustomAttributes(Module* *element*) []	Returns an array of all custom attributes applied to the specified module.
static Attribute* GetCustomAttributes(Module* *element*, bool *inherited*) []	Returns an array of all custom attributes applied to the specified module.
static Attribute* GetCustomAttributes(Module* *element*, Type* *attrType*) []	Returns an array of custom attributes of the specified type of applied to the specified module.
static Attribute* GetCustomAttributes(Module* *element*, Type* *attrType*, bool *inherited*) []	Returns an array of custom attributes of the specified type applied to the specified module.
static Attribute* GetCustomAttributes(MemberInfo* *element*) []	Returns an array of all custom attributes applied to the specified class member.
static Attribute* GetCustomAttributes(MemberInfo*, bool *inherited*) []	Returns an array of all custom attributes applied to the specified class member.
static Attribute* GetCustomAttributes(MemberInfo*, Type* *attrType*) []	Returns an array of custom attributes of the specified type applied to the specified class member.
static Attribute* GetCustomAttributes(MemberInfo*, Type* *attrType*, bool *inherited*) []	Returns an array of custom attributes of the specified type applied to the specified class member.
static Attribute* GetCustomAttributes(ParameterInfo* *element*) []	Returns an array of all custom attributes applied to the specified class member parameter.
static Attribute* GetCustomAttributes(ParameterInfo* *element*, bool *inherited*) []	Returns an array of all custom attributes applied to the specified class member parameter.

<Continued on Next Page>

<Table 4.3 Continued>

Operator	Description
static Attribute* GetCustomAttributes(ParameterInfo* *element,* **Type*** *attrType***) []**	Returns an array of custom attributes of the specified type applied to the specified class member parameter.
static Attribute* GetCustomAttributes(ParameterInfo* *element,* **Type*** *attrType,* **bool** *inherited***) []**	Returns an array of custom attributes of the specified type applied to the specified class member parameter.
virtual bool IsDefaultAttribute()	Returns **true** if the attribute contains the default value. You can override this method to provide support for attribute values.
static bool IsDefined(Assembly* *element,* **Type*** *attrType***)**	Returns **true** if the attribute of the specified type is applied to the specified assembly.
static bool IsDefined(Assembly* *element,* **Type*** *attrType,* **bool** *inherited***)**	Returns **true** if the attribute of the specified type is applied to the specified assembly.
static bool IsDefined(Module* *element,* **Type*** *attrType***)**	Returns **true** if the attribute of the specified type is applied to the specified module.
static bool IsDefined(Module* *element,* **Type*** *attrType,* **bool** *inherited***)**	Returns **true** if the attribute of the specified type is applied to the specified module.
static bool IsDefined(MemberInfo* *element,* **Type*** *attrType***)**	Returns **true** if the attribute of the specified type is applied to the specified class member.
static bool IsDefined(MemberInfo* *element,* **Type*** *attrType,* **bool** *inherited***)**	Returns **true** if the attribute of the specified type is applied to the specified class member.
static bool IsDefined(ParameterInfo* *element,* **Type*** *attrType***)**	Returns **true** if the attribute of the specified type is applied to the specified class member parameter.
static bool IsDefined(ParameterInfo* *element,* **Type*** *attrType,* **bool** *inherited***)**	Returns **true** if the attribute of the specified type is applied to the specified class member parameter.

NOTE: *The* **inherited** *parameter specifies whether to search the ancestors of the* **element** *for the occurrence of the attribute. The* **inherited** *parameter is ignored for assemblies and modules.*

| **virtual bool Match(Object*** *obj***)** | Returns **true** if the current attribute is equal to the attribute specified by the *obj*. You can override this method to provide support for attribute values. |

AttributeUsage Attribute

When defining a custom attribute class, you must use the **AttributeUsage** attribute to specify additional attribute information including the allowable attribute targets. The **AttributeUsage** attribute has the following syntax:

```
[AttributeUsage(targets, AllowMultiple=BooleanValue, Inherited=BooleanValue)]
```

The **AttributeUsage** attribute parameters are defined as follows:

* *targets*: Specifies the attribute target flags. The target constants can be combined using logical OR and are defined in the **AttributeTargets** enumeration. Possible values include **All**, **Assembly**, **Class**, **Constructor**, **Delegate**, **Enum**, **Event**, **Field**, **Interface**, **Method**, **Module**, **Parameter**, **Property**, **ReturnValue**, and **Struct.**

* *AllowMultiple*: Indicates if the attribute can be applied to the same target several times. The following example illustrates how you can apply the **SomeAttribute** attribute to the class definition twice:

```
[SomeAttribute("abc"), SomeAttribute("xyz")]
__gc class TestClass {
};
```

* *Inherited*: Indicates if the attribute is inherited by derived classes/overloaded members.

Specifying Attribute Targets

Applying an attribute to a class, structure, enumeration, member, parameter, field, event, interface, or property definition is easy. You simply insert the attribute in square brackets in front of the appropriate definition. Applying attributes to return values is trickier, however. To apply an attribute to the method return value, you must use the **returnvalue** keyword to prefix the attribute and apply the attribute to the method definition. Here is an example:

```
__gc class TestClass {
   [returnvalue:SomeAttribute]
   int TestMethod();
};
```

To apply attributes to the current module or assembly, you must use the **returnvalue**, **assembly**, or **module** keywords to prefix the attribute name and apply attributes to the global scope (i.e., terminate the attribute block enclosed in square brackets with a semicolon):

```
[assembly:SomeAttribute];
[module:SomeAttribute];
```

Attribute Initialization

When defining a custom attribute class, you can define the attribute constructors and properties. The attribute constructors provide *positional syntax* (see Chapter 2), while the public attribute properties provide *name/value syntax* for initializing the attribute. In actuality, you can combine both positional and name/value syntax for initializing the attribute. You can use one of the attribute constructors to initialize the required data and follow the complement constructor syntax with optional name/value property initialization list. The only rule to remember is that the positional syntax must always precede the name/value syntax.

As an example, suppose that you have an attribute **MyAttribute** that has two properties, **Param** and **Text,** and supplies two constructors as shown here:

```
[AttributeUsage(All)]
__gc class MyAttribute: public Attribute {
public:
    MyAttribute();
    MyAttribute(int param);
    __property int get_Param();
    __property void set_Param(int);
    __property String* get_Text();
    __property void set_Text(String*);
};
```

Given this attribute definition, the following **MyAttribute** initialization scenarios are legal:

```
[MyAttribute] // Uses the default constructor
public __gc class TestClass1 { ... };

[MyAttribute(10)] // Uses the second constructor
public __gc class TestClass1 { ... };

[MyAttribute(Param=10, Text="abc")] // Uses the default constructor
public __gc class TestClass1 { ... };

[MyAttribute(10, Text="abc")] // Uses the second constructor
public __gc class TestClass1 { ... };

[My(10, Text="abc")] // Uses the second constructor
public __gc class TestClass1 { ... };
```

The last definition uses the *short* name "**My**" to refer to the attribute. If a custom attribute class name ends with an "Attribute" suffix, you can omit the suffix when applying the attribute. If the runtime cannot find the attribute using the name specified in the attribute block, it thinks that the specified name was the short name, appends the "Attribute" suffix to the short name, and repeats the search.

As with custom attributes, you can apply predefined .NET Framework Class Library attributes using any legal combination of positional and name/value syntax and refer to attributes in the attribute blocks using their short or the full names.

> **NOTE:** The attribute short names are allowed only in the attribute blocks.

BitConverter Class

Certain operations such as data packing, compression, and conversion between little-endian/big-endian formats require access to numeric types at the byte level. The .NET Framework Class Library supports byte-level access to integral types by means of the **BitConverter** class:

```
Object
|- BitConverter

Attributes: none.
Abstract: No
Sealed: Yes
Implemented Interfaces: none
```

The **BitConverter** class has no constructors and is entirely comprised of static members such as **GetBytes** and **To**_TYPE_ for converting numeric types to/from the arrays of bytes. Also, the **BitConverter** class supplies the **IsLittleEndian** property that is set to **true** if the current hardware architecture utilizes little-endian number representation (x86 architecture is little-endian).

> Little-Endian and Big-Endian Formats
> _Little-Endian_ format indicates that the least significant byte in a word is stored before the most significant byte: WORD = LSB | MSB.
>
> _Big-Endian_ format indicates that the least significant byte in a word is stored before the most significant byte: WORD = MSB | LSB.

The complete set of the **BitConverter** class fields and methods is presented in Tables 4.4 through 4.5.

Table 4.4 **BitConverter** class fields.

Field	Description
static bool IsLittleEndian	Contains a **true** value if the underlying computer architecture uses little-endian data representation.

Table 4.5 **BitConverter** class methods.

Method	Description
static __int64 DoubleToInt64Bits(double _value_**)**	Converts the specified double-precision floating-point number to a 64-bit integer.
static double Int64BitsToDouble(__int64 _value_**)**	Converts the specified 64-bit integer to a double-precision floating-point number.
static unsigned char GetBytes(bool _value_**) __gc[]**	Returns the specified value as an array of bytes.
static unsigned char GetBytes(__wchar_t _value_**) __gc[]**	Returns the specified value as an array of bytes.

<Continued on Next Page>

<Table 4.5 Continued>

Method	Description
static unsigned char GetBytes(double *value***) __gc[]**	Returns the specified value as an array of bytes.
static unsigned char GetBytes(short *value***) __gc[]**	Returns the specified value as an array of bytes.
static unsigned char GetBytes(int *value***) __gc[]**	Returns the specified value as an array of bytes.
static unsigned char GetBytes(__int64 *value***) __gc[]**	Returns the specified value as an array of bytes.
static unsigned char GetBytes(float *value***) __gc[]**	Returns the specified value as an array of bytes.
static unsigned char GetBytes(unsigned short *value***) __gc[]**	Returns the specified value as an array of bytes.
static unsigned char GetBytes(unsigned int *value***) __gc[]**	Returns the specified value as an array of bytes.
static unsigned char GetBytes(unsigned __int64 *value***) __gc[]**	Returns the specified value as an array of bytes.
static bool ToBoolean(unsigned char __gc[] *array***, int** *index***)**	Returns a Boolean value represented by *array* elements starting at the index *index*.
static __wchar_t ToChar(unsigned char __gc[] *array***, int** *index***)**	Returns a Unicode character represented by two consecutive *array* elements starting at the index *index*.
static double ToDouble(unsigned char __gc[] *array***, int** *index***)**	Returns a double-precision floating-point number represented by eight consecutive *array* elements starting at the index *index*.
static short ToInt16(unsigned char __gc[] *array***, int** *index***)**	Returns a 16-bit integer represented by two consecutive *array* elements starting at the index *index*.
static int ToInt32(unsigned char __gc[] *array***, int** *index***)**	Returns a 32-bit integer represented by four consecutive *array* elements starting at the index *index*.
static __int64 ToInt64(unsigned char __gc[] *array***, int** *index***)**	Returns a 64-bit integer represented by eight consecutive *array* elements starting at the index *index*.
static float ToSingle(unsigned char __gc[] *array***, int** *index***)**	Returns a single-precision floating-point number represented by four consecutive *array* elements starting at the index *index*.
static String* ToString(unsigned char __gc[] *array***)**	Converts the specified *array* into a string format with each array element represented by a hexadecimal number separated by dashes, e. g., 00-A8-CF .
static String* ToString(unsigned char __gc[] *array***, int** *index***)**	Converts the specified *array* starting at the index *index* into a string format.
static String* ToString(unsigned char __gc[] *array***, int** *index***, int** *length***)**	Converts the *length* elements of the specified *array* starting at the index *index* into a string format.

<Continued on Next Page>

<Table 4.5 Continued>

Method	Description
static unsigned short ToUInt16(unsigned char __gc[] *array*, int *index*)	Returns an unsigned short value represented by two *array* elements starting at the index *index* (non-CLS compliant).
static unsigned int ToUInt32(unsigned char __gc[] *array*, int *index*)	Returns a 32-bit unsigned integer represented by four consecutive *array* elements starting at the index *index* (non-CLS compliant).
static unsigned __int64 ToUInt64(unsigned char __gc[] *array*, int *index*)	Returns a 64-bit unsigned integer represented by eight consecutive *array* elements starting at the index *index* (non-CLS compliant).

Buffer Class

Occasionally, you may need to access arrays of managed types as if they were arrays of primitive types. For example, if you want to encrypt data stored in a managed array, you will need to access the array data at a direct byte level. To accomplish this, you should use the System namespace **Buffer** class, which has this inheritance diagram:

```
Object
|- Buffer
```

```
Attributes: none.
Abstract: No
Sealed: Yes
Implemented Interfaces: none
```

The **Buffer** class has no constructors and is entirely comprised of static members copying data from one managed array to another and for performing direct byte-level read and write operations on managed arrays. Table 4.6 lists the methods for the **Buffer** class.

Table 4.6 **Buffer** class methods.

Method	Description
static void BlockCopy(Array* *src*, int *srcOffs*, Array* *dest*, int *destOffs*, int *count*)	Copies the count bytes from *src[srcOffc]* to *dest[destOffs]*.
static int ByteLength(Array* *array*)	Returns the length in bytes of the specified *array*.
static unsigned char GetByte(Array* *array*, int *index*)	Returns a byte from the specified index in the *array*.
static void SetByte(Array* *array*, int *index*, unsigned char *value*)	Sets a byte at the specified index in the *array*.

Convert Class

Converting among various data types can be tricky. First of all, to convert one type to another, a meaningful conversion principle is applied. If such conversion is supported, your class can implement the **IConvertible** interface to provide a concrete conversion between your type and the desired target type.

The .NET Framework Class Library supplies the **Convert** class to make the data type conversion easier. This class supplies static methods for facilitating conversion between primitive types. The **Convert** class inheritance diagram is the following:

```
Object
|- Convert

Attributes: none.
Abstract: No
Sealed: Yes
Implemented Interfaces: none
```

The **Convert** class provides **ToBoolean**, **ToByte**, **ToChar**, **ToDateTime**, **ToDecimal**, **ToDouble**, **ToInt16**, **ToInt32**, **ToInt64**, **ToSByte**, **ToSingle**, **ToString**, **ToUInt16**, **ToUInt32**, and **ToUint64** methods with numerous overloads that correspond to the source values of different types. The source value type can be one of the following: **bool**, **unsigned char**, **__wchar_t**, **DateTime**, **Decimal**, **double**, **short**, **int**, **__int64**, **Object***, **char**, **float**, **String***, **unsigned short**, **unsigned int**, or **unsigned __int64**.

In addition, the **Convert** class supports converting **String** values to and from Base 64 encoding, which is frequently used for binary data transmission over the Internet.

> **Base 64 Encoding**
> The Base 64 encoding uses characters 'A..'Z','a'..'z','0'..'9','+','/-' to represent numbers from 0 to 63. The '=' character has no value and is used as white space. Internet communication frequently relies on the Base 64 encoding for operations such as transmitting binary e-mail attachments.

The **Convert** class fields and methods are summarized in Tables 4.7 through 4.8.

Table 4.7 **Convert** class fields.

Field	Description
static Object* DBNull	Database NULL-value constant.

Table 4.8 **Convert** class methods.

Method	Description
static Object* ChangeType(Object* *object*, Type* *type*),	
static Object* ChangeType(Object* *object*, TypeCode *type*)	Converts the ***object*** to the type ***type*** and returns the converted object. The ***object*** must implement the **IConvertible** interface.
static Object* ChangeType(Object* *object*, Type* *type*, IFormatProvider	Converts the object to the type ***type*** using the supplied interface. The object must implement the **IConvertible** interface.
static Object* ChangeType(Object* *object*, TypeCode* *type*, IFormatProvider* *provider*)	Converts the object to the type ***type*** using the supplied **IFormatProvider** interface. The object must implement the **IConvertible** interface.
static unsigned char FromBase64CharArray (__wchar_t *array* __gc[], int *index*, int *length*) __gc[]	Converts the length elements of the ***array*** starting at the index ***index*** from the Base 64 encoding into an equivalent ASCII character array.
static unsigned char FromBase64String(String* *str*) __gc[]	Converts the specified string from the Base 64 encoding into an equivalent ASCII character array.
static TypeCode GetTypeCode(Object* *object*)	Returns the **TypeCode** for the specified object.
static bool IsDBNull(Object* *object*)	Returns true if the specified object is **DBNull**.
static int ToBase64CharArray(unsigned char *src* __gc[], int *srcIndex*, int *length*, __wchar_t *dest* __gc[], int *destIndex*)	Converts the length ASCII characters from the ***src*** array starting at the index ***srcIndex*** into Base 64 encoded Unicode characters in the ***dest*** array starting at the ***destIndex*** index.
static String* ToBase64String(unsigned char *array* __gc[])	Converts the specified ASCII character ***array*** into a Base 64-encoded Unicode string.
static String* ToBase64String(unsigned char *array* __gc[], int *index*, int *length*)	Converts the length characters in the ASCII character ***array*** starting at the index ***index*** into a Base 64 encoded Unicode string.
static *TYPE2* To*TYPE2*(*TYPE1* *value*)	Converts the value from the type *TYPE1* into an equivalent value of type *TYPE2*. Possible values of *TYPE2* are: **Boolean, Byte, Char, DateTime, Decimal, Double, Int16, Int32, Int64, SByte, Single, String, UInt16, UInt32,** and **UInt65.** Possible values of *TYPE1* are: **bool, unsigned char, __wchar_t, DateTime, Decimal, double, short, int, __int64, Object*, char, float, String*, unsigned short, unsigned int,** and **unsigned __int64.**

<Continued on Next Page>

<Table 4.8 Continued>

Method	Description
static *TYPE* **To**_TYPE_**(Object*** *object*, **IFormatProvider*** *provider*)	Converts the specified object into an equivalent value of type *TYPE* using the specified **IFormatProvider** interface. Possible values of *TYPE* are all primitive types.
static *TYPE* **To**_TYPE_ **(String*** *str*, **IFormatProvider*** *provider*)	Converts the *str* string into an equivalent value of type *TYPE* using the specified **IFormatProvider** interface. Possible values of *TYPE* are all primitive types.

Environment Class

The .NET Framework provides the **Environment** class to provide access to such information as environment variables, process command line arguments, and system paths:

```
Object
|- Environment

Attributes: None
Abstract: No
Sealed: Yes
Implemented Interfaces: None
```

The **Environment** class has no constructors and contains only static properties and methods. These methods include the **CurrentDirectory** property for getting and setting the current directory, the **GetCommandLineArgs** method for retrieving the process command line arguments, the **GetEnvironmentVariable** method for retrieving the value of a specified environment variable, the **ExpandEnvironmentVariables** method for formatting text strings that contain names of the environment variables enclosed in '%'-characters (e.g., '%PATH%'), and others. The complete set of the **Environment** class properties and methods is presented in Tables 4.9 through 4.10.

Table 4.9 **Environment** class properties (all static).

Get/Set	Type	Property	Description
Get	**String***	**CommandLine**	Returns the process command line.
Get/Set	**String***	**CurrentDirectory**	Returns or sets the current directory.
Get/Set	**int**	**ExitCode**	Returns or sets the process exit code.
Get	**bool**	**HasShutdownStarted**	Returns **true** if the CLR is shutting down.
Get	**String***	**MachineName**	Returns the NetBIOS name of the local system.
Get	**String***	**NewLine**	Returns the new line string (e.g., CR/LF pair).

<Continued on Next Page>

<Table 4.9 Continued>

Get/Set	Type	Property	Description
Get	Operating System*	OSVersion	Returns the **Operating System** object identifying the current platform (i.e., **Win32NT**, **Win32S**, or **Win32Windows**) and the OS version number.
Get	String*	StackTrace	Returns current stack trace.
Get	String*	SystemDirectory	Returns the system directory path.
Get	int	TickCount	Returns the number of milliseconds elapsed since the system booted.
Get	String*	UserDomainName	Returns the current user application domain name.
Get	bool	UserInteractive	Returns **true** if the current process is running in user interactive mode.
Get	String*	UserName	Returns the current thread user account name.
Get	Version*	Version	Returns the CLR version information.
Get	__int64	WorkingSet	Returns the number of bytes of physical memory allocated for the current process.

Table 4.10 **Environment** class methods.

Method	Description
static void Exit(int *exitCode*)	Terminates this process with the specified exit code.
static String* ExpandEnvironmentVariables(String* *str*)	Replaces the environment variables embedded in the specified string with their actual values. An environment variable name must be enclosed in percent signs, e.g. ,%LIBPATH%.
static String* GetCommandLineArgs() __gc[]	Returns an array of command line arguments of the current process.
static String* GetEnvironmentVariable(String* *variable*)	Returns the value of the specified environment variable.
static IDictionary* GetEnvironmentVariables()	Returns a dictionary of all environment variables and their values.
String* GetFolderPath(Environment.SpecialFolder *folder*)	Gets the path to the specified system special folder.
static String* GetLogicalDrives() __gc[]	Returns an array of the logical drives on the current system.

Special Folders

The **Environment** class provides the **GetFolderPath** method for retrieving paths of the special system folders. The method accepts an argument of type **Environment.SpecialFolder**, which can accept one of the following values: **ApplicationData**, **CommonApplicationData**, **CommonProgramFiles**, **Cookies**, **DesktopDirectory**, **Favorites**, **History**, **InternetCache**, **LocalApplicationData**, **Personal**, **ProgramFiles**, **Programs**, **Recent**, **SendTo**, **StartMenu**, **Startup**, **Startup,** and **Templates**.

Uniform Resource Identifiers

Similarly to file paths that are used for locating files and directories on the file system, *Uniform Resource Identifiers* (URI) are used for locating resources on the Internet, intranet or local area network. URIs encompass *Uniform Resource Locators* (URLs), which represent links to WWW and FTP sites and network paths expressed in the Universal Naming Convention form (UNC).

> **NOTE:** Although in theory the terms URI and URL are different, in actuality, both terms are often used interchangeably.

The general format of a URI consists of six parts and has the following syntax:

```
scheme://host:port/path?query#fragment
```

The concrete URI syntax depends on the URI scheme (*file, ftp, gopher, http, https, mailto,* or *news*). Some URI parts may not be applicable to a particular scheme. In the .NET Framework URIs are represented by means of the **Uri** class:

```
Object
|- MarshalByRefObject
   |- Uri

Attributes: Serializable
Abstract: No
Sealed: No
Implemented Interfaces: ISerializable
```

Similarly to the **String** class, the **Uri** class is immutable. Internally URIs are stored in the *escaped* format, i.e., blanks are replaced with the %20 character and all ASCII characters with values greater than 127 will be converted into hexadecimal form.

The **Uri** class provides constructors for initializing URIs from strings, base and relative paths (see Table 4.11), static read-only fields that define the URI separator character and scheme strings (see Table 4.12), properties corresponding to the URI parts (see Table 4.13), and methods for parsing, checking, encoding, and decoding URI text (see Table 4.14).

Table 4.11 **Uri** class constructors.

Constructor	Description
Uri(String* *str***)**	Constructs a URI based on the specified string.
protected: Uri(SerializationInfo* *info***, StreamingContext** *context***)**	Constructs a URI based on the specified serialization information.
Uri(String* *str***, bool** *dontEscape***)**	Constructs a URI based on the specified string. Sets the *dontEscape* parameter to **true** if the URI is already escaped.
Uri(Uri* *baseUri***, String*** *RelativeUri***)**	Constructs a URI from a specified base and relative URIs.
Uri(Uri* *baseUri***, String*** *RelativeUri***, bool** *dontEscape***)**	Constructs a URI from a specified base and relative URIs. Sets the *dontEscape* parameter to **true** if the URI is already escaped.

Table 4.12 **Uri** class fields.

Field	Description
static String* SchemeDelimiter	Delimiter for separating the communication protocol scheme from the address portion of the URI (://).
static String* UriSchemeFile	Represents a pointer to a local file (file).
static String* UriSchemeFtp	Represents a File Transfer Protocol - FTP (ftp).
static String* UriSchemeGopher	Represents a gopher protocol (gopher).
static String* UriSchemeHttp	Represents a HyperText Transfer Protocol - HTTP (http).
static String* UriSchemeHttps	Represents a secure HTTP (https).
static String* UriSchemeMailto	Represents a Simple Mail Network Protocol - SMNP (mailto).
static String* UriSchemeNews	Represents a Network News Transfer Protocol - NNTP (news).
static String* UriSchemeNntp	Represents a Network News Transfer Protocol - NNTP (nntp).

Table 4.13 **Uri** class properties.

Get/Set	Type	Property	Description
Get	String*	AbsolutePath	Returns the absolute path of the URI.
Get	String*	AbsoluteUri	Returns the absolute URI.
Get	String*	Authority	Returns the DNS host name or IP address including the port number (if available) portion of the URI.
Get	String*	Fragment	Returns an escaped URI fragment if any (i.e., name past # sign in the URI).
Get	String*	Host	Returns the DNS host name, or IP address of the URI.
Get	UriHostNameType	HostNameType	Returns the URI host name type.
Get	bool	IsDefaultPort	Returns **true** if the URI uses a default port for the specified protocol.
Get	bool	IsFile	Returns **true** if the URI represents a pointer to a local file.
Get	bool	IsLoopback	Returns **true** if the URI host is localhost or 127.0.0.1 (i.e., local system).
Get	bool	IsUnc	Returns **true** if the URI represents a UNC network name (i.e., \\helix\Data\).
Get	String*	LocalPath	Returns an OS file name corresponding to file URI.
Get	String*	PathAndQuery	Returns the path and query portion of the URI.
Get	int	Port	Returns URI port.
Get	String*	Query	Returns URI query portion.
Get	String*	Scheme	Returns URI scheme.
Get	String*[]	Segments	Returns an array of URI segments.
Get	bool	UserEscaped	Returns **true** if the URI was escaped before the URI object was constructed.
Get	String*	UserInfo	Returns user name and password information encoded in the URI.

Table 4.14 **Uri** class methods.

Method	Description
static UriHostNameType CheckHostName(String* *name*)	Returns URI host type (**Basic**, **Dns**, **IPv4**, **IPv6,** or **Unknown**).
static bool CheckSchemeName(String* *schemeName*)	Returns **true** if the host name is valid.
protected: static String* EscapeString(String* *str*)	Escapes the specified string in a URI manner.
static int FromHex(__wchar_t *digit*)	Converts the specified hexadecimal digit (0..F) into an integer.
String* GetLeftPart(UriPartial *part*)	Returns **Scheme**, **Authority**, or **Path** portion of the URI.
static String* HexEscape(__wchar_t *chr*)	Escapes the specified Unicode character by converting it into a hexadecimal equivalent suitable for usage in URIs.
static __wchar_t HexUnescape(String* *str*, int *index*)	Converts a portion of the specified string starting from the index *index* from the escaped format into the unescaped Unicode string.
static bool IsHexDigit(__wchar_t *chr*)	Returns **true** if the specified character is a valid hex digit.
static bool IsHexEncoding(String* *str*, int *index*)	Returns **true** if a portion of the specified string starting at the index *index* represents a hexadecimal encoding (i.e., %0A0B%F0).
String* MakeRelative(Uri* *baseUri*)	Converts the current URI into a relative form by comparing with the specified base URI. If the specified base URI does not actually represent a base for the current URI, the absolute current URI is returned.

UriBuilder Class

As with **String** objects, **Uri** objects are immutable. To facilitate construction and modification of URIs, the .NET Framework Class Library provides the **UriBuilder** class, which has the following inheritance diagram:

```
Object
|- UriBuilder

Attributes: None
Abstract: No
Sealed: No
Implemented Interfaces: None
```

The **Uri** class supplies constructors for initializing URIs based on URI parts such as scheme, host, port, path, and query string (see Table 4.15), and get/set properties corresponding to individual URI parts (see Table 4.16).

The typical **UriBuilder** class usage scenario involves constructing a **UriBuilder** object, modifying the individual URI parts accessible as the **UriBuilder** properties, and obtaining the resulting URI using the **Uri** property.

Table 4.15 **UriBuilder** class constructors.

Constructor	Description
UriBuilder()	Default constructor.
UriBuilder(String* *uri***)**	Constructs a **UriBuilder** object based on the specified URI string.
UriBuilder(Uri* *uri***)**	Constructs a **UriBuilder** object based onf the specified URI.
UriBuilder(String* *scheme***, String*** *host***)**	Constructs a **UriBuilder** object based on the specified URI components.
UriBuilder(String* *scheme***, String*** *host***, int** *port***)**	Constructs a **UriBuilder** object based on the specified URI components.
UriBuilder(String* *scheme***, String*** *host***, int** *port***, String*** *path***)**	Constructs a **UriBuilder** object based on the specified URI components.
UriBuilder(String* *scheme***, String*** *host***, int** *port***, String*** *path***, String*** *query***)**	Constructs a **UriBuilder** object based on the specified URI components.

Table 4.16 **UriBuilder** class properties.

Get/Set	Type	Property	Description
Get/Set	**String***	**Fragment**	Returns or sets the fragment portion of the URI.
Get/Set	**String***	**Host**	Returns or sets the URI host name.
Get/Set	**String***	**Password**	Returns or sets the URI password.
Get/Set	**String***	**Path**	Returns or sets the URI path.
Get/Set	**String***	**int Port**	Returns or sets the URI port.
Get/Set	**String***	**Query**	Returns or sets the URI query.
Get/Set	**String***	**Scheme**	Returns or sets the URI scheme.
Get	**Uri***	**Uri**	Returns a **Uri** object constructed by the **UriBuilder**.
Get/Set	**String***	**UserName**	Returns or sets the URI user name.

Garbage Collector

The garbage collector is the key component for the CLR. The .NET Framework Class Library allows you to control the garbage collector by means of the **GC** class:

```
Object
|- GC
```

```
Attributes: None
Abstract: No
Sealed: Yes
Implemented Interfaces: None
```

If you recall from Chapter 2, garbage collector is a separate process that executes periodically to reclaim memory that is no longer used. When the garbage collector kicks in it scans all object references to identify objects eligible for garbage collection. If the object cannot be referenced from running code, the garbage collector reclaims the memory used by the object and compacts the managed heap.

In some cases, however, the garbage collection procedure becomes more complex. Some objects implement the **Finalize** method and require *finalization*. If an object requires finalization, it is not immediately discarded by the garbage collector. Instead, the garbage collector schedules the object for finalization by placing the object into an internal *F-reachable queue*. Objects queued up in the F-reachable queue are not considered garbage and cannot be collected by the garbage collector. The F-reachable queue is processed by yet another thread that calls the object's **Finalize** methods and removes the object's pointer from the F-reachable queue. Once the object pointer is removed from the F-reachable queue, the finalized object becomes true garbage that can be removed by the garbage collector on the next run.

Still, the situation can get even more complex. The garbage collector will *resurrect* the object if the object's **Finalize** method creates a new reachable reference to the object (i.e., by initializing a global static variable with the **this** pointer). A resurrected object is not eligible for garbage collection and will stay alive until all references to the object become Null references or go out of scope. When the resurrected object becomes unreachable, the garbage collector will once again schedule the object for finalization and the whole process repeats.

The **GC** class allows controlling the garbage collector behavior by allowing the following actions:

* *Forcing garbage collection*: You can force immediate garbage collection by calling the **GC::Collect** method. Forcing garbage collection may be necessary to free and compact managed heap memory prior to allocation of a big chunk of memory, although excessive calls to the **GC::Collect** method will dramatically reduce performance of the code.

* *Suppressing finalization*: If an object implements the **Finalize** method and requires finalization, you can instruct the garbage collector by calling the **GC::SuppressFinalize** method to bypass the object's finalization and garbage-collect the object the "fast" way.

> **NOTE:** Typically, object's **Finalize** method releases critical resources. If the object's critical resources have already been released, you can instruct the garbage collector to bypass finalization for the object and thus improve the performance of your code.

*   *Re-enabling finalization*: If finalization for an object was suppressed by calling the **GC::SuppressFinalize** method, you can re-enable the finalization for the object by calling the **GC::ReRegisterForFinalize** method.

*   *Waiting for pending finalizers*: You can suspend the current thread by calling the **GC::WaitForPendingFinalizers** method, which blocks execution until the **Finalize** methods are called for all objects in the F-reachable queue.

The complete set of the garbage collector properties and methods is listed in Tables 4.17 through 4.18.

Table 4.17 **GC** class properties (all static).

Get/Set	Type	Property	Description
Get	**int**	**MaxGeneration**	Returns the maximum number of generations the garbage collector supports.

Table 4.18 **GC** class methods.

Method	Description
static void Collect()	Forces garbage collection.
static void Collect(int *generation***)**	Forces garbage collection.
static int GetGeneration(Object* *obj***)**	Returns the current generation number of an object.
static int GetGeneration(WeakReference* *obj***)**	Returns the current generation number of an object.
static __int64 GetTotalMemory(bool *forceFullCollection***)**	Returns the number of bytes currently allocated. The *forceFullCollection* parameter specifies whether to perform garbage collection prior to returning the amount of allocated memory.
static void KeepAlive(Object* *obj***)**	Prevents the specified object from being garbage collected.
static void ReRegisterForFinalize(Object* *obj***)**	Requests that the system call the **Finalize** method for the specified object, for which **SuppressFinalize** has previously been called.
static void SuppressFinalize(Object* *obj***)**	Requests that the system not call the **Finalize** method for the specified object.
static void WaitForPendingFinalizers()	Suspends the current thread until the garbage collector executes **Finalize** methods for all objects pending finalization in the finalizer thread.

Weak References

Managed objects become eligible for garbage collection when they can no longer be referenced by running code. The object remains protected from garbage collection while there exists a direct or indirect reference to it. Such reference is called *strong references*. In addition to ordinary strong references, the .NET Framework defines *weak references* implemented by means of the class library **WeakReference** class:

```
Object
|- WeakReference
```

Attributes: **Serializable**
Abstract: No
Sealed: No
Implemented Interfaces: **ISerializable**

Weak references allow you to access objects they represent, but unlike strong references, they do not protect objects from being garbage collected. A weak reference allows you to track its target until the target is garbage collected. When a garbage collection occurs a weak reference automatically becomes a Null reference.

Alternatively, a weak reference can be configured for tracking objects past finalization. Some objects can be *resurrected* by the garbage collector, if their **Finalize** method creates a new valid reference to the object (e.g., by initializing a global variable with a pointer to **this**). The **WeakReference** class constructors and properties are listed in Tables 4.19 and 4.20.

Table 4.19 **WeakReference** class constructors.

Constructor	Description
WeakReference(Object* *target*)	Constructs a **WeakReference** object for the specified target.
WeakReference(Object* *target*, bool *track*)	Constructs a **WeakReference** object tracking the specified target. The **track** parameter indicates whether the target should be tracked past finalization.
WeakReference(SerializationInfo* *info*, StreamingContext *context*)	Constructs a **WeakReference** object using the serialization information.

Table 4.20 **WeakReference** class properties (all virtual).

Get/Set	Type	Property	Description
Get	**bool**	**IsAlive**	Returns **true** if there are strong references to the target and the target is not eligible for garbage collection.
Get/Set	**Object***	**Target**	Returns or sets the weak reference target object.
Get	**bool**	**TrackResurrection**	Returns **true** to indicate that the target should be tracked past finalization.

Immediate Solutions

Creating Custom Attributes

Follow these steps to define a custom attribute class:

1.   Derive a new custom attribute class from the **Attribute**.
2.   Apply the **AttributeUsage** attribute to the class declaration and specify the attribute target.
3.   Define the custom attribute constructors and properties as needed.

Once you define the attribute and implement its constructors, properties, and methods, you can apply the attribute to targets in your code.

The following code example demonstrates how a custom attribute type, **TestAttribute**, can be defined. **TestAttribute** can be applied to class and member declarations and can be repeated multiple times (**AttributeUsage(Class|Method, AllowMultiple=true)**). The attribute provides the default constructor, a constructor accepting an integer parameter, and the public **Param** property:

```
#using <mscorlib.dll>
using namespace System;
using namespace System::Reflection;

// Custom attribute class
[AttributeUsage(Class|Method, AllowMultiple=true)]
public __gc class TestAttribute: public Attribute {
public:
    TestAttribute() { ParamData = 10; }
    TestAttribute(int param) { ParamData = param; }
    __property int get_Param() { return ParamData; }
    __property void set_Param(int param) { ParamData = param; }
private:
    int ParamData;
};

// Attribute target class
[Test, Test(8)]
public __gc class TestClass {
public:
    [Test(Param=5)]
    TestClass() {}
    // [Test] is equivalent to [TestAttribute]
    [TestAttribute]
    void TestMethod() {}
};
```

The **TestAttribute** attribute usage is demonstrated by applying the attribute to the sample **TestClass**. The attribute is applied to the **TestClass** class definition twice; to the default constructor, and to the **TestMethod** method.

Obtaining Attribute Information

If you want to query attribute information at runtime, you can use the **Attribute::GetAttribute/Attribute::GetAttributes** static methods, which allow retrieving all attributes applied to a specified type or class member. The code example shown next defines the **GetAttributes** routine that reports attribute information on a specified type, including attributes applied to class members. The code performs the following steps:

1. Retrieves the array of attributes applied to a specified type using the **Attribute::GetCustomAttributes** method.

2. If the returned array of attributes is not empty, reports the names of the attributes applied to the type.

3. Retrieves the array of class members using the **Type::GetMethods** method.

4. For each class member, retrieves the array of attributes using the **Attribute::GetCustomAttributes** method.

If the returned array of attributes is not empty, reports the names of the attributes applied to the member.

> NOTE: The **Type::GetMethods** method returns the array of objects of type **MemberInfo**, which is defined in the System::Reflection namespace.

```
#using <mscorlib.dll>
using namespace System;
using namespace System::Reflection;

// Attribute recovery function
void GetAttributes(Type* type)
{
    // 1. Get class attributes
    Attribute* Attributes[] = Attribute::GetCustomAttributes(type);
    if ( Attributes == 0 || !Attributes->Count )
        Console::WriteLine("Type {0}: no attributes", type->Name);
    else
    {
        Console::Write("Type {0}: ", type->Name);
        // 2. Report attribute names
        for ( int i = 0; i < Attributes->Count; i++ )
            Console::Write("[{0}]; ", Attributes[i]->GetType()->Name);
        Console::WriteLine();
    }

    // 3. Get class members
    MemberInfo* MemberInfo[] = type->GetMethods();
    for ( int i = 0; i < MemberInfo->Count; i++ )
    {
        // 4. Get member attributes
        Attributes = Attribute::GetCustomAttributes(MemberInfo[i]);
```

```
        if ( Attributes == 0 || !Attributes->Count )
          Console::WriteLine("{0}::{1}(): no attributes",
                type->Name, MemberInfo[i]->Name);
        else
        {
            Console::Write("{0}::{1}(): ",
                type->Name, MemberInfo[i]->Name);
            // 5. Report attribute info
            for ( int i = 0; i < Attributes->Count; i++ )
                Console::Write("[{0}]; ", Attributes[i]->GetType()->Name);
            Console::WriteLine();
        }
    }
}

void main()
{
    // Report class attributes
    GetAttributes(__typeof(String));
}
```

Accessing Numeric Types on Byte Level

To access numeric types at the byte level to perform encryption/decryption, packing, or endian-conversion, you should use the **BitConverter** class. The code example provided next illustrates little-endian to big-endian conversion of a 32-bit integer. First, the code converts the **i32** integer variable into an array of bytes using the **BitConverter::GetBytes** method. Then, the order of the array bytes is reversed. Lastly, the rearranged array is converted back to a 32-bit integer using the **BitConverter::ToInt32** method:

```
#using <mscorlib.dll>
using namespace System;

void main()
{
    int i32 = 0x01020304;
    // 1. Convert 32-bit integer to array of bytes
    unsigned char bytes __gc[] = BitConverter::GetBytes(i32);
    // 2. Swap bytes
    unsigned char b1 = bytes[1], b0 = bytes[0];
    bytes[0] = bytes[3];
    bytes[1] = bytes[2];
    bytes[2] = b1;
    bytes[3] = b0;
    // 3. Convert byte array to 32-bit integer
    i32 = BitConverter::ToInt32(bytes, 0);
    Console::WriteLine("{0:X}", __box(i32));
}
```

Accessing Managed Arrays on Byte Level

To access managed arrays of primitive types at the byte level, you should use the **Buffer** class. The following code example illustrates how to copy bytes from one managed array to another with subsequent modification of the first byte in the destination array:

1.   First, the source array size in bytes is obtained using the **Buffer::ByteLength** method.
2.   Next, the source array bytes are copied to the destination array using the **Buffer::BlockCopy** method.
3.   Finally, the first byte in the destination array is set to 255 using the **Buffer::SetByte** method.

```
#using <mscorlib.dll>
using namespace System;

void main()
{
    Int32 Array1[] = new Int32[10];
    Int32 Array2[] = new Int32[20];

    // 1. Get the array length
    int Size = Buffer::ByteLength(Array2);
    // 2. Copy one array to another
    Buffer::BlockCopy(Array2, 0, Array1, 0, Size);
    // 3. Modify the first bye in the array
    Buffer::SetByte(Array1, 0, 255); //Array[0] = 255
}
```

Converting Types

To convert between primitive types, including "lossy" conversion, or to convert text characters to and from Base 64 encoding, you should use the **Convert** class. The following code sample illustrates how you use the Convert class to perform these actions:

1.   Converts ASCII character array into a base 64-encoded **String** using the **Convert::ToBase64String** method.
2.   Converts the encoded **String** back into an ASCII character array using the **Convert::FromBase64String** method.
3.   Performs "lossy" conversion of a floating-point value into an integer value using the **Convert::ToInt32** method.

```
#using <mscorlib.dll>
using namespace System;

void main()
{
    // Source text
    unsigned char s __gc[] = {'T','h','i','s',' ','i','s',' ','a',
        ' ','t','e','s','t'};
```

```
   // 1. Convert text to base-64 encoding
   String* Base64Str = Convert::ToBase64String(s);
   // 2. Convert text from base-64 encoding
   s = Convert::FromBase64String(Base64Str);

   float floatA = 3.2f;
   // 3. Execute lossy float-to-int conversion
   int intA = Convert::ToInt32(floatA);
}
```

Implementing Custom Type Conversion

To provide support for custom type conversion in a user-defined class, you must have your class implement the **IConvertible** interface. The **IConvertible** interface defines the **ToType** method for converting the class value into an arbitrary type and numerous **To***TYPE* methods for converting the class value into primitive types.

When implementing the **IConvertible** interface you *must* provide bodies for all interface methods. If a meaningful conversion to a primitive type cannot be defined, the conversion method should throw a **FormatException** exception. To support conversion of the class value into another user-defined type, you should have the **ToType** method to perform custom conversion necessary to convert the value as well as type checking.

A sample program demonstrating custom conversion is shown next. The code defines two types: **FullAge** and the **Age**. The **FullAge** class implements the **IConvertible** interface to support **FullAge** to **Age** conversion. The **ToType** method performs type checking and returns a new instance of the **Age** class if the **conversionType** parameter is of type **Age**. Otherwise, the method throws a **FormatException** exception. Both the **FullAge** and the **Age** classes override the **ToString** method to provide a custom string representation for the age values.

The main program instantiates a **FullAge** object and performs conversion to **Age** type using the **Convert::ChangeType** method. When the **Convert::ChangeType** method is called, the framework invokes the **FullAge::ToType** method, which performs type checking and creates a new instance of the **Age** class.

```
#using <mscorlib.dll>
using namespace System;

// Age class: Years
__gc struct Age {
   Age(int years)
   {
      Years = years;
   }
   String* ToString()
   {
      return String::Concat(Years.ToString(), " years");
   }
   int Years;
};
```

```
// Full Age class: Years & Month
__gc struct FullAge: public IConvertible {
   FullAge(int years, int month)
   {
      Years = years;
      Month = month;
   }
   int Years;
   int Month;
   String* ToString()
   {
      return String::Concat(Years.ToString(), " years ",
         Month.ToString(), " month");
   }
   String* ToString(IFormatProvider*)
   {
      return ToString();
   }
   // Conversion methods
   Object* ToType(Type* conversionType, IFormatProvider*)
   {
      if ( conversionType == __typeof(Age) )
         return new Age(Years);
      else
         throw new FormatException();
   }
   TypeCode GetTypeCode()
   {
      return TypeCode::Int32;
   }
   bool ToBoolean(IFormatProvider*)
   {
      throw new FormatException();
      return false;
   }
   unsigned char ToByte(IFormatProvider*)
   {
      throw new FormatException();
      return 0;
   }
   __wchar_t ToChar(IFormatProvider*)
   {
      throw new FormatException();
      return 0;
   }
   DateTime ToDateTime(IFormatProvider*)
```

```
    {
        throw new FormatException();
        return 0;
    }
    Decimal ToDecimal(IFormatProvider*)
    {
        throw new FormatException();
        return 0;
    }
    double ToDouble(IFormatProvider*)
    {
        throw new FormatException();
        return 0;
    }
    short ToInt16(IFormatProvider*)
    {
        throw new FormatException();
        return 0;
    }
    int ToInt32(IFormatProvider*)
    {
        throw new FormatException();
        return 0;
    }
    __int64 ToInt64(IFormatProvider*)
    {
        throw new FormatException();
        return 0;
    }
    signed char ToSByte(IFormatProvider*)
    {
        throw new FormatException();
        return 0;
    }
    float ToSingle(IFormatProvider*)
    {
        throw new FormatException();
        return 0;
    }
    unsigned short ToUInt16(IFormatProvider*)
    {
        throw new FormatException();
        return 0;
    }
    unsigned int ToUInt32(IFormatProvider*)
    {
```

```
        throw new FormatException();
        return 0;
   }
   unsigned __int64 ToUInt64(IFormatProvider*)
   {
        throw new FormatException();
        return 0;
   }
};

void main()
{
   // 1. Instantiate FullAge object
   FullAge* MyAge = new FullAge(26, 6);
   Console::WriteLine("My age: {0}", MyAge);

   // 2. Instantiate Age object by converting from FullAge
   Age* ShortAge = dynamic_cast<Age*>(Convert::ChangeType(MyAge,
       __typeof(Age)));
   Console::WriteLine("Converted age: {0}", ShortAge);
}
```

Obtaining Environment Information

To obtain information on environment variables, process command line arguments, and system paths, you should use the **Environment** class. The following code example shows how to use the **Environment** class to perform these actions:

1.   Reports current directory, machine name, user name using the **Environment** class **CurrentDirectory**, **MachineName**, and **UserName** properties.

2.   Retrieves the PATH environment variable using the **Environment::ExpandEnvironmentVariables** method.

3.   Retrieves the command line arguments using the **Environment::GetCommandLineArgs** method.

4.   Changes the current directory by setting the **Environment::CurrentDirectory** property.

```
#using <mscorlib.dll>
using namespace System;
void main()
{
   // 1. Report environment information
   Console::WriteLine("Current Directory: {0}", Environment::CurrentDirectory);
   Console::WriteLine("Machine name: {0}", Environment::MachineName);
   Console::WriteLine("Current User: {0}", Environment::UserName);
   // 2. Report PATH environment variable
   Console::WriteLine(Environment::ExpandEnvironmentVariables(
       "PATH is: %PATH%"));
```

```
// 3. Report command line arguments
String* CmdLine[] = Environment::GetCommandLineArgs();
for ( int i = 0; i < CmdLine->GetLength(0); i++ )
    Console::WriteLine(CmdLine[i]);
// 4. Change current directory
Environment::CurrentDirectory = "C:\\";
}
```

Using Uniform Resource Identifiers

To represent Uniform Resource Identifiers (URIs) or Uniform Resource Locators (URLs), you should use the **Uri** class. Because the **Uri** class represents an immutable URI it is more convenient to use **Uri** objects in conjunction with the **UriBuilder** class, which supports building new and modifying existing URIs. The following code example demonstrates how to use the **Uri** and **UriBuilder** classes to perform these steps:

1.   Creates a **UriBuilder** object for an HTTP URL using the constructor.

2.   Obtains a **Uri** from the **UriBuilder** object using the **UriBuilder::Uri** property.

3.   Creates a new **Uri** object using the constructor.

4.   Initializes the **UriBuilder** object with the **Uri** using the constructor.

5.   Modifies the URI information by setting the **UriBuilder::Path**, **UserName** and **Password** properties.

6.   Obtains the modified URI using the **UriBuilder::Uri** property.

```
#using <mscorlib.dll>
#using <system.dll>
using namespace System;

void main()
{
    // 1. Create a new UriBuilder
    UriBuilder* myBuilder = new UriBuilder("http", "www.ultramax-music.com");
    // 2. Convert to URI
    Uri* myUri = myBuilder->Uri;


    // 3. Creates a Uri for FTP URL
    Uri* someUri = new Uri("ftp://Gems3D.com");
    // 4. Initializes the UriBuilder with the Uri
    myBuilder = new UriBuilder(someUri);
    // 5. Modifies an existing URI by adding path, user name and password
    myBuilder->Path = "Download/Gems3D.exe";
    myBuilder->UserName = "Joe_Hacker";
    myBuilder->Password = "go";
    // 6. Produce a new URI
    someUri = myBuilder->Uri;
    Console::WriteLine(someUri);
}
```

> **NOTE:** The **Uri/UriBuilder** classes are defined in system.dll, thus, if you want to reference these classes, you must include the **#using <system.dll>** statement in your code.

Forcing Garbage Collection

To force immediate garbage collection, you should call the **GC::Collect** method. Keep in mind, however, that immediate garbage collection does not result in immediate finalization of unused objects. Finalization is managed by another thread that is independent of the garbage-collector process. To force the completion of pending finalizers, you can call the **GC::WaitForPendingFinalizers** method.

To better understand manual garbage collection and controlled finalization, consider the code example shown next. The code defines the **TestClass** class, which declares a destructor. If you recall Chapter 2, the destructor of a managed type is converted by the compiler into the **Finalize** method. Thus, the **TestClass** requires finalization. To create an instance of the **TestClass**, the **CreateTestClass** function is defined. When the main program calls the **CreateTestClass** function, a **TestClass** object is created. The newly created object is quickly "orphaned" when the function returns and thus becomes eligible for garbage collection.

> **NOTE:** If you attempt to orphan an object by making the object go out of scope, in actuality the object will not be orphaned until the function that orphaned it returns.

The main program forces garbage collection by calling the **GC::Collect** method. At this point the **TestClass** object is scheduled for finalization, but the **Finalize** method (i.e., the destructor) is not yet called. To force the execution of the **TestClass** destructor, the main program calls the **GC::WaitForPendingFinalizers** method, which blocks the execution of the main program thread and forces the finalization thread to execute the **TestClass::Finalize** method.

```
#using <mscorlib.dll>
using namespace System;

__gc class TestClass {
    // Destructor makes object to require finalization
    ~TestClass()
    {
        Console::WriteLine("TestClass::Finalize");
    }
};

void CreateTestClass()
{
    TestClass* myClass = new TestClass();
}

int main()
{
    // 1. Creates objects
    CreateTestClass();
    // Objects go out of scope and become eligible for GC

    // 2. Report free memory
    Console::WriteLine("Total bytes allocated: {0}",
        __box(GC::GetTotalMemory(false)));
```

```
// 3. Force garbage collection for the objects
   GC::Collect();

   // Report free memory
   Console::WriteLine("Total bytes allocated: {0}",
      __box(GC::GetTotalMemory(false)));

   // 4. Wait until the objects are finalized
   GC::WaitForPendingFinalizers();
   return 0;
}
```

Suppressing Finalization

If your object acquires important resources that must be released in a predictable manner, your class should implement the **IDisposable** interface and supply the **Dispose** method. It is a common practice to call the **Dispose** method from the class's destructor to ensure that the resources are released when the object is garbage collected. To prevent calling the **Dispose** method twice, you should suppress the finalization for your class by calling the **GC::SuppressFinalize** from the class's **Dispose** method. The **GC::SuppressFinalize** call prevents the garbage collector from calling your object's **Finalize** method (i.e., C++ destructor) when the object is garbage collected.

The code example shown next demonstrates the definition of the **TestClass** class, which implements the **IDisposable** interface. The class provides a destructor and the **Dispose** method, which calls the **GC::SuppressFinalize** to avoid double disposing.

```
#using <mscorlib.dll>
using namespace System;

__gc class TestClass: public IDisposable {
public:
   void Dispose()
   {
      Console::WriteLine("TestClass::Dispose");
      // Free resources
      // ...
      // Suppress finalization
      GC::SuppressFinalize(this);
   }
   ~TestClass()
   {
      Console::WriteLine("TestClass::~TestClass");
      Dispose();
   }
};

void main()
```

```
{
    // 1. Create object
    TestClass* MyClass = new TestClass();
    // 2. Dispose
    MyClass->Dispose();
}
```

If you comment out the **MyClass->Dispose()** statement, the **MyClass** object will be finalized normally and the **TestClass** destructor will be called.

Protecting Unmanaged Pointers to Managed Objects

The garbage collector can effectively track only managed references to managed objects. If you are interoperating with unmanaged code that uses references to managed objects, you can explicitly direct the garbage collector not to dispose of a particular managed object that still may be used by an unmanaged code by calling the **GC::KeepAlive** method.

The **GC::KeepAlive** method does not actually do anything. Instead, it forces a reference to the managed object to appear in the code. Thus, the **GC::KeepAlive** method must be called *at the end* of the code where you want to ensure the existence of the unmanaged object:

```
// Create unmanaged object
MyObject* obj = new MyObject();
// Call unmanaged code
CallCOMDll(obj);
// ...
// Insert KeepAlive to keep obj valid until this point
GC::KeepAlive(obj);
// OK, obj may be disposed if a garbage collection occurs past this point
```

Using Weak References

To keep track of objects eligible for garbage collection without preventing them from being garbage collected, you should use *weak references*. Weak references are implemented by means of the **WeakReference** class. You can inspect a weak reference to the object to determine whether the object was garbage collected and no longer accessible. If the object has not yet been destroyed, you can convert the weak reference to a strong reference using the **WeakReference::Target** property to temporarily or permanently protect the object from being garbage collected.

The code example shown next demonstrates how to instantiate a weak reference and convert the weak reference to a strong reference. The code performs the following actions:

1. Creates a weak reference by calling the **CreateWeakRef** function.

2. The **CreateWeakRef** function creates an instance of the **Object** class, initializes and returns a weak reference to the **Object** using the **WeakReference** constructor. When the **CreateWeakRef** function returns, the **Object** goes out of scope and becomes eligible for garbage collection.

3.   Inspects the weak reference's **IsAlive** property to see if the associated object has not yet been destroyed.

4.   Creates a strong reference from the weak reference by storing the **Target** object pointer in a local variable.

```
#using <mscorlib.dll>
using namespace System;

WeakReference* CreateWeakRef()
{
    Object* Obj = new Object();
    // 2. Initialize the weak reference with a pointer to an object
    return new WeakReference(Obj);
}

void main()
{
    // 1. Create weak reference
    WeakReference* WeakRef = CreateWeakRef();

    // 3. Is the weak reference is pointing to the alive object?
    if ( WeakRef->IsAlive )
    {
        // 4. Create strong reference
        Object* StrongRef = WeakRef->Target;
        Console::WriteLine("Object is still alive: {0}",
            StrongRef->ToString());
    }
}
```

Multithreaded Programming with .NET

QUICK JUMPS

CHAPTER 5

Multithreaded Programming with .NET

In Depth

Multithreading is the ability of your code to perform multiple computations simultaneously. Unlike *multitasking*, multithreading requires that a single program perform various tasks in parallel. Multitasking, on the other hand, requires that an operating system execute multiple programs or tasks in parallel. Both multitasking and multithreading have become important features of software development. While multitasking is transparently supported by most operating systems, you get to decide whether to use multithreading or not when you write your own code.

The .NET Framework Class Library provides all the tools in the System::Threading namespace you need to write multithreaded code. In this chapter, you will learn how to write multithreaded .NET programs, how to create and manage threads, how to implement thread-safe access to shared resources, how to use programmable timers, and how to issue interprocess notifications.

The System::Threading Namespace Hierarchy

The System::Threading namespace contains classes representing execution threads, thread pools, timers, and various synchronization objects such as mutexes, wait handles, interlocks, and so on. It may seem strange but the .NET Framework Class Library supplies a second namespace related to multithreaded programming—System::Timers. The System::Timers serves a single purpose: to provide a **Timer** component compatible with visual designers.

The System::Threading namespace general classes, exceptions, value types, delegates, and enumerations are listed in Tables 5.1 through 5.5. The combined System::Threading and System::Timers namespace class hierarchy is shown in Figure 5.1.

Table 5.1 System::Threading namespace general classes.

Class	Description
AutoResetEvent	Notifies one or more waiting threads that an event has occurred. The **AutoResetEvent** event remains signaled until a single waiting thread is released.
Interlocked	Provides locking mechanism for modifying variables shared among multiple threads.
ManualResetEvent	Notifies one or more waiting threads that an event has occurred. The **ManualResetEvent** event must be set or reset manually.
Monitor	Provides a mechanism for critical section synchronization.

<Continued on Next Page>

<Table 5.1 Continued>

Class	Description
Mutex	Provides mutually exclusive access to shared resources (similar to the MFC **CMutex**).
ReaderWriterLock	Defines the locking mechanism supporting single-writer/multiple-reader access.
RegisteredWaitHandle	Represents a registered with the **ThreadPool::RegisterWaitForSingleObject** method **WaitHandle** object.
Thread	Represents an execution thread (similar to the MFC **CWinThread**).
ThreadExceptionEventArgs	Represents data for the **ThreadException** event.
ThreadPool	Represents a pool of general-purpose threads that can process asynchronous I/O and respond to timer events and other notifications.
Timeout	Contains a single **int Infinite** field (=-1) corresponding to an infinite amount of time.
Timer	Provides a mechanism for executing class methods at specified intervals of time.
WaitHandle	The abstract base class for **AutoResetEvent**, **ManualResetEvent**, and **Mutex**.

Table 5.2 System::Threading namespace exceptions.

Exception	Description
SynchronizationLockException	Represents an exception thrown when a synchronized method is called from an unsynchronized code.
ThreadAbortException	Represents an exception thrown when a **Thread** is terminated via the **Abort** method.
ThreadInterruptedException	Represents an exception thrown when a **Thread** is interrupted by calling the **interrupt** method while the thread is in the **WaitSleepJoin** state.
ThreadStateException	Represents an exception thrown when the code requests a particular operation of a **Thread** that can not be performed due to the current thread state (i.e., resuming a thread that has been terminated).

Table 5.3 System::Threading namespace value types.

Value Type	Description
LockCookie	Represents a locked cookie for the single-writer/multiple-reader access.
NativeOverlapped	Represents a managed equivalent of the Win32 **OVERLAPPED** structure. Normally, you would never use this class directly. The structure contains **EventHandle**, **InternalHigh**. **InternalLow**, **OffsetHigh**, and **OffsetLow int** fields. The **EventHandle** contains a handle of the event object, which will be signaled when the I/O operation completes. The **OffsetHigh** and **OffsetLow** fields contain the offset from the beginning of the file at which to start the data transfer. The **InternalHigh**. **InternalLow** fields are reserved.

Table 5.4 System::Threading namespace delegates.

Delegate	Description
void IOCompletionCallback(unsigned int *errorCode*, unsigned int *numBytes*, NativeOverlapped* *overlapped*)	A delegate for handling I/O completion notifications.
void ThreadExceptionEventHandler(Object* *sender*, ThreadExceptionEventArgs* *e*)	A delegate for handling the **ThreadException** events for the **System::Windows::Forms::Application** objects.
void ThreadStart()	Main **Thread** routine delegate.
void TimerCallback(Object* *state*)	A delegate for handling **Timer** events (similar to the MFC **WM_TIMER** event handler).
void WaitCallback(Object* *state*)	A delegate for registered **WaitHandle** objects, which is called when a **WaitObject** is signaled.
void WaitOrTimerCallback (Object* *state*, bool *timeOut*)	A delegate for registered **WaitHandle** objects, which is called when a **WaitObject** is signaled or timed out (*timeout*=**true**).

Table 5.5 System::Threading namespace enumerations.

Enumeration	Flags	Description
ApartmentState apartment), **STA**		Defines apartment state constants for a **Thread**: **MTA** (multithreaded (single-threaded apartment), or **Unknown**.
ThreadPriority **Highest**, **Lowest**,		Defines priority constants for a **Thread**: **AboveNormal**, **BelowNormal**, and **Normal**.
ThreadState		Defines a **Thread** state combinable flags:
*	**Aborted**:	The thread is aborted by calling the **Abort** method.
*	**AbortRequested**:	The thread is about to be stopped by calling the **Abort** method.
*	**Background**:	The thread executes on the background.
*	**Running**:	The thread is currently executing.
*	**Stopped**:	The thread is stopped.
*	**StopRequested**:	The thread is about to be stopped by calling the **Stop** method.
*	**Suspended**:	The thread is suspended by calling the **Suspend** method.
*	**SuspendRequested**:	The thread is about to be suspended by calling the **Suspend** method.
*	**Unstared**:	The thread is created but has not been started yet.
*	**WaitSleepJoin**:	The thread is asleep after calling the **Sleep** method or the thread is joining or waiting for another thread by calling the **Join** or **Wait** methods.

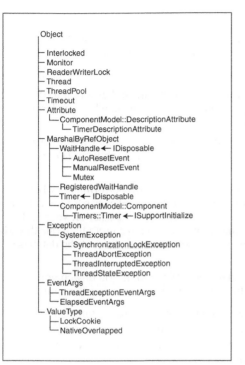

```
  Object
  ├─ Interlocked
  ├─ Monitor
  ├─ ReaderWriterLock
  ├─ Thread
  ├─ ThreadPool
  ├─ Timeout
  ├─ Attribute
  │   └─ ComponentModel::DescriptionAttribute
  │       └─ TimerDescriptionAttribute
  ├─ MarshalByRefObject
  │   ├─ WaitHandle ◄─ IDisposable
  │   │   ├─ AutoResetEvent
  │   │   ├─ ManualResetEvent
  │   │   └─ Mutex
  │   ├─ RegisteredWaitHandle
  │   ├─ Timer ◄─ IDisposable
  │   └─ ComponentModel::Component
  │       └─ Timers::Timer ◄─ ISupportInitialize
  ├─ Exception
  │   └─ SystemException
  │       ├─ SynchronizationLockException
  │       ├─ ThreadAbortException
  │       ├─ ThreadInterruptedException
  │       └─ ThreadStateException
  ├─ EventArgs
  │   ├─ ThreadExceptionEventArgs
  │   └─ ElapsedEventArgs
  └─ ValueType
      ├─ LockCookie
      └─ NativeOverlapped
```

Figure 5.1 The combined System::Threading and System::Timers namespace class hierarchy.

Pros and Cons of Multithreading

When writing a .NET program, you may end up using multiple threads without realizing it. For instance, when you read a file using asynchronous I/O, the Common Language Runtime will automatically create a new thread for you to perform the asynchronous I/O request. Or, when you write a GUI application that uses Windows Forms the CLR will automatically create a GUI message pump thread that waits for user input events and user messages to dispatch to your application code.

In addition to using multiple threads transparently provided by the CLR, you get to decide if you want to create your own *worker threads* for executing portions of your code in parallel. Unlike GUI threads, worker threads usually do not implement message pumps but instead perform some useful utility or computational task.

Reasons Against Using Threads

Programming is hard but parallel programming is *much* harder. It is like dating several people at the same time: You've got to manage your schedule to avoid collisions, keep all your dates happy, and manage your scarce cash without letting any of the relationships crash. Before trying to implement multithreaded programming features, you should understand the potential difficulties that you may encounter:

* *Programming difficulties*: Designing and maintaining a multithreaded program is much harder than designing and maintaining a single-threaded program because you must debug the thread's code when it is running in parallel with other threads and make sure that the threads do not interfere with each other in adverse and unpredictable ways. The unpredictability and sporadic nature of multithreaded software glitches may drive you nuts and your project off-schedule.

* *Decreased performance*: Since most computers have only one CPU, multiple threads will not directly improve performance. In fact, having too many threads running on a single CPU will *decrease* overall system performance due to the overhead associated with maintaining threads and switching among different threads. Every time a thread switch occurs the operating system must save the context and state of the currently executing thread and load the state and context of the next thread in the execution queue.

* *Competition for resources*: Multiple threads may decrease overall system performance even further by competing for scarce resources such as file handles. Also, the overhead of sharing resources such as shared variables or shared files with section locks may decrease performance. One thread may have to wait for another thread to release a lock on a file or another shared resource. In some cases competition for shared resources may cause a program crash. An example of this would be when a thread attempts to acquire a shared resource, but fails to gain access, and you forgot to insert a check for such failure. Deadlocks are another problem that you need to watch out for. (Two or more threads may create a circular dependency on the same shared resource and fall in an infinite wait loop.)

My best advice is to think carefully before you rush into implementing a multithreaded coding project.

Reasons for Using Threads

Multithreading does offer certain benefits to software developers despite the overhead of maintaining and switching threads and the difficulties associated with multithreaded programming. Some of the reasons you should consider multithreading are when you need to:

* *Perform several tasks simultaneously*: We have high expectation for our software and expect it to do everything at once (i.e., downloading, decoding, and playing background MP3 music while rendering a 3D scene).

* *Provide high responsiveness*: It is generally considered a bad practice to block user input when your program is performing a noncritical task (i.e., you should be able to keep browsing while an HTML page is still downloading);

* *Improve performance of blocking code:* Multiple threads *do* allow you to improve performance when there are blocking sections of your code that depend on slow external resources however paradoxical this may sound. For instance, if you connect to a remote database server to perform a transaction your code may block other operations until the transaction completes. This allows you to have more than one thread running to recover CPU cycles which would otherwise be lost while the code is waiting on the database transaction to complete.

* *Improve software scalability*: Some computers *do* have more than one CPU and, if you design your code to take advantage of additional CPUs by creating additional threads, you will be ahead of the game.

Perhaps you can find more reasons for using multiple threads but there are alternatives to using threads. You should keep in mind that modern CPUs are *always* single threaded, at least for the time being. Although all CPUs provide the means for multithreading, including instructions for switching tasks and managing task context, the majority of thread/task associated processing is performed in software.

Alternatives to Using Threads

Some of the alternatives to using threads include:

* *Interrupts*: An interrupt breaks the execution of the normal program flow by invoking an interrupt handling routine. Interrupts are typically generated by hardware in response to certain events, such as keyboard input or arrival of data packets to the network interface card buffer. Software interrupts also occur but they are really no different than subroutine calls in the sense that code-generated software interrupts happen predictably—code initiates them explicitly by calling a specific **INT** instruction. Hardware interrupts, on the other hand, occur sporadically. Hardware interrupts are usually handled by the OS, which abstracts them and generates messages dispatched to the user application message pump. For example, a key stroke interrupt is passed to a user interface program as a WM_KEYDOWN event on the Win32 platform.

* *Timers*: You can schedule background tasks to be executed in chunks on recurring intervals. For instance, you could use a timer to decode and play an MP3 file in the background.

* *Queuing*: Queuing is a frequently overlooked alternative for improving software responsiveness. When implementing service requests, for example, you typically would create a new thread for each request so that the next request can start processing immediately without having to wait for a previous one to complete. Components such as web servers must provide high responsiveness and create multiple threads for processing simultaneous requests. Queuing techniques, on the other hand, involve storing the incoming requests in a queue and processing the requests in a single thread. Queuing offers an improved performance in comparison to multithreading when the request-processing code contains little or no blocking sections and can return only the *whole* result. Consider a situation where you have a component that returns a chart in response to an HTTP request. The component will not work any faster nor will you improve the component's responsiveness by creating 100 threads for handling 100 incoming requests.

After all, a partially completed chart will not enhance the user's experience. But if you queue the requests, cut out the threading overhead, and process the requests back-to-back in a single thread, you will produce charts faster.

Personally, I find queuing to be the most viable alternative to multithreading because of its simple single-threaded design and improved performance due to the lack of multithreading overhead and costly competition for shared resources. Queuing does, however, has its limitations. You should not use queuing as a replacement for multithreading if:

* *Your code has lots of blocking sections*: You should never waist CPU cycles by waiting. You also shouldn't exhaust server capacity on dummy check-and-wait loops.

* *Your code can produce partial results*: A user doesn't have to wait for a request to be processed completely if he or she can be satisfied with partial results. A classic example is returning database query results or downloading HTML pages. If a query returns many rows or if the requested HTML page is large, it may take a while to return all the data back to the user and the user will be happy with partial results that he or she can view while the rest of the data is still being transmitted. If you implement such a query using queuing, other users would have to wait until the first user receives all of his or her data, which may take a very long time. The multithreaded approach, however, will allow all concurrent users to start receiving data almost immediately, and the overhead of multithreading will be unnoticed because users will be busy examining the data that they receive.

Threads

Threads in the .NET Framework are represented by the **Thread** class as shown here:

```
System::Object
|- System::Threading::Thread
```

```
Attributes: None
Abstract: No
Sealed: Yes
Implements Interfaces: None
```

The **Thread** class constructors, properties, and methods are summarized in Tables 5.6 through 5.8.

Table 5.6 **Thread** class constructors.

Constructor	Description
Thread(ThreadStart* *start***)**	Constructs a new thread object using the specified notification event delegate called when the thread is started.

Table 5.7 **Thread** class properties.

Get/Set	Type	Property	Description
Get/Set	**ApartmentState**	**ApartmentState**	Gets or sets the apartment state of the thread.
Get	**Context***	**CurrentContext**	Contains a pointer to the thread's current execution context.
Get/Set	**CultureIndo***	**CurrentCulture**	Gets or sets the current culture information for the thread.
Get/Set	**IPrincipal***	**CurrentPrincipal**	Gets or sets the thread's current principal for the role-based security.
Get	**static Thread***	**CurrentThread**	Contains a pointer to the current thread.
Get/Set	**CultureInfo***	**CurrentUICulture**	Gets or sets current culture information for the Resource Manager.
Get	**bool**	**IsAlive**	Contains **true** if the thread is executing.
Get	**bool**	**IsBackground**	Contains **true** if the thread is executing with the background priority.
Get	**bool**	**IsThreadPoolThread**	Contains **true** if the thread belongs to a thread pool.
Get/Set	**String***	**Name**	Gets or sets the name of the thread.
Get/Set	**ThreadPriority**	**Priority**	Gets or sets the thread priority.
Get	**ThreadState**	**ThreadState**	Contains the current state of the thread.

Table 5.8 **Thread** class methods.

Method	Description
void Abort()	Throws a **ThreadAbortException** exception to initiate a thread termination sequence.
void Abort(Object* *stateInfo*)	Throws a **ThreadAbortException** exception to initiate a thread termination sequence. The *stateInfo* parameter represents user-defined data.
static LocalDataStoreSlot* *AllocateDataSlot*()	Allocates an unnamed data slot.
static LocalDataStoreSlot* AllocateNamedDataSlot(String* *name*)	Allocates a data slot with the specified name.
static void FreeNamedDataSlot(String* *name*)	Releases a data slot with the specified name.
static Object* GetData(LocalDataStoreSlot* *slot*)	Retrieves data from the specified slot.
static AppDomain* GetDomain()	Returns a pointer to the current application domain.
static int GetDomainID()	Returns the unique identifier of the current application domain.
static LocalDataStoreSlot* GetNamedDataSlot(String* *name*)	Looks up a named data slot using the specified name.
void Interrupt()	Interrupts the thread that is in the **WaitSleepJoin** state.
void Join()	Blocks the calling thread until the thread whose **Join** method is called terminates.

<Continued on Next Page>

<Table 5.8 Continued>

Method	Description
bool Join(int *milliseconds***)**	Blocks the calling thread no longer than the specified number of milliseconds or until the thread whose **Join** method is called terminates.
bool Join(TimeSpan *timeout***)**	Blocks the calling thread no longer than the specified timeout or until the thread whose **Join** method is called terminates.
static void ResetAbort()	Cancels an **Abort** request initiated for the current thread.
void Resume()	Resumes execution of the previously suspended thread.
static void SetData(LocalDataStoreSlot* *slot***, Object*** *data***)**	Sets the data in the specified slot of the current thread.
static void Sleep(int *milliseconds***)**	Suspends execution of the current thread for the specified number of milliseconds.
static void Sleep(TimeSpan *timeout***)**	Suspends execution of the current thread for the specified timeout.
static void SpinWait(int *times***)**	Forces the current thread to wait for the specified number of times.
void Start()	Initiates execution of the tread.
void Suspend()	Suspends execution of the thread.
~Thread()	Destructor.

The thread class allows you to create new threads as well as control and obtain information on the current thread by calling the **Thread** class static methods and properties (i.e., **Thread::CurrentThread**).

Every running thread must be associated with a **ThreadStart** routine containing the code for a thread to execute. A thread will remain running until the associated **ThreadStart** routine returns or until you **Abort** the thread manually. It is perfectly okay to have multiple threads executing the same **ThreadStart** routine.

Thread States

Once you create a thread, the thread takes on a life of its own and operates like a finite state engine. At any moment, the thread can be in one of the states defined by the **ThreadState** enumeration, and transitions between states can occur based on the external or internal events, including events induced by calling methods on the thread instance. Figure 5.2 depicts a thread object state diagram. When you create a thread object, the thread is initiated in the **Unstarted|Stopped** state. Once you start a thread by calling the **Start** method, the thread transits to the **Running** state and remains in the **Running** state until the thread routine terminates, the thread is suspended by calling the **Suspend** method, the thread falls asleep via the **Sleep** method, the thread is waiting on another thread to terminated via the **Join** method, or the thread is waiting on a critical section via the **Wait** method. From the **WaitSleepJoin** state, a thread can return to the running state either naturally (i.e., when the **Sleep/Wait/Join** timeout expires, or the **Wait/Join** succeeds) or be forced into a running state by another thread calling the **Interrupt** method.

If another thread is attempting to terminate the thread by calling the **Abort** method, the thread first transits to the **AbortRequested** state from which it can either return to the **Running** state by resetting the abort request via the **ResetAbort** method or submit to the abort request and terminate (i.e., transit into the **Aborted|Stopped** state).

The **StopRequested** states are used internally by the CLR.

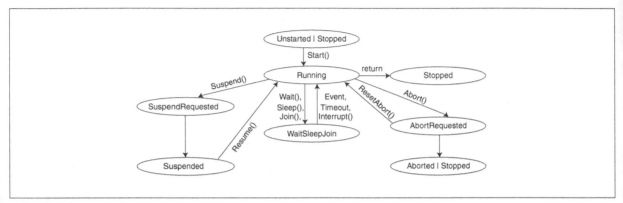

Figure 5.2. Thread state diagram.

Background Threads

A thread can be either foreground or background. **Background** threads are different from foreground threads only in the way the program terminates. If the main program thread spawns foreground threads, the CLR *will not terminate* the program when the program mail thread exists—it will wait for all foreground threads to terminate. If the main program thread spawns background threads, the CLR *will attempt terminating* the program when the program mail thread exits by dispatching the **Abort** requests to the background threads.

> **NOTE:** You can get or set the background status of the thread by getting or setting the Boolean **Background** thread property.

Thread Local Store

CLR provides threads with local data store, which is organized in *slots*. Two types of local data store slots are available: named and unnamed. You are free to decide whether to allocate an unnamed data slot (via the **AllocateDataSlot** method) to store private data, or to allocate a named slot (via the **AllocateNamedDataSlot** method). Unnamed data slots are released automatically, while public named data slots must be released manually by calling the **FreeNamedDataSlot** method.

> **NOTE:** Unmanaged code must rely on the **TlsAlloc**, **TlsFree**, **TlsGetValue**, and **TlsSetValue** Platform SDK functions to manage thread-local storage (TLS).

Thread Local Static Fields

If a class that has a static field is used by multiple threads, any thread can modify the value of the static field and other threads would be able to see the changes. Such sharing of class static fields among multiple threads may not be desirable and can have adverse effects on your code. To avoid potential problems you can mark a class static field with the **ThreadStatic** attribute, which indicates that each thread should use *its own* copy of the class static field. Thus, changes made to the static field on one thread will not be visible in another thread. In other words, the **ThreadStatic** attribute allows you to achieve class *static field isolation*.

> **NOTE:** The **ThreadStatic** attribute is equivalent to the **__declspec(thread)** unmanaged declaration.

Thread Synchronization

Rarely, a program creates multiple threads that execute in total isolation and do not communicate in some way. A more realistic scenario involves threads that interoperate and access shared resources, typically objects, variables, or arrays. When there are multiple threads accessing the same shared resource, you should provide means for *synchronizing* the access to the shared resource. The last thing you want to happen is to mess up your shared data having one thread to accidentally undo the changes made by another thread or, equally bad, to modify the data when another thread is in the middle of using the data under the assumption that the data would not change. Thus, you must use some form of thread synchronization to resolve the nightmares of simultaneous data access.

Critical Sections

The most common scenario for thread synchronization is to ensure that only one thread at a time can perform operations on shared critical data. Good programming practice dictates that you should group all operations on shared critical data in one section or in as few sections as possible. The sections of multithreaded code that perform operations on critical data are called *critical sections*. For instance, inserting new elements into a sorted list in a multithreaded program should be done in a critical section, otherwise a list may end up being corrupt or unsorted. You should create a class method for inserting elements in a sorted list and mark the method as a critical section in one of the following ways:

*   *Use a context-bound object*: If you derive your class from the **ContextBoundObject,** you can apply the **System::Runtime::Remoting::Contexts::SynchronizationAttribute** to a class to indicate that the class methods are synchronized.

*   *Use the **MethodImpl** attribute*: If you apply the **MethodImpl (Synchronized)** attribute to a method, the method can be executed only by one thread at a time.

*   *Use manual synchronization*: You can synchronize a method manually by means of the **WaitHandle**, **Monitor**, or **Mutex** objects.

The **Synchronization** attribute supplies a variety of options for defining the desired synchronization behavior of the method. The Synchronization constructors are listed in Table 5.19.

Table 5.9 **Synchronization** attribute constructors.

Constructor	Description
SynchronizationAttribute()	Indicates that only one thread at a time can execute object methods.
SynchronizationAttribute(bool *reentry*)	Indicates that only one thread at a time can execute object methods but a method reentry is permitted if a method blocks.
SynchronizationAttribute(int *flags*)	Specifies class synchronization options.
SynchronizationAttribute(int *flags*, bool *reentry*)	Specifies class synchronization options and reentry properties.

You can initialize a **Synchronization** attribute using the following flags:

*   **NOT_SUPPORTED**: Indicates that an instance of the class cannot be created in a synchronized context.

*   **REQUIRED**: Indicates that an instance of the class can be created only in a synchronized context.

*   **REQUIRED_NEW**: Indicates that an instance of the class can be created only in a synchronized context, and should use a new instance of the synchronization property each time.

*   **SUPPORTED**: Indicates that an instance of the class can be created in both synchronized and non-synchronized contexts.

Context-Bound Objects

Context-Bound objects are objects that reside in a particular context (i.e., synchronization context) and are governed by the context rules. Context rules usually represent additional code automatically wrapped around a context-bound object instance to enforce the desired object behavior (like automatic synchronization) in a particular context. Objects that are not context bound (i.e., all other objects) are called *agile* objects.

Manual Thread Synchronization

The **Synchronization** attribute makes all methods of a class synchronized and the **MethodImpl(Synchronized)** makes an individual method of a class synchronized. For a finer level of control over synchronization, you can use wait handles, mutexes, or **Monitor** objects to synchronize small sections of your code.

Wait Handles

A wait handle represents the simplest case of synchronization. A wait handle corresponds to the underlying OS synchronization object that can be in two states: Signaled and nonsignaled. Wait handles can be used to synchronize multiple threads in the following way: One thread acquires a wait handle and other threads are blocking by waiting on the wait handle. The waiting threads will be resumed as soon as the first thread sets the wait handle into a signaled state.

The .NET Framework implements a generic wait handle by means of the **WaitHandle** abstract base class as shown here:

```
System::Object
|- System::MarshalByRefObject
   |- System::Threading::WaitHandle


Attributes: None
Abstract: Yes
Sealed: No
Implements Interfaces: IDisposable
```

The **WaitHandle** class constructors, fields, properties, and methods are summarized in Tables 5.10 through 5.13.

Table 5.10 **WaitHandle** class constructors.

Method	Description
WaitHandle()	Default constructor.

Table 5.11 **WaitHandle** class fields.

Field	Description
static IntPtr InvalidHandle	Represents a constant indicating an invalid handle.
const int WaitTimeout	Represents a constant indicating that the **WaitAny** method returned due to the timeout expiration.

Table 5.12 **WaitHandle** class properties (all virtual).

Get/Set	Type	Property	Description
Get/Set	**IntPtr**	**Handle**	Gets or sets the handle of the **WaitHandle** object.

Table 5.13 **WaitHandle** class methods.

Method	Description
virtual void Close()	Releases resources held by the **WaitHandle** object.
protected: virtual void Dispose(bool *disposing*)	Releases the resources held by the **WaitHandle** object. If the *disposing* parameter is set to **true**, both managed and unmanaged resources are disposed.
~WaitHandle()	Destructor (behaves similarly to the **Close** and **Dispose**).
void IDisposable::Dispose()	Required by the **IDisposable** interface releases resources held by the **WaitHandle** object.
static bool WaitAll(WaitHandle* *waitHandles*[])	Waits until all objects in the specified array are signaled and returns **true** if successful or **false** if the thread received a request to abort.
static bool WaitAll(WaitHandle* *waitHandles*[], int *milliseconds*, bool *exitContext*)	Waits no more than the *milliseconds* milliseconds for all objects in the specified array to change into a signaled state and returns **true** if successful or **false** if the thread received a request to abort. The *exitContext* parameter indicates whether to exit the synchronization domain before the wait and re-enter the domain after the wait.

<Continued on Next Page>

<Table 5.13 Continued>

Method	Description
static bool WaitAll(WaitHandle* *waitHandles*[], TimeSpan *timeout*, bool *exitContext*)	Waits no longer than the specified amount of time for all objects in the specified array to change into a signaled state and returns **true** if successful or **false** if the thread received a request to abort. The *exitContext* parameter indicates whether to exit the synchronization domain before the wait and re-enter the domain after the wait.
static bool WaitAny(WaitHandle* *waitHandles*[])	Waits until one of the objects in the specified array is signaled and returns **true** if successful or **false** if the thread received a request to abort.
static bool WaitAny(WaitHandle* *waitHandles*[], int *milliseconds*, bool *exitContext*)	Waits no more than the *milliseconds* milliseconds for any object in the specified array to change into a signaled state and returns **true** if successful or **false** if the thread received a request to abort. The *exitContext* parameter indicates whether to exit the synchronization domain before the wait and re-enter the domain after the wait.
static bool WaitAny(WaitHandle* *waitHandles*[], TimeSpan *timeout*, bool *exitContext*)	Waits no longer than the specified amount of time for any object in the specified array to change into a signaled state and returns **true** if successful or **false** if the thread received a request to abort. The *exitContext* parameter indicates whether to exit the synchronization domain before the wait and re-enter the domain after the wait.

NOTE: *WaitAll* and *WaitAny* methods throw an **NotSupprotedException** exception if you supply more than 64 wait handles in the **waitHandles** array.

Method	Description
virtual bool WaitOne()	Waits until the **WaitHanlde** object is signaled and returns **true** if successful or **false** if the thread received a request to abort.
virtual bool WaitOne(int *milliseconds*, bool *exitContext*)	Waits no more than the *milliseconds* milliseconds for the **WaitHanlde** object to become signaled and returns **true** if successful or **false** if the thread received a request to abort. The *exitContext* parameter indicates whether to exit the synchronization domain before the wait and re-enter the domain after the wait.

<Continued on Next Page>

<Table 5.13 Continued>

Method	Description
virtual bool WaitOne(TimeSpan *timeout*, bool *exitContext*)	Waits no more than the specified amount of time for the **WaitHanlde** object to become signaled and returns **true** if successful or **false** if the thread received a request to abort. The *exitContext* parameter indicates whether to exit the synchronization domain before the wait and re-enter the domain after the wait.

The main purpose of a wait handle is to allow waiting (blocking) on the handle or the array of handles until the handle (or all handles) in the array of handles is signaled.

Manual and Automatic Wait Handles

The .NET Framework implements two concrete wait handle classes: **AutoResetEvent** and **ManualResetEvent**:

```
System::Object
|- System::MarshalByRefObject
    |- System::Threading::WaitHandle
        |- System::Threading::AutoResetEvent
        |- System::Threading::ManualResetEvent


Attributes: None
Abstract: No
Sealed: Yes
Implements Interfaces: None
```

The **AutoResetEvent / ManualResetEvent** class constructors and methods are summarized in Tables 5.14 through 5.15.

Table 5.14 **AutoResetEvent / ManualResetEvent** class constructors.

Constructor	Description
AutoResetEvent(bool *signaled*)	Constructs an **AutoResetEvent** object, which is signaled or nonsignaled depending on the value of the *signaled* parameter.
ManualResetEvent(bool *signaled*)	Constructs an **ManualResetEvent** object, which is signaled or nonsignaled depending on the value of the *signaled* parameter.

Table 5.15 **AutoResetEvent / ManualResetEvent** class methods.

Method	Description
bool Reset()	Sets the state of the event object to nonsignaled.
bool Set()	Sets the state of the event object to signaled.

The difference between the **AutoResetEvent** and **ManualResetEvent** classes is subtle, yet important. When an **AutoResetEvent** handle is signaled and a thread or threads waiting on the handle are resumed, the handle is automatically set to a nonsignaled state (*reset*). On the other hand, a **ManualResetEvent** handle will stay signaled when the waiting thread(s) resume execution and will remain signaled until a manual reset by means of the **Reset** method.

Mutexes

Mutexes are one of the most commonly used synchronization objects. Mutex is short for *mutual exclusion*. Mutexes implement a locking mechanism that allows only one thread at a time to acquire a lock on a mutex and suspends all other threads that attempt to acquire a lock on the same mutex until the first thread explicitly releases the lock. Mutexes are usually supported by the underlying OS directly and are represented by the OS wait handles. In the .NET Framework class library mutexes are implemented by the **Mutex** class, which has the following inheritance diagram:

```
System::Object
|- System::MarshalByRefObject
    |- System::Threading::WaitHandle
        |- System::Threading::Mutex

Attributes: None
Abstract: No
Sealed: Yes
Implements Interfaces: None
```

The **Mutex** class constructors and methods are summarized in Tables 5.16 through 5.17.

Table 5.16 **Mutex** class constructors.

Constructor	Description
Mutex()	Default constructor.
Mutex(bool *initiallyOwned*)	Constructs a **Mutex** object. The *initiallyOwned* parameter indicates whether the calling state should have the initial ownership of the mutex.
Mutex(bool *initiallyOwned*, String* *name*)	Constructs a **Mutex** object with the specified name. The *initiallyOwned* parameter indicates whether the calling state should have the initial ownership of the mutex.
Mutex(bool *initiallyOwned*, String* *name*, bool* *createdNew*)	Constructs a **Mutex** object with the specified name. The *initiallyOwned* parameter indicates whether the calling state should have the initial ownership of the mutex. The *createdNew* parameter will contain **true** if the thread was able to acquire the initial ownership of the mutex.

NOTE: *If you want to create a **Mutex** object by name and the specified mutex name is already used by another process or thread, you should not set the initiallyOwned parameter to **true** or you will not be able to determine whether your thread has the initial ownership of the mutex. If you want to set the initiallyOwned parameter to **true** anyway, you should use the third **Mutex** constructor overload and examine the **createdNew** return value to determine whether the thread has gotten the initial ownership of the specified mutex.*

Table 5.17 **Mutex** class methods.

Method   Description

void ReleaseMutex()	Makes the calling thread release the ownership of the mutex. You must release the ownership of the mutex as many times as you acquired ownership of the mutex. The mutex is automatically released (signaled) when the thread, which acquired its ownership, terminates normally.

If you want to use mutexes for interprocess/interthread communication, you should create named mutexes. Named mutexes are shared among threads/processes. When a thread attempts to create a mutex with a name that corresponds to an already existing mutex, the existing mutex object is returned.

The **Mutex** class is similar to the MFC **CMutex** class encapsulating a Win32 mutex handle, except for the traditional **Lock/Unlock** methods that the **Mutex** class supplies.

> **NOTE:** If a thread owns a mutex and nevertheless requests the ownership of the mutex by calling the **WaitOne** method; to release the ownership of the mutex, the thread would have to call the **ReleaseMutex** method as many times as it requested the ownership of the mutex. If a thread owning a mutex terminates, it automatically releases the ownership of the mutex.

Monitors

Although monitors are very similar to mutexes they cannot be referenced by name and require a user-supplied object to be used for synchronization. Also, monitors do not correspond to the OS objects, but instead represent a fully-portable CLR-managed construct for thread synchronization. To implement monitors, the .NET Framework Class Library supplies the all-static class **Monitor**, which has the following inheritance diagram:

```
System::Object
|- System::Threading::Monitor

Attributes: None
Abstract: No
Sealed: Yes
Implements Interfaces: None
```

The **Monitor** class methods are summarized in Table 5.18.

Table 5.18 **Monitor** class methods.

Method	*Description*
static void Enter(Object* obj)	Acquires an exclusive lock on the specified object. If another thread holds an exclusive lock on the object, the current thread is blocked until the other thread releases the lock.
static void Exit(Object* obj)	Releases an exclusive lock on the specified object.

<Continued on Next Page>

<Table 5.18 Continued>

Method	Description
static void Pulse(Object* *obj***)**	Moves the next thread in line for the lock on the specified object into the ready queue. When the thread that acquired the lock on the specified object releases the lock, the next thread in the ready queue acquires the lock on the object.
static void PulseAll(Object* *obj***)**	Moves all threads waiting in line for the lock on the specified object into the ready queue.
static bool TryEnter(Object* *obj***)**	Attempts to acquire an exclusive lock on the specified object and returns **true** if the lock was successfully acquired. Unlike the **Enter** method, the **TryEnter** method does not block the execution of the current thread.
static bool TryEnter(Object* *obj***, int** *milliseconds***)**	Attempts to acquire an exclusive lock on the specified object and returns **true** if the lock was successfully acquired. If another thread holds an exclusive lock on the object, the execution of the current thread is blocked no longer than the specified number of milliseconds.
static bool TryEnter(Object* *obj***, TimeSpan** *timeout***)**	Attempts to acquire an exclusive lock on the specified object and returns **true** if the lock was successfully acquired. If another thread holds an exclusive lock on the object, the execution of the current thread is blocked no longer than the specified timeout.
static bool Wait(Object* *obj***)**	Temporarily releases the lock on the specified object and reacquires the lock as soon as another thread invokes the **Pulse** or **PulseAll** method on the specified object.
static bool Wait(Object* *obj***, int** *milliseconds***)**	Temporarily releases the lock on the specified object and attempts to reacquire the lock as soon as another thread invokes the **Pulse** or **PulseAll** method on the specified object. The method blocks no longer than the specified number of milliseconds and returns **true** if the lock was successfully reacquired.
static bool Wait(Object* *obj***, TimeSpan** *timeout***)**	Temporarily releases the lock on the specified object and attempts to reacquire the lock as soon as another thread invokes the **Pulse** or **PulseAll** method on the specified object. The method blocks no longer than the specified timeout and returns **true** if the lock was successfully reacquired.

<Continued on Next Page>

<Table 5.18 Continued>

Method	Description
static bool Wait(Object* *obj*, int *milliseconds*, bool *exitContext*)	Temporarily releases the lock on the specified object and attempts to reacquire the lock as soon as another thread invokes the **Pulse** or **PulseAll** method on the specified object. The method blocks no longer than the specified number of milliseconds and returns **true** if the lock was successfully reacquired. If the *exitContext* is set to **true** then the current thread exists the synchronization domain before the **Wait** and re-enters it after the **Wait**.
static bool Wait(Object* *obj*, TimeSpan *timeout*, bool *exitContext*)	Temporarily releases the lock on the specified object and attempts to reacquire the lock as soon as another thread invokes the **Pulse** or **PulseAll** method on the specified object. The method blocks no longer than the specified timeout and returns **true** if the lock was successfully reacquired. If the *exitContext* is set to **true** then the current thread exists the synchronization domain before the **Wait** and re-enters it after the **Wait**.

Any object can serve as a lock for the **Monitor** class. To acquire a lock on the object, you should call the **Enter** or **TryEnter** method. To release a lock on the object, the **Exit** method should be used. To release the lock on the object completely a thread must call the **Exit** method as many times as it called the **Enter** method.

The CLR maintains two queues for monitored objects:

* *Ready queue*: Contains threads in line to acquire the lock on the monitored object (e.g., threads that called **Enter** on the already locked object).
* *Waiting queue*: Contains threads waiting on the object by means of the **Wait** method.

> **WARNING!** Threads from the waiting queue do not propagate to the ready queue automatically.

A typical scenario involves multiple threads trying to gain access to the same locked object and threads that are ready to acquire the lock reside in the ready queue. In some cases a thread that gained the lock on the monitored object may wish to release the lock temporarily (by calling the **Wait** method) and yield the monitored object to another thread from the ready queue. The thread, which called the **Wait** method, is moved to the waiting queue. The thread will remain in the waiting queue until another thread calls the **Pulse** or **PulseAll** method to move a single thread or all threads from the waiting queue to the ready queue.

If a thread specified a timeout as a parameter to the **Wait** method, the thread will be automatically moved to the ready queue when the timeout expires.

> **NOTE:** If the ready queue is empty but there are threads in the waiting queue, the threads in the waiting queue will remain inactive and will not be able to acquire the lock on the monitored object until you explicitly move them from the ready queue to the waiting queue by calling the **Pulse/PulseAll** method.

MFC programmers will find the **Monitor** class similar to the MFC **CCriticalSection** class.

Thread Pools

The **Thread** class gives you all the power for manual thread management at the cost of, well, manual thread management. Sometimes, you just want to schedule a parallel operation or perform an asynchronous wait on a wait handle without being burdened by the manual thread management technicalities. To relieve you from the hassles of manual thread management and to improve performance of frequently used multithreading tasks, the CLR provides a *thread pool* for each application domain. A thread pool comprises a collection of worker threads and a queue for storing work requests, which can include:

*   Asynchronous I/O requests

*   System::Net socket connections

*   Timers callbacks

*   Registered wait operation callbacks

*   User work items

A thread pool picks an unprocessed request from the request queue and assigns it to an idle thread. If all threads in the thread pool are busy, the thread pool will create a new thread unless the number of threads in the pool has reached the CLR-defined maximum. Otherwise, the requests will not be processed until one of the threads becomes idle again.

> **NOTE:** All threads in the thread pool are background threads executing with default priority.

The .NET Framework Class Library encapsulates an application domain thread pool in the all-static **ThreadPool** class:

```
System::Object
|- System::Threading::ThreadPool

Attributes: None
Abstract: No
Sealed: Yes
Implements Interfaces: None
```

The **ThreadPool** class methods are summarized in Tables 5.19.

Table 5.19 **ThreadPool** class methods.

Method	Description
static bool BindHandle(IntPtr *handle*)	Binds the specified OS handle to the thread pool.
static void GetAvailableThreads(int* *workerThreads*, int* *completionPortThreads*)	Retrieves the current number of worker and asynchronous I/O threads in the thread pool.
static void GetMaxThreads(int* *workerThreads*, int* *completionPortThreads*)	Retrieves the maximum number of worker and asynchronous I/O threads in the thread pool.

<Continued on Next Page>

<Table 5.19 Continued>

Method	Description
static bool QueueUserWorkItem(WaitCallback* *callBack***)**	
static bool QueueUserWorkItem(WaitCallback* *callBack***, Object*** *state***)**	Queues a user work item to the thread pool. The specified callback is called with the specified *state* parameter when a thread in the thread pool picks up the worker item.
static RegisteredWaitHandle* RegisterWaitForSingleObject (WaitHandle* *waitObject***, WaitOrTimerCallback*** *callBack***, Object*** *state***, int** *milliseconds***, bool** *executeOnlyOnce***)**	
static RegisteredWaitHandle* RegisterWaitForSingleObject (WaitHandle* *waitObject***, WaitOrTimerCallback*** *callBack***, Object*** *state***, __int64** *milliseconds***, bool** *executeOnlyOnce***)**	
static RegisteredWaitHandle* RegisterWaitForSingleObject (WaitHandle* *waitObject***, WaitOrTimerCallback*** *callBack***, Object*** *state***, TimeSpan** *timeout***, bool** *executeOnlyOnce***)**	
static RegisteredWaitHandle* RegisterWaitForSingleObject (WaitHandle* *waitObject***, WaitOrTimerCallback*** *callBack***, Object*** *state***, unsigned int** *milliseconds***, bool** *executeOnlyOnce***)**	Registers the *callBack* delegate to wait on the specified **WaitHandle** until the handle is signaled or the specified timeout expires. If the *executeOnlyOnce* parameter is set to **true**, the delegate is invoked only once when the *waitObject* is signaled for the first time, otherwise, the delegate is invoked every time the *waitObject* is signaled.
static bool UnsafeQueueUserWorkItem(WaitCallback* *callBack***, Object*** *state***)**	Queues a user work item to the thread pool. This method is similar to the **QueueUserWorkItem** method except that the **UnsafeQueueUserWorkItem** method does not propagate the calling stack onto the worker thread.

<Continued on Next Page>

<Table 5.19 Continued>

Method	Description
static RegisteredWaitHandle* UnsafeRegisterWaitForSingleObject(WaitHandle* *waitObject*, WaitOrTimerCallback* *callBack*, Object* *state*, int *milliseconds*, bool *executeOnlyOnce*)	
static RegisteredWaitHandle* UnsafeRegisterWaitForSingleObject (WaitHandle* *waitObject*, WaitOrTimerCallback* *callBack*, Object* *state*, __int64 *milliseconds*, bool *executeOnlyOnce*)	
static RegisteredWaitHandle* UnsafeRegisterWaitForSingleObject (WaitHandle* *waitObject*, WaitOrTimerCallback* *callBack*, Object* *state*, TimeSpan *timeout*, bool *executeOnlyOnce*)	
static RegisteredWaitHandle* UnsafeRegisterWaitForSingleObject(WaitHandle* *waitObject*, WaitOrTimerCallback* *callBack*, Object* *state*, unsigned int *milliseconds*, bool *executeOnlyOnce*)	Registers the *callBack* delegate to wait on the specified **WaitHandle** until the handle is signaled or the specified timeout expires. If the *executeOnlyOnce* parameter is set to **true** the delegate is invoked only once when the *waitObject* is signaled for the first time, otherwise, the delegate is invoked every time the *waitObject* is signaled. This method is similar to the **RegisterWaitForSingleObject** method except that the **UnsafeRegisterWaitForSingleObject** method does not propagate the calling stack onto the worker thread.

A thread pool is automatically created in an application domain when you queue a work item by calling the **ThreadPool::QueueUserWorkItem**, create a timer, or register a wait operation by calling the **RegisterWaitForSingleObject** or the **UnsafeRegisterWaitForSingleObject** method of the **ThreadPool** class.

Wait Notification Callbacks

Besides queuing work items, you can use the **ThreadPool** to register callbacks to respond to wait notifications. Suppose that you have a shared resource represented by a **WaitHandle,** which you want to acquire. Rather than block your main thread waiting on the handle to become signaled, you can register a callback routine that will be called when the **WaitHandle** of interest is signaled. This approach leaves your code free to continue normal processing and be notified about the availability of the shared resource asynchronously.

The .NET Framework Class Library supports registration of wait handle callbacks by means of the **RegisteredWaitHandle** class as shown here:

```
System::Object
|- System::MarshalByRefObject
   |- System::Threading::RegisteredWaitHandle
```

```
Attributes: None
Abstract: No
Sealed: Yes
Implements Interfaces: None
```

The **RegisteredWaitHandle** class methods are summarized in Tables 5.20.

Table 5.20 **RegisteredWaitHandle** class methods.

Method	Description
bool Unregister(WaitHandle* *waitObject***)**	Terminates a registered wait operation initiated by the **ThreadPool::RegisterWaitForSingleObject** method.
~ RegisteredWaitHandle()	Destructor.

You do not instantiate **RegisteredWaitHandle** objects directly. Instead, a pointer to a **RegisteredWaitHandle** object is returned when you register your callback routine by calling the **RegisterWaitForSingleObject** or the **UnsafeRegisterWaitForSingleObject** method of the **ThreadPool** class.

Performance of Thread Processing

When you create a thread manually, the thread receives the same security privileges as the parent thread. When you use a thread pool, however, the threads in the thread pool execute under different system security privileges. To ensure that a worker item/wait callback executes using the correct security privileges, the **ThreadPool** captures the caller's stack to perform security checks when the queued worker item/wait callback actually executes. Needless to say, additional security checks come at a cost of reduced performance. If you are sure that your work item/wait request cannot violate system security, you can instruct the **ThreadPool** to bypass the security checks by calling the **UnsafeQueueUserWorkItem** or the **UnsafeRegisterWaitForSingleObject** method when scheduling a work item or registering a wait callback.

Interlocked Exchange

A special case of thread synchronization involves implementation of a thread-safe concurrent modification of numeric fields. Consider a situation when you have a large data set and you need to count records matching a specified search criteria. For better performance, you could devise a divide-and-conquer algorithm, create multiple threads for searching portions of the data set, and maintain a single integer count variable, which individual search threads can update. In such a situation it is extremely important to ensure that the count variable is incremented in a thread-safe way. In the worst case, you may end up with an incorrect result caused by several threads writing a new value to the count field simultaneously and overwriting each others result.

Using a full-blow thread synchronization with mutexes or critical sections for such a simple task is total overkill. Fortunately, the .NET Framework class library provides us with just the tool we need: the **Interlocked** class. This class implements a thread-safe increment, decrement, and assignment to a shared integer or floating-point field. The **Interlocked** class has the following inheritance diagram:

```
System::Object
|- System::Threading::Interlocked

Attributes: None
Abstract: No
Sealed: Yes
Implements Interfaces: None
```

The **Interlocked** class methods are summarized in Table 5.21.

Table 5.21 **Interlocked** class methods.

Method	Description
static int CompareExchange(int* *var1*, int *value*, int *var2*)	
static Object* CompareExchange(Object** *var1*, Object* *value*, Object* *var2*)	
static float CompareExchange(float* *var1*, float *value*, float *var2*)	Compares the *var1* with the *var2*, replaces the *var1* with the *value* if *var1* = *var2* and returns the original value of the *var1*.
static int Decrement(int* *var*)	
static __int64 Decrement(__int64* *var*)	Decrements the specified variable by one and returns the decremented value.
static int Exchange(int* *var*, int *value*)	
static Object* Exchange(Object** *var*, Object* *value*)	
static float Exchange(float* *var*, float *value*)	Sets the *var* to the specified value and returns the previous value of the variable.
static int Increment(int* *location*)	
static __int64 Increment(__int64* *location*)	Increments the specified variable by one and returns the decremented value.

The **Interlocked** class consists exclusively of static members. The **Interlocked** class encompasses functionality provided by the **Interlocked**_XYZ_ Platform SDK functions.

Single-Writer/Multiple-Reader Access

Another special case of thread synchronization deals with single-writer/multiple-reader semantics. Consider the following scenario: You want to implement an MP3 download site with a real-time music popularity chart sorted by the number of downloads. Whenever somebody downloads an MP3 song, your code must update the chart instantaneously to reflect the new position of the song being downloaded. Since download requests coming from different IP addresses are usually handled by different threads, you must ensure that the code, which is writing to the music chart, is thread-safe. That is, only one thread at a time should be able to write the chart. At the same time multiple users should be able to view the chart simultaneously, and the chart viewing should also be thread-safe. The code should not allow the chart data to be read if it is still being used by a writer. You must also balance between the read and write requests so that none of these operations will be blocked indefinitely.

Fortunately, the .NET Framework relives you of the troubles of implementing a single-writer/multiple-reader access by supplying the **ReaderWriterLock** class:

```
System::Object
|- System::Threading::ReaderWriterLock

Attributes: None
Abstract: No
Sealed: Yes
Implements Interfaces: None
```

The **ReaderWriter** class constructors, properties, and methods are summarized in Tables 5.22 through 5.24.

Table 5.22 **ReaderWriter** class constructors.

Constructor	Description
ReaderWriterLock()	Default constructor.

Table 5.23 **ReaderWriter** class properties.

Get/Set	Type	Property	Description
Get	**bool**	**IsReaderLockHeld**	Contains **true** if the current thread holds the reader lock.
Get	**bool**	**IsWriterLockHeld**	Contains **true** if the current thread holds the writer lock.
Get	**int**	**WriterSeqNum**	Contains the writer sequence number.

Table 5.24 **ReaderWriter** class methods.

Method	Description
void AcquireReaderLock(int *milliseconds*)	Attempts to acquire the reader lock. The current thread execution is blocked no longer than the specified number of milliseconds.
void AcquireReaderLock(TimeSpan *timeout*)	Attempts to acquire the reader lock. The current thread execution is blocked no longer than the specified timeout.
void AcquireWriterLock(int *milliseconds*)	Attempts to acquire the writer lock. The current thread execution is blocked no longer than the specified number of milliseconds.
void AcquireWriterLock(TimeSpan *timeout*)	Attempts to acquire the writer lock. The current thread execution is blocked no longer than the specified timeout.

NOTE: The current thread will deadlock if it has the reader lock and attempts to acquire the writer deadlock. To avoid the potential deadlock use the UpgradeToWriterLock method.

bool AnyWritersSince(int *seqNum*)	Returns **true** if there were intermediate writers since the specified sequence number.
void DowngradeFromWriterLock(LockCookie* *lockCookie*)	Restores the thread status to its state before the call to the **UpgradeToWriterLock**.
LockCookie ReleaseLock()	Releases the lock regardless of the number of times the thread acquired the lock.
void ReleaseReaderLock()	Releases the reader or writer lock held by the current thread.
void ReleaseWriterLock()	Releases the writer lock held by the current thread. If the current thread holds the reader lock rather than the writer lock, an **ApplicationException** exception is thrown.
void RestoreLock(LockCookie* *lockCookie*)	Restores the thread status to the state before the call to the **ReleaseLock**.
LockCookie UpgradeToWriterLock(int *milliseconds*)	Attempts to upgrade the reader lock to the writer lock. The current thread execution is blocked no longer than the specified number of milliseconds.
LockCookie UpgradeToWriterLock(TimeSpan *timeout*)	Attempts to upgrade the reader lock to the writer lock. The current thread execution is blocked no longer than the specified timeout.

Threads involved in the single-writer/multiple-reader scenario should share the same instance of the **ReaderWrite** object and acquire necessary thread-safe reader/writer access by calling the **AcquireReaderLock** or the **AcquireWriterLock** method on the object instance.

Timers

Timers can be used as an alternative to multithreading for performing recurring background tasks, such as polling, music synthesis, or animation rendering. The .NET Framework Class Library supports timer functionality by providing the **Timer** class as shown here:

```
System::Object
|- System::MarshalByRefObject
    |- System::Threading::Timer
```

```
Attributes: None
Abstract: No
Sealed: Yes
Implements Interfaces: IDisposable
```

The **Timer** class constructors and methods are summarized in Tables 5.25 through 5.26.

Table 5.25 **Timer** class constructors.

Constructor	Description
Timer(TimerCallback* *callback*, Object* *state*, int *dueTime*, int *period*)	
Timer(TimerCallback* *callback*, Object* *state*, __int64 *dueTime*, __int64 *period*)	
Timer(TimerCallback* *callback*, Object* *state*, TimeSpan *dueTime*, TimeSpan *period*)	
Timer(TimerCallback* *callback*, Object* *state*, unsigned int *dueTime*, unsigned int *period*)	Constructs a **Timer** object using the specified callback delegate. The *state* parameter represents a user-defined data passed to the *callback* delegate. You can specify the timer *period* in milliseconds or as a **TimeSpan**. The *dueTime* parameter specifies the initial delay for starting the timer.

Table 5.26 **Timer** class methods.

Method	Description
bool Change(int *dueTime*, int *period*)	
bool Change(__int64 *dueTime*, __int64 *period*)	
bool Change(TimeSpan *dueTime*, TimeSpan *period*)	
bool Change(unsigned int *dueTime*, unsigned int *period*)	Changes the timer interval and period. Returns **true** if the timer object has not been disposed.
__sealed void Dispose()	Releases the resources used by the **Timer** object.
bool Dispose(WaitHandle* *notifyObject*)	Releases the resources used by the **Timer** object and signals the specified *notifyObject* that the timer has been disposed of.
~Timer()	Destructor.

> **NOTE:** The **System::Threading::Timer** class represents an OS independent timer mechanism managed by the CLR.

The **Timer** callbacks are implemented as worker threads that execute on the thread pool. The **System::Threading::Timer** timers are also referred to as *server timers*. To use a timer, you must define a callback method to be called by **Timer** objects on regularly scheduled intervals. The timer ceases operation when you dispose the object.

System::Timers Namespace

In addition to OS-independent timers, the CLR supports OS-dependent timers implemented as messages sent to the client application. An examples includes the WM_TIMER Win32 message that is dispatched to a client application in response to the **SetTimer** Platform SDK function. The OS-dependent message-driven timers are intended primarily to be used with GUI/Windows Forms applications. For that matter, the .NET Framework reserved a separate namespace for an OS-dependent timer component—System::Timers. The System::Timers namespace defines just two classes: a single attribute and a single delegate (see Tables 5.27 through 5.29). This delegate is designed to support a timer component implemented by the **Timer** class.

Table 5.27 System::Timers namespace classes.

Class	Description
ElapsedEventArgs	Represents data for the **Elapsed** event.
Timer	Fires recurring **Elapsed** events.

Table 5.28 System::Timers namespace attributes.

Attribute	Description
TimersDescription	An attribute for specifying textual description of a timer class.

Table 5.29 System::Timers namespace delegates.

Delegate	Description
void ElapsedEventHandler(Object* *sender*, **ElapsedEventArgs*** *e*)	A delegate for handling the **Elapsed** event of the **Timer** class.

System::Timers::Timer Class

The **System::Timers::Timer** class is similar to the **System::Threading::Timer** class, except that the former implements a OS-dependent timer, and the latter implements a CLR-supported timer. The **System::Timers::Timer** timers are also referred to as *Windows timers*. The **System::Timers::Timer** class has the following inheritance diagram:

```
System::Object
|- System::MarshalByRefObject
   |- System::Threading::Timer

Attributes: None
Abstract: No
Sealed: Yes
Implements Interfaces: IDisposable
```

The **Timer** class constructors, properties, methods, and events are summarized in Tables 5.30 through 5.33.

Table 5.30 **System::Threading::Timers::Timer** class constructors.

Constructor	Description
Timer()	Default constructor.
Timer(double *interval***)**	Constructs a **Timer** object, which will fire the **Elapsed** events on the specified interval in milliseconds.

Table 5.31 **System:: Timers::Timer** class properties.

Get/Set	Type	Property	Description
Get/Set	**bool**	**AutoReset**	Gets or sets a value indicating whether the **Timer** object should fire the **Elapsed** event recurrently or only once.
Get/Set	**bool**	**Enabled**	Gets or sets a value indicating whether the **Timer** object is allowed to fire the **Elapsed** events.
Get/Set	**double**	**Interval**	Gets or sets the **Timer** interval.
Get/Set	**ISite***	**Site**	Gets or sets the component site.
Get/Set	**ISynchronizeInvoke***	**SynchronizingObject**	Gets or sets the object for marshalling event-handler calls.

Table 5.32 **System:: Timers::Timer** class methods.

Method	Description
__sealed void BeginInit()	Begins the **Timer** initialization.
void Close()	Releases the resources use by the **Timer** object.
protected: void Dispose(bool *disposing*)	Releases the resources use by the **Timer** object.
__sealed void EndInit()	Ends the **Timer** initialization. The **BeginInit** / **EndInit** methods prevent the **Timer** object from being used until it is fully initialized.
void Start()	Starts the timer.
void Stop()	Stops the timer.

Table 5.33 **System:: Timers::Timer** class events.

Method	Description
ElapsedEventHandler* Elapsed	The event is fired when the recurring **Interval** elapses.

Unlike the **System::Threading::Timer** class, the **System::Timers::Timer** class contains **Start** and **Stop** methods for starting and stopping the timer and the **Enabled** property for controlling if a timer is allowed to fire the **Elapsed** events. Also, the **System::Threading::Timer** class requires explicitly hooking a timer event handler to the **Elapsed** delegate. Thus, you can modify the **System::Threading::Timer::Elapsed** event handler *after* an object was instantiated. At the same time, the **System::Timers::Timer** class does not allow modification of the timer callback method after a timer object is instantiated.

> NOTE: The OS-independent **System::Threading::Timer** timers are generally more accurate than the OS-dependent **System::Timers::Timer** timers, which accuracy is limited to 55 milliseconds.

Synchronized Method

As you probably noticed from the previous chapters, many .NET classes contain **Synchronized** methods for generating thread-safe copies of a class instance. The synchronized object instances returned by a **Synchronized** method represent a very convenient alternative to using manual synchronization. If you want operations on your object to be thread-safe, it is easier to obtain a thread-safe copy of the object by calling the **Synchronized** method than messing around with manual synchronization.

On the other hand, not all classes expose the **Synchronized** method. If that is the case, you have no other choice but to resort to manual synchronization.

Immediate Solutions

Creating Threads

Follow these steps to create an execution thread:

1.   Define a thread method by either creating a new class or adding to an existing class a method (static or instance) of type **void**. This method should be defined to accept no parameters.

2.   Create a new **Thread** object and pass a delegate to the thread method as a parameter.

3.   Call the **Start** method the instance of the **Thread** object to start the thread execution.

When creating threads keep in mind that:

*   A thread routine must always be a member of the class. Nonmember functions are not allowed, unlike with MFC/Platform SDK programming.

*   A thread will not start executing until you call the **Start** method on the thread object.

*   A program will not terminate until all nonbackground threads terminate. (Background threads will terminate automatically when the main program thread terminates.)

To show you how to create and manipulate a basic thread, I've provided the following code example. This code performs the following operations:

1.   Obtains the current thread pointer by querying the **Thread::CurrentThread** property.

2.   Reports the current thread information including culture, name, background status, priority, and state.

3.   Creates a new worker thread using the **Thread** constructor.

4.   Starts a worker thread.

5.   Suspends a worker thread.

6.   Waits until the thread status is changed to **Suspended**.

7.   Resumes a worker thread.

```cpp
#using <mscorlib.dll>
using namespace System;
using namespace System::Threading;

__gc struct ThreadClass {
    // Worker thread routine
    static void WorkerThread()
    {
        Console::Write("...");
        Thread::Sleep(1000);
    }
};

void main()
{
    // 1. Obtain current thread pointer
    Thread* CurrentThread = Thread::CurrentThread;

    // 2. Report current thread information
    Console::WriteLine("Apartment state: {0}",
        __box(CurrentThread->ApartmentState));
    Console::WriteLine("        Culture: {0}", CurrentThread->CurrentCulture);
    Console::WriteLine("      Principal: {0}", CurrentThread->CurrentPrincipal);
```

```
    Console::WriteLine("                Name: {0}", CurrentThread->Name);
    Console::WriteLine("   Background? {0}",
        __box(CurrentThread->IsBackground));
    Console::WriteLine("            Priority: {0}", __box(CurrentThread->Priority));
    Console::WriteLine("            State: {0}",
        __box(CurrentThread->ThreadState));

    // 3. Create new worker thread
    Thread* myThread = new Thread(new ThreadStart(0,
        &ThreadClass::WorkerThread));

    // 4. Start worker thread
    myThread->Start();

    if ( myThread->IsAlive )
    {
        Console::WriteLine("myThread State: {0}", __box(myThread->ThreadState));

        // 5. Suspend worker thread
        myThread->Suspend();
        // 6. Wait/Sleep until the worker thread is suspended
        while ( !(myThread->ThreadState & ThreadState::Suspended) )
            Thread::Sleep(100);

        // 7. Resume worker thread
        myThread->Resume();
    }
}
```

Aborting Threads

Occasionally, you may want to terminate a running thread prematurely. For instance, you may want to terminate all non-background threads when your program must exit. You can terminate a thread in one of two ways:

*   You can implement a thread method that periodically queries a status variable and returns if the status variable is set. (This approach is frequently used by MFC/Platform SDK developers.)

*   You can terminate a thread by invoking the **Abort** method on the thread object.

The advantage of the second approach is that it allows you to terminate *any* thread. The potential disadvantage is that you may not be able to terminate a thread because a thread can reset the abort request by calling the **ResetAbort** method. When the **Abort** method is called a **ThreadAbortException** exception is thrown on the thread being aborted. Thus, when developing a thread method, you should enclose a thread code in a **try/catch** block to capture abort requests represented by **ThreadAbortException** exceptions. To submit to an abort request, take no action in the **catch** block. To defy the abort request, on the other hand, you should call the **Thread::ResetAbort** method and your thread execution will continue normally.

The code example presented next demonstrates these actions:

1. The worker thread routine handles the abort requests.
2. Attempts are made to abort a worker thread by calling the **Abort** method.
3. The process waits for a timeout period for the worker thread to abort.
4. The code forces the worker thread to abort.
5. The program main thread is blocked until the worker thread terminates by calling the **Join** method.

```cpp
#using <mscorlib.dll>
using namespace System;
using namespace System::Threading;


__gc struct ThreadClass {
    // 1. Worker thread routine handling abort requests
    static void WorkerThread()
    {
        while ( true )
        {
            try {
                Console::Write(".");
                Thread::Sleep(100);
            }
            catch(Exception* e) {
                // Check to see if this is a ThreadAbortException
                ThreadAbortException* abortExcep =
                    dynamic_cast<ThreadAbortException*>(e);
                if ( abortExcep )
                    // Cancel the abort request
                    if ( abortExcep->ExceptionState != S"Must exit!" )
                    {
                        Thread::ResetAbort();
                        Console::WriteLine("WorkerThread: AbortReset...");
                    }
                    else
                        Console::WriteLine("WorkerThread: Aborting...");
            }
        }
    }
};

void main()
{
    // Create a new worker thread
    Thread* myThread = new Thread(new ThreadStart(0,
        &ThreadClass::WorkerThread));
```

```
    // Start the worker thread
    myThread->Start();

    // 2. Attempt to abort the worker thread
    myThread->Abort();
    // 3. Wait until the thread is stopped, but no longer than 3 sec
    int Count = 0;
    while ( !(myThread->ThreadState & ThreadState::Stopped) && Count < 30 )
    {
        Thread::Sleep(100);
        Count++;
    }

    // 4. Force the worker thread termination
    myThread->Abort(S"Must exit!");

    // 5. Blocks current thread until the worker terminates
    myThread->Join();
    Console::Write("WorkerThread terminated...");
}
```

You may be surprised to see the **while** loop outside of the **try/catch** block in the **WorkerThread** method. The **while** loop must be placed here if you want to be able to recover from the abort requests. Even if you reset the abort request, the next statement executed is the first statement following the catch block. Thus, to ensure that the thread will keep running, you must nest the **try/catch** block inside of an infinite (or otherwise controlled) loop.

You can supply additional information to the **Abort** method, which is stored in the **ExceptionState** property of the **ThreadAbortException** exception. The code example above examines the **ExceptionState** information to determine whether the abort request was significant enough to be honored.

Using Thread Local Storage

Thread local storage (TLS) provides a means for storing data that you intend to keep private to the thread. To store dynamically allocated data, you should use thread data slots. To store static data, on the other hand, you can use static variables marked with the **ThreadStatic** attribute.

Here are the steps to follow to read or write data from an unnamed thread data slot:

1.   Allocate a new data slot using the **AllocateDataSlot** method and store the **LocalDataStoreSlot** pointer to the allocated data slot, which you will need to supply to the **GetData/SetData** methods for reading or writing data from the data slot.

2.   Write data to the data slot using the **Thread::SetData** method.

3.   Read data from the data slot using the **Thread::GetData** method.

If you want to allocate a named data slot, the steps are slightly different:

1.   Allocate a new data slot using the **AllocateNamedDataSlot** method, or obtain a pointer to an existing data slot by calling the **GetNamedDataSlot** method.

2.   Write data to the data slot using the **Thread::SetData** method.

3.   Read data from the data slot using the **Thread::GetData** method or the **GetNamedDataSlot** method.

4.   Free the name data slot by invoking the **FreeNamedDataSlot** when you no longer need it.

Consider the following code example to see how you can use the thread local storage feature:

```cpp
#using <mscorlib.dll>
using namespace System;
using namespace System::Threading;

__gc struct ThreadClass {
   [ThreadStatic]
   static int tsInt;
   static int sharedInt;

   static void WorkerThread1()
   {
       // 1. Allocate unnamed TLS
       LocalDataStoreSlot* tlsPrivate = Thread::AllocateDataSlot();
       // 2. Write data to unnamed TLS
       Thread::SetData(tlsPrivate, S"Private Data");

       // 3. Allocate named TLS
       LocalDataStoreSlot* tlsPublic = Thread::AllocateNamedDataSlot("Public");
       // 4. Write data to named TLS
       Thread::SetData(tlsPublic, new String(S"Public Data"));

       // 5. Read data from named TLS
       Object* data = Thread::GetData(Thread::GetNamedDataSlot("Public"));
       Console::WriteLine("WorkerThread1, Public TLS: {0}", data);

       // Write data to trhead-status and shared static variables
       tsInt = 123;
       Console::WriteLine("WorkerThread1, tsInt = {0}", __box(tsInt));
       sharedInt = 456;

       // 6. Free named TLS
       Thread::FreeNamedDataSlot("Public");
   }
   static void WorkerThread2()
   {
       // Wait until shared variable is set
```

```
   // (also synchronizes threads)
   while ( sharedInt != 456 ) {
      Thread::Sleep(100);
   };

   // Check the thread-static variable
   Console::WriteLine("WorkerThread2, tsInt = {0}", __box(tsInt));

   // Read data from named TLS
   Object* data = Thread::GetData(Thread::GetNamedDataSlot("Public"));
   Console::WriteLine("WorkerThread2, Public TLS: {0}", data);
   }
};

void main()
{
   // Create two worker threads
   Thread* myThread1 = new Thread(new ThreadStart(0,
      &ThreadClass::WorkerThread1));
   Thread* myThread2 = new Thread(new ThreadStart(0,
      &ThreadClass::WorkerThread2));

   // Start threads
   myThread1->Start();
   myThread2->Start();
   myThread2->Join();
}
```

The code example above initiates two concurrent threads: **WorkerThread1** and **WorkerThread2**. The **WorkerThread1** thread creates both a named and unnamed data slot, modifies the thread-static variable **tsInt**, and modifies the global static variable **sharedInt**. The **WorkerThread2** thread attempts to read the named data slot allocated by the first thread and inspects the values of the thread static and global static variables **tsInt** and **sharedInt**.

As a result, the **WorkerThread2** thread does not see the changes made by the first thread to the thread-static variable **tsInt**, nor can it retrieve the data written by the first thread to the named data slot.

Synchronizing Classes using the **Synchronization** Attribute
The easiest way to synchronize all instance methods of a class is to derive a class from the **ContextBoundObject** class and mark a derived class with the **Synchronization** attribute. The following code example demonstrates how to use the class synchronization feature:

```
#using <mscorlib.dll>
using namespace System;
using namespace System::Threading;
using namespace System::Runtime::Remoting::Contexts;
```

```
// Synchronized class
[Synchronization]
__gc struct PrintClass: public ContextBoundObject {
   void PrintNumbers()
   {
      for ( int i = 0; i < 3; i++ )
      {
         Console::WriteLine(__box(i));
         Thread::Sleep(100);
      }
   }
};


__gc class ThreadClass {
public:
   ThreadClass(PrintClass* print)
   {
      printClass = print;
   }
   void WorkerThread()
   {
      if ( printClass )
         printClass->PrintNumbers();
   }
private:
   PrintClass* printClass;
};

void main()
{
   PrintClass* printClass = new PrintClass;
   ThreadClass* threadClass = new ThreadClass(printClass);
   // Create two worker threads
   Thread* myThread1 = new Thread(new ThreadStart(threadClass,
      &ThreadClass::WorkerThread));
   Thread* myThread2 = new Thread(new ThreadStart(threadClass,
      &ThreadClass::WorkerThread));
   // Start threads
   myThread1->Start();
   myThread2->Start();
}
```

The output for this program is:

```
0
1
2
0
1
2
```

The **PrintClass** has been synchronized ensuring that no two threads can execute the **PrintNumbers** method on the same **PrintClass** object simultaneously. Instead, the calls to the **PrintNumbers** method are queued by the CLR and processed serially. However, if you create two instances of the **PrintClass** object and have the threads invoke the **PrintNumbers** on different **PrintClass** instances, the requests will be processed concurrently because methods invoked on different instances are not synchronized by the **Synchronization** attribute.

Synchronizing Instance and Static Methods using the **MethodImpl** Attribute

To synchronize individual instance methods of a class or to synchronize static class methods, you should use the **MethodImpl** attribute defined in the System::Runtime::CompilerServices namespace. Simply apply the **MethodImpl(Synchronized)** attribute to an instance or static class method that you want to synchronize. The code example provided next illustrates how you use the **MethodImpl** attribute on the static **PrintNumbers** method:

```
#using <mscorlib.dll>
using namespace System;
using namespace System::Threading;
using namespace System::Runtime::CompilerServices;

// Synchronized class
__gc struct PrintClass {
    [MethodImpl(Synchronized)]
    static void PrintNumbers()
    {
        for ( int i = 0; i < 10; i++ )
        {
            Console::WriteLine(__box(i));
            Thread::Sleep(100);
        }
    }
};

__gc struct ThreadClass {
    static void WorkerThread()
    {
        PrintClass::PrintNumbers();
```

```
   }
};

void main()
{
   // Create two worker threads
   Thread* myThread1 = new Thread(new ThreadStart(0,
       &ThreadClass::WorkerThread));
   Thread* myThread2 = new Thread(new ThreadStart(0,
       &ThreadClass::WorkerThread));
   // Start threads
   myThread1->Start();
   myThread2->Start();
}
```

Synchronizing Code Sections Using Mutexes

Sometimes synchronizing entire methods is impractical and can adversely affect the performance of multithreaded code. This can be the case when the majority of code in a multithreaded method can execute in parallel, except for a tiny portion that must be executed serially. To improve performance, you should synchronize only the section of the code that requires synchronization. This can be accomplished by using the .NET **Mutex** class. To force a section of the code to execute serially follow these steps:

1.   Create a named **Mutex** object.

2.   Immediately before the code section that you wish to synchronize, acquire a lock on the mutex by calling the **WaitOne** method on the mutex object. (If another thread has already acquired the lock on the mutex, the current thread will block until the other thread releases the lock.)

3.   Immediately after exiting the synchronized code section, release the lock on the mutex by calling the **ReleaseMutex** method on the mutex object.

The code example shown next demonstrates code synchronization by using the **Mutex** object:

```
#using <mscorlib.dll>
using namespace System;
using namespace System::Threading;

__gc struct PrintClass {
   // Synchronized method
   static void PrintNumbers()
   {
       // BEGIN NON-SYNCHRONIZED CODE
       for ( int i = 0; i < 3; i++ )
       {
           Console::WriteLine(new String('A' + i, 1));
           Thread::Sleep(100);
```

```
        }
        // END NON-SYNCHRONIZED CODE

        // Create named mutex
        Mutex* myMutex = new Mutex(false, "PrintNumbers");
        // Wait until mutex is signaled
        myMutex->WaitOne();

        // BEGIN SYCHRONIZED CODE
        for ( i = 0; i < 3; i++ )
        {
            Console::WriteLine(__box(i));
            Thread::Sleep(100);
        }
        // END SYCHRONIZED CODE

        // Reset the mutex
        myMutex->ReleaseMutex();
    }
};

void main()
{
    // Create two worker threads
    Thread* myThread1 = new Thread(new ThreadStart(0,
        &PrintClass::PrintNumbers));
    Thread* myThread2 = new Thread(new ThreadStart(0,
        &PrintClass::PrintNumbers));
    // Start threads
    myThread1->Start();
    myThread2->Start();    // Start threads
    myThread1->Start();
    myThread2->Start();
}
```

The **PrintNumbers** method contains both a nonsynchronized code section, which prints letters A through C, and a synchronized code section, which prints numbers 1 through 3. The program produces the following output:

```
A
A
B
B
C
C
1
2
3
1
2
3
```

Synchronizing Critical Code Sections Using Monitors

You can use the .NET **Monitor** class if you prefer to use an OS-independent synchronization mechanism to synchronize sections of your code. The **Monitor** class allows you to implement critical code sections that can be executed by only one thread at a time. Here are the steps you should follow to implement a critical code section using the **Monitor** class:

1.   Create a dummy synchronization object for monitoring a critical section.

2.   Immediately before entering the critical section, invoke the **Monitor::Enter** method to acquire the lock on the synchronization object, which you created in Step 1. (If another thread already has acquired the lock on the critical section, the current thread will block until the other thread releases the lock.)

3.   Immediately after exiting the critical section invoke the **Monitor::Exit** method to release the lock.

The code shown next is similar to the example presented in the previous section, except that the code uses the **Monitor** class rather than a **Mutex** object:

```
#using <mscorlib.dll>
using namespace System;
using namespace System::Threading;

__gc struct PrintClass {
    PrintClass()
    {
        SyncObject = new String("");
    }
    // Synchronized method
    void PrintNumbers()
    {
        // BEGIN NON-CRITICAL CODE
        for ( int i = 0; i < 3; i++ )
```

```
    {
        Console::WriteLine(new String('A' + i, 1));
        Thread::Sleep(100);
    }
    // END NON- CRITICAL CODE

        // Enter the critical section
        Monitor::Enter(SyncObject);

        // BEGIN CRITICAL SECTION
        for ( i = 0; i < 3; i++ )
        {
            Console::WriteLine(__box(i));
            Thread::Sleep(100);
        }
        // END CRITICAL SECTION

        // Leave the critical section
        Monitor::Exit(SyncObject);
    }
private:
    // Monitor synchronization object
    String* SyncObject;
};

void main()
{
    PrintClass* printClass = new PrintClass();
    // Create two worker threads
    Thread* myThread1 = new Thread(new ThreadStart(printClass,
        &PrintClass::PrintNumbers));
    Thread* myThread2 = new Thread(new ThreadStart(printClass,
        &PrintClass::PrintNumbers));
    // Start threads
    myThread1->Start();
    myThread2->Start();
}
```

The **PrintClass** class uses **SyncObject** to monitor the critical section in the **PrintNumbers** routine. The program produces the same output as the program in the previous section.

Synchronizing Threads Using Wait Handles

The **ManualResetEvent** and **AutoResetEvent** classes provide a simple way to synchronize threads: Simply pass a non-signaled wait handle to a thread and make the thread wait until another thread signals the wait handle.

This code example illustrates multithreaded console input processing using wait handles. One thread reads console input, and another thread capitalizes the text and prints it on the console:

```
#using <mscorlib.dll>
using namespace System;
using namespace System::Threading;


__gc class ThreadClass {
public:
   ThreadClass()
   {
      TextReady = new AutoResetEvent(false);
   }
   // Reads console input
   void WorkerThread1()
   {
      do {
         Text = Console::ReadLine();
         // Signal the wait handle
         TextReady->Set();
      } while ( Text->CompareTo("exit") );
   }
   // Prints console input in upper case
   void WorkerThread2()
   {
      do {
         //  Wait for handle to be signaled
         TextReady->WaitOne();
         // Resetting the wait handle is unnecessary because it is AUTO
         //TextReady->Reset();
          Console::WriteLine(Text->ToUpper());
      } while ( Text->CompareTo("exit") );
   }
private:
   String* Text;
   AutoResetEvent* TextReady;
};


void main()
{
   // Create worker threads with manual wait handles
```

```
ThreadClass* threadClass = new ThreadClass();
Thread* thread1 = new Thread(new ThreadStart(threadClass,
    &ThreadClass::WorkerThread1));
Thread* thread2 = new Thread(new ThreadStart(threadClass,
    &ThreadClass::WorkerThread2));

// Start worker threads
thread1->Start();
thread2->Start();
}
```

The **ThreadClass** defines two thread methods: **WorkerThread1** for reading console input and **WorkerThread2** for printing the uppercased text on the console. Also, the class defines a **TextReady** auto-reset wait handle, which is used to synchronize the threads in the following way: The **WorkerThread1** signals the wait handle when it finishes reading console input and the **WorkerThread2** waits until the **TextReady** is signaled. Both threads exit when you type "exit."

Instead of an auto-reset wait handle, you can also use the manual-reset handle wait handle in the code example above. Besides changing the data type of the **TextReady** field from the **AutoResetEvent** to the **MaualResetEvent,** you would have to uncomment the **TextReady->Reset**() statement in the **WorkerThread2** because a **MaualResetEvent** handle is not reset automatically when the **WaitOne** operation completes.

Queuing Worker Threads in the Thread Pool

Thread pools provide an efficient and easy way for scheduling background worker threads. To schedule a new worker thread on the thread pool, simply invoke the **ThreadPool::QueueUserWorkItem** method with a delegate pointing to a thread method that you want to initiate. The code example shown next schedules two thread pool threads on the **WorkerClass::SearchFor** method for concurrent searching of nonoverlapping sections of the **List** array for a specified string pattern:

```
#using <mscorlib.dll>
#using <mscorlib.dll>
using namespace System;
using namespace System::Threading;
using namespace System::Collections;

// Multithreaded string search class
__gc class WorkerClass {
public:
    WorkerClass(String* list[], int fromIndex, int toIndex,
        ArrayList* result)
    {
        List = list;
        FromIndex = fromIndex;
        ToIndex = toIndex;
        Result = result;
```

```
        // Create wait handle
        Ready = new AutoResetEvent(false);
    }
    // Worker thread method
    void SearchFor(Object* pattern)
    {
        String* Pattern = dynamic_cast<String*>(pattern);

        if ( Pattern )
        {
            // Search for all strings in the list matching the specified pattern
            for ( int i = FromIndex; i <= ToIndex; i++ )
                if ( List[i]->EndsWith(Pattern) )
                    Result->Add(List[i]);
        }
        // Signal the event
        Ready->Set();
    }
    // Wait handle
    AutoResetEvent* Ready;
private:
    String* List __gc[];
    int FromIndex, ToIndex;
    ArrayList* Result;
};

void main()
{
    // The list to search through
    String* List[] = {"Consequential - Classical", "Asteroid - Techno",
        "EnTrance - Trance", "Sweet Harp - Classical", "Good Life - Mood Music",
        "Fatalism - Techno", "Automatic - Dance", "Dance Track #1 - Dance",
        "The Call of Stars - Electronica", "My Heart is Stone Cold - Techno"};
    // The list of matches
    ArrayList* Result = new ArrayList;

    // Create worker classes
    WorkerClass* myClass1 = new WorkerClass(List, 0, 4, Result);
    WorkerClass* myClass2 = new WorkerClass(List, 5, 9, Result);

    // Queue work requests item into the thread pool
    ThreadPool::QueueUserWorkItem(new WaitCallback(myClass1,
        WorkerClass::SearchFor), S"Techno");
    ThreadPool::QueueUserWorkItem(new WaitCallback(myClass2,
        WorkerClass::SearchFor), S"Techno");
```

```
    // Wait for the search to complete
    WaitHandle* Handles[] = {myClass1->Ready, myClass2->Ready};
    WaitHandle::WaitAll(Handles);

    Console::WriteLine("Techno Compositions:");
    // Print the results
    for ( int i = 0; i < Result->Count; i++ )
        Console::WriteLine(Result->Item[i]);
}
```

The main program waits by blocking on the **WaitHandle::WaitAll(Handles)** statement until the threads terminate and prints the search results. Since each thread searches half of the **List** array in parallel, the program will offer improved performance on the multiprocessor system.

Registering Wait Notification Callbacks

The thread pool can be used for asynchronous processing of wait handle notifications in addition to executing worker threads. You can register a particular class method to execute when a specified wait handle is signaled. Scheduling wait handle notification callbacks is a viable alternative to creating dummy threads, which block until the wait handle is signaled, to perform a one-time task. To register a wait handle notification, you use the **ThreadPool::RegisterWaitForSingleObject** method, as show in this example:

```
#using <mscorlib.dll>
using namespace System;
using namespace System::Threading;

__gc struct WorkerClass {
    // Wait handle callback
    static void Callback(Object* obj, bool timeout)
    {
        Console::WriteLine("CallbackEvent called", obj);
    }
};

void main()
{
    // Create wait handle
    AutoResetEvent* CallbackEvent = new AutoResetEvent(false);

    // Register wait handle callback
    ThreadPool::RegisterWaitForSingleObject(CallbackEvent,
        new WaitOrTimerCallback(0, WorkerClass::Callback),
        0, Timeout::Infinite, false);

    // Signal the wait handle and fire the notification callback
    CallbackEvent->Set();

    // Delay
    Thread::Sleep(500);
}
```

Implementing Interlocked Access/Modification of Shared Numeric Variables

To ensure a thread-safe increment, decrement, or modification of a shared numeric variable, you should use the interlocked increment, decrement, or exchange operations implemented by means of the .NET **Interlocked** class. The following code example initiates two threads that increment a shared integer variable in a small **while** loop using the **Interlocked::Increment** method to ensure a predictable result:

```cpp
#using <mscorlib.dll>
using namespace System;
using namespace System::Threading;


__gc class ThreadClass {
public:
    ThreadClass(int* pvalue)
    {
        pValue = pvalue;
    }
    // Worker thread routine
    void WorkerThread()
    {
        while ( *pValue < 16 )
        {
            // Non-safe increment (may yield the same number twice)
            //*pValue = *pValue + 1;
            Interlocked::Increment(pValue);
            Console::WriteLine(pValue->ToString());
            Thread::Sleep(100);
        }
    }
private:
    int* pValue;
};


void main()
{
    // Shared variable
    int myValue = 0;

    // Create worker threads
    Thread* myThread1 = new Thread(new ThreadStart(new ThreadClass(&myValue),
        &ThreadClass::WorkerThread));
    Thread* myThread2 = new Thread(new ThreadStart(new ThreadClass(&myValue),
        &ThreadClass::WorkerThread));

    // Start worker threads
    myThread1->Start();
```

```
    myThread2->Start();

    // Wait for all threads to terminate
    myThread1->Join();
    myThread2->Join();
}
```

If you comment out the **Interlocked::Increment(pValue)** statement in the **WorkerThread** method and uncomment the ***pValue = *pValue + 1** statement, which is not thread-safe, the code may print the same number twice thus illustrating how the increment operation of one thread is undone by the increment operation of another thread. If you replace the ***pValue = *pValue + 1** statement with the **(*pValue)++** statement, chances are that the code will produce the correct results every time, but I would not count on it. A good compiler implements an integer increment operation in a single CPU instruction (e.g., **INC [pValue]**). Obviously, a single CPU instruction *always* represents an interlocked operation because no two threads can process the same CPU instruction at the same time. However, relying on the assumption that the **(*pValue)++** operation will always translate in a single CPU instruction means assuming too much about a Microsoft product without any assurance on the Microsoft's part, which is, needless to say, reckless.

Implementing Single-Writer/Multiple-Reader Access to Shared Data

Single-writer/multiple reader locking mechanisms can be very useful when you have multiple threads that both read and write the same shared data. The single-writer/multiple reader lock, implemented by the .NET **ReaderWriterLock** class, ensures that only one thread at a time can write the data, and it can write the data only when nobody is reading it.

Follow these steps to successfully (without deadlocks) implement a single-writer/multiple reader multithreaded access to shared data:

1.   Allocate a new **ReaderWriterLock** object to be shared among threads.

2.   *To modify the shared data,* first acquire the writer lock by invoking the **AcquireWriterLock** method on the lock object and, once you are done writing the data, release the writer lock by invoking the **ReleaseWriterLock** method.

3.   *To read the shared data,* first acquire the reader lock by invoking the **AcquireReaderLock** method on the lock object and, once you are done reading the data, release the reader lock by invoking the **ReleaseReaderLock** method.

4.   *To modify the shared data immediately after reading it,* invoke the **UpgradeToWriterLock** method to transform the current reader lock into a writer lock and, once you are done writing, transform the writer lock back into the reader lock by invoking the **DowngradeFromWriterLock** method.

The code example shown next demonstrates how to use the **ReaderWriterLock** class by creating three threads— a single normal-priority **ReadSongName** thread, which reads a song title typed by the user and inserts it into a shared **PlayList** array, and two background threads. These threads are named –**BroadcastSong**, which polls the **PlayList** array searching for a particular song style (i.e., techno and classical) to broadcast. Once a song is broadcasted it is removed from the **PlayList**. The program exits when the user types "exit" in place of a song name.

Listing 5.1 Sample program illustrating the usage of the ReaderWriterLock class

```
#using <mscorlib.dll>
using namespace System;
using namespace System::Threading;
using namespace System::Collections;

// Multithreaded string search class
__gc class PlatListClass {
public:
    PlatListClass(ArrayList* list)
    {
        PlayList = list;
        // Create wait handle
        Ready = new AutoResetEvent(false);
        // 1. Create reader/write lock
        Lock = new ReaderWriterLock;
    }
    // Worker thread method
    void BroadcastSong(Object* pattern)
    {
        String* Pattern = dynamic_cast<String*>(pattern);

        if ( Pattern )
            while ( true )
            {
                // 2. Acquire reader lock for reading the play list
                Lock->AcquireReaderLock(Timeout::Infinite);

                // Search for all songs in the play list matching the
                // specified pattern
                for ( int i = 0; i < PlayList->Count; i++ )
                    if ( static_cast<String*>(PlayList->Item[i])->
                        EndsWith(Pattern) )
                    {
                        // Do something to broadcast the song
                        // ...
                        Thread::Sleep(50);
                        Console::WriteLine("{0} is broadcasted", PlayList->Item[i]);

                        // 3. Upgrade to write lock to remove the broadcasted song
                        // from the play list
                        LockCookie Cookie = Lock->UpgradeToWriterLock(
                                Timeout::Infinite);
```

```
                        // Remove the song from the play list
                        PlayList->RemoveAt(i-);

                        // 4. Restore the reader lock
                        Lock->DowngradeFromWriterLock(&Cookie);
                    }
                // 5. Release reader lock for reading the play list
                Lock->ReleaseReaderLock();
                Thread::Sleep(50);
            }
        }
    void ReadSongName()
    {
        String* SongName;
        Console::WriteLine("Enter song name:");
        while ( true )
        {
            // Read a song name
            SongName = Console::ReadLine();
            if ( SongName->CompareTo(S"exit") == 0 ) break;

            // 6. Acquire writer lock
            Lock->AcquireWriterLock(Timeout::Infinite);

            // Insert song name into the play list
            PlayList->Add(SongName);
            PlayList->Sort();

            // 7. Release writer lock
            Lock->ReleaseWriterLock();
        }
    }
    // Wait handle
    AutoResetEvent* Ready;
private:
    ArrayList* PlayList;
    ReaderWriterLock* Lock;
};

void main()
{
    ArrayList* PlayList = new ArrayList;

    // Creat worker classes
    PlatListClass* myClass = new PlatListClass(PlayList);
```

```
    // Queue work requests item into the thread pool
    ThreadPool::QueueUserWorkItem(new WaitCallback(myClass,
        PlatListClass::BroadcastSong), S"Techno");
    ThreadPool::QueueUserWorkItem(new WaitCallback(myClass,
        PlatListClass::BroadcastSong), S"Classical");

    // Create normal-priority thread for inputting song names
    Thread* InputThread = new Thread(new ThreadStart(myClass,
        PlatListClass::ReadSongName));
    InputThread->Start();

    // Wait for the input thread to terminate
    InputThread->Join();

    // Print the contents of the list (i.e. unplayed songs)
    Console::WriteLine("Unplayed songs in the list:");
    for ( int i = 0; i < PlayList->Count; i++ )
        Console::WriteLine(PlayList->Item[i]);
}
```

Using CLR Timers

You can use the **System::Threading::Timer** class to schedule a recurring background processing that should occur on regular time intervals. Follow these steps to initiate and manage a timer:

1.   Create new **Timer** object and supply a **TimerCallback**-compatible class method that you want to associate with the timer. The timer will start immediately, unless you specify the *dueTime* parameter in the **Timer** constructor to set the initial delay for starting the timer.

Destroy the timer when it is no longer needed by invoking the **Dispose** method on the timer object.

The following code example demonstrates a countdown from 9 to 0 implemented as a timer event. The timer is automatically destroyed when the countdown reaches zero:

```
#using <mscorlib.dll>
using namespace System;
using namespace System::Threading;

// Countdown data
__gc struct CountdownClass {
    CountdownClass(int count)
    {
        Count = count;
        // Wait handle
        Ready = new AutoResetEvent(false);

        // 1. Create countdown timer with 500ms = 0.5 sec interval
```

```
        CountdownTimer = new Timer(new TimerCallback(this,
            CountdownClass::Countdown), 0, 0, 500);
    }
    // Timer method
    void Countdown(Object* obj)
    {
        // Output countdown
        Console::Write("{0}\r", __box(-Count));

        if ( Count == 0 )
        {
            Console::Write("GO!");
            // 2. Dispose the timer when countdown reaches zero
            CountdownTimer->Dispose();
            // Signal the wait handle
            Ready->Set();
        }
    }
    AutoResetEvent* Ready;
    Timer* CountdownTimer;
    int Count;
};

void main()
{
    // Countdown data for counting from 10 to 0
    CountdownClass* Countdown = new CountdownClass(10);

    // Wait for the countdown
    Countdown->Ready->WaitOne();
}
```

Using OS/Windows Forms Timers

To schedule a recurring background processing in a GUI/Windows Forms application, you should use the
System::Timers::Timer class. This class represents an OS-dependent timer (i.e., WM_TIMER event on Win32
platforms) and is optimized to be used with Windows Forms applications and visual design components.

Here are the steps to follow for initiating and managing a timer:

1. Create a new **Timer** object with a specified interval.
2. Attach an **ElapsedEventHandler** to the timer object **Elapsed** event.
3. Start the timer by invoking the **Start** method.

Stop the timer when you no longer need it by calling the **Stop** method.

The following code example demonstrates a countdown from 9 to 0 implemented as a timer event. The timer is automatically stopped when the countdown reaches zero:

```cpp
#using <mscorlib.dll>
#using <system.dll>
using namespace System;
using namespace System::Threading;
using namespace System::Timers;

// Countdown data
__gc struct CountdownClass {
   CountdownClass(int count)
   {
      Count = count;
     // Wait handle
     Ready = new AutoResetEvent(false);
     // Set StopTime to max value
     StopTime = DateTime::MaxValue;

      // 1. Create countdown timer with 500ms = 0.5 sec interval
     CountdownTimer = new System::Timers::Timer(500);

      // 2. Hookup the Elapsed event
     CountdownTimer->Elapsed += new ElapsedEventHandler(this,
         CountdownClass::Countdown);
     // 3. Start the countdown
     CountdownTimer->Start();
   }
   // Timer method
   void Countdown(Object* obj, ElapsedEventArgs* e)
   {
     // Check to see if Stop() was already called
     if ( e->SignalTime < StopTime )
   {
        // Output countdown
        Console::Write("{0}\r", __box(-Count));

        if ( Count == 0 )
        {
           Console::Write("GO!");
           // Get stop time
           StopTime = DateTime::Now;
           // 4. Stop the timer when countdown reached zero
           CountdownTimer->Stop();
           // Signal the wait handle
```

```
            Ready->Set();
        }
    }
}
DateTime StopTime;
AutoResetEvent* Ready;
System::Timers::Timer* CountdownTimer;
int Count;
};

void main()
{
    // Countdown data for counting from 10 to 0
    CountdownClass* Countdown = new CountdownClass(10);

    // Wait for the countdown
    Countdown->Ready->WaitOne();
}
```

NOTE: The **System::Timers::Timer** class has a unique behavior. If you stop a timer by invoking the **Stop** method, the timer event may occur one more time before ceasing completely. This behavior is due to the fact that the **Stop** method may be actually invoked on a different thread from the timer callback method, and due to the thread timing, the timer callback may be processed prior to the **Stop** method taking effect. To eliminate the undesired last firing of the timer callback, take notice of the time when you call the **Stop** method, and compare the stop time with the current time in the timer callback method. If the stop time is less than the current time (i.e., the stop was invoked *before* the callback method was called), do no processing and return. The example above illustrates this technique.

CHAPTER 6

Using .NET Collections

QUICK JUMPS

CHAPTER 6

Using .NET Collections

In Depth

Collections lists, hash tables, dictionaries, queues, and stacks are essential for developing well-organized applicatic The .NET Framework Class Library provides two namespaces for managing collections: System::Collections and System::Collections::Specialized. The System::Collections namespace supplies base collection classes and generic collection interfaces, while the System::Collections::Specialized namespace provides concrete implementations of basic collection classes and dictionaries of **String** objects. You'll find that this chapter contains reference to all important classes residing in the System::Collections and System::Collections::Specialized namespaces. So I will be presenting numerous tables summarizing constructors, fields, properties, and methods of each class. You will learn how to work with built-in collection objects such as lists, queues, dictionaries, stacks, etc. and create your own collections by extending base .NET Framework classes.

The System::Collections Namespace

If you have programmed with MFC before, you should be familiar with basic collections such as **CArray** or **CList**. Collections are also widely used throughout the Visual C++ Standard Template Library (STL). Virtually any programming project requires some collection programming, and no programming toolkit is complete without collection support. Naturally, the .NET Framework supports collections and uses collection classes extensively as containers and for method parameters. In the .NET Framework, the core collection functionality is implemented by means of base collection classes and interfaces defined in the System::Collections namespace. There are five types of collections directly supported by the .NET Framework:

* *Lists*: Collections of objects where an individual element can be accessed by means of an integer index.

* *Dictionaries*: Collections of key/value pairs where an individual element can be accessed by means of a key.

* *Hash tables*: A special kind of dictionary where key/value pairs are stored in a direct address table and can be retrieved very efficiently using indices.

* *Queues*: Collections where individual elements are accessed based on the first-in/first-out principle. (Random access of queue elements is not allowed.)

* *Stacks*: Collections where individual elements are accessed based on the last-in/first-out principle. (Random access of stack elements is not allowed.)

Each of these collection types has a base class and sometimes a base interface or a set of associated interfaces defined in the System::Collections namespace. The System::Collections namespace classes and structures are listed in Tables 6.1 and 6.2, and the combined System::Collections and System::Collections::Specialized namespace class hierarchy is shown in Figure 6.1.

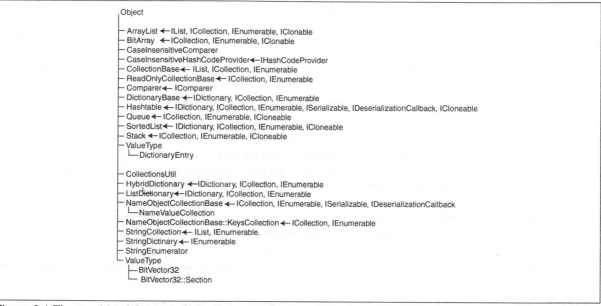

Figure 6.1 The combined System::Collections and System::Collections::Specialized namespace class hierarchy.

Table 6.1 System::Collections namespace classes.

Class	Description
ArrayList	Implements a dynamic array (similar to MFC **CArray**).
BitArray	Implements an array of bit flags.
CaseInsensitiveComparer	Implements the case-insensitive object comparison needed for sorting objects in ordered collections.
CaseInsensitiveHashCodeProvider	Implements a case-insensitive hash function.
CollectionBase	Abstract base class for all .NET collection class.
Comparer	Implements the case-sensitive object comparison needed for sorting objects in ordered collections.
DictionaryBase	Abstract base class for all .NET dictionary classes.
Hashtable	Implements a hash table.
Queue	Implements first-in/first-out (FIFO) queue.
ReadOnlyCollectionBase	Abstract base class for all .NET read-only collections.
SortedList	Implements a sorted collection/dictionary.
Stack	Implements a last-in/first-out (LIFO) stack.

Table 6.2 System::Collections namespace structures (value types).

Structure	Description
DictionaryEntry	Represents a dictionary entry consisting of a key/value pair.

The System::Collections::Specialized Namespace

While the System::Collections namespace primarily provides generic collection classes, many of which are abstract, the System::Collections::Specialized namespace provides concrete implementations of the collection classes optimized for **String*** elements, **String*/String***, or **String*/Object*** key/value pairs. The System::Collections::Specialized namespace classes and value types are listed in Table 6.3 and 6.4, and the namespace hierarchy is illustrated in Figure 6.1.

Table 6.3 System::Collections::Specialized namespace classes.

Class	Description
CollectionsUtil	A utility class for creating case-insensitive hash tables or sorted lists.
HybridDictionary	Implements a **ListDictionary**/**Hashtable** hybrid by automatically switching the internal collection representation from the **ListDictionary** to the **Hashtable** when the collection becomes sufficiently large.
NameObjectCollectionBase	Abstract base class for all .NET collections storing **String*/Object*** name/value pairs.
NameObjectCollectionBase::KeysCollection	Implements a collection of **String*** keys for the **NameObjectCollectionBase** collection.
NameValueCollection	Implements a sorted collection of **String*/String*** pairs.
StringCollection	Implements a generic collection of **String** objects.
StringDictinary	Implements a generic dictionary of **String** objects.
StringEnumerator	Implements a simple **StringCollection** enumerator.

Table 6.4 System::Collections::Specialized namespace value types.

Structure	Description
BitVector32	Represents a collection of bit flags or tiny integers packed in a 32-bit integer.
BitVector32::Section	Represents a section (group of bits) of a **BitVector32** that can contain a tiny integer.

Base Interfaces

Collection functionality is too generic to be expressed in base classes. Therefore, the .NET Framework defines a set of base interfaces describing features (e.g., properties and methods) common to all collection types regardless of the particular implementation. The System::Collections namespace defines the following base interfaces:

* **ICollection:** Supplies **Count** and synchronization properties for collection classes.

* **IComparer**: Provides the **int CompareTo(Object* a, Object* b)** method for object comparison.

* **IDictionary**: Defines dictionary-specified properties and methods.

* **IDictionaryEnumerator**: Defines properties for retrieving key/value information from a dictionary element.

* **IEnumerable**: Provides the **IEnumerator* GetEnumerator()** method for retrieving a collection's enumerator.

* **IEnumerator:** Supplies methods for navigating collection elements.

* **IHashCodeProvider**: Provides the **int GetHashCode(Object* *obj*)** method for calculating an object's hash code.

* **IList:** Supplies methods necessary for adding, inserting, and removing elements in a list.

The System::Collections namespace hierarchy is shown on Figure 6.2.

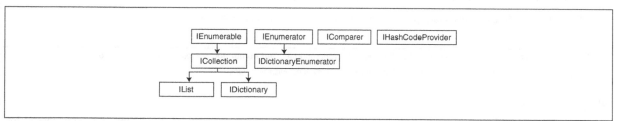

Figure 6.2 System::Collections namespace interface hierarchy.

ICollection Interface

The **ICollection** interface represents a generic collection interface implemented by many .NET Framework classes including **Array**, **ArrayList**, and some Windows Forms, ADO.NET, and XML classes. The **ICollection** inherits from the **IEnumerable** interface. The **ICollection** interface properties and methods are summarized in Tables 6.5 and 6.6.

Table 6.5 **ICollection** interface properties.

Get/Set	Type	Property	Description
Get	**int**	**Count**	Returns the number of elements in the collection.
Get	**bool**	**IsSynchronized**	Returns **true** if the access to the collection elements is thread-safe.
Get	**Object***	**SyncRoot**	Returns the synchronization object for the collection.

NOTE: *In general, access to collection elements is not thread-safe: One thread can modify collection elements while another thread is enumerating them, thus causing unpredictable results. When developing a thread-safe collection class, you should implement the **IsSynchronized** property to return **true** and the **SyncRoot** property to return a pointer to the .NET synchronization object, which can be used to lock or unlock the collection.*

Table 6.6 **ICollection** interface methods.

Method	Description
void CopyTo(Array* *array*, int *index*)	Copies all elements of the collection into the specified array starting at the specified *index*.

IEnumerator Interface

The **IEnumerator** interface allows forward-navigating collections that do not provide a means for direct access to collection elements. The **IEnumerator** interface defines a single property and two methods (see Tables 6.7 and 6.8).

Table 6.7 **IEnumerator** interface properties.

Get/Set	Type	Property	Description
Get	**Object***	**Current**	Returns the current element in the collection.

Table 6.8 **IEnumerator** interface methods.

Method	Description
bool MoveNext()	Moves the enumerator to the next element in the collection.
void Reset()	Sets the enumerator position to point to the first element in the collection.

*NOTE: When you obtain a pointer to an enumerator object using the **IEnumerable::GetEnumerator** method, you must invoke the **MoveNext** before accessing the **Current** property of the **IEnumerator**. (The **Current** property is not initially populated.)*

IList Interface

The **IList** interface defines the functionality of a *list*— a collection where individual elements can be accessed by means of an index. This is illustrated in Figure 6.3.

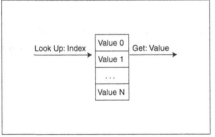

The **IList** interface accumulates more functionality than any other System::Collection interface by combining the indexed access and element insertion and removal capabilities with the **ICollection** and **IEnumerable** interfaces from which it inherits. The **IList** interface properties and methods are summarized in Tables 6.9 and 6.10.

Figure 6.3 List collection architecture. List elements can be accessed by index or sequentially.

Table 6.9 **IList** interface properties.

Get/Set	Type	Property	Description
Get	**bool**	**IsFixedSize**	Returns **true** if the list has a fixed number of entries.
Get	**bool**	**IsReadOnly**	Returns **true** if the list is read-only.
Get/Set	**Object***	**Item(int *index*)**	Gets or sets a list element at the specified index.

Table 6.10 **IList** interface methods.

Method	Description
int Add(Object* *element*)	Adds an element to the list.
void Clear()	Removes all elements from the list.
bool Contains(Object* *element*)	Returns **true** if the specified object is present in the list.
int IndexOf(Object* *element*)	Returns the index of the specified object or -1 if the element is not in the list.
void Insert(int *index*, Object* *element*)	Inserts an object at the specified index in the list.
void Remove(Object* *element*)	Removes the specified object from the list.
void RemoveAt(int *index*)	Removes an element at the specified index from the list.

ArrayList Class

All managed arrays are implicitly derived from the **System::Array** class, which represents a fixed-size array that does not allow you to add or remove elements. If you want to use dynamic arrays that can grow or shrink in size and support element insertion and removal, you should use the **ArrayList** class as defined here:

```
System::Object
|- System::Collections::ArrayList

Attributes: Serializable
Abstract: No
Sealed: No
Implemented Interfaces: IList, ICollection, IEnumerable, IClonable
```

The **ArrayList** class supports a full range of operations on elements in the dynamic array including:

* *Adding elements*: **Add** and **AddRange** methods.
* *Removing elements*: **Remove** and **RemoveRange** methods.
* *Searching elements*: **BinarySearch**, **Contains**, **IndexOf**, **LastIndexOf** methods.
* *Sorting elements*: **Sort** method.

The **ArrayList** class constructors, properties, and methods are summarized in Tables 6.11 through 6.13.

Table 6.11 **ArrayList** class constructors.

Constructor	Description
ArrayList()	Default constructor.
ArrayList(ICollection* obj)	Constructs an **ArrayList** object by copying elements from the specified collection object.
ArrayList(int count)	Creates an **ArrayList** object initially capable of containing **count** elements.

Table 6.12 **ArrayList** class properties (all virtual).

Get/Set	Type	Property	Description
Get/Set	**int**	**Capacity**	Gets or sets the number of elements that a dynamic array can contain.
Get	**int**	**Count**	Contains the number of elements in the **ArrayList**.
Get	**bool**	**IsFixedSize**	Contains **true** if the **ArrayList** has a fixed number of entries.
Get	**bool**	**IsReadOnly**	Contains **true** if the **ArrayList** is read-only.
Get/Set	**Object***	**Item(int index)**	Gets or sets an array element at the specified index.
Get	**bool**	**IsSynchronized**	Contains **true** if the access to the **ArrayList** elements is thread-safe.
Get	**Object***	**SyncRoot**	Contains the synchronization object for the **ArrayList**.

Table 6.13 **ArrayList** class methods.

Member	Description
static ArrayList* Adapter(IList* list)	Converts the specified list into an **ArrayList** object.
virtual int Add(Object* value)	Adds an object to the end of the **ArrayList** collection.
virtual void AddRange(ICollection* coll)	Adds all elements of the specified collection to the **ArrayList**.
virtual int BinarySearch(Object* element) **virtual int BinarySearch(Object* element, IComparer* comparer)** **virtual int BinarySearch(int index, int count, Object* element, IComparer* comparer)**	Performs a binary search on sorted **ArrayList** and returns the index of the **element** or -1 if the element is not found. You can specify optional comparer interface and use optional **index** and **count** arguments to search only a portion of the **ArrayList**.
virtual void Clear()	Removes all elements from the **ArrayList**.
virtual Object* Clone()	Creates a shallow copy of the **ArrayList**.
virtual bool Contains(Object* element)	Returns **true** if the specified element exists in the **ArrayList**.

<Continued on Next Page>

<Table 6.13 Continued>

Member	Description
virtual void CopyTo(Array* *array*) **virtual void CopyTo(Array* *array*, int *destIndex*)** **virtual void CopyTo(int *srcIndex*, Array* *array*, int *destIndex*, int *count*)**	Copies the **ArrayList** to the *array*. You can use optional *srcIndex, destIndex,* and *count* parameters to copy only a portion of the source **ArrayList** to the destination array.
static ArrayList* FixedSize(ArrayList* *list*) **static IList* FixedSize(IList* *list*)**	Creates a fixed-size copy of the **ArrayList** object.
virtual IEnumerator* GetEnumerator() **virtual IEnumerator* GetEnumerator(int *index*, int *count*)**	Creates an enumerator for the **ArrayList**. You can specify optional *index* and *count* parameters to enumerate only a portion of the **ArrayList**.
virtual ArrayList* GetRange(int *index*, int *count*)	Creates a new **ArrayList** object containing *count* elements starting at the index *index* of the original **ArrayList**.
virtual int IndexOf(Object* *element*) **virtual int IndexOf(Object* *element*, int *index*)** **virtual int IndexOf(Object* *element*, int *index*, int *count*)**	Returns the index of the *element* or -1 if the *element* is not found in the **ArrayList**. You can use optional *index* and *count* arguments to search only a portion of the **ArrayList**.
virtual void Insert(int *index*, Object* *element*)	Inserts the specified element at the specified index in the **ArrayList**.
virtual void InsertRange(int *index*, ICollection* *coll*)	Inserts all elements of the specified collection into the **ArrayList** starting at the index *index*.
virtual int LastIndexOf(Object* *element*) **virtual int LastIndexOf(Object* *element*, int *index*)** **virtual int LastIndexOf(Object* *element*, int *index*, int *count*)**	Searches no more than the *count* elements of the **ArrayList** backwards starting at the index *index* and returns the index of the *element* or -1 if the *element* is not found in the **ArrayList**.

<Continued on Next Page>

<Table 6.13 Continued>

Member	Description
static ArrayList* ReadOnly(ArrayList* *list*)	
static IList* ReadOnly (IList* *list*)	Creates a read-only copy of the **ArrayList** object.
virtual void Remove(Object* *element*)	Removes the **element** from the **ArrayList**.
virtual void RemoveRange(int *index*, **int** *count*)	Removes the **count** elements from the **ArrayList** starting at the index **index**.
static ArrayList* Repeat(Object* *obj*, **int** *count*)	Creates a new **ArrayList** object containing the **count** copies of the specified object.
virtual void Reverse()	
virtual void Reverse(int *index*, **int** *count*)	Reverses the order of elements in the **ArrayList**. You can use optional **index** and **count** arguments to reverse only a portion of the **ArrayList**.
virtual void SetRange(int *index*, **ICollection*** *coll*)	Overwrites elements of the **ArrayList** starting at the index **index** with the elements of the specified collection.
virtual void Sort()	
virtual void Sort(IComparer* *comparer*)	
virtual void Sort(int *index*, **int** *count*, **IComparer*** *comparer*)	Sorts the **ArrayList**. You can use optional **index**, **count**, and **comparer** arguments to sort only a portion of the **ArrayList** using the specified comparer.
static ArrayList* Synchronized(ArrayList* *list*)	
static IList* Synchronized(IList* *list*)	Returns a synchronized copy of the specified **list** object.
virtual Array* ToArray()	
virtual Array* ToArray(Type* *type*),	Converts the **ArrayList** into **Array** of the specified type (if any).
virtual void TrimToSize()	Sets the **Capacity** to the **Count** of elements in the **ArrayList**.

CollectionBase Class

The .NET Framework provides an abstract base class **CollectionBase** representing a generic strongly typed collection:

```
System::Object
|- System::Collections::CollectionBase
```

Attributes: **Serializable**
Abstract: Yes
Sealed: No
Implemented Interfaces: **IList, ICollection, IEnumerable**

The **CollectionBase** class implements all methods of the **IList**, **Icollection**, and **IEnumerable** interfaces and defines numerous **On***XYZ* methods for handling events such as inserting, removing, or modifying the collection elements. You can override the **On***XYZ* methods in a derived class to perform custom processing such as data validation. (The **On***XYZ* methods should throw an exception to indicate an unsuccessful operation.) The **CollectionBase** class constructors, properties, and methods are summarized in Tables 6.14 through 6.16.

Table 6.14 **CollectionBase** class constructors.

Constructor	Description
protected: CollectionBase()	Default constructor.

Table 6.15 **CollectionBase** class properties.

Get/Set	Type	Property	Protected	Description
Get	**int**	**Count**	No	Contains the number of elements in the collection.
Get	**ArrayList***	**InnerLIst**	Yes	Provides direct access to the collection elements.
Get	**IList***	**List**	Yes	Provides indirect (i.e., notification-causing) access to the collection elements.

NOTE: *The collection calls **On***XYZ* notification methods when operations such as adding or removing elements are performed on the **List** property. When the same operations are performed on the **InnerList** property, the notification methods are not called.*

Table 6.16 **CollectionBase** class methods.

Method	Description
__sealed void Clear()	Removes all elements from the collection.
__sealed IEnumerator* GetEnumerator()	Returns the collection's enumerator object.
void ICollection::CopyTo(Array* *array***, int** *index***)**	Copies all elements of the collection into the specified array starting at the index *index*.

<Continued on Next Page>

<Table 6.16 Continued>

Method	Description
int IList.Add(Object* *element*)	Adds an element to the collection.
bool IList::Contains(Object* *element*)	Returns **true** if the specified object is present in the collection.
int IList::IndexOf(Object* *element*)	Returns the index of the specified object or -1 if the element is not in the collection.
void IList::Insert(int *index*, Object* *element*)	Inserts an object at the specified index in the collection.
void IList::Remove(Object* *element*)	Removes the specified object from the collection.
protected: virtual void OnClear()	The method can be overridden by a derived class to perform additional processing when the **Clear** method is called.
protected: virtual void OnClearComplete()	The method can be overridden by a derived class to perform additional processing when the **Clear** method completes.
protected: virtual void OnInsert(int *index*, Object* *element*)	The method can be overridden by a derived class to perform additional processing when the **Insert** method is called.
protected: virtual void OnInsertComplete(int *index*, Object* *element*)	The method can be overridden by a derived class to perform additional processing when the **Insert** method completes.
protected: virtual void OnRemove(int *index*, Object* *element*)	The method can be overridden by a derived class to perform additional processing when the **Insert** method is called.
protected: virtual void OnRemoveComplete(int *index*, Object* *element*)	The method can be overridden by a derived class to perform additional processing when the **Insert** method completes.
protected: virtual void OnSet(int *index*, Object* *oldElement*, Object* *newElement*)	The method can be overridden by a derived class to perform additional processing before a collection element is set. The *newElement* parameter contains the new value of the element to be set, while the *oldElement* parameter contains the current value of the collection element.
protected: virtual void OnSetComplete(int *index*, Object* *oldElement*, Object* *newElement*)	The method can be overridden by a derived class to perform additional processing after a collection element is set. The *newElement* parameter contains the new value of the element to be set, while the *oldElement* parameter contains the old value of the collection element.

<Continued on Next Page>

<Table 6.16 Continued>

Method	Description
protected: virtual void OnValidate(Object* *element*)	Override this method to prevent certain elements from being added to the collection. The default implementation prevents Null references from being added.
__sealed void RemoveAt(int *index*)	Removes a collection element at the specified index.

Although the **CollectionBase** class does not contain pure abstract methods, it does not allow public access to its **List** or **InnerList** properties. Thus, you must derive your own class from the **CollectionBase** and supply your own methods for updating elements in the collection.

ReadOnlyCollectionBase Class

The **CollectionBase** class supports the full range of collection functionality including adding and removing elements. If you want to restrict access to your collection to read-only, you should derive your collection class from the **ReadOnlyCollectionBase**, which only allows you to initialize the collection and enumerate the collection elements. The **ReadOnlyCollectionBase** class has the following inheritance diagram:

```
System::Object
|- System::Collections::ReadOnlyCollectionBase
```

```
Attributes: Serializable
Abstract: Yes
Sealed: No
Implemented Interfaces: ICollection, IEnumerable
```

As with the **CollectionBase** class, the **ReadOnlyCollectionBase** does not allow direct access to the collection element. (The **InnerList** property is protected.) Thus, in order to implement a read-only collection, you must derive your own class from the **ReadOnlyCollectionBase**. The **CollectionBase** class constructors, properties, and methods are listed in Tables 6.17 through 6.19.

Table 6.17 **ReadOnlyCollectionBase** class constructors.

Constructor	Description
protected: ReadOnlyCollectionBase()	Default constructor.

Table 6.18 **ReadOnlyCollectionBase** class properties.

Get/Set	Type	Property	Protected	Description
Get	**int**	**Count**	No	Contains the number of elements in the collection.
Get	**ArrayList***	**InnerList**	Yes	Provides direct access to the collection elements.

Table 6.19 **ReadOnlyCollectionBase** class methods.

Method	Description
__**sealed IEnumerator* GetEnumerator()**	Returns an enumerator for iterating trough the collection.
void ICollection::CopyTo(Array* array, int index)	Copies all collection elements to the specified one-dimensional array starting at the specified **index**.

String Collections

A collection of strings is the most common type of collection. The .NET Framework provides a concrete implementation of a collection of strings by means of the **StringCollection** class as shown here:

```
System::Object
|- System::Collections::Specialized::StringCollection


Attributes: Serializable
Abstract: No
Sealed: No
Implemented Interfaces: IList, IEnumerable
```

The **StringCollection** class provides its own set of methods with the same names as the **IList** interface methods but accepting only **String*** parameters. (The **IList** interface methods use **Object*** parameters.) You can still use the methods provided by the **IList** interface if you explicitly qualify them (e.g., **MyStringCollection->IList::Add(MyStr)**). Keep in mind that if you attempt to add elements to the **StringCollection** other than of type **String***, the **StringCollection** class will throw an exception. The **StringCollection** class constructors, properties, and methods are summarized in Tables 6.20 through 6.22.

Table 6.20 **StringCollection** class constructors.

Constructor	Description
StringCollection()	Default constructor.

Table 6.21 **StringCollection** class properties.

Get/Set	Type	Property	Description
Get	**int**	**Count**	Contains the number of elements in the collection.
Get	**bool**	**IsReadOnly**	Always contains **false**.
Get	**bool**	**IsSynchronized**	Always contains **false**.
Get/Set	**String***	**Item(int index)**	Gets or sets a string at the specified index.
Get	**Object***	**SyncRoot**	Returns a synchronization object for the string collection.

Table 6.22 **StringCollection** class methods.

Method	Description
int Add(String* *str***)**	Adds a string to the end of the string collection.
void AddRange(String* __gc[] *array***)**	Adds strings from the specified array to the end of the string collection.
__sealed void Clear()	Removes all strings from the string collection.
bool Contains(String* *str***)**	Returns **true** if the specified string is present in the string collection.
void CopyTo(String* __gc[] *array***, int** *index***)**	Copies all strings from the string collection into the specified array starting at the specified *index*.
StringEnumerator* GetEnumerator()	Returns the string collection enumerator object.
void ICollection::CopyTo(Array* *array***, int** *index***)**	Copies all elements from the collection into the specified array starting at the specified *index*.
IEnumerable* Enumerable.GetEnumerator()	Returns the collection enumerator object.
int IList::Add(Object* *element***)**	Adds an element to the end of the collection.
bool IList::Contains(Object* *element***)**	Returns **true** if the specified object is present in the collection.
int IList::IndexOf(Object* *element***)**	Returns the index of the specified object or -1 if the element is not in the collection.
void IList::Insert(int *index***, Object*** *element***)**	Inserts an object at the specified index in the collection.
void IList::Remove(Object* *element***)**	Removes the specified object from the collection.
int IndexOf(String* *str***)**	Returns the index of the specified string or -1 if the string is not found in the string collection.
void Insert(int *index***, String*** *str***)**	Inserts a string at the specified index in the string collection.
void Remove(String* *str***)**	Removes the specified string from the string collection.
__sealed void RemoveAt(int *index***)**	Removes a string at the specified index from the string collection.

StringEnumerator Class

The .NET Framework provides a special enumerator for navigating string collections—**StringEnumerator**. You might find this surprising but the **StringEnumerator** does not implement the **IEnumerator** interface because it has to provide its own **Current** property of type **String*** and not of type **Object*** as required by the **IEnumerator** interface. The **StringEnumerator** class inheritance diagram is shown next:

```
System::Object
|- System::Collections::Specialized::StringEnumerator


Attributes: None.
Abstract: No
Sealed: No
Implemented Interfaces: None
```

The **StringEnumerator** class properties and methods are listed in Tables 6.23 and 6.24.

Table 6.23 **StringEnumerator** class properties.

Get/Set	Type	Property	Description
Get	**String***	**Current**	Returns the current string of the string collection.

Table 6.24 **StringEnumerator** class methods.

Method	Description
bool MoveNext()	Moves the enumerator to the next element in the string collection.
void Reset()	Sets the enumerator position to point to the first element in the string collection.

Collections of Sorted Name/Value Pairs

Database application developers often deal with ordered lists of key/value pairs implementing look up tables. A list of *name/value* pairs, where *name* is expressed as a **String*** and *value* is expressed as an **Object*,** represent a special common case of the key/value pair list. The .NET Framework provides a semiconcrete implementation of the name/value list by means of the **NameObjectCollectionBase** specialized collection class:

```
System::Object
|- System::Collections::Specialized::NameObjectCollectionBase

Attributes: Serializable
Abstract: Yes
Sealed: No
Implemented Interfaces: ICollection, IEnumerable, ISerializable,
    IDeserializationCallback
```

The **NameObjectCollectionBase** class constructors, properties, and methods are summarized in Tables 6.25 through 6.27.

Table 6.25 **NameObjectCollectionBase** class constructors.

Constructor	Description
protected: NameObjectCollectionBase()	Default constructor.
protected: NameObjectCollectionBase(int *capacity*)	

protected: NameObjectCollectionBase
      (IHashCodeProvider* *hashProvider*,
      IComparer* *comparer*)	

protected: NameObjectCollectionBase(int *capacity*,
      IHashCodeProvider* *hashProvider*,
      IComparer* *comparer*)
	Constructs the **NameObjectCollectionBase** object capable of containing the *capacity* elements initially. Optional *hashProvider* and *comparer* arguments allow specifying custom hash function and comparer objects.

protected: NameObjectCollectionBase(SerializationInfo* *info*, StreamingContext *context*)	Constructs the **NameObjectCollectionBase** object using the specified serialization information.

*NOTE: The capacity of a **NameObjectCollectionBase** object grows automatically as you add new elements to the list.*

Table 6.26 **NameObjectCollectionBase** class properties.

Get/Set	Type	Property	Virtual	Protected	Description
Get	int	Count	Yes	No	Contains the number of elements in the collection.
Get/Set	bool	IsReadOnly	No	Yes	Gets or sets the read-only flag for the collection.
Get	NameObject CollectionBase:: KeysCollection*	Keys	Yes	No	Contains the keys of the **NameObjectCollectionBase** collection.

Table 6.27 **NameObjectCollectionBase** class methods.

Method	Description
protected: void BaseAdd(String* *name*, Object* *value*)	Adds the specified *name*/*value* pair to the collection.
protected: void BaseClear()	Removes all elements from the collection.
protected: Object* BaseGet(int *index*)	
protected: Object* BaseGet(String* *name*)	Returns the value from the collection identified by the specified *name* or *index*.

*NOTE: The **BaseGet** method may return a Null reference in two cases: (1) when there are no name/value pairs in the collection with a specified name, or (2) when the found name/value pair contains a Null value. The **BaseGet** method does not provide means for differentiating between the two scenarios.*

<Continued on Next Page>

<Table 6.27 Continued>

Method	Description
protected: String* BaseGetAllKeys() __gc[]	Returns an array of all names in the collection.
protected: Object* BaseGetAllValues() __gc[]	
protected: Object* BaseGetAllValues(Type* *type*) __gc[]	Returns an array of all values in the collection. Optional *type* argument allows specifying the resulting array type.
protected: String* BaseGetKey(int *index*	Returns the name from the collection at the specified index.
protected: bool BaseHasKeys()	Returns **true** if the collection contains name/value pairs with non-Null names.
protected: void BaseRemove(String* *name*)	Removes one ore more name/value pairs from the collection corresponding to the specified *name*.
protected: void BaseRemoveAt(int *index*)	Removes a single element at the specified index from the collection.
protected: void BaseSet(int *index*, Object* *value*)	
protected: void BaseSet(String* *name*, Object* *value*)	Sets the value of the first name/value pair identified by the specified *name* or *index*.
__sealed IEnumerator* GetEnumerator()	Returns an enumerator, which allows navigating name strings of the **NameObjectCollectionBase** collection.
virtual void GetObjectData(SerializationInfo* *info*, StreamingContext *context*)	Returns the object data as required by the **ISerializable** interface to serialize the object.
void ICollection::CopyTo(Array* *array*, int *index*)	Copies all elements of the collection into the specified array starting at the index *index*.
virtual void OnDeserialization(Object* *sender*)	Implements a deserialization event handler as required by the **ISerializable** interface.

Internally, the **NameObjectCollectionBase** class utilizes a hash table to store the data. If no specific hash provider is specified, the **NameObjectCollectionBase** class uses the **CaseInsensitiveHashCodeProvider** by default and the **CaseInsensitiveComparer** to compare the keys (i.e., **String** names) of the list elements for element lookup and sorting.

NameObjectCollectionBase::KeysCollection Class

You may occasionally need to extract just the keys (names) from the key/value pair collection to build a component such as a drop down list of names for a GUI user interface. While the **NameObjectCollectionBase::Keys** property allows retrieving the collection of keys from a **NameObjectCollectionBase** list object, the .NET Framework provides a specialized **NameObjectCollectionBase::KeysCollection** collection for managing such lists. The **NameObjectCollectionBase::KeysCollection** class inheritance diagram is shown here:

```
System::Object
|- System::Collections::Specialized::NameObjectCollectionBase::KeysCollection
```

```
Attributes: None.
Abstract: No
Sealed: No
Implemented Interfaces: ICollection, IEnumerable
```

The **NameObjectCollectionBase::KeysCollection** class properties and methods are listed in Tables 6.28 and 6.29.

Table 6.28 **NameObjectCollectionBase::KeysCollection** class properties.

Get/Set	Type	Property	Description
Get	**int**	**Count**	Contains the number of elements in the collection.
Get	**String***	**Item(int *index*)**	Returns the element of the collection at the specified index.

Table 6.29 **NameObjectCollectionBase::KeysCollection** class methods.

Method	Description
virtual String* Get(int *index*)	Returns the key of the **KeysCollection** at the specified index (similar to the **Item** property).
__sealed IEnumerator* GetEnumerator()	Returns an enumerator object for the **KeysCollection** collection.
void ICollection::CopyTo(Array* *array*, int *index*)	Copies all elements of the **KeysCollection** into the specified array starting at the index *index*.

String Lookup Collections

String lookup collection are very similar to dictionaries and can be used to store **String*/String*** name/value pairs. The string lookup collections are represented in the .NET Framework by means of the **NameObjectCollectionBase** specialized collection class, which has the following inheritance structure:

```
System::Object
|- System::Collections::Specialized::NameObjectCollectionBase
   |- System::Collections::Specialized::NameValueCollection
```

Attributes: **Serializable**
Abstract: No
Sealed: No
Implemented Interfaces: None

The **NameValueCollection** class is very similar to the **NameValueCollection** class, except that the **NameValueCollection** class is not an abstract class. It supplies concrete **Add**, **Get**, and **Remove** methods for managing elements in the collection. The **NameValueCollection** class constructors, properties, and methods are summarized in Tables 6.30 through 6.32.

Table 6.30 **NameValueCollection** class constructors.

Constructor	Description
NameValueCollection()	Default constructor.
NameValueCollection(int *capacity*)	Constructs the **NameValueCollection** object capable of initially holding the *capacity* elements.
NameValueCollection(NameValueCollection* *coll*)	
NameValueCollection(int *capacity*, NameValueCollection* *coll*)	Constructs the **NameValueCollection** by copying entries from the specified collection. The optional *capacity* argument specifies the initial capacity of the collection, which is automatically extended if it is less than the number of elements in the source collection.
NameValueCollection(IHashCodeProvider* *hashProvider*, IComparer* *comparer*)	
NameValueCollection(int *capacity*, IHashCodeProvider* *provider*, IComparer* *comparer*)	Constructs the **NameValueCollection** object with the initial capacity *capacity* using the specified hash code provider and comparer objects.
NameValueCollection(SerializationInfo* *info*, StreamingContext *context*)	Constructs the **NameValueCollection** object based on the specified serialization information.

Table 6.31 **NameValueCollection** class properties.

Get/Set	Type	Property	Virtual	Description
Get	**String*[]**	**AllKeys**	Yes	Contains a string array of all keys of the **NameValueCollection**.
Get	**String***	**Item(int *Index*)**	No	Returns the **NameValueCollection** element at the specified index.
Get/Set	**String***	**Item(String* *key*)**	No	Gets or sets the value of an element identified by the specified key. If you specify a key that does not exist in the collection when setting an item, a new key/value pair will be added to the collection.

Table 6.32 **NameValueCollection** class methods.

Method	Description
void Add(NameValueCollection* *coll*)	Copies entries from the specified **NameValueCollection** into the current collection.
virtual void Add(String* *key*, String* *value*)	Adds the specified key/value pair to the **NameValueCollection**.
void Clear()	Removes all elements from the **NameValueCollection** collection.
void CopyTo(Array* *dest*, int *index*)	Copies all elements from the **NameValueCollection** into the specified array starting at the index *index*.
virtual String* Get(int *index*)	
virtual String* Get(String* *key*)	Returns a string of comma-separated values of all the **NameValueCollection** elements identified by the specified *index* or *key*.
virtual String* GetKey(int *index*)	Returns the key of the **NameValueCollection** element at the specified index.
virtual String* GetValues(int *index*) __gc[]	
virtual String* GetValues(String* *key*) __gc[]	Returns an array of values of the **NameValueCollection** elements identified by the specified *name* or *key*.
bool HasKeys()	Returns true if the **NameValueCollection** contains entries with non-Null keys.
protected: void InvalidateCachedArrays()	Releases extra memory by resetting cached arrays to Null pointers. (Arrays returned by the **AllKeys** property are automatically cached by the **NameValueCollection** object for better performance.)
virtual void Remove(String* *key*)	Removes elements from the **NameValueCollection** identified by the specified key.
virtual void Set(String* *key*, String* *value*)	Sets the value of a **NameValueCollection** element identified by the specified key.

Object Comparison Support

The .NET Framework supplies the base **IComparer** interface for comparing objects. The interface defines a single **CompareTo** method:

```
int CompareTo(Object* obj1, Object* obj2);
```

When implemented by a class, the method must return less than 0 if the current **obj1** is less than **obj2**. It will return a value of 0 if two objects are equal, or greater than 0 if **obj1** is greater than **obj2**.

Comparer and CaseInsensitiveComparer Classes

The .NET Framework supplies two default classes—**Comparer** and **CaseInsensitiveComparer**—for performing both case-sensitive and case-insensitive object comparisons required for ordering objects in sorted collections:

```
System::Object
|- System::Collections::Comparer
|- System::Collections::CaseInsensitiveComparer
```

```
Attributes: Serializable
Abstract: No
Sealed: Yes
Implemented Interfaces: IComparer
```

Both the **Comparer** and the **CaseInsensitiveComparer** classes have the same fields and methods, which are summarized in Tables 6.33 and 6.34. The **Comparer** class has no constructors. The **CaseInsensitiveComparer** class constructors are listed in Table 6.35.

Table 6.33 **Comparer/CaseInsensitiveComparer** class Fields.

Field	Description
static Comparer* Default	Returns an always-available instance of the **Comparer** class.

Table 6.34 **Comparer/CaseInsensitiveComparer** class methods.

Method	Description
__sealed int Compare(Object* obj1, Object* obj2)	Compares two objects and returns < 0 if *obj1* < *obj2*, 0 if *obj1* = *obj2*, or > 0 if *obj1* > *obj2*.

Table 6.35 **CaseInsensitiveComparer** class constructors.

Constructor	Description
CaseInsensitiveComparer()	Default constructor.
CaseInsensitiveComparer(CultureInfo* cultureInfo)	Constructs a case insensitive comparer using the specified culture information.

Dictionaries

A dictionary is a collections of key/value pairs where an individual element can be accessed by means of a key, which can be of any type. Figure 6.4 shows the dictionary collection architecture. Notice that the dictionary elements can be accessed by index, key, or sequentially.

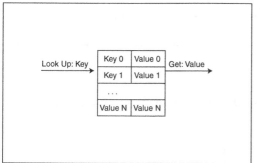

Figure 6.4 Dictionary collection architecture.

NOTE: The main difference between dictionaries and collections of key/value pairs is that dictionaries do not allow multiple entries with the same key while collections do. Thus, for a particular key, a dictionary can contain at most one value, while a collection can contain multiple values corresponding to the same key.

The core dictionary functionality is defined in the .NET Framework by means of the **IDictionary** interface. The **IDictionary** interface is a base interface for .NET dictionary objects including **Hashtable**, **ListDictionary**, and **SortedList**. The **IDictionary** interface inherits from the **ICollection** and **IEnumerable** interfaces. Its properties and methods are summarized in Tables 6.36 and 6.37.

Table 6.36 **IDictionary** interface properties.

Get/Set	Type	Property	Description
Get	**bool**	**IsFixedSize**	Returns **true** if the dictionary has a fixed number of entries.
Get	**bool**	**IsReadOnly**	Returns **true** if the dictionary is read-only.
Get/Set	**Object***	**Item(Object* Key)**	Gets or sets a dictionary element specified by the *key*. If you specify a key that does not exist in the dictionary when setting an item, a new key/value pair will be added to the collection.
Get	**ICollection***	**Keys**	Returns the collection of dictionary keys.
Get	**ICollection***	**Values**	Returns the collection of dictionary values.

Table 6.37 **IDictionary** interface methods.

Method	Description
void Add(Object* key, Object* value)	Adds the specified *key*/*value* pair to the dictionary.
void Clear()	Removes all elements from the dicitonary.
bool Contains(Object* key)	Returns **true** if the specified element is found in the dictionary.
void Remove(Obect* key)	Removes element identified by *key* form the dictionary.
void CopyTo(Array* array, int index)	Copies all elements of the dictionary into the specified array starting at the index *index*. The destination array must be sufficiently big to accommodate all dictionary elements, otherwise an exception is thrown.

IDictionaryEnumerator Interface

The **IDictionaryEnumerator** interface is intended to enumerate dictionaries. The **IDictionaryEnumerator** interface inherits from the **IEnumerable** interface and supplies additional **Key** and **Value** properties for retrieving key/value information from a dictionary entry. The **IDictionaryEnumerator** interface properties are listed in Table 6.38.

Table 6.38 **IDictionaryEnumerator** interface properties.

Get/Set	Type	Property	Description
Get	**DictionaryEntry**	**Entry**	Returns a key/value pair of the current dictionary entry.
Get	**Object***	**Key**	Returns the key of the current dictionary entry.
Get	**Object***	**Value**	Returns the value of the current dictionary entry.

DictionaryBase Class

The .NET Framework Class Library supplies the abstract base class **DictionaryBase** to support the core dictionary functionality:

```
System::Object
|- System::Collections::DictionaryBase


Attributes: Serializable
Abstract: Yes
Sealed: No
Implemented Interfaces: IDictionary, ICollection, IEnumerable
```

The **DictionaryBase** class implements all the methods of the **IDictionary** interface and supplies numerous **On**XYZ methods for handling events associated with addition, modification, and removal of key/value pairs to and from the dictionary. Although the **DictionaryBase** class has no pure virtual method, the class is defined as an abstract class because it does not allow direct access to the internal **Dictionary** collection, which is protected. To use dictionary functionality, you should derive your own class from the **DictionaryBase**. The **DictionaryBase** class constructors, properties, and methods are listed in Tables 6.39 through 6.41.

Table 6.39 **DictionaryBase** class constructors.

Constructor	Description
protected: DictionaryBase()	Default Constructor.

Table 6.40 **DictionaryBase** class properties.

Get/Set	Type	Property	Protected	Description
Get	**int**	**Count**	No	Contains the number of entries in the dictionary.
Get	**IDictionary***	**Dictionary**	Yes	Provides the notification-causing access to the dictionary collection. If you modify elements returned by the **Dictionary** property, appropriate **On**XYZ notifications are called.
Get	**Hashtable***	**InnerHashtable**	Yes	Provides direct access to the dictionary collection. If you modify elements returned by the **InnerHashtable** property, the **On**XYZ notifications are *not* called.

Table 6.41 **DictionaryBase** class methods.

Method	Description
__sealed void Clear()	Removes all entries from the dictionary.
__sealed void CopyTo(Array* *array*, **int** *index***)**	Copies all dictionary elements to the specified array starting at the specified index. The destination array must be large enough to accommodate all dictionary entries or an exception will be thrown.
__sealed IDictionaryEnumerator* GetEnumerator()	Returns the dictionary enumerator for the dictionary.
void IDictionary::Add(Object* *key*, **Object*** *value***)**	Adds a new entry to the dictionary. If the specified key already exists, the old entry is overwritten with the new entry.
bool IDictionary::Contains(Object* *key***)**	Returns **true** if the specified *key* exists in the dictionary.
void IDictionary::Remove(Object* *key***)**	Removes the specified *key* from the dictionary.
IEnumerator* IEnumerable::GetEnumerator()	Returns the enumerator object for the dictionary.
protected: virtual void OnClear()	Called when the **Clear** method is invoked in the **Dictionary** property.
protected: virtual void OnClearComplete()	Called when the **Clear** method invoked in the **Dictionary** property completes.
protected: virtual Object* OnGet(Object* *key*, **Object*** *value***)**	Called before an entry is retrieved from the **Dictionary** property (i.e., using **Dictionary->Item[***key***]**).
protected: virtual void OnInsert(Object* *key*, **Object*** *value***)**	Called before an entry is inserted into the **Dictionary** property (i.e., using **Dictionary->Item[***key***] =** *value* because the *key* did not exists in the dictionary).
protected: virtual void OnInsertComplete(Object* *key*, **Object*** *value***)**	Called after an entry is inserted into the **Dictionary** property (i.e., using **Dictionary->Item[***key***] =** *value*).
protected: virtual void OnRemove(Object* *key*, **Object*** *value***)**	Called before an entry is removed from the **Dictionary** property (i.e., using **Dictionary->Remove(***key***)**).
protected: virtual void OnRemoveComplete(Object* *key*, **Object*** *value***)**	Called after an entry is removed from the **Dictionary** property (i.e., using **Dictionary->Remove(***key***)**).

<Continued on Next Page>

<Table 6.41 Continued>

Method	Description
protected: virtual void OnSet(Object* *key*, Object* oldValue, Object* *newValue*)	Called before a value of a dictionary entry is updated using the **Dictionary** property (i.e., Dictionary->Item[*key*] = *value*).
protected: virtual void OnSetComplete(Object* *key*, Object* oldValue, Object* *newValue*)	Called after a value of a dictionary entry is updated using the **Dictionary** property (i.e., Dictionary->Item[*key*] = *value*).
protected: virtual void OnValidate(Object* *key*, Object* *value*)	Override this method to implement a type-safe dictionary by verifying the type of the specified *value* and throwing an **ArgumentException** if the *value* is of incompatible type.

DictionaryEntry Class

The .NET Framework supplies a special enumerator interface called **IdictionaryEnumerator** for enumerating dictionary entries. The **IDictionaryEnumerator** allows you to retrieve dictionary entries into the **DictionaryEntry** structure that represents a key/value pair. The **DictionaryEntry** value type has the following inheritance structure:

```
System::Object
|- System::ValueType
   |- System::Collections::DictionaryEntry

Attributes: Serializable
Abstract: None
Sealed: No
Implements Interfaces: None
```

The **DictionaryEntry** value type constructors and properties are listed in Tables 6.42 and 6.43.

Table 6.42 **DictionaryEntry** value type constructors.

Constructor	Description
DictionaryEntry(Object* *key*, Object* *value*)	Constructs a dictionary entry.

Table 6.43 **DictionaryEntry** value type properties.

Get/Set	Type	Property	Description
Get/Set	Object*	Key	Gets or sets the key of the dictionary entry.
Get/Set	Object*	Value	Gets or sets the value of the dictionary entry.

ListDictionary and HybridDictionary Classes

The .NET Framework Class Library was designed with performance in mind. Because the collection classes, such as dictionaries, are frequently used by developers to represent various data structures, it is critical to be able to extract maximum performance from collections. This is especially the case when executing key-lookup operations. Fortunately, the .NET Framework Class Library contains additional specialized collection classes optimized for different purposes:

* **ListDictionary**: Concrete implementation of a dictionary optimized for 10 or less entries.

* **HybridDictionary**: Concrete implementation of a dictionary optimized for large numbers of entries. (The **HybridDictionary** automatically switches internal data representation from **ListDictionary** to **Hashtable** when the number of elements is greater than 10.)

The inheritance structure for the **ListDictionary** and **HybridDictionary** classes is shown here:

```
System::Object
|- System::Collections::Specialized::ListDictionary
|- System::Collections::Specialized::HybridDictionary
```

Attributes: **Serializable**

Abstract: None

Sealed: No

Implements Interfaces: **IDictionary, ICollection, IEnumerable**

No special actions are required when using the **ListDictionary** or **HybridDictionary** objects. You simply use them like any other dictionary and you will reap the benefits of the improved performance automatically. The **ListDictionary/HybridDictionary** class constructors, properties, and methods are summarized in Tables 6.44 through 6.47.

Table 6.44 **ListDictionary** class constructors.

Constructor	Description
ListDictionary()	Default constructor.
ListDictionary(IComparer* *comparer*)	Constructs a list dictionary using the specified comparer.

Table 6.45 **HybridDictionary** class constructors.

Constructor	Description
HybridDictionary()	Default constructor.
HybridDictionary(bool *caseInsensitive*)	Constructs a dictionary object that uses case-sensitive or case-insensitive hashing and comparison depending on the value of the *caseInsensitive* parameter.
HybridDictionary(int *capacity*)	
HybridDictionary(int *capacity*, bool *caseInsensitive*)	Creates a dictionary with the specified initial capacity. If the specified capacity is grater than 10, the dictionary automatically switches into a **Hashtable** mode. The optional *caseInsensitive* argument switches between case-sensitive and case-insensitive hash function.

Table 6.46 **ListDictionary/HybridDictionary** class properties.

Get/Set	Type	Property	Description
Get	**int**	**Count**	Contains the number of entries in the dictionary.
Get	**bool**	**IsFixedSize**	Always contains **false**.
Get	**bool**	**IsReadOnly**	Always contains **false**.
Get	**bool**	**IsSynchronized**	Always contains **false**.
Get/Set	**Object***	**Item(Object* *key*)**	Gets or sets a dictionary value corresponding to the specified key. If you specify a key that does not exist in the dictionary when setting an item, a new key/value pair will be added to the collection.
Get	**ICollection***	**Keys**	Returns a collection of dictionary keys.
Get	**Object***	**SyncRoot**	Returns the dictionary synchronization object.
Get	**ICollection***	**Values**	Returns a collection of dictionary values.

Table 6.47 **ListDictionary**/**HybridDictionary** class methods.

Method	Description
__sealed void Add(Object* *key*, Object* *value*)	Adds a new key/value pair to the dictionary.
__sealed void Clear()	Removes all entries in the dictionary.
__sealed bool Contains(Object* *key*)	Returns **true** if the specified key is found in the dictionary.
__sealed void CopyTo(Array* *array*, int *index*)	Copies all dictionary elements to the specified array starting at the specified index. The destination array must be large enough to accommodate all dictionary entries or an exception will be thrown.
__sealed IDictionaryEnumerator* GetEnumerator()	Returns the dictionary enumerator for the dictionary object.
IEnumerator* IEnumerable::GetEnumerator()	Returns the enumerator for the dictionary object.
__sealed void Remove(Object* *key*)	Removes an entry with the specified key from the dictionary.

StringDictionary class

String dictionaries (i.e., dictionaries containing **String***/**String*** pairs) represent a common special case of dictionary. The .NET Framework provides a specialized implementation of a string dictionary by means of the **StringDictionary** class. Unlike other dictionary classes, the **StringDictionary** class does not implement the **IDictionary** interface because the **IDictionary** interface does not provide the desired type safety. It simply allows **Object*** pointers for dictionary keys and values. The **StringDictionary** class goes a step further and requires **String*** pointers for dictionary keys and values. The **StringDictionary** class inheritance structure is as follows:

```
System::Object
|- System::Collections::Specialized::StringDictionary
```

Attributes: **Serializable**

Abstract: No

Sealed: No

Implements **IEnumerable**

The **StringDictionary** dictionary internally implements a case-insensitive hash table and is very similar to the **ListDictionary**/**HybridDictionary** classes except that the **StringDictionary** class members (including the **Item** indexer property) accept **String** pointers rather than generic **Object** pointers. The **StringDictionary** class constructors, properties, and methods are listed in Tables 6.48 through 6.50.

Table 6.48 **StringDictionary** class constructors.

Constructor	Description
StringDictionary()	Default constructor.

Table 6.49 **StringDictionary** class properties (all virtual).

Get/Set	Type	Property	Description
Get	**int**	**Count**	Contains the number of entries in the dictionary.
Get	**bool**	**IsFixedSize**	Always contains **false**.
Get	**bool**	**IsReadOnly**	Always contains **false**.
Get	**bool**	**IsSynchronized**	Always contains **false**.
Get/Set	**String***	**Item(String* *key*)**	Gets or sets a dictionary value corresponding to the specified key. If you specify a key that does not exist in the dictionary when setting an item, a new key/value pair will be added to the collection.
Get	**ICollection***	**Keys**	Returns a collection of dictionary keys.
Get	**Object***	**SyncRoot**	Returns the dictionary synchronization object.
Get	**ICollection***	**Values**	Returns a collection of dictionary values.

Table 6.50 **StringDictionary** class methods.

Method	Description
virtual **Add(String* key, String* value)**	Adds a new key/value pair to the dictionary.
virtual **Clear()**	Removes all entries from the dictionary.
virtual bool ContainsValue(String* key)	Returns true if the specified value is found in the dicitonary.
virtual **Contains**Key(**String* key**)	Returns **true** if the specified key is found in the dictionary.
virtual **void CopyTo(Array* array, int index)**	Copies all dictionary elements to the specified array starting at the specified index. The destination array must be large enough to accommodate all dictionary entries or an exception will be thrown.
virtual **IDictionaryEnumerator* GetEnumerator()**	Returns the dictionary enumerator for the dictionary object.
IEnumerator* IEnumerable::GetEnumerator()	Returns the enumerator for the dictionary object.
virtual **void Remove(String* key)**	Removes an entry with the specified key from the dictionary.

SortedList Class

The .NET Framework Class Library provides you with the convenience of setting up sorted lists by providing the **SortedList** class:

```
System::Object
|- System::Collections::SortedList
```

```
Attributes: Serializable
Abstract: No
Sealed: No
Implemented Interfaces: IDictionary, ICollection, IEnumerable, ICloneable
```

This class is equivalent to the **ArrayList** class, except that it stores key/value pairs and automatically sorts elements as you add them to the list. The **SortedList** class supplies the **Item** indexer property for accessing the collection elements by key. The complete summary of the **SortedList** class constructors, properties, and methods is given in Tables 6.51 through 6.53.

Table 6.51 **SortedList** Class Constructors.

Constructor	Description
SortedList()	Default constructor.
SortedList(int *capacity***)**	Constructs a sorted list with the specified initial capacity.
SortedList(IComparer* *comparer***)**	
SortedList(int *capacity***, IComparer*** *comparer***)**	Constructs a sorted list that uses the specified comparer. The optional *capacity* argument specifies the initial capacity of the list.
SortedList(IDictionary* *dictionary***)**	
SortedList(int *capacity***, IDictionary*** *dictionary***)**	Constructs a sorted list with the specified capacity by copying elements from the specified dictionary. The optional *capacity* argument specifies the initial capacity of the list.

Table 6.52 **SortedList** class properties (all virtual).

Get/Set	Type	Property	Description
Get/Set	**int**	**Capacity**	Gets or sets the number of elements the sorted list can contain.
Get	**int**	**Count**	Contains the number of elements in the sorted list.
Get	**bool**	**IsFixedSize**	Contains **true** if the **SortedList** is fixed-size (the default is **false**).
Get	**bool**	**IsReadOnly**	Contains **true** if the **SortedList** is read-only (the default is **false**).
Get	**bool**	**IsSynchronized**	Contains **true** if the **SortedList** is thread safe (the default is **false**).
Get/Set	**Object***	**Item(Object*** *Key***)**	Gets or sets a sorted list element identified by the specified key. If you specify a key that does not exist in the list when setting an item, a new key/value pair will be added to the collection.
Get	**ICollection***	**Keys**	Returns a collection of the sorted list keys.
Get	**Object***	**SyncRoot**	Returns a synchronization object for the sorted list.
Get	**ICollection***	**Values**	Returns a collection of the sorted list values.

Table 6.53 **SortedList** class methods.

Method	Description
virtual void Add(Object* *key***, Object*** *value***)**	Adds the specified key/value pair to the sorted list.
virtual void Clear()	Removes all elements from the sorted list.
virtual Object* Clone()	Creates a copy of the sorted list object.
virtual bool Contains(Object* *key***)**	Returns **true** if the sorted list contains an element with the specified key.
virtual bool ContainsKey(Object* *key***)**	Same as the **Contains** method
virtual bool ContainsValue(Object* *value***)**	Returns **true** if the sorted list contains an element with the specified value.
virtual void CopyTo(Array* *dest***, int** *index***)**	Copies all elements from the sorted list into the specified array starting at the index *index*.

<Continued on Next Page>

<Table 6.53 Continued>

Method	Description
virtual Object* GetByIndex(int *index*)	Returns the value of a sorted list element at the specified index.
virtual IDictionaryEnumerator* GetEnumerator()	Returns the dictionary enumerator for the sorted list object.
virtual Object* GetKey(int *index*)	Returns the key of a sorted list element at the specified index.
virtual IList* GetKeyList()	Returns a read-only list of the keys of the sorted list elements.
virtual IList* GetValues()	Returns a read-only list of the values of the sorted list elements.
virtual IEnumerator* IEnumerable::GetEnumerator()	Returns the enumerator for the sorted list object.
virtual int IndexOfKey(Object* *key*)	Returns the index of the sorted list element identified by the key.
virtual int IndexOfValue(Object* *value*)	Returns the index of the sorted list element identified by the value.
virtual void Remove(Object* *key*)	Removes the elements from the sorted list identified by the specified key.
virtual void RemoveAt(int *index*)	Removes an element from the sorted at the specified index.
virtual void SetByIndex(int *index*, Object* *value*)	Sets the sorted list element at the specified index to the specified value.
static SortedList* Synchronized(SortedList* *list*)	Returns a thread-safe version of the sorted list.
virtual void TrimToSize()	Releases extra memory by setting the sorted list capacity to match the number of elements in the list.

Hash Tables

Suppose that you have a collection of key/value pairs containing N elements. To find an element in the collection corresponding to a particular key, you could search the entire collection and compare the key of each element with the search key. This would require $O(N)$ operations. To make the search more efficient you could implement a hashing scheme. For each key in the table a unique integer in the range of $1..M$ $(M>N)$—hash value—could be calculated and placed in the table at the index corresponding to its hash value. Then, the key-lookup operation becomes trivial: You calculate the hash value of a search key and return an element of the table located at the calculated index (or Null if the corresponding slot in the table is empty). The key-lookup operation on a hash table requires $O(1)$ operations, roughly N-times faster (for sufficiently large N) than the ordinary lookup involving traversal of the entire table.

Calculating hash values involves devising a *hash function* capable of converting keys from a specified range into unique integers. Devising a good hash function can be difficult. On one hand, the range of hash values should not exceed the number of elements in the table so that we would not have to waist memory on empty table slots. On the other hand, it is not always possible to map all keys into unique integers. Thus, *collisions* may occur. If that happens, some hash table entries may contain more than one element. Nevertheless, the key-lookup operation remains very efficient: Calculate the hash value of a search key and check to see if the corresponding table entry contains more than one element. If it does, compare keys of all elements in the list with the search key and return the matching element. The number of operations for a key-lookup on a hash table involving collisions is greater than O(1) but still much less than O(N), if the N is sufficiently large.

In the .NET Framework a hashtable is a special case of dictionary where key/value pairs are stored in a direct address table and can be retrieved very efficiently using indices corresponding to hash values of their keys. This is illustrated in Figure 6.5.

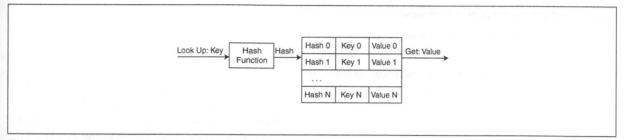

Figure 6.5 Hash table collection architecture.

Hashtable Class

The .NET Framework Class Library supports hash tables by means of the **Hashtable** class as shown here:

```
System::Object
|- System::Collections::Hashtable
```

Attributes: **Serializable**

Abstract: No

Sealed: No

Implements Interfaces: **IDictionary, ICollection, IEnumerable, ISerializable, IDeserializationCallback, ICloneable**

This class provides numerous constructors for initializing hash tables using various dictionary objects, hash code providers, and comparer interfaces. The class supplies a public **Item** indexer property for accessing hash table elements by key. The **Hashtable** class constructors, properties, and methods are summarized in Tables 6.54 through 6.56.

Table 6.54 **Hashtable** class constructors.

Constructor	Description
Hashtable()	Default constructor.
Hashtable(int *capacity*)	
Hashtable(int *capacity*, float *loadFactor*)	
Hashtable(int *capacity*, IHashCodeProvider* *provider*, IComparer* *comparer*)	
Hashtable(int *capacity*, float *loadFactor*, IHashCodeProvider* *provider*,IComparer* *comparer*)	Constructs a hash table with the specified initial capacity. Optional *loadFactor*, *provider,* and *comparer* arguments specify the hash table load factor (0.1 < *loadFactor* < 1.0), hash code provider and comparer objects.

<Continued on Next Page>

<Table 6.54 Continued>

Constructor	Description
Hashtable(IDictionary* *dict***)**	
Hashtable(IDictionary* *dict***, float** *loadFactor***)**	
Hashtable(IDictionary* *dict***, IHashCodeProvider*** *provider***,** **IComparer*** *comparer***)**	
Hashtable(IDictionary* *dict***, float** *loadFactor***, IHashCodeProvider*** *provider***, IComparer*** *comparer***)**	Constructs a hash table by copying elements of the specified dictionary. Optional *loadFactor*, *provider,* and *comparer* arguments specify the hash table load factor ($0.1 <$ *loadFactor* < 1.0), hash code provider and comparer objects.
Hashtable(IHashCodeProvider* *provider***, IComparer*** *comparer***)**	Constructs a hash table using the specified hash code provider and comparer interfaces.
Hashtable(SerializationInfo* *info***, StreamingContext** *context***)**	Constructs a hash table using the specified serialization information.

Hash Table Load Factor

The *hash table load factor* specifies the ratio of elements in a hash table to the number of slots. The load factor is applicable to hash tables utilizing imperfect hash functions that cannot map all the elements in the table into unique integers, thus producing collisions. In practice, most hash functions are imperfect.

Specifying the load factor provides means for selecting the tradeoff between memory consumption and lookup performance. In general, smaller load factors speed up hash table lookup by spreading hash table elements thin and reducing the number of collisions. (Most hash table slots will have a single element.) Larger load factors result in compact hash tables with slower look-ups due to the increased number of collisions (i.e., some hash table slots may contain more than one element).

Table 6.55 **Hashtable** class properties.

Get/Set	Type	Property	Virtual	Description
Get/Set	**IComparer***	**Comparer**	No	Gets or sets the comparer for the hash table.
Get	**int**	**Count**	Yes	Contains the number of elements in the hash table.
Get/Set	**IHashCodeProvider**	**hcp**	No	Gets or sets the hash code provider for the hash table.
Get	**bool**	**IsFixedSize**	Yes	Contains **true** if the hash table is fixed-size. (The default is **false**.)
Get	**bool**	**IsReadOnly**	Yes	Contains **true** if the hash table is read-only. (The default is **false**.)

<Continued on Next Page>

<Table 6.55 Continued>

Get/Set	Type	Property	Virtual	Description
Get	**bool**	**IsSynchronized**	Yes	Contains **true** if the hash table is thread-safe (The default is **false**.)
Get/Set	**String***	**Item(Object* *key*)**	Yes	Gets or sets a hash table element identified by the specified key. If you specify a key that does not exist in the hash table when setting an item, a new key/value pair will be added to the hash table.
Get	**ICollection***	**Keys**	Yes	Returns a collection of keys of the hash table.
Get	**Object***	**SyncRoot**	Yes	Returns a synchronization object for the hash table.
Get	**ICollection***	**Values**	Yes	Returns a collection of values of the hash table.

Table 6.56 **Hashtable** class methods.

Method	Description
virtual void Add(Object* *key*, Object* *value*)	Adds the specified key/value pair to the hash table.
virtual void Clear()	Removes all elements from the hash table.
virtual Object* Clone()	Creates a copy of the hash table.
virtual bool Contains(Object* *key*)	Returns **true** if the hash table contains an element with the specified key.
virtual bool ContainsKey(Object* *key*)	Same as the **Contains** method.
virtual bool ContainsValue(Object* *value*)	Returns **true** if the hash table contains an element with the specified value.
virtual void CopyTo(Array* *dest*, int *index*)	Copies all elements from the hash table into the specified array starting at the index *index*.
virtual IDictionaryEnumerator* GetEnumerator()	Returns the enumerator for the hash table.
protected: virtual int GetHash(Object* key)	Returns a hash of the specified key.
virtual void GetObjectData(SerializationInfo* *info*, StreamingContext *context*)	Retrieves the object data as required by the **ISerializable** interface.
virtual IEnumerator* IEnumerable::GetEnumerator()	Returns the enumerator for the hash table.
protected: virtual bool KeyEquals(Object* *element*, Object* *key*)	Returns **true** if the specified element is equal to the specified key. If the *element* implements the **IComparer** interface, it is used to compare the objects. Otherwise, **Object::Equals** is invoked to perform the comparison.
virtual void OnDeserialization(Object* *sender*)	Handles the object deserialization event.

<Continued on Next Page>

<Table 6.56 Continued>

Method	Description
virtual void Remove(Object* *key*)	Removes elements from the hash table identified by the specified key.
static Hashtable* Synchronized(Hashtable* *hashtable*)	Returns a thread-safe copy of the specified hash table.

*NOTE: The **Hashtable::Item** property does not allow you to distinguish whether the specified key does not exist in the hash table or whether the associated element simply contains a Null value. In both cases, the **Item** property returns Null. To check whether a particular key exists in a hash table, use the **Contains** or **ContainsKey** methods.*

Case-Insensitive Hash Code Provider

The **Hashtable** class requires a hash code provider for converting key values into hash values. The .NET Framework supplies a default hash code provider named **CaseInsensitiveHashCodeProvider** that generates hash codes based on string values:

```
System::Object
|- System::Collections::CaseInsensitiveHashCodeProvider
```

```
Attributes: Serializable
Abstract: No
Sealed: No
Implemented Interfaces: IHashCodeProvider
```

The **CaseInsensitiveHashCodeProvider** disregards case when comparing strings or generating hash code values. The class constructors, properties, and methods are listed in Tables 6.57 through 6.59.

Table 6.57 **CaseInsensitiveHashCodeProvider** class constructors.

Constructor	Description
CaseInsensitiveHashCodeProvider()	Default constructor.
CaseInsensitiveHashCodeProvider(CultureInfo* *cultureInfo*)	Constructs a case-insensitive hash code provider object using the specified culture information.

Table 6.58 **CaseInsensitiveHashCodeProvider** class properties.

Get/Set	Type	Property	Description
Get	**static CaseInsensitiveHashCodeProvider***	**Default**	Returns an always-available instance of the **CaseInsensitiveHashCodeProvider** class.

Table 6.59 **CaseInsensitiveHashCodeProvider** class methods.

Method	Description
__sealed int GetHashCode(Object* *obj*)	Generates a hash code for the specified object.

The **CaseInsensitiveHashCodeProvider** class supplies a single **GetHashCode** method that generates a hash code for a specified object. The method uses the supplied object's **ToString** method to obtain the string representation of the object value, which is used to calculate the hash code. In most cases, you will use the default instance of the **CaseInsensitiveHashCodeProvider** class provided by the **Default** property. But you can also create a new instance of the **CaseInsensitiveHashCodeProvider** and supply the desired culture information:

```
// Create a case insensitive hash code provider for Dutch language
Hashtable* hashtable = new Hashtable(10,
    new CaseInsensitiveHashCodeProvider(new CultureInfo("nl")),
    new CaseInsensitiveComparer(new CultureInfo("nl")));
```

Queues

As you know, queues are collections where individual elements are accessed based on the first-in/first-out principle as shown in Queue elements cannot be accessed randomly.

The .NET Framework implements LIFO queues by means of the **Queue** class as shown here:

```
System::Object
|- System::Collections::Queue
```

```
Attributes: Serializable
Abstract: No
Sealed: No
Implements Interfaces: ICollection, IEnumerable, ICloneable
```

The **Queue** class implements two basic operations on the queue—*enqueuing* and *dequeuing* elements by means of the **Enqueue** and **Dequeue** methods. Also, the **Queue** class provides the **Peek** method for retrieving the object at the beginning of the queue without dequeuing it. The **Queue** class constructors, properties, and methods are summarized in Tables 6.60 through 6.62.

Table 6.60 **Queue** class constructors.

Constructor	Description
Queue()	Default constructor
Queue(ICollection* *coll*)	Constructs a queue and initializes it by copying elements from the specified collection.
Queue(int *capacity*)	
Queue(int *capacity*, float *growBy*)	Constructs a queue with the specified initial capacity. The queue will grow automatically as you add more elements without dequeuing them. The queue will grow by the ***growBy*** * 100 percent (1 < ***growBy*** < 10).

Table 6.61 **Queue** class properties (all virtual).

Get/Set	Type	Property	Description
Get	**int**	**Count**	Returns the number of objects in the queue.
Get	**bool**	**IsSynchronized**	Returns **true** if the **Queue** is synchronized.
Get	**Object***	**SyncRoot**	Returns a synchronization object for the **Queue**.

Table 6.62 **Queue** class methods.

Method	Description
virtual void Clear()	Removes all elements from the queue.
virtual Object* Clone()	Creates a copy of the queue.
virtual void Contains(Object* *element*)	Returns **true** if the specified element is in the queue.
virtual void CopyTo(Array* *array*, int *index*)	Copies all dictionary elements to the specified array starting at the specified index. The destination array must be large enough to accommodate all dictionary entries or an exception will be thrown.
virtual Object* Dequeue()	Removes and returns an object at the beginning of the queue.
virtual void Enqueue(Object* *element*)	Places the specified element in the queue.
virtual IEnumerator* GetEnumerator()	Returns the enumerator for the queue.
virtual Object* Peek()	Returns an object at the beginning of the queue without removing it.
static Queue* Synchronized(Queue * *queue*)	Returns a thread-safe copy of the queue object.
virtual Object* ToArray() __gc[]	Returns an array of objects stored in the queue.
virtual void TrimToSize()	Releases extra memory by setting the queue capacity to match the number of elements in the queue.

*TIP: The **Queue** class provides a static **Synchronized** method for returning a thread-safe version of the queue object. You must use this method to obtain a thread-safe pointer to queue, which can be used for concurrent element enqueuing or dequeuing.*

Stacks

Stacks are collections where individual elements are accessed based on the last-in/first-out principle. Random access of stack elements is not allowed.

The .NET Framework implements FIFO stacks by means of the **Stack** class:

```
System::Object
|- System::Collections::Stack
```

```
Attributes: Serializable
Abstract: No
Sealed: No
Implements Interfaces: ICollection, IEnumerable, ICloneable
```

The **Stack** class supports two basic stack operations: *pushing* and *popping* objects, which are implemented as **Push** and **Pop** methods. As an added benefit, the **Stack** class allows you to retrieve the object at the top of stack without popping it by means of the **Peek** method. The complete summary of the **Stack** class constructors, properties, and methods is provided in Tables 6.63 through 6.65.

Table 6.63 **Stack** class constructors.

Constructors	Description
Stack()	Default constructor.
Stack(ICollection* *coll*)	Constructs a stack object and initializes it with elements of the specified collection.
Stack(int *capacity*)	Constructs a stack object with the specified initial capacity.

Table 6.64 **Stack** class properties (all virtual).

Get/Set	Type	Property	Description
Get	**int**	**Count**	Contains the number of elements in the stack.
Get	**bool**	**IsSynchronized**	Returns **true** if the stack is synchronized.
Get	**Object***	**SyncRoot**	Returns a synchronization object of the stack.

Table 6.65 **Stack** class methods.

Method	Description
virtual void Clear()	Removes all elements from the stack.
virtual Object* Clone()	Creates a copy of the stack object.
virtual void Contains(Object* *element*)	Returns **true** if the specified element is in the stack.
virtual void CopyTo(Array* *array*, int *index*)	
virtual IEnumerator* GetEnumerator()	Returns the enumerator for the **Stack**.
virtual Object* Peek()	Returns an object at the top of the stack without popping it.
virtual Object* Pop()	Returns an object at the top of the stack by popping it.
virtual void Push(Object* *element*)	Pushes the specified object into the **Stack**.
static Stack* Synchronized(Stack* *stack*)	Returns a thread-safe copy of the **Stack** object.
virtual Object* ToArray() __gc[]	Returns an array of objects stored in the **Stack**.

CollectionsUtil Class

As an added benefit the **System::Collections::Specialized** namespace provides an additional class called **CollectionsUtil** that is not really a collection. The **CollectionsUtil** class has no constructors and contains static-only members for quick and easy instantiation of **Hashtable** and **SortedList** objects. This is the only function of this utility class. The **CollectionsUtil** class inheritance diagram is as follows:

```
System::Object
|- System::Collections::Specialized::CollectionsUtil
```

```
Attributes: None
Abstract: No
Sealed: No
Implemented Interfaces: None
```

The **CollectionsUtil** class methods are listed in Table 6.66.

Table 6.66 **CollectionsUtil** class methods.

Method	Description
static Hashtable* CreateCaseInsensitiveHashtable()	Creates a case-insensitive hash table collection.
static Hashtable* CreateCaseInsensitiveHashtable(IDictionary* *dict*)	Converts the specified dictionary into a case-insensitive hash table.
static Hashtable* CreateCaseInsensitiveHashtable(int *capacity*)	Creates a case-insensitive hash table with the specified capacity.
static SortedList* CreateCaseInsensitiveSortedList()	Creates a case-insensitive **SortedList** collection.

BitArray class

Bit fields in integer variables are often used to represent status flags or error codes. The .NET Framework Class Library implements variable length bit fields by means of the **BitArray** class as shown here:

```
System::Object
|- System::Collections::BitArray
```

```
Attributes: Serializable
Abstract: No
Sealed: Yes
Implemented Interfaces: ICollection, IEnumerable, IClonable
```

The **BitArray** class is different than the **ArrayList** in the sense that you cannot add or remove elements from a bit array by calling **Add/Remove** methods. Instead the **BitArray** class supports the **Length** property, which can be used to get or set the number of bits a bit array can hold. The **BitArray** class supports the following common operations:

*   *Setting bit values*: **Set/SetAll** methods.
*   *Performing bitwise logical operations*: **And**, **Not**, **Or**, and **Xor** methods.

The **BitArray** class constructors, properties, and methods are summarized in Tables 6.67 through 6.69.

Table 6.67 **BitArray** class constructors.

Constructor	Description
BitArray(BitArray* *bitArray*)	Copy constructor.
BitArray(bool __gc[] *values*)	
BitArray(int __gc[] *values*)	
BitArray(unsigned char __gc[] *values*)	Constructs a bit array by copying bits from the specified array of Boolean, integer, or byte values.
BitArray(int *length*)	
BitArray(int *length*, bool *defaultValue*)	Constructs a bit array containing the *length* bits. Optional *defaultValue* argument allows initializing array bits with zeros (**false**) or ones (**true**).

Table 6.68 **BitArray** class properties.

Get/Set	Type	Property	Description
Get	**int**	**Count**	Contains the number of bits in the **BitArray**.
Get	**bool**	**IsReadOnly**	Always returns **false**.
Get	**bool**	**IsSynchronized**	Always returns **false**.
Get/Set	**bool**	**Item(int *index*)**	Gets or sets a bit at the specified index.
Get/Set	**int**	**Length**	Gets or sets the number of bits in the array (similar to **Count**).
Get	**Object***	**SyncRoot**	Returns the synchronization object for the **BitArray**.

Table 6.69 **BitArray** class methods.

Member	Description
BitArray* And(BitArray* *array*)	Creates a new bit array by performing logical AND operation on the bits of the current bit array and the bits of the specified bit array.
__sealed Object* Clone()	Creates a shallow copy of the **BitArray**.
__sealed void CopyTo(Array* *array*, int *index*)	Copies all elements of the **BitArray** into the specified array starting at the index *index*.
bool Get(int *index*)	Returns a bit at the specified index.
__sealed IEnumerator* GetEnumerator()	Returns an enumerator object for the **BitArray**.

<Continued on Next Page>

<Table 6.69 Continued>

Member	Description
BitArray* Not()	Creates a new bit array by inverting the bits (i.e., logical NOT) of the current bit array.
BitArray* Or(BitArray* *array*)	Creates a new bit array by performing a logical OR operation on the bits of the current bit array and the bits of the specified array.
void Set(int *index* bool *value*)	Sets a bit array bit at the specified index.
void SetAll(bool *value*)	Sets all bits in the bit array to the specified value.
BitArray* Xor(BitArray* *array*)	Creates a new bit array by performing a logical XOR operation on the bits of the current bit array and the bits of the specified array.

Arrays of 32-bit

While the **BitArray** class provides great versatility, using it for most purposes is overkill. Fortunately, the .NET Framework Class Library provides a more efficient bit array implementation: the **BitVector32** class. This class represents a collection of bits packed in a 32-bit integer. Unlike the **BitArray** class, **BitVector32** is a fixed-size value type:

```
System::Object
|- System::ValueType
   |- System::Collections::Specialized::BitVector32

Attributes: None
Abstract: No
Sealed: No
Implemented Interfaces: None
```

The **BitVector32** class supplies two **Item** indexer properties for setting or getting values of individual bits and values of groups of bits in the bit array (i.e., *bit sections*). The **BitVector32** class constructors, properties, and methods are summarized in Tables 6.70 through 6.72.

Table 6.70 **BitVector32** value type constructors.

Constructor	Description
BitVector32(BitVector32 *value*)	Copy constructor.
BitVector32(int *value*)	Constructs a **BitVector32** object using the specified 32-bit integer.

Table 6.71 **BitVector32** value type properties.

Get/Set	Type	Property	Description
Get	int	**Data**	Returns a 32-bit integer representation of the **BitVector32** object.
Get/Set	int	**Item(BitVector32::Section *section*)**	Gets or sets a subset of bits in the **BitVector32** object.
Get/Set	bool	**Item(int *bit*)**	Gets or sets a specified bit in the bit array.

Table 6.72 **BitVector32** class methods.

Method	Description
static int CreateMask()	Creates a mask for isolating the first bit in the **BitVector32** object. The method will always return 1 on little-endian systems.
static int CreateMask(int *previous*)	Creates a mask for isolating the next bit in the **BitVector32** object. The *previous* parameter must specify a mask isolating the previous bit of the **BitVector32**.
static Section CreateSection(short *maxValue*)	Creates the first **BitVector32::Section** window into the **BitVector32** object. The number of bits in the section is determined based off the *maxValue* parameter. Note that there must be enough bits in the section to represent the specified *maxValue*.
static Section CreateSection(short *maxValue*, BitVector32::Section *previous*)	Creates the next **BitVector32::Section** window into the **BitVector32** object. The *previous* parameter must specify a previous section.
static String* ToString(BitVector32 *value*)	Converts the specified **BitVector32** value into a string representation.

*NOTE: The **CreateMask** method represents an architecture-independent way of isolating a particular bit in a **BitVector32** object by taking into account little-endian or big-endian architecture of the target system.*

Bit Sections

Bit flags in status words are frequently grouped in sections. To represent a section encompassing a number of consecutive bits, the .NET Framework provides a **BitVector32::Section** value type:

```
System::Object
|- System::ValueType
   |- System::Collections::Specialized::BitVector32::Section

Attributes: None
Abstract: No
Sealed: No
Implemented Interfaces: None
```

The main purpose of the **BitVector32::Section** class is to serve as a key into the **BitVector32** collection. Rather than accessing bits in a **BitVector32** object individually, you can create a **BitVector32::Section** object corresponding to a block of consecutive bits and get or set the value of the bit block easily using the **BitVector32::Item** indexer property. The **BitVector32::Section** class properties and methods are listed in Tables 6.73 and 6.74.

Table 6.73 **BitVector32::Section** value type properties.

Get/Set	Type	Property	Description
Get	**short**	**Mask**	Contains the mask isolating the bit section.
Get	**short**	**Offset**	Contains the offset from the beginning of the bit vector where the bit section begins.

Table 6.74 **BitVector32::Section** value type methods.

Method	Description
static String* ToString(BitVector32::Section *value*)	Converts the specified **BitVector32::Section** value into a string representation.

Immediate Solutions

Creating Dynamic Arrays, Adding and Removing Elements

All **__gc** arrays are implicitly derived from the **Array** class that represents a fixed-size collection. If you want to create an array that can grow or shrink in size, you should instantiate a dynamic array object represented by the **ArrayList** class and invoke the **Add** and **Remove** methods to add or remove elements from the dynamic array.

The code example shown next illustrates how to use the **ArrayList** class to create a simple dynamic array. The code performs the following steps:

1. Creates an **ArrayList** object with an initial capacity of 10 elements using the **ArrayList** constructor.

2. Adds elements to the dynamic array using the **Add** method.

3. Inserts new elements into the dynamic array at index 0 using the **Insert** method.

4. Accesses the dynamic array elements using the **Item** indexer property.

5. Removes the element at index 1 from the dynamic array using the **RemoveAt** method (the array size shrinks by one element).

6. Removes element '2' from the dynamic array using the **Remove** method (the array size shrinks by one element). Note that the integer element '2' is boxed when supplied to the **Remove** method: Unlike fixed-size arrays dynamic arrays can store only **__gc** objects represented by **__gc** pointers, hence all primitive types stored in a dynamic array *must* be boxed.

7. Prints the dynamic array contents.

8.   Removes all elements from the dynamic array using the **Clear** method.

```
#using <mscorlib.dll>
using namespace System;
using namespace System::Collections;


void main()
{
    // 1. Create an ArrayList
    ArrayList* myArray = new ArrayList(10);
    // 2. Add elements to the ArrayList
    for ( int i = 0; i < myArray->Capacity; i++ )
        myArray->Add( __box(10 - i));

    // 3. Inserts new element at index 0
    myArray->Insert(0, __box(33));

    // 4. Output element #0
    Console::WriteLine("myArray[0]={0}", myArray->Item[0]);

    // 5. Remove the element #1 from the ArrayList
    myArray->RemoveAt(1);

    // 6. Remove the element '2' from the ArrayList
    myArray->Remove( __box(2));

    // 7. Output the ArrayList
    for ( int i = 0; i < myArray->Count; i++ )
        Console::WriteLine(myArray->Item[i]);

    // 8. Removes all elements from the ArrayList
    myArray->Clear();
}
```

The code example above calls the **Insert**, **Remove,** and **RemoveAt** methods implemented by the **ArrayList** class as prescribed by the **IList** interface. Although ordinary fixed-size **__gc** arrays implement the same **IList** interface, all **IList** methods intended for adding or removing array elements throw the **NotSupportedException** exception when called on a fixed-size array object.

> **NOTE:** Unlike fixed-size arrays represented by the **Array** class, dynamic arrays and the **ArrayList** class do not support the [] operator. Thus one *must* use the **ArrayList::Item** property to access the dynamic array elements.

Converting Between Dynamic and Fixed Arrays

Fixed-size **__gc** arrays are more common throughout the .NET Framework than dynamic **ArrayList** arrays. While the fixed-size **__gc** arrays are simple and efficient, dynamic arrays are more powerful and more convenient to work with. Fortunately, the .NET Framework Class Library allows converting between dynamic and fixed-size array and back.

The easiest way to convert a fixed size array into a dynamic array is to pass the fixed-size array as an explicitly qualified **IList** pointer to the **ArrayList** constructor (see Table 6.11).

To convert a dynamic array into a fixed-size __gc array one should invoke the **ArrayList::ToArray** method or cop the dynamic array elements into an existing fixed-size array using the **ArrayList::CopyTo** method.

The code example shown next illustrates the above techniques by performing these steps:

1. Instantiate fixed-size array of ints using the __**gc new** operator.

2. Convert the fixed-size array into a dynamic array by instantiating an **ArrayList** object using the fixed-size array as a parameter to the **ArrayList** constructor. The fixed-size array has to be explicitly cast to the **ICollection** pointer when supplied as a parameter to the **ArrayList** constructor.

3. Alternatively, the fixed-size array elements can be added into an existing dynamic array using the **AddRange** method as demonstrated in Step 4.

4. Add a new element to the dynamic array using **Add** method.

5. Convert the dynamic array into a fixed array using the **ToArray** method. Since the **ToArray** method returns a generic **Array** pointer, the method return value must be explicitly cast into a desired fixed-size __gc array type. Moreover, the desired __gc array type *must* be specified as a __**typeof** parameter to the **ToArray** method and match the type involved in the explicit method return value casting. If the two types are incompatible the resulting __gc array pointer will be Null.

6. Allocate a new __gc array of ints for storing dynamic array elements.

7. Copies dynamic array elements into the newly allocated __gc array using the **CopyTo** method. The destination __gc array must be large enough to hold the number of dynamic array elements specified as a parameter to the **CopyTo** method, otherwise the **ArgumentException** will occur.

```
#using <mscorlib.dll>
using namespace System;
using namespace System::Collections;

void main()
{
    // 1. Instantiate fixed array
    int FixedArray __gc[] = new int __gc[10];

    // 2. Initializes ArrayList from Array
    ArrayList* DynamicArray = new
        ArrayList(dynamic_cast<ICollection*>(FixedArray));

    DynamicArray->Clear();
    // 3. Alternatively, initialize by copying fixed-size array elements
    DynamicArray->AddRange(dynamic_cast<ICollection*>(FixedArray));

    // 4. Add new element
    DynamicArray->Add(__box(12));
```

```
    // 5. Convert back, now FixedArray has 10+1 = 11 elements
    FixedArray = dynamic_cast<int __gc[]>(DynamicArray->ToArray(__typeof(int)));

    // 6. Allocate new array for  holding dynamic array elements
    int NewArray __gc[] = new int __gc[DynamicArray->Count];
    // 7. Copy elements from dynamic array to fixed array
    DynamicArray->CopyTo(0, NewArray, 0, DynamicArray->Count);
}
```

Resizing Fixed-Size Arrays

Dynamic arrays can be used to resize fixed-size arrays. To achieve the goal, one can initialize a dynamic array with a pointer to a fixed-size array, use the **ArrayList** methods to add or remove array elements, and convert the dynamic array back to fixed-size using the **ArrayList::ToArray** method. This approach is illustrated by the **GrowByOne** helper function presented in the solution below:

```
#using <mscorlib.dll>
using namespace System;
using namespace System::Collections;

// Increases the size of a fixed array by one element
int GrowByOne(int SrcArray __gc[], int NewElement) __gc[]
{
    ArrayList* DestArray = new ArrayList(dynamic_cast<ICollection*>(SrcArray));
    DestArray->Add(__box(NewElement));
    return dynamic_cast<int __gc[]>(DestArray->ToArray(__typeof(int)));
}

void main()
{
    // 1. Instantiate fixed array
    int FixedArray __gc[] = new int __gc[10];

    // 2. Grow fixed-array by one element
    FixedArray = GrowByOne(FixedArray, 12);
}
```

In the **main** routine the **GrowByOne** helper function is called to insert an additional element in the fixed-size array of ints. It is worth pointing out that the original fixed-size array is not actually modified: The **GrowByOne** function in fact creates a new array containing all the original fixed-size array elements plus an extra one. Thus, you should resort to such practice sparingly to avoid excessive memory fragmentation and reduced performance due to increased time required for garbage collecting the unused original instances of fixed-size arrays.

Locating Dynamic Array Elements

Dynamic arrays provide ample means for locating array elements. **IndexOf** and **LastIndexOf** methods allow locating first and last occurrences of a specified element in the array. Similarly, the **Contains** method allows verifying whether a specified element is contained in the array.

To practice locating dynamic array elements consider the following simple code example, which performs the following actions:

1. Creates and initializes an **ArrayList** object with boxed integer values descending from 10 to 1.

2. Verifies that the array contains integer element '9' by means of the **Contains** method. As usual, the integer must be before it can be supplied as parameter to the **Contains** method. For improved performance the code creates a boxed instance of the element '9' to avoid redundant boxing later in the code.

3. Retrieves the index of the first occurrence of the element '9' in the dynamic array using the **IndexOf** method. If the specified element is not found the **IndexOf** method returns -1.

```
#using <mscorlib.dll>
using namespace System;
using namespace System::Collections;

void main()
{
    // 1. Create and Initialize ArrayList
    ArrayList* myArray = new ArrayList(10);
    for ( int i = 0; i < myArray->Capacity; i++ )
        myArray->Add(__box(10 - i));

    Object* myElement = __box(9);

    // 2. Lookup element '9'
    if ( myArray->Contains(myElement) )
        Console::WriteLine("myArray contains element=9");
    else
        Console::WriteLine("myArray does not contain element=9");

    // 3. Retrieve index of element '9'
    int index = myArray->IndexOf(myElement);
    if ( index > -1 )
        Console::WriteLine("Index of the element=9 is {0}", __box(index));
}
```

Sorting and Searching Sorted Dynamic Arrays

Dynamic arrays implemented as instances of the **ArrayList** class support sorting and searching by means of the **Sort** and **BinarySearch** methods. The **BinarySearch** method can be used for fast searching of sorted arrays. The binary search requires only $O(\log_2(N))$ operations, where N represents the number of elements in the array. You can compare this to ordinary linear searches which work on both sorted and unsorted arrays but require O(N) operations. The binary search algorithm is considerably more efficient than a linear search and it should be used on large *sorted* arrays (the **BinarySearch** method has no effect when the array is unsorted). The code example shown next shows you how to use the **ArrayList** to sort and search and array. The actual steps performed include:

1. Create and initializes an **ArrayList** object with a sample set of city names.

2. Sort the array by means of the **Sort** method using the default case-insensitive comparer object (**CaseInsensitiveComparer::Default**).

3. Perform binary search on the sorted array using the **BinarySearch** method.

4. Perform case-sensitive binary search using the **BinarySearch** method with the **CaseInsensitiveComparer**.

```
#using <mscorlib.dll>
using namespace System;
using namespace System::Collections;

void main()
{
    // 1. Initialize ArrayList
    ArrayList* myArray = new ArrayList(10);
    myArray->Add(S"Smolensk");
    myArray->Add(S"Moscow");
    myArray->Add(S"Zelenograd");
    myArray->Add(S"Tulsa");

    // 2. The array must be sorted in order for the BinarySearch method to work
    myArray->Sort(CaseInsensitiveComparer::Default);
    for ( int i = 0; i < myArray->Count; i++ )
        Console::WriteLine(myArray->Item[i]);

    // 3. Search
    int index = myArray->BinarySearch(S"SMOLENSK");
    if ( index < 0 )
    {
        // 4. Case-sensitive binary search
        index = myArray->BinarySearch(S"SMOLENSK",
            CaseInsensitiveComparer::Default);
        if ( index > -1 )
            Console::WriteLine("SMOLENSK is found at index {0}", __box(index));
    }
}
```

WARNING! The **BinarySearch** method fails to locate an array element if the array is not sorted. For instance, if you comment out the **Sort** statement in the code example above, the **BinarySearch** method will fail to retrieve the index of "SMOLENSK" element. However, the **BinarySearch** method *may* work if the array is partially organized. The success of a binary search is based on the assumption the source data is properly organized, and the **BinarySearch** method makes no checks to verify that the array is indeed sorted.

Deriving Custom Collection Classes

You should derive your own class from the **CollectionBase** class to implement a custom collection class. To understand how to use the **CollectionBase** class, consider the following code example that shows how to derive a new collection class from the **CollectionBase**. The code also shows you how to implement the **OnInsert** and **OnSet** collection event handlers to prohibit inserting elements other than **int** and setting existing collection elements to values of type other than **int**:

```cpp
#using <mscorlib.dll>
using namespace System;
using namespace System::Collections;

// Instantiate a class from CollectionBase
__gc class MyColl: public CollectionBase {
public:
    MyColl() : CollectionBase() {}
    void Set(int Index, Object* value)
    {
        List->Item[Index] = value;
    }
    void InnerSet(int Index, Object* value)
    {
        InnerList->Item[Index] = value;
    }
    virtual void OnInsert(int index, Object* element)
    {
        if ( element->GetType() != __typeof(int) )
            throw new Exception("Only integers allowed!");
    }
    virtual void OnSet(int index, Object* oldElement, Object* newElement)
    {
        if ( newElement->GetType() != __typeof(int) )
            throw new Exception("Only integers allowed!");
    }
    // Prevent ints < 10 from being added into collection
    virtual void OnValidate(Object* element)
    {
        if ( element->GetType() == __typeof(int) &&
            *dynamic_cast<__box int*>(element) < 10 )
            throw new Exception("Integers less than 10 are not allowed!");
    }
};

void main()
{
    // Create two arrays of 16 bits each
```

```
MyColl* myColl = new MyColl();
myColl->Add(__box(20));
myColl->Add(__box(30));
Console::WriteLine("{0} elements in the collection", __box(myColl->Count));

// Will throw an exception
try {
    myColl->Add(new String("test"));
}
catch(Exception* e) {
    Console::WriteLine(e);
}
// Will throw an exception
try {
    myColl->Set(0, new String("test"));
}
catch(Exception* e) {
    Console::WriteLine(e);
}
// Will not throw an exception
myColl->InnerSet(0, new String("test"));
// Will throw an exception
try {
    myColl->Add(__box(9));
}
catch(Exception* e) {
    Console::WriteLine(e);
}
myColl->Add(__box(11));

// Enumerate collection elements
IEnumerator* enumerator = myColl->GetEnumerator();
while ( enumerator->MoveNext() )
    Console::WriteLine(enumerator->Current);
}
```

The **MyColl** class is derived from the **CollectionBase**. It supplies two methods for setting collection elements: **Set** and **InnerSet**. The **Set** method uses the **List** property for setting the collection elements. When you use the method, the **OnSet** notification method will be called. The **InnerSet** method, on the other hand, uses the **InnerList** property. When you use this method, no notification will be generated.

The **MyColl** class overrides the **OnSet** and **OnValidate** methods for enforcing type safety and performing custom validation. Both methods throw an exception if the inserted element has the type other than **int**. Also, the **OnValidate** method throws an exception if the inserted integer has a value greater than 10.

The main program that follows the **MyColl** class definition demonstrates how you can add elements to the collection using the **Add** method and set the element values using the **Set/InnerSet** methods. When the **Add** method is invoked, the **OnValidate** handler is fired to perform type and value validation. When the **Set** method is called, the **OnSet** method is fired to perform type validation. The **InsertSet** method, however, bypasses all validation and type checking and successfully adds **String** value to the integer collection.

Working with String Collections

To implement a collection of strings, you can instantiate a **StringCollection** object. Then, you can add elements to the collection using the **Add** method and enumerate the strings using the **IStringEnumerator** class. The code example shown next demonstrates how to:

1. Create a collection of strings using the **StringCollection** constructor.

2. Add strings to the collection using the **Add** method.

3. Insert a string at the beginning of the collection using the **Insert** method.

4. Forward-navigate the collection strings using the **IStringEnumerator** interface. While the **MoveNext** method returns **true**, the current element is accessed using the **Current** enumerator property.

```
#using <mscorlib.dll>
#using <system.dll>
using namespace System;
using namespace System::Collections::Specialized;


void main()
{
    // 1. Create a collection of strings
    StringCollection* myColl = new StringCollection();
    // 2. Add strings to the collection
    myColl->Add(S"Resurrection");
    myColl->Add(S"Techno/Classical");
    // 3. Insert a strings at the beginning of the collection
    myColl->Insert(0, S"UltraMax Music");
    // 4. Enumerate strings in the collection
    IStringEnumerator* enumerator = myColl->GetEnumerator();
    while ( enumerator->MoveNext() )
        Console::WriteLine(enumerator->Current);
}
```

> **NOTE:** When navigating collections using the **IEnumerator** interface or **StringEnumerator** class, one should remember to call the enumerator's **MoveNext** method prior to accessing the enumerator's **Current** property. This may seem counter-intuitive to database application developers, which are accustomed to working with ADO record sets. Unlike opening ADO record set, the .NET Framework enumerator interface does not automatically fetch the first collection element into the **Current** property when the enumerator is created.

Using Collections of Sorted Name/Value Pairs

To use a collection of string/value pairs, you must derive your own class from the **NameObjectCollectionBase**. To do this, you should provide public **Add**, **Set**, **GetByIndex**, **GetByName**, and, perhaps, other methods to ensure the type safety if the collection is strongly typed. The code example shown next demonstrates a derivation of the **MyColl** collection class corresponding to a generic loosely typed collection. The **MyColl** class supplies the **Add**, **Set**, **GetByIndex**, and **GetByName** methods that simply invoke the protected base class methods **BaseAdd**, **BaseSet**, and **BaseGet**. The main program illustrates how to use the name/value collection and performs these actions:

1. Creates the custom collection using the default constructor.
2. Adds initial data to the collection using the **Add** method.
3. Sets the element value by name using the **Set** method.
4. Retrieves the element value by index using the **GetByIndex** method.
5. Looks up the element value by name using the **GetByName** method.
6. Copies the collection of keys into an array using the **GetAllKeys** method.

```
#using <mscorlib.dll>
#using <system.dll>
using namespace System;
using namespace System::Collections::Specialized;

__gc class MyColl: public NameObjectCollectionBase {
public:
    MyColl() : NameObjectCollectionBase() {}
    void Add(String* name, Object* value)
    {
        BaseAdd(name, value);
    }
    void Set(String* name, Object* value)
    {
        BaseSet(name, value);
    }
    Object* GetByIndex(int index)
    {
        return BaseGet(index);
    }
    Object* GetByName(String* name)
    {
        return BaseGet(name);
    }
};


void main()
{
    // 1. Create a collection of name/value pairs
    MyColl* myColl = new MyColl();
    // 2. Add name/value pairs to the collection
    myColl->Add("Alaska", __box(1));
    myColl->Add("Oklahoma", __box(2));
```

```
myColl->Add("Arizona", __box(3));
// 3. Sets the new value for "Oklahoma"
myColl->Set("Oklahoma", __box(20));
// 4. Retrieve the value by index
Console::WriteLine(myColl->GetByIndex(0));
// 5. Lookup by the value name (key)
Console::WriteLine(myColl->GetByName("Oklahoma"));

// 6. Retrieve names as an array of strings
String* keyArray __gc[] = myColl->GetAllKeys();
}
```

Creating String Lookup Collections

You should use the .NET **NameValueCollection** specialized collection, to implement a string look-up table that is similar to the MFC **CMapStringToString** class. The following code example shows how to use the **NameValueCollection** class to perform these steps:

1. Create a **NameValueCollection** object with initial capacity of 10 elements using the constructor.

2. Add **String/String** pairs to the collection using the **Add** method.

3. Retrieve values (i.e., conducts look up) from the collection by index and by name using the **Get** method, and by name using the **Item** property.

4. Retrieve the key value using the **GetKey** method.

5. Set the new element value using the **Set** method and the **Item** property.

6. Add a new name/value pair to the collection by using the **Item** property and supplying the key that is not found in the collection. (The **Item** property adds new key/value pairs automatically.)

```
#using <mscorlib.dll>
#using <system.dll>
using namespace System;
using namespace System::Collections;
using namespace System::Collections::Specialized;


void main()
{
    // 1. Create a collection of name/value pairs
    NameValueCollection* myColl = new NameValueCollection(10);
    // 2. Add elements to the collection
    myColl->Add(S"Gems 3D", S"Cool");
    myColl->Add(S"Jumbo Gems", S"Nice");
    myColl->Add(S"Gem Master", S"Sweet");

    // 3. Retrieve values
    Console::WriteLine("Jumbo Gems is {0}", myColl->Get(1));
    Console::WriteLine("Gem Master is {0}", myColl->Get(S"Gems Master"));
    Console::WriteLine("Gems 3D is {0}", myColl->Item[S"Gems 3D"]);
```

```
    // 4. Retrieve key
    Console::WriteLine(myColl->GetKey(0));

    // 5. Set values
    myColl->Set(S"Gems 3D", S"The coolest ever");
    myColl->Item[S"Gem Master"] = S"Not that cool";
    // 6. Add new key/value pair to the collection
    myColl->Item[S"Quake"] = S"Rated R";
}
```

Creating Custom Comparer Objects

The .NET Framework supplies the **CaseInsensitiveComparer** class for performing case-insensitive comparisons of string representations of objects. When the comparison of object string representations implicitly obtained using the **ToString** method cannot yield acceptable results, you should implement a custom comparer class tailored to compare objects of a particular type. To be able to use the custom comparer class with standard sorted collections, such as **SortedList**, the custom comparer class must implement the **IComparer** interface.

To illustrate custom object comparison consider the following situation: You have a class named **Age** containing the number of years and month. To sort objects of type **Age,** you must compare both year and month portions of the age. To implement the comparison, you can define a custom **AgeComparer** class as follows:

```
#using <mscorlib.dll>
using namespace System;
using namespace System::Collections;

// Age object
__gc struct Age {
    Age(int years, int month)
    {
        Years = years;
        Months = month;
    }
    String* ToString()
    {
        return String::Concat(Years.ToString(), S" years, ",
            Months.ToString(), S" months");
    }
    int Years, Months;
};

// Age compare
__gc class AgeComparer: public IComparer {
```

```
    int Compare(Object* x, Object* y)
    {
        Age* age1 = __try_cast<Age*>(x);
        Age* age2 = __try_cast<Age*>(y);
        if ( age1->Years > age2->Years ||
            age1->Years == age2->Years && age1->Months > age2->Months )
            return 1;
        if ( age1->Years == age2->Years && age1->Months == age2->Months )
            return 0;
        else
            return -1;
    }
};

void main()
{
    // 1. Create a sorted list
    SortedList* list = new SortedList(new AgeComparer());
    // 2. Add elements that will be automatically ordered
    list->Add(new Age(26, 6), S"Max");
    list->Add(new Age(25, 11), S"Veronica");
    list->Add(new Age(3, 2), S"Vlad");

    // 3. Retrieve values from the sorted order
    for ( int i = 0; i < list->Count; i++ )
        Console::WriteLine("{0,20} : {1}", list->GetKey(i),list->GetByIndex(i));
}
```

The **AgeComparer** class implements the **IComparer** interface and provides the **Compare** method, which returns 0 when the two **Age** objects are equal. It returns 1 if the first age is greater than the second age and returns -1 otherwise. The method performs type checking using the **__try_cast** operator and throws an exception if one attempts to compare objects of a type other than **Age**.

Working with Dictionaries

The .NET Framework does not supply a concrete class for a loosely typed dictionary. To use dictionaries in your code, you must derive your own class from the **DictionaryBase** class. Fortunately, to create a concrete loosely typed dictionary implementation it is sufficient to write a very basic wrapper around the **DictionaryBase** without overriding any methods. The code example shown next illustrates how to derive a custom loosely typed dictionary class from the **DictionaryBase**. The code also shows the basic techniques involved for working with dictionaries in general. The code performs the following actions:

1.   Derives a custom dictionary class named **MyDictionary** from the **DictionaryBase**.
2.   Instantiates a **MyDictionary** object using the default constructor.
3.   Adds elements to the dictionary.

4.　　　Conducts element lookup by name using the **Item** property.

5.　　　Copies the dictionary **Keys** collection into the **keys**.

6.　　　Copies the dictionary **Values** collection into the **values**.

7.　　　Enumerates dictionary entries using the **IDictionaryEnumerator** interface.

```cpp
#using <mscorlib.dll>
using namespace System;
using namespace System::Collections;
// 1. Derive custom dictionary
__gc class MyDictionary: public DictionaryBase {
public:
   MyDictionary() : DictionaryBase() {}
};

void main()
{
   // 2. Instantiate custom dictionary object
   MyDictionary* dict = new MyDictionary();
   // 3. Add elements
   dict->Add(S"OK", S"Oklahoma");
   dict->Add(S"TX", S"Texas");
   dict->Add(S"DM", S"Depeche Mode");
   // 4. Lookup value by name
   Object* Value = dict->Item[S"TX"];

   String* keys __gc[] = new String*[10];
   // 5. Extract keys (the target array must be large enough)
   dict->Keys->CopyTo(keys, 0);

   String* values __gc[] = new String*[10];
   // 6. Extract values (the target array must be large enough)
   dict->Values->CopyTo(values, 0);

   // 7. Enumerate dictionary entries
   IDictionaryEnumerator* enumerator = dict->GetEnumerator();
   while ( enumerator->MoveNext() )
      Console::WriteLine("{0} : {1}", enumerator->Entry.Key,
         enumerator->Entry.Value);
}
```

> **NOTE:** The **DictionaryBase** class does not ensure type safety. Thus, there is nothing in the **DictionaryBase** class stopping you from adding values of different types to the dictionary. To ensure type safety of the dictionary, you must override the **DictionaryBase**::**On**XYZ methods to implement custom type verification. The simplest way to ensure type safety is to use the **__try_cast** operator when casting the **DictionaryBase**::**On**XYZ method parameters.

Using String Dictionaries

The .NET Framework supplies the concrete dictionary class named **StringDictionary**, which supports name/value pairs expressed by **String** objects. You can use this class in the same way that you use the **NameValueCollection** class except that in the case of the **StringDictionary**, both the key and the value must be of type **String**. The following code example shows how to set up a string dictionary and perform the following steps:

1. Create a **StringDictionary** object using the default constructor.

2. Add key/value strings to the dictionary using the **Add** method.

3. Conduct case-insensitive lookup using the **Contains** method.

4. Retrieve the dictionary value by name using the **Item** property.

```
#using <mscorlib.dll>
using namespace System;
using namespace System::Collections::Specialized;

void main()
{
    // 1. Create a string dictionary
    StringDictionary* dict = new StringDictionary();
    // 2. Add key/value pairs to the dictionary
    dict->Add(S"OK", S"Oklahoma");
    dict->Add(S"TX", S"Texas");
    dict->Add(S"DM", S"Depeche Mode");
    // 3. Conduct case-insensitive lookup
    if ( dict->Contains(S"ok") )
        // 4. Retrieve the element value by name
        Console::WriteLine(dict->Item[S"ok"]);
}
```

Using Sorted Lists

To maintain automatically sorted lists of name/value pairs, you should use the **SortedList** class. The following code example shows how to use the **SortedList** class to perform these operations.

1. The **SortedList** class is created using the default constructor.

2. Name/value pairs are added to the list using the **Add** method. The elements are sorted as they are added.

3. The sorted list is navigated by iterating through all elements and retrieving element keys and values by index using the **GetKey/GetByIndex** methods.

```
#using <mscorlib.dll>
using namespace System;
using namespace System::Collections;

void main()
```

```
{
    // 1. Create a sorted list
    SortedList* list = new SortedList();
    // 2. Add elements to the sorted list
    list->Add(S"EnTrance", S"Melodic Trance");
    list->Add(S"Asteroid", S"Acid Techno");
    list->Add(S"Good Life", S"Mood Music");
    list->Add(S"Consequential", S"Symphonic Electronica");

    // 3. Retrieve values from the sorted list
    for ( int i = 0; i < list->Count; i++ )
        Console::WriteLine("{0,15} : {1}", list->GetKey(i),
            list->GetByIndex(i));
}
```

Using Hash Tables

You should instantiate **Hashtable** objects if you want to use hash tables for speedy element lookup in your code. The code presented next shows you how to use the **Hashtable** class to perform these actions:

1.   Instantiate a case-insensitive hash table using the **Hashtable** constructor.

2.   Add elements to the hash table using the **Add** method.

3.   Conduct the hash table look up using the **Item** property.

```
#using <mscorlib.dll>
using namespace System;
using namespace System::Collections;

void main()
{
    // 1. Create a hash table
    Hashtable* hashtable = new Hashtable(10,
        CaseInsensitiveHashCodeProvider::Default,
        CaseInsensitiveComparer::Default);
    // 2. Add elements to the hash table
    hashtable->Add(S"Vlad", S"Fomitchev");
    hashtable->Add(S"Max", S"Fomitchev");
    hashtable->Add(S"Veronica", S"Grigorashvily");
    // 3. Retrieve value by name (case insensitive)
    Console::WriteLine("Vlad's last name {0}", hashtable->Item[S"VLAD"]);
}
```

Using Queues

You should use the .NET **Queue** class to implement FIFO data queues. The **Queue** class allows you to add and remove elements to and from the queue using the **Enqueue** and **Dequeue** methods. The **Queue** class also provides the **Peek** method for retrieving the object at the beginning of the queue without dequeuing it. The following code example shows you how to use the **Queue** class to perform these actions:

1.   Create a **Queue** object using the default constructor.

2.   Add elements to the queue using the **Enqueue** method.

3.   Create a thread-safe version of the queue using the **Synchronized** method.

4.   Retrieve the first element from the queue using the **Dequeue** method.

```cpp
#using <mscorlib.dll>
using namespace System;
using namespace System::Collections;

void main()
{
    // 1. Create queue
    Queue* queue = new Queue();
    // 2. Put elements into the queue
    queue->Enqueue(S"Apples");
    queue->Enqueue(S"Oranges");
    queue->Enqueue(S"Tomatoes");
    // 3. Create a synchronized version of the queue
    queue = Queue::Synchronized(queue);
    if ( queue->IsSynchronized )
        // 4. Retrieve the first element from the queue
        Console::WriteLine("First element in queue was: {0}",
            queue->Dequeue());
}
```

Using Stacks

You should use the .NET **Stack** class to implement LIFO data stacks. The **Stack** class allows you to add and remove elements to and from the stack using the **Push** and **Pop** methods. The **Stack** class also provides the **Peek** method for retrieving an object on the top of the stack without popping the object. The following code example shows you how to use the **Stack** class to perform these steps:

1.   Create a **Stack** object using the default constructor.

2.   Add elements to the stack using the **Push** method.

3.   Retrieve the element on the top of the stack using the **Peek** method without popping the stack.

4.   Retrieve the element on the top of the stack using the **Push** method.

```cpp
#using <mscorlib.dll>
using namespace System;
using namespace System::Collections;

void main()
```

```
{
    // 1. Create stack
    Stack* stack = new Stack();
    // 2. Push elements to stack
    stack->Push(S"Apples");
    stack->Push(S"Oranges");
    stack->Push(S"Tomatoes");
    // 3. Peek at the element at the top of stack
    if ( stack->Peek() == S"Tomatoes" )
        // 4. Pop the element
        Console::WriteLine("The top element in stack is '{0}'", stack->Pop());
}
```

Instantiating Collection Objects with the **CollectionsUtil** Class

You can use the **CollectionsUtil** class to instantiate the case-insensitive **Hashtable** and **SortedList** objects as demonstrated in the code sample shown here:

```
#using <mscorlib.dll>
#using <system.dll>
using namespace System;
using namespace System::Collections;
using namespace System::Collections::Specialized;

void main()
{
    // 1. Create a case-insensitive sorted list
    SortedList* myList = CollectionsUtil::CreateCaseInsensitiveSortedList();
    // Equivalent to
    SortedList* myList2 = new SortedList(CaseInsensitiveComparer::Default);

    // 2. Create a case-insensitive hash table
    Hashtable* hashtable = CollectionsUtil::CreateCaseInsensitiveHashtable();
    // Equivalent to
    Hashtable* hashtable2 = new Hashtable(
        CaseInsensitiveHashCodeProvider::Default,
        CaseInsensitiveComparer::Default);
}
```

The **CollectionsUtil** is used solely for convenience and calling the **CreateCaseInsensitiveSortedList** and **CreateCaseInsensitiveHashtable** pair is equivalent to creating the **SortedList** and **Hashtable** objects using the corresponding constructors.

Using Bit Arrays

You can use the **BitArray** class to work with bit fields packed in integer variables. The following code example illustrates how to:

1. Create **BitArray** objects using the **BitArray** constructor.

2. Perform a logical bitwise OR operation on two bit arrays.

3. Access and set individual bits in the array using the **Item** indexer and the **Set** method.

4. Expand the array size to 32 bit using the **Length** property.

5. Catch exceptions thrown as a result of bitwise OR operation on two bit arrays of mismatched size.

```
#using <mscorlib.dll>
using namespace System;
using namespace System::Collections;

void main()
{
    // 1. Create two arrays of 16 bits each
    BitArray* myArray1 = new BitArray(16, false);
    BitArray* myArray2 = new BitArray(16, true);

    // 2. Perform Logical bitwise OR on two arrays
    myArray1 = myArray1->Or(myArray2);
    // 3. If bit #7 is set
    if ( myArray1->Item[7] )
        // Reset bit #7
        myArray1->Set(7, false);

    // 4. Expand array to 32 bits
    if ( myArray1->Length < 32 )
        myArray1->Length = 32;

    // 5. Will throw an exception because array sizes do not match
    try {
        myArray1 = myArray1->Or(myArray2);
    }
    catch(Exception* e) {
        Console::WriteLine(e->Message);
    }
}
```

> **WARNING!** A logical operation (OR, AND, XOR) on bit arrays of mismatched size will throw an exception.

Working with Bit Flags and Bit Sections

You should use the **BitVector32** class if you want to work with bit fields packed in a 32-bit integer. This class allows you to access and set individual bits in the integer using the **Item** indexer property. You can also access and set groups of consecutive bits by creating bit sections (**BitVector32::Section** value type) and use them as indexes for the **Item** indexer property. To understand how the **BitVector32** class is used, consider the following code example, which performs these steps:

1.　Creates a bit vector using the **BitVector32** constructor.

2.　Outputs the bit vector value using the implicit **ToString** conversion.

3.　Resets the bit #7 using the **Item** property.

4.　Creates the first bit section big enough to hold the value of 30 using the **BitVector32::CreateSection** method. (The section spans bits 0 through 5.)

5.　Creates the second bit section big enough to hold the value of 60 using the **BitVector32::CreateSection** method. (The section spans bits 6 through 12.)

6.　Sets the new values of the bit sections using **BitVector32::Item** indexer property with the sections supplied as indexes.

```
#using <mscorlib.dll>
using namespace System;
using namespace System::Collections::Specialized;


void main()
{
    // 1. Create a 32-bit array
    BitVector32* flags = new BitVector32(128);
    // 2. Output bit vector value
    Console::WriteLine("flags={0:X8}", flags);
    // 3. Reset the bit #7
    flags->Item[7] = false;

    // 4. Create the first 4-bit section
    BitVector32::Section a = flags->CreateSection(30);
    Console::WriteLine("Section a: offset={0}, mask={1:X}", a.Offset, a.Mask);

    // 5. Create the second 5-bit section
    BitVector32::Section b = flags->CreateSection(60, a);
    Console::WriteLine("Section b: offset={0}, mask={1:X}", b.Offset, b.Mask);

    // 6. Update section values in the BitVector32
    flags->Item[a] = 0x10;
    flags->Item[b] = 0x20;
    Console::WriteLine("flags={0}", flags->ToString("X8"));
}
```

.NET File and Stream I/O

QUICK JUMPS

CHAPTER 7

.NET File and Stream I/O

In Depth

The .NET Framework Class Library provides two namespaces dedicated to file and stream I/O: System::IO for managing files, directories, and binary and text streams, and System::IO::IsolatedStorage for managing storage isolated by a particular user, application domain, or assembly. In this chapter, you will learn how to work with .NET I/O, including creating, copying, reading and writing files and directories, storing and retrieving data from binary and text streams, detecting file system changes, implementing asynchronous I/O, and managing isolated storage.

You'll find that this chapter contains reference to all of the essential classes residing in the System::IO and System::IO::IsolatedStorage namespaces; thus, be prepared to see a lot of tables summarizing constructors, fields, properties, methods, and events of each class.

System::IO Namespace Hierarchy

The System::IO namespace contains classes representing files, directories, paths, file system events, and streams, including streams for reading and writing binary, text, and numeric data, and streams mapped to memory buffers. The System::IO namespace general classes, stream classes, attributes, exceptions, value types, and delegates are listed in Tables 7.1 through 7.7, respectively. The combined System::IO and System::IO::IsolatedStorage namespace class hierarchy is shown in Figure 7.1, which follows the tables. It may catch you as a surprise but most of the stream classes in the System::IO namespace are not derived from the same base class.

Table 7.1 System::IO namespace general classes.

Class	Description
Directory	Provides static methods for manipulating directories: creating, deleting, renaming, moving, querying, and modifying creation and last access times, listing files, and subdirectories, and so on.
DirectoryInfo	Used to represent a particular file-system directory and perform operations on the directory, including creating, deleting, renaming, and so on. The **DirectoryInfo** class provides the same amount of functionality as the **Directory** class.
ErrorEventArgs	Represents data for the **FileSystemWatcher::Error** event.
File	Provides static methods for manipulating files: creating, deleting, renaming, moving, querying and modifying creation and last access times, and opening file streams for reading, writing, or both.
FileInfo	Used to represent a particular file and perform operations on the file, including creating, deleting, or opening file streams. The **FileInfo** class provides the same amount of functionality as the **File** class.
FileSystemEventArgs	Represents data for the **FileSystemWatcher** directory notification events: **Changed**, **Created**, and **Deleted**.
FileSystemInfo	Base class for **FileInfo** and **DirectoryInfo** classes.

<Continued on Next Page>

<Table 7.1 Continued>

Class	Description
FileSystemWatcher	A class for monitoring directory changes. The class can fire events when files are added or removed to or from a directory being watched, or when existing files change in size, last access date/time, and so on.
Path	Encapsulates platform-independent file path operations.
RenamedEventArgs	Represents data for the **FileSystemWatcher::Renamed** event.

Table 7.2 System::IO namespace stream classes.

Class	Description
BinaryReader	Reads primitive data types as binary values using a specific encoding.
BinaryWriter	Writes primitive data types as binary values using a specific encoding.
BufferedStream	Implements buffered stream reading and writing intended to improve I/O performance.
FileStream	Generic file read/write stream supporting both synchronous and asynchronous operations.
MemoryStream	Implements a read/write stream mapped to a memory buffer.
Stream	Abstract base class for all streams.
StreamReader	Reads text using a specific encoding.
StreamWriter	Writes text using a specific encoding.
StringReader	Reads text from a **StringBuilder** object.
StringWriter	Writes text to a **StringBuilder** object.
TextReader	Abstract base class for reading text.
TextWriter	Abstract base class for writing text.

Table 7.3 System::IO namespace attributes.

Attribute	Description
IODescriptionAttribute	An attribute for specifying textual descriptions of an I/O class or stream.

Table 7.4 System::IO namespace exceptions.

Exception	Description
EndOfStreamException	Represents an exception thrown when one attempts reading past the end of a stream.
DirectoryNotFoundException	Represents an exception thrown when one attempts accessing a nonexistent directory.
FileLoadException	Represents an exception thrown when an assembly file is found but can't be loaded due to a system error other than security exception.
FileNotFoundException	Represents an exception thrown when one attempts accessing a nonexistent file.
InternalBufferOverflowException	Represents an exception thrown by a **FileSystemWatcher** object when too many changes occur in a short period of time and the internal **FileSystemWatcher** buffer overflows.
IOException	Represents a generic I/O error exception.
PathTooLongException	Represents an exception thrown when a path name exceeds the maximum allowable length.

Table 7.5 System::IO namespace value types.

Value Type	Description
WaitForChangedResult	Represents a structure used by the **FileSystemWatcher::WaitForChanged** method, indicating particular file-system changes to watch.

Table 7.6 System::IO namespace delegates.

Delegate	Description
void ErrorEventHandler(Object* *sender*, **ErrorEventArgs*** *e*)	A delegate for handling the **Error** events of the **FileSystemWatcher** class.
void FileSystemEventHandler(Object* *sender*, **FileSystemEventArgs*** *e*)	A delegate for handling the **Changed**, **Created**, or **Deleted** events of the **FileSystemWatcher** class.
void RenamedEventHandler(Object* *sender*, **RenamedEventArgs*** *e*)	A delegate for handling the **Renamed** events of the **FileSystemWatcher** class.

Table 7.7 System::IO namespace enumerations.

Enumeration	Flags	Description
FileAccess	Yes	Defines file access constants: **Read**, **ReadWrite**, and **Write**.
FileAttributes	Yes	Defines file and directory attributes: **Archive**, **Compressed**, **Device**, **Directory**, **Encrypted**, **Hidden**, **Normal**, **NotContentIndexed**, **Offline**, **ReadOnly**, **ReparsePoint**, **SparseFile**, **System**, and **Temporary**.
FileMode	No	Defines constants for opening a file: **Append**, **Create**, **CreateNew**, **Open**, **OpenOrCreate**, and **Truncate**.
FileShare	Yes	Defines constants for sharing an open file among **FileStreams**: **Inheritable**, **None** (i.e., file cannot be shared), **Read**, **ReadWrite**, and **Write**.
NotifyFilters	Yes	Defines constants used by the **FileSystemWatcher** class to identify which changes to track: **Attributes**, **CreationTime**, **DirectoryName**, **FileName**, **LastAccess**, **LastWrite**, **Security**, and **Size**.
SeekOrigin	No	Defines file stream seeking constants: **Begin**, **Current**, and **End**.
WatcherChangeTypes	Yes	Defines constants used by the **FileSystemWatcher** to identify changes that may occur to a file or directory: **All**, **Changed**, **Created**, **Deleted**, and **Renamed**.

Files and Directories

The System::IO namespace supplies two sets of classes representing files and directories:

* *File* and *Directory* *classes*: Provide an inventory of static methods for manipulating files and directories as you would using Win32 API.

* *FileInfo* and *DirectoryInfo* *classes*: Provide instance methods for manipulating files and directories as you would using the MFC **CFile** class.

Two sets of file and directory classes are provided for a reason—*efficiency*. Static methods of the **File** and **Directory** classes offer improved performance in comparison with instance methods of the **FileInfo** and **DirectoryInfo** classes because you do not have to allocate **File/Directory** objects first. On the other hand, the **FileInfo** and **DirectoryInfo** classes offer the convenience of object-oriented programming by providing means for encapsulating a file or directory. Thus, you can supply a **FileInfo/DirectoryInfo** object as a parameter to a function, which can invoke instance methods to manipulate the encapsulated file or directory.

There is another important difference between all-static **File** and **Directory** classes and instance-based **FileInfo** and **DirectoryInfo** objects. The **File** and **Directory** classes can refer only to *existing* files and directories, whereas the **FileInfo**

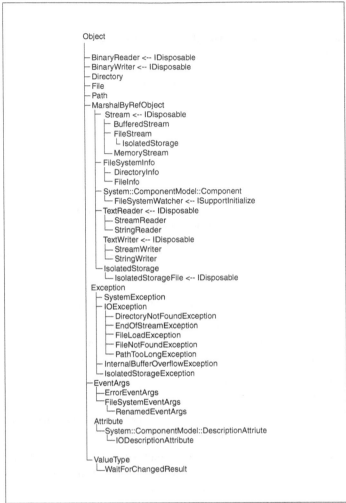

Figure 7.1 The combined System::IO and System::IO::IsolatedStorage namespace class hierarchy.

and **DirectoryInfo** objects can refer to files and folders that do not exist. Thus, it is okay to initialize a **FileInfo** or a **DirectoryInfo** object with a name that does not exist and create the actual file or folder later. However, if you attempt to call the **FileInfo** or **DirectoryInfo** methods that require an underlying object to exist (i.e., querying last write time with **LastWriteTime**), a **FileNotFoundException** or a **DirectoryNotFoundException** will be thrown.

The **Directory** Class

The **Directory** class provides static methods for manipulating directories and has the following inheritance structure:

```
System::Object
|- Syste::IO::Directory
```

```
Attributes: None
Abstract: No
Sealed: Yes
Implements Interfaces: None
```

The **Directory** class methods are summarized in Table 7.8.

Table 7.8 **Directory** class methods.

Method	Description
static DirectoryInfo* CreateDirectory(String* *path*)	Creates a new directory.
static void Delete(String* *dir*)	
static void Delete(String* *dir*, bool *recursive*)	Deletes a specified directory. To delete a nonempty directory, set the optional *recursive* parameter to **true**.
static bool Exists(String* *dir*)	Returns **true** if the specified directory exists.
static DateTime GetCreationTime(String* *dir*)	Returns the creation date/time of the specified directory.
static String* GetCurrentDirectory()	Returns the name of the current working directory.
static String* GetDirectories(String* *dir*) __gc[]	
static String* GetDirectories(String* *dir*, String* *mask*) __gc[]	Returns the array of names of subdirectories in the specified directory. Use the optional *mask* parameter to specify a search mask.
static String* GetDirectoryRoot(String* *dir*)	Returns the volume name or the root directory name for the specified directory.
static String* GetFiles(String* *dir*) __gc[]	
static String* GetFiles(String* *dir*, String* *mask*) __gc[]	Returns the array of file names in the specified directory. Uses the optional *mask* parameter to specify a search mask..
static String* GetFileSystemEntries(String* *dir*) __gc[]	
static String* GetFileSystemEntries(String* *dir*, String* *mask*) __gc[]	Returns the array of files and subdirectories in the specified directory. Use the optional *mask* parameter to specify a search mask.
static DateTime GetLastAccessTime(String* *dir*)	Returns the date and time the specified directory was last accessed.

<Continued on Next Page>

<Table 7.8 Continued>

Method	Description
static DateTime GetLastWriteTime(String* *dir*)	Returns the date and time the specified directory was last written to.
static String* GetLogicalDrives() __gc[]	Returns the array of logical drive names (i.e., drive letters).
static DirectoryInfo* GetParent(String* *dir*)	Retrieves the parent directory for the specified path.
static void Move(String* *srcDir*, String* *destDir*)	Moves a file or a directory to a new location.
static void SetCreationTime(String* *dir*, DateTime *time*)	Sets the creation date/time for the specified directory.
static void SetCurrentDirectory(String* *dir*)	Sets the current working directory to the specified path.
static void SetLastAccessTime(String* *dir*, DateTime *time*)	Sets the date and time at which the specified directory was last accessed.
static void SetLastWriteTime(String* *dir*, DateTime *time*)	Sets the date and time a directory was last written to.

File Class

The **File** class provides static methods for manipulating files and has the following inheritance structure:

```
System::Object
|- Syste::IO::File

Attributes: None
Abstract: No
Sealed: Yes
Implements Interfaces: None
```

The **File** class methods are summarized in Table 7.9

Table 7.9 **File** class methods.

Method	Description
static StreamWriter* AppendText(String* *path*)	Creates a **StreamWriter** for appending UTF-8 encoded text to the specified existing file.
static void Copy(String* *src*, String* *dest*)	
static void Copy(String* *src*, String* *dest*, bool *overwrite*)	Copies the *src* file to the *dest* file. The optional *overwrite* parameter controls whether the destination file is overwritten if it already exists.

<Continued on Next Page>

<Table 7.9 Continued>

Method	Description
static FileStream* Create(String* *path*)	
static FileStream* Create(String* *path*, int *bufferSize*)	Creates a new file and opens it for reading and writing. The optional ***bufferSize*** parameter specifies the I/O buffer size for file reading/writing.
static StreamWriter* CreateText(String* *path*)	Creates a new file and opens it for writing UTF-8 encoded text.
static void Delete(String* *path*)	Deletes the specified file. (An exception is not thrown if the specified file does not exist.)
bool Exists(String* *path*)	Returns **true** if the specified file exists.
static FileAttributes GetAttributes(String* *path*)	Returns the **FileAttributes** of the specified file.
static DateTime GetCreationTime(String* *path*)	Returns the creation date/time of the specified file.
static DateTime GetLastAccessTime(String* *path*)	Returns the date and time in which the specified file was last accessed.
static DateTime GetLastWriteTime(String* *path*)	Returns the date and time the specified file was last written to.
static void Move(String* *src*, String* *dest*)	Moves the ***src*** file to the ***dest*** file, which can be on another volume or UNC name.
static FileStream* Open(String* *path*, FileMode *mode*)	
static FileStream* Open(String* *path*, FileMode *mode*, FileAccess *access*)	
static FileStream* Open(String* *path*, FileMode *mode*, FileAccess *access*, FileShare *share*)	Creates or opens the specified file. Optional ***access*** and ***share*** arguments allow specifying the desired file access and file-sharing mode. By default, a file is open for reading/writing in exclusive mode
static FileStream* OpenRead(String* *path*)	Opens the specified existing file for reading.
static StreamReader* OpenText(String* *path*)	Opens the specified existing file for reading UTF-8 encoded text.
static FileStream* OpenWrite(String* *path*)	Opens the specified existing file for writing.
static void SetAttributes(String* *path*, FileAttributes *attributes*)	Sets the attributes of the specified file.
static void SetCreationTime(String* *path*, DateTime *time*)	Sets the creation date/time of the specified file.
static void SetLastAccessTime(String* *path*, DateTime *time*)	Sets the date and time in which the specified file was last accessed.
static void SetLastWriteTime(String* *path*, DateTime *time*)	Sets the date and time that the specified file was last written to.

File System Objects

The **FileSystemInfo** is an abstract base class for the **FileInfo** and **DirectoryInfo** classes. The **FileSystemInfo** represents a generic file system object (file or directory) and has the following inheritance structure:

```
System::Object
|-System::MarshalByRefObject
  |- System::IO::FileSystemInfo
```

```
Attributes: Serializable
Abstract: Yes
Sealed: No
Implements Interfaces: None
```

The **FileSystemInfo** class constructors, fields, properties, and methods are summarized in Tables 7.10 through 7.13.

Table 7.10 **FileSystemInfo** class constructors.

Constructor	Description
protected: FileSystemInfo(String* *path*)	Default constructor.

Table 7.11 **FileSystemInfo** class fields.

Field	Description
protected: String* FullPath	Fully qualified path of the file system object.
protected: String* OriginalPath	Original path of the file system object (possibly relative) specified by the user.

Table 7.12 **FileSystemInfo** class properties.

Get/Set	Type	Property	Virtual	Description
Get/Set	**FileAttributes**	**Attributes**	No	Contains attributes of the file system object.
Get/Set	**DateTime**	**CreationTime**	No	Gets or sets the date and time the file system object was created.
Get	**bool**	**Exists**	Yes	Contains **true** if the directory represented by the **DirectoryInfo** object exists.
Get	**String***	**Extension**	No	Contains the extension of the file system object name.
Get	**String***	**FullName**	No	Contains full path of the file system object.
Get/Set	**DateTime**	**LastAccessTime**	No	Gets or sets the date and time the file system object was last accessed.
Get/Set	**DateTime**	**LastWriteTime**	No	Gets or sets the date and time the file system object was last written.
Get	**String***	**Name**	Yes	Contains the file system object name.

Table 7.13 **FileSystemInfo** class methods.

Field	Description
virtual void Delete() = 0	Deletes the file system object.
void Refresh()	Refreshes the state of the file system object to pick up the changes caused by the recent modifications and repopulates the **FileSystemInfo** properties.

For the most part, you will not be using the **FileSystemInfo** class directly, except for the situations when you must enumerate both files and subdirectories residing in a particular directory. (The **DirectoryInfo::GetFileSystemEntries** method enumerates both files and subdirectories by returning an array of pointers to **FileSystemInfo** objects.)

DirectoryInfo Class

The **DirectoryInfo** class encapsulates a file system directory and provides instance methods for manipulating directory objects. The class inheritance structure is as follows:

```
System::Object
|-System::MarshalByRefObject
  |- System::IO::FileSystemInfo
      |- System::IO::DirectoryInfo

Attributes: Serializable
Abstract: No
Sealed: Yes
Implements Interfaces: None
```

The **DirectoryInfo** class constructors, properties, and methods are summarized in Table 7.14 through 7.16.

Table 7.14 **DirectoryInfo** class constructors.

Method	Description
DirectoryInfo(String* *path*)	Constructs a **DirectoryInfo** object for the specified path.

Table 7.15 **DirectoryInfo** class properties.

Get/Set	Type	Property	Virtual	Description
Get	**bool**	**Exists**	Yes	Contains **true** if the directory represented by the **DirectoryInfo** object exists.
Get	**String***	**Name**	Yes	Contains the directory name (e.g., Gems 3D for the C:\Program files\Gems 3D path).
Get	**DirectoryInfo***	**Parent**	No	Contains a pointer to the parent directory object or Null if the current directory *is* the root directory.
Get	**DirectoryInfo***	**Root**	No	Contains a pointer to the root directory object of the current **DirectoryInfo** object.

Table 7.16 **DirectoryInfo** class methods.

Method	Description
void Create()	Creates a new directory if the directory does not already exist.
DirectoryInfo* CreateSubdirectory(String* *path*)	Creates a subdirectory on the specified path. The subdirectory must be on the same volume or UNC name as the current **DirectoryInfo** path.
void Delete()	
void Delete(bool *recursive*)	Deletes the directory. To delete a nonempty directory set the optional *recursive* parameter to **true**.
String* GetDirectories() __gc[]	
String* GetDirectories(String* *mask*) __gc[]	Returns the array of names of subdirectories located in the directory represented by the **DirectoryInfo** object. Use the optional *mask* parameter to specify a search mask.
String* GetFiles() __gc[]	
String* GetFiles(String* *mask*) __gc[]	Returns the array of file names directory located in the directory represented by the **DirectoryInfo** object. Use the optional *mask* parameter to specify a search mask..
String* GetFileSystemInfos() __gc[]	
String* GetFileSystemInfos(String* *mask*) __gc[]	Returns the array of files and subdirectories located in the directory represented by the **DirectoryInfo** object. Use the optional *mask* parameter to specify a search mask.
void MoveTo(String* *path*)	Moves the directory to a new location. The directory will become a subdirectory on the specified path. If a directory with the same name already exists on the specified path, an **IOException** exception is thrown.

FileInfo Class

The **FileInfo** class encapsulates a file and provides instance methods for manipulating file objects. The class inheritance structure is as follows:

```
System::Object
|-System::MarshalByRefObject
  |- System::IO::FileSystemInfo
     |- System::IO::FileInfo
```

```
Attributes: Serializable
Abstract: No
Sealed: Yes
Implements Interfaces: None
```

The **FileInfo** class constructors, properties, and methods are summarized in Tables 7.17 through 7.18.

Table 7.17 **FileInfo** class constructors.

Method	Description
FileInfo(String* *path*)	Constructs a **FileInfo** object for the specified path.

Table 7.18 **FileInfo** class properties.

Get/Set	Type	Property	Virtual	Description
Get	**DirectoryInfo***	**Directory**	No	Contains a pointer to the parent directory of the file.
Get	**String***	**DirectoryName**	No	Contains the directory portion of the fie's path.
Get	**bool**	**Exists**	Yes	Contains **true** if the file represented by the **FileInfo** object exists.
Get	**__int64**	**Length**	No	Contains the size of the file.
Get	**String***	**Name**	Yes	Contains the file name (e.g., Gems3D.exe for the C:\Program files\Gems 3D\Gems3D.exe path).

Table 7.19 **FileInfo** class methods.

Method	Description
StreamWriter* AppendText()	Creates a **StreamWriter** for appending UTF-8 encoded text to the current file.
void CopyTo(String* *dest*)	
void CopyTo(String* *dest*, bool *overwrite*)	Copies the current file to the ***dest*** file. The optional ***overwrite*** parameter controls whether the destination file is overwritten if it already exists.
FileStream* Create()	Creates the file and opens it for reading and writing. If the file already exists, its contents are erased.
StreamWriter* CreateText()	Creates the file and opens it for writing UTF-8 encoded text.
void Delete()	Deletes the current file if it exists.
void MoveTo(String* *dest*)	Moves the current file to the ***dest*** file.
FileStream* Open(FileMode *mode*)	
FileStream* Open(FileMode *mode*, FileAccess *access*)	
FileStream* Open(FileMode *mode*, FileAccess *access*, FileShare *share*)	Creates or opens the file. Optional ***access*** and ***share*** arguments allow specifying the desired file access and file sharing mode. By default a file is open for reading/writing in exclusive mode.
FileStream* OpenRead()	Opens the file for reading.
StreamReader* OpenText()	Opens the file for reading UTF-8 encoded text.
FileStream* OpenWrite(String* *path*)	Opens the file for writing.

Streams

Unlike the MFC **CFile** class, both the **File** and **FileInfo** classes do not allow reading or writing data from files directly. Instead, the .NET Framework provides a set of *stream* classes implementing reading and writing operations from files, optimized for various tasks at hand like reading or writing binary or text data. You would think that there ought to be more similarity between the .NET streams and the Standard C++ streams. After all, both allow you to store and retrieve data from a store. The truth is that the two are no more similar than American and Russian cars: Both can move people around, but the latter requires a sledge hummer to get started. The difference between the .NET streams and the Standard C++ streams is that most .NET streams support random access and seeking, yet none of them support Standard C++ >> and << serialization operators. Thus, if you are going to use the .NET streams, you better get used to calling **Read** and **Write** methods.

All .NET I/O streams are derived from a single abstract base class named **Stream**, which has the following inheritance structure:

```
System::Object
|- System::MarshalByRefObject
   |- System::IO::Stream

Attributes: No
Abstract: Yes
Sealed: No
Implements Interfaces: Idisposable
```

The **Stream** class constructors, fields, properties, and methods are listed in Tables 7.20 through 7.23.

Table 7.20 **Stream** class constructors.

Constructor	Description
protected: Stream()	Default constructor.

Table 7.21 **Stream** class fields.

Field	Description
static Stream* Null	A stream that is not associated with any storage.

Table 7.22 **Stream** class properties (all pure virtual).

Get/Set	Type	Property	Description
Get	**bool**	**CanRead**	Contains **true** if the stream supports reading.
Get	**bool**	**CanSeek**	Contains **true** if the stream supports seeking.
Get	**bool**	**CanWrite**	Contains **true** if the stream supports writing.
Get	**__int64**	**Length**	Contains the length of the stream in bytes.
Get/Set	**__int64**	**Position**	Gets or sets the current read/write position in the stream.

Table 7.23 **Stream** class methods.

Method	Description
virtual IAsyncResult* BeginRead(unsigned char *array* **__gc[],** **int** *offset***, int** *numBytes***, AsyncCallback*** *userCallback***, Object*** *state***)**	Initiates an asynchronous read operation. The *userCallback* delegate is called when the read request completes with the *state* object passed as a parameter.
virtual IAsyncResult* BeginWrite(unsigned char *array* **__gc[], int** *offset***, int** *numBytes***, AsyncCallback*** *userCallback***, Object*** *stateObject***)**	Initiates an asynchronous write operation. The *userCallback* delegate is called when the write request completes with the *state* object passed as a parameter.
virtual void Close()	Closes the file (if any) and releases any resources associated with the stream.
protected: virtual WaitHandle* CreateWaitHandle()	Creates a wait handle used by asynchronous stream I/O operations.
virtual int EndRead(IAsyncResult* *result***)**	Waits for the specified pending asynchronous read request to complete.
virtual void EndWrite(IAsyncResult* *result***)**	Waits for the specified pending asynchronous write request to complete.
virtual void Flush() = 0	If the stream implements buffered I/O, this forces the content of the buffer to be written to the underlying device.
virtual void IDisposable::Dispose()	Disposes the stream.
virtual int Read(__in unsigned char* *array* **__gc[], int** *offset***, Int** *count***) = 0**	Reads the *count* bytes from the stream into the specified array at the specified index and returns the number of bytes read, or 0 if the end of stream was reached.
virtual int ReadByte()	Reads and returns a byte from the stream, or -1 if the end of stream was reached.
virtual __int64 Seek(__int64 *offset***, SeekOrigin** *origin***) = 0**	Sets the current read/write position to the specified value.
virtual void SetLength(__int64 *length***) = 0**	Sets the length of the stream to the specified value. The stream must support writing (**CanWrite == true**) in order for the **SetLength** method to have effect.
virtual void Write(unsigned char *array* **__gc[], int** *offset***, int** *count***) = 0**	Writes to the stream the *count* bytes from the specified array at the specified index.
virtual void WriteByte(unsigned char *value***)**	Writes the specified byte to the stream.

All **Stream** class properties and most methods are pure virtual and must be implemented in a derived class. Derived classes override **CanRead**, **CanWrite**, and **CanSeek** methods to offer a range of operations applicable to a particular stream. Thus, you should query one of the **Can***XYZ* properties before attempting to read, write, or seek on an unknown stream. If you are too lazy to check the supported stream operations, your program may get too lazy to work properly and throw a **NotSupportedException** exception.

To get a better grasp of what streams the System::IO namespace has to offer, consider the following stream class selection guide:

*   **FileStream** class: Use for *reading and writing binary data from files.*

*   **BinaryReader/BinaryWriter** classes: Use for *reading or Write numeric data types from files.*

*   **StreamReader/StreamWriter** classes: Use for *reading or writing text from files.*

*   **StringReader/StringWriter** classes: Use for *reading or writing text from memory buffers.*

*   **MemoryStream** class: Use for *reading or writing binary data from memory buffers.*

File Streams

The **FileStream** class represents a generic stream for reading/writing byte arrays from files. The **FileStream** class inherits directly from the **Stream** class and overrides all of its methods:

```
System::Object
|- System::MarshalByRefObject
   |- System::IO::Stream
      |- System::IO::FileStream


Attributes: None
Abstract: No
Sealed: No
Implements Interfaces: None
```

The **FileStream** class constructors, properties, and methods are summarized in Tables 7.24 through 7.26.

Table 7.24 **FileStream** class constructors.

Constructor	Description
FileStream(String* *path*, **FileMode** *mode*)	
FileStream(String* *path*, **FileMode** *mode*, **FileAccess** *access*)	
FileStream(String* *path*, **FileMode** *mode*, **FileAccess** *access*, **FileShare** *share*)	
FileStream(String* *path*, **FileMode** *mode*, **FileAccess** *access*, **FileShare** *share*, **int** *bufferSize*)	
FileStream(String* *path*, **FileMode** *mode*, **FileAccess** *access*, **FileShare** *share*, **int** *bufferSize*, **bool** *isAsync*)	Constructs a **FileStream** object by creating or opening the specified file. Optional *mode* parameter specifies whether a file should be opened or created (**Create**, **Open**, **OpenOrCreate**, etc.). Optional *access* parameter specifies whether a file should be open for reading, writing, or both. Optional *share* parameter specifies file sharing options. Optional *bufferSize* parameter specifies I/O buffer size (the default is 8192). Optional *isAsync* parameter specifies whether the file should be open for asynchronous I/O (e.g., overlapped I/O in Windows NT—see **FILE_FLAG_OVERLAPPED** flag used by the **CreateFile** API call).
FileStream(IntPtr *handle*, **FileAccess** *access*)	
FileStream(IntPtr *handle*, **FileAccess** *access*, **bool** *ownsHandle*)	
FileStream(IntPtr *handle*, **FileAccess** *access*, **bool** *ownsHandle*, **int** *bufferSize*)	
FileStream(IntPtr *handle*, **FileAccess** *access*, **bool** *ownsHandle*, **int** *bufferSize*, **bool** *isAsync*)	Constructs a **FileStream** object by using the specified file **HANDLE**. (The handle must be obtained using the **FileOpen** or **FileCreate** Win32 API calls.) Optional *access* parameter specifies whether a file should be open for reading, writing, or both. Optional *ownsHandle* parameter indicates whether the stream should own the file handle. (If the stream owns the file handle, you should not read or write from or to the file directly without calling the **Flush** or **Close** methods on the stream first.) Optional *bufferSize* parameter specifies a file buffer size. (The default is 8192.) Optional *isAsync* parameter specifies whether the file should be open for asynchronous I/O.

Table 7.25 **FileStream** class properties (all virtual).

Get/Set	Type	Property	Description
Get	**IntPtr**	**Handle**	Contains the OS file handle. (**HANDLE** is returned by the **CreateFile** or **OpenFile** Win32 API calls.)
Get	**bool**	**IsAsync**	Contains **true** if the **FileStream** was opened for asynchronous I/O.
Get	**String***	**Name**	Contains the **FileStream** file path.

Table 7.26 **FileStream** class methods.

Method	Description
virtual void Lock(__int64 *position*, **__int64** *length*)	Locks a section of the file to prevent access by other processes.
virtual void Unlock(__int64 *position*, **__int64** *length*)	Unlocks a section of the file to allow access by other processes.

Under the Windows operating system, the **FileStream** class encapsulates the Win32 File I/O API, represented by the **OpenFile**, **ReadFile**, **WriteFile,** and other methods. For that matter, a **FileStream** object can be initialized using either a file path or a Win32 file **HANDLE**. The **FileStream** class also fully supports asynchronous I/O by means of the **BeginRead**, **BeginWrite**, **EndRead**, and **EndWrite** methods. For better performance, the **FileStream** constructor can accept a Boolean parameter (*isAsync*), indicating whether the underlying file should be opened for asynchronous I/O. If you do not specify the *isAsync* parameter, the asynchronous I/O will still work, although its performance will be diminished.

The **FileStream** class is tightly linked to the **File** and the **FileInfo** classes—both can instantiate new **FileStream** objects by means of the **AppendText**, **Create**, **CreateText**, **Open**, **OpenRead**, **OpenWrite**, and **OpenText** methods.

Asynchronous I/O

When working with streams, keep in mind that file I/O is a time-consuming operation. Typically, a file read/write operation will block your program execution until the data is read or written from the stream. Thus, if you are reading 50 megs of data from a CD-ROM, your program will freeze until the I/O request completes. To avoid unnecessary stalls and improve the performance of your code, you should use the *asynchronous* I/O. Here are a few examples in which an asynchronous I/O will be beneficial:

* *Reading data with subsequent processing*: It makes no sense to wait for the complete data set to load if you can process it in chunks. For example, if you are compressing a wave file, you can read chunks of the file asynchronously and process each chunk individually as soon as the corresponding I/O request completes.

* *Data dumping*: If your program generates data and dumps it to a file, you can write the data asynchronously.

* *Backing up data*: Stream write operations intended to back up data on the background should be handled asynchronously.

You should not use asynchronous I/O if:

* *Multiple threads are writing to the same stream*: To guarantee the desired order of write operations, you should write synchronously on a synchronized instance of a stream.

* *Writing data with subsequent read*: If you write data to a stream and read it back later in your code, you should write your data synchronously. Otherwise, you may attempt to read the data, which was not yet written.

* *Writing critical data with subsequent modification*: If you save a user document asynchronously, a user should not be able to modify the document until the write operation completes. Otherwise, a modified version of the document may be written, not the original one.

The **Stream** class supports both synchronous (blocking) I/O and asynchronous I/O. The **Read** and **Write** methods are synchronous, while the asynchronous I/O is supported by means of the **BeginRead/BeginWrite** methods accepting an **AsyncCallback** delegate for handling I/O complete notifications and returning the **IAsyncResult** pointer to the initiated asynchronous I/O request.

To force the *blocking* (synchronous completion) of an asynchronous I/O operation, you can call the **EndRead/EndWrite** methods with an **IAsyncResult** of the I/O request that you want to complete synchronously.

> **NOTE:** If you initiate multiple asynchronous I/O requests, the I/O request completion order may be unpredictable.

For a detailed example of an asynchronous I/O, see "Using Asynchronous I/O" in the "Immediate Solutions" section of this chapter.

Buffered Streams

I/O operations can be very expensive and take anywhere from microseconds to a few seconds to complete. Thus, you should use I/O operations sparingly. Alternatively, you can use buffered I/O to improve your stream read/write performance. The .NET Framework Class Library supports the buffered I/O by means of the **BufferedStream** class, which is a concrete sealed implementation of the **Stream** class. The **BufferedStream** class implements an internal buffer for storing data before writing and for reading data in chunks. The bigger the internal buffer, the more efficient stream reading and writing can potentially be. The **BufferedStream** class inheritance diagram is shown here:

```
System::Object
|- System::MarshalByRefObject
    |- System::IO::Stream
        |- System::IO::BufferedStream

Attributes: Serializable
Abstract: No
Sealed: Yes
Implements Interfaces: None
```

The **BufferedStream** class constructors are listed in Table 7.27.

Table 7.27 **BufferedStream** class constructors.

Constructor	Description
BufferedStream (Stream* stream)	
BufferedStream(Stream* *stream*, int *bufferSize*)	Constructs a buffered stream. Optional ***bufferSize*** parameter allows specifying the desired I/O buffer size. (The default buffer size is 4096 bytes)

Typically, the OS implements internal buffering and caching for file I/O operations. Thus, normal file read/write requests are already buffered, and it makes little sense to add even more buffering. You should use the **BufferedStream** class only if you experience unusual performance degradation when reading/writing from certain streams. If the performance hit is due to the inefficient I/O, the **BufferedStream** class will take care of the problem.

> **NOTE:** Data that you write to the **BufferedStream** object may not show up in the underlying stream until you explicitly flush it by calling the **Flush** method.

Text Streams

Text I/O is arguably the most common type of file I/O. The slew of new human-readable data formats, including XML, make text I/O even more important. The .NET supports text I/O by providing two abstract base classes for writing and reading text streams—**TextWriter** and **TextReader**. The **TextWriter** class has the following inheritance diagram:

```
System::Object
|- System::MarshalByRefObject
   |- System::IO::TextWriter


Attributes: Serializable
Abstract: Yes
Sealed: No
Implements Interfaces: IDisposable
```

The **TextWriter** class constructors, fields, properties, and methods are listed in Tables 7.28 through 7.31.

Table 7.28 **TextWriter** class constructors.

Constructor	Description
protected: TextWriter()	Default constructor.
protected: TextWriter(IFormatProvider* *provider*)	Constructs a **TextWriter** stream using the specified format provider.

Table 7.29 **TextWriter** class fields.

Field	Description
static TextWriter* Null	Represents a **TextWriter** stream that is not associated with any storage.

Table 7.30 **TextWriter** class properties (all virtual).

Get/Set	Type	Property	Description
Get	**Encoding***	**Encoding**	Returns the text writer stream encoding.
Get	**IFormatProvider***	**FormatProvider**	Returns the format provider used by the stream.
Get/Set	**String***	**NewLine**	Gets or sets the new line terminator character sequence.

Table 7.31 **TextWriter** class methods.

Method	Description
virtual void Close()	Closes the file and releases any resources associated with the current stream.
protected: void Dispose(bool *disposing***)**	Releases managed and, if the disposing is set to **true**, unmanaged resources of the text stream.
virtual void Flush()	Writes the data to the underlying stream and flushes the text stream buffer.
virtual void IDisposable::Dispose()	Disposes the stream.
static TextWriter* Synchronized(TextWriter * stream)	Creates a thread-safe copy of the specified text writer stream.
virtual void Write(bool *value***)**	
virtual void Write(__wchar_t *value***)**	
virtual void Write(Decimal *value***)**	
virtual void Write(double *value***)**	
virtual void Write(int *value***)**	
virtual void Write(__int64 *value***)**	
virtual void Write(Object* *value***)**	
virtual void Write(float* *value***)**	
virtual void Write(String* *value***)**	
virtual void Write(unsigned int* *value***)**	
virtual void Write(unsigned __int64* *value***)**	Writes the specified value to the text stream.
virtual void Write(__wchar_t *buffer* **__gc[])**	Writes the array of Unicode characters to the stream.
virtual void Write(__wchar_t* *buffer***, int** *index***, int** *count***)**	Writes to the text stream a section of the Unicode character ***buffer*** identified by the ***index*** and ***count*** arguments.
virtual void Write(String* *format***, Object*** *arg***)**	
virtual void Write(String* *format***, Object*** *arg***, Object*** *arg2***)**	
virtual void Write(String* *format***, Object*** *arg***, Object*** *arg2***, Object*** *arg3***)**	Writes a formatted string to the stream.
virtual void Write(String* *format***, Object*** *args* **__gc[])**	Writes a formatted string to the stream.
virtual void WriteLine()	Writes a line terminator new line character to the stream.

<Continued on Next Page>

<Table 7.31 Continued>

Method	Description
virtual void WriteLine(bool *value*)	
virtual void WriteLine(__wchar_t *value*)	
virtual void WriteLine(Decimal *value*)	
virtual void WriteLine(double *value*)	
virtual void WriteLine(int *value*)	
virtual void WriteLine(__int64 *value*)	
virtual void WriteLine(Object* *value*)	
virtual void WriteLine(float* *value*)	
virtual void WriteLine(String* *value*)	
virtual void WriteLine(unsigned int* *value*)	
virtual void WriteLine(unsigned __int64* *value*)	Writes to the text stream the specified value followed by the new line character.

*NOTE: The **TextWriter** class **Write** and **WriteLine** methods for writing **unsigned int** and **unsigned __int64** values are not CLS-compliant.*

Method	Description
virtual void WriteLine(__wchar_t *buffer* __gc[])	Writes to the stream the array of Unicode characters followed by the new line character.
virtual void WriteLine(__wchar_t* *buffer*, int *index*, int *count*)	Writes to the text stream a section of the Unicode character **buffer** identified by the **index** and **count** arguments followed by the new line character.
virtual void WriteLine(String* *format*, Object* *arg*)	
virtual void WriteLine(String* *format*, Object* *arg*, Object* *arg2*)	
virtual void WriteLine(String* *format*, Object* *arg*, Object* *arg2*, Object* *arg3*)	Writes to the stream a formatted string followed by the new line character.
virtual void WriteLine(String* *format*, Object* *args* __gc[])	Writes to the stream a formatted string followed by the new line character.

TextReader Class

The **TextReader** complements the **TextWriter** class by providing functionality for reading from a text stream. The **TextReader** class has the following inheritance diagram:

```
System::Object
|- System::MarshalByRefObject
   |- System::IO::TextReader
```

```
Attributes: Serializable
Abstract: Yes
Sealed: No
Implements Interfaces: IDisposable
```

The **TextReader** class constructors, fields, and methods are listed in Tables 7.32 through 7.34.

Table 7.32 **TextReader** class constructors.

Constructor	Description
protected: TextReader()	Default constructor.

Table 7.33 **TextReader** class fields.

Field	Description
static TextReader* Null	Represents a **TextReader** stream that is not associated with any storage.

Table 7.34 **TextReader** class methods.

Method	Description
virtual void IDisposable::Dispose()	Disposes the stream.
virtual int Peek()	Returns the next character from the stream without updating the stream position, or -1 if there are no more characters in the stream.
virtual int Read()	Reads and returns the next character from the stream, or -1 if there are no more characters in the stream.
virtual int ReadBlock(__in __wchar_t* *buffer* __gc[], int *index*, int *count*)	Reads the ***count*** Unicode characters from the stream and writes them to the specified ***buffer*** at the specified ***index*** and returns the number of characters read.
virtual String* ReadLine()	Reads a new-line-character terminated line of text from the stream.
virtual String* ReadToEnd()	Reads all data from the stream from the current position until the end of stream.
static TextReader* Synchronized(TextReader* stream)	Creates a thread-safe copy of the specified text reader stream.

Unlike **TextWriter**, which allows writing different data types to a text stream, **TextReader** supports reading individual characters (**Read** method) or newline-character terminated text lines (**ReadLine** method). Thus, if you wrote any numeric values to the text stream, you can read them back as text and convert to the appropriate numeric type manually (e.g., using the **Convert::String2***XYZ* method).

> **NOTE:** For more information on converting textual representations of primitive types back to primitive types see the Converting Types immediate solution in Chapter 4.

Text Encodings

Everybody has worked with text streams at some point. If you've used text streams in a Standard C++ program, you've probably dealt with ASCII streams. Java programmers deal mostly with Unicode streams. Well, with .NET you've got a choice of weapons—you can specify a desired character encoding for your stream:

* *ASCII*: Each character is encoded using a single byte; thus, the encoding can represent up to 256 characters (best for English).

* *Unicode*: Each character is encoded using 2 bytes; thus, the encoding can represent up to 65536 characters. (English characters are interleaved with space-wasting zeros.)

* *UTF-7*: (UCS Transformation Format) This 7-bit form was designed to efficiently transmit Unicode text via an e-mail system that recognized only ASCII characters. The UTF-7 encoding maps Unicode characters into sequences of 7-bit US ASCII characters.

* *UTF-8*: (UCS Transformation Format) This 8-bit form allows encoding Unicode characters in the range, 0..127, in a single byte, while other Unicode characters will take more than one byte to encode.

Each encoding listed here has a corresponding **Encoding**-based class defined for it—**ASCIIEncoding**, **UnicodeEncoding**, **UTF7Encoding**, and **UTF8Encoding**. The encoding classes are defined in the System::Text namespace. You must create an instance of the **StreamReader/StreamWriter** class to use a specific encoding in your text stream. If you want to encode binary values, you must create an instance of the **BinaryReader/BinaryWriter** class. (See the "Writing Encoded Text Streams" section in "Immediate Solutions" for more information.)

7-bit Encoded Format

If you don't care about a particular encoding and want to use streams to read/write binary data, you can save disk space by choosing the *7-bit encoded integer format*. The 7-bit encoded format allows for the storing of integers representing small values very compactly. The 8th bit of each byte written indicates whether there are more bytes to follow. Thus, if an integer represents a value under 128, only 1 byte is required to store the value in the stream. If the integer represents a value under 16384, 2 bytes are required, and so on.

To use the 7-bit encoded format, you must create instances of the **BinaryReader** or **BinaryWriter** streams and read/write integer values using the **Read7BitEncodedInt/Write7BitEncodedInt** methods.

Encoded Text Stream Writer

The **StreamWriter** class supports writing text using a particular encoding. The **StreamWriter** class inheritance diagram is shown here:

```
System::Object
|- System::MarshalByRefObject
   |- System::IO::TextWriter
      |- System::IO::StreamWriter
```

```
Attributes: Serializable
Abstract: No
Sealed: No
Implements Interfaces: none
```

The **StreamWriter** class constructors, properties, and methods are summarized in Tables 7.35 through 7.38.

Table 7.35 **StreamWriter** class constructors.

Constructor	Description
StreamWriter(Stream* *stream*)	
StreamWriter(Stream* *stream*, Encoding* *encoding*)	
StreamWriter(Stream* *stream*, Encoding* *encoding*, int *bufferSize*)	Constructs the encoded text writer stream based off the specified stream. Optional *encoding* and *bufferSize* arguments allow specifying the desired stream encoding and I/O buffer size. The default encoding is UTF-8.
StreamWriter(String* *path*)	
StreamWriter(String* *path*, bool *append*)	
StreamWriter(String* *path*, bool *append*, Encoding* *encoding*)	
StreamWriter(String* *path*, bool *append*, Encoding* *encoding*, int *bufferSize*)	Constructs a text writer stream for the specified file *path*. Optional *append*, *encoding* , and *bufferSize* arguments allow specifying whether to overwrite or append an existing file, what encoding to use and the desired I/O buffer size. The default encoding is UTF-8.

Table 7.36 **StreamWriter** class fields.

Field	Description
static StreamWriter* Null	A **StreamWriter** stream that is not associated with any storage.

Table 7.37 **StreamWriter** class properties (all virtual).

Get/Set	Type	Property	Description
Get/Set	**bool**	**AutoFlush**	Gets or sets a value, indicating whether to flush the stream buffer after each **Write/WriteLine** operation.
Get	**Stream***	**BaseStream**	Returns a pointer to the underlying stream.
Get	**Encoding***	**CurrentEncoding**	Returns the current encoding for the stream.

Table 7.38 **StreamWriter** class methods.

Method	Description
~StreamWrite()	Destructor.

Encoded Text Stream Reader

The **StreamReader** class compliments the **StreamWriter** class by providing functionality for reading text in a particular encoding from text files. The **StreamReader** class inheritance diagram is shown here:

```
System::Object
|- System::MarshalByRefObject
   |- System::IO::TextReader
      |- System::IO::StreamReader


Attributes: Serializable
Abstract: No
Sealed: No
Implements Interfaces: none
```

The **StreamReader** class constructors, properties, and methods are summarized in Tables 7.39 through 7.42.

Table 7.39 **StreamReader** class constructors.

Constructor	Description
StreamReader(Stream* *stream*)	
StreamReader(Stream* *stream*, bool *detect*)	
StreamReader(Stream* *stream*, Encoding* *encoding*)	
StreamReader(Stream* *stream*, Encoding* *encoding*, bool *detect*)	
StreamReader(Stream* *stream*, Encoding* *encoding*, bool *detect*, int *bufferSize*)	Constructs a text stream reader based off the specified stream. Optional *encoding*, *detect* , and *bufferSize* arguments allow specifying the source stream encoding, whether to automatically detect the source stream encoding, and the desired I/O buffer size. The user-specified encoding is selected only if the **StreamReader** fails to figure out the source stream encoding.
StreamReader(String* *path*)	
StreamReader(String* *path*, bool *detect*)	
StreamReader(String* *path*, Encoding* *encoding*)	
StreamReader(String* *path*, Encoding* *encoding*, bool *detect*)	
StreamReader(String* *path*, Encoding* *encoding*, bool *detect*, int *bufferSize*)	Constructs a text stream reader for the specified file *path*. Optional *encoding*, *detect* , and *bufferSize* arguments allow specifying the source stream encoding, whether to automatically detect the source stream encoding, and the desired I/O buffer size. The user-specified encoding is selected only if the **StreamReader** fails to figure out the source stream encoding.

Table 7.40 **StreamReader** class fields.

Field	Description
static StreamReader* Null	A **StreamReader** that is not associated with any storage.

Table 7.41 **StreamReader** class properties (all virtual).

Get/Set	Type	Property	Description
Get	**Stream***	**BaseStream**	Returns a pointer to the underlying stream.
Get	**Encoding***	**CurrentEncoding**	Returns the current encoding for the stream.

Table 7.42 **StreamReader** class methods.

Method	Description
void DiscardBufferedData()	Discards the contents of the stream buffer.

In-Memory Text Streams

You may need to create temporary streams, which are not mapped to any backing store, for reading and writing text strings. Such streams can be very useful for list processing or textual data parsing. To support the storage-less text streams, the .NET Framework supplies two classes:

* *StringWriter*–for writing **String**s into an in-memory text stream.

* *StringReader*–for reading **String**s from an in-memory text stream.

StringWriter Class

The **StringWriter** class supports writing strings to memory stream and is derived from the **TextWriter** class:

```
System::Object
|- System::MarshalByRefObject
   |- System::IO::TextWriter
      |- System::IO::StringWriter


Attributes: Serializable
Abstract: No
Sealed: No


Implements Interfaces: none
```

This class overrides all methods of the **TextWriter** class and supplies a few methods and properties of its own. The class constructors, fields, properties, and methods are listed in Tables 7.43 through 7.46.

Table 7.43 **StringWriter** class constructors.

Constructor	Description
StringWriter()	Default constructor.
StringWriter(StringBuilder* *buffer*)	
StringWriter(IFormatProvider* *provider*)	
StringWriter(StringBuilder* *buffer*, IFormatProvider* *provider*)	Constructs the **StringWriter** stream using the specified **StringBuilder** buffer and/or the specified format provider.

Table 7.44 **StringWriter** class fields.

Field	Description
static StreamWriter* Null	Represents a **StreamWriter** stream that is not associated with any storage.

Table 7.45 **StringWriter** class properties (all virtual).

Get/Set	Type	Property	Description
Get	**Encoding***	**Encoding**	Returns the encoding of the **StringWriter** stream.

Table 7.46 **StringWriter** class methods.

Method	Description
virtual StringBuilder* GetStringBuilder()	Retrieves the underlying **StringBuilder** object.
String* ToString()	Returns characters written to the current string so far.

The **StringWriter** class implements an internal buffer using a **StringBuilder** object. You can supply your own **StringBuilder** buffer as a parameter to the **StringWriter** constructor. You can also obtain a pointer to the class' internal **StringBuilder** buffer by calling the **GetStringBuilder** method. Finally, you can use the **ToString** method to obtain the **String** representation of data written to a **StringWriter** stream.

StringReader Class

The **StringReader** class compliments **StringWriter** by providing functionality for reading **String**s from in-memory text streams. The **StringReader** class is derived from **TextReader**:

```
System::Object
|- System::MarshalByRefObject
    |- System::IO::TextReader
        |- System::IO::StringReader

Attributes: Serializable
Abstract: No
Sealed: No
Implements Interfaces: none
```

This class overrides all methods of the **TextReader** class and does not supply any new methods of its own. The class has a single constructor (Table 7.47), which accepts a pointer to the source string.

Table 7.47 **StringReader** class constructors.

Constructor	Description
StringReader(String* *str*)	Constructs a **StringReader** stream reading from the specified string.

Streams for Reading/Writing Primitive Data Types

Although reading and writing text streams provides means for creating human-readable data, textual representation of numeric data is not very efficient. For compact data representation, you can use the **FileStream** class, which allows reading/writing arrays of bytes. Unfortunately, the **FileStream** class does not support reading/writing numeric value types other than the arrays bytes. Although you can use the **BitCoverter** class to convert numeric types to and from the arrays of bytes, this approach seems like a hassle and is not very efficient. For efficient reading and writing of numeric data types, you should use the other stream classes as shown here:

* *BinaryWriter*—for writing numeric values.

* *BinaryReader*—for reading numeric values.

Both classes can read/write numeric values in binary form. On top of that, the **BinaryWriter/BinaryReader** classes allow for specifying a desired encoding for the resulting binary stream to limit the stream character set or to obtain binary data representation suitable for e-mail or HTTP transmission.

BinaryWriter Class

The **BinaryWriter** class supports writing numeric data types to a file and has the following inheritance diagram:

```
System::Object
|- System::IO::BinaryWriter


Attributes: None
Abstract: No
Sealed: No


Implements Interfaces: IDisposable
```

The **BinaryWriter** class constructors, fields, properties, and methods are listed in Tables 7.48 through 7.51.

Table 7.48 **BinaryWriter** class constructors.

Constructor	Description
BinaryWriter()	Default constructor.
BinaryWriter(Stream* *stream*)	
BinaryWriter(Stream* *stream*, Encoding* *encoding*)	Constructs a **BinaryWriter** object based off the specified stream. Optional *encoding* argument allow specifying the desired stream encoding. The default encoding is UTF-8.

Table 7.49 **BinaryWriter** class fields.

Field	Description
static BinaryWriter* Null	Represents a Null stream, which is not mapped to any storage.
protected: Stream* OutStream	Contains the **Stream** object passed in the constructor (same as the **BaseStream** property).

Table 7.50 **BinaryWriter** class properties (all virtual).

Get/Set	Type	Property	Description
Get	**Stream***	**BaseStream**	Contains the **Stream** object passed in the constructor.

Table 7.51 **BinaryWriter** class methods.

Method	Description
virtual void Close()	Closes the writer stream by calling **Dispose(true)**.
protected: virtual void Dispose(bool *disposing*)	Releases managed and, if the *disposing* is set to true, unmanaged resources.
void IDisposable::Dispose()	Required by the **IDisposable** interface.
virtual __int64 Seek(int *offset*, SeekOrigin *origin*)	Sets the current writing position to the specified offset from the specified origin.
virtual void Write(bool *value*)	
virtual void Write(unsigned char *value*)	
virtual void Write(__wchar_t *value*)	
virtual void Write(Decimal *value*)	
virtual void Write(double *value*)	
virtual void Write(short *value*)	
virtual void Write(int *value*)	
virtual void Write(__int64 *value*)	
virtual void Write(char *value*)	
virtual void Write(float *value*)	
virtual void Write(String* *value*)	
virtual void Write(unsigned short *value*)	
virtual void Write(unsigned int *value*)	
virtual void Write(unsigned __int64 *value*)	Writes the specified primitive-type value to the stream.

NOTE: *The **BinaryWriter** class methods for writing **char**, **unsigned short**, **unsigned int** and **unsigned __int64** values are not CLS-compliant.*

Method	Description
virtual void Write(unsigned char __gc[] *array*)	
virtual void Write(unsigned char *array* __gc[], int *index*, int *count*)	Writes the specified *array* of bytes to the stream. Optional *index* and *count* arguments allow specifying the section of the array to write.
virtual void Write(__wchar_t __gc[] *array*)	
virtual void Write(__wchar_t *array* __gc[], int *index*, int *count*)	Writes the specified *array* of Unicode characters to the stream. Optional *index* and *count* arguments allow specifying the section of the array to write.
protected: void Write7BitEncodedInt(int *value*)	Writes an integer to the stream in 7-bit encoded format.

BinaryReader Class

The **BinaryReader** class supports reading numeric data types from a file and has the following inheritance diagram:

```
System::Object
|- System::IO::BinaryReader
```

```
Attributes: None
Abstract: No
Sealed: No
Implements Interfaces: IDisposable
```

The **BinaryReader** class constructors, properties, and methods are listed in Tables 7.52 through 7.54.

Table 7.52 BinaryReader class constructors.

Constructor	Description
BinaryReader(Stream* *stream*)	
BinaryReader(Stream* *stream*, Encoding* *encoding*)	Constructs a **BinaryReader** objects based off the specified stream. Optional ***encoding*** argument allows specifying the source stream encoding. The default encoding is UTF-8.

Table 7.53 BinaryReader class properties (all virtual).

Get/Set	Type	Property	Description
Get	**Stream***	**BaseStream**	Contains the **Stream** object passed in the constructor.

Table 7.54 BinaryReader class methods.

Method	Description
virtual void Close()	Closes the reader stream.
protected: virtual void Dispose(bool *disposing*)	Releases managed and, if the ***disposing*** is set to true, unmanaged resources.
protected: virtual void FillBuffer(int *numBytes*)	Fills the internal buffer with the specified number of bytes read from the stream.
void IDisposable::Dispose()	Required by the **IDisposable** interface.
virtual int PeekChar()	Returns the next character from the stream without updating the stream position, or -1 if there are no more characters in the stream.
virtual int Read()	Reads and returns the next character from the stream, or -1 if there are no more characters in the stream.
virtual int Read(unsigned char *buffer* __gc[], int *index*, int *count*)	Reads the ***count*** bytes from the stream and writes them to the specified buffer at the specified index.

<Continued on Next Page>

<Table 7.54 Continued>

Method	Description
virtual int Read(__wchar_t *buffer* __gc[], int *index,* int *count*)	Reads the *count* Unicode characters from the stream and writes them to the specified buffer at the specified index.
protected: int Read7BitEncodedInt()	Reads a 32-bit integer in a 7-bit encoded format.
virtual bool ReadBoolean()	
virtual unsigned char ReadByte()	
virtual __wchar_t ReadChar()	
virtual Decimal ReadDecimal()	
virtual double ReadDouble()	
virtual short ReadInt16()	
virtual int ReadInt32()	
virtual __int64 ReadInt64()	
virtual char ReadSByte()	
virtual float ReadSingle()	
virtual String* ReadString()	
virtual unsigned short ReadUInt16()	
virtual unsigned int ReadUInt32()	
virtual unsigned __int64 ReadUInt64()	Reads a primitive value from the stream.
virtual unsigned char ReadBytes(int *count*) __gc[]	Reads the specified *count* of bytes from the stream into an array.
virtual __wchar_t ReadChars(int *count*) __gc[]	Reads the specified *count* of Unicode characters from the stream into an array.

NOTE: *The current read position automatically advances after each stream read operation.*

The **BinaryWriter/BinaryReader** classes allow for specifying a desired encoding in their constructors. If the encoding is not specified, the default UTF-8 encoding is used.

In-Memory Binary Streams

Reading and writing from a file stream requires considerable overhead. If you want to use a stream to store temporary data, you should consider using memory streams, which are not mapped to any permanent storage. Using a memory stream instead of a file stream will boost your code's performance considerably because reading and writing data from a memory buffer is a much less costly operation than reading and writing data from a disk file. The .NET Framework implements memory streams by means of the **MemoryStream** class. The

MemoryStream class inherits from the **Stream** class and overrides and implements all of the **Stream** class methods. The **MemoryStream** class inheritance diagram is shown here:

```
System::Object
|- System::MarshalByRefObject
   |- System::IO::Stream
      |- System::IO::MemoryStream
```

```
Attributes: Serializable
Abstract: No
Sealed: Yes
Implements Interfaces: None
```

The **MemoryStream** class constructors, properties, and methods are listed in Tables 7.55 through 7.57.

Table 7.55 **MemoryStream** class constructors.

Constructor	Description
MemoryStream()	Creates a variable-length **MemoryStream**.
MemoryStream(int *capacity*)	Creates a variable-length **MemoryStream** with the specified initial capacity.
MemoryStream(unsigned char *buffer* **__gc[])**	
MemoryStream(unsigned char *buffer* **__gc[], bool** *writable*)	
MemoryStream(unsigned char *buffer* **__gc[], int** *index*, **int** *count*)	
MemoryStream(unsigned char *buffer* **__gc[], int** *index*, **int** *count*, **bool** *writable*)	
MemoryStream(unsigned char *buffer* **__gc[], int** *index*, **int** *count*, **bool** *writable*, **bool** *visible*)	Creates a fixed-length memory stream based of the specified byte *buffer*. Optional *writable* argument determines if the memory stream is writable or read-only. Optional *index* and *count* arguments indicate a section of the *buffer* to be used with the memory stream. Optional *visible* argument controls whether the internal memory stream buffer is accessible by means of the **GetBuffer** method.

Table 7.56 **MemoryStream** class properties (all virtual).

Get/Set	Type	Property	Description
Get	**bool**	**CanRead**	Always contains **true**.
Get	**bool**	**CanSeek**	Always contains **true**.
Get	**bool**	**CanWrite**	Contains **true** if the memory stream was created with the *writable*=**true** (default).
Get/Set	**int**	**Capacity**	Gets or sets the number of bytes allocated for the memory stream.
Get	**__int64**	**Length**	Contains the length of the stream in bytes. The length of a fixed-length stream cannot be greater than the size of the buffer supplied to the **MemoryStream** constructor.
Get/Set	**__int64**	**Position**	Gets or sets the current read/write position in the stream.

Table 7.57 **MemoryStream** class methods.

Method	Description
void Close()	Closes the memory stream. Closing the stream does not prevent you from accessing the memory stream buffer using the **GetBuffer** or **ToArray** methods.
void Flush()	Overrides **Stream::Flush** so that no action is performed.
virtual unsigned char GetBuffer() __gc[]	Returns an internal buffer of a variable-length stream or the supplied buffer of a fixed-length memory stream. The **GetBuffer** throws an **UnauthorizedAccessException** exception if the memory stream was constructed with the *visible*=**false**.
int Read(__in unsigned char* array __gc[], int offset, int count)	Reads the *count* bytes from the memory stream into the specified array at the specified index and returns the number of bytes read, or 0 if the end of stream was reached.
Int ReadByte()	Reads and returns a byte from the memory stream, or -1 if the end of stream was reached.
__int64 Seek(__int64 offset, SeekOrigin origin)	Sets the current read/write position to the specified value.
void SetLength(__int64 length)	Sets the length of the memory stream. If the memory stream is fixed-length, you must specify the length lesser than the size of the byte array used to construct the stream. Otherwise a **NotSupportedException** exception is thrown.
virtual unsigned char ToArray() __gc[]	Returns a copy of the memory stream buffer.
void Write(unsigned char array __gc[], int index, int count)	Writes (to the memory stream) the *count* bytes from the specified *array* at the specified *index*. The memory stream must be constructed with the *writable*=**true** to support writing. Variable-length memory streams are automatically extended if the writing occurs at the end of the stream.
void WriteByte(unsigned char value)	Writes the specified byte *value* to the memory stream.
virtual void WriteTo(Stream* stream)	Writes the entire contents of the memory stream to another *stream*.

NOTE: When using fixed-length streams, you cannot set the length of the stream to a value greater than the length of the underlying byte array. The **SetLength** method will throw a **NotSupportedException** exception. However, you can truncate the stream by specifying the **Length** values less than the underlying array size.

File System Paths

The .NET Framework Class Library supplies an all-static utility class named **Path** that implements platform- and OS-independent path operations, such as parsing, modifying, and combining paths. The **Path** class has the following inheritance diagram:

```
System::Object
|- System::IO::Path

Attributes: Serializable
Abstract: No
Sealed: Yes
Implements Interfaces: None
```

The **Path** class fields and methods are listed in Tables 7.58 through 7.59.

Table 7.58 **Path** class fields.

Field	Description
static __wchar_t AltDirectorySeparatorChar	Contains a platform-specific alternate directory separator character (e.g., / for Windows).
static __wchar_t DirectorySeparatorChar	Contains a platform-specific directory separator character (e.g., / for Windows).
static __wchar_t InvalidPathChars __gc[]	Contains a list of characters that cannot be used in path names (e.g., < , > , |, etc.).
static __wchar_t PathSeparator	Contains a path separator character: ; .
static __wchar_t VolumeSeparator	Contains a volume separator character (e.g., : for Windows).

Table 7.59 **Path** class methods.

Method	Description
static String* ChangeExtension(String* *path*, String* *extension*)	Changes the extension in the specified *path* string with the specified *extension*.
static String* Combine(String* *path1*, String* *path2*)	Combines two paths into one path. The function is useful for appending relative paths or file names to a root path.
static String* GetDirectoryName(String* *path*)	Returns the directory name portion of the specified *path*.
static String* GetExtension(String* *path*)	Returns the file extension portion of the specified *path*.

<Continued on Next Page>

<Table 7.59 Continued>

Method	Description
static String* GetFileName(String* *path*)	Returns the file name portion of the specified *path*.
static String* GetFileNameWithoutExtension(String* *path*)	Returns the file name without the extension of the specified *path*.
static String* GetFullPath(String* *path*)	Returns the absolute path for the specified *path* relative to the current working directory.
static String* GetPathRoot(String* *path*)	Returns the root directory for the specified *path* (e.g., returns C:\ for C:\Gems 3D\Gems.exe).
static String* GetTempFileName()	Creates a zero-length unique temporary file and returns its name.
static String* GetTempPath()	Returns the system temporary folder path (e.g., C:\Windows\Temp).
static bool HasExtension(String* *path*)	Returns **true** if the specified file name contains an extension.
static bool IsPathRooted(String* *path*)	Returns **true** if the specified path is absolute.

NOTE: The **Path** class does not perform path checking and, therefore, can represent existing and nonexistent paths. If you use a path string without a trailing slash (\), the path is considered a file name. A path with a trailing slash is considered a directory name. However, if you combine two paths, the first path is *always* considered a directory name.

Watching File System Changes

Software integration projects frequently involve linking legacy systems with new systems, where legacy systems produce or consume data represented by disk files. To determine whether a legacy application has produced or needs new data, developers used to poll a particular directory for changes. Needless to say, polling is not the best way to detect directory changes. The .NET Framework Class Library supplies a more elegant solution by providing a **FileSystemWatcher** class. The **FileSystemWatcher** class can be configured to detect desired file system changes (e.g., creation of new files in a specified directory) and fire notification events.

The **FileSystemWatcher** class saves you the hassle of directory polling and provides asynchronous change notifications. The drawback of the **FileSystemWatcher** class is that it can detect file system changes only on Windows NT systems (Windows 9x family is not supported). The **FileSystemWatcher** class has the following inheritance diagram:

```
System::Object
|- System::MarshalByRefObject
   |- System::ComponentModel::Component
      |- System::IO::FileSystemWatcher


Attributes: Serializable
Abstract: No
Sealed: Yes
Implements Interfaces: ISupportInitialize
```

The **FileSystemWatcher** class constructors, properties, methods, and events are listed in Tables 7.60 through 7.63.

Table 7.60 **FileSystemWatcher** class constructors.

Constructor	Description
FileSystemWatcher()	Default constructor.
FileSystemWatcher(String* *path*)	
FileSystemWatcher(String* *path*, String* *filter*)	Constructs a **FileSystemWatcher** object for monitoring the specified *path*. Optional *filter* argument allows specifying a mask for monitoring only selected files.

Table 7.61 **FileSystemWatcher** class properties.

Get/Set	Type	Property	Virtual	Description
Get/Set	**bool**	**EnableRaisingEvents**	No	Gets or sets a value indicating whether the **FileSystemWatcher** object will fire notification events.
Get/Set	**String***	**Filter**	No	Gets or sets a filter specifying which files to be monitored (e.g., * for all files, or *.xml for XML files).

<Continued on Next Page>

<Table 7.61 Continued>

Get/Set	Type	Property	Virtual	Description
Get/Set	**bool**	**IncludeSubdirectories**	No	Gets or sets a value indicating whether to monitor subdirectories on the specified path.
Get/Set	**int**	**InternalBufferSize**	No	Gets or sets the internal buffer size (in bytes) for storing information on the file system changes. If the buffer is too small, some of the file system changes information may be lost.
Get/Set	**NotifyEvents**	**NotifyFilter**	No	Gets or sets the filter, specifying which events to monitor.
Get/Set	**String***	**Path**	No	Gets or sets the path to monitor.
Get/Set	**ISite***	**Site**	**No**	Gets or sets the component site.
Get/Set	**ISynchronizeInvoke***	**SynchronizingObject**	No	Gets or sets the event handler marshaller object.

Table 7.62 **FileSystemWatcher** class methods.

Method	Description
__sealed void BeginInit()	Begins the initialization of the **FileSystemWatcher** object used by a form or another component.
protected: void Dispose(bool *disposing*)	Releases managed and, if the disposing is set to **true**, unmanaged resources.
__sealed void EndInit()	Ends the initialization of the **FileSystemWatcher** object used by a form or another component.
protected: void OnChanged(FileSystemEventArgs* *e*)	Called when the size, attributes, last access time, last modified time, or security permissions change on a file or directory being monitored. The default implementation raises the **Changed** event.
protected: void OnCreated(FileSystemEventArgs* *e*)	Called when a new file or subdirectory is created on the path being monitored. The default implementation raises the **Created** event.
protected: void OnDeleted(FileSystemEventArgs* *e*)	Called when a file or subdirectory is deleted on the path being monitored. The default implementation raises the **Deleted** event.
protected: void OnError(ErrorEventArgs* *e*)	Raises the **Error** event.
protected: void OnRenamed(RenamedEventArgs* *e*)	Called when a new file or subdirectory is renamed on the path being monitored. The default implementation raises the **Renamed** event.
WaitForChangedResult WaitForChanged(WatcherChangeTypes *eventType*)	Waits indefinitely for the specified event type to occur.

<Continued on Next Page>

<Table 7.62 Continued>

Method	Description
WaitForChangedResult WaitForChanged (WatcherChangeTypes *eventType*, int *timeout*)	Waits no longer than *timeout* milliseconds for the specified event type to occur.

Table 7.63 **FileSystemWatcher** class events.

Event	Description
FileSystemEventHandler* Changed	The event is raised when the size, attributes, last access time, last modified time, or security permissions change on a file or directory being monitored.
FileSystemEventHandler* Created	The event is raised when a new file or subdirectory is created on the path being monitored.
FileSystemEventHandler* Deleted	The event is raised when a new file or subdirectory is deleted on the path being monitored.
ErrorEventHandler* Error	The event is called when an error occurs (i.e., the internal buffer overflows or an I/O exception occurs).
RenamedEventHandler* Renamed	The event is raised when a new file or subdirectory is renamed on the path being monitored.

WARNING! The **FileSystemWatcher** class can detect file system changes only on Windows NT systems (Windows 9x family is not supported).

When copying or moving files or directories, keep in mind that several notification events may be caused by a single file operation. For instance, if you move a file from one subdirectory to another, the **Deleted** and the **Created** events may be fired. To enable a **FileSystemWatcher** object to fire events, you must hook up event handlers. Thus, you must create your own class exposing methods compatible with the **FileSystemEventHandler**, **RenamedEventHandler**, or **ErrorEventHandler** event delegates. The delegate signatures are:

```
void FileSystemEventHandler(Object* sender, FileSystemEventArgs* e);
void ErrorEventHandler(Object* sender, ErrorEventArgs* e);
void RenamedEventHandler(Object* sender, RenamedEventArgs* e);
```

The **FileSystemEventArgs** and **ErrorEventArgs** classes derive from the **EventArgs** class, while the **RenamedEventArgs** classes derive from the **FileSystemEventArgs** class. The **FileSystemEventArgs**, **ErrorEventArgs**, and **RenamedEventArgs** class constructors, properties, and methods are listed in Tables 7.64 through 7.68.

Table 7.64 **FileSystemEventArgs** class constructors.

Constructor	Description
FileSystemEventArgs(WatcherChangeTypes *changeType*, String* *directory*, String* *file*)	Constructs a **FileSystemEventArgs** object indicating that the *changeType* event occurred on a *file* in a *directory*.

Table 7.65 **FileSystemEventArgs** class properties.

Get/Set	Type	Property	Description
Get	**WatcherChangeTypes**	**ChangeType**	Contains the change type.
Get	**String***	**FullPath**	Contains the full path of the affected file or directory.
Get	**String***	**Name**	Contains the name of the affected file or directory.

Table 7.66 **RenamedEventArgs** class constructors.

Constructor	Description
RenamedEventArgs(WatcherChangeTypes *changeType*, String* *directory*, String* *newName*, String* *oldName*)	Constructs a **RenamedEventArgs** object indicating that the *oldName* file or directory was renamed into the *newName*.

Table 7.67 **RenamedEventArgs** class properties.

Get/Set	Type	Property	Description
Get	**String***	**OldFullPath**	Contains the old full path of the renamed file or directory.
Get	**String***	**OldName**	Contains the old name of the renamed file or directory.

Table 7.68 **ErrorEventArgs** class constructors.

Constructor	Description
ErrorEventArgs(Exception* *e*)	Constructs an **ErrorEventArgs** object using the specified exception.

Table 7.69 **ErrorEventArgs** class methods.

Method	Description
virtual Exception* GetException()	Returns the exception that caused the **FileSystemWatcher::Error** event.

Isolated Storage

Microsoft .NET Framework puts a great deal of focus on security. To achieve tight security and smooth side-by-side execution of different programs or assemblies (some of which could have originated from Internet remote file share), it is important to ensure that the software modules do not interfere with each other by snooping on file I/O or by accidentally writing into the same location. .NET ensures smooth side-by-side assembly execution by enforcing I/O security permissions and providing *isolated storage*. While I/O security permissions specify whether a particular assembly is allowed to read or write from local storage at all, the isolated storage provides a means for ensuring that, if an assembly must read or write data to the local storage, the data is going to be written to a private location isolated from storage used by other assemblies. For example, downloadable components, such as ActiveX controls, by default do not have rights to perform file I/O on the local system unless the file I/O is directed to the isolated storage.

An isolated storage location is just a directory on the system, typically called "Application Data." Because isolated storage is only a directory, it should not be used to store sensitive information such as unencrypted passwords because trusted code can easily read the contents of isolated storage directories and discover the sensitive information.

The .NET Framework supports isolated storage by means of the System::IO::IsolatedStorage namespace. The System::IO::IsolatedStorage namespace classes, exceptions, interfaces, and enumerations are listed in Tables 7.70 through 7.73.

Table 7.70 System::IO::IsolatedStorage namespace classes.

Class	Description
IsolatedStorage	Abstract base class for all isolated storage implementations.
IsolatedStorageFile	Represents an isolated storage location, which can contain files and directories.
IsolatedStorageFileStream	Isolated storage file stream supporting reading and writing.

Table 7.71 System::IO::IsolatedStorage namespace exceptions.

Exception	Description
IsolatedStorageException	Thrown when an isolated storage error occurs.

Table 7.72 System::IO::IsolatedStorage namespace interfaces.

Interface	Description
INormalizeForIsolatedStorage	Exposes the **Object* Normalize()** method for retrieving the name of the isolated store or the stream to which the name of the isolated store was serialized.

Table 7.73 System::IO::IsolatedStorage namespace enumerations.

Enumeration	Flags	Description
IsolatedStorageScope	Yes	Defines levels of isolation for the **IsolatedStorage** class: **Assembly**, **Domain**, **None**, **Roaming**, and **User**.

Isolated Storage Levels

When you create an isolated storage object using the **IsolatedStorageFile** class, you must specify a desired *level of isolation*. The **IsolatedStorageScope** enumeration defines combinable flags for all possible levels of isolation. Isolated storage is always isolated by the user. Thus, no two assemblies executed under different user accounts can share isolated storage. In addition to isolation by the user, the isolated storage can be:

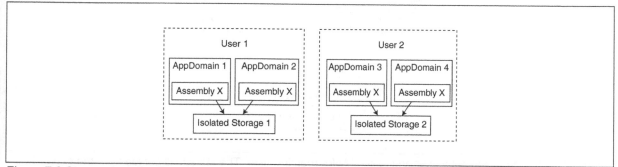

Figure 7.2 Storage isolation by user and assembly. The storage is shared among application domains.

*   *Isolated by assembly* (**IsolatedStorageScope::Domain**): An assembly is used by several applications and must store data, which is not application-specific (see Figure 7.2). An example of assembly-specific data is dial-up parameters used by a remote-access DLL shared among multiple applications.

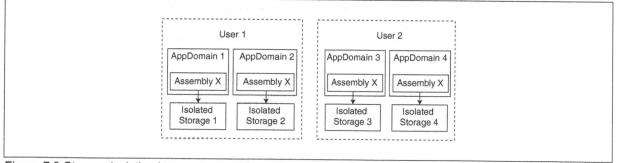

Figure 7.3 Storage isolation by user, assembly, and domain. The storage is private to each application domain.

*   *Isolated by domain and assembly* (**IsolatedStorageScope::Assembly**): A shared assembly must store data, which is application–specific (see Figure 7.3). For instance, a window layout component should store window size and position-specific information for each GUI application that uses it.

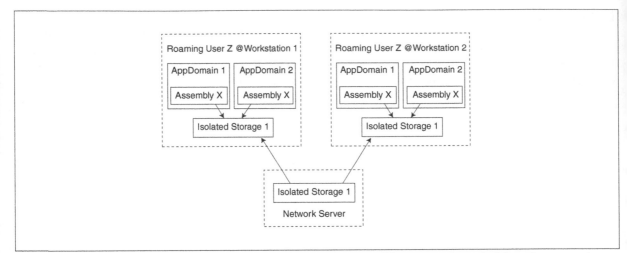

Figure 7.4 Storage isolation by user and assembly for roaming user. The storage is copied from the server to each workstation a user logs in to.

* *Roaming* (**IsolatedStorageScope::Roaming**): Roaming isolated storage can be used by roaming users to retrieve their settings (see Figures 7.4 and 7.5). Windows NT, Windows 2000, and some Windows 98 systems support roaming user profiles. When a roaming user logs in, his or her personal preferences are restored no matter which workstation on the network he or she logs in to. Thus, if a roaming user executes an application, which writes data to a roaming isolated storage, logs off, then logs in on another workstation, the data written to the roaming isolated storage will be downloaded to the roaming isolated storage on the other workstation.

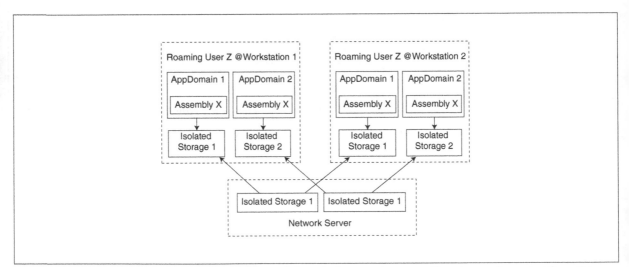

Figure 7.5 Storage isolation by user, assembly, and domain for roaming user. The storage is copied from the server to each workstation a user logs in to.

IsolatedStorage Class

To support the core isolated storage functionality, the System::IO::IsolatedStorage namespace supplies an abstract base class **IsolatedStorage** as defined here

```
System::Object
|- System::MarshalByRefObject
   |- System::IO::IsolatedStorage::IsolatedStorage
```

```
Attributes: none
Abstract: Yes
Sealed: No
Implements Interfaces: none
```

The **IsolatedStorage** class constructors, properties, and methods are listed in Tables 7.74 through 7.76.

Table 7.74 IsolatedStorage class constructors.

Constructor	Description
protected: IsolatedStorage()	Default constructor.

Table 7.75 IsolatedStorage class properties.

Get/Set	Type	Property	Virtual	Description
Get	**Object***	**AssemblyIdentity**	No	Contains the assembly identity used to scope the isolated storage.
Get	**__int64**	**CurrentSize**	Yes	Contains the size of the isolated storage.
Get	**Object***	**DomainIdentity**	No	Contains the domain identity used to scope the isolated storage.
Get	**__int64**	**MaximumSize**	Yes	Contains the maximum size of the isolated storage.
Get	**IsolatedStorageScope**	**Scope**	No	Contains the scope of the isolated storage.
Get	**__wchar_t**	**SeparatorExternal**	Yes	Contains a backslash character (\) used to separate directories in a path name.
Get	**__wchar_t**	**SeparatorInternal**	Yes	Contains a period character (.).

Table 7.76 **IsolatedStorage** class methods.

Method	Description
protected: virtual IsolatedStoragePermission* GetPermission(PermissionSet* *ps*) = 0	Must return the isolated storage permissions.
protected: void InitStore(IsolatedStorageScope *scope*, Type* *domainEvidenceType*, Type* *assemblyEvidenceType*)	Initializes the isolated storage for the specified assembly in the specified domain.
public: virtual void Remove() = 0	Must remove all the data in the isolated storage.

Isolated Storage Files

The **IsolatedStorageFile** class provides methods for manipulating isolated storage files and directories. This class is similar to the **FileInfo** class, except that all the files and directories managed by the **IsolatedStorageFile** class are confined to the isolated storage directory defined by the requested level of isolation. The **IsolatedStorageFile** class does not allow you to access files or directories outside the isolated storage and will throw an exception if you undertake such an attempt. The **IsolatedStorageFile** class has the following inheritance diagram:

```
System::Object
|- System::MarshalByRefObject
   |- System::IO::IsolatedStorage::IsolatedStorage
      |- System::IO::IsolatedStorage::IsolatedStorageFile


Attributes: none
Abstract: No
Sealed: Yes
Implements Interfaces: IDisposable
```

The **IsolatedStorageFile** class does not have constructors. The **IsolatedStorage** methods are listed in Table 7.77.

Table 7.77 **IsolatedStorageFile** class methods.

Method	Description
void Close()	Closes the isolated storage file.
void CreateDirectory(String* *path*)	Creates an isolated storage directory.
void DeleteDirectory(String* *path*)	Deletes an isolated storage directory.
void DeleteFile(String* *path*)	Deletes an isolated storage file.
__sealed void Dispose()	Disposes the isolated storage.
~IsolatedStorageFile()	Destructor.
String* GetDirectoryNames(String* *mask*) __gc[]	Returns an array of isolated storage directories matching the specified mask.

<Continued on Next Page>

<Table 7.77 Continued>

Method	Description
static IEnumerator* GetEnumerator(IsolatedStorageScope *scope***)**	Returns an enumerator for enumerating the isolated storage stores with the specified scope.
String* GetFileNames(String* *mask***) __gc[]**	Returns an array of isolated storage files matching the specified mask.
protected: IsolatedStoragePermission* GetPermission(PermissionSet* *ps***)**	Returns the isolated storage permissions.
static IsolatedStorageFile* GetStore(IsolatedStorageScope *level*, **Object*** *domainIdentity*, **Object*** *assemblyIdentity*)	
static IsolatedStorageFile* GetStore(IsolatedStorageScope *level*, **Type*** *domainEvidenceType*, **Type*** *assemblyEvidenceType*)	
static IsolatedStorageFile* GetStore(IsolatedStorageScope *level*, **Evidence*** *domainEvidence*, **Type*** *domainEvidenceType*, **Evidence*** *assemblyEvidence*, **Type*** *assemblyEvidenceType*)	Creates an isolated storage file with the desired *level* of isolation using the specified domain and assembly evidence.
static IsolatedStorageFile* GetUserStoreForAssembly()	Returns an isolated storage file corresponding to the current assembly.
static IsolatedStorageFile* GetUserStoreForDomain()	Returns an isolated storage file corresponding to the current domain.
void Remove()	Removes all files and directories from the isolated storage. You should not access the isolated storage properties after calling this method, as an **InvalidOperationException** exception will be thrown.
static void Remove(IsolatedStorageScope *scope***)**	Removes any isolated storage with the specified scope, including all isolated storage files and directories.

Isolated Storage Streams

The **IsolatedStorageFileStream** class represents a **FileStream**-based stream for reading/writing binary data from isolated storage files. The **IsolatedStorageFileStream** class has the following inheritance diagram:

```
System::Object
|- System::MarshalByRefObject
   |- System::IO::Stream
      |- System::IO::FileStream
         |- System::IO::IsolatedStorage::IsolatedStorageFileStream
Attributes: none
Abstract: No
Sealed: Yes
Implements Interfaces: None
```

The **IsolatedStorageFileStream** class methods are listed in Table 7.78. The **IsolatedStorageFileStream** overrides all methods of the **FileStream** class and does not define any original methods. For a summary of the **Stream** and **FileStream** methods, see Tables 7.23 and 7.26, respectively.

Table 7.78 **IsolatedStorageFileStream** class constructors.

Constructor	Description
IsolatedStorageFileStream(String* *path*, FileMode *mode*)	
IsolatedStorageFileStream(String* *path*, FileMode *mode*, IsolatedStorageFile* *isf*)	
IsolatedStorageFileStream(String* *path*, FileMode *mode*, FileAccess *access*)	
IsolatedStorageFileStream(String* *path*, FileMode *mode*, FileAccess *access*, IsolatedStorageFile* *isf*)	
IsolatedStorageFileStream(String* *path*, FileMode *mode*, FileAccess *access*, FileShare *share*)	
IsolatedStorageFileStream(String* *path*, FileMode *mode*, FileAccess *access*, FileShare *share*, IsolatedStorageFile* *isf*)	
IsolatedStorageFileStream(String* *path*, FileMode *mode*, FileAccess *access*, FileShare *share*, int *bufferSize*)	
IsolatedStorageFileStream(String* *path*, FileMode *mode*, FileAccess *access*, FileShare *share*, int *bufferSize*, IsolatedStorageFile* *isf*)	Constructs the isolated storage file stream object by creating or opening a file on the specified ***path***. Optional ***mode*** argument specifies whether a file should be opened or created (**Create**, **Open**, **OpenOrCreate**, etc.). Optional ***access*** argument specifies whether a file should be open for reading, writing, or both. Optional ***share*** parameter specifies file sharing options. Optional ***isf*** argument allows specifying an **IsolatedStorageFile** object associated with the stream.

Immediate Solutions

Using **Directory** Class: Retrieving and Changing Current Directory, Obtaining Directory Information

All-static **Directory** class represents a convenient wrapper for directory management API. Because the **Directory** class is static one must always supply the name of the target directory when invoking **Directory** class methods. Fortunately, using this class is a no-brainer. The following code example illustrates how to:

1. Retrieve the current working directory name using the **GetCurrentDirectory** method.

2. Retrieve directory creation, last access, and last write time using the **GetCreationTime**, **GetLastAccessTime** and **GetLastWriteTime** methods.

3. Change current directory using the **SetCurrentDirectory** method.

Here is the code that performs all of these operations:

```
#using <mscorlib.dll>
using namespace System;
using namespace System::IO;

void main()
{
    // 1. Get current directory
    String* CurrentDir = Directory::GetCurrentDirectory();
    Console::WriteLine("Current directory: {0}", CurrentDir);

    // 2. Obtain directory information
    Console::WriteLine("   Creation time: {0}",
        Directory::GetCreationTime("Test").ToString());
    Console::WriteLine("Last access time: {0}",
        Directory::GetLastAccessTime("Test").ToString());
    Console::WriteLine(" Last write time: {0}",
        Directory::GetLastWriteTime("Test").ToString());

    // 3. Change directory
    Directory::SetCurrentDirectory("..");
}
```

As you can see from the code, the **Directory** class fully supports "." and ".." specifiers for current and parent directory names.

> **NOTE:** If you specify an invalid directory name when calling the **Directory** class methods, a **DirectoryNotFoundException** exception will be thrown.

Using **Directory** Class: Listing Contents, Creating, Renaming, Deleting Directories

All-static **Directory** class allows performing full spectrum of operations on directories, including creating, renaming, deleting, listing contents, etc. The only rule to remember is that you have to specify the target directory name when invoking **Directory**-class methods. The following code example illustrates how to:

1. List files in a directory using the **GetFiles** method.

3. Create a directory if it doesn't exist using the **Exists** and **CreateDirectory** methods.

6. Rename directory using the **Move** method.

7. Delete a directory with all of its contents using the **Delete** method.

Here is the code that performs all of these operations:

```
#using <mscorlib.dll>
using namespace System;
using namespace System::IO;

void main()
{
    // 1. List all files in the current directory
    String* Files __gc[] = Directory::GetFiles(".");
    for ( int i = 0; i < Files->Count; i++ )
        Console::WriteLine(Files[i]);

    // 2. Create a directory if it does not exist
    if ( !Directory::Exists("Test") )
        Directory::CreateDirectory("Test");

    // 3. Rename directory
    Directory::Move("Test", "Test2");

    // 4. Delete directory including subdirectories
    Directory::Delete("Test2", true);
}
```

Using **DirectoryInfo** Class: Initializing, Obtaining Directory Information, Creating Directories and Subdirectories

While the all-static **Directory** class is convenient for working with random directories, its instance-based counterpart **DirectoryInfo** is intended for managing a particular directory. Thus, in order to use a **DirectoryInfo** object, you must instantiate it with the **new** operator and initialize it with a directory name. Then you can start invoking instance methods on the **DirectoryInfo** object to perform desired directory operations.

Unlike with the all-static **Directory** class, you do not have to specify a valid directory name when creating a **DirectoryInfo** object—you can specify a new directory name and actually create the new directory by calling the **Create** method at a later time. Keep in mind, however, that if you attempt to use the directory before you create it, a **DirectoryNotFoundException** will be thrown. Also, if the directory associated with the **DirectoryInfo** object does not exist, the **DirectoryInfo** properties will not be initialized until you create the directory by calling the **Create** method.

The following code example shows how to:

1. Instantiate a **DirectoryInfo** object using the **DirectoryInfo** constructor.
2. Verify that the directory exists using the **Exists** method.
2. Create the directory using the **Create** method.
3. Obtain the directory's parent and root information using the **DirectoryInfo**'s **Parent** and **Root** properties.
4. Create a subdirectory using the **CreateSubdirectory** method.
5. Rename a directory.
6. Initialize a new instance of the **DirectoryInfo** class by creating a new directory using the **CreateDirectory** method.

Here is the code that performs all of these operations:

```
#using <mscorlib.dll>
using namespace System;
using namespace System::IO;

void main()
{
    // 1. Initialize a DirectoryInfo object
    DirectoryInfo* dir = new DirectoryInfo("Test");
    // 2. Verify that the directory exists
    if ( !dir->Exists )
        Console::WriteLine("The directory does not exist yet");
    // 3. Create the directory
    dir->Create();

    // 4. Obtain directory information
    Console::WriteLine("Parent: {0}", dir->Parent);
    Console::WriteLine("  Root: {0}", dir->Root);

    // 5. Create a subdirectory
    dir->CreateSubdirectory("SubDir");

    // 6. Initialize another DirectoryInfo object
    dir = Directory::CreateDirectory("Test2");
}
```

Using **DirectoryInfo** Class: Listing Directory Contents, Renaming, Deleting Directories

The instance-based **DirectoryInfo** class is fully equivalent to the all-static **Directory** class in terms of operations that it can perform on directories. Such operations include listing directory contents, renaming, removing directories, and creating subdirectories. The following code example shows how to:

1. Instantiate a **DirectoryInfo** object.

2. List the directory contents using the **GetFileSystemInfos** method. The **GetFileSystemInfos** retrieves both files and subdirectories. To limit your selection just to files, use the **GetFiles** methods; to subdirectories, use **GetDirectories** methods. Also, you can specify optional file mask to limit your selection even further. In the example below, the "*.cpp" mask is specified to limit the selection to files and subdirectories with cpp-extension.

3. Rename the directory using the **MoveTo** method.

4. Delete the directory using the **Delete** method. To delete a nonempty directory, you must set the optional *recursive* argument of the **Delete** method to **true**. Otherwise, an exception will be thrown if you attempt deleting a directory, which is not empty.

Here is the code that performs all of these operations:

```cpp
#using <mscorlib.dll>
using namespace System;
using namespace System::IO;

void main()
{
    // 1. Initialize a DirectoryInfo object
    DirectoryInfo* dir = new DirectoryInfo("Test");

    // 2. List all files and directories
    FileSystemInfo* info __gc[] = dir->GetFileSystemInfos("*.cpp");
    for ( int i = 0; i < info->Count; i++ )
        Console::WriteLine(info[i]);

    // 3. Rename the directory
    dir->MoveTo("Test3");

    // 4. Delete the directory including subdirectories
    dir->Delete(true);
}
```

Using **File** Class: Creating Files, Obtaining File Information

All-static **File** class represents a convenient wrapper for file management API. Because the **File** class is static, one must always supply the name of the target file when invoking **File**-class methods. Besides managing files on the file system level, the **File** class allows you to open files for reading or writing and creating streams using **AppendText**, **Open**, **Create**, **OpenRead,** or **OpenWrite** methods. The following code example illustrates how to:

1. Verify file existence using the **Exist** method.

2. Create a new file using the **Create** method. The **Create** method not just creates a file, but also opens a file for writing by returning a pointer to the **FileStream** object.

6. Retrieves the file creation time, last write time, and attributes using the **GetCreationTime**, **GetLastWriteTime** and **GetAttributes** methods.

The code example is as follows:

```
#using <mscorlib.dll>
using namespace System;
using namespace System::IO;

void main()
{
   // 1. Verify file existence
   if ( !File::Exists("Test.txt") )
   {
      // 2. Create new file
      FileStream* stream = File::Create("Test.txt");
      stream->Close();
   }

   // 3. Retrieve file information
   Console::WriteLine("   Creation time: {0}",
      File::GetCreationTime("Test.txt").ToString());
   Console::WriteLine(" Last write time: {0}",
      File::GetLastWriteTime("Test.txt").ToString());
   Console::WriteLine("      Attributes: {0}",
      __box(File::GetAttributes("Test.txt")));
}
```

Using **File** Class: Copying, Moving Files, and Modifying File Attributes

The all-static **File** class allows performing full spectrum of operations on files, including copying, renaming, deleting, and modifying attributes. Just like with the all-static **Directory** class, you must specify the target file name when invoking **File**-class methods. The following code example illustrates how to:

1. Modify file attributes using the **SetAttributes** method.

2. Copy a file into a new file using the **Copy** method. You can use the **Copy** method to copy a file over an existing file if you set the optional overwrite *argument* to **true**. Keep in mind, however, that read-only files cannot be overwritten with the **Copy** method as the framework throws the **IOException**.

3. Rename a file using the **Move** method. The **Move** method throws an exception if the target file already exists.

4.   Remove read-only attribute from a file using the **SetAttributes** method and delete the file using the **Delete** method. (The **Delete** method cannot remove read-only files).

The code example is as follows:

```
#using <mscorlib.dll>
using namespace System;
using namespace System::IO;

void main()
{
    // 1. Set Read-Only attribute
    File::SetAttributes("Test.txt", FileAttributes::ReadOnly);

    // 2. Copy file
    File::Copy("Test.txt", "Test2.txt");
    // Copy and overwrite: will fail, because the file is ReadOnly
    try {
        File::Copy("Test.txt", "Test2.txt", true);
    }
    catch(Exception* e) {
        Console::WriteLine(e->Message);
    }

    // 3. Move file: will throw an exception because file already exists
    try {
        File::Move("Test.txt", "Test2.txt");
    }
    catch(Exception* e) {
        Console::WriteLine(e->Message);
    }

    // 4. Delete files: remove Read-Only attributes first
    File::SetAttributes("Test.txt", Normal);
    File::Delete("Test.txt");
    File::SetAttributes("Test2.txt", Normal);
    File::Delete("Test2.txt");
}
```

NOTE: The **File** class throws an exception if you attempt to move or delete a file marked with a read-only attributes.

Using **FileInfo** Class: Initializing, Retrieving File Properties

While the all-static **File** class is convenient for working with random files, its instance-based counterpart **FileInfo** is intended for managing a particular file. For instance, you can use the **FileInfo** object to pass a file as a parameter to a function or method call. To use a **FileInfo** object, you must instantiate it with the **new** operator and initialize it with a file name. Then you can start invoking instance methods on the **FileInfo** object to perform desired file operations.

Unlike with the all-static **File** class, you do not have to specify a valid file name when creating a **FileInfo** object—you can specify a new file name and actually create the file by calling the **Create** method at a later time. Keep in mind, however, that if you attempt to use the file before you create it, a **FileNotFoundException** will be thrown. Also, if the file associated with the **FileInfo** object does not exist, the **FileInfo** properties will not be initialized until you create the file by calling the **Create** method.

The following code example illustrates how to:

1. Instantiate a **FileInfo** object using the **FileInfo** constructor.

2. Create a new file using the **Create** method and write some data to file using the **FileStream** object returned by the **Create** method. (The **Create** method not just creates a file but also opens it for writing.)

3. Retrieve the name and the directory path of the newly created file using the **DirectoryName** and **Name** properties.

4. Attempt retrieving the file length using the **Length** property. Despite the fact that the file is already created, the **Length** property throws the **FileNotFoundException**, because the file did not originally exist when the **FileInfo** object was initialized.

5. To overcome the difficulty, one must call the **Refresh** method to force the **FileInfo** object to pickup the latest file system changes pertaining to the associated file.

6. Retrieve the file length and some other properties again. This time, no exception will be thrown.

Here is the code example:

```
#using <mscorlib.dll>
using namespace System;
using namespace System::IO;

void main()
{
    // 1. Initialize a FileInfo object
    FileInfo* file = new FileInfo("Test.txt");
    if ( !file->Exists )
       Console::WriteLine("The file does not exist yet.");

    // 2. Create a new file
    FileStream* stream = file->Create();
    stream->WriteByte(123);
    stream->Close();

    // 3. Obtain file information
    Console::WriteLine("Directory name: {0}", file->DirectoryName);
    Console::WriteLine("      File name: {0}", file->Name);

    // 4. Will throw an exception because the file did not exist when
    // the file object was initialized
    try {
       Console::WriteLine("         Length: {0} byte(s)",
```

```
            __box(file->Length));
}
catch(Exception* e) {
    Console::WriteLine(e->Message);
}

    // 5. Must refresh in order to pick up changes
    file->Refresh();

    // 6. Obtain file length, full name and extension
    Console::WriteLine("        Length: {0} byte(s)", __box(file->Length));
    Console::WriteLine("      FullName: {0}", file->FullName);
    Console::WriteLine("     Extension: {0}", file->Extension);
}
```

Using **FileInfo** Class: Modifying File Properties, Renaming and Deleting Files

The instance-based **FileInfo** class is fully equivalent to the all-static **File** class in terms of operations that it can perform on files. Such operations include getting/setting file attributes, renaming, and deleting files. The following code example shows how to:

1.   Instantiate a **FileInfo** object using the **FileInfo** constructor.

2.   Verify file existence using the **Exists** property. (The **Exists** is initialized when a **FileInfo** object is instantiated.)

3.   Modify the file last access time by setting the **LastAccessTime** property.

4.   Rename file using the **Move** method.

5.   Delete file using the Delete method.

Here is the code example:

```
#using <mscorlib.dll>
using namespace System;
using namespace System::IO;

void main()
{
    // 1. Initialize a FileInfo object
    FileInfo* file = new FileInfo("Test.txt");

    // 2. Verify file existence
    if ( !file->Exists )
    {
        Console::WriteLine("The file does not exist.");
        return;
    }
```

```
   // 3. Modify last access time
   file->LastAccessTime = DateTime::Today;

   // 4. Rename the file
   file->MoveTo("Test2.txt");

   // 5. Delete the file
   file->Delete();
}
```

Reading and Writing Files

To read or write from file binary data represented as an array of bytes, you should use the **FileStream** class. You can open a file for reading or writing in one of two ways:

* Create a new instance of the **FileStream** class and specify the file name, file creation mode (i.e., **CreateNew**, **OpenOrCreate**, and so on), desired file access (**Read**, **ReadWrite**, or **Write**), and file sharing options in the **FileStream** constructor parameters (see Table 7.24);

* Use the **File/FileInfo Create** or **Open** methods (see Table 7.9).

Both approaches are absolutely equivalent.

The following code example demonstrates how to:

1. Instantiate a **FileStream** object by means of the **File** class.
2. Instantiate a **FileStream** object using the constructor.
3. Write data to the file stream.
4. Change the stream read/write position.
5. Read data from the stream.

Here's the code example:

```
#using <mscorlib.dll>
using namespace System;
using namespace System::IO;

void main()
{
   // 1. Create a file and open a file stream
   FileStream* stream = File::Create("Test.txt");
   stream->Close();

   // 2. Open or Create a file using the constructor
   stream = new FileStream("Test.txt", FileMode::OpenOrCreate,
            FileAccess::ReadWrite, FileShare::None, 1024);
```

```
    // Report stream name
    Console::WriteLine(stream->Name);

    // 3. Write a single byte
    stream->WriteByte(123);
    // Write buffer
    unsigned char buffer __gc[] = new unsigned char __gc[128];
    stream->Write(buffer, 0, buffer->Count);

    // 4. Seek
    if ( stream->CanSeek )
    {
        stream->Position = 0;
        // The same as above
        stream->Seek(0, SeekOrigin::Begin);
    }

    // 5. Read a single byte
    unsigned char b = stream->ReadByte();
    // Read buffer
    int BytesRead = stream->Read(buffer, 0, (int)stream->Length);

    // Close stream
    stream->Close();
}
```

NOTE: You must explicitly close a stream using the **Close** method when you no longer need the stream. If you forget to close the stream, the stream will not be released until the garbage collector finalizes it.

Reading Files Asynchronously

Asynchronous I/O is often used due to potential performance improvements resulting from the elimination of blocking on synchronous I/O calls. When implementing asynchronous I/O, keep in mind that there is an overhead associated with asynchronous I/O. When reading small amounts of data from files (less than 64K on Windows), you will achieve better performance using synchronous I/O. Large chunks of data should be read asynchronously, on the other hand.

Converting an existing program to use asynchronous I/O could be a difficult task because you would have to redesign the code to eliminate data dependencies and, perhaps, to utilize pipelined processing. Also, you need to make sure that your code does not issue multiple asynchronous I/O requests simultaneously because the completion order of the simultaneous I/O requests may be unpredictable. A typical scenario for asynchronous I/O is asynchronous reading of a large file. You can boost the performance of your code by reading data in chunks and processing each chunk individually without having to wait for the entire file to load.

To implement an asynchronous file reader, we'll create a class named **AsyncReader** and define a callback routine named **ReadCallback** for handling the read request completion notifications. The **ReadCallback** method must be defined as **void ReadCallback(IAsyncResult*** *Result***)** to be compatible with the

AsyncCallback delegate.The general asynchronous file reading strategy is as follows:

1. Initiate the first read request.
2. Initiate the next read request when the request completes and the callback method is called.
3. Continue the chain until the end of file is reached.

Listing 7.1 illustrates an implementation of the **AsyncReader** class. The class defines two properties:

*   The Boolean **IsFinished** to indicate if the class finished reading a file.
*   **Data** to provide access to the buffer holding the read file data.

In the **AsyncReader** constructor, the class initializes the **readCallback** delegate with the pointer to the **ReadCallback** method. The **readCallback** delegate is later used by the **AsyncReader::BeginRead** method to initiate the first asynchronous read request on the specified file. The **AsyncReader::BeginRead** method initializes the **Stream** member with a new instance of a **FileStream** object and calls the **BeginRead** on the stream.

The **ReadCallback** method reports the number of bytes read by the previous requests and initiates a new asynchronous read request if the stream position is less than the stream length (**Stream->Position < Stream->Length**). Otherwise, the **bFinished** flag is set to **true** to indicate that the file has been read, and the stream is closed to release the file handle.

A small program accompanying the **AsyncReader** class definition illustrates how to use the **AsyncReader** class as it waits until the **IsFinished** property is set to **true**. The **AsyncReader** class also implements the **IDisposable** interface and defines a destructor, the **Dispose** method. This destructor is provided for convenience so you could manually close the stream and terminate the pending read request. The **Dispose** method sets the **bDisposing** flag so that a pending **ReadCallback** routine does not initiate a new asynchronous read request and terminates the pending read request synchronously by calling the **EndRead** method.

Listing 7.1 **AsyncReader** class for reading files asynchronously.

```
#using <mscorlib.dll>
using namespace System;
using namespace System::IO;

// Asynchronous file reader
gc class AsyncReader: public IDisposable {
public:
   AsyncReader()
   {
      readCallback = new AsyncCallback(this, &AsyncReader::ReadCallback);
      bFinished = false;
   }
   void BeginRead(String* fileName, int chunkSize)
   {
      bFinished = false;
      bDisposing = false;
```

```cpp
        ChunkSize = chunkSize;

        // Open file stream
        Stream = new FileStream(fileName, FileMode::Open, FileAccess::Read,
            FileShare::Read, chunkSize, true);

        // Allocate buffer
        if ( Stream->Length )
        {
            OldPosition = 0;
            Buffer = new unsigned char __gc[(int)Stream->Length];

            // Start reading first chunk
            __int64 RemainingBytes = Stream->Length - Stream->Position;
            AsyncResult = Stream->BeginRead(Buffer, (int)Stream->Position,
                RemainingBytes > ChunkSize ? ChunkSize : (int)RemainingBytes,
                readCallback, 0);
        }
        else
            // Zero-length file
            bFinished = true;
    }
    void ReadCallback(IAsyncResult* Result)
    {
        if ( !bDisposing )
        {
            // Report the number of bytes read
            Console::WriteLine("{0} bytes read...",
                __box(Stream->Position - OldPosition));
            OldPosition = Stream->Position;
            // Read next chunk
            __int64 RemainingBytes = Stream->Length - Stream->Position;
            // EOF is not yet reached?
            if ( RemainingBytes > 0 )
                AsyncResult = Stream->BeginRead(Buffer, (int)Stream->Position,
                    RemainingBytes > ChunkSize ? ChunkSize : (int)RemainingBytes,
                    readCallback, 0);
            else
            {
                Console::WriteLine("Finished reading file {0}", Stream->Name);
                // Close the stream
                Stream->Close();
                Stream = 0;
                bFinished = true;
            }
        }
```

```
    }
    __property bool get_IsFinished()
    {
        return bFinished;
    }
    __property unsigned char get_Data() __gc[]
    {
        return Buffer;
    }
    // Close stream in case the reading is terminated prematurely
    void Dispose()
    {
        if ( Stream )
        {
            bDisposing = true;
            // End a pending read request
            if ( AsyncResult )
            {
                Console::WriteLine("File reading aborted.");
                Stream->EndRead(AsyncResult);
                Stream->Close();
                Stream = 0;
                bFinished = true;
            }
        }
    }
    ~AsyncReader()
    {
        Dispose();
    }
private:
    bool bFinished, bDisposing;
    AsyncCallback* readCallback;
    IAsyncResult* AsyncResult;
    FileStream* Stream;
    unsigned char Buffer __gc[];
    int ChunkSize;
    __int64 OldPosition;
};

void main()
{
    // Instantiate notification class and a callback delegate
    AsyncReader* asyncReader = new AsyncReader();

    // Read file asynchronously
```

```
asyncReader->BeginRead("Test.txt", 16384);

// Wait
while ( !asyncReader->IsFinished )
{
    System::Threading::Thread::Sleep(100);
    // Uncomment this to test aborting the asynchronous reading
    //asyncReader->Dispose();
}
}
```

NOTE: The **Read** method throws an exception when reading a zero-size array or when attempting to read more bytes than the array can accommodate.

Writing Encoded Text Streams

If you need to write text to a file, you should use the .NET Framework Class Library **StreamWriter** class. You can either instantiate a **StreamWriter** object directly by means of the **new** operator or by invoking the **AppendText** or **CreateText** methods on the **File** class or a **FileInfo** object. If you instantiate a **StreamWriter** object directly, you can specify a desired encoding in the constructor's *encoding* parameter. If no encoding is specified, or you used the **AppendText** or **CreateText** methods to instantiate a text stream, the default UTF-8 encoding will be used. The following code example illustrates these steps:

1. Creates a new text file for writing using the **File::CreateText** method.
2. Appends text to an existing text file using the **File::AppendText** method.
3. Appends UTF-8 encoded text to an existing file.
4. Appends UTF-7 encoded text to an existing file.
5. Appends Unicode encoded text to an existing file.

The code sample is as follows:

```
#using <mscorlib.dll>
using namespace System;
using namespace System::IO;
using namespace System::Text;

void main()
{
    // 1. Create a text stream
    StreamWriter* stream = File::CreateText("Test.txt");
    // Write text
    stream->WriteLine("First Line");
    stream->WriteLine("Second Line");
    stream->Close();

    // 2. Append the text file
```

```
stream = File::AppendText("Test.txt");
   stream->WriteLine(__box(123));
   stream->WriteLine(__box(456.789));
   stream->Close();

   // 3. Append the existing text file with UTF-8 encoded text
   stream = new StreamWriter("Test.txt", true, new UTF8Encoding());
   stream->WriteLine("UTF8-Encoded text: Çüéâ");
   stream->Close();
   // 4. Append the existing text file with UTF-7 encoded text
   stream = new StreamWriter("Test.txt", true, new UTF7Encoding());
   stream->WriteLine("UTF7-Encoded text: Çüéâ");
   stream->Close();
   // 5. Append the existing text file with UTF-8 encoded text
   stream = new StreamWriter("Test.txt", true, new UnicodeEncoding());
   stream->WriteLine("Unicode-Encoded text: Çüéâ");
   stream->Close();
}
```

Reading Encoded Text Streams

To read text from a file, you should use the .NET Framework Class Library **StreamReader** class. This class supports reading text using a particular encoding. You can either instantiate a **StreamReader** object directly by using the **new** operator or by invoking the **OpenText** method of the **File** or **FileInfo** classes. If you instantiate a **StreamReader** object directly, you can specify a desired encoding in the constructor's *encoding* parameter, or you can set the *detect* parameter to **true** to select the proper encoding automatically. To select the proper encoding, the **StreamWriter** examines the first 3 bytes in the stream. If you wrote the stream using different encodings, the **StreamWriter** will recognize only the first encoding in the stream.

If you don't specify a particular encoding in the **StreamWriter** constructor, or you used the **OpenText** method to instantiate a text stream, the default UTF-8 encoding is used. The following code example performs these steps:

1. Opens an existing text file for reading using the **File::OpenText** method.
2. Checks to see if there is any text in the file and reading all text from the file.
3. Reads UTF-7 encoded text.
4. Reads UTF-8 encoded text.
5. Reads Unicode encoded text.

Here is the complete code example:

```
#using <mscorlib.dll>
using namespace System;
using namespace System::IO;
using namespace System::Text;


void main()
```

```
{
    // 1. Open a text stream
    StreamReader* stream = File::OpenText ("Test.txt");


    String* s;
    // 2. Check if there is anything in the stream
    if ( stream->Peek() != -1 )
    {
        // Read text
        while (s = stream->ReadLine() )
            Console::WriteLine(s);
    }
    stream->Close();

    // 3. Try UTF-8 Encoding
    stream = new StreamReader("Test.txt", new UTF8Encoding());
    // Read text
    while (s = stream->ReadLine() )
        Console::WriteLine(s);
    stream->Close();

    // 4. Try UTF-7 Encoding
    stream = new StreamReader("Test.txt", new UTF7Encoding());
    // Read text
    while (s = stream->ReadLine() )
        Console::WriteLine(s);
    stream->Close();

    // 5. Try Unicode encoding
    stream = new StreamReader("Test.txt", new UnicodeEncoding());
    // Read text
    while (s = stream->ReadLine() )
        Console::WriteLine(s);
    stream->Close();
}
```

NOTE: Text written using one culture information/encoding may not always be readable using another culture/encoding the **StreamReader** class may throw an exception if the stream contains characters not supported by the current encoding and/or culture.

Reading and Writing Primitive Data Types

If you want to store primitive data types, such as integer or floating-point values, in a file compactly, you should store them in binary form. The .NET Framework supports reading/writing primitive data types in binary form by means of the **BinaryReader** and **BinaryWriter** classes. The **BinaryReader/BinaryWriter** classes allow specifying a desired encoding for the resulting binary stream to confine stream characters to a particular character set or to obtain binary data representation suitable for e-mail or HTTP transmission.

To create a stream for reading/writing primitive data types in binary form, you must obtain a pointer to a **FileStream** object (i.e., by creating a new **FileStream** or by invoking the **File::Create** method) and supply it to the **BinaryReader/BinaryWriter** constructor. Then, you can use the **Read/Write** methods of the **BinaryReader/BinaryWriter** classes to read/write binary data from the file stream.

The following code example illustrates how to:

1.   Create a **BinaryWriter** stream with the UTF-8 encoding.
2.   Write binary data to a **BinaryWriter** stream.
3.   Create a **BinaryReader** stream with the UTF-8 encoding.
4.   Read data from a **BinaryReader** stream.

The code sample is as follows:

```
#using <mscorlib.dll>
using namespace System;
using namespace System::IO;

void main()
{
    // 1. Create a file and a BinaryWriter
    FileStream* stream = File::Create("Test.dat");
    BinaryWriter* writer = new BinaryWriter(stream);

    int a = 123;
    float b = 456.789f;
    unsigned char c __gc[] = {'t','e','x','t'};
    // 2. Write binary data
    writer->Write(a);
    writer->Write(b);
    writer->Write(c);
    writer->Close();
    stream->Close();

    // 3. Open a file and a BinaryReader
    stream = File::OpenRead("Test.dat");
    BinaryReader* reader = new BinaryReader(stream);

    // 4. Read data
    a = reader->ReadInt32();
    b = reader->ReadSingle();
    c = reader->ReadBytes(4);
    writer->Close();
    stream->Close();
}
```

WARNING! If you write binary data using one encoding, you should read it back using the same encoding. Otherwise, a **BinaryReader** stream may read the data incorrectly or even throw an exception if unrecognized characters are found in the stream.

Reading and Writing In-Memory Text Streams

If you want to implement a temporary in-memory stream for reading/writing **String** objects, you should use the .NET **StringReader/StringWriter** classes. Using this class makes it easy to perform the following operations:

* *Creating a memory text stream:* Simply create a new instance of the **StringWriter** class and use the **Write/WriteLine** methods to write text and numeric data to the stream.

* *Obtaining data written to a memory text stream:* Invoke the **ToString** method of the **StringWriter** object.

* *Reading data from a memory text stream:* Simply create an instance of the **StringReader** class and supply a pointer to a **String** object representing the source data. Then, use the **Read/ReadLine** methods to read individual characters or new-line-character terminated text strings.

To see how both the **StringWriter** and **StringReader** classes are used, examine this sample code:

```cpp
#using <mscorlib.dll>
using namespace System;
using namespace System::IO;
using namespace System::Text;

void main()
{
    // 1. Create an in-memory text stream
    StringWriter* writer = new StringWriter();

    // 2. Write text to StringWriter
    writer->WriteLine("First Line");
    writer->WriteLine("Second Line");
    writer->WriteLine(__box(123));
    writer->WriteLine(__box(123.456));
    writer->Close();

    // 3. Get the combined text as a StringBuilder
    StringBuilder* text = writer->GetStringBuilder();
    Console::WriteLine(text);

    // 4. Read strings from the String buffer
    StringReader* reader = new StringReader(text->ToString());
    String* s;
    // 5. Read text
    while (s = reader->ReadLine() )
        Console::WriteLine(s);
    reader->Close();
}
```

The code example above demonstrates how to:

1.   Create in-memory text streams using the default **StringWriter** constructor.
2.   Write various data types to the **StringWriter** stream using the default format provider.
3.   Obtain a pointer to the stream's internal **StringBuilder** buffer and print the buffer contents on the console.
4.   Create a **StringReader** stream for reading **Strings** from the **StringBuilder** buffer.

Read new-line-character terminated text lines from the **StringReader** stream.

> **NOTE:** You can specify your own format provider object, implementing the **IFormatProvider** interface to convert primitive value types to **Strings** as they are written to a **StringWriter** stream. However, you cannot supply a custom parser to automatically parse out the custom-formatted primitive value types as they are read from a **StringReader** stream. In this case, you would have to manually parse the strings read.

Reading and Writing In-Memory Binary Streams

To implement a temporary in-memory stream for reading or writing binary data, you use the .NET **MemoryStream** class. Here, you simply create a new **MemoryStream** object and invoke **Read/Write** methods to read/write arrays of bytes from stream to manipulate an in-memory binary stream. Depending on a particular **MemoryStream** constructor overload (see Table 7.55) that you use to create the memory stream, you can instantiate either a fixed-length stream that uses a specified buffer, or a variable-length stream that can grow as you write data to it.

The following code example demonstrates how to:

1.   Create a variable-length memory stream.
2.   Write data to a memory stream.
3.   Change the length of a variable-length memory stream.
4.   Read data from a memory stream.
5.   Write directly to the memory stream buffer.
6.   Create a read-only fixed-length memory stream with inaccessible buffer.
7.   Obtain a copy of the memory stream buffer using the **ToArray** method.

The code sample is as follows:

```
#using <mscorlib.dll>
using namespace System;
using namespace System::IO;

void main()
{
    // 1. Create a variable-length memory stream
    MemoryStream* stream = new MemoryStream(128);

    // 2. Write to memory stream
```

```
unsigned char buffer __gc[] = new unsigned char __gc[128];
stream->Write(buffer, 0, buffer->Count);

// 3. Change length
stream->SetLength(256);

// 4. Read data back
stream->Position = 0;
stream->Read(buffer, 0, 128);
stream->Close();

// 5. Access the buffer directly
stream->GetBuffer()[0] = 100;

// 6. Create a fixed-length memory stream with inaccessible buffer
stream = new MemoryStream(buffer, 0, buffer->Count, false, false);

// Write to memory stream fails because the stream is not writable
try {
    stream->Write(buffer, 0, buffer->Count);
}
catch(Exception* e) {
    Console::WriteLine(e->Message);
}

// Increasing the stream length fails because buffer is fixed-length
try {
    stream->SetLength(256);
}
catch(Exception* e) {
    Console::WriteLine(e->Message);
}

// 7. ToArray works
unsigned char array __gc[] = stream->ToArray();
// But GetBuffer fails because the buffer is inaccessible
try {
    array = stream->GetBuffer();
}
catch(Exception* e) {
        Console::WriteLine(e->Message);
}
}
```

Working with Paths

You should use the all-static **Path** class to parse or concatenate file-system path strings. The **Path** class is, for the most part, straightforward. For a list of the available **Path** class fields and methods, see Tables 7.58 and 7.58. The following code example demonstrates how to:

1. Parse a path to obtain directory and file names by means of the **GetDirectoryName/GetFileName** methods.

2. Combine two paths by means of the **Combine** method.

3. Obtain a temporary folder name and create a unique temporary file name by means of the **GetTempPath/GetTempFileName** methods.

Here is the code example:

```
#using <mscorlib.dll>
using namespace System;
using namespace System::IO;

void main()
{
    String* myPath = "D:\\Program files\\Helix";

    // 1. Get path info (Helix is considered a file name at this point)
    Console::WriteLine("Directory: {0}", Path::GetDirectoryName(myPath));
    Console::WriteLine("File name: {0}", Path::GetFileName(myPath));

    // 2. Append file name
    myPath = Path::Combine(myPath, "Gems3D.exe");
    Console::WriteLine("Full path: {0}", Path::GetFullPath(myPath));
    Console::WriteLine("File name: {0}", Path::GetFileName(myPath));
    Console::WriteLine("Extension: {0}", Path::GetExtension(myPath));

    // 3. Temp files
    Console::WriteLine(" Temp dir: {0}", Path::GetTempPath());
    Console::WriteLine("Temp name: {0}", Path::GetTempFileName());
}
```

Detecting File System Changes

Directory polling is frequently used to detect the addition of files in a directory or changes in file sizes or last access dates on a particular path. But directory polling is not very efficient because a lot of CPU cycles are wasted on running the query-check-sleep loop used in a typical polling process. Fortunately, a more efficient and elegant technique is available for detecting file system changes of any kind. You can use the **FileSystemWatcher** class to hook up notification callbacks associated with a desired type of file system change on a specified path (i.e., addition or deletion of files, changes in file sizes, or changes in file attributes).

Here are the steps you follow to set up file system notifications using the **FileSystemWatcher** class:

1. Create a new **FileSystemWatcher** object and specify a path to monitor and the extension of files being monitored (e.g., *.exe).

2. Create notification callback methods, which will be called when file system events of interest occur.

3. Hook up the notification callback methods to the **FileSystemWatcher** object as you normally hook up multicast delegates.

The **FileSystemWatcher** object will be able to start firing events as soon as you hook up event handlers. To disable the event firing by a **FileSystemWatcher** object, either dispose the **FileSystemWatcher** object or disassociate event handlers as you disassociate multicast event delegates. You can also set the **EnableRaisingEvents** property of the **FileSystemWatcher** object to **false** if you want to temporarily suspend event firing.

Study the following code to see how the **FileSystemWatcher** class is used:

```
#using <mscorlib.dll>
#using <system.dll>
using namespace System;
using namespace System::IO;

// Class for handling new file notifications
__gc class MyClass {
public:
    void MoveToTemp(Object* sender, FileSystemEventArgs* e)
    {
        try {
            // Create TEMP folder
            if ( !Directory::Exists("Temp") )
                Directory::CreateDirectory("Temp");

            // Move the new file to the temp folder
            Directory::Move(e->Name, Path::Combine("Temp", e->Name));

            // Report the action
            Console::WriteLine("File {0} move to TEMP folder", e->Name);
        }
        catch(Exception* e) {
            Console::WriteLine("ERROR: {0}", e->Message);
        }
    }
};

void main()
{
    // 1) Watch *.txt files in the current directory
```

```
FileSystemWatcher* watcher = new FileSystemWatcher(
    Directory::GetCurrentDirectory(), "*.txt");
watcher->EnableRaisingEvents = true;

// 2) Detect new files and move the to the TEMP folder
watcher->Created += new FileSystemEventHandler(new MyClass(),
    &MyClass::MoveToTemp);

// Create some new files
FileStream* stream = File::Create("Test1.txt");
stream->Close();
stream = File::Create("Test2.txt");
stream->Close();
// 3) Wait for events
watcher->WaitForChanged(WatcherChangeTypes::Created);
}
```

This code example creates a class called **MyClass,** which exposes a single **MoveToTemp** method listening to the **Created** event notifications. The **MoveToTemp** method is compatible with the **Created** event signature defined by the **FileSystemEventHandler*** delegate. The **MoveToTemp** method moves newly created files on the path being watched into a TEMP folder. The file system event notifications are not fired immediately. Thus, the last statement in the program is a call to the **WaitForChanged** method that halts the program execution until at least one **Created** event occurs.

> **NOTE:** You must include the **#using <system.dll>** statement in your code to use the **FileSystemWatcher** class.

Working with Isolated Storage

You should store your assembly private data in the *isolated storage* to ensure that your assembly does not accidentally corrupt data written by another assembly. From the OS-perspective, an isolated storage is a file system directory intended to store data that belongs to a particular application or, more precisely, to a particular isolation level (i.e., user/domain or user/domain/assembly combination).

It is good programming practice to store your assembly data in the isolated storage because assemblies running from a network or downloaded from the Internet by default are denied access to the local file system except for the isolated storage directory. This is done for security reasons to deprive low-trusted code from the opportunity for an intentional or accidental malice.

Using isolated storage is similar to using regular files, directories, and streams other than confinement to a specific OS folder. Follow these steps for manipulating isolated storage:

1. Create a new **IsolatedStorageFile** object and specify the desired level of isolation in the **IsolatedStorageFile** constructor.

2. Create or delete isolated storage directories by calling the **IsolatedStorageFile** object methods, such as **CreateDirectory** or **DeleteDirectory**.

3. To read or write data from isolated storage files, create a new **IsolatedStorageFileStream** object and specify a file name, file access, and an isolated storage pointer in the **IsolatedStorageFileStream** constructor.

4. Use the **IsolatedStorageFileStream** object as you would use an ordinary **FileStream** object.

The following code example shows you how to use the isolated storage scoped by the current user, assembly, and domain. The code illustrates how to:

1. Instantiate an **IsolatedStorageFile** object scoped by the current user, assembly, and domain by means of the **GetUserStoreForDomain** method.

2. Report assembly and domain identities.

3. Create a new isolated storage file using the **IsolatedStorageFileStream** class and write some text to it using the **StreamWriter**.

4. Create a new isolated storage directory by means of the **CreateDirectory** method.

5. Enumerate isolated storage directories by means of the **GetFileNames** method.

6. Enumerate isolated storage files by means of the **GetDirectoryNames** method.

7. Report isolated storage usage.

8. Remove isolated storage for the specified scope by deleting its files and directories by calling the **Remove** method.

```cpp
#using <mscorlib.dll>
using namespace System;
using namespace System::IO;
using namespace System::IO::IsolatedStorage;

void main()
{
    // 1. Create an IsolatedStorage object for current user,
    // domain and assembly
    IsolatedStorageFile* is = IsolatedStorageFile::GetUserStoreForDomain();

    // 2. Report XML identities and current size
    Console::WriteLine("Assembly Identity: {0}", is->AssemblyIdentity);
    Console::WriteLine("  Domain Identity: {0}", is->DomainIdentity);
    Console::WriteLine("Current Size: {0}", __box(is->CurrentSize));

    // 3. Create a new isolated storage file
    IsolatedStorageFileStream* stream = new IsolatedStorageFileStream(
        "Test.txt", FileMode::OpenOrCreate, is);
    StreamWriter* writer = new StreamWriter(stream);
    writer->WriteLine("Line 1");
    writer->WriteLine("Line 2");
    writer->Close();
    stream->Close();
```

```
    // 4. Create a new isolated storage directory
    is->CreateDirectory("Test");

    // 5. Enumerate Isolated Storage directories
    String* Directories __gc[] = is->GetDirectoryNames("*");
    for ( int i = 0; i < Directories->Count; i++ )
        Console::WriteLine(Directories[i]);

    // 6. Enumerate Isolated Storage files
    String* Files __gc[] = is->GetFileNames("*");
    for ( int i = 0; i < Files->Count; i++ )
        Console::WriteLine(Files[i]);

    // 7. Report isolated storage size
    Console::WriteLine("Current Size: {0}", __box(is->CurrentSize));
    Console::WriteLine("Maximum Size: {0}", __box(is->MaximumSize));

    // 8. Remove isolated storage for this user, domain and assembly
    is->Remove();
    // Storage is released at this point
}
```

The **IsolatedStorageFile** identities, such as **AssemblyIdentity** and **DomainIdentities,** are usually represented as URLs pointing to the location of the isolated storage assembly and domain (e.g., file://C:/Projects/.NET/IoTest/Debug/IoTest.exe in the example above). When the isolated storage identity URLs are printed on console, they are outpu as XML. You can specify the appropriate URLs as the **GetStore** method parameters to access the isolated storage of another assembly/application domain::

```
is = IsolatedStorageFile::GetStore(
    (IsolatedStorageScope)(IsolatedStorageScope::User|
    IsolatedStorageScope::Assembly|IsolatedStorageScope::Domain),
    new System::Security::Policy::Url(
        "file://C:/Projects/.NET/IoTest/Debug/IoTest.exe"),
    new System::Security::Policy::Url(
        "file://C:/Projects/.NET/IoTest/Debug/IoTest.exe"));
```

Your code must have sufficient security privileges to access the isolated storage of other assembles/applications. Code running under an Administrator account has the necessary security permission by default.

CHAPTER 8

ADO.NET: DataSets, DataTables, and XML

QUICK JUMPS

CHAPTER 8

ADO.NET: DataSets, DataTables, and XML

In Depth

Microsoft .NET Framework implements relational data and database access by means of ADO.NET. If you are already familiar with ActiveX Data Objects—ADO—be prepared to learn a whole lot more as ADO.NET represents a considerable improvement over ADO. If you are not very familiar with ADO, this chapter will give you a head start.

ADO.NET

ADO.NET is a collection of objects designed to represent structured relational data, to enforce data integrity and to provide means for storing/retrieving structured data from extraneous storage such as databases, data files, or XML. Conceptually there are two major top-level components in the ADO.NET architecture (see Figure 8.1):

*   *Datasets*: Represent hierarchical view of the data isolated from the underlying storage.

*   *.NET Data Providers*: Represent interface between datasets and the data storage, which can be a database storage.

The .NET Data Providers (discussed in detail in Chapter 9) are responsible for populating datasets with data and for saving changes made to data in datasets to the underlying database, while datasets merely constitute a pool of data in memory.

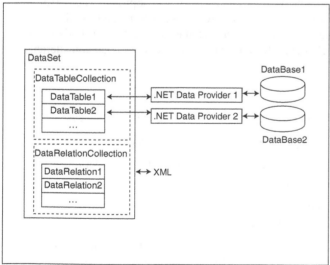

Figure 8.1. Major components of ADO.NET architecture: dataset and data provider.

Thus, ADO.NET clearly separates data management/processing code from data retrieval code. Such architecture goes well inline with the common programming axiom that behooves us to separate data from code. Data changes frequently while code does not. Thus, to simplify and improve code maintenance you should separate data from code and maintain both independently. This approach is opposite to *hardcoding*, which refers to mixing code with data. By separating data management/processing code from data retrieval code ADO.NET not just improves the organization of code by grouping similar functionality together, but also allows developers write applications that are are totally independent from the underlying data source: simply plug in a different set of classes in the data retrieval code, and you can switch from text files to SQL Server, or to XML streams.

ADO vs. ADO.NET

Those of you who are familiar with ADO by now must be wonder??? how is ADO.NET different from ADO. The truth is that the difference is quite substantial. For the most part ADO provides object-oriented interface for accessing database data and cannot be used if a database connection is unavailable. ADO.NET, on the other hand, can be used for *reliably* maintaining fully relational data in memory and does not require any database connectivity unless you want to store your data permanently. By saying *reliably* I mean the ADO.NET capacity to enforce referential integrity and impose constrains on relational data located in memory. This is an important advantage of ADO.NET over ADO, which makes ADO.NET look and feel like small but fully programmable RDBMS core: Developers can design their own tables, establish relationships, and rely on the framework to maintain the data wholeness.

Another advantage of ADO.NET over ADO is that ADO.NET datasets do not care where the actual data come from. Thus, ADO.NET allows constructing complex relational datasets, which join data that physically resides in diverse and possibly incompatible data sources. For example, with ADO.NET it is possible to describe a structure that relies on lists of employees stored in SQL Server database, employee records stored in text files and employee e-mail addresses located in Outlook. Regardless of the fact that pieces of data come from different databases ADO.NET allows enforcing referential integrity and imposes constrains on hereto unified heterogeneous data. This is the power that ADO does not have.

There are some similarities between ADO and ADO.NET, too. You will find that ADO.NET contains familiar **Connection, Command,** and **Parameter** classes. But this is pretty much where the similarity ends: In comparison with ADO, equivalent ADO.NET classes expose substantially different properties and methods. To bridge the gap between ADO and ADO.NET, Microsoft equipped some of the ADO.NET classes with additional methods that accept pointers to legacy ADO objects. This was done in order to facilitate integration between new ADO.NET and existing ADO applications.

If you are considering porting your existing ADO code to ADO.NET and concerned about ADO.NET performance, don't be. One of the top priorities put into the design of ADO.NET was improving the performance of ADO. ADO.NET does not use database cursors because the cursors are database-specific and usually very resource intensive. ADO.NET almost exclusively relies on standard SQL statements (e.g., SELECT, INSERT, UPDATE) for exchanging database data. In ADO.NET, the performance of data access has been considerably tuned up.

ADO.NET Namespaces

ADO.NET is implemented in the .NET Framework Class Library with the following five namespaces:

* *System::Data*: Implements core functionality of ADO.NET including the **DataSet** class.
* *System::Data::Common*: Implements functionality shared among ADO.NET data providers.
* *System::Data::OleDb*: Implements OLE DB data provider.
* *System::Data::SqlClient*: Implements SQL Server data provider.
* *System::Data::SqlTypes*: Defines SQL Server native data types.

A sixth namespace, *System::Data::ODBC*, is also provided. This namespace is supplied as a standalone download. The System::Data::ODBC namespcace implements ODBC data provider for ADO.NET.

System::Data Namespace Hierarchy

The System::Data namespace contains core ADO.NET classes such as **DataSet**, **DataTable**, **DataRow**, **DataColumn**, and so on that represent generic data, which is laid out in memory and isolated from a particular data source. The System::Data namespace general classes, attributes, exceptions, interfaces, delegates, and enumerations are listed in Tables 8.1 through 8.6, respectively. The System::Data namespace class hierarchy is shown in Appendix E.

Table 8.1 System::Data Namespace General Classes.

Class	Description
Constraint	Abstract base class representing constraints that can be enforced on one or more **DataColumn** objects.
ConstraintCollection	Implements a collection of constraints contained in a **DataTable**.
DataColumn	Implements a data column in a **DataTable**.
DataColumnChangeEventArgs	Represents data for the **ColumnChanging** event.
DataColumnCollection	Implements a collection of **DataColumn** objects contained in a **DataTable**.
DataRelation	Implements a parent/child relationship between two **DataTable** objects.
DataRelationCollection	Implements a collection of **DataRelation** objects contained in a **DataSet**.
DataRow	Implements a row of data in a **DataTable**.
DataRowChangeEventArgs	Represents data for the **RowChanged**, **RowChanging**, **OnRowDeleting**, and **OnRowDeleted** events.
DataRowCollection	Implements a collection of data rows contained in a **DataTable**.
DataRowView	Implements a custom view of a **DataRow**.
DataSet	Implements an in-memory set of data.
DataTable	Implements a table of in-memory data.
DataTableCollection	Implements a collection of tables contained in a **DataSet**.
DataView	Implements a custom view of a **DataTable** optimized for sorting, filtering, searching, editing, and navigation.
DataViewManager	Implements a default **DataViewSettingCollection** for each **DataTable** in a **DataSet**.
DataViewSetting	Implements the default settings for the default **DataView** of a **DataTable** in a **DataSet**.
DataViewSettingCollection	Implements a read-only collection of **DataViewSetting** objects for each **DataTable** in a **DataSet**.
FillErrorEventArgs	Represents data for the **FillError** event of a **DbDataAdapter**.
ForeignKeyConstraint	Implements a foreign key constraint enforced on a set of columns in a primary key/foreign key relationship.
InternalDataCollectionBase	Abstract base class for ADO.NET collections.

<Continued on Next Page>

<Table 8.1 Continued>

Class	Description
MergeFailedEventArgs	Represents data for the **MergeFailedEventHandler** delegate fired when a target and source **DataRow** have the same primary key value, and constraints are enforced.
PropertyCollection	Implements a collection of user-defined properties that can be added to **DataColumn**, **DataSet**, or **DataTable**.
StateChangeEventArgs	Represents data for the state change event of a .NET data provider.
TypedDataSetGenerator	A utility class for generating strongly typed **DataSet** objects.
UniqueConstraint	Implements a unique constraint that requires a set of columns to contain unique values.

Table 8.2 System::Data Namespace Attributes.

Attribute	Description
DataSysDescription	A visual designer attribute for specifying textual description of data objects.

Table 8.3 System::Data Namespace Exceptions.

Exception	Description
ConstraintException	Represents an exception thrown when a constraint is violated.
DataException	Represents a general ADO.NET exception.
DBConcurrencyException	Represents an exception thrown by the **DataAdapter** during the update operation if the number of rows affected is zero.
DeletedRowInaccessibleException	Represents an exception thrown when one attempts an action on a **DataRow** that has been deleted.
DuplicateNameException	Represents an exception thrown when more than one object with the same name is added to a **DataSet**-related object.
EvaluateException	Represents an exception thrown when the **Expression** property of a **DataColumn** is syntactically correct but cannot be evaluated.
InRowChangingEventException	Represents an exception thrown when the **EndEdit** method is called from the **RowChanging** event.
InvalidConstraintException	Represents an exception thrown when a data relation cannot be accessed or created.
InvalidExpressionException	Represents an exception thrown when adding a **DataColumn** that contains an invalid **Expression** to a **DataColumnCollection**.
MissingPrimaryKeyException	Represents an exception thrown when accessing a row in a table that has no primary key.
NoNullAllowedException	Represents an exception thrown when inserting a Null value into a column that does not allow Nulls (i.e., **AllowDBNull** is set to **false**).
ReadOnlyException	Represents an exception thrown when changing the value of a read-only column.
RowNotInTableException	Represents an exception thrown when trying to perform an operation on a **DataRow** that is not in a **DataTable**.

<Continued on Next Page>

<Table 8.3 Continued>

Class	Description
StrongTypingException	Represents an exception thrown by a strongly typed **DataSet** when the user accesses **DBNull** value.
SyntaxErrorException	Represents an exception thrown when the **Expression** property of a **DataColumn** contains a syntax error.
TypedDataSetGeneratorException	Represents an exception thrown when a name conflict occurs while generating a strongly typed **DataSet**.
VersionNotFoundException	Represents an exception thrown when attempting to return a version of a **DataRow** that has been deleted.

Table 8.4 System::Data Namespace Interfaces

Interface	Description
IColumnMapping	Base interface for associating a data source column with a **DataSet** column (implemented by the **DataColumnMapping** class).
IColumnMappingCollection	Base interface for collections of **DataColumnMapping** objects (implemented by the **DataColumnMappingCollection**).
IDataAdapter	Base interface for mapping actions used to fill, refresh, and update a **DataSet** from a data source.
IDataParameter	Base interface for implementing database command (**Command** object) parameters.
IDataParameterCollection	Base interface for collections of database command parameters.
IDataReader	Base interface for reading one or more forward-only streams of result sets obtained by executing a command on a data source (implemented by the **DataReader** class).
IDataRecord	Base interface for accessing column values within each row of a **DataReader**.
IDbCommand	Base interface for database commands: SELECT, INSERT, DELETE, UPDATE (Implemented by the **Command** class).
IDbConnection	Base interface used by ADO.NET data providers to connect to a data source.
IDbDataAdapter	Base interface implementing command-related properties that are used to fill a **DataSet** and update a data source (implemented by .NET data providers that access relational databases).
IDbDataParameter	Base interface for implementing database command (**Command** object) parameters.
IDbTransaction	Base interface for implementing database transactions.
ITableMapping	Base interface for mapping a data source table to a table in a **DataSet** (implemented by the **DataTableMapping** class).
ITableMappingCollection	Base interface for collections of **DataTableMapping** objects (implemented by the **DataTableMappingCollection** class).

Table 8.5 System::Data Namespace Delegates

Delegate	Description
void DataColumnChangeEventHandler(Object* *sender*, DataColumnChangeEventArgs* *e*)	A delegate for handling the **ColumnChanging** event of the **DataTable** class.
void DataRowChangeEventHandler(Object* *sender*, DataRowChangeEventArgs* *e*)	A delegate for handling the **RowChanging**, **RowChanged**, **RowDeleting**, and **RowDeleted** events of the **DataTable** class.
void FillErrorEventHandler(Object* *sender*, FillErrorEventArgs* *e*)	A delegate for handling the **FillError** event of the **DbDataAdapter** class.
void MergeFailedEventHandler(Object* *sender*, MergeFailedEventArgs* *e*)	A delegate for handling the **Merge-Failed** event of the **DatSet** class.
void StateChangeEventHandler(Object* *sender*, StateChangeEventArgs* *e*)	A delegate for handling the **StateChange** event of the **OleDbConnection** class.

Table 8.6 System::Data Namespace Enumerations

Enumeration	Description
AcceptRejectRule	Defines constants**, Cascade** and **None**, specifying an action to be taken with regard to child rows when a parent row is modified or deleted by means of the **AcceptChanges/RegectChanges** method and a **ForeignKeyConstraint** is enforced.
CommandBehavior	Defines constants specifying the results and the effect of a query command on the database: **CloseConenction**, **Default**, **KeyInfo**, **SchemaOnly**, **SequentialAccess**, **SingleResult**, and **SingleRow**.
CommandType	Defines constants specifying how a database command should be interpreted: **StoredProcedure**, **TableDirect** (i.e., the command contains a comma-separated list of table names), or **Text** (SQL generic command).
ConnectionState	Defines connection state constants used by the **State** property of the **OleDbConnection** class: **Broken**, **Closed**, **Connecting**, **Executing**, **Fetching**, and **Open**.
DataRowAction	Defines flags describing an action performed on a **DataRow**: **Add**, **Change**, **Commit**, **Delete**, **Nothing**, and **Rollback**.
DataRowState	Defines flags used by the **RowState** property to describe the state of a **DataRow**: **Added**, **Deleted**, **Detached**, **Modified**, and **Unchanged**.
DataRowVersion	Defines constants describing the version of a **DataRow**: **Current**, **Default**, **Original**, and **Proposed**.
DataViewRowState	Defines flags used by the **RowStateFilter** property of a **DataRow** object to describe the version of the **DataRow** data: **Added**, **CurrentRows**, **Deleted**, **ModifiedCurrent**, **ModifiedOriginal**, **None**, **OriginalRows**, and **Unchanged**.

<Continued on Next Page>

<Table 8.6 Continued>

Class	Description
DbType	Defines parameter, field or property data type constants: **AnsiString, AnsiStringFixedLength, Binary, Boolean, Byte, Currency, Data, DateTime, Decimal, Double, Guid, Int16, Int32, Int64, Object, SByte, Single, String, StringFixedLength, Time, UInt16, UInt32, UInt64,** and **VarNumeric.**
IsolationLevel	Defined flags specifying transaction locking behavior: **Chaos, ReadCommitted, ReadUncommitted, RepeatableRead, Serializable,** and **Unspecified.**
MappingType	Defines constants for specifying **DataColumn** XML mappings: **Attribute, Element, Hidden,** and **SimpleContent.**
MissingMappingAction	Defines constants for specifying what action should be taken when a mapping is missing from a source table or a source column: **Error, Ignore,** and **Passthrough.**
MissingSchemaAction	Defines constants for specifying what action should be taken when adding data to the **DataSet** and the required **DataTable** or **DataColumn** is missing: **Add, AddWithKey, Error,** and **Ignore.**
ParameterDirection	Defines constants for specifying database command parameter types: **Input, InputOutput, Output,** and **ReturnValue.**
PropertyAttributes	Defines constants for specifying property attributes: **NotSupported, Optional, Read, Required,** and **Write.**
Rule	Defines constants for specifying what action to be taken when enforcing a **ForeignKeyConstraint**: **Cascade, None, SetDefault,** and **SetNull.**
SchemaType	Defines constants specifying how to handle existing schema mappings when performing a **FillSchema** operation: **Mapped** and **Ignored.**
SqlDbType	Defines SQL Server data types constants: **BigInt, Binary, Bit, Char, DateTime, Decimal, Float, Image, Int, Money, NChar, NText, NVarChar, Real, SmallDateTime, SmallInt, SmallMoney, Text, Timestamp, TinyInt, UniqueIdentifier, VarBinary, VarChar,** and **Variant.**
StatementType	Defines constants specifying the SQL query type used by the **OleDbRowUpdatedEventArgs, OleDbRowUpdatingEventArgs, SqlRowUpdatedEventArgs,** and **SqlRowUpdatingEventArgs** classes: **Delete, Insert, Select,** and **Update.**
UpdateRowSource	Defines constants specifying how database command results are applied to the row being updated: **Both, FirstReturnedRecord, None,** and **OutputParameters.**
UpdateStatus	Defines constants specifying what action to take with regard to the current and remaining rows during a **DbDataAdapter::Update** operation: **Continue, ErrorsOccured, SkipRemainingRows,** and **SkipCurrentRow.**
XmlReadMode	Defines constants specifying how to read data and a relational schema from XML into a **DataSet**: **Auto, DiffGram, Fragment, IgnoreSchema, InferSchema,** and **ReadSchema.**
XmlWriteMode	Defines constants specifying how to write data and a relational schema from a **DataSet** to XML: **DiffGram, IgnoreSchema,** and **WriteSchema.**

DataSet Class

Dataset is the key component of the ADO.NET architecture. In the .NET Framework datasets are implemented by means of the **DataSet** class, which has the following inheritance structure:

```
System::Object
|- System::ComponentModel::MarshalByValueComponent
   |- System::Data::DataSet
```

Attributes: **Serializable**
Abstract: No
Sealed: No
Implements Interfaces: **IListSource, ISupportInitialize, ISerializable**

A **DataSet** object represents a collection of data stored in one or more **DataTable** objects, which are organized in a **DataTableCollection**. If a **DataSet** represents hierarchal data it must contain a description of parent/child relationships between data tables represented by **DataRelation** objects organized in a **DataRelationCollection** (see Figure 8.1). The organization of data represented by a **DataSet**, including names and types of data fields in data tables and relationships between tables, are referred to as *dataset schema*. The actual data in **DataTable** objects of a **DataSet** can be loaded from one or more data sources interfaced with the **DataSet** by means of .NET Data Providers, or they can be loaded directly from an XML file. The **DataSet** class constructors, properties, methods, and events are summarized in Tables 8.7 through 8.10.

Table 8.7 **DataSet** class constructors.

Constructor	Description
DataSet()	Default constructor.
DataSet(String* *name*)	Constructs a **DataSet** object with the specified name.
protected: DataSet(SerializationInfo* *info*, StreamingContext *context*)	Constructs a **DataSet** using the specified serialization information.

Table 8.8 **DataSet** class properties.

Get/Set	Type	Property	Description
Get/Set	**bool**	**CaseSensitive**	Gets or sets a Boolean value indicating whether string comparisons within **DataTable** objects contained in the **DataSet** must be case-sensitive.
Get/Set	**String***	**DataSetName**	Gets or sets the **DataSet** object name.
Get	**DataViewManager***	**DefaultViewManager**	Contains a pointer to a collection of default **DataView** settings for each **DataTable** in the **DataSet**.
Get/Set	**bool**	**EnforceConstraints**	Gets or sets a Boolean value indicating whether constraints should be enforced when updating the **DataSet**.

<Continued on Next Page>

<Table 8.8 Continued>

Get/Set	Type	Property	Description
Get/Set	**PropertyCollection***	**ExtendedProperties**	Contains a pointer to the collection of user-defined properties of the **DataSet**.
Get	**bool**	**HasErrors**	Contains **true** if the **DataSet** contains errors in any of the rows of any of the tables.
Get/Set	**CultureInfo***	**Locale**	Gets or sets the locale information for comparing strings within the data tables of the **DataSet**.
Get/Set	**String***	**Namespace**	Gets or sets the **DataSet** XML namespace (**xmlns** attribute).
Get/Set	**String***	**Prefix**	Gets or sets an XML prefix that aliases the namespace of the **DataSet**. The **DataSet** is designated by the **<Prefix:DataSetName xmlns= Namespace >** tag in the XML document.
Get	**DataRelationCollection***	**Relations**	Contains a pointer to parent/child relations between the **DataSet** data tables.
Get	**DataTableCollection***	**Tables**	Contains a pointer to the collection of the **DataSet** data tables.

Table 8.9 **DataSet** class methods.

Method	Description
void AcceptChanges()	Commits any pending changes made to the **DataSet**.
void Clear()	Clears the **DataSet** by removing all rows from all data tables.
virtual DataSet* Clone()	Creates a structural copy of the **DataSet** without copying data.
DataSet* Copy()	Creates both structural and data copy of the **DataSet**.
DataSet* GetChanges()	
DataSet* GetChanges(DataRowState *rowStates*)	Creates a copy of the **DataSet** that contains changes made to the **DataSet** since it was last loaded, or since the **AcceptChanges** method was called. Optional *rowStates* argument allows specifying a particular type changes to retrieve.
String* GetXml()	Returns text corresponding to the XML representation of the data stored in the **DataSet**.
String* GetXmlSchema()	Returns text corresponding to the XSD schema of the data stored in the **DataSet**.
bool HasChanges()	
bool HasChanges(DataRowState *rowStates*)	Returns **true** if the **DataSet** has been modified. Optional *rowStates* argument allows specifying a particular type of changes to query the data set for.

<Continued on Next Page>

<Table 8.9 Continued>

Method	Description
void InferXmlSchema(Stream* *stream*, String* *nsArray* __gc[])	
void InferXmlSchema(String* *fileName*, String* *nsArray* __gc[])	
void InferXmlSchema(TextReader* *reader*, String* *nsArray* __gc[])	
void InferXmlSchema(XmlReader* *reader*, String* *nsArray* __gc[])	Infers the **DataSet** schema from the structure of an XML document contained in the specified file or stream. The *nsArray* parameter specifies an array of namespace URIs to be excluded from the schema inference.
void Merge(DataRow* *rows*[])	
void Merge(DataTable* *table*)	
void Merge(DataSet* *dataSet*)	
void Merge(DataSet* *dataSet*, bool *preserveChanges*)	
void Merge(DataRow* *rows*[], bool *preserveChanges*, MissingSchemaAction *missingSchemaAction*)	
void Merge(DataSet* *dataSet*, bool *preserveChanges*, MissingSchemaAction *missingSchemaAction*)	
void Merge(DataTable* *table*, bool *preserveChanges*, MissingSchemaAction *missingSchemaAction*)	Merges the **DataSet** with the specified array of data rows, data table, or dataset. Optional *preserveChanges* and *missingSchemaAction* arguments control whether to keep the changes made to the **DataSet** and how to handle incompatibility between the **DataSet** and the data being merged.
protected public: virtual void OnPropertyChanging(PropertyChangedEventArgs* *event*)	Fires the **OnPropertyChanging** event.
protected: virtual void OnRemoveRelation(DataRelation* *relation*)	Invoked when a **DataTable**, which is a part of **DataRelation**, is about to be removed from the **DataSet**. You can override this method to restrict the removal of tables from the **DataSet**.
protected: virtual void OnRemoveTable(DataTable* *table*)	Invoked when a **DataTable** is about to be removed from the **DataSet**.
protected public: void RaisePropertyChanging(String* *name*)	Fires a notification indicating that a **DataSet** property with the specified name is about to change.

<Continued on Next Page>

<Table 8.9 Continued>

Method	Description
XmlReadMode ReadXml(Stream* *stream*)	
XmlReadMode ReadXml(String* *fileName*)	
XmlReadMode ReadXml(TextReader* *reader*)	
XmlReadMode ReadXml(XmlReader* *reader*)	
XmlReadMode ReadXml(Stream* *stream*, XmlReadMode *mode*)	
XmlReadMode ReadXml(String* *fileName*, XmlReadMode *mode*)	
XmlReadMode ReadXml(TextReader* *reader*, XmlReadMode *mode*)	
XmlReadMode ReadXml(XmlReader* *reader*, XmlReadMode *mode*)	Reads an XML schema (including tables, relations, and constraints) and data from the specified stream or file. Optional *mode* argument specifies how to interpret the source XML file schema. By default the **DataSet** is automatically extended to match the source XML schema. If the two schemas are incompatible or conflicting the exception is raised.
void ReadXmlSchema(Stream* *stream*)	
void ReadXmlSchema(String* *fileName*)	
void ReadXmlSchema(TextReader* *reader*)	
void ReadXmlSchema(XmlReader* *reader*)	Reads an XML schema (including tables, relations, and constraints) from the specified stream or file and extends the **DataSet** accordingly.
virtual void RejectChanges()	Rolls-back changes made to the **DataSet** since it was created, or since the **AcceptChanges** was called.
virtual void Reset()	Resets the **DataSet** to its original state.
protected: virtual bool ShouldSerializeRelations()	Returns **true** if the **DataSet** should serialize its **Relations** property.
virtual bool ShouldSerializeTables()	Returns **true** if the **DataSet** should serialize its **Tables** property.

<Continued on Next Page>

<Table 8.9 Continued>

Method	Description
void WriteXml(Stream* *stream*)	
void WriteXml(String* *fileName*)	
void WriteXml(TextWriter* *writer*)	
void WriteXml(XmlWriter* *writer*)	
void WriteXml(Stream* *stream*, XmlWriteMode *mode*)	
void WriteXml(String* *fileName*, XmlWriteMode *mode*)	
void WriteXml(TextWriter* *writer*, XmlWriteMode *mode*)	
void WriteXml(XmlWriter* *writer*, XmlWriteMode *mode*)	Writes to the specified stream or file the XML schema (including tables, relations, and constraints) of the **DataSet**. Optional *mode* argument specifies whether to write data only (**IgnoreSchema**), or write xdata and **DataSet** schema (**WriteSchema**), or that the data written corresponds to an XML diffgram (**DiffGram**).
void WriteXmlSchema(Stream* *stream*)	
void WriteXmlSchema(String* *fileName*)	
void WriteXmlSchema(TextWriter* *writer*)	
void WriteXmlSchema(XmlWriter* *writer*)	Writes the **DataSet** schema in the XSD standard to the specified XML stream or file.

Table 8.10 **DataSet** class events.

Event	Description
MergeFailedEventHandler* MergeFailed	Fired when the **Merge** method fails because a **DataRow** in the DataSet, **DataTable**, or **DataRow** array being merged with the **DataSet** have the same primary key value as an existing **DataRow** in the **DataSet**, and the **EnforceConstraints** property is set to **true**.

NOTE: The **DataSet** class does not have dedicated methods for managing data tables and data relations. To add/remove data tables and relations to a **DataSet** object, you must invoke appropriate methods on the **Tables** and the **Relations** collection properties of the **DataSet** object.

Dataset Merging

It is possible to merge datasets that have identical or almost identical schemas. Dataset merging is helpful when adding new data or updating existing data in a dataset. If the schemas of the current dataset and the dataset, data table, or rowset that is being merged are different, the **DataSet** class will attempt to reconcile the schemas by adding new columns and tables to the current **DataSet** object. You can specify the desired missing schema action by supplying the **MissingSchemaAction** parameter to the **Merge** method:

* **Add**: Automatically add new columns to the dataset.

* **AddWithKey**: Add new columns and accompanying primary key information to the dataset.

* **Error**: Abort the merging and throw a **SystemException** exception.

* **Ignore**: Ignore new columns.

New rows that are being merged to the data set are compared against existing rows by the primary key to detect which existing dataset rows need updating, and which new rows should be added. If you invoked the **Merge** method with the *preserveChanges* parameter set to **true,** the modified dataset rows will not be updated—only new rows will be added or unmodified dataset rows will be updated.

During the process of dataset merging, the constraints are disabled. If the merging violates any of the existing constraints, the **DataSet** class disables the constraints by resetting the **EnforceConstraints** property and throws the **ConstraintException**. Data rows that violated the constraints are marked with the error flag and the dataset **HasErrors** property is set to **true**. Thus, the code is left to decide what to do with the merged rows that violated the constraints. The **EnforceConstraints** property will stay reset.

XML Documents, XSD Schemas, and Datasets

XML plays an important role in .NET, in part because web services rely on XML to serialize their data, but mainly because XML has gained the recognition as a universal data interchange format. Since XML is virtually ubiquitous, chances are that your application will need to accept XML data. For that reason, the **DataSet** class fully supports XML and allows reading and writing XML data as well as XSD schemas. When writing **DataSet** data to an XML document, the **DataSet** schema is translated into an XSD schema inlined in the XML document. The XSD schema specifies the relational structure of the **DataSet**, column data types, and constraints.

The easiest way to obtain the XML representation of the data stored in the **DataSet** or the XSD schema of the **DataSet** data is to call the **GetXml/GetXmlSchema** methods. Although these methods are very simple, they are not as efficient as their counterparts that write XML/XSD data to a file or a stream (see the next section).

Writing XML Data

You can export a **DataSet** data as XML using the **WriteXml** method. To specify exactly how you want to write XML data, you can set the **XmlWriteMode** parameter of the **WriteXml** method to one of the following values:

* **DiffGram**: Writes the dataset as a **DiffGram** that contains only rows that changed and includes both the original and the new values of the columns that changed.

* **IgnoreSchema**: Writes only XML data but does not write XSD schema. (If a **DataSet** is empty nothing will be written.)

* **WriteSchema**: Writes both the **DataSet** data and the relational structure as an inline XSD schema. (If the **DataSet** has no data, the XSD schema will still be written.) This option is the default.

DataRow Changes and XML DiffGrams

The **DataSet's** primary function is to represent a cache of data. More often than not, a **DataSet** stores a copy of data that comes from a database or from a remote location. Since a **DataSet** only caches data that is physically stored elsewhere, a need arises to synchronize the **DataSet** with the original data, or to synchronize datasets that store copies of the same data. The **DataSet** class provides the **GetChanges** method and internally keeps track of modified, added, and deleted rows by maintaining several versions of the **DataSet** data corresponding to different row states (**DataRowState** enumeration). This is done to reconcile changes made to the same data by various datasets or to implement an efficient delta-update of the cached or physical data:

* **Added**: Adds a new row.

* **Deleted**: Deletes a row using the **Delete** method.

* **Detached**: Detaches a newly created row that has not been added to any **DataTable**.

* **Modified**: Modifies a row.

* **Unchanged**: Unmodifies a row.

DataRow states are kept until the **AcceptChanges** method is called. The **AcceptChanges** method changes the state of new and modified rows to **Unchanged**. When calling the **GetChanges** method you can specify the desired **DataRowState** you are interested in. Thus, you can use the **GetChanges** method to obtain only new, modified, or deleted rows. Once you obtain an array of **DataSet** rows that have changed using the **GetChanges** method, you can merge the resulting data rows with another **DataSet** of similar structure using the **Merge** method. The **Merge** method will attempt to apply the delta changes done to the original **DataSet** to the data stored in the current **DataSet**, including adding, deleting, or modifying rows. (The rows are matched by the primary key.)

If you must transmit the delta-changes obtained using the **GetChanges** method, chances are you will be required to use XML. If this is the case you can serialize or persist the delta-changes in an *XML DiffGram*. An XML DiffGram is an XML document of special format, which indicates which dataset rows were modified, added, or deleted, as well as what columns were changed for modified rows. You can store delta-changes in an XML DiffGram using the **WriteXml** method with the **XmlWriteMode** parameter set to **DiffGram**. Also, you can read the XML DiffGram using the **ReadXml** with the **XmlReadMode** parameter set to **DiffGram**. Once the DiffGram is read, you can apply the delta-changes to the current dataset data.

Reading XML Data

You can import an XML document into a **DataSet** by calling the **ReadXml** method. Keep in mind the following when importing XML data:

* The **ReadXml** method will throw an exception if the XML document contains an inline XSD schema and the data types in the XSD schema do not match the data types of columns that already exist in the **DataSet**.

* The **DataSet** schema can be extended to accommodate the data being loaded if the XSD schema and the current **DataSet** schema data types match, but the **DataSet** is missing some fields or relationships. If the existing **DataSet** structure differs too much from the schema of the XML document that it cannot be extended through inference, the **ReadXml** method will throw an exception.

When loading XML documents in a dataset you can supply an additional **XmlReadMode** parameter to the **ReadXml** method. The parameter accepts the following values defined in the **XmlReadMode** enumeration:

* **Auto**: Automatically detects the type of data being read and switches to **DiffGram** when the XML data corresponds to a DiffGram, **ReadSchema** when the XML document has in-line schema, or **InferSchema** when the XML document does not have a schema. This is the default option.

*   **DiffGram:** Reads and merges DiffGram data. The XML DiffGram document must have been previously written by the **WriteXml** method and must have the same schema as the current **DataSet**, or the **ReadXml** method may fail.

*   **Fragment:** Reads the XML document, which represents a result of a "FOR XML" query generated by the SQL Server.

*   **IgnoreSchema:** Ignores the inline schema of the XML document and uses the current **DataSet** schema. XML data that cannot be converted to accommodate the current **DataSet** schema is discarded.

*   **InferSchema:** Ignores the inline schema of the XML document, infers the schema from the XML document structure, and extends the current **DataSet** schema by adding new tables/columns.

*   **ReadSchema:** Reads inline schema of the XML document. (New tables/columns are not added if the **DataSet** already has a schema.)

Reading/Writing XSD Schemas

In addition to reading/writing XML data from a **DataSet**, you can read/write just the **DataSet** schema as a standard XSD. You can read/write a **DataSet** schema using the **ReadXmlSchema/WriteXmlSchema** methods. The **ReadXmlSchema** method creates a new schema for an empty **DataSet**. Thus, you can call this method to specify the **DataSet** schema for reading data from schemaless/structureless XML documents.

Inferring Schemas

Use the **InferXmlSchema** method to modify the current schema of a **DataSet** based on the structure of the specified XML document. The **InferXmlSchema** method will add new tables/columns to the **DataSet**. Since the **InferXmlSchema** method ignores the inline XML document schema, all newly added columns will be of type **String**. Also, you can specify an array of namespace URIs that you want to ignore when inferring a **DataSet** schema, thus taking into account only a desired portion of the XML document.

DataTable Class

Individual data tables that represent actual data stored in a dataset are implemented by means of the ADO.NET **DataTable** class, which has the following inheritance structure:

```
System::Object
|- System::ComponentModel::MarshalByValueComponent
   |- System::Data::DataTable
```

Attributes: **Serializable**

Abstract: No

Sealed: No

Implements Interfaces: **IListSource, ISupportInitialize, ISerializable**

DataTable objects possess a fairly complex internal structure; as shown in Figure 8.2. They contain the following elements:

*   Collections of **DataRelation** objects corresponding to child relations of the table.

*   Collections of **DataRelation** objects corresponding to parent relations of the table.

*   Collections of **DataRow** objects corresponding to rows of data in the table.

*   Collections of constraints (both unique and foreign keys).

*   Collections of **DataColumn** objects corresponding to the table columns in the database.

*   **DefaultView** object corresponding to a filtered and/or sorted version of the data table data.

*   **PrimaryKey** array corresponding to **DataColumn** objects that together comprise the primary key of the table. (The array can contain a single **DataColumn** if the primary key corresponds to a single column.)

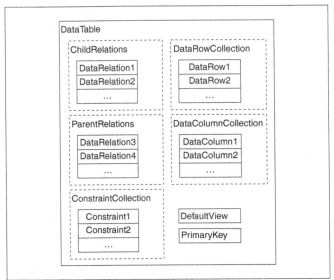

The collections of **DataRelation**, **DataRow**, and **DataColumn** objects are implemented by means of the **DataRelationCollection**, **DataRowCollection**, and **DataColumnCollection** collection classes.

The **DataTable** class constructors, properties, methods, and events are summarized in Tables 8.11 through 8.14.

Figure 8.2. **DataTable** class architecture.

Table 8.11 **DataTable** class constructors.

Constructor	Description
DataTable()	Default constructor.
DataTable(String* *name*)	Constructs a **DataTable** object using the specified table name.
protected: DataTable(SerializationInfo* *info*, StreamingContext *context*)	Constructs a **DataTable** object using the specified serialization information.

Table 8.12 **DataTable** class properties.

Get/Set	Type	Property	Description
Get/Set	**bool**	**CaseSensitive**	Gets or sets a Boolean value indicating whether string comparisons within the **DataTable** must be case-sensitive.
Get	**DataRelationCollection***	**ChildRelations**	Contains a pointer to the collection of child relations of the **DataTable**.
Get	**DataColumnCollection***	**Columns**	Contains a pointer to the collection of table columns.

<Continued on Next Page>

<Table 8.12 Continued>

Get/Set	Type	Property	Description
Get	ConstraintCollection*	Constraints	Contains a pointer to the collection of constraints.
Get	DataSet*	DataSet	Contains a pointer to the **DataSet** that the **DataTable** belongs to.
Get	DataView*	DefaultView	Contains a pointer to a customized view of the table data, which may include filtering and/or sorting.
Get/Set	String*	DisplayExpression	Gets or sets the expression that is used by visual designers to represent the table in the user interface.
Get	PropertyCollection*	ExtendedProperties	Contains a pointer to the collection of user-defined properties.
Get	bool	HasErrors	Contains **true** if the **DataSet** contains errors in any of the rows in any of the tables.
Get/Set	CultureInfo*	Locale	Gets or sets the locale information for comparing strings within the data tables of the **DataSet**.
Get/Set	int	MinimumCapacity	Gets or sets the initial size of the **DataTable**.
Get/Set	String*	Namespace	Gets or sets the **DataSet** XML namespace (**xmlns** attribute).
Get	DataRelationCollection*	ParentRelations	Contains a pointer to the collection of parent relations of the **DataTable**.
Get/Set	String*	Prefix	Gets or sets an XML prefix that aliases the **DataTable** records: The table data rows are written as **<Prefix:TableName xmlns:Namespace=** *DataSetNamespace* **>** XML tags.
Get/Set	DataColumn*[]	PrimaryKey	Gets or sets the array of columns that comprise the primary key of the **DataTable**.
Get	DataRowCollection*	Rows	Contains a pointer to the collection of table data rows.
Get/Set	String*	TableName	Gets or sets the name of the **DataTable**.

Table 8.13 **DataTable** class methods.

Method	Description
void AcceptChanges()	Commits any pending changes made to the **DataTable**.
__sealed void BeginInit()	Begins the initialization of the **DataTable** that is used on a form or used by another component (Windows Forms).
void BeginLoadData()	Begins loading data by turning off notifications, index maintenance, and constraints.
void Clear()	Removes all data rows from the **DataTable**.
virtual DataTable* Clone()	Creates a structural copy of the **DataTable** (the data is not cloned).
Object* Compute(String* *expression*, String* *filter*)	Computes the specified aggregate expression on the current rows that satisfy the specified filter criteria.

<Continued on Next Page>

<Table 8.13 Continued>

Method	Description
DataTable* Copy()	Creates both structural and data copy of the **DataTable**.
__sealed void EndInit()	Ends the initialization of the **DataTable** that is used on a form or used by another component (Windows Forms).
void EndLoadData()	Ends loading data by turning on notifications, index maintenance, and constraints.
DataTable* GetChanges()	
DataTable* GetChanges(DataRowState *rowStates*)	Creates a copy of the **DataTable** only containing changes made since it was last loaded, or since the **AcceptChanges** method was called. Optional *rowStates* argument allows specifying a particular type changes to retrieve.
DataRow* GetErrors()[]	Returns an array of **DataRow** objects that contain errors.
void ImportRow(DataRow* *row*)	Copies the specified **DataRow** into the **DataTable**, preserving any property settings, as well as original and current values.
DataRow* LoadDataRow(Object* *values* __gc[], bool a*cceptChanges*)	Finds and updates a specific row. If no matching row is found, a new row is created using the specified values. If the *acceptChanges* is set to **true** the changes are automatically accepted by invoking the **AcceptChanges** method.
DataRow* NewRow()	Creates a new **DataRow** with the same schema as the table.
protected: virtual DataRow* NewRowFromBuilder(DataRowBuilder* *builder*)	Creates a new row from an existing row using the specified **DataRowBuilder**.
protected: virtual void OnColumnChanged(DataColumnChangeEventArgs* *e*)	Fires the **ColumnChanged** event.
protected: virtual void OnColumnChanging(DataColumnChangeEventArgs* *e*)	Fires the **ColumnChanging** event.
protected public: virtual void OnPropertyChanging(PropertyChangedEventArgs* *e*)	Fires the **PropertyChanging** event.
protected public: virtual void OnRemoveColumn(DataColumn* *column*)	Invoked when a **DataColumn** is being removed from the **DataTable**.
protected: virtual void OnRowChanged(DataRowChangeEventArgs* *e*)	Fires the **RowChanged** event.
protected: virtual void OnRowChanging(DataRowChangeEventArgs* *e*)	Fires the **RowChanging** event.
protected: virtual void OnRowDeleted(DataRowChangeEventArgs* *e*)	Fires the **RowDeleted** event.

<Continued on Next Page>

<Table 8.13 Continued>

Method	Description
protected: virtual void OnRowDeleting(DataRowChangeEventArgs* e)	Fires the **RowDeleting** event.
void RejectChanges()	Rolls back changes made to the table since it was loaded, or the last time **AcceptChanges** was called.
virtual void Reset()	Resets the **DataTable** to the original state.
DataRow* Select()[]	
DataRow* Select(String* *filterExpression*)[]	
DataRow* Select(String* *filterExpression*, String* *sort*)[]	
DataRow* Select(String* *filterExpression*, String* *sort*, DataViewRowState *recordStates*)[]	Returns the array of data table rows. Optional *filterExpression* and *sort* and arguments allow specifying expressions for limiting and sorting the resulting data rows. Optional *recordStates* argument allows including only rows in a specified state (i.e., deleted, modified, unchanged, etc.).
String* ToString()	Returns concatenated **TableName** and **DisplayExpression**.

Table 8.14 **DataTable** class events.

Event	Description
DataColumnChangeEventHandler* ColumnChanged	Fired after a column value has been changed.
DataColumnChangeEventHandler* ColumnChanging	Fired when a column value is about to change.
DataRowChangeEventHandler* RowChanged	Fired after a table row has been changed successfully.
DataRowChangeEventHandler* RowChanging	Fired when a table row is about to change.
DataRowChangeEventHandler* RowDeleted	Fired after a table row has been deleted.
DataRowChangeEventHandler* RowDeleting	Fired when a table row is about to be deleted.

A **DataTable** object usually has a name stored in the **TableName** property. If you do not specify a name for a **DataTable** object, it will be assigned a default name, (e.g., "TABLE1"). The name of a **DataTable** object does not necessarily correspond to the name of the actual database table. Instead, the property is used for identifying data tables in the data table collections and for writing XML documents.

As with the **DataSet** class, the **DataTable** class possesses the **Profix** and **Namespace** properties that may come in handy for writing XML data. Both the **Profix** and the **Namespace** properties allow you to specifying the XML namespace when saving a table or a dataset as an XML document.

Selecting Rows

To select **DataRows** from a **DataTable** you can either access the rows directly using the **Rows** property, or you can execute a separate SELECT operation on the table by invoking the **Select** method. The advantage of the **Select** method is that you can optionally specify filter and sort expressions as well as limit the result set by specifying a particular row status flag—a constant from the **DataViewState** enumeration:

* **Added**: Newly added rows since last SELECT.

* **CurrentRows**: Current rows including unchanged and newly added.

* **Deleted**: Deleted rows.

* **ModifiedCurrent**: Modified current rows.

* **ModifiedOriginal**: Modified original rows.

* **None**: The **Select** returns no rows.

* **OriginalRows**: Unchanged and deleted rows.

* **Unchanged**: Unchanged rows.

You can combine flags to retrieve more than one version of the **DataTable** rows.

Primary Keys

A **DataTable** object may or may not contain a *primary key*—a value uniquely identifying each row in the table. Primary keys are used for row lookup and for parent/child relationships. Information about the **DataTable** primary key is stored in the **PrimaryKey** property, which is defined as an array of **DataColumn** objects. In most cases the primary key is defined by a single column. In this case the **PrimaryKey** array will contain a single element. But in some cases a primary key may be represented by a collection of columns that when combined yield a unique value for each row in the **DataTable**. Such primary keys are called *composite*. For instance, an "Area Code" column combined with a "Phone Number" column can be used as a composite primary key for a nation-wide telephone directory.

Aggregate Expressions

The **DataTable** class allows you to calculate aggregate expressions (e.g., COUNT, SUM, MIN, MAX) on a data table by means of the **Compute** method. To do this you simply specify the expression in the *expression* parameter and a filter expression (which is similar to the SQL WHERE clause) in the *filter* parameter (if any). The aggregate expression will be evaluated and returned without affecting the state of the **DataTable**.

DataTable Notifications

The **DataTable** class provides six notification events: **RowChanging**, **RowChanged**, **ColumnChanging**, **ColumnChanged**, **RowDeleting**, and **RowDeleted**. These events are fired when individual columns or entire rows are modified or deleted. You can hook up custom event handlers to the **DataTable** events to perform custom column/row data validation, reject changes made to the **DataTable** if the validation fails, or restrict deletion of rows from the **DataTable**.

There is an important difference between *-ing* and *–ed* events: The *ing*-events are raised *before* the change/delete action is committed and the *ed*-events are raised *after* the change/delete action is committed. In general, you still have an opportunity to undo an undesired action *before* the action is committed. Thus, you should perform data validation in the *ing*-event handlers. The **DataTable** event handlers rely on the **DataRowChangeEventArgs** and

DataColumnChangeEventArgs classes to supply data on the notification events, which properties are listed in Tables 8.15 through 8.16.

Table 8.15 **DataRowChangeEventArgs** class properties.

Get/Set	Type	Property	Description
Get	**DataRowAction**	**Action**	Describes the data row action, which cause the event.
Get	**DataRow***	**Row**	Contains a pointer to the affected row.

Table 8.16 **DataColumnChangeEventArgs** class properties.

Get/Set	Type	Property	Description
Get	**DataColumn***	**Column**	Contains a pointer to the affected column.
Get/Set	**Object***	**ProposedValue**	Gets or sets the proposed column value. You can set the **ProposedValue** to a new value to perform a *correcting silent* validation.
Get	**DataRow***	**Row**	Contains a pointer to the row to which the affected column belongs.

The **Action** property of the **DataRowChangeEventArgs** class can contain one of the following values:

* **Add**: A row has been or is being added.
* **Change**: A row has been or is being changed.
* **Commit**: A row has been or is being committed (e.g., the **AcceptChanges** method was called).
* **Delete**: A row has been or is being deleted.
* **Nothing**: A row has not been changed.

Rollback: Row changes have been or are being rejected (e.g., the **RejectChanges** method was called).

> **NOTE:** If you do not use **BeginEdit/EndEdit** methods to modify a **DataRow**, the **RowChanging/RowChanged** notification events are fired as soon as you modify a row column. If you enclose the changes to a **DataRow** with the **BeginEdit/EndEdit** block, the **RowChanging/RowChanged** notification events are fired when the **EndEdit** is called.

Data Table Collections

Data tables in a **DataSet** object are not stored in an array. Instead, they are kept in a special container called –**DataTableCollection** and they are implemented as the **DataSet::Tables** property. The **DataTableCollection** class is one of many special-purpose collection classes in the System::Data namespace. All special-purpose collections in the System::Data namespace, such as **DataTableCollection**, **DataColumnCollection**, or

DataRowCollection are derived from the same base class **InternalDataCollectionBase**, hence the **DataTableCollection** class inheritance diagram looks like this:

```
System::Object
|- System::Data::InternalDataCollectionBase
   |- System::Data::DataTableCollection
```

Attributes: **Serializable**
Abstract: No
Sealed: No
Implements Interfaces: None

The **InternalDataCollectionBase** implements the **ICollection** and **IEnumerable** interfaces and has no members of particular interest. Quite the contrary, the **DataTableCollection** class has a number of useful properties and methods, including the **Item** indexer capable of retrieving individual **DataTable** objects from the collection by table name or by index and numerous **Add** and **Remove** method overloads for creating and adding new **DataTable** objects to the collection, and for removing them. For a summary of the **DataTableCollection** class properties, methods, and events see Tables 8.17 through 8.19.

Table 8.17 **DataTableCollection** class properties.

Get/Set	Type	Property	Virtual	Description
Get	**DataTable***	**Item(int *index*)**	No	Returns a **DataTable** object at the specified index.
Get	**DataTable***	**Item(String* *name*)**	No	Returns a **DataTable** object with the specified name.
Get	**ArrayList***	**List**	Yes	Contains the list of all **DataTable** objects in the collection.

Table 8.18 **DataTableCollection** class methods.

Method	Description
virtual DataTable* Add()	Adds a new **DataTable** to the collection.
virtual void Add(DataTable* *table*)	Adds the specified **DataTable** to the collection.
virtual DataTable* Add(String* *name*)	Adds a new **DataTable** with the specified name to the collection.
void AddRange(DataTable* *tables*[])	Adds the specified array of **DataTable** objects to the collection.
bool CanRemove(DataTable* *table*)	Returns **true** if the specified **DataTable** can be removed from the collection.
void Clear()	Removes all tables from the collection.
bool Contains(String* *name*)	Returns **true** if a **DataTable** with the specified name is in the collection.
virtual int IndexOf(DataTable* *table*)	
virtual int IndexOf(String* *tableName*)	Returns the index of **DataTable**.

<Continued on Next Page>

<Table 8.18 Continued>

Method	Description
protected: virtual void OnCollectionChanged(CollectionChangeEventArgs* e)	Fires the **OnCollectionChanged** event.
protected public: virtual void OnCollectionChanging(CollectionChangeEventArgs* e)	Fires the **OnCollectionChanging** event.
void Remove(DataTable* *table*)	
void Remove(String* *name*)	
void RemoveAt(int *index*)	Removes the specified **DataTable** from the collection.

Table 8.19 **DataTableCollection** class events.

Event	Description
CollectionChangeEventHandler* CollectionChanged	Fired after a **DataTable** is added or removed from the collection.
CollectionChangeEventHandler* CollectionChanging	Fired when a **DataTable** is about to be added or removed from the collection.

Most of the System::Data namespace special-purpose collections implement the **OnCollectionChanging** and **OnCollectionChanged** methods that fire the **CollectionChanging** and **CollectionChanged** events by default before and after the collection is modified (i.e., when a new element is added or removed from the collection). You can override the **OnCollectionChanging** and **OnCollectionChanged** methods to implement additional validation and restrict the addition or removal of elements from the collection by throwing an exception. To indicate a particular action that caused the **CollectionChanging** or **CollectionChanged** events, the framework supplies a **CollectionChangeEventArgs** parameter to the event handlers. The **CollectionChangeEventArgs** structure has two useful properties:

* **Action**: Set to one of the **CollectionChangeAction** enumeration constants: **Add**, **Refresh**, or **Remove**.

* **Element**:Set to a pointer to the object that was added or removed from the collection.

DataColumn Class

If you recall from Figure 8.2, which depicted the **DataTable** class architecture, each data table object contains a collection of data columns. Each data column object corresponds to a database table field or an expression (which can be a combination of columns or an aggregate function). A data column is represented by means of the **DataColumn** class, which has the following inheritance structure:

```
System::Object
|- System::ComponentModel::MarshalByValueComponent
   |- System::Data::DataColumn

Attributes: None
Abstract: No
Sealed: No
Implements Interfaces: None
```

Similarly to a database field, a **DataColumn** object is characterized by name and type. You can specify both name and type of a **DataColumn** as a parameter to the **DataColumn** constructor. The **DataColumn** class constructors, properties, and methods are summarized in Tables 8.20 through 8.22.

Table 8.20 **DataColumn** class constructors.

Constructor	Description
DataColumn()	Default constructor.
DataColumn(String* *name***)**	
DataColumn(String* *name***, Type*** *dataType***)**	
DataColumn(String* *name***, Type*** *dataType***, String*** *expression***)**	
DataColumn(String* *name***, Type*** *dataType***, String*** *expression***, MappingType** *type***)**	Constructs a **DataColumn** with the specified *name*. Optional *dataType*, *expression* and *type* arguments allow specifying the column data type, expression, and XML mapping type (i.e. **Attribute**, **Element**, **Hidden**, or **SimpleContent**). The default column data type is **String**.

Table 8.21 **DataColumn** class properties.

Get/Set	Type	Property	Virtual	Description
Get/Set	**bool**	**AllowDBNull**	No	Gets or sets a Boolean value indicating whether the column can contain Null values.
Get/Set	**bool**	**AutoIncrement**	No	Gets or sets a Boolean value indicating whether the column value automatically increments when a new row is added.
Get/Set	**__int64**	**AutoIncrementSeed**	No	Gets or sets the starting value of an **AutoIncrement** column.
Get/Set	**__int64**	**AutoIncrementStep**	No	Gets or sets the increment step used by an **AutoIncrement** column.
Get/Set	**String***	**Caption**	No	Gets or sets the caption for the column used by visual designers (Windows Forms).
Get/Set	**MappingType**	**ColumnMapping**	Yes	Gets or sets the XML **MappingType** of the column.
Get/Set	**String***	**ColumnName**	No	Gets or sets the name of the column.
Get/Set	**Type***	**DataType**	No	Gets or sets the column data type.
Get/Set	**Object***	**DefaultValue**	No	Gets or sets the default value for the column used for initializing the column in a new **DataRow**.
Get/Set	**String***	**Expression**	No	Gets or sets the column expression.
Get	**PropertyCollection***	**ExtendedProperties**	No	Contains a pointer to the collection of user-defined propertied of the column.

<Continued on Next Page>

<Table 8.21 Continued>

Get/Set	Type	Property	Virtual	Description
Get	**int**	**MaxLength**	No	Gets or sets the maximum length of a text column.
Get/Set	**String***	**Namespace**	No	Gets or sets the **xmlns** namespace of the **DataColumn**.
Get	**int**	**Ordinal**	No	Contains the index of the column in the **DataColumnCollection** collection.
Get/Set	**String***	**Prefix**	No	Gets or sets an XML prefix that aliases the namespace of the **DataColumn**.
Get/Set	**bool**	**ReadOnly**	No	Gets or sets a Boolean value indicating whether the column can be modified after a row has been added to the table.
Get	**DataTable***	**Table**	No	Contains a pointer to the **DataTable** to which the column belongs to.
Get/Set	**bool**	**Unique**	No	Gets or sets a Boolean value indicating whether the column values in each data row of the data table must be unique.

Table 8.22 **DataColumn** class methods.

Method	Description
protected public: virtual void OnPropertyChanging(PropertyChangedEventArgs* *event*)	Fires the **OnPropertyChanging** event.
protected public: void RaisePropertyChanging(String* *name*)	Sends a notification that the specified **DataColumn** property is about to change.

Data Column Collections

DataColumn objects are stored in a **DataTable** object in the **DataColumnCollection**. The **DataColumnCollection** class has the following inheritance structure:

```
System::Object
|- System::Data::InternalDataCollectionBase
   |- System::Data::DataColumnCollection
```

Attributes: **Serializable**
Abstract: No
Sealed: No
Implements Interfaces: None

The **DataColumnCollection** class properties, methods, and events are listed in Tables 8.23 through 8.25.

Table 8.23 **DataColumnCollection** class properties.

Get/Set	Type	Property	Virtual	Description
Get	**DataColumn***	**Item(int *index*)**	No	Returns a **DataColumn** object at the specified index.
Get	**DataColumn***	**Item(String* *name*)**	No	Returns a **DataColumn** object with the specified name.
Get	**ArrayList***	**List**	Yes	Contains the list of all **DataColumn** objects in the collection.

Table 8.24 **DataColumnCollection** class methods.

Method	Description
virtual void Add(DataColumn* *column*)	Adds the specified **DataColumn** to the collection.
virtual DataColumn* Add()	
virtual DataColumn* Add(String* *name*)	
virtual DataColumn* Add(String* *name*, Type* *type*)	
virtual DataColumn* Add(String* *name*, Type* *type*, String* *expression*)	Creates and adds a new **DataColumn** to the collection. Optional *name*, *type,* and *expression* arguments allow specifying column name, data type, and expression.
void AddRange(DataColumn* *columns*[])	Adds the specified array of **DataColumn** objects to the collection.
bool CanRemove(DataColumn* *column*)	Returns **true** if the specified **DataColumn** can be removed from the collection.
void Clear()	Removes all columns from the collection.
bool Contains(String* *name*)	Returns **true** if a **DataColumn** with the specified name is in the collection.
virtual int IndexOf(DataColumn* *column*)	
virtual int IndexOf(String* *name*)	Returns the index of a specified **DataColumn** in the collection.
protected: virtual void OnCollectionChanged(CollectionChangeEventArgs* *e*)	Fires the **OnCollectionChanged** event.
protected public: virtual void OnCollectionChanging(CollectionChangeEventArgs* *e*)	Invoked when a **DataColumn** is about to be added or removed from the collection.
void Remove(DataColumn* *column*)	
void Remove(String* *name*)	Removes a specified **DataColumn** from the collection.
void RemoveAt(int *index*)	Removes from the collection a **DataColumn** at the specified index.

Table 8.25 **DataColumnCollection** class events.

Event	Description
CollectionChangeEventHandler* CollectionChanged	Fires after a **DataColumn** is added or removed from the collection.

The most useful of all **DataColumnCollection** class properties are the **Item** indexers, which allow you to retrieve a **DataColumn** from a **DataColumnCollection** by name or by ordinal (i.e., index). Also, you can use the **Add** method to create and add a new **DataColumn** to a **DataColumnCollection**. You do this by simply specifying the column name and optionally the column data type and expression as parameters to the **Add** method. When you add or remove data columns from the **DataColumnCollection**, the class fires the **CollectionChanged** event, which you can use for notification purposes or for restricting addition or removal of elements to or from the collection.

DataRow Class

The actual data is stored in a **DataTable** in data rows. Each data row corresponds to an individual record in the table. Data rows are implemented in the .NET Framework by means of the **DataRow** class:

```
System::Object
|- System::Data::DataRow

Attributes: Serializable
Abstract: No
Sealed: No
Implements Interfaces: None
```

The **DataRow** class properties and methods are summarized in Tables 8.26 through 8.27.

Table 8.26 **DataRow** class properties.

Get/Set	Type	Property	Description
Get	**bool**	**HasErrors**	Contains **true** if the **DataRow** has errors.
Get/Set	**Object***	**Item(String* *columnName*)**	Gets or sets data stored in the **DataRow** column with the specified name.
Get/Set	**Object***	**Item(String* *columnName*, DataRowVersion *version*)**	Gets or sets data with the specified name stored in the specified version of the **Data Row**.
Get/Set	**Object***	**Item(DataColumn* *column*)**	Gets or sets data stored in the specified **DataRow** column.
Get/Set	**Object***	**Item(DataColumn* *column*, DataRowVersion *version*)**	Gets or sets data of the specified column stored in the specified version of the **DataRow**.
Get/Set	**Object***	**Item(int *columnIndex*)**	Gets or sets data stored in the **DataRow** column with the specified ordinal/index.

<Continued on Next Page>

<Table 8.26 Continued>

Get/Set	Type	Property	Description
Get/Set	**Object***	**Item(int *columnIndex*, DataRowVersion *version*)**	Gets or sets data of a column with the specified ordinal/index stored in the specified version of the **DataRow**.
Get/Set	**Object* __gc[]**	**ItemArray**	Gets or sets all column values of the **DataRow**.
Get/Set	**String***	**RowError**	Gets or sets the custom error description for the **DataRow**.
Get	**DataRowState**	**RowState**	Contains the current state of the **DataRow** with respect to the **DataRowCollection**.
Get	**DataTable***	**Table**	Contains a pointer to the **DataTable** to which the **DataRow** belongs to.

NOTE: *The **Item** indexer, which accepts more than one parameter (index) must be accessed using **Get_Item/Set_Item** methods.*

Table 8.27 **DataRow** class methods.

Method	Description
void AcceptChanges()	Commits changes made to the **DataRow** since the last time **AcceptChanges** was called.
void BeginEdit()	Begins editing of the **DataRow**.
void CancelEdit()	Cancels editing of the **DataRow** without saving changes.
void ClearErrors()	Clears all errors in the DataRow, including the **RowError** and the column errors.
void Delete()	Deletes the **DataRow**.
void EndEdit()	Ends editing of the **DataRow** and saves changes.
DataRow* GetChildRows(DataRelation* *relation*)[]	
DataRow* GetChildRows(String* *relation*)[]	
DataRow* GetChildRows(DataRelation* *relation*, DataRowVersion *version*)[]	
DataRow* GetChildRows(String* *relation*, DataRowVersion *version*)[]	Returns the array of child rows for the specified data relation. Optional *version* argument allows specifying which version of data rows (i.e., **Current**, **Default**, **Original,** or **Proposed**) to retrieve.
String* GetColumnError(DataColumn* *column*)	
String* GetColumnError(int *columnIndex*)	
String* GetColumnError(String* *columnName*)	Returns the error description for the specified column.

<Continued on Next Page>

<Table 8.26 Continued>

Method	Description
Method	*Description*
DataColumn* GetColumnsInError()[]	Builds and returns an array of columns that have errors.
DataRow* GetParentRow(DataRelation* *relation***)**	
DataRow* GetParentRow(String* *relation***)**	
DataRow* GetParentRow(DataRelation* *relation***, DataRowVersion** *version***)**	
DataRow* GetParentRow(String* *relation***, DataRowVersion** *version***)**	Returns the parent row for the specified data relation. Optional *version* argument allows specifying which *version* of data rows (i.e., **Current**, **Default**, **Original**, or **Proposed**) to retrieve.
DataRow* GetParentRows(DataRelation* *relation***)[]**	
DataRow* GetParentRows(String* *relation***)[]**	
DataRow* GetParentRows(DataRelation* *relation***, DataRowVersion** *version***)[]**	
DataRow* GetParentRows(String* *relationName***, DataRowVersion** *version***)[]**	Returns the array of parent rows for the specified data relation. Optional version argument allows specifying which *version* of data rows (i.e., **Current**, **Default**, **Original,** or **Proposed**) to retrieve.
bool HasVersion(DataRowVersion *version***)**	Returns **true** if the specified version of the **DataRow** exists.
bool IsNull(DataColumn* *column***)**	
bool IsNull(int *columnIndex***)**	
bool IsNull(String* *columnName***)**	
bool IsNull(DataColumn* *column***, DataRowVersion** *version***)**	Returns **true** if the specified column is NULL. Optional *version* argument indicates which version of the data row (i.e., **Current**, **Default**, **Original**, or **Proposed**) to examine.
void RejectChanges()	Rolls back changes made to the **DataRow** since the **AcceptChanges** was last called.
void SetColumnError(DataColumn* *column***, String*** *error***)**	
void SetColumnError(int *columnIndex***, String*** *error***)**	
void SetColumnError(String* *columnName***, String*** *error***)**	Sets the error description for the specified column.
protected: void SetNull(DataColumn* *column***)**	Sets the specified column to NULL.
void SetParentRow(DataRow* *parentRow***)**	
void SetParentRow(DataRow* *parentRow***, DataRelation*** *relation***)**	Sets the parent row of the **DataRow**. Optional *relation* argument allows specifying a data relation to which the parent row belongs.

NOTE: You will never create **DataRow** objects directly. Instead, you should rely on the System::Data class methods to construct the **DataRow** objects for you as needed.

Data Row Versions

The **DataRow** class has a numerous **Item** indexer properties, which allow retrieving data stored in columns of the **DataRow**. You can retrieve column data by specifying the column name or ordinal/index. Also, you can specify the desired version of the **DataRow** to retrieve the data from. The following versions of a **DataRow** objects available (defined in the **DataRowVersion** enumeration): **Current**, **Default**, **Original**, and **Proposed**. The **DataRow** version pertains to the way row data changes in the **DataRow** as you modify it (see Figure 8.3).

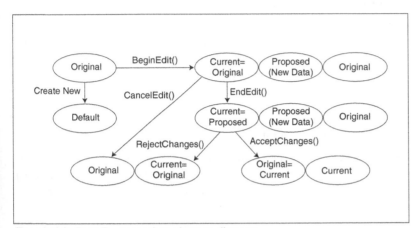

Figure 8.3. **DataRow** version change diagram.

When you first fetch a row, the **DataRow** status is **Original**. Once you begin editing by calling the **BeginEdit** method, the **DataRow** two new versions of the **DataRow** are created: **Current** (which contains the same column values as the **Original**) and the **Proposed**. If you end editing by invoking the **EndEdit** method, the **Current** version becomes identical to the **Proposed** version. Then, if you accept the changes by invoking the **AcceptChanges** method, the **Original** version becomes equivalent to the **Current** and the **Proposed** version is discarded. Alternatively, if you reject the changes by calling the **RejectChanges** method, the **Current** version becomes equivalent to the **Original**, and the **Proposed** version is once again discarded. As you can see, the Original version of the **DataRow** is available at all times. Lastly, if you create a new **DataRow**, the **Default** version is available containing the default values of data columns.

Data Row Collections

DataRow objects are stored in the **Rows** property of the **DataTable** class. The **DataTable::Rows** property represents a collection of **DataRow** objects implemented by means of the **DataRowCollection** class, which has the following inheritance structure:

```
System::Object
|- System::Data::InternalDataCollectionBase
   |- System::Data::DataRowCollection
```

Attributes: **Serializable**
Abstract: No
Sealed: No
Implements Interfaces: None

The **DataRowCollection** class properties and methods are summarized in Tables 8.28 through 8.29.

Table 8.28 **DataRowCollection** class properties.

Get/Set	Type	Property	Virtual	Description
Get	**DataRow***	**Item(int *index*)**	No	Returns a **DataRow** object at the specified index.
Get	**ArrayList***	**List**	Yes	Contains the list of all **DataRow** objects in the collection.

Table 8.29 **DataRowCollection** class methods.

Method	Description
virtual void Add(DataRow* *row*)	Adds the specified **DataRow** to the collection.
virtual DataRow* Add(Object* *values*[])	Creates a new **DataRow** using the specified values and adds it to the collection.
void Clear()	Removes all data rows from the collection.
bool Contains(Object* *pkValue*)	Returns **true** if there is a **DataRow** with the primary key matching the specified value.
bool Contains(Object* *pkValues*[])	Returns **true** if there is a **DataRow** in the collection with the composite primary key matching the specified values.
DataRow* Find(Object* *pkValue*)	Looks up and returns a **DataRow** with the primary key matching the specified value.
DataRow* Find(Object* *pkValues*[])	Looks up and returns a **DataRow** with the composite primary key matching the specified values.
void InsertAt(DataRow* *row*, int *index*)	Inserts the specified **DataRow** at the specified index into the collection.
void Remove(DataRow* *row*)	Removes the specified **DataRow** from the collection.
void RemoveAt(int *index*)	Removes the **DataRow** at the specified index from the collection.

The **DataRowCollection** class has the **Item** indexer property for retrieving **DataRow** objects by index. Also, the **DataRowCollection** class has **Contains** and **Find** methods that allow looking up a particular row in a **DataTable**'s **DataRowCollection** given the primary key value (or the array of values for a composite primary key). The **Contains** and **Find** methods provide a very easy and convenient means for searching tables for a particular row designated by a specified primary key without having to requery the entire dataset.

Describing Relations Between Tables

Representing complex hierarchal data usually requires inserting more than one **DataTable** in a **DataSet**. If you have more than one table in a **DataSet** you must specify relations between tables to describe the hierarchy of data. The hierarchy of data is described by means of parent/child relations among primary key/foreign key columns in parent and child tables. You can describe three types of relations:

* *Simple*: A single-column primary key in a parent table linked to a single-column foreign key in a child table.

* *composite*: A composite (i.e., multicolumn) primary key in a parent table linked to a composite foreign key in a child table.

* *Nested*: Simple or composite parent/child relation optimized for XML document representation. When converted to XML, child tables in nested relations appear as nested entities. This gives the XML document a structural view that you can easily interpret visually without having to analyze the document XSD schema. Child tables participating in non-nested relations will be written as separate top-level XML entities.

To describe a parent/child relation between two columns located in different tables, you should use the ADO.NET **DataRelation** class:

```
System::Object
|- System::Data::DataRelation
```

Attributes: **Serializable**
Abstract: No
Sealed: No
Implements Interfaces: None

DataRelation class constructors and properties are summarized in Tables 8.30 through 8.31.

Table 8.30 **DataRelation** class constructors.

Constructor	Description
DataRelation(String* *relationName*, DataColumn* *parent*, DataColumn* *child*)	
DataRelation(String* *relationName*, DataColumn* *parent*, DataColumn* *child*, bool *createConstraints*)	Constructs a data relation object with the specified name, using the specified parent and child columns. Optional *createConstraints* argument indicates whether to create a **ForeignKeyConstraint** necessary to enforce the created parent/child relation.
DataRelation(String* *relationName*, DataColumn* *parents*[], DataColumn* *children*[])	
DataRelation(String* *relationName*, DataColumn* *parenTs*[], DataColumn* *children*[], bool *createConstraint*)	Constructs a composite data relation with the specified name, using the specified arrays of parent and child columns. Optional *createConstraints* argument indicates whether to create a **ForeignKeyConstraint** necessary to enforce the created parent/child relation.
DataRelation(String* *relationName*, String* *parentTable*, String* *childTable*, String* *parentColumns*[], String* *childColumns*[], bool *nested*)	Constructs a composite or nested data relation with the specified name, for the specified parent and child tables, using the specified arrays of parent and child column names.

Table 8.31 **DataRelation** class properties (all virtual).

Get/Set	Type	Property	Description
Get	DataColumn*	ChildColumns	Contains a pointer to child columns of the **DataRelation**.
Get	ForeignKeyConstraint*	ChildKeyConstraint	Contains a pointer to the foreign key constraint of the **DataRelation**.
Get	DataTable*	ChildTable	Contains a pointer to the child table of the **DataRelation**.
Get	DataSet*	DataSet	Contains a pointer of the data set to which the **DataRelation** belongs.
Get	PropertyCollection*	ExtendedProperties	Contains a pointer to the collection of custom properties of the **DataRelation**.
Get/Set	bool	Nested	Gets or sets a Boolean value indicating whether the **DataRelation** is nested.
Get	DataColumn*	ParentColumns	Contains a pointer to the parent columns of the **DataRelation**.
Get	UniqueConstraint*	ParentKeyConstraint	Contains a pointer to the unique constraint that ensures that the values in the parent columns are unique.
Get	DataTable*	ParentTable	Contains a pointer to the parent table of the **DataRelation**.
Get/Set	String*	RelationName	Gets or sets the name of the **DataRelation**.

To create a new data relation, use the **DataRelation** class constructor. You simply supply pointers to parent and child **DataColumn** objects or names of parent and child columns as parameters to the appropriate **DataRelation** constructor overload. Unless you explicitly set the *createConstraints* constructor parameter to **false**, the necessary constraints will be created automatically to ensure the integrity of data in the tables bound by the **DataRelation**.

Data Relation Collections

Data relations among **DataTables** are stored in the **Relations** property of a **DataSet** object, which is a collection. The collection of data relations is implemented in ADO.NET by means of the **DataRelationCollection** class, which has the following inheritance structure:

```
System::Object
|- System::Data::InternalDataCollectionBase
    |- System::Data::DataRelationCollection

Attributes: Serializable
Abstract: Yes
Sealed: No
Implements Interfaces: None
```

The **DataRelationCollection** class constructors, properties, methods, and events are summarized in Tables 8.32 through 8.35.

Table 8.32 **DataRelationCollection** class constructors.

Constructor	Description
protected: DataRelationCollection()	Default constructor.

Table 8.33 **DataRelationCollection** class properties (all virtual).

Get/Set	Type	Property	Description
Get	**DataRelation***	**Item(String* *name*)**	Returns a **DataRelation** with the specified name.
Get	**DataRelation ***	**Item(int *index*)**	Returns a **DataRelation** at the specified index.

Table 8.34 **DataRelationCollection** class methods.

Method	Description
void Add(DataRelation* *relation*)	Adds the specified **DataRelation** to the collection.
virtual DataRelation* Add(String* *name*, DataColumn* *parent*, DataColumn* *child*)	
virtual DataRelation* Add(String* *name*, DataColumn* *parent*, DataColumn* *child*, bool *createConstraints*)	Creates a parent/child relation with the specified name, for the specified columns and adds it to the collection. Optional *createConstraints* argument indicates whether to create a **ForeignKeyConstraint** necessary to enforce the created parent/child relation.
virtual DataRelation* Add(String* *name*, DataColumn* *parents*[], DataColumn* *children*[])	
virtual DataRelation* Add(String* *name*, DataColumn* *parents*[], DataColumn* *children*[], bool *createConstraints*)	Creates a composite parent/child relation for the specified arrays of parent/child columns and adds it to the collection. Optional *createConstraints* argument indicates whether to create a **ForeignKeyConstraint** necessary to enforce the created parent/child relation.
virtual DataRelation* Add(DataColumn* *parent*, DataColumn* *child*)	Creates a parent/child relation for the specified columns and adds it to the collection.
virtual DataRelation* Add(DataColumn* *parents*[],DataColumn* *children*[])	Creates a composite parent/child relation for the specified arrays of parent/child columns and adds it to the collection.
virtual void AddRange(DataRelation* *relations*[])	Adds all relations in the specified array to the collection.
virtual bool CanRemove(DataRelation* *relation*)	Returns **true** if the specified relation can be removed from the collection.
virtual void Clear()	Removes all relations from the collection.

<Continued on Next Page>

<Table 8.34 Continued>

Method	Description
virtual bool Contains(String* *name***)**	Returns **true** if the specified relation is found in the collection.
protected: virtual DataSet* GetDataSet()	Returns the **DataSet** to which the **DataRelationCollection** applies.
virtual int IndexOf(DataRelation* *relation***)**	
virtual int IndexOf(String* *name***)**	Returns the index of the specified relation.
protected: virtual void **OnCollectionChanged(CollectionChangeEventArgs*** *e***)**	Fires the **CollectionChanged** event after a new relation is added to or removed from the collection.
protected: virtual void **OnCollectionChanging(CollectionChangeEventArgs*** *e***)**	Invoked before a new relation is added to or removed from the collection
void Remove(DataRelation* *relation***)**	
void Remove(String* *name***)**	
void RemoveAt(int *index***)**	Removes the specified relation from the collection.

Table 8.35 **DataRelationCollection** class events.

Method Description

CollectionChangeEventHandler* CollectionChanged	The event is fired whenever relations are added or removed from the collection.

The **DataRelationCollection** class allows creating and adding data relations to the collection all in one shot by means of the **Add** method. The **Add** method has numerous overloads that allow creating simple or composite data relations. You can optionally generate foreign key constraints necessary to enforce a parent/child relation being added to the collection by setting the *createConstraints* constructor parameter to **true**.

Constraints

Database tables rarely exist without any constraints imposed on the table columns. Similarly ADO.NET **DataTable** objects may require constraints imposed on column values. The two most common types of column constraints are:

* *Unique column constraint*: Ensures that all rows in the table contain different values in the column on which the unique constraint is enforced.

* *Foreign key constraint*: Enforces the integrity of a parent/child table relation by matching the foreign key values in the child table against the primary key in the parent table and allowing foreign key values only in the range of the primary key values.

All types of constraints implemented in the ADO.NET must be derived from a single abstract base class named **Constraint**:

```
System::Object
|- System::Data::Constraint


Attributes: Serializable
Abstract: Yes
Sealed: No
Implements Interfaces: None
```

The **Constraint** class constructors and properties are listed in Tables 8.36 through 8.37.

Table 8.36 **Constraint** class constructors.

Constructor	Description
protected: Constraint()	Default constructor.

Table 8.37 **Constraint** class properties.

Get/Set	Type	Property	Virtual	Description
Get/Set	**String***	**ConstraintName**	Yes	Gets/sets the constraint name.
Get	**PropertyCollection***	**ExtendedProperties**	No	Contains a collection of user-defined constraint properties.
Get	**DataTable***	**Table**	Yes	Points to a **DataTable** object to which the constraint applies.

Foreign Key Constraints

Foreign key constraints, which enforce the integrity of parent/child table relationships, are implemented in the ADO.NET be means of the **ForeignKeyConstraint** class:

```
System::Object
|- System::Data::Constraint
   |- System::Data::ForeignKeyConstraint


Attributes: Serializable
Abstract: No
Sealed: No
Implements Interfaces: None
```

The **ForeignKeyConstraint** class constructors and methods are summarized in Tables 8.38 through 8.39.

Table 8.38 **ForeignKeyConstraint** class constructors.

Constructor	Description
ForeignKeyConstraint(DataColumn* *parentColumn*, **DataColumn*** *childColumn*)	
ForeignKeyConstraint(String* *name*, **DataColumn*** *parentColumn*, **DataColumn*** *childColumn*)	Constructs a **ForeignKeyConstraint** with the specified name by associating the specified parent column (foreign key) with the specified child column (primary key).
ForeignKeyConstraint(DataColumn* *parentColumns[]*, **DataColumn*** *childColumns[]*)	
ForeignKeyConstraint(String* *constraintName*, **DataColumn*** *parentColumns[]*, **DataColumn*** *childColumns[]*)	Constructs a **ForeignKeyConstraint** with the specified name by associating the specified array of parent columns (composite foreign key) with the specified array of child columns (composite primary key).
ForeignKeyConstraint(String* *name*, **String*** *parentTable*, **String*** *parentColumns[]*, **String*** *childColumns[]*, **AcceptRejectRule** *acceptRejectRule*, **Rule** *deleteRule*, **Rule** *updateRule*)	Constructs a **ForeignKeyConstraint** with the specified name for the specified parent table by associating the specified array of parent columns (composite foreign key) with the specified array of child columns (composite primary key). The *acceptRejectRule*, *deleteRule*, and *updateRule* parameters specify rules for handling actions violating the constraint.

Table 8.39 **ForeignKeyConstraint** class properties (all virtual).

Get/Set	Type	Property	Description
Get/Set	**AcceptRejectRule**	**AcceptRejectRule**	Gets or sets the action that should be taken when the **AcceptChanges** method is involved on a **DataTable** to which the constraint applies.
Get	**DataColumn*[]**	**Columns**	Contains a pointer to the array of child columns of the **ForeignKeyConstraint**.
Get/Set	**Rule**	**DeleteRule**	Gets or sets the action that should be taken when a row is deleted from the **DataTable** to which the constraint applies.
Get	**DataColumn***	**RelatedColumns**	Contains a pointer to the array of parent columns of the **ForeignKeyConstraint**.
Get	**DataTable***	**RelatedTable**	Contains a pointer to the parent table of the **ForeignKeyConstraint**.
Get	**DataTable***	**Table**	Contains a pointer to the child table of the **ForeignKeyConstraint**.
Get/Set	**Rule**	**UpdateRule**	Gets or sets the action that should be taken when a row is updated in the **DataTable** to which the constraint applies.

To create a foreign key constraint, you can create a **ForeignKeyConstraint** object using one of the **ForeignKeyConstraint** constructor overloads. You must supply pointers to parent and child columns of the **ForeignKeyConstraint** to the constructor. The **ForeignKeyConstraint** constructors accept both single parent/child **DataColumn** objects and arrays of parent/child columns for foreign key constraints enforced on composite primary/foreign keys.

Constraint Rules

When specifying foreign key constraints, you may want to specify rules for handling changes in the primary key values of the parent table that is a part of a parent/child relationship. Consider the following example: You maintain a World Map database and you have a "Country" table that lists all countries in the world, a "Capital" table that contains the capitals of all countries along with the information on sites and tourist attractions. You designated a "Country Name" column as the primary key of the "Country" table. The same column exists in the "Capital" table and represents a foreign key into the "Country" table. Since the "Country"/"Capital" tables logically participate in the parent/child relationship and you recognize the need for data integrity, you created an appropriate **DataRelation** and imposed a **ForeignKeyConstraint** on the "Country Name" column in the "Capital."

Everything was fine until in 1991 the Soviet Union collapsed and was largely replaced by the Russian Federation. Now you have to go back to the World Map database and change the value of the primary key for "USSR" to "Russian Federation." But what's going to happen with the contents of the "Capital" child table?

Fortunately, ADO.NET allows you to specify rules for such situations. When you create a **ForeignKeyConstraint** you can set the *acceptRejectRule* parameter to one of the values from the **AcceptRejectRule** enumeration:

* **Cascade**: Propagate primary key changes across the relationships (thus, the "Country Name" column in the "Capital" table will be automatically modified to "Russian Federation").

* **None**: No action taken (thus a **ConstraintException** will be thrown and you will not be able to change the country name from "USSR" to "Russian Federation" because the change will violate the foreign key constraint imposed on the table).

Similarly you can specify rules for deleting and updating data rows in tables bound by parent/child relationships by specifying the *deleteRule* and the *updateRule* parameter values from the **Rule** enumeration in the **ForeignKeyConstraint** constructor:

* **Cascade**: If you modify the primary key value in a parent table, the foreign key values in child tables will be updated accordingly. If you delete a row from the parent table, all rows in the child tables that reference the deleted parent row will be deleted (thus if the president of the United States commands Arnold Schwartzenegger to defeat Taliban, and later, after Arnold's glorious victory, annexes Afghanistan to exile all Java programmers to Kandahar, deleting a row for "Afghanistan" from the "Country" table will cause the deletion of the row for "Kabul" from the "Capital" table).

* **None**: No action is taken and a **ConstraintException** is thrown.

* **SetDefault:** Set the affected child table foreign key columns to default values (you may create a dummy country called "Orphaned" in the "Country" table, and set the default value of the "Country" column in the "Capital" table to "Orphaned," once you delete or modify the name of a country in the "Country" table, a child record in the "Capital" table will automatically link to the "Orphaned" country; later you can process the "Orphaned" "Capital"-table rows manually, say to specify a new name of the country capital.

* **SetNull**: Set the affected child table foreign key columns to NULLs. You can rely on NULL values in the foreign keys to clean up orphaned rows in child tables manually.

Unique Constraints

Unique constraints are typically imposed on foreign key columns to ensure that there are no two primary keys with the same value to avoid ambiguous relations. The unique constraint is implemented by means of the **UniqueConstraint** class a shown here

```
System::Object
|- System::Data::Constraint
    |- System::Data::UniqueConstraint
```

Attributes: **Serializable**
Abstract: No
Sealed: No
Implements Interfaces: None

The **UniqueConstraint** class constructors and properties are summarized in Tables 8.40 and 8.41.

Table 8.40 **UniqueConstraint** class constructors.

Constructor	Description
UniqueConstraint(DataColumn* *column*)	
UniqueConstraint(DataColumn* *column*, bool *isPK*)	Constructs the unique constraint for the specified *column*. Optional *isPK* argument indicates whether the constraint is for a primary key.
UniqueConstraint(DataColumn* *columns*[])	
UniqueConstraint(DataColumn* *columns*[], bool *isPK*)	Constructs the unique composite constraint using the specified array of *columns*. Optional *isPK* argument indicates whether the constraint is for a primary key.
UniqueConstraint(String* *constraintName*, DataColumn* *column*)	
UniqueConstraint(String* *constraintName*, DataColumn* *column*, bool *isPK*)	Constructs named unique constraint for the specified *column*. Optional *isPK* argument indicates whether the constraint is for a primary key.
UniqueConstraint(String* *constraintName*, DataColumn* *columns*[])	
UniqueConstraint(String* *constraintName*, DataColumn* *columns*[], bool *isPK*)	Constructs named unique composite constraint using the specified array of *columns*. Optional *isPK* argument indicates whether the constraint is for a primary key.
UniqueConstraint(String* *constraintName*, String* *columnNames*[], bool *isPK*)	Constructs named unique composite constraint for the specified array of columns, indicating whether the constraint is for a composite primary key.

Table 8.41 **UniqueConstraint** class properties (all virtual).

Get/Set Type		Property	Description
Get	DataColumn*[]	Columns	Contains a pointer to the array of columns to which the **UniqueConstraint** applies.
Get	bool	IsPrimaryKey	Contains **true** if the UniqueConstraint applies to a primary key column.
Get	DataTable*	Table	Contains a pointer to a **DataTable** to which the **UniqueConstraint** belongs.

To create a unique constraint, you can create a **UniqueConstraint** object using one of the **UniqueConstraint** constructor overloads. You must supply a pointer to a **DataColumn** or a pointer to an array of **DataColumn** objects to which the unique constrain shall apply.

Although unique constraints are usually enforced on primary keys, you can enforce a unique constraint on any column or set of columns. Thus, you can supply an *isPK* parameter to the **UniqueConstraint** constructor to indicate whether this constraint applies to a primary key. Also, you can query the **IsPrimaryKey** property to check whether the constraint applies to a primary key.

Constraint Collections

Constraints applicable to a **DataTable** are stored in the **Constraints** property of the **DataTable** class, which is implemented as a collection of constraints. The collection of constraints is represented by the ADO.NET **ConstraintCollection** class, which has the following inheritance structure:

```
System::Object
|- System::Data::InternalDataCollectionBase
   |- System::Data::ConstraintCollection
```

```
Attributes: Serializable
Abstract: No
Sealed: No
Implements Interfaces: None
```

The **ConstraintCollection** class properties, methods, and events are summarized in Tables 8.42 through 8.44.

Table 8.42 **ConstraintCollection** class properties (all virtual).

Get/Set	Type	Property	Protected	Description
Get	Constraint*	Item(String* *name*)	No	Returns a constraint with the specified name.
Get	Constraint*	Item(int *index*)	No	Returns a constraint at the specified index.
Get	ArrayList*	List	Yes	Contains the list of all constraints stored in the **ConstraintCollection**.

Table 8.43 **ConstraintCollection** class methods.

Method	Description
void Add(Constraint* *constraint*)	Adds the specified **Constraint** object to the collection.
virtual Constraint* Add(String* *constraintName*, **DataColumn*** *column*, **bool** *isPK*)	Constructs and adds to the collection a new **UniqueConstraint** with the specified name, for the specified **DataColumn**, indicating whether the constraint is for a primary key.
virtual Constraint* Add(String* *constraintName*, **DataColumn*** *columns[]*, **bool** *isPK*)	Constructs and adds to the collection a new composite **UniqueConstraint** with the specified name, for the specified array of columns, indicating whether the constraint is for a composite primary key.
virtual Constraint* Add(String* *constraintName*, **DataColumn*** *pkColumn*, **DataColumn*** *fkColumn*)	Constructs and adds to the collection a new **ForeignKeyConstraint** with the specified name, for the specified primary key/foreign key columns.
virtual Constraint* Add(String* *constraintName*, **DataColumn*** *pkColumns[]*, **DataColumn*** *fkColumns[]*)	Constructs and adds to the collection a new composite **ForeignKeyConstraint** with the specified name, for the specified array of primary key/foreign key columns.
void AddRange(Constraint* *constraints[]*)	Copies the elements of the specified array of constraints to the end of the **ConstraintCollection**.
bool CanRemove(Constraint* *constraint*)	Returns **true** if the specified constraint can be removed from the collection.
void Clear()	Removes all constraints from the collection.
bool Contains(String* *name*)	Returns **true** if the specified constraint is found in the collection.
int IndexOf(Constraint* *constraint*)	
int IndexOf(String* *name*)	Returns the index of the specified constraint in the collection.
protected: virtual void OnCollectionChanged(CollectionChangeEventArgs* *e*)	Raises the **CollectionChanged** event.
void Remove(Constraint* *constraint*)	
void Remove(String* *name*)	Removes the specified constraint from the collection.

Table 8.44 **ConstraintCollection** class events.

Method	Description
CollectionChangeEventHandler* CollectionChanged	The event is fired whenever a constraint is added or removed from the collection.

The **ConstraintCollection** class has the **Item** indexer property that allows you to retrieve constraints from the collection by name or by index. You would typically create new constraints and add them to the **ConstraintCollection** by using the **ConstraintCollection::Add** method. There are many different overloads of the **Add** method for creating/adding unique and foreign key constraints to the collection. The **Add** method overloads are similar to the **ForeignKeyConstraint** and **UniqueConstraint** class constructors.

Views

Although the **DataTable** class represents rows of data and provides a means for accessing the data, it does not provide means for viewing the data or for building a subset of data based on some criteria. Database developers frequently use database view to specify the desired representation of a database table data, including applying filter and sort criteria. ADO.NET provides similar functionality by means of the **DataView** class. The **DataView** class allows filtering and sorting data stored in a **DataTable** and has the following inheritance structure:

```
System::Object
|- System::ComponentModel::MarshalByValueComponent
   |- System::Data::DataView


Attributes: None
Abstract: No
Sealed: No
Implements Interfaces: IBindingList, IList, ICollection, IEnumerable, ITypedList, ISupportInitialize
```

The **DataView** class constructors, properties, methods, and events are summarized in Tables 8.45 through 8.48.

Table 8.45 **DataView** class constructors.

Constructor	Description
DataView()	Default constructor.
DataSet(DataTable* *table***)**	
DataView(DataTable* *table***, String*** *rowFilter***, String*** *sort***, DataViewRowState** *rowState***)**	Constructs a **DataView** object for the specified *table*. Optional *rowFilter*, *sort* and *rowState* arguments allow specifying row filter and sort expressions, and which **DataTable** rows to include in the view.

Table 8.46 **DataView** class properties.

Get/Set	Type	Property	Description
Get/Set	**bool**	**AllowDelete**	Gets or sets a Boolean value indicating whether data rows can be deleted from the **DataView**.
Get/Set	**bool**	**AllowEdit**	Gets or sets a Boolean value indicating whether existing data rows can be modified in the **DataView**.
Get/Set	**bool**	**AllowNew**	Gets or sets a Boolean value indicating whether data rows can be added to the **DataView**.

<Continued on Next Page>

<Table 8.46 Continued>

Get/Set	Type	Property	Description
Get/Set	**bool**	**ApplyDefaultSort**	Gets or sets a Boolean value indicating whether to sort the **DataView** by the primary key.
Get	**int**	**Count**	Contains the number of rows in the **DataView** after the **RowFilter** and **RowStateFilter** have been applied.
Get	**DataViewManager***	**DataViewManager**	Contains the **DataViewManager** associated with the **DataView**.
Get	**bool**	**IsOpen**	Contains **true** if the data source is currently open by means of the **Open** method.
Get	**DataRowView***	**Item(int** *index***)**	Returns a row of data at the specified index from the **DataView**.
Get/Set	**String***	**RowFilter**	Gets or sets the expression for filtering rows in the **DataView**.
Get/Set	**DataViewRowState**	**RowStateFilter**	Gets or sets the row state filter for filtering rows in the **DataView**.
Get/Set	**String***	**Sort**	Gets or sets the expression for sorting rows in the **DataView**.
Get/Set	**DataTable***	**Table**	Gets or sets a **DataTable** to which the **DataView** applies.

Table 8.47 DataView class methods.

Method	Description
virtual DataRowView* AddNew()	Adds a new row to the **DataView**.
protected: void Close()	Closes the **DataView**.
protected: virtual void ColumnCollectionChanged(Object* *sender*, **CollectionChangeEventArgs*** *e***)**	Invoked after a **DataColumnCollection** has been changed.
void Delete(Int *index***)**	Deletes a row at the specified index from the **DataView**.
protected: void Dispose(bool *disposing***)**	Disposes the **DataView** object.
int Find(Object* *key***)**	Finds a row in the **DataView** using the specified sort key value and returns the row index or —1 if no rows were found.
int Find(Object* *key* **__gc[])**	Finds a row in the **DataView** using the specified array of sort keys and returns the row index or —1 if no rows were found. This method should be used if more than one data column was used in the **Sort** expression.
DataRowView* FindRows(Object* *key***) []**	Returns an array of **DataRowView** objects matching the specified sort key value.
DataRowView* FindRows(Object* *key* **__gc[]) []**	Returns an array of **DataRowView** objects matching the specified sort key values. This method should be used if more than one data column was used in the **Sort** expression.

NOTE: *Unlike the* **Find** *method of the* **DataRow** *class, which searches data rows by the primary key, the* **Find**/**FindRows** *methods of the* **DataView** *class search by the sort key. If no sort key is specified, then the* **DataView** *rows are searched by the primary key.*

<Continued on Next Page>

<Table 8.47 Continued>

Method	Description
protected: virtual void IndexListChanged(Object* sender, ListChangedEventArgs* e)	Invoked after a **DataView** has been changed successfully.
protected: virtual void OnListChanged(ListChangedEventArgs* e)	Fires the **ListChanged** event.
protected: void Open()	Opens the **DataView**.

Table 8.48 **DataView** class events.

Event	Description
__sealed ListChangedEventHandler* ListChanged	Fired when the list managed by the **DataView** changes.

NOTE: Unlike SQL data views, ADO.NET data views always contain the same set of columns as the underlying DataTable.

A **DataView** object is characterized by the following three important properties:

* **RowFilter**: An expression for filtering rows in the **DataTable** (e.g., sName LIKE 'Veronica *').

* **Sort**: An expression for sorting rows in the **DataTable**. The **Sort** expression can contain one or more comma-separated column names optionally followed by ASC for ascending sort order, or DESC for descending sort order. If none is specified, the ascending sort order is assumed (e.g., a sort expression "sName, iAge DESC" will sort data rows by name in ascending and by age in descending order). If no sort expression is specified, table rows are sorted by the primary key values.

* **RowStateFilter**: A state of **DataTable** rows that the **DataView** object will operate on.

As far as the **DataView** class is concerned, a **DataTable** rows can be in one of the following states defined in the **DataViewRowState** enumeration:

* **Added**: A new row is added to the **DataTable** (e.g., by invoking **Rows->Add** on a **DataTable** object).

* **CurrentRows:** Unmodifies original, new, and modified rows.

* **Deleted**: Delete rows by means of the **Delete** method. (The **Remove** method does not mark rows as deleted but merely removes them from the collection of rows.)

* **ModifiedCurrent**: Modifies rows from the **Current** version of the **DataTable** rows.

* **ModifiedOriginal**: Modifies rows from the **Original** version of the **DataTable**, corresponding to the modified rows in the **Current** version. (See also the "Data Row Versions" section in this chapter.)

* **None**: No rows.

* **OriginalRows**: Restores rows from the **Original** version of the **DataTable**, including modified and deleted rows.

* **Unchanged**: Unmodifies current rows.

Thus, the **DataView** class allows you to select specific kinds of rows from a particular version of the **DataTable** data. To obtain a customized view of the **DataTable** data, you can create a new **DataView** object by means of the **new** operator and supply the desired **RowFilter** and **Sort** expressions. You can also supply the

DataViewRowState state as a parameter to the **DataView** constructor. Alternatively, you can use the **DefaultView** property of a **DataTable** object and set the **RowFilter, Sort**, and **RowStateFilter** properties to any desired values.

The **DataView** class is similar to the **DataTable** class in the sense that you can modify and navigate **DataView** rows as you would a **DataTable** rows. For instance, you can add a new row to a **DataView** by invoking the **AddNew** method. On the other hand, the **DataView** class allows you to specify the allowable range of actions on data view rows by setting **AllowDelete**, **AllowEdit**, and **AllowNew** properties. In the extreme case, you can completely lock down a **DataView** by setting all these properties to **false**.

DataRowView Class

The **DataView** class provides the **Item** indexer property that allows you to retrieve individual data rows from the **DataView**. The total number of data rows in a **DataView** is stored in the **DataView::Count** property. The **DataView** rows are somewhat different from the **DataTable** rows, hence they are represented by a different class—**DataRowView**:

```
System::Object
|- System::Data::DataRowView
```

Attributes: none

Abstract: No

Sealed: No
Implements Interfaces: **ICustomTypeDescriptor, IEditableObject, IDataErrorInfo**

The **DataRowView** class properties and methods are listed in Tables 8.49 through 8.50.

Table 8.49 **DataRowView** class properties.

Get/Set	Type	Property	Description
Get	**DataView***	**DataView**	Contains a pointer to the **DataView** to which the **DataRowView** belongs.
Get	**bool**	**IsEdit**	Contains **true** if the **DataRowView** is in edit mode.
Get	**bool**	**IsNew**	Contains **true** if the **DataRowView** corresponds to a newly created row.
Get/Set	**Object***	**Item(int** *index***)**	Gets or sets a **DataRowView** column value at the specified index.
Get/Set	**Object***	**Item(String*** *columnName***)**	Gets or sets the value of a **DataRowView** column with the specified name.
Get	**DataRow***	**Row**	Contains a pointer to the **DataRow** associated with the **DataRowView**.
Get	**DataRowVersion**	**RowVersion**	Contains the version description for the associated **DataRow**.

Table 8.50 **DataRowView** class methods.

Method	Description
__sealed void BeginEdit()	Begins row editing.
__sealed void CancelEdit()	Cancels row editing without saving changes.
DataView* CreateChildView(DataRelation* *relation*)	
DataView* CreateChildView(String* *relationName*)	Creates and returns a **DataView** for the child table, which is a part of the specified data relation.
void Delete()	Deletes a data row.
__sealed void EndEdit()	Ends row editing and saves the changes.

As with the **DataRow** class, the **DataRowView** class allows you to access row column values by name or by index using the **Item** indexer property. You can also use a **DataRowView** object to obtain a pointer to the corresponding **DataRow** object by means of the **Row** property.

> **NOTE:** If a **DataView** does not allow you to delete rows (i.e., the **AllowDelete** property is set to **false**), an attempt to delete a **DataRowView** by means of invoking the **Delete** method on the **DataRowView** will throw an exception. However, if you obtain a pointer to the underlying **DataRow** by accessing the **Row** property of the **DataRowView** object, the attempt to delete a row by invoking the **Delete** method on the **DataRow** directly will succeed provided that it does not violate any constraints.

Default Data View Settings

Each **DataTable** has a default **DataView** exposed as the **DefaultView** property. The **DefaultView** property provides means for centralized management of filtering and sorting data tables in a **DataSet**. To modify the default **DataView** settings of a data table in a **DataSet**, you should use the **DataSet::DefaultViewManager** property to specify a new **RowFilter**, **Sort**, or **RowStateFilter** properties to be used by the **DefaultView** of the **DataTable**. The **DefaultViewManager** represents an object that stores **DataView** settings for each **DataTable** in a **DataSet**, and the ADO.NET provides a special class for this purpose—**DataViewManager**:

```
System::Object
|- System::ComponentModel::MarshalByValueComponent
   |- System::Data::DataViewManager

Attributes: none
Abstract: No
Sealed: No
Implements Interfaces: IBindingList, IList, ICollection, IEnumerable, ITypedList
```

The **DataViewManager** class provides a **CreateDataView** helper function for generating **DataView** objects for a specified **DataTable** besides storing default **DataView** settings. The **DataViewManager** class constructors, properties, methods, and events are summarized in Tables 8.51 through 8.54.

Table 8.51 **DataViewManager** class constructors.

Constructor	Description
DataViewManager()	Default constructor.
DataViewManager(DataSet* *dataSet*)	Constructs a **DataViewManager** for the specified **DataSet**.

Table 8.52 **DataViewManager** class properties.

Get/Set	Type	Property	Description
Get/Set	**DataSet***	**DataSet**	Gets or sets a pointer to the **DataViewManager** dataset.
Get	**DataViewSettingCollection***	**DataViewSettings**	Contains a pointer to the collection of the **DataView** settings used by the **DataViewManager**.

Table 8.53 **DataViewManager** class methods.

Method	Description
DataView* CreateDataView(DataTable* *table*)	Creates a new **DataView** for the specified **DataTable**.
protected: virtual void OnListChanged(ListChangedEventArgs* *e*)	Fires the **ListChanged** method.
protected: virtual void RelationCollectionChanged(Object* *sender*, CollectionChangeEventArgs* *e*)	Invoked when a **DataRelation** is added or removed from the **DataRelationCollection**.
protected: virtual void TableCollectionChanged(Object* *sender*, CollectionChangeEventArgs* *e*)	Invoked when a **DataTable** is added to or removed from the **DataTableCollection**.

Table 8.53 **DataViewManager** class events.

Event	Description
__sealed ListChangedEventHandler* ListChanged	Fired when a data row is added or deleted from the **DataView** managed by the **DataViewManager**.

DataViewSetting Class

The **DataViewManager** class requires yet another class to store default **DataView** settings—**DataViewSetting**:

```
System::Object
|- System::Data::DataViewSetting
```

Attributes: **Serializable**
Abstract: No
Sealed: No
Implements Interfaces: None

The **DataViewSetting** class serves a single purpose of providing storage for **DataView** properties. For that matter the **DataViewSetting** class has no constructors, methods, or events, but has only a set of properties corresponding to the **DataView** class properties (see Table 8.55).

Table 8.55 **DataViewSetting** class properties.

Get/Set	Type	Property	Description
Get/Set	**bool**	**ApplyDefaultSort**	Gets or sets a Boolean value indicating whether to sort the **DataView** by the primary key.
Get	**DataViewManager***	**DataViewManager**	Contains a pointer to the **DataViewManager** of the **DataView**.
Get/Set	**String***	**RowFilter**	Gets or sets the filter expression for filtering the **DataView** rows.
Get/Set	**DataViewRowState**	**RowStateFilter**	Gets or sets the **DataViewRowState** filter for limiting the view to contain only rows with the specified state.
Get/Set	**String***	**Sort**	Gets or sets the sort expression for sorting the **DataView** rows.
Get	**DataTable***	**Table**	Contains a pointer to the **DataTable** to which the **DataView** applies.

Data View Setting Collection

The **DataViewManager** provides access to individual **DataViewSetting** objects in the **DataViewSetting** property, implemented by means of the **DataViewSettingCollection** class as shown here:

```
System::Object
|- System::Data::DataViewSettingCollection


Attributes: Serializable
Abstract: No
Sealed: No
Implements Interfaces: ICollection, IEnumerable
```

The **DataViewSettingCollection** class has no constructors or original methods. The **DataViewSettingCollection** class properties are listed in Table 8.56.

Table 8.56 **DataViewSettingCollection** class properties.

Get/Set	Type	Property	Virtual	Description
Get	**bool**	**IsReadOnly**	No	Contains **true** if the collection is read-only.
Get/Set	**DataViewSetting***	**Item(DataTable* *table*)**	Yes	Gets or sets a **DataViewSetting** for the specified **DataTable**.
Get	**DataViewSetting***	**Item(String* *tableName*)**	Yes	Returns a **DataViewSetting** for the **DataTable** with the specified name.
Get/Set	**DataViewSetting***	**Item(int *index*)**	Yes	Gets or sets a **DataViewSetting** at the specified index.

As with any other ADO.NET collection class, the **DataViewSettingCollection** class provides the **Item** indexer property for accessing **DataViewSetting** objects by **DataTable** name or by index. To modify the default **DataView** properties of a **DataTable** in a **DataSet**, simply obtain a **DataViewSetting** pointer for the **DataTable** and set the desired **DefaultView** properties. Modifying the default **DataView** properties by means of the **DataViewManager** class does not offer any particular advantages unless you are working with Windows Forms and want to display the contents of the **DataSet** tables in a **DataGrid** control. The **DataGrid** control requires a pointer to a **DataViewManager** class to display multiple data tables.

Immediate Solutions

Creating Tables, Adding Columns, and Specifying Primary Keys

You should use the ADO.NET **DataTable** class if you need to represent a table of in-memory data. You can create a new instance of the **DataTable** class using the **DataTable** constructor. To specify the **DataTable** schema you add columns using the **Columns** collection **Add** method. The following code example demonstrates how to:

1. Create a **DataTable** object using the **DataTable** constructor.

2. Add columns to the **DataTable** using the **Columns** collection **Add** method.

3. Create a column using the **DataColumn** constructor.

4. Set the default column value using the **DefaultValue** column property.

5. Create a composite primary key using the **DataTable::PrimaryKey** property.

```
#using <mscorlib.dll>
#using <system.dll>
#using <system.data.dll>
using namespace System;
using namespace System::Data;


void main()
{
   // 1. Create "Player" table
   DataTable* PlayerTable = new DataTable("Player");


   // 2. Add/create a column using Columns collection
   DataColumn* FirstNameColumn = PlayerTable->Columns->Add("First Name",
      __typeof(String));
   // 3. Create a column using the constructor
   DataColumn* LastNameColumn = new DataColumn("Last Name", __typeof(String));
   PlayerTable->Columns->Add(LastNameColumn);
   PlayerTable->Columns->Add("Email", __typeof(String));
   PlayerTable->Columns->Add("LoggedOn", __typeof(DateTime));
   DataColumn* ActiveColumn = PlayerTable->Columns->Add("Active",
      __typeof(bool));


   // 4. Set default column value
   ActiveColumn->DefaultValue = __box(true);
```

```
// 5. Create composite primary key
DataColumn* PrimaryKey[] = {FirstNameColumn, LastNameColumn};
PlayerTable->PrimaryKey = PrimaryKey;
}
```

> **NOTE:** You must import system.dll and system.data.dll assemblies in order to work with **DataTable** objects, or your code will not compile.

In this example the columns "First Name" and "Last Name" form a composite primary key. Thus, you can not have two rows in the "Player" table with the same First Name/Last Name combination.

Using Expressions in Data Columns

You can use the **Expression** property of the **DataColumn** class to define *calculated columns* as shown here:

```
MyDataSet->Tables("Sales")->Columns("OrderCost")->Expression =
    "Price*Quantity";
```

Alternatively, you can use the **Expression** property to define *aggregate columns*:

```
MyDataSet->Tables("Sales")->Columns("TotalCost")->Expression =
    "SUM(Price*Quantity)";
```

In both cases you must supply a correct expression for calculating the column value. The following rules apply to specifying **DataColumn** expressions:

1. Columns must be referred to by the **ColumnName**.
2. Text strings must be enclosed in single quotes (e.g., User = 'Vlad').
3. Special characters in column names, such as ',', \,[], and so on must be "escaped" when used in the **Expression**. Thus, if you have a column named HiScore[1] you should escape it like [HiScore\[1\]].
4. Date values must be enclosed by '#'characters, (e.g., dtPurchaseDate = #1/12/01#).
5. The following SQL operators are recognized: <, >, <=, >=, <> =, IN, LIKE, + (arithmetic and for string concatenation), -, *, % (modulus), AND, OR, NOT.
6. The '*' and '%'characters identify any number of character combinations and any single character respectively, in the LIKE expression(e.g., sName LIKE '%ax Fomit*' matches 'Max Fomitchev', but you cannot put the '*' character in the middle of text).
7. You can reference columns in a child table by preceding the child column name with a 'Child.' string (e.g., "Child.Score"). If you have more than one child table you should use the following syntax for referencing child columns: Child(*RelationName*).*ColumnName*.
8. The following aggregate functions are permitted: **Sum, Avg, Min, Max, Count, StdDev** (statistical standard deviation), and **Var** (statistical variance).

9. The following miscellaneous functions are permitted:

* **Len(*expr*)**: Calculates the length in characters of the specified string.

* **IsNull(*expr*, *newExpr*)**: rReplaces the specified expression with the new expression if the expression evaluates to NULL.

* **IIF(*expr*, *trueExpr*, *falseExpr*)**: Replaces the expression with the *trueExpr* if the expression evaluates to TRUE, or *falseExpre* if the expression evaluates to FALSE.

* **Substring(*expr*, *start*, *length*)**: Returns a substring of the *length* characters starting at the index *start* from the specified textual expression.

NOTE: The functions and operators used in the expressions are evaluated by the .NET Framework, not by the database.

Adding/Navigating Rows and Computing Aggergate Expressions

Once you create a **DataTable** you would probably want to add data to it. Here are the steps to follow to add data to a **DataTable**:

1. Invoke the the **DataTable::NewRow** method to create a new **DataRow** object with the same schema as the table.

2. Set the column values of the new row using the **Item** indexer of the **DataRow**. You can access columns by name or by index (ordinal).

3. Add the new row to the **DataTable** using the **Add** method of the **DataTable::Rows** collection.

To navigate data rows in a **DataTable** simply iterate through the **DataTable::Rows** collection and access individual rows by index using the **Rows** collection **Item** indexer. You can also compute an aggregate expression such as COUNT, SUM, or AVG on a **DataTable** by invoking the **Compute** method. The process of adding rows to a **DataTable** and iterating through the **DataTable** rows is illustrated in the following example:

```
#using <mscorlib.dll>
#using <system.dll>
#using <system.data.dll>
using namespace System;
using namespace System::Data;

void main()
{
   // Create "Player" table
   DataTable* PlayerTable = new DataTable("Player");
   // Add/create a column using Columns collection
   DataColumn* FirstNameColumn = PlayerTable->Columns->Add("First Name",
      __typeof(String));
   DataColumn* LastNameColumn = PlayerTable->Columns->Add("Last Name",
      __typeof(String));
   PlayerTable->Columns->Add("Email", __typeof(String));
   PlayerTable->Columns->Add("LoggedOn", __typeof(DateTime));
   DataColumn* ActiveColumn = PlayerTable->Columns->Add("Active",
```

```
    __typeof(bool));
// Set default column value
ActiveColumn->DefaultValue = __box(true);
// Create composite primary key
DataColumn* PrimaryKey[] = {FirstNameColumn, LastNameColumn};
PlayerTable->PrimaryKey = PrimaryKey;

// 1. Create new row
DataRow* NewRow = PlayerTable->NewRow();

// 2. Set row data
NewRow->Item["First Name"] = S"Max";
NewRow->Item["Last Name"] = S"Fomitchev";
NewRow->Item["Email"] = S"fomitchev@home.com";
NewRow->Item["LoggedOn"] = __box(DateTime::Now);

// 3. Add data row to the DataTable
PlayerTable->Rows->Add(NewRow);

NewRow = PlayerTable->NewRow();
NewRow->Item["First Name"] = S"Veronica";
NewRow->Item["Last Name"] = S"Grigorashvily";
NewRow->Item["Email"] = S"nika@VeronicasArt.com";
NewRow->Item["LoggedOn"] = __box(DateTime::Now);
PlayerTable->Rows->Add(NewRow);

NewRow = PlayerTable->NewRow();
NewRow->Item["First Name"] = S"Vlad";
NewRow->Item["Last Name"] = S"Fomitchev";
NewRow->Item["Email"] = S"n/a";
NewRow->Item["LoggedOn"] = __box(DateTime::Now);
PlayerTable->Rows->Add(NewRow);

// 4. Navigate DataTable rows
for ( int i = 0; i < PlayerTable->Rows->Count; i++ )
{
    // 5. Check the default column value, Unbox the value type
    bool __gc* active = static_cast<__box bool*>(PlayerTable->Rows->
        Item[i]->Item[4]);
    Console::WriteLine("Player {0}: {1} {2}, {3}", __box(i),
        PlayerTable->Rows->Item[i]->Item[0],
        PlayerTable->Rows->Item[i]->Item[1],
        *active ? S"Active" : S"Inactive");
}

// 6. Computing an expression
```

```
Object* count = PlayerTable->Compute("COUNT([Last Name])",
    "[Last Name]='Fomitchev'");
Console::WriteLine("There are {0} players with Last Name 'Fomitchev'",
    count);
}
```

> **NOTE:** When evaluating the COUNT expression on a **DataTable** you must supply a column name as a parameter to the COUNT function. COUNT(*) expression is not permitted.

This code example checks the value of the "Active" table column, which is of type **bool**. The "Active" column has the default value of **true**. Since data columns of a **DataTable** can store only values of type **Object***, the value of the "Active" column has to be unboxed to be converted back to the **bool** value type.

Adding/Deleting Rows and Handling **DataTable** Notifications

If you have a **DataTable** that already contains data you can modify or delete existing rows or add new rows to the **DataTable**. Also, you can hook up custom event handlers to the **DataTable** events to perform custom column and row data validation and reject changes made to the **DataTable** if the validation fails. You can also restrict deleting of rows from the **DataTable**. Consider the code example presented in Listing 8.1. The sample program creates and populates the "Player" table, and hooks up **RowChanging/RowChanged** and **RowDeleting/RowDeleted** event handlers (step 1). The **RowChanging** event is associated with the **RowChanging** method of the **EventClass**, which performs custom data validation. Namely, the **RowChanging** method examines the value of the "First Name" column of the modified **DataRow** and rejects changes if the column value contains blanks. This operation is accomplished by calling the **RejectChanges** method and throwing an exception. The **RowChanging** method validates the data only when the changes are committed—the **Action** property of the **DataRowChangeEventArgs** event handler parameter is set to **DataRowAction::Commit**.

The steps completed by the program displayed in Listing 8.1 are as follows:

1. Hook up **RowChanging/RowChanged** and **RowDeleting/RowDeleted** event handlers to the **PlayerTable**.

2. Locate a row corresponding to the primary key (i.e., First Name/Last Name combination) of "Vlad"/"Fomitchev" using the **Rows** collection **Find** method.

3. Modify the **DataRow** by setting the "First Name" and "LoggedOn" column values by means of the **Item** accessor property and accept the changes by invoking the **AcceptChanges** method. The **RowChanging/RowChanged** events are fired separately for each modified column as soon as a new value is assigned to a column.

4. Modify the **DataRow** and group changes by using the **BeginEdit/EndEdit** methods.

5. Modify the **DataRow** by setting the "First Name" column to "Maxim Igorevitch" to test the validation. As soon as the **AcceptChanges** is called, the **EventClass::RowChanging** method detects validation errors, rejects changes by calling the **RejectChanges** method, and throws an exception. (If you throw an exception but do not invoke the **RejectChanges** method, the changes to the row will persist.)

6. Modify the **DataRow** again and display the **Original** and **Proposed** versions of the **DataRow** and roll back the changes by calling the **CancelEdit** method.

7. Delete the first row in the **DataTable** by invoking the **Delete** method.

Listing 8.1 Sample program illustrating updating, deleting rows in a **DataTable,** and handling **DataTable** notification events to perform custom data validation.

```cpp
#using <mscorlib.dll>
#using <system.dll>
#using <system.data.dll>
using namespace System;
using namespace System::Data;

// DataTable Event Handler class
__gc struct EventClass {
    static void RowChanging(Object* sender,
        DataRowChangeEventArgs* e)
    {
        Console::WriteLine("Row is being changed: {0}", GetAction(e->Action));
        // Validate changes: MUST be in DataRowChanging
        if ( e->Action == DataRowAction::Commit )
        {
            // Get current values of the First Name/Last Name columns
            String* FirstName = dynamic_cast<String*>(e->Row->Item["First Name"]);
            String* LastName = dynamic_cast<String*>(e->Row->Item["Last Name"]);
            // Disallow blanks in First Name/Last Name
            if ( FirstName->IndexOf(' ') > -1 ||
                LastName->IndexOf(' ') > -1 )
            {
                // Rollback changes
                e->Row->RejectChanges();
                // Throw an exception
                throw new Exception(
                    "Blanks are not allowed in First Name/Last Name.");
            }
        }
    }
    static void RowChanged(Object* sender,
        DataRowChangeEventArgs* e)
    {
        Console::WriteLine("Row has changed: {0}", GetAction(e->Action));
    }
    static void RowDeleting(Object* sender,
        DataRowChangeEventArgs* e)
    {
        Console::WriteLine("Row is being deleted");
    }
    static void RowDeleted(Object* sender,
        DataRowChangeEventArgs* e)
```

```
      {
          Console::WriteLine("Row has been deleted");
      }
      // Get tectual descriptions for row actions
      static String* GetAction(DataRowAction Action)
      {
          // Report current action
          switch ( Action ) {
             case DataRowAction::Add:
                 return S"added";
                 break;
             case DataRowAction::Change:
                 return S"change";
                 break;
             case DataRowAction::Commit:
                 return S"committed";
                 break;
             case DataRowAction::Rollback:
                 return S"rolled back";
                 break;
             default:
                 return S"other or none";
          }
      }
};

void main()
{
    // Create DataTable
    DataTable* PlayerTable = new DataTable("Players");
    // Add columns
    DataColumn* colFirstName = PlayerTable->Columns->Add("First Name",
        __typeof(String));
    DataColumn* colLastName = PlayerTable->Columns->Add("Last Name",
        __typeof(String));
    PlayerTable->Columns->Add("LoggedOn", __typeof(DateTime));
    // Create composite primary key
    DataColumn* primaryKey[] = {colFirstName, colLastName};
    PlayerTable->PrimaryKey = primaryKey;

    // Add initial data
    DataRow* NewRow = PlayerTable->NewRow();
    NewRow->Item["First Name"] = S"Max";
    NewRow->Item["Last Name"] = S"Fomitchev";
    NewRow->Item["LoggedOn"] = __box(DateTime::Now);
    PlayerTable->Rows->Add(NewRow);
```

```
NewRow = PlayerTable->NewRow();
NewRow->Item["First Name"] = S"Veronica";
NewRow->Item["Last Name"] = S"Grigorashvily";
NewRow->Item["LoggedOn"] = __box(DateTime::Now);
PlayerTable->Rows->Add(NewRow);

NewRow = PlayerTable->NewRow();
NewRow->Item["First Name"] = S"Vlad";
NewRow->Item["Last Name"] = S"Fomitchev";
NewRow->Item["LoggedOn"] = __box(DateTime::Now);
PlayerTable->Rows->Add(NewRow);

// 1. Hookup row event notifications
PlayerTable->RowChanging += new DataRowChangeEventHandler(0,
    EventClass::RowChanging);
PlayerTable->RowChanged += new DataRowChangeEventHandler(0,
    EventClass::RowChanged);
PlayerTable->RowDeleting += new DataRowChangeEventHandler(0,
    EventClass::RowDeleting);
PlayerTable->RowDeleted += new DataRowChangeEventHandler(0,
    EventClass::RowDeleted);

// 2. Find a row by the primary key
String* pkValues[] = {"Vlad", "Fomitchev"};
DataRow* myRow = PlayerTable->Rows->Find(pkValues);

Console::WriteLine("\n-Make Changes-----");
// 3. Modify existing data
myRow->Item["First Name"] = S"Vladislav";
NewRow->Item["LoggedOn"] = __box(DateTime::Today);
myRow->AcceptChanges();

Console::WriteLine("\n-Bunch changes-----");
// 4. Bunch changes
myRow->BeginEdit();
myRow->Item["First Name"] = S"Vladislav";
NewRow->Item["LoggedOn"] = __box(DateTime::Today);
myRow->EndEdit();
myRow->AcceptChanges();

Console::WriteLine("\n-Cancel changes-----");
// 5. Reject changes due to validation
try {
    myRow->Item["First Name"] = S"Vladislav Maximovitch";
    myRow->AcceptChanges();
```

```
    }
    catch(Exception* e) {
        Console::WriteLine("ERROR: {0}", e->Message);
    }

    Console::WriteLine("\n-Versions————");
    // Begin editing...
    myRow->BeginEdit();
    myRow->Item["First Name"] = S"Horsik";
    // 6. Get the original & proposed version of the column
    if ( myRow->HasVersion(DataRowVersion::Original) )
        Console::WriteLine("Original First 4Name: {0}",
            myRow->get_Item(0, DataRowVersion::Original));
    if ( myRow->HasVersion(DataRowVersion::Proposed) )
        Console::WriteLine("Proposed First Name: {0}",
            myRow->get_Item(0, DataRowVersion::Proposed));
    // Cancel editing...
    myRow->CancelEdit();

    Console::WriteLine("\n-Delete row————-");
    // 7. Delete a row
    PlayerTable->Rows->Item[0]->Delete();

    Console::WriteLine("\n-Table contents————");
    // Show the DataTable contents
    for ( int i = 0; i < PlayerTable->Rows->Count; i++ )
        Console::WriteLine("Player {0}: {1} {2}", __box(i),
            PlayerTable->Rows->Item[i]->Item[0],
            PlayerTable->Rows->Item[i]->Item[1]);
}
```

Creating Datasets, Adding Tables, and Establishing Relations

If you want to represent a hierarchial set of data you should use the ADO.NET **DataSet** class. The **DataSet** class allows you to create data objects that contain multiple **DataTable** objects organized by means of data relations. Follow these steps to create a **DataSet** object corresponding to a hierarchal data structure:

1.   Create a **DataSet** object using the **DataSet** constructor.

2.   Add tables to the **DataSet** using the **Add** method of the **DataSet::Tables** property.

3.   Add columns to **DataTable** objects.

4.   Establish relations between data tables by adding **DataRelation** objects, specifying related columns in parent and child tables, to the the **Relations** property of the **DataSet**.

> **NOTE:** To use the **DataSet** class you must insert the **#using <system.xml.data.dll>** statement in your code to import the XML stream classes referenced by the **DataSet** class.

The code example shown next creates a **DataSet** object and adds two tables to it: A parent table called "Player" and a child table called "Score." The tables are linked by means of the one-to-many relation:

```cpp
#using <mscorlib.dll>
#using <system.dll>
#using <system.data.dll>
#using <System.Xml.dll>
using namespace System;
using namespace System::Data;

void main()
{
    // 1. Create DataSet
    DataSet* MyDataSet = new DataSet("Game Data");

    // 2. Add tables to the DataSet
    MyDataSet->Tables->Add("Player");
    MyDataSet->Tables->Add("Score");

    // 3. Add columns to the 1st table
    DataTable* PlayerTable = MyDataSet->Tables->Item["Player"];
    DataColumn* FirstNameColumn1 = PlayerTable->Columns->Add("First Name",
        __typeof(String));
    DataColumn* LastNameColumn1 = PlayerTable->Columns->Add("Last Name",
        __typeof(String));
    PlayerTable->Columns->Add("Email", __typeof(String));
    // Create composite primary key
    DataColumn* PrimaryKey[] = {FirstNameColumn1, LastNameColumn1};
    PlayerTable->PrimaryKey = PrimaryKey;

    // 3. Add columns to the 2nd table
    DataTable* ScoreTable = MyDataSet->Tables->Item["Score"];
    DataColumn* FirstNameColumn2 = ScoreTable->Columns->Add("First Name",
        __typeof(String));
    DataColumn* LastNameColumn2 = ScoreTable->Columns->Add("Last Name",
        __typeof(String));
    ScoreTable->Columns->Add("Points", __typeof(int));

    // 4. Establish a one-to-many relation between "Player" and "Score"
    DataColumn* ForeignKey[] = {FirstNameColumn2, LastNameColumn2};
    MyDataSet->Relations->Add("Player-Score", PrimaryKey, ForeignKey);

    // Convert the relation to one-to-one by applying a unique constraint
    //MyDataSet->Tables->Item["Score"]->Constraints->Add("Unique",
        ForeignKey, true);
}
```

NOTE: To convert the one-to-many relation between Player and Score tables into a one-to-one relation, make the First Name / Last Name columns in the Score table a primary key, or apply a unique constraint on the columns. (See the last line in the code example, which is commented out.)

Navigating Hierarchal Datasets

If you have a **DataSet** object representing a hierarchial data structure, you can navigate its entire hierarchy by iterating through data rows and child relations. To navigate the rows of a top-level **DataSet** table, including the rows of child tables, you should use the **ChildRows** and **ChildRelations** properties of the **DataTable** class. To better understand a **DataSet** navigation examine the sample program shown in Listing 8.2. The program creates a simple hierarchal **DataSet** containing two tables, "Player" and "Score," and establishes a one-to-many relation between the tables. The program implements **DataSet** navigation by traversing individual rows using the **TraverseRow** function. The **TraverseRow** function traverses a row of a **DataTable** and descends the hierarchy to traverse child rows of the current row.

The **TraverseRow** function forforms the following actions:

*   Indents the output by keeping track of the current hierarchy level.

*   Prints the table name (**Table->TableName** property) and row number information, which is supplied as a function parameter.

*   For each column in the row (**Table->Columns** collection):

    *   Obtains the column name using the **Table->Columns->   Item[i]->ColumnName** property.

    *   Verifies if the current table is a part of a child relation and if it is, the function examines the foreign key of the child relation to determine if the current column is a part of it.

    *   If the current column is not a part of the foreign key of the child relation, the column value is printed in the format *ColumnName=value*. (The test on the foreign key is performed for the sake of obtaining a cleaner XML-like output not cluttered with repetitive foreign key values.)

*   For each child relation of the current table (**Table->ChildRelations** collection):

    *   Obtain the array of child rows of the current row using the **GetChildRows** method.

    *   For each child row of the current row, recursively call the **TraverseRow** function by supplying a pointer to the child row to traverse, as well as the pointer to the current child relation, row number, and next level number.

Listing 8.2 Sample program demonstrating the traversal of a hierarchal **DataSet**.

```cpp
#using <mscorlib.dll>
#using <system.dll>
#using <system.data.dll>
#using <System.Xml.dll>
using namespace System;
using namespace System::Data;

// Function for traversing DataRows
void TraverseRow(DataRow* Row, DataRelation* ChildRelation,
```

```
    int RowNumber, int Level)
{
    // Indent for nested output
    String* Indent = new String(' ', Level);

    // Output table name and row #
    Console::Write("{0}{1} {2}: ", Indent, Row->Table->TableName, __box(RowNumber + 1));

    bool FirstColumn = true;
    // For each column of the row output column name=column value pairs
    for ( int i = 0; i < Row->Table->Columns->Count; i++ )
    {
        // Get column name
        String* ColumnName = Row->Table->Columns->Item[i]->ColumnName;

        int j = 0, Count = 0;
        // Exclude columns that are part of the relation
        if ( ChildRelation != 0 )
        {
            Count = ChildRelation->ChildColumns->Count;
            for ( j = 0; j < Count; j++ )
                if ( ChildRelation->ChildColumns[j]->ColumnName == ColumnName )
                    break;
        }
        if ( j >= Count )
        {
            // Output column separator
            if ( !FirstColumn )
                Console::Write("\t");
            else
                FirstColumn = false;
            Console::Write("{0}={1}", ColumnName, Row->Item[i]);
        }
    }
    Console::WriteLine();

    // For each child relation of the table
    for ( i = 0; i < Row->Table->ChildRelations->Count; i++ )
    {
        // Get child relation name
        DataRelation* ChildRelation = Row->Table->ChildRelations->Item[i];

        // Get rows of the child relation
        DataRow* ChildRow[] = Row->GetChildRows(ChildRelation);
        for ( int j = 0; j < ChildRow->Count; j++ )
            TraverseRow(ChildRow[j], ChildRelation, j, Level + 1);
```

```
       }
}

void main()
{
    // 1. Create DataSet
    DataSet* MyDataSet = new DataSet("Game Data");
    MyDataSet->ReadXml("myDatSet nested with schema.xml");

    // 2. Get the first table in the DataSet assuming that it is at the row
    // of the data hierarchy
    DataTable* RootTable = MyDataSet->Tables->Item[0];

    // 3. Traverse the DataSet assuming that it has a tree structure
    // with a single root
    for ( int i = 0; i < RootTable->Rows->Count; i++ )
        TraverseRow(RootTable->Rows->Item[i], 0, i, 0);
}
```

Creating Unique and Foreign Key Constraints

Constraints are necessary for enforcing data integrity. The ADO.NET supports two kinds of constraints:

*   *Unique*: Applicable for primary keys and foreign keys in one-to-one relationships.

*   *Foreign key*: Ensures that a child record in a parent/child relation is not orphaned and points to a valid (existing) parent row.

If you create a **DataTable** and specify primary key column(s), the unique constraint is automatically created on the table. Similarly, if you create a **DataRelation**, a foreign key constraint is automatically created on the child table. However, you can set the constraints manually, as demonstrated in the code example presented next.

The code example does the following:

1. Creates a unique constraint on the "Player" table to enforce the uniqueness of the the primary key columns.

2. Creates a foreign key constraint on the "Score" table to enforce the integrity of the parent/child **DataRelation**.

3. Tests the unique constraint by attempting to insert a duplicate value into the "First Name"/"Last Name" columns in the "Player" table.

4. Tests the foreign key constraint by attempting to set the "First Name"/"Last Name" columns in the "Score" tables to a value that is not found in the parent "Player" table.

5. Deletes a row from the parent "Player" table to demonstrate a cascade delete from the child table.

6. Invokes the **Select** method on the child "Score" table to make sure that the child row was in fact deleted.

```
#using <mscorlib.dll>
#using <system.dll>
```

```
#using <system.data.dll>
#using <System.Xml.dll>
using namespace System;
using namespace System::Data;

void main()
{
    // Create DataSet
    DataSet* MyDataSet = new DataSet("Game Data");
    // Add tables to the DataSet
    MyDataSet->Tables->Add("Player");
    MyDataSet->Tables->Add("Score");

    // Add columns to 1st table
    DataTable* PlayerTable = MyDataSet->Tables->Item["Player"];
    DataColumn* FirstNameColumn1 = PlayerTable->Columns->Add("First Name",
        __typeof(String));
    DataColumn* LastNameColumn1 = PlayerTable->Columns->Add("Last Name",
        __typeof(String));
    PlayerTable->Columns->Add("Email", __typeof(String));

    DataColumn* PrimaryKey[] = {FirstNameColumn1, LastNameColumn1};
    // 1. Add a unique constraint
    PlayerTable->Constraints->Add("PlayerPK", PrimaryKey, true);
    // (Same as creating the composite primary key)
    //PlayerTable->PrimaryKey = PrimaryKey;

    // Add columns to 2nd table
    DataTable* ScoreTable = MyDataSet->Tables->Item["Score"];
    DataColumn* FirstNameColumn2 = ScoreTable->Columns->Add("First Name",
        __typeof(String));
    DataColumn* LastNameColumn2 = ScoreTable->Columns->Add("Last Name",
        __typeof(String));
    ScoreTable->Columns->Add("Points", __typeof(int));

    DataColumn* ForeignKey[] = {FirstNameColumn2, LastNameColumn2};
    // 2. Add a forign key constraint
    //ScoreTable->Constraints->Add("PlayerFK", PrimaryKey, ForeignKey);
    // (Same as establish a data relation)
    MyDataSet->Relations->Add("Player-Score", PrimaryKey, ForeignKey);

    // 3. Test the unique constraint
    // OK
    DataRow* NewRow = PlayerTable->NewRow();
    NewRow->Item["First Name"] = S"Max";
    NewRow->Item["Last Name"] = S"Fomitchev";
```

```
PlayerTable->Rows->Add(NewRow);
// OK
NewRow = PlayerTable->NewRow();
NewRow->Item["First Name"] = S"Veronica";
NewRow->Item["Last Name"] = S"Grigorashvily";
PlayerTable->Rows->Add(NewRow);
// Violates constraint - will fail
try {
    NewRow = PlayerTable->NewRow();
    NewRow->Item["First Name"] = S"Max";
    NewRow->Item["Last Name"] = S"Fomitchev";
    PlayerTable->Rows->Add(NewRow);
}
catch(Exception* e) {
    Console::WriteLine("ERROR: {0}", e->Message);
}


// 4. Test the foreign key constraint
// OK
NewRow = ScoreTable->NewRow();
NewRow->Item["First Name"] = S"Max";
NewRow->Item["Last Name"] = S"Fomitchev";
NewRow->Item["Points"] = __box(100);
ScoreTable->Rows->Add(NewRow);
// Violates constraint - will fail
try {
    NewRow = ScoreTable->NewRow();
    NewRow->Item["First Name"] = S"Maxim";
    NewRow->Item["Last Name"] = S"Fomitchev";
    NewRow->Item["Points"] = __box(200);
    ScoreTable->Rows->Add(NewRow);
}
catch(Exception* e) {
    Console::WriteLine("ERROR: {0}", e->Message);
}


// 5. Delete a row in the parent table to initiate a cascade delete
// in the child table
String* PKValues[] = {"Max", "Fomitchev"};
DataRow* Row = PlayerTable->Rows->Find(PKValues);
Row->Delete();


// 6. Look for child row, which is supposed to be deleted
if ( ScoreTable->
    Select("[First Name]='Max' AND [Last Name]='Fomitchev'")->Count )
    Console::WriteLine("Child row is still there");
```

```
    else
        Console::WriteLine("Child row is removed");
}
```

> **NOTE:** The code in this example will behave exactly the same if you comment out the constraint definitions and uncomment the **PrimaryKey** and **DataRelation** definitions.

Writing Dataset Data/Schema as XML/XSD Documents

The **DataSet** class provides **ReadXml/WriteXml** and **ReadXmlSchema/WriteXmlSchema** methods for reading/writing dataset data and schema. Using these methods is a no brainer. For greater versatility, the **DataSet** and **DataTable** classes allow you to specify namespace names and prefixes (**Namespace** and **Prefix** properties), as well as indicating whether to nest child relations (**Nested** property). To illustrate writing dataset data as XML, consider the code example presented next, which writes a relational **DataSet** to an XML file and performs the following tasks:

1. Creates a DataSet containing two tables, "Player" and "Score," bound by a parent/child relation, and populates the tables with sample data.

2. Enables nesting for the "Player-Score" relation by setting the **Nested** property of the relation to **true**. Once the nesting is turned on, child "Score" records will appear nested within parent "Player" records in the resulting XML file.

3. Writes the entire **DataSet** to an XML file without schema using the **WriteXml** method with the **XmlWriteMode** parameter set to the **IgnoreSchema**.

4. Writes the **DataSet** schema to an XSD file using the **WriteXmlSchema** method.

5. Writes the entire **DataSet** to an XML file with schema using the **WriteXml** method with the **XmlWriteMode** parameter set to the **WriteSchema**.

6. Disables nesting for the "Player-Score" relation by setting the **Nested** property of the relation to **false**. Once the nesting is turned off, child "Score" records will appear on the same level as parent "Player" records, and the relation between the two tables can be inferred only by examining the document inline XSD schema.

7. Writes the unnested **DataSet** to an XML file with and without schema using the **WriteXml** method.

8. Specifies the **DataSet** namespace using the dataset's **Namespace** property.

9. Specifies **DataTable**'s prefixes and writes the **DataSet** to an XML file.

```
#using <mscorlib.dll>
#using <system.dll>
#using <system.data.dll>
#using <System.Xml.dll>
using namespace System;
using namespace System::Data;

void main()
{
    // 1. Create DataSet
    DataSet* MyDataSet = new DataSet("Game_Data");
    // Add tables to the DataSet
```

```
MyDataSet->Tables->Add("Player");
MyDataSet->Tables->Add("Score");

// Add columns to 1st table
DataTable* PlayerTable = MyDataSet->Tables->Item["Player"];
DataColumn* FirstNameColumn1 = PlayerTable->Columns->Add("First_Name",
    __typeof(String));
DataColumn* LastNameColumn1 = PlayerTable->Columns->Add("Last_Name",
    __typeof(String));
PlayerTable->Columns->Add("Email", __typeof(String));
// Create composite primary key
DataColumn* PrimaryKey[] = {FirstNameColumn1, LastNameColumn1};
PlayerTable->PrimaryKey = PrimaryKey;

// Add columns to 2nd table
DataTable* ScoreTable = MyDataSet->Tables->Item["Score"];
DataColumn* FirstNameColumn2 = ScoreTable->Columns->Add("First_Name",
    __typeof(String));
DataColumn* LastNameColumn2 = ScoreTable->Columns->Add("Last_Name",
    __typeof(String));
ScoreTable->Columns->Add("Points", __typeof(int));

// Establish a data relation
DataColumn* ForeignKey[] = {FirstNameColumn2, LastNameColumn2};
MyDataSet->Relations->Add("Player-Score", PrimaryKey, ForeignKey);

// Add initial data to 1st table
DataRow* newRow = PlayerTable->NewRow();
newRow->Item["First_Name"] = S"Max";
newRow->Item["Last_Name"] = S"Fomitchev";
PlayerTable->Rows->Add(newRow);

newRow = PlayerTable->NewRow();
newRow->Item["First_Name"] = S"Veronica";
newRow->Item["Last_Name"] = S"Grigorashvily";
PlayerTable->Rows->Add(newRow);

newRow = PlayerTable->NewRow();
newRow->Item["First_Name"] = S"Vlad";
newRow->Item["Last_Name"] = S"Fomitchev";
PlayerTable->Rows->Add(newRow);

// Add initial data to 2st table
newRow = ScoreTable->NewRow();
newRow->Item["First_Name"] = S"Max";
newRow->Item["Last_Name"] = S"Fomitchev";
```

```
newRow->Item["Points"] = __box(100);
ScoreTable->Rows->Add(newRow);
newRow = ScoreTable->NewRow();
newRow->Item["First_Name"] = S"Max";
newRow->Item["Last_Name"] = S"Fomitchev";
newRow->Item["Points"] = __box(200);
ScoreTable->Rows->Add(newRow);

newRow = ScoreTable->NewRow();
newRow->Item["First_Name"] = S"Veronica";
newRow->Item["Last_Name"] = S"Grigorashvily";
newRow->Item["Points"] = __box(999);
ScoreTable->Rows->Add(newRow);

// 2. Enable table nesting
MyDataSet->Relations->Item["Player-Score"]->Nested = true;

// 3. Write DataSet as XML without schema
MyDataSet->WriteXml("myDatSet nested.xml", XmlWriteMode::IgnoreSchema);

// 4. Write DataSet as XML with schema
MyDataSet->WriteXml("myDatSet nested with schema.xml",
    XmlWriteMode::WriteSchema);

// 5. Write DataSet XSD schema
MyDataSet->WriteXmlSchema("myDatSet.xsd");

// 6. Disable table nesting
MyDataSet->Relations->Item["Player-Score"]->Nested = false;

// 7. Write not nested tables as XML with and without schema
MyDataSet->WriteXml("myDatSet.xml", XmlWriteMode::IgnoreSchema);
MyDataSet->WriteXml("myDatSet with schema.xml", XmlWriteMode::WriteSchema);

// 8. Specify DataSet namespace
MyDataSet->Namespace = "Gems3D";

// 9. Specify DataTable prefixes
MyDataSet->Tables->Item["Player"]->Prefix = "UserData";
MyDataSet->Tables->Item["Score"]->Prefix = "GameData";
MyDataSet->WriteXml("myDatSet with namespace.xml",
    XmlWriteMode::IgnoreSchema);
MyDataSet->WriteXml("myDatSet with namespace and schema.xml",
    XmlWriteMode::WriteSchema);
}
```

Saving/Loading Dataset Changes as an XML DiffGram

XML DiffGrams provide a convenient way to persist delta-changes made to a **DataSet**. Follow these steps to store dataset changes in an XML DiffGram:

1. Modify **DataSet** data but do not commit the changes by calling the **AcceptChanges** method.

2. Write XML DiffGram using the **WriteXml** method with the **XmlWriteMode** parameter set to **DiffGram**.

To apply the persisted delta-changes in the XML DiffGram changes to a **DataSet**:

1. Load the XML DiffGram into a **DataSet** using the **ReadXml** method with the **XmlReadMode** parameter set to **DiffGram**.

2. Apply the loaded delta-changes using the **AcceptChanges** method.

Alternatively, you can create a new **DataSet** for holding the delta-changes and load an XML data into this new **DataSet**. Then, you can merge the new **DataSet** with another **DataSet** using the **Merge** method and, consequently, apply the **DiffGram** changes to the **DataSet** on which instance the **Merge** method was invoked. The code example below illustrates the first approach.

```
#using <mscorlib.dll>
#using <system.dll>
#using <system.data.dll>
#using <System.Xml.dll>
using namespace System;
using namespace System::Data;

// Function for traversing DataRows
void TraverseRow(DataRow*, DataRelation*, int, int);

void main()
{
   // Create DataSet
   DataSet* myDataSet = new DataSet("Game_Data");
   // Add DataTable to the DataSet
   myDataSet->Tables->Add("Player");

   // Add columns to DataTable
   DataTable* PlayerTable = myDataSet->Tables->Item["Player"];
   DataColumn* FirstNameColumn = PlayerTable->Columns->Add("First_Name",
       __typeof(String));
   DataColumn* LastNameColumn = PlayerTable->Columns->Add("Last_Name",
       __typeof(String));
   PlayerTable->Columns->Add("Email", __typeof(String));
   // Create composite primary key
   DataColumn* PrimaryKey[] = {FirstNameColumn, LastNameColumn};
   PlayerTable->PrimaryKey = PrimaryKey;
```

```
// Specify Initial Data
DataRow* NewRow = PlayerTable->NewRow();
NewRow->Item["First_Name"] = S"Max";
NewRow->Item["Last_Name"] = S"Fomitchev";
PlayerTable->Rows->Add(NewRow);

NewRow = PlayerTable->NewRow();
NewRow->Item["First_Name"] = S"Veronica";
NewRow->Item["Last_Name"] = S"Grigorashvily";
PlayerTable->Rows->Add(NewRow);

NewRow = PlayerTable->NewRow();
NewRow->Item["First_Name"] = S"Vlad";
NewRow->Item["Last_Name"] = S"Fomitchev";
PlayerTable->Rows->Add(NewRow);
// 1. Accept changes end establish a point of reference for GetChanges()
myDataSet->AcceptChanges();

// 2. Do changes
PlayerTable->Rows->Item[0]->Delete();     // Delete
PlayerTable->Rows->Item[2]->Item[S"First_Name"] = S"Vladislav";     // Modify
Object*   NewRowData[] = {S"Vladimir", S"Lenin", S"mausoleum@RedSquare.ru"};
PlayerTable->LoadDataRow(NewRowData,
   false/*do not accept changes*/);     // Add new

// 3. Write DataSet as XML without schema
myDataSet->WriteXml("myDatSet changes.xml", XmlWriteMode::DiffGram);

// 4. Reject changes
myDataSet->RejectChanges();
// Show DataSet contents
for ( int i = 0; i < PlayerTable->Rows->Count; i++ )
   TraverseRow(PlayerTable->Rows->Item[i], 0, i, 0);
Console::WriteLine();

// 5. Load changes from the XML DiffGram
myDataSet->ReadXml("myDatSet changes.xml");
myDataSet->AcceptChanges();
// Show DataSet contents
for ( int i = 0; i < PlayerTable->Rows->Count; i++ )
   TraverseRow(PlayerTable->Rows->Item[i], 0, i, 0);
}
```

Loading/Inferring Dataset Schemas from XSD and XML Documents

Most applications deal with data stored in some known format. The requirements of interoperability with other applications and, most importantly, compatibility with various data formats may impose a requirement on your application to understand data stored in partially known, or in totally unknown formats. Fortunately, ADO.NET supports loading **DataSet** data in an unknown format provided that the data is represented by an XML document. There are two common scenarios for initializing a **DataSet** with an XML data:

* *The structure of the data is completely unknown*: In this case, the **DataSet** schema can be loaded from the XSD schema or inferred from the structure of the XML document.

* *The structure of the data is partially unknown*: In this case, the **DataSet** schema can be extended to accommodate new columns and tables found in the XML document.

In the first case, you can use the **ReadXmlSchema** method to create the **DataSet** structure from an XSD or an XML file, which contains the inlined schema. You can also load both schema and data in the same time by invoking the **ReadXml** method. The second scenario is more interesting because you can write code to load only data that matches the current **DataSet** schema, or you can write code to extend the **DataSet** schema to accommodate all data found in the XML document.

If you want just to read data matching the current **DataSet** schema, you should use the **ReadXml** method. If you want to extend the **DataSet** schema, however, you should use the **InferXmlSchema** method. Strictly speaking, you can use the **ReadXml** to infer the XML schema and load the data at the same time if you supply the **InferSchema** value in the **XmlReadMode** parameter to the method.

> NOTE: If you are going to infer a schema from an XML document, which was written without nesting child tables (**Nested** property set to **false**), the **DataSet** class will not be able to reconstruct parent/child relationships and all tables loaded from XML will appear as top-level.

To illustrate reading **DataSet** schema and loading data from an XML document, consider the code example shown next, which does the following:

1.   Loads a schema into an empty **DataSet** from an XSD document using the **ReadXmlSchema** method.

2.   Loads an XML document into the **DataSet**, which now has schema, using the **ReadXml** method. Since the **DataSet** already has a schema, you can load a schemaless non-nested XML files preserving the data relations specified by the **DataSet** schema.

3.   Creates a second **DataSet**, which has incomplete schema information—two tables with no columns or relationships.

4.   Extends the schema of the second **DataSet** using the **InferXmlSchema** method and loads data using the **ReadXml** method. The XML file used to infer the **DataSet** schema has nested tables; therefore, the original **DataSet** structure is restored properly including data relations.

> NOTE: The **InferXmlSchema** and **ReadXml** method calls in step 4 can be combined in just one **ReadXml** call with the **XmlReadMode::InferSchema** parameter specified.

```
#using <mscorlib.dll>
#using <system.dll>
#using <system.data.dll>
#using <System.Xml.dll>
```

```
using namespace System;
using namespace System::Data;

// Function for traversing DataRows
void TraverseRow(DataRow*, DataRelation*, int, int);

void main()
{
    // Create DataSet
    DataSet* MyDataSet = new DataSet("Game_Data");

    // 1. Load the DataSet schema from XSD
    MyDataSet->ReadXmlSchema("myDatSet.xsd");

    // 2. Read schema-less XML into the DataSet
    MyDataSet->ReadXml("myDatSet.xml", XmlReadMode::IgnoreSchema);
    DataTable* RootTable = MyDataSet->Tables->Item[0];
    // Show DataSet content
    for ( int i = 0; i < RootTable->Rows->Count; i++ )
        TraverseRow(RootTable->Rows->Item[i], 0, i, 0);

    Console::WriteLine();
    // 3. Create new data set with some schema
    DataSet* MyDataSet2 = new DataSet("Game_Data");
    MyDataSet2->Tables->Add("Player");
    MyDataSet2->Tables->Add("Score");

    // 4. Read schema from the XML document
    MyDataSet2->InferXmlSchema("myDatSet nested.xml", 0);
    MyDataSet2->ReadXml("myDatSet nested.xml");
    // Same as
    //MyDataSet2->ReadXml("myDatSet nested.xml", XmlReadMode::InferSchema);
    RootTable = MyDataSet2->Tables->Item[0];
    // Show DataSet content
    for ( int i = 0; i < RootTable->Rows->Count; i++ )
        TraverseRow(RootTable->Rows->Item[i], 0, i, 0);
    // Report "Points" column type
    Console::WriteLine("Type of ""Points"" is {0}",
        MyDataSet2->Tables->Item["Score"]->Columns->Item["Points"]->DataType);
}
```

WARNING! The **InferXmlSchema** method can restore the structure of a **DataSet**, including tables, columns, and data relations, but it cannot restore column data types because the datatype information is stored in the XML schema, which is ignored by the **InferXmlSchema** method.

Creating Data Views

To limit the contents of a **DataTable** to a subset of rows matched or sorted according to specified criteria, you should use the **DataView** class. The **DataView** class allows you to create customized views of rows in a **DataTable** by specifying desired sort and filter expressions. Here are the steps you should follow to create a **DataView** on a **DataTable**:

1. Create a **DataView** object using the **DataView** constructor and specify the target **DataTable**.

2. You can supply sort and filter expressions as parameters to the constructor, or you can set them later by modifying the **Sort** and **RowFilter** properties of the **DataView** object.

3. Iterate through the **DataView** result set using the **DataView::Item** indexer property.

The following code example illustrates the usage of the **DataView** class. The code performs the following operations:

1. Loads the "Player" table into the **DataSet** from an XML file and outputs the original table rows (i.e., unordered and unfiltered data).

2. Creates a **DataView** for the "Player" table and includes only current rows with the Last_Name='Fomitchev', ordered by First_Name descending.

3. Reports the number of rows in the "Player" table matching the specified criteria using the **DataView::Count** property.

4. Outputs the matching "Player" table rows using the **DataView::Item** accessor.

```
#using <mscorlib.dll>
#using <system.dll>
#using <system.data.dll>
#using <System.Xml.dll>
using namespace System;
using namespace System::Data;

void main()
{
   // Create DataSet
   DataSet* myDataSet = new DataSet("Game_Data");
   // 1. Read data from XML document
   myDataSet->ReadXml("myDatSet with schema.xml");
   DataTable* PlayerTable = myDataSet->Tables->Item["Player"];
   // Show DataSet content
   for ( int i = 0; i < PlayerTable->Rows->Count; i++ )
      Console::WriteLine("Player {0}: {1} {2}",
         __box(i), PlayerTable->Rows->Item[i]->Item["First_Name"],
         PlayerTable->Rows->Item[i]->Item["Last_Name"]);

   // 2. Create a view of the data
   DataView* MyView = new DataView(PlayerTable, "Last_Name='Fomitchev'",
      "First_Name DESC", DataViewRowState::CurrentRows);
```

```
    Console::WriteLine();
    // 3. Report row count in the view
    Console::WriteLine("{0} rows in the view", __box(MyView->Count));

    // 4. Show DataView content
    for ( int i = 0; i < MyView->Count; i++ )
        Console::WriteLine("Player {0}: {1} {2}", __box(i),
            MyView->Item[i]->Item["First_Name"],
            MyView->Item[i]->Item["Last_Name"]);
}
```

Specifying Default View Settings

To specify settings of the **DefaultView** of a **DataTable** in a **DataSet** you should use the **DefaultViewManager** class. An instance of the **DefaultViewManager** is provided by the **DataSet** class in the **DefaultViewManager** property. The **DefaultViewManager** property allows you to modify the **DefaultView** settings of any data table in the **DataSet** by means of the **DataViewSettings** collection. The **DataViewSettings** collection provides the **Item** accessor, which allows you to retrieve the **DevaultViewSetting** object for a specified **DataTable** in the **DataSet**.

The following code example demonstrates how to modify the **DefaultView** settings of a **DataTable** in a **DataSet**. The code does the following:

1. Loads the "Player" table into the **DataSet** from an XML file and displays the original table contents (i.e., unordered and unfiltered data).
2. Obtains the **DataViewSetting** pointer for the "Player" table using the **DefaultViewManager::DataViewSettings** property.
3. Modifies the **DataViewSetting** by including only current rows with Last_Name='Fomitchev', ordered by First_Name descending.
4. Reports the number of rows in the "Player" table matching the specified criteria using the **DefaultView::Count** property.
5. Prints the matching "Player" table rows using the **DefaultView::Item** accessor.

> **NOTE:** You do not have to **Open** or **Close** the **DataView** to execute the query. The view refreshes automatically as soon as you change its view settings.

```
#using <mscorlib.dll>
#using <system.dll>
#using <system.data.dll>
#using <System.Xml.dll>
using namespace System;
using namespace System::Data;
void main()
{
    // Create DataSet
```

```
DataSet* MyDataSet = new DataSet("Game_Data");
// 1. Read data from XML document
MyDataSet->ReadXml("myDatSet with schema.xml");
DataTable* PlayerTable = MyDataSet->Tables->Item["Player"];
// Show DataSet content
for ( int i = 0; i < PlayerTable->Rows->Count; i++ )
    Console::WriteLine("Player {0}: {1} {2}",
        __box(i), PlayerTable->Rows->Item[i]->Item["First_Name"],
        PlayerTable->Rows->Item[i]->Item["Last_Name"]);

// 2. Obtain the DataViewSetting pointer for the "Player" table
DataViewSetting* ViewSettings =
    MyDataSet->DefaultViewManager->DataViewSettings->Item["Player"];
// 3. Modify default view parameters for the "Player" table
ViewSettings->RowFilter = "Last_Name='Fomitchev'";
ViewSettings->Sort = "First_Name DESC";

Console::WriteLine();
// 4. Report row count in the DefaultView
Console::WriteLine("{0} rows in the view",
    __box(PlayerTable->DefaultView->Count));

// 5. Show DataView content
for ( int i = 0; i < PlayerTable->DefaultView->Count; i++ )
    Console::WriteLine("Player {0}: {1} {2}", __box(i),
        PlayerTable->DefaultView->Item[i]->Item["First_Name"],
        PlayerTable->DefaultView->Item[i]->Item["Last_Name"]);
}
```

CHAPTER 9

ADO.NET: OLE DB and SQL Server Data Providers

QUICK JUMPS

CHAPTER 9

ADO.NET: OLE DB and SQL Server Data Providers

In Depth

ADO.NET provides a means for both representing in memory pools of relational data (**DataSet/DataTable** classes) and for populating these pools with database data. The latter task is accomplished by ADO.NET data providers. In this chapter you will learn how to use ADO.NET data providers in general (System::Data::Common namespace) and OLE DB (System::Data::OleDb) and SQL Server (System::Data::SqlServer) providers, specifically to retrieve and update database data.

Similarly to ADO, ADO.NET relies on various data providers (such as OLE DB, ODBC.NET, or SQL Server) for retrieving database data. Unlike ADO, ADO.NET exposes a set of provider-specific classes, including Commands, Connections, Data Columns, Data Adapters, and so on which effectively encapsulate provider-specific data access technicalities and leverage the same uniform functionality for populating, updating, and synchronizing generic ADO.NET data objects with database data.

ADO.NET Data Providers

ADO.NET data providers offer means for populating data tables in a **DataSet** object with database or any other external in origin data. Thus, ADO.NET data providers serve as an interface between an in-memory cache of data represented by a **DataSet** object and the actual data store. To better understand this you might want to review Figure 8.1 presented in Chapter 8.

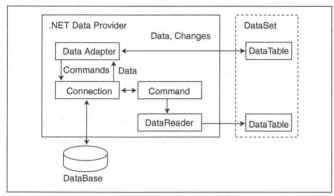

Figure 9.1 ADO.NET data provider architecture.

A **DataSet** object can be linked to multiple data providers connecting to various databases or data sources. From the **DataSet** point of view, the data can come from anywhere and be stored in any manner. The data provider's job is to fetch the data, stick it in a **DataTable** in the **DataSet**, and propagate changes made to the data in the **DataSet** back to the physical storage. An ADO.NET data provider consists of the following components (see Figure 9.1):

*   **Connection** *object*: Represents a database connection, which provides a physical path to the data.

*   **Command** *object*: Represents a unit operation on database/data source data.

*   **DataAdapter** *object*: Translates data changes, such as selecting, inserting, updating, and deleting data rows into database commands.

*   **DataReader** *object*: Provides means for reading streams of database data.

This architecture is shared among all ADO.NET data providers. The base classes supporting the ADO.NET provider architecture are implemented in the System::Data::Common namespace, while all the base interfaces are defined in the System::Data namespace.

The three most common types of ADO.NET data providers include:

* *OLE DB provider*: Implements access to OLE DB data sources (defined in the System::Data::OleDb namespace).

* *SQL Server provider*: Implements access to SQL Server databases (defined in the System::Data::OleDb namespace).

* *ODBC provider*: Implements access to ODBC data sources (defined in the System::Data::ODBC namespace).

NOTE: ADO.NET data provider for ODBC is not a part of the standard .NET Framework distribution. The ODBC provider is available as a free download from the Microsoft site.

Tables 9.1 and 9.2 summarize System::Data::Common namespace classes and attributes. The combined System::Data::Common, System::Data::OleDb, and System::Data::SqlClient namespace class hierarchy is shown in Appendix F.

Table 9.1 System::Data::Common namespace classes.

Class	Description
DataAdapter	Provides means for maintaining sync between a **DataTable** and a database table.
DataColumnMapping	Maps database table columns to **DataTable** columns.
DataColumnMappingCollection	Implements a collection of **DataColumnMapping** objects for the **DataTableMapping** class.
DataTableMapping	Maps a database table to a **DataTable** in a **DataSet**.
DataTableMappingCollection	Implements a collection of **DataTableMapping** objects for the **DataAdapter** class.
DbDataAdapter	Provides means for maintaining sync between a **DataTable** and a database table, including generation of database commands.
DBDataPermission	Provides support for data access security permissions.
RowUpdatedEventArgs	Represents data for the **RowUpdated** event of an ADO.NET data provider.
RowUpdatingEventArgs	Represents data for the **RowUpdating** event of an ADO.NET data provider.

Table 9.2 System::Data::Common Namespace Attributes

Attribute	Description
DBDataPermissionAttribute	Provides support for code access security when working with ADO.NET data providers.

OLE DB and SQL Server Data Providers

Usually a one-to-one correspondence exists between System::Data::Common, System::Data::OleDb, and System::Data::SqlServer classes with the System::Data::Common namespace providing abstract base classes for concrete implementations for the OLE DB and SQL Server Data Providers. Plus, a base interface defined in the System::Data namespace is available for each base data provider class. To mirror this, I've organized this chapter as follows: For each key data provider component, the base interface (if any) is discussed first, then the common class from the System::Data::Common namespace is introduced (if any). Finally, the concrete implementations in OLE DB and SQL Server providers are considered together.

Much similarity exists between OLE DB and SQL Server classes. Similar classes differ only by prefix: **OleDb-** or **Sql-**. For instance, the implementation of database connection classes for OLE DB and SQL Server is represented by the **OleDbConnection** and **SqlConnection** classes. Moreover, the only difference between the provider classes is found in property or method parameter data types in most cases: **OleDb**-classes are used for OLE DB provider and **Sql**-classes for SQL Server provider. Tables 9.3 through 9.7 summarize the System::Data::OleDb and System::Data::SqlClient namespaces general classes, attributes, exceptions, delegates, and enumerations indicating matching OLE DB and SQL Server classes.

Table 9.3 System::Data::OleDb and System::Data::SqlClient namespace general classes.

OLE DB Class	SQL Server Class	Description
OleDbCommand	**SqlCommand**	Implements a SQL statement or stored procedure.
OleDbCommandBuilder	**SqlCommandBuilder**	Generates UPDATE, INSERT, and DELETE commands based on a specified SELECT command.
OleDbConnection	**SqlConnection**	Implements an ADO.NET data connection.
OleDbDataAdapter	**SqlDataAdapter**	Implements a data adapter, which can be used to fill datasets with database data or to update database with dataset data.
OleDbDataReader	**SqlDataReader**	Implements a forward-only stream for reading data rows from a result set produced by executing a database command.
OleDbError	**SqlError**	Represents an ADO.NET data provider error or warning information.
OleDbErrorCollection	**SqlErrorCollection**	Implements a collection of error objects.
OleDbInfoMessageEventArgs	**SqlInfoMessageEventArgs**	Represents data for the **InfoMessage** event.
OleDbParameter	**SqlParameter**	Implements a database command parameter.
OleDbParameterCollection	**SqlParameterCollection**	Implements a collection of database commands.
OleDbPermission	**SqlClientPermission**	Represents data permissions used by ADO.NET data providers.
OleDbRowUpdatedEventArgs	**SqlDbRowUpdatedEventArgs**	Represents data for the **RowUpdated** event.
OleDbRowUpdatingEventArgs	**SqlDbRowUpdatedEventArgs**	Represents data for the **RowUpdating** event.
OleDbSchemaGuid	n/a	Represents an OLE DB data source schema table.
OleDbTransaction	**SqlTransaction**	Implements a data transaction.

Table 9.4 System::Data::OleDb and System::Data::SqlClient namespace attributes.

OLE DB Attribute	SQL Server Attribute	Description
OleDbPermissionAttribute	**SqlClientPermissionAttribute**	Provides support for code access security when working with ADO.NET data providers.

Table 9.5 System::Data::OleDb and System::Data::SqlClient namespace exceptions.

OLE DB Exception	SQL Server	Description
OleDbException	**SqlException**	Represents an exception thrown when an ADO.NET data provider returns a warning or error as a result of the current data operation.

Table 9.6 System::Data::OleDb and System::Data::SqlClient namespace delegates.

OLE DB Delegate	SQL Server Delegate	Description
OleDbInfoMessage-EventHandler(Object* *sender*, OleDbInfoMessageEventArgs* *e*)	**void SqlInfoMessage-EventHandler(Object* *sender*, SqlInfoMessage-EventArgs* *e*)**	A delegate for handling the **InfoMessage** event raised by a data connection object.
void OleDbRowUpdated-EventHandler(Object* *sender*, OleDbRow-UpdatedEventArgs* *e*)	**void SqlRowUpdatedEvent-Handler(Object* *sender*, SqlRowUpdatedEventArgs* *e*)**	A delegate for handling the **RowUpdated** event raised by a data adapter object.
void OleDbRowUpdating-EventHandler(Object* *sender*, OleDbRowUpdatingEventArgs* *e*)	**void SqlRowUpdating-EventHandler(Object* *sender*, SqlRowUpdatingEventArgs* *e*)**	A delegate for handling the **RowUpdating** event raised by a data adapter object.

Table 9.7 System::Data::OleDb and System::Data::SqlClient namespace enumerations.

OLE DB Enumeration	SQL Server Enumeration	Description
OleDbLiteral	n/a	Defines constants for literals used in OLE DB commands, data values, and database objects.
OleDbType	n/a	Defines constants for specifying column data types for **OleDbParameter** objects.

Database Connections

ADO.NET database connection objects represent a path to physical data. To exchange data with an ADO.NET data provider, you *must* create a connection object corresponding to a unique session with a desired database or data source. Also, ADO.NET database connection objects provide a means for performing data transactions.

IDbConnnection Interface

The functionality shared among all ADO.NET data provider connections is specified by the **IDbConnnection** interface, which is defined in the System::Data namespace. The **IDbConnnection** interface properties and methods are listed in Tables 9.8 and 9.9. The **IDbConnnection** interface provides a means for specifying connection strings (data provider-specific database or data source connection information) and initiating data transactions.

Table 9.8 **IDbConnnection** interface properties.

Get/Set	Type	Property	Description
Get/Set	**String***	**ConnectionString**	Gets or sets the database/data source connection string.
Get	**int**	**ConnectionTimeout**	Contains a timeout in seconds specifying the maximum allowable time to wait when attempting to establish a database or data source connection.
Get	**String***	**Database**	Contains the name of the connection's current database/data source.
Get	**ConnectionState State**		Contains the connection state information.

Table 9.9 **IDbConnnection** class methods.

Method	Description
IDbTransaction* BeginTransaction()	
IDbTransaction* BeginTransaction(IsolationLevel *level*)	Begins a database transaction. Optional *level* argument allows specifying the transaction isolation level.
void ChangeDatabase(String* *databaseName*)	Specifies a new database name for an open connection object.
void Close()	Closes the database or data source connection.
IDbCommand* CreateCommand()	Creates and returns a command object associated with the connection.
void Open()	Opens a database or data source connection.

Connection States

At any point of time a connection object can be in one of the following states, defined in the **ConnectionState** enumeration:

* **Broken**: The connection was open for a while, and then was lost.

* **Closed**:The connection is closed.

* **Connecting**: The connection object is in the process of being established.

* **Executing**: The connection object is executing a command.

* **Fetching**: The connection object is retrieving data.

* **Open**: The connection is open and idle.

OleDbConnection and SqlConnection Classes

The implementations of the connection object for OLE DB and SQL Server ADO.NET data providers are provided by the **OleDbConnection** and **SqlConnection** classes. Both classes implement the **IDbConnection** interface and have the following inheritance structure:

```
System::Object
|- System::MarshalByRefObject
    |- System::ComponentModel::Component
        |- System::Data::OleDb::OleDbConnection
        |- System::Data::SqlClient::SqlConnection


Attributes: none
Abstract: No
Sealed: Yes
Implements Interfaces: ICloneable, IDbConnection
```

The **OleDbConnection** class constructors, properties, methods, and events are summarized in Tables 9.10 through 9.13. The **SqlConnection** class constructors, properties, methods, and events are summarized in Tables 9.14 through 9.17.

Table 9.10 **OleDbConnection** class constructors.

Constructor	Description
OleDbConnection()	Default constructor.
OleDbConnection(String* *connectionString*)	Constructs the **OleDbConnection** object using the specified connection string.

Table 9.11 **OleDbConnection** class properties.

Get/Set	Type	Property	Description
Get	**String***	**DataSource**	Contains the OLE DB data source name.
Get	**String***	**Provider**	Contains the OLE DB provider name.
Get	**String***	**ServerVersion**	Contains the version of the server to which the OLE DB client is connected.

Table 9.12 **OleDbConnection** class methods.

Method	Description
OleDbTransaction* BeginTransaction()	
OleDbTransaction* BeginTransaction(IsolationLevel *isolationLevel*)	Begins a database transaction. Optional *level* argument allows specifying the transaction isolation level.
OleDbCommand* CreateCommand()	Creates and returns an **OleDbCommand** object associated with the **OleDbConnection**.
DataTable* GetOleDbSchemaTable(Guid *schema*, Object* *restrictions*[])	Returns the specified schema information from the data source after applying the specified restrictions.
static void ReleaseObjectPool()	Disposes the pool of OLE DB connections.

Table 9.13 **OleDbConnection** class events.

Event	Description
OleDbInfoMessageEventHandler* InfoMessage	Fired when the OLE DB provider sends a warning or an informational message.
StateChangeEventHandler* StateChange	Fired when the state of the connection changes.

Table 9.14 **SqlConnection** class constructors.

Constructor	Description
SqlConnection()	Default constructor.
SqlConnection(String* *connectionString*)	Constructs the **SqlConnection** object using the specified connection string.

Table 9.15 **SqlConnection** class properties.

Get/Set	Type	Property	Description
Get	**String***	**DataSource**	Contains the name of the SQL Server data source.
Get	**int**	**PacketSize**	Contains the size (in bytes) of network packets used to communicate with the SQL Server database.
Get	**String***	**ServerVersion**	Contains the version of the SQL Server to which the client is connected.
Get	**String***	**WorkstationId**	Contains a workstation ID identifying the client computer.

Table 9.16 **SqlConnection** class methods.

Method	Description
SqlTransaction* BeginTransaction()	
SqlTransaction* BeginTransaction(IsolationLevel *level*)	
SqlTransaction* BeginTransaction(String* *name*)	
SqlTransaction* BeginTransaction(IsolationLevel *level*, String* *name*)	Begins a database transaction. Optional *level* and *name* arguments allow specifying the transaction isolation level and name.
SqlCommand* CreateCommand()	Creates and returns an **SqlCommand** object associated with the **SqlConnection**.

Table 9.17 **SqlConnection** class events.

Event	Description
SqlDbInfoMessageEventHandler* InfoMessage	Fired when the provider sends a warning or an informational message.
StateChangeEventHandler* StateChange	Fired when the state of the connection changes.

Data Adapters

ADO.NET data adapter objects represent a link between **DataSet/DataTable** objects and database data. The ADO.NET data adapter architecture is depicted in Figure 9.2. A data adapter object contains the following principal components:

*   ***TableMappings*** *collection*, which associates database tables **DataTable** objects in the corresponding **DataSet**;

*   ***SelectCommand, InsertCommand, UpdateCommand,*** *and* ***DeleteCommand*** *objects*, which represent commands issued by the data adapter to maintain the sync between the **DataSet/DataTable** data and the database.

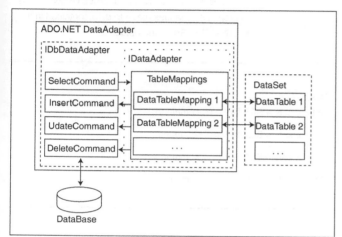

A data adapter performs two functions:

1. Fills a **DataSet** object with database data upon request. The data adapter requests database data by executing the **SelectCommand** and uses the **TableMappings** collection to map database tables/columns into **DataTable/DataColumn** objects of the **DataSet**.

2. Propagates changes made to data in the **DataSet** back to the database by executing appropriate INSERT, UPDATE, and DELETE commands on the database connection. Once again, the data adapter uses **TableMappings** collection to figure out which columns/rows in which physical tables were changed, inserted, or deleted.

Figure 9.2 The ADO.NET data adapter architecture.

IDataAdapter and IDbDataAdapter Interfaces

The core functionality shared among ADO.NET data adapters is specified by the **IDataAdapter** and **IDbDataAdapter** interfaces defined in the System::Data namespace:

```
System::Data::IDataAdapter
|- System::Data::IDbDataAdapter
```

The **IDataAdapter** interface properties and methods are summarized in Tables 9.18 and 9.19. The **IDbDataAdapter** interface adds only four more data command properties to the **IDataAdapter** interface as listed in Table 9.20.

Table 9.18 **IDataAdapter** interface properties.

Get/Set	Type	Property	Description
Get/Set	**MissingMappingAction**	**MissingMappingAction**	Gets or sets an action to be taken when there are source tables or column that are not mapped to any **DataTable/DataColumn** objects.
Get/Set	**MissingSchemaAction**	**MissingSchemaAction**	Gets or sets an action to be taken when there are relations between source tables that are not mapped to any **DataRelation** objects in the **DataSet**.
Get	**ITableMappingCollection***	**TableMappings**	Contains a pointer to the collection of data table mapping objects.

Table 9.19 **IDataAdapter** interface methods.

Method	Description
int Fill(DataSet* *dataSet*)	Fills the specified **DataSet** with the database data.
DataTable* FillSchema(DataSet* *dataSet*, SchemaType *schemaType*)[]	Extends the **DataSet** schema by creating and adding to the **DataSet** new **DataTable** objects matching the schema of the **DataAdapter** data.
IDataParameter* GetFillParameters()[]	Returns an array of parameters used by the **DataAdapter** SELECT command.
int Update(DataSet* *dataSet*)	Executes INSERT, UPDATE, or DELETE commands to propagate changes made to data contained in the specified **DataSet** to the database.

Table 9.20 **IDbDataAdapter** interface properties.

Get/Set	Type	Property	Description
Get/Set	**IDbCommand***	**DeleteCommand**	Gets or sets a SQL DELETE command.
Get/Set	**IDbCommand***	**InsertCommand**	Gets or sets a SQL INSERT command.
Get/Set	**IDbCommand***	**SelectCommand**	Gets or sets a SQL SELECT command.
Get/Set	**IDbCommand***	**UpdateCommand**	Gets or sets a SQL UPDATE command.

Missing Mapping Action

When a data adapter is filling a **DataSet** with database data, it may appear that the **DataSet** is missing a **DataTable** corresponding to database data being loaded. Alternatively, if the target **DataTable** is present in the **DataSet**, it may not have all columns necessary to accommodate the database data. You can specify the desired missing mapping action by setting the **MissingMappingAction** property of a data adapter object to one of the following values (defined in the **MissingMappingAction** enumeration):

*   **Error**: Throws an exception if there are missing tables/columns in the **DataSet**.
*   **Ignore**: Ignores missing tables/columns.
*   **Passthrough**: Automatically adds new **DataTable/DataColumn** objects to the **DataSet** to accommodate the database data.

Missing Schema Action

You can specify a desired missing schema action (i.e., an action to be taken if the target dataset misses tables and relations between tables) by setting the **MissingSchemaAction** property of a data adapter to one of the following values (defined in the **MissingSchemaAction** enumeration):

*   **Add**: Adds missing **DataTable**, **DataColumn,** and **DataRelation** objects to the **DataSet**.
*   **AddWithKey**: Adds missing tables, columns, and data relations and create necessary primary and foreign keys to enforce data integrity.
*   **Error**: Throws an exception if there are missing tables/columns in the **DataSet**.
*   **Ignore**: Ignores missing tables, columns, or data relations.

DataAdapter and DbDataAdapter Classes

ADO.NET supplies two common classes, **DataAdapter** and **DbDataAdapter**, that serve as abstract base classes for all concrete implementations of ADO.NET data adapters:

```
System::Object
|- System::MarshalByRefObject
   |- System::ComponentModel::Component
      |- System::Data::Common::DataAdapter::IDataAdapter
         |- System::Data::Common::DbDataAdapter::IClonable

Attributes: none
Abstract: Yes
Sealed: No
```

Surprisingly, the **DbDataAdapter** class does not implement the **IDbDataAdapter** interface, which is instead directly implemented by the **OleDbDataAdapter** and the **SqlDataAdapter** classes. The **DataAdapter** class properties are listed in Table 9.21, and the **DbDataAdapter** class methods and events are summarized in Tables 9.22 and 9.23.

Table 9.21 **DataAdapter** class properties.

Get/Set	Type	Property	Description
Get/Set	**bool**	**AcceptChangesDuringFill**	Gets or sets a Boolean value indicating whether to call the **AcceptChanges** method on a **DataRow** after it's been added to the **DataTable**.
Get/Set	**bool**	**ContinueUpdateOnError**	Gets or sets a Boolean value indicating whether to throw an exception when an error is encountered during a **DataRow** update.
Get	**DataTableMappingCollection***	**TableMappings**	Contains a pointer to the collection of data **DataTableMapping** objects.

Table 9.22 **DbDataAdapter** class methods.

Method	Description
protected: virtual RowUpdatedEventArgs* CreateRowUpdatedEvent(DataRow* *dataRow*, IDbCommand* *command*, StatementType *statementType*, DataTableMapping* *tableMapping*) = 0	Creates a new **RowUpdatedEventArgs** object using the specified parameters.
protected: virtual RowUpdatingEventArgs* CreateRowUpdatingEvent(DataRow* *dataRow*, IDbCommand* *command*, StatementType *statementType*, DataTableMapping* *tableMapping*) = 0	Creates a new **RowUpdatingEventArgs** object using the specified parameters.
protected: void Dispose(bool *disposing*)	Disposes the **DbDataAdapter** object.
int Fill(DataSet* *dataSet*)	
int Fill(DataSet* *dataSet*, String* *srcTable*)	
int Fill(DataSet* *dataSet*, int *startRow*, int *maxRows*, String* *srcTable*)	Fills the specified *dataSet* with database data. Optional *srcTable* argument allows specifying **DataSet** table to fill. Optional *startRow* and *maxRows* arguments allow specifying a section of the **DataSet** to fill.
protected: virtual int Fill(DataSet* *dataSet*, String* *srcTable*, IDataReader* *dataReader*, int *startRow*, int *maxRows*)	Fills the table *srcTable* in the specified *dataSet* with database data, using the specified data reader.
protected: virtual int Fill(DataSet* *dataSet*, int *startRow*, int *maxRows*, String* *srcTable*, IDbCommand* *command*, CommandBehavior *behavior*)	Fills the table *srcTable* in the specified *dataSet* with database data, by executing the specified *command*, using the specified command *behavior*.

*NOTE: The **Fill** method overloads that accept **maxRows** and **startRow** parameters process only a portion of rows returned by the data adapter SELECT command: No more than the **maxRows** rows starting at the row index **startRow** are filled. If **maxRows** =0, then all rows starting from the specified index are filled.*

Method	Description
int Fill(DataTable* *dataTable*)	Fills the specified **DataTable** with database data.
protected: virtual int Fill(DataTable* *dataTable*, IDataReader* *dataReader*)	Fills the specified **DataTable** with database data, using the specified data reader.
protected: virtual int Fill(DataTable* *dataTable*, IDbCommand* *command*, CommandBehavior *behavior*)	Fills the specified **DataTable** by executing the specified command, using the specified command behavior.

<Continued on Next Page>

<Table 9.22 Continued>

Method	Description
DataTable* FillSchema(DataSet* *dataSet*, SchemaType *schemaType*) []	Extends the **DataSet** schema by creating and adding to the **DataSet** new **DataTable** objects matching the schema of the data adapter data returned by the data adapter SELECT command.
DataTable* FillSchema(DataSet* *dataSet*, SchemaType *schemaType*, String* *srcTable*) []	Extends the schema of a **DataTable** identified by the specified source table mapping in the specified **DataSet** to match the schema of the data adapter data.
protected: virtual DataTable* FillSchema(DataSet* *dataSet*, SchemaType *schemaType*, IDbCommand* *command*, String* *srcTable*, CommandBehavior *behavior*)	Extends the schema of a **DataTable** identified by the specified source table mapping in the specified **DataSet** to match the schema of the data adapter data by executing the specified command, using the specified command behavior.
DataTable* FillSchema(DataTable* *dataTable*, SchemaType *schemaType*)	Extends the schema of the specified **DataTable** to match that of the data adapter data.
protected: virtual DataTable* FillSchema(DataTable* *dataTable*, SchemaType *schemaType*, IDbCommand* *command*, CommandBehavior *behavior*)	Extends the schema of the specified **DataTable** to match the schema of the data adapter data by executing the command, using the specified command behavior.
protected: virtual void OnFillError(FillErrorEventArgs* *value*)	Fires the **FillError** event.
protected: virtual void OnRowUpdated(RowUpdatedEventArgs* *value*) = 0	Invoked after a data row is updated in the database.
protected: virtual void OnRowUpdating(RowUpdatingEventArgs* *value*) = 0	Invoked before a data row is updated in the database.
int Update(DataRow* *dataRows*[])	Executes INSERT, UPDATE, or DELETE commands on the data connection for each inserted, updated, or deleted row in the specified array of **DataRow** objects.
protected: virtual int Update(DataRow* *dataRows*[], DataTableMapping* *mapping*)	Executes INSERT, UPDATE, or DELETE commands on the data connection for each inserted, updated, or deleted row in the specified array of **DataRow** objects, for the specified **DataTableMapping**.
int Update(DataSet* *dataSet*)	
int Update(DataSet* *dataSet*, String* *srcTable*)	Executes INSERT, UPDATE, or DELETE commands on the data connection for each inserted, updated, or deleted row in the *dataSet*. Optional *srcTable* argument allows which data table in the *dataSet* to update.
int Update(DataTable* *dataTable*)	Executes INSERT, UPDATE, or DELETE commands on the data connection for each inserted, updated, or deleted row in the specified *dataTable*.

Table 9.23 **DbDataAdapter** class events.

Event	Description
FillErrorEventHandler* FillError	Fired when an error occurs during the **Fill** operation.

Filling Datasets

When filling a **DataSet** or a **DataTable** with the database data by calling the **Fill** method, the **DbDataAdapter** class executes the **SelectCommand** on the data connection to retrieve database data. Then, the database data is stored in the specified **DataSet/ DataTable,** and missing columns, tables, and data relations are processed according to the settings of the **MissingSchemaAction** and **MissingMappingAction** properties of the **DbDataAdapter**. When invoking the **Fill** method, you can also specify a different SELECT command (in the *command* parameter to the **Fill** method) to be used for selecting data, instead of the default **SelectCommand**. You can also specify a desired command behavior in the *behavior* parameter. The *behavior* parameter can be set to one of the following values defined **CommandBehavior** enumeration:

* **CloseConnection**: Closes the database connection when the command is executed and the **DataReader** object is closed.

* **Default**: Equivalent to calling the **ExecuteReader** method.

* **KeyInfo**: Retrieves column and primary key information (no rows selected).

* **SchemaOnly**: Retrieves table schema information (no rows selected).

* **SequentialAccess**: Provides a mechanism for the **DataReader** to load rows with columns containing large binary values: Rather than loading the entire row, the **SequentialAccess** flag enables the **DataReader** to load row data on demand as a binary stream. (You can call the **GetBytes/GetChars** methods to retrieve **DataRow** bytes at the specified index.)

* **SingleResult**: Query shall return a single result set.

* **SingleRow**: Query shall return a single data row (additional rows are ignored).

NOTE: The **Fill** method uses the primary key to match up database data rows with the existing data rows in a DataSet.

Also, when filling datasets you can specify which data table in the dataset to fill in the *srcTable* parameter to the **Fill** method. The *srcTable* argument is usually case-insensitive. However, if there is more than one data table in the dataset, which names differ by case only, the case of the source table in the *srcTable* argument must match exactly the source table name. Otherwise, the framework will create and add a new table to the dataset.

Same rules apply to updating datasets with the **Update** method, except that the framework throws an exception when there is more than one table in the dataset with names differing only by case, and the *srcTable* parameter to the **Update** method utilizes the spelling, which case does not exactly correspond to the case of any table names in the dataset.

FillError Event

The **FillError** event is fired when an error occurs during the execution of the **Fill** method. Typically a **Fill** error is caused by incompatible data type of the source and **DataSet** column. The **FillErrorEventHandler** delegate uses the **FillErrorEventArgs** class to provide information on the **Fill** error. The **FillErrorEventArgs** class has the following properties:

*   **Continue**: Gets or sets a Boolean value indicating whether to continue the **Fill** operation.

*   **DataTable**: Contains a pointer to a **DataSet** data table being filled.

*   **Errors**: Gets or sets exceptions generated by the ADO.NET data provider.

*   **Values**: Contains a pointer to an array of database values for the row being filled.

If you handle the **FillError** event you have the power to abort the **Fill** operation by setting the **Continue** property to **false**.

OleDbDataAdapter and SqlDataAdapter Classes

The concrete implementations of the data adapter objects for OLE DB and SQL Server data providers are represented by the **OleDbDataAdapter** and **SqlDataAdapter** classes. Both classes implement the **IDbDataAdapter** interface and derive from the **DbDataAdapter** class:

```
System::Object
|- System::MarshalByRefObject
   |- System::ComponentModel::Component
      |- System::Data::Common::DataAdapter
         |- System::Data::Common::DbDataAdapter
            |- System::Data::OleDb::OleDbDataAdapter
            |- System::Data::SqlClient::SqlDataAdapter

Attributes: none
Abstract: None
Sealed: Yes
Implements Interfaces: IDbDataAdapter
```

The **OleDbDataAdapter** class constructors, properties, methods, and events are summarized in Tables 9.24 through 9.27. The **SqlDataAdapter** class constructors, properties, and events are listed in Tables 9.28 through 9.30. As you can see from the tables, constructors, properties, and events of the **OleDbDataAdapter** and **SqlDataAdapter** classes differ only by data types: the OLE DB provider uses **OleDb**-types, while the SQL Server provider uses the **Sql**-types.

Table 9.24 **OleDbDataAdapter** class constructors.

Constructor	Description
OleDbDataAdapter()	Default constructor.
OleDbDataAdapter(OleDbCommand* *selectCommand***)**	Constructs the **OleDbDataAdapter** object using the specified SELECT command.
OleDbDataAdapter(String* *selectCommand,* **OleDbConnection*** *connection***)**	Constructs the **OleDbDataAdapter** object using the specified SELECT command and the specified OLE DB connection.
OleDbDataAdapter(String* *selectCommand,* **String*** *connectString***)**	Constructs the **OleDbDataAdapter** object using the specified SELECT command and the specified OLE DB connection string.

Table 9.25 **OleDbDataAdapter** class properties.

Get/Set	Type	Property	Description
Get/Set	**OleDbCommand***	**DeleteCommand**	Gets or sets the DELETE command.
Get/Set	**OleDbCommand***	**InsertCommand**	Gets or sets the INSERT command.
Get/Set	**OleDbCommand***	**SelectCommand**	Gets or sets the SELECT command.
Get/Set	**OleDbCommand***	**UpdateCommand**	Gets or sets the UPDATE command.

Table 9.26 **OleDbDataAdapter** class methods.

Method	Description
int Fill(DataTable* *dataTable***, Object*** *ADORecordSet***)**	Fills the specified **DataTable** from the specified ADO recordset.
int Fill(DataSet* *dataSet***, Object*** *ADORecordSet***, String*** *srcTable***)**	Fills the specified table in the specified **DataSet** from the specified ADO recordset.

Table 9.27 **OleDbDataAdapter** class events.

Event	Description
OleDbRowUpdatedEventHandler* **RowUpdated**	Fired after a row is updated by the **Update** method.
OleDbRowUpdatingEventHandler* **RowUpdating**	Fired before a row is updated by the **Update** method.

Table 9.28 **SqlDataAdapter** class constructors.

Constructor	Description
SqlDataAdapter()	Default constructor.
SqlDataAdapter(SqlCommand* *selectCommand***)**	Constructs the **SqlDataAdapter** object using the specified SELECT command.
SqlDataAdapter(String* *selectCommand***, SqlConnection*** *connection***)**	Constructs the **SqlDataAdapter** object using the specified SELECT command and the specified SQL Server connection.
SqlDataAdapter(String* *selectCommand***, String*** *connectString***)**	Constructs the **SqlDataAdapter** object using the specified SELECT command and the specified SQL connection string.

Table 9.29 **SqlDataAdapter** class properties.

Get/Set	Type	Property	Description
Get/Set	**SqlCommand***	**DeleteCommand**	Gets or sets the DELETE command.
Get/Set	**SqlCommand***	**InsertCommand**	Gets or sets the INSERT command.
Get/Set	**SqlCommand***	**SelectCommand**	Gets or sets the SELECT command.
Get/Set	**SqlCommand***	**UpdateCommand**	Gets or sets the UPDATE command.

Table 9.30 **SqlDataAdapter** class events.

Event	Description
SqlRowUpdatedEventHandler* RowUpdated	Fired after a row is updated by the **Update** method.
SqlRowUpdatingEventHandler* RowUpdating	Fired before a row is updated by the **Update** method.

RowUpdating and **RowUpdated** Events

The data adapter **Update** method fires the **RowUpdating** and **RowUpdated** events for each modified row *before* a row is updated in the database and *after* a row is updated. When the **RowUpdated** event is raised, the modified **DataSet** row will already contain new data loaded as a result of the UPDATE command. You can use the **RowUpdating** and **RowUpdated** events to monitor data row changes and to handle the **Update** errors like primary or foreign key or other constraint violations. The RowUpdating and RowUpdated event handlers are implemented using different delegate types for OLE DB and SQL Server data providers: OleDbRowUpdatingEventHandler/OleDbRowUpdatedEventHandler and SqlRowUpdatingEventHandler/SqlRowUpdatedEventHandler. However, the delegates use event arguments OleDbRowUpdatingEventArgs/OleDbRowUpdatedEventArgs and SqlRowUpdatingEventArgs/SqlRowUpdatedEventArgs that are very similar. The *ing*-event arguments derive from the RowUpdatingEventArgs defined in the System::Data::Common namespace and has the following properties:

* **Command**: Gets or sets a pointer to the database command that caused the event.

* **Errors:** Gets or sets exceptions generated by the ADO.NET data provider.

* **StatementType**: Gets the **Command's** statement type: **Delete**, **Insert**, **Select**, or **Update** (constants defined in the **StatementType** enumeration).

* **Status**: Gets or sets the **UpdateStatus** of the **Command**: **Continue**, **ErrorsOccurred**, **SkilAllRemainingRows**, or **SkipCurrentRow** (constants defined in the **UpdateStatus** enumeration).

* **TableMapping**: Gets a pointer to the **DataTableMapping** used by the **Update**.

The *ed*-event arguments derived from the **RowUpdatedEventArgs** are defined in the System::Data::Common namespace. The **RowUpdatedEventArgs** has the same properties as the **RowUpdatingEventArgs** and provides an additional property of type **DataRow***, which contains new data of the updated data row. The only difference between the **OleDb**- and **Sql**-prefixed event arguments is in the data type of the **Command** property: **OleDb**-classes use **OleDbCommand** pointer, while **Sql**-classes use **SqlCommand** pointer.

Bridge between ADO and ADO.NET

The **OleDbDataAdapter** class supplies two additional overloads of the **Fill** method that accept a pointer to an ADO recordset or record object as a parameter. These overloads allow populating **DataSet/DataTable** objects with data copied from a specified ADO recordset or ADO record object. The pointer to an ADO recordset or record must be obtained using .NET COM interop services.

Table Mappings

An integral part of an ADO.NET data reader object is a collection of table mappings, which specifies associations between database tables and **DataSet** tables. To describe a mapping of a source table to a **DataSet** table, you must specify names of both tables as well as define the mappings of source columns to the **DataSet** columns (see Figure 9.3). The source columns can be selectively mapped to **DataSet** columns, and the column names do not have to match.

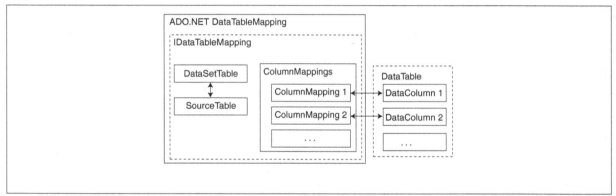

Figure 9.3 The ADO.NET table mapping object architecture.

There is no difference in table mappings among ADO.NET data providers, hence all providers use a single common class to describe table mappings—**DataTableMapping**, which is defined in the System::Data::Common namespace and has the following inheritance structure:

```
System::Object
|- System::MarshalByRefObject
   |- System::Data::Common::DataTableMapping

Attributes: none
Abstract: No
Sealed: Yes
Implements Interfaces: ITableMapping, ICloneable
```

The **DataTableMapping** class constructors, properties, and methods are summarized in Tables 9.31 through 9.33.

Table 9.31 **DataTableMapping** class constructors.

Constructor	Description
DataTableMapping()	Default constructor.
DataTableMapping(String* *sourceTable*, String* *datasetTable*)	
DataTableMapping(String* *sourceTable*, String* *datasetTable*, DataColumnMapping* *columnMappings*[])	Constructs a **DataTableMapping** object mapping the specified data source table into the specified **DataSet** table. Optional *columnMappings* argument allows specifying correspondence between individual *sourceTable* and *datasetTable* columns.

Table 9.32 **DataTableMapping** class properties.

Get/Set	Type	Property	Description
Get	**DataColumnMappingCollection***	**ColumnMappings**	Contains the collection of column mappings for a **DataTable** to which the **DataTableMapping** applies.
Get/Set	**String***	**DataSetTable**	Gets or sets the name of the destination **DataSet** table to which the table mapping applies.
Get/Set	**String***	**SourceTable**	Gets or sets the name of the source table to which the table mapping applies.

Table 9.33 **DataTableMapping** class methods.

Method	Description
DataColumnMapping* GetColumnMappingBySchemaAction(String* *sourceCol*, MissingMappingAction *mappingAction*)	Returns a **DataColumnMapping** for the specified source column using the specified *mappingAction*.
DataTable* GetDataTableBySchemaAction(DataSet* *dataSet*, MissingSchemaAction *schemaAction*)	Returns the current **DataTable** for the specified **DataSet** using the specified *schemaAction* value.

Table Mapping Collections

Table mapping objects are stored in the **TableMappings** collection of the ADO.NET **DbDataAdapter** class. The **TableMappings** property is a specialized collection of type **DataTableMappingCollection** defined in the System::Data::Common namespace:

```
System::Object
|- System::MarshalByRefObject
   |- System::Data::Common::DataTableMappingCollection

Attributes: none
Abstract: No
Sealed: Yes
Implements Interfaces: ITableMappingCollection, IList, ICollection, IEnumerable
```

The **DataTableMappingCollection** class constructors, properties, and methods are listed in Tables 9.34 through 9.36.

Table 9.34 **DataTableMappingCollection** class constructors.

Constructor	Description
DataTableMappingCollection()	Default constructor.

Table 9.35 **DataTableMappingCollection** class properties.

Get/Set	Type	Property	Description
Get/Set	**DataTableMapping***	**Item(int *index*)**	Gets/sets the table mapping at the specified index.
Get/Set	**DataTableMapping ***	**Item(String* *sourceTable*)**	Gets/sets the table mapping for the specified source table.

Table 9.36 **DataTableMappingCollection** class methods.

Method	Description
DataTableMapping* Add(String* *sourceTable*, String* *datasetTable*)	Creates and adds to the collection a new mapping of the specified source table to the specified **DataSet** table.
void AddRange(DataTableMapping* *mappings*[])	Adds the specified array of data table mappings to the collection.
bool Contains(String* *sourceTable*)	Returns **true** if the collection contains a mapping for the specified source table.
DataTableMapping* GetByDataSetColumn(String* *datasetTable*)	Returns a pointer to the table mapping object corresponding to the specified **DataSet** table or Null if the collection contains no mappings for the specified table.
static DataTableMapping* GetTableMappingBySchemaAction(Data-TableMappingCollection* *tableMappings*, String* *sourceTable*, String* *datasetTable*, MissingMappingAction*mappingAction*)	Returns from the **DataColumnMappingCollection** a **DataTableMapping** for the specified source table/**DataSet** table pair using the specified *mappingAction*.
int IndexOf(String* *sourceTable*)	Returns the index of the table mapping for the specified source table.
int IndexOfDataSetTable (String* *datasetTable*)	Returns the index of the **DataTableMapping** for the specified **DataSet** table.
void RemoveAt(String* *sourceTable*)	Removes a table mapping for the specified source table from the collection.

The most useful members of the **DataTableMappingCollection** class are the **Item** indexer, which allows retrieving **DataTableMapping** objects by source table name and the **Add** method, which allows constructing and adding new **DataTableMapping** objects to the collection, provided that you specify the source and the **DataSet** table names.

Data Column Mappings

An ADO.NET column mapping describes a one-to-one correspondence between a column in a database table and a column in a **DataTable** object. An ADO.NET column mapping is implemented by means of **DataColumnMapping**, which is used by all .NET data providers. The **DataColumnMapping** class is defined in the System::Data::Common namespace and has the following inheritance structure:

```
System::Object
|- System::MarshalByRefObject
   |- System::Data::Common::DataColumnMapping
```

```
Attributes: none
Abstract: No
Sealed: Yes
Implements Interfaces: IColumnMapping, ICloneable
```

The **DataColumnMapping** class constructors, properties, and methods are summarized in Tables 9.37 through 9.39.

Table 9.37 **DataColumnMapping** class constructors.

Constructor	Description
DataColumnMapping()	Default constructor.
DataColumnMapping(String* *sourceColumn*, String* *datasetColumn*)	Constructs a **DataColumnMapping** object associating the specified source column with the specified dataset column.

Table 9.38 **IColumnMapping** interface properties.

Get/Set	Type	Property	Description
Get/Set	**String***	**DataSetColumn**	Gets or sets the name of the destination column in a **DataSet**.
Get/Set	**String***	**SourceColumn**	Gets or sets the name of the data the source column in a database.

Table 9.39 **DataColumnMapping** class methods.

Method	Description
DataColumn* GetDataColumnBySchemaAction(DataTable* *dataTable*, Type* *dataType*, MissingSchemaAction *schemaAction*)	Returns a **DataColumn** of the specified type from the specified **DataTable** using the specified **MissingSchemaAction**. If a **DataColumn** of the specified data type does not exist in the collection and the *schemaAction* parameter is set to **Add**, a new data column is created; otherwise, an exception is thrown (*schemaAction* **Error**) or no action is taken (*schemaAction*=**Ignore**).

Data Column Mapping Collections

DataColumnMapping objects are stored in the **ColumnMappings** collection of the **DataTableMapping** class. The **ColumnMappings** collection is a specialized collection of type **DataColumnMappingCollection**, defined in the System::Data::Common namespace:

```
System::Object
|- System::MarshalByRefObject
   |- System::Data::Common::DataColumnMappingCollection

Attributes: none
Abstract: No
Sealed: Yes
Implements Interfaces: IColumnMappingCollection, IList, ICollection, IEnumerable
```

The **DataColumnMappingCollection** class constructors, properties, and methods are summarized in Tables 9.40 through 9.42.

Table 9.40 **DataColumnMappingCollection** class constructors.

Constructor	Description
DataColumnMappingCollection()	Default constructor.

Table 9.41 **DataColumnMappingCollection** class properties.

Get/Set	Type	Property	Description
Get/Set	**DataColumnMapping***	**Item(int *index*)**	Gets or sets the column mapping at the specified index.
Get/Set	**DataColumnMapping***	**Item(String* *sourceColumn*)**	Gets or sets the column mapping for the specified source column.

Table 9.42 **DataColumnMappingCollection** class methods.

Method	Description
DataColumnMapping* Add(String* *sourceCol*, String* *datasetCol*)	Creates and adds to the collection a new mapping of the specified source column to the specified **DataSet** column.
void AddRange(DataColumnMapping* *mappings*[])	Adds to the array of data column mappings to the collection.
bool Contains(String* *sourceCol*)	Returns **true** if the collection contains a mapping for the specified source column.
DataColumnMapping* GetByDataSetColumn(String* *datasetCol*)	Returns a pointer to the column mapping object for the specified **DataSet** column or Null if the collection contains no mappings for the specified **DataSet** column.

<Continued on Next Page>

<Table 9.42 Continued>

Method	*Description*
static DataColumnMapping* **GetColumnMappingBySchemaAction(DataColumnMappingCollection*** *columnMappings*, **String*** *sourceColumn*, **MissingMappingAction** *mappingAction***)**	Returns a **DataColumnMapping** from the specified **DataColumnMappingCollection**, using the specified source column name and *mappingAction*.
int IndexOf(String* *sourceCol***)**	Returns the index of the column mapping for the specified source column.
int IndexOfDataSetColumn(String* *datasetCol***)**	Returns the index of the **DataColumnMapping** for the specified **DataSet** column.
void RemoveAt(String* *sourceCol***)**	Removes a column mapping for the specified source column from the collection.

The **DataColumnMappingCollection** class supplies the **Item** indexer property, which allows retrieving **DataColumnMapping** objects at a specified index in the collection, or for a specified source table column name. The **Add** method automatically constructs and adds a new **DataColumnMapping** object to the collection using a specified source and **DataSet** column names.

Database Commands

An ADO.NET data adapter object communicates with a database by means of database commands. A database command encapsulates a textual expression containing one or more database commands written in the DBMS management language (usually SQL). A database command can accept input parameters and return data in output parameters (see Figure 9.4). Hence the command contains a collection of command parameters specifying input/output data for the command. The five most common types of database commands are SELECT, UPDATE, INSERT, DELETE, and stored procedure calls. Individual SQL commands can be grouped together to execute sequentially in a batch. In this case the command may return more than one result set corresponding to the results produced by each command in the batch.

IDbCommand Interface

The common functionality for database commands used by all ADO.NET data providers is specified by the **IDbCommand** interface defined in the System::Data namespace. The **IDbCommand** interface properties and methods are summarized in Tables 9.43 and 9.44.

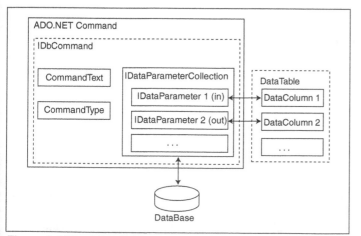

Figure 9.4 The ADO.NET command object architecture.

Table 9.43 **IDbCommand** interface properties.

Get/Set	Type	Property	Description
Get/Set	**String***	**CommandText**	Gets or sets the command text (SQL statement, stored procedure, and so on).
Get/Set	**int**	**CommandTimeout**	Gets or sets the timeout in seconds to wait for the command to execute. Zero indicates infinite timeout. If the timeout expires before the command completes an exception is thrown.
Get/Set	**CommandType**	**CommandType**	Gets or sets the command type (**Text**, **TableDirect**, or **StoredProcedure**).
Get/Set	**IDbConnection***	**Connection**	Gets or sets the command database connection.
Get	**IDataParameterCollection***	**Parameters**	Contains a pointer to the command parameter collection.
Get/Set	**IDbTransaction***	**Transaction**	Gets or sets the transaction in which the command executes.
Get/Set	**UpdateRowSource**	**UpdatedRowSource**	Gets or sets the value indicating how affected data rows should be updated in the **DataSet** as a result of the **Update** method being called on the **DbDataAdapter** object.

Table 9.44 **IDbCommand** interface methods.

Method	Description
void Cancel()	Aborts the execution of the command.
IDbDataParameter* CreateParameter()	Creates a new command parameter object.
int ExecuteNonQuery()	Executes the command and returns the number of affected rows.
IDataReader* ExecuteReader() **IDataReader* ExecuteReader(CommandBehavior** *behavior***)**	Executes the command and constructs a data reader object for reading the result set. Optional *behavior* argument allows specifying the desired database command behavior.
Object* ExecuteScalar()	Executes the command and returns the first column of the first row in the result set.
void Prepare()	Prepares a command for execution.

If a command corresponds with a SELECT statement, you can execute the command and read data rows returned by the query using the **ExecuteReader** method. If the command returns a single result (e.g., SELECT COUNT(*) FROM *TableName*), you can execute the command and read the result using the **ExecuteScalar** method. Database commands can be executed as a part of a database transaction. For that matter, the

IDbCommand interface defines the **Transaction** property, which contains a pointer to a database transaction to which the command belongs.

Command Types
The **CommandType** property of the **IDbCommand** interface specified the type of the database command and can be set to one of the following values defined in the **CommandType** enumeration:

* **StoredProcedure**: The **CommandText** contains the name of a stored procedure.

* **TableDirect**: The **CommandText** contains a comma-separated list of table names that will be joined for the SELECT query.

* **Text**: The **CommandText** contains a generic SQL statement (default).

Update Commands
When you invoke the **Update** method on a **DbDataAdapter**, changes made to the **DataSet** data rows will propagate to the database by means of the **DbDataAdapter** executing UPDATE, INSERT, and DELETE commands for each affected **DataRow** in the **DataSet**. Besides affecting the database, the **Update** method also affects the changed rows in the **DataSet** by reloading modified rows with database data. You can specify a desired effect of the **Update** method on the modified **DataSet** rows by setting the **UpdateRowSource** property to one of the following values (defined in the **UpdateRowSource** enumeration):

* **Both**: Modified **DataSet** rows are updated using data returned by the UPDATE command and then updated with the values of the UPDATE command output parameters mapped to data columns (if any).

* **FirstReturnedRecord**: Modified **DataSet** rows are updated using the first row returned by the UPDATE command (if any).

* **None**: Modified **DataSet** rows are not updated.

* **None OutputParameters**: Modified **DataSet** rows are updated with the values of the UPDATE command output parameters mapped to data columns (if any).

> **NOTE:** The DbDataAdapter::Update method fires the **OnRowUpdating** and **OnRowUpdated** events. When the **OnRowUpdated** is raised, the modified **DataSet** row will already contain new data loaded as a result of the UPDATE command.

OleDbCommand and **SqlClientCommand** Classes
The concrete implementations of the data command objects for OLE DB and SQL Server data providers are represented by the **OleDbCommand** and **SqlClientCommand** classes. Both classes implement the **IDbCommand** interface:

```
System::Object
|- System::MarshalByRefObject
   |- System::ComponentModel::Component
      |- System::Data::OleDb::OleDbCommand
      |- System::Data::SqlClient::SqlCommand

Attributes: None
Abstract: No
Sealed: Yes
Implements Interfaces: ICloneable, IDbCommand
```

The **OleDbCommand** class constructors, properties, and methods are summarized in Tables 9.46 through 9.47. The **SqlCommand** class constructors, properties, and methods are presented in Tables 9.48 through 9.50.

Table 9.45 **OleDbCommand** class constructors.

Constructor	Description
OleDbCommand()	Default constructor.
OleDbCommand(String* *command*)	
OleDbCommand(String* *command*, OleDbConnection* *connection*)	
OleDbCommand(String* *command*, OleDbConnection* *connection*, OleDbTransaction* *transaction*)	Constructs an **OleDbCommand** using the specified *command* text. Optional *connection* argument allows specifiying the database connection on which to execute the command. The optional **transaction** argument forces the command to execute within the scope of the specified transaction.

Table 9.46 **OleDbCommand** class properties.

Get/Set	Type	Property	Description
Get/Set	**OleDbConnection***	**Connection**	Gets or sets the command OLE DB data connection.
Get/Set	**bool**	**DesignTimeVisible**	Gets or sets a Boolean value indicating whether the command should be visible in a Windows Forms control.
Get	**OleDbParameterCollection***	**Parameters**	Contains a pointer to the command parameter collection.
Get/Set	**OleDbTransaction***	**Transaction**	Gets or sets the transaction in which the **OleDbCommand** executes.

Table 9.47 **OleDbCommand** class methods.

Method	Description
OleDbParameter* CreateParameter()	Creates a new **OleDbParameter** object.
OleDbDataReader* ExecuteReader()	
OleDbDataReader* ExecuteReader(CommandBehavior *behavior*)	Executes the command and constructs a **OleDbDataReader** object for reading the result set. Optional *behavior* argument allows specifying the desired database command behavior.
void ResetCommandTimeout()	Resets the **CommandTimeout** property to the default value.

Table 9.48 **SqlCommand** class constructors.

Constructor	Description
SqlCommand()	Default constructor.
SqlCommand(String* *command*)	
SqlCommand(String* *command*, SqlConnection* *connection*)	
SqlCommand(String* *command*, SqlConnection* *connection*, SqlTransaction* *transaction*)	Constructs a **SqlCommand** using the specified *command* text. Optional *connection* argument allows specifying the database connection on which to execute the command. The Optional *transaction* argument forces the command to execute within the scope of the specified transaction.

Table 9.49 **SqlCommand** class properties.

Get/Set	Type	Property	Description
Get/Set	**SqlConnection***	**Connection**	Gets or sets the command SQL Server connection.
Get/Set	**bool**	**DesignTimeVisible**	Gets or sets a Boolean value indicating whether the command should be visible in a Windows Forms control.
Get	**SqlParameterCollection***	**Parameters**	Contains a pointer to the command parameter collection.
Get/Set	**SqlTransaction***	**Transaction**	Gets or sets the transaction in which the **SqlCommand** executes.

Table 9.50 **SqlCommand** class methods.

Method	Description
SqlParameter* CreateParameter()	Creates a new **SqlParameter** object.
SqlDataReader* ExecuteReader()	
SqlDataReader* ExecuteReader(CommandBehavior *behavior*)	Executes the command and constructs a **SqlDataReader** object for reading the result set. Optional *behavior* argument allows specifying the desired database command behavior.
XmlReader* ExecuteXmlReader()	Executes the **SqlCommand** and reads the result set as XML.
void ResetCommandTimeout()	Resets the **CommandTimeout** property to the default value.

The **OleDbCommand** and **SqlCommand** classes, for the most part, provide implementations of the **IDbCommand** interface methods and properties using data types specific to OLE DB and SQL Server data providers (e.g., **OleDb**- or **Sql**-prefixed types).

The **SqlCommand** class supplies an additional original method named **ExecuteXmlReader**, which supports the SQL Server capability of returning query results as XML stream.

Database Command Parameters

Depending on the command type, a command may require *input* parameters for specifying information necessary to complete the command statement, or *output* parameters needed for storing the command results. For instance, if you build a SELECT query command you may want to specify input WHERE clause parameters, e.g., "SELECT * FROM Music WHERE GenreID=?." Or, if you execute a stored procedure you should be able to retrieve the stored procedure return value plus the values of the output parameters if any. ADO.NET provides parameter objects for implementing database command parameters. The command parameter objects can also associate command parameters with **DataSet** columns for retrieving/storing parameter values.

IDataParameter Interface

Functionality shared among command parameters used by different ADO.NET data providers is specified by the **IDataParameter/IDbDataParameter** interfaces defined in the System::Data namespace:

```
System::Data::IDataParameter
|- System::Data::IDbDataParameter
```

The **IDataParameter** interface properties are listed in Table 9.51, and the **IDbDataParameter** interface properties are presented in Table 9.52.

Table 9.51 **IDataParameter** interface properties.

Get/Set	Type	Property	Description
Get/Set	**DbType**	**DbType**	Gets/ sets the parameter data type.
Get/Set	**ParameterDirection**	**Direction**	Gets or sets the parameter direction: **Input**, **InputOutput**, **Output**, or **ReturnValue**.
Get	**bool**	**IsNullable**	Gets or sets a Boolean value indicating whether the parameter can be set to **DBNull** value.
Get/Set	**String***	**ParameterName**	Gets or sets the parameter name.
Get/Set	**String***	**SourceColumn**	Gets or sets the name of the **DataSet** column mapped to the parameter **Value** property.
Get/Set	**DataRowVersion**	**SourceVersion**	Gets or sets the **DataRowVersion** to use when loading the parameter **Value** property.
Get/Set	**Object***	**Value**	Gets or sets the parameter value.

Table 9.52 **IDbDataParameter** interface properties.

Get/Set	Type	Property	Description
Get/Set	**char**	**Precision**	Gets or sets the precision of numeric parameters.
Get/Set	**char**	**Scale**	Gets or sets the scale of numeric parameters.
Get/Set	**char**	**Size**	Gets or sets the number of characters in text parameters.

The most important characteristics of a command parameter are parameter type (**DbType** property as presented in Table 8.6 in Chapter 8), **ParameterName**, and **Direction**. The **Direction** property can be set to one of the following values defined in the **ParameterDirection** enumeration: **Input**, **InputOutput**, **Output**, or **ReturnValue**. Optionally you can set the **SourceColumn** name to specify the parameter mapping to a **DataSet** column.

OleDbParameter and SqlParameter Classes

The implementations of the data command parameter objects for OLE DB and SQL Server data providers are represented by the **OleDbParameter** and **SqlParameter** classes. Both classes implement the **IDataParameter** and **IDbDataParameter** interfaces:

```
System::Object
|- System::MarshalByRefObject
    |- System::Data::OleDb::OleDbParameter
    |- System::Data::SqlClient::SqlParameter


Attributes: Serializable
Abstract: No
Sealed: Yes
Implements Interfaces: IDbDataParameter, IDataParameter, ICloneable
```

The **OleDbParameter** class constructors and properties are listed in Tables 9.53 and 9.54. The **SqlParameter** class constructors and properties are listed in Tables 9.55 and 9.56.

Table 9.53 **OleDbParameter** class constructors.

Constructor	Description
OleDbParameter()	Default constructor.
OleDbParameter(String* *name*, **Object*** *value*)	Constructs a **OleDbParameter** with the specified *name* and *value*.
OleDbParameter(String* *name*, **OleDbType** *type*)	
OleDbParameter(String* *name*, **OleDbType** *type*, **int** *size*)	
OleDbParameter(String* *name*, **OleDbType** *type*, int *size*, **String*** *sourceColumn*)	Constructs a **OleDbParameter** with the specified *name* and data *type*. Optional *size* and *sourceColumn* arguments allow specifying the parameter size in characters and the **DataSet** column name to which the parameter is assigned.
OleDbParameter(String* *name*, **OleDbType** *type*, int *size*, **ParameterDirection** *direction*, **bool** *isNullable*, **unsigned char** *precision*, **unsigned char** *scale*, **String*** *datasetColumn*, **DataRowVersion** *datasetRowVersion*, **Object*** *value*)	A constructor that allows you to specify all **OleDbParameter** properties.

Table 9.54 **OleDbParameter** class properties.

Get/Set	Type	Property	Description
Get/Set	**OleDbType**	**OleDbType**	Gets or sets the OLE DB parameter type.

Table 9.55 **SqlParameter** class constructors.

Constructor	Description
SqlParameter()	Default constructor.
SqlParameter(String* *name*, **Object*** *value*)	Constructs a **SqlParameter** with the specified name and value.
SqlParameter(String* *name*, **SqlDbType** *type*)	
SqlParameter(String* *name*, **SqlDbType** *type*, **int** *size*)	
SqlParameter(String* *name*, **SqlDbType** *type*, **int** *size*, **String*** *sourceColumn*)	Constructs a **SqlParameter** with the specified *name* and data *type*. Optional *size* and *sourceColumn* arguments allow specifying the parameter size in characters and the **DataSet** column name to which the parameter is assigned.
SqlParameter(String* *name*, **SqlDbType** *type*, **int** *size*, **ParameterDirection** *direction*, **bool** *isNullable*, **unsigned char** *precision*, **unsigned char** *scale*, **String*** *datasetColumn*, **DataRowVersion** *dataserRowVersion*, **Object*** *value*)	A constructor that allows you to specify all **SqlParameter** properties.

Table 9.56 **SqlParameter** class properties.

Get/Set	Type	Property	Description
Get/Set	**SqlDbType**	**SqlDbType**	Gets or sets the SQL Server parameter type.

For the most part **OleDbParameter/SqlParameter** classes supply numerous constructor overloads for initializing parameter objects.

Identifying Command Parameters

The two common scenarios for using command parameters are:

* *Specifying parameters for WHERE clauses.*
* *Specifying parameters for stored procedures.*

When specifying parameters for WHERE clauses, there is an important difference between **OleDbCommand** parameters and **SqlCommand** parameters: **OleDbCommand** identifies parameters either by name or by order (i.e., using question mark signs '?'), while the **SqlCommand** always identifies parameters by name. The following two examples illustrate the same SELECT statement, which uses a WHERE clause parameter, formatted for the use with OLE DB and SQL Server commands:

*   OLE DB: SELECT * FROM Music WHERE Genre=?

*   SQL Server: SELECT * FROM Music WHERE Genre=@Genre

NOTE: A preferred method of identifying parameters is by name because it is supported by both OLE DB and SQL Server ADO.NET providers.

When specifying parameters to stored procedures you *must* always use the parameter names preceded with a '@' character and the command parameter names *must* match the names of the stored procedure parameters specified in the stored procedure definition. The physical order of command parameters in the **Parameters** collection does not matter. A parameter corresponding to the return value of a stored procedure is identified by the "RETURN_VALUE" name.

Parameter Collections

Parameter objects are stored in ADO.NET command objects in the **Parameters** property. The **Parameters** property corresponds to a specialized collection, which implements the **IDataParameterCollection** interface defined in the System::Data namespace. The **IDataParameterCollection** interface combines the **IList**, **ICollection,** and **IEnumerable** interfaces and specifies command parameter collection functionality shared among ADO.NET data providers. The original **IDataParameterCollection** interface properties and methods are summarized in Tables 9.57 and 9.58.

Table 9.57 Original **IDataParameterCollection** interface properties.

Get/Set	Type	Property	Description
Get	**Object***	**Item(String* *parameterName*)**	Returns the parameter at the specified index.

Table 9.58 Original **OleDbDataReader** class methods.

Method	Description
bool Contains(String* *parameterName*)	Returns **true** if the collection contains a parameter with the specified name.
int IndexOf(String* *parameterName*)	Returns the index of the specified parameter or -1 if the parameter is not in the collection.
void RemoveAt(String* *parameterName*)	Removes the specified parameter from the collection.

OleDbParameterCollection and SqlParameterCollection Classes

The implementations of the command parameter collections for OLE DB and SQL Server data providers are represented by the **OleDbParameterCollection** and **SqlParameterCollection** classes, which implement the **IDbDataParameter IDataParameterCollection** interface:

```
System::Object
|- System::MarshalByRefObject
    |- System::Data::SqlClient::OleDbParameterCollection
    |- System::Data::SqlClient::SqlParameterCollection
```

Attributes: None
Abstract: No
Sealed: Yes
Implements Interfaces: **IDataParameterCollection, IList, ICollection, IEnumerable**

The **OleDbParameterCollection** class properties and methods are summarized in Tables 9.59 and 9.60, and the properties and methods of the **SqlParameterCollection** class are summarized in Tables 9.61 and 9.62.

Table 9.59 **OleDbParameterCollection** class properties.

Get/Set	Type	Property	Description
Get	**OleDbParameter***	**Item(int *index*)**	Returns the parameter at the specified index.
Get	**OleDbParameter***	**Item(String* *parameterName*)**	Returns the parameter with the specified name.

Table 9.60 **OleDbParameterCollection** class methods.

Method	Description
OleDbParameter* Add(OleDbParameter* *value*)	Adds the specified **OleDbParameter** to the collection.
OleDbParameter* Add(String* *parameterName*, Object* *value*)	Creates and adds to the collection a new parameter with the specified parameter name and initial value.
OleDbParameter* Add(String* *name*, OleDbType *type*)	
OleDbParameter* Add(String* *name*, OleDbType *type*, int *size*)	
OleDbParameter* Add(String* *name*, OleDbType *type*, int *size*, String* *sourceColumn*)	Creates and adds to the collection a new parameter with the specified *name* and data *type*. Optional *size* and *sourceColumn* arguments allow specifying the parameter size in characters and the **DataSet** column name to which the parameter is assigned.

Table 9.61 **SqlParameterCollection** class properties.

Get/Set	Type	Property	Description
Get	SqlParameter*	Item(int *index*)	Returns the parameter at the specified index.
Get	SqlParameter*	Item(String* *Name*)	Returns the parameter with the specified name.

Table 9.62 **SqlParameterCollection** class methods.

Method	Description
SqlParameter* Add(SqlParameter* *value*)	Adds the specified **OleDbParameter** to the collection.
SqlParameter* Add(String* *parameterName*, Object* *value*)	Creates and adds to the collection a new parameter with the specified parameter name and initial value.
SqlParameter* Add(String* *name*, SqlType *type*)	
SqlParameter* Add(String* *name*, SqlType *type*, int *size*)	
SqlParameter* Add(String* *name*, SqlType *type*, int *size*, String* *sourceColumn*)	Creates and adds to the collection a new parameter with the specified *name* and data *type*. Optional *size* and *sourceColumn* arguments allow specifying the parameter size in characters and the **DataSet** column name to which the parameter is assigned.

Both the **OleDbParameterCollection** and **SqlParameterCollection** classes supply the **Item** indexer property for retrieving from the collection parameter objects with a specified name or index. Also, both classes provide numerous **Add** method overloads for constructing and adding new parameter objects to the parameter collection.

Database Command Builders

The **DbDataAdapter** class uses four command properties: **SelectCommand**, **UpdateCommand**, **InsertCommand**, and **DeleteCommand** to reconcile changes made to the **DataSet** with the database data. The **DbDataAdapter** class (or any provider-specific data adapter classes) does not automatically generate the required UPDATE, INSERT, and DELETE commands, however, and it is always a responsibility of a developer to specify the **SelectCommand** (i.e., a SELECT statement for retrieving database data). To save developers the hassle of generating INSERT, UPDATE, and DELETE commands the ADO.NET provides command builder classes, which construct **UpdateCommand**, **InsertCommand**, and **DeleteCommand** objects based on a specified **SelectCommand**.

Command builder objects are not mandated by the ADO.NET, therefore, there is no common base interface or base class for this purpose. Instead OLE DB and SQL Server data providers implement their own **OleDbCommandBuilder** and **SqlCommandBuilder** classes that are very similar, yet have no common root in the ADO.NET class hierarchy.

OleDbCommandBuilder and SqlCommandBuilder Classes

The **OleDbCommandBuilder** and **SqlCommandBuilder** classes implement no common interfaces and have the following inheritance diagram:

```
System::Object
|- System::MarshalByRefObject
    |- System::ComponentModel::Component
        |- System::Data::OleDb::OleDbCommandBuilder
        |- System::Data::SqlClient::SqlCommandBuilder
```

```
Attributes: none
Abstract: No
Sealed: Yes
Implements Interfaces: None
```

OleDbCommandBuilder class constructors, properties, and methods are summarized in Tables 9.63 through 9.65. The **SqlCommandBuilder** class constructors, properties, and methods are listed in Tables 9.66 through 9.68.

Table 9.63 **OleDbCommandBuilder** class constructors.

Constructor	Description
SqlCommandBuilder()	Default constructor.
SqlCommandBuilder(OleDbDataAdapter* *adapter***)**	Constructs an **OleDbCommandBuilder** object using the specified data adapter.

Table 9.64 **OleDbCommandBuilder** class properties.

Get/Set	Type	Property	Description
Get/Set	**OleDbDataAdapter***	**DataAdapter**	Gets/sets the data adapter for the **OleDbCommandBuilder** object.
Get/Set	**String***	**QuotePrefix**	Gets or sets the beginning character or characters to use when specifying OLE DB object names (e.g., table or column names) that contain characters such as spaces.
Get/Set	**String***	**QuoteSuffix**	Gets or sets the ending character or characters to use when specifying OLE DB object names (e.g., table or column names) that contain characters such as spaces.

Table 9.65 **OleDbCommandBuilder** class methods.

Method	Description
static void DeriveParameters(OleDbCommand* *command***)**	Populates the specified **OleDbCommand** object's **Parameters** collection with parameter information for a stored procedure specified in the command.
protected: void Dispose(bool *disposing***)**	Disposes the **OleDbCommandBuilder** object.

<Continued on Next Page>

<Table 9.65 Continued>

Method	Description
OleDbCommand* GetDeleteCommand()	Builds and returns the DELETE command.
OleDbCommand* GetInsertCommand()	Builds and returns the INSERT command.
OleDbCommand* GetUpdateCommand()	Builds and returns the UPDATE command.
void RefreshSchema()	Refreshes the database schema information used by the command builder to generate INSERT, UPDATE, or DELETE statements. You should call this method whenever the associated SELECT statement is changed.

Table 9.66 **SqlCommandBuilder** class constructors.

Constructor	Description
SqlCommandBuilder()	Default constructor.
SqlCommandBuilder(SqlDataAdapter* adapter)	Constructs a **SqlCommandBuilder** object using the specified data adapter.

Table 9.67 **SqlCommandBuilder** class properties.

Get/Set	Type	Property	Description
Get/Set	**SqlDataAdapter***	**DataAdapter**	Gets or sets the data adapter for the **SqlCommandBuilder** object.
Get/Set	**String***	**QuotePrefix**	Gets or sets the beginning character or characters to use when specifying SQL Server object names (e.g., table or column names) that contain characters such as spaces.
Get/Set	**String***	**QuoteSuffix**	Gets or sets the ending character or characters to use when specifying SQL Server object names (e.g., table or column names) that contain characters such as spaces.

Table 9.68 **SqlCommandBuilder** class methods.

Method	Description
static void DeriveParameters(SqlCommand* command)	Populates the specified **SqlCommand** object's **Parameters** collection with parameter information for a stored procedure specified in the command.
protected: void Dispose(bool disposing)	Disposes the **SqlCommandBuilder** object.
SqlCommand* GetDeleteCommand()	Builds and returns the DELETE command.
SqlCommand* GetInsertCommand()	Builds and returns the INSERT command.
SqlCommand* GetUpdateCommand()	Builds and returns the UPDATE command.
void RefreshSchema()	Refreshes the database schema information used by the command builder to generate INSERT, UPDATE, or DELETE statements. You should call this method whenever the associated SELECT statement is changed.

Both the **OleDbCommandBuilder** and **SqlCommandBuilder** classes require a pointer to a **DbDataAdapter** object, which is needed to obtain a **SelectCommand** text. Given a SELECT command text, an **OleDbCommandBuilder/SqlCommandBuilder** object can generate necessary INSERT, DELETE, and UPDATE SQL statements that can be obtained using the **GetInsertCommand**, **GetUpdateCommand,** or **GetDeleteCommand** methods. Then you can update the **DbDataAdapter**'s **InsertCommand**, **UpdateCommand,** and **DeleteCommand** properties with the commands produced by the command builder object.

If you change the **DbDataAdapter**'s **SelectCommand** at a later time you can obtain the updated **InsertCommand**, **UpdateCommand,** and **DeleteCommand** properties by invoking the **RefreshSchema** method on the **OleDbCommandBuilder/SqlCommandBuilder** object.

Deriving Stored Procedure Parameters

The **OleDbCommandBuilder** and **SqlCommandBuilder** classes supply a useful **DeriveParameters** method, which allows discovering parameters of a specified store procedure command. Simply create a stored procedure command by specifying the store procedure name and setting the command type to **StoredProcedure** and invoke the **DeriveParameters** method. The method will query the database and automatically populate the command's **Parameters** collection with command parameter objects corresponding to the stored procedure parameters including the return value.

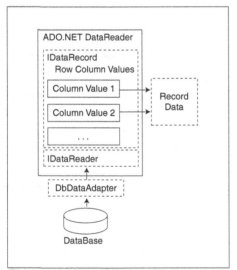

Figure 9.5 ADO.NET data reader architecture.

Data Readers

There are two ways in which you can retrieve data from a database: by creating a **DbDataReader** object and invoking the **Fill** method to populate a **DataSet**, or by executing a data command directly on the connection and navigating the command result set using a *data reader* object. An ADO.NET data reader provides a means of forward-only navigation of the command result set and means of accessing values of individual columns in the current row of the command result set. The ADO.NET data reader architecture is illustrated in Figure 9.5.

In the .NET Framework the functionality shared among all ADO.NET data readers is specified by means of two interfaces:

* **IDataReader** supports forward-only navigation of a command result set.

* **IDataRecord** supports retrieving column values of the current row in the result set, including converting to various data types.

Both interfaces are defined in the System::Data namespace. The **IDataReader** interface properties and methods are listed in Tables 9.69 and 9.70, while the **IDataRecord** interface properties and methods are given in Tables 9.71 and 9.72

Table 9.69 **IDataReader** interface properties.

Get/Set	Type	Property	Description
Get	int	**Depth**	Contains the nesting depth of the current row for hierarchal result sets.
Get	bool	**IsClosed**	Contains **true** if the data reader is closed.
Get	int	**RecordsAffected**	Contains the number of rows changed, inserted, or deleted by the SQL command, which created the data reader.

Table 9.70 **IDataReader** interface methods.

Method	Description
void Close()	Closes the data reader.
DataTable* GetSchemaTable()	Returns a **DataTable** that corresponding to the data reader schema.
bool NextResult()	Reads the next result set if the command that created the data reader corresponds to a batch of SQL statements.
bool Read()	Reads the next data row in the current result set.

Table 9.71 **IDataRecord** interface properties.

Get/Set	Type	Property	Description
Get	**int**	**FieldCount**	Contains the number of columns in the current row.
Get	**Object***	**Item(String* *colName*)**	Returns the value of the column with the specified name.
Get	**Object***	**Item(int *colIndex*)**	Returns the value of the column at the specified index.

Table 9.72 **IDataRecord** interface methods.

Method	Description
bool GetBoolean(int *colIndex*)	Returns the value of the specified column as a Boolean.
unsigned char GetByte(int *colIndex*)	Returns the value of the specified column as a byte.
__int64 GetBytes(int *colIndex*, __int64 *fieldOffset*, unsigned char *buffer* __gc[], int *bufferOffset*, int *length*)	Copies the *length* bytes from the specified column starting at the index *fieldOffset* into the specified buffer starting at the **bufferOffset**. The method returns the number of unread bytes remaining in the field. To obtain the field size in bytes you can call the **GetBytes** method and specify Null in the buffer pointer parameter.
__wchar_t GetChar(int *colIndex*)	Returns the value of the specified column as a character.
__int64 GetChars(int *colIndex*, __int64 *fieldoffset*, __wchar_t *buffer* __gc[], int *bufferOffset*, int *length*)	Copies the *length* characters from the specified column starting at the index *fieldOffset* into the specified buffer starting at the **bufferOffset**. The method returns the number of unread characters remaining in the field. To obtain the count of characters in the field you can call the **GetChars** method and specify Null in the buffer pointer parameter.

<Continued on Next Page>

<Table 9.72 Continued>

Method	Description
IDataReader* GetData(int *colIndex*)	Returns the value of the specified columns as a **IDataReader** pointer.
String* GetDataTypeName(int *colIndex*)	Returns data type information of the specified column.
DateTime GetDateTime(int *colIndex*)	Returns the value of the specified column as **DateTime**.
Decimal GetDecimal(int *colIndex*)	Returns the value of the specified column as **Decimal**.
double GetDouble(int *colIndex*)	Returns the value of the specified column as **double**.
Type* GetFieldType(int *colIndex*)	Returns the type of the specified column.
float GetFloat(int *colIndex*)	Returns the value of the specified column as **float**.
Guid GetGuid(int *colIndex*)	Returns the value of the specified column as **Guid**.
short GetInt16(int *colIndex*)	Returns the value of the specified column as **short**.
short GetInt32(int *colIndex*)	Returns the value of the specified column as **int**.
short GetInt64(int *colIndex*)	Returns the value of the specified column as **__int64**.
String* GetName(int *colIndex*)	Returns the name of the specified column.
int GetOrdinal(String* *colName*)	Returns the index of the specified column.
String*GetString(int *colIndex*)	Returns the value of the specified column as **String**.
Object*GetValue(int *colIndex*)	Returns the value of the specified column as **Object**.
int GetValue(Object* *values* __gc[])	Copies values of all columns in the current record into the specified array and returns the number of array elements (i.e., record columns).
bool IsDBNull(int *colIndex*)	Returns **true** if the specified column is Null.

Sequential Access to Row Data

The **IDataRecord** interface provides the **GetBytes** method, which allows reading the specified column as stream by requesting data on demand. The **GetBytes** method can be used for retrieving Binary Large OBjects (BLOB) on demand. Rather than retrieving the entire row and potentially wasting memory and network bandwidth on loading undesired binary data, you can set the **CommandBehavior** to **SequentialAccess**. Then you can invoke the **GetBytes** method to bytes of the current data row as a stream.

> Warning! The GetBytes method allows reading as many bytes as you want starting from whatever column index you want. Keep in mind, however, that if a data reader is configured for SequentialAccess, once you request the data for a particular column you can no longer request data for the previous column in the row.

OleDbDataReader and SqlDataReader Classes

The concrete implementations of the ADO.NET data reader objects for OLE DB and SQL Server data providers are represented by the **OleDbDataReader** and **SqlDataReader** classes, which implement both the **IDataReader** and the **IDataRecord** interfaces:

```
System::Object
|- System::MarshalByRefObject
    |- System::Data::OleDb::OleDbDataReader
    |- System::Data::SqlClient::SqlDataReader
```

```
Attributes: none
Abstract: no
Sealed: Yes
Implements Interfaces: IDataReader, IDataRecord, IEnumerable, IDisposable
```

The **OleDbDataReader** and **SqlDataReader** classes have no original methods of special interest.

Database Transactions

Database operations in most applications are grouped in transactions. Transactions ensure that all or none data changes requested by commands participating in a transaction succeed. ADO.NET fully supports transactions and specifies common transaction functionality by means of the **IDbTransaction** interface, defined in the System::Data namespace. The **IDbTransaction** interface properties and methods are summarized in Tables 9.73 and 9.74. The **IDbTransaction** interface defines only two methods, **Commit** and **Rollback,** for committing/cancelling the transaction.

Table 9.73 **IDbTransaction** interface properties.

Get/Set	Type	Property	Description
Get	**IDbConnection***	**Connection**	Contains a pointer to the database connection on which a transaction is performed.
Get	**IsolationLevel**	**IsolationLevel**	Contains the isolation level of the transaction.

Table 9.74 **IDbTransaction** interface methods.

Method	Description
void Commit()	Commits the database transaction.
void Rollback()	Rolls back the database transaction.

Data Transaction Levels

ADO.NET supports the following levels of database transactions (**IsolationLevel** enumeration):

* **Chaos**: The current transaction cannot overwrite any pending changes made by highly isolated transactions.

* **ReadCommitted**: Shared locks are held while the data is being read to avoid reading uncommitted data, but another user can change the data before the end of the transaction, resulting in nonrepeatable reads or phantom data.

* **ReadUncommitted**: An uncommitted data can be read, meaning that no shared locks are issued and no exclusive locks are honored.

* **RepeatableRead**: Locks are placed on all data that is used in a query, preventing other users from updating the data (prevents nonrepeatable reads).

* **Serializable**: A range lock is placed on the dataset, preventing other users from updating or inserting rows into the dataset until the transaction is complete.

* **Unspecified**: The level cannot be determined.

OleDbTransaction and SqlDbTransaction Classes

The concrete implementations of the transaction objects for the OLE DB and the SQL Server data providers are represented by means of the **OleDbTransaction** and **SqlDbTransaction** classes, both of which implement the **IDbTransaction** interface:

```
System::Object
|- System::MarshalByRefObject
   |- System::Data::SqlClient::OleDbTransaction
   |- System::Data::SqlClient::SqlTransaction

Attributes: None
Abstract: No
Sealed: Yes
Implements Interfaces: IDbTransaction, IDisposable
```

The **OleDbTransaction** class properties and methods are summarized in Tables 9.75 and 9.76, and the **SqlTransaction** class properties and methods are listed in Tables 9.77 and 9.78.

Table 9.75 **OleDbTransaction** class properties.

Get/Set	Type	Property	Description
Get	**OleDbConnection***	**Connection**	Specifies the connection object to associate with the transaction.

Table 9.76 **OleDbTransaction** class methods.

Method	Description
OleDbTransaction* Begin()	
OleDbTransaction* Begin(IsolationLevel *level*)	Creates a nested transaction. Optional *level* argument allows specifying the desired transaction isolation level.
void Rollback()	Rolls back the transaction.
~OleDbTransaction()	Destructor.

Table 9.77 **SqlTransaction** class properties.

Get/Set	Type	Property	Description
Get	**SqlConnection***	**Connection**	Specifies the connection object to associate with the transaction.

Table 9.78 **SqlTransaction** class methods.

Method	Description
void Rollback(String* *savePointName*)	Rolls back the transaction changes incurred since the specified savepoint.
void Save(String* *savePointName*)	Creates a savepoint in the transaction.

The OLE DB Data Provider supports nested transactions with lower level transactions initiated using the **OleDbTransaction::Begin** method. The SQL Server Data Provider supports transaction *savepoints*. A savepoint can be used to identify a portion of the current transaction which can be rolled back using the **Rollback** method (i.e., rather than undoing the whole transaction you can undo the changes made since a specified savepoint).

Immediate Solutions

Creating Database Connection String

Making a connection to a database or data source is straightforward by using the **ConnectionString** property to setup a connection string. The key here is that you must set the connection string *prior* to opening a database connection by calling the **Open** method, and the **ConnectionString** may not be modified until the connection is closed. A connection string represents a sequence of semicolon-separated "*keyword=value*" pairs describing the database connection parameters. The actual format of a connection string depends on the ADO.NET data provider used, although the framework supplies the following keywords recognized by most (if not all) providers:

* *Data Source* or *Server* or *Address* or *Addr*: Data source name or database server name or address.

* *Datababse* or *Initial Catalog*: Database file or database name to connect to.

* *User ID* or *UID*: User name for user authentication.

* *Password* or *PWD*: Password for user authentication.

* *Connection Timeout* or *Connect Timeout*: Max number of seconds allotted for establishing a database connection.

* *Pooling*: Indicates whether to use connection pooling (set to *true*) or not (set to *false*), the default is *true*.

Below are a couple of examples of database connection strings for connecting to MS Access database via OLEDB provider and for connecting to a SQL Server database via SQL Server provider:

```
"Provider=Microsoft.Jet.OLEDB.4.0; Data Source=UltramaxMusic.mdb"
"Data Source=localhost; Database=Music; UID=UltraMax; PWD=Resurrection"
```

Creating an OLE DB Connection String

OLE DB connection string must contain an additional keyword: *Provider*. The following OLE DB providers are supported by the .NET OLE DB provider:

* *MSDAORA*: Provider for Oracle.

* *Microsoft.Jet.OLEDB.4.0*: Provider for Microsoft Jet databases (i.e., MS Access).

* *SQLOLEDB*: Provider for SQL Server.

* *MSDataShape*: Microsoft Data Shaping Service provider.

> **NOTE:** OLE DB Provider for ODBC (MSDASQL) is not supported by the .NET OLE DB data provider. To connect to ODBC data sources, you must use the ODBC .NET Data provider available as a free download from Microsoft site.

Here's an example of how you set up an OLE DB connection string to connect to an MS Access database UltramaxMusic.mdb, which is password protected:

```
"Provider=Microsoft.Jet.OLEDB.4.0; Data Source=UltramaxMusic.mdb; UID=Admin; PWD=Admin"
```

Creating a SQL Server Connection String

The ADO.NET data provider for SQL Server understands the following additional connection starting parameters:

* *Integrated Security* or *Trusted_Connection*: Indicates if the connection should be secure (set to *trusted* or *sspi*) or not (set to *false*).

* *Network Library* or *Net*: Specifies SQL Server connection protocol:
  * *dbnmpntw*-Named Pipes
  * *dbmsrpcn*-Multiprotocol
  * *dbmsadsn*-Apple Talk
  * *dbmsgnet*-VIA
  * *dbmsipcn*-Shared Memory
  * *dbmsspxn*-IPX/SPX
  * *dbmssocn*-TCP/IP (default)

* *Packet Size*: Specifies SQL Server packet size in bytes (default is 8192).

* *Workstation ID*: Client workstation ID (default is local computer name).

Here's an example of how you set up a SQL Server connection string for connecting to a remote SQL Server database using TCP/IP and trusted connection (trusted connection means that the credentials of the currently logged-in user will be used to authenticate the SQL Server connectivity request):

```
"Data Source=10.10.10.164; Database=Music; Net=dbmssocn; Integrated Security=trusted"
```

Alternatively, you can disable integrated security and explicitly specify SQL Server login and password:

```
"Data Source=10.10.10.164; Database=Music; Net=dbmssocn; Integrated Security=false; UID=UltraMax;
PWD=Resurrection"
```

If you decide not to use integrated security, you must create a new SQL Server user (e.g., using the SQL Server Enterprise Manager) that you will use for authentication.

Controlling Connection Pooling

Database connections closed with the **Close** method are usually not destroyed immediately to improve performance. Instead, the framework maintains a pool of active connections and draws connection objects from the pool. Thus, if you close a database connection using the **Close** method, the database connection will not be closed but it will be added to the pool. If at a later time your code or another application requests a database connection, the framework first conducts a search on the connection pool to see if there are active connections with the matching connection string. If a matching connection is found, it is returned to the requester. If one is not found a new connection is created.

> WARNING! **If you do not explicitly** Close **or** Dispose **a connection, it will not be returned to the connection pool and thus will not be reused.**

The connection pool helps eliminate the wait associated with opening and closing database connections. This encourages a programming practice where you create connection objects when you need to read or write database data and dispose of the connection as soon as you done are reading or writing the data. An alternative approach would be to create a single connection and keep it open for the lifetime of the application. Unfortunately, this defeats the purpose of the connection pools and is not recommended for server components, which can be instantiated multiple times (i.e., components serving web requests).

You can control connection pooling by specifying the *Pooling* keyword in a connection string. If you set the *Pooling* parameter in a connection string to *false* the corresponding connection will not be pooled.

Also, you can also control the lifetime of an individual connection in the pool by setting the *Connection Lifetime* value in the connection string. When a connection is returned to the connection pool, its lifetime is calculated by subtracting the connection creation time, and the connection is returned to the pool if its calculated lifetime is less than the *Connection Lifetime* value specified in the connection string.

You may wish to reduce the connection lifetime to minimize the number of open database connections. The side effect of this is that you can potentially improve database server performance, since the server would not have to maintain large numbers of unused but open connections and can release the associated resources.

Here is an example of a SQL Server connection string that sets the connection lifetime to 100 seconds and draws the connection object from the pool (if the appropriate connection object cannot be found in the pool, a new connection will be created and added to the pool):

```
"Data Source=localhost; Database=master; UID=sa; PWD=; Connection Lifetime=100; Pooling=true"
```

> **NOTE:** When designing your connect string for connection pooling keep in mind that open connections are retrieved from the pool by conducting a search on the connection string text. Thus, to take advantage of the connection pooling you must use the same connection string every time you connect to the database. If you modify the original connection string (e.g., by adding more or specifying different connection parameters) a new connection object will be created and added to the pool.

Creating Database Connections

To retrieve data from a database you must establish a database connection by instantiating a connection object corresponding to a desired ADO.NET data provider (e.g., OLE DB or SQL Server), specify a connection string containing the name of the database/data source and optionally database/catalog, user name and password information, and open the connection using the **Open** method. The code example shown next demonstrates how to open OLE DB and SQL Server connections and performs the following steps:

1. Creates a connection to a MS Access database using the **OleDbConnection** class.
2. Hooks-up a handler to the **InfoMessage** event for reporting OLE DB provider errors and notification messages.
3. Opens the OLE DB data connection using the **OleDbConnection::Open** method.
4. Creates a connection to a SQL Server 7.0 database using the **SqlConnection** class.
5. Opens the SQL Server connection using the **SqlConnection::Open** method.
6. Reports the SQL Server connection information including database name, server version, and workstation I
7. Closes database connections by calling the **Close** method.

```
#using <mscorlib.dll>
#using <system.dll>
#using <system.data.dll>
using namespace System;
using namespace System::Data::OleDb;
using namespace System::Data::SqlClient;


// Event handler class
__gc struct MyEventHandler {
    static void OleDbInfoMessage(Object* sender, OleDbInfoMessageEventArgs* e)
    {
        Console::WriteLine(e->Message);
    }
};


void main()
```

```cpp
{
    OleDbConnection* MyOleDbConnection;
    SqlConnection* MySqlConnection;
    try {
        // 1. Create OLE DB connection for ODBC MS Access driver
        MyOleDbConnection = new OleDbConnection(
            "Provider=Microsoft.Jet.OLEDB.4.0;\
            Data Source=MyDatabase.mdb");

        // 2. Hook up the InfoMessage delegate
        MyOleDbConnection->InfoMessage += new OleDbInfoMessageEventHandler(0,
            MyEventHandler::OleDbInfoMessage);

        // 3. Open OLE DB connection
        MyOleDbConnection->Open();

        // 4. Create SQL Server connection
        MySqlConnection = new SqlConnection("Data Source=localhost;\
            Database=Music; UID=UltraMax; PWD=Resurrection");

        // 5. Open SQL Server the connection
        MySqlConnection->Open();

        // 6. Report SQL Server connection information
        Console::WriteLine("        Database: {0}", MySqlConnection->Database);
        Console::WriteLine("      DataSource: {0}", MySqlConnection->DataSource);
        Console::WriteLine(" ServerVersion: {0}",
            MySqlConnection->ServerVersion);
        Console::WriteLine("Workstation ID: {0}",
            MySqlConnection->WorkstationId);
    }
    catch(Exception* e) {
        Console::WriteLine(e->Message);
    }
    __finally {
        // 7. Close connections
        if ( MyOleDbConnection ) MyOleDbConnection->Close();
        if ( MySqlConnection ) MySqlConnection->Close();
    }
}
```

NOTE: All database operations in the code sample shown here are performed inside of a try-catch block with the database connections being closed in the __**finally** block. It is important to close database connections using the **Close** or **Dispose** methods when you no longer use them so that the connection can be returned to the connection pool. Although the garbage collector will eventually close the connection when finalizing the connection object, the connection will not be returned to the pool until the garbage collection occurs.

Creating and Executing Database Commands

The easiest way to interact with a database is by executing database commands corresponding to desired SQL statements. To issue a database command you must instantiate an ADO.NET data provider command object, initialize it with the command text, and execute the command using one of the **ExecuteReader**, **ExecuteNonQuery**, or **ExecuteScalar** methods. The sample code shown next demonstrates instantiation and execution of OLE DB commands and performs the following steps:

1. Creates and opens an OLE DB connection to MS Access database.

2. Creates an OLE DB command using the **OleDbConnection::CreateCommand** method and initializes the **CommandText** with a SQL SELECT statement.

3. For demonstration purposes, creates an OLE DB command using the **OleDbCommand** constructor with the command text supplied as the constructor parameter.

4. Executes the command to obtain a single result using the **ExecuteScalar** method.

5. Changes the command text, executes a nonquery DELETE command that does not return any results, and reports the number of affected (deleted) records.

```
#using <mscorlib.dll>
#using <system.dll>
#using <system.data.dll>
using namespace System;
using namespace System::Data::OleDb;

void main()
{
    OleDbConnection* MyOleDbConnection;
    try {
        // 1. Create OLE DB connection for MS Access database
        MyConnection = new OleDbConnection(
            "Provider=Microsoft.Jet.OLEDB.4.0;\
            Data Source=UltraMax-Music.mdb");
        MyConnection->Open();

        // 2. Create command and specify command text
        OleDbCommand* MyCommand = MyConnection->CreateCommand();
            MyCommand->CommandText = "SELECT COUNT(*) FROM Music";

        // 3. Or create command using the constructor
        MyCommand = new OleDbCommand("SELECT COUNT(*) FROM Music", MyConnection);

        // 4. Execute command to obtain single value
        Object* Count = MyCommand->ExecuteScalar();
        Console::WriteLine("There are {0} songs in the Music table", Count);

        // 5. Change command text
        MyCommand->CommandText = "DELETE FROM Music WHERE Genre='Neoclassical'";
```

```
        // Execute non-query command
        int RecordsAffected = MyCommand->ExecuteNonQuery();
        Console::WriteLine("{0} songs were deleted from the Music table",
            __box(RecordsAffected));
    }
    catch(Exception* e) {
        Console::WriteLine(e->Message);
    }
    __finally {
        MyConnection->Close();
    }
}
```

> **NOTE:** The **ExecuteScalar** method returns the value of the first column in the first row of the command result set and thus can be used with commands that return multiple rows.

Creating and Executing Parameterized Commands

Database commands frequently rely on parameters to specify additional information such as query limits or new column values for an inserted row. In OLE DB commands, parameters are identified either by a question mark ('?') or by '@'-prefixed name, e.g., '@Genre'. SQL Server command parameters are always identified by '@' prefixed name. Once you construct a command object and specify a command text referring to parameter names, you must instantiate parameter objects and add them to the **Parameters** collection of the command. The parameter name and type must match the parameter name and type in the command text. (The parameter type is inferred from the database schema.) You must assign values to all input parameters involved in the parameterized command prior to executing the command.

The code example shown next demonstrates how to create commands with parameters and specify parameter values. The code performs the following steps:

1. Creates an **OleDbCommand** that uses a parameter named "@Genre."

2. For demonstration purposes, constructs an **OleDbParameter** object named "@Genre" using the constructor, sets the parameter **Direction** to **Input**, and sets the parameter **Value**.

3. Adds the parameter to the command **Parameters** collection using the **Add** method.

4. Executes the command and prints the result of the parameterized query.

```
#using <mscorlib.dll>
#using <system.dll>
#using <system.data.dll>
using namespace System;
using namespace System::Data;
using namespace System::Data::OleDb;

void main()
{
    OleDbConnection* MyConnection;
```

```
try {
    // Create OLE DB connection for MS Access database
    MyConnection = new OleDbConnection(
        "Provider=Microsoft.Jet.OLEDB.4.0;\
        Data Source=UltraMax-Music.mdb");
    MyConnection->Open();
    // Create Command
    OleDbCommand* MyCommand = new OleDbCommand(
        "SELECT COUNT(*) FROM Music WHERE Genre=@Genre",
        MyConnection);

    // 1. Create command parameter using constructor
    OleDbParameter* Parameter = new OleDbParameter("@Genre",
        OleDbType::Char);
    // 2. Set parameter direction and value
    Parameter->Direction = ParameterDirection::Input;
    Parameter->Value = S"Techno/Classical";

    // 3. Add parameter to the Command
    MyCommand->Parameters->Add(Parameter);

    // 4. Execute command
    Object* Count = MyCommand->ExecuteScalar();
    // Report parameter value
    Console::WriteLine("Count = {0}", Count);
}
catch(Exception* e) {
    Console::WriteLine(e->Message);
}
__finally {
    MyConnection->Close();
}
}
```

NOTE: If you forget to specify a value of an input parameter, the framework will throw an exception when you execute the command. To set the parameter value to database NULL, you must initialize the parameter **Value** property with **DBNull**, not C++ null or zero.

Invoking Stored Procedures

Follow these steps to invoke a stored procedure:

1. Create a command object with **CommandText** set to the stored procedure name and **CommandType** set to **StoredProcedure**.

2. Create command parameters manually or derive them automatically by calling the **DeriveParameters** method. If you create parameters manually, you must specify '@'-prefixed parameter names that match the names of the stored procedure parameters. If a stored procedure returns a value, you must create an additional parameter named "RETURN_VALUE" of type **ReturnValue** and add it to the **Parameters**

collection of the command.

3.	Specify values for all parameters of type **Input** and **InputOutput** and execute the command using the **ExecuteScalar**, **ExecuteReader**, or **ExecuteNonQuery** methods. The **Output** parameters and the return value parameter will receive values when the call completes.

The code example shown next demonstrates how to invoke a SQL Server stored procedure called "GetMusicByGenre." The procedure accepts a single input parameter, "@Genre," and returns a single value. First, the **DeriveParameters** method is used to obtain parameter information. Then, for demonstration purposes, the **Parameters** collection is cleared using the **Clear** method and the parameters are added manually. Finally, the command is executed using the **ExecuteNonQuery** method and the value of the "RETURN_VALUE" parameter is displayed.

```
#using <mscorlib.dll>
#using <system.dll>
#using <system.data.dll>
#using <system.xml.dll>
using namespace System;
using namespace System::Data;
using namespace System::Data::SqlClient;

void main()
{
    SqlConnection* MyConnection;
    try {
        // 1. Create OLE DB connection for MS Access database
        MyConnection = new SqlConnection("Data Source=localhost;\
            Database=Music; UID=UltraMax; PWD=Resurrection");
        MyConnection->Open();

        // 2. Create Command for store procedure
        SqlCommand* MyCommand = new SqlCommand("GetMusicByGenre",
            MyConnection);
        MyCommand->CommandType = CommandType::StoredProcedure;

        // 3. Derive stored procedure parameter information automatically
        SqlCommandBuilder::DeriveParameters(MyCommand);

        // 4. Report parameter information
        for ( int i = 0; i < MyCommand->Parameters->Count; i++ )
            Console::WriteLine("Name={0}; Type={1}; Direction={2}",
                MyCommand->Parameters->Item[i]->ParameterName,
                __box(MyCommand->Parameters->Item[i]->DbType),
                __box(MyCommand->Parameters->Item[i]->Direction));

        // 5. Clear parameter collection to add parameters manually
        MyCommand->Parameters->Clear();
```

```
    // 6. Add input parameter
    MyCommand->Parameters->Add("@Genre", SqlDbType::Char);
    MyCommand->Parameters->Item["@Genre"]->Value = S"Techno/Classical";

    // 7. Add return value parameters
    SqlParameter* RetValParameter = new SqlParameter("RETURN_VALUE",
        SqlDbType::Int);
    RetValParameter->Direction = ParameterDirection::ReturnValue;
    MyCommand->Parameters->Add(RetValParameter);

    // 8. Execute command
    MyCommand->ExecuteNonQuery();

    // 9. Report count returned by the stored procedure
    Console::WriteLine("Count = {0}",
        MyCommand->Parameters->Item["RETURN_VALUE"]->Value);
}
catch(Exception* e) {
    Console::WriteLine(e->Message);
}
__finally {
    MyConnection->Close();
}
}
```

Using Data Readers to Retrieve Database Data

Typically, a database SELECT command produces a result set, which can contain one or more data rows with each row containing one or more data columns. To read the command result set, you can create a data reader object using the command's **ExecuteReader** method. Then, you can forward-navigate the data reader rows using the **Read** method and obtain column values using the **GetValue** method. To illustrate reading a command result set data rows consider the code example below, which performs the following actions:

1. Creates an OLE DB command and executes it using the **ExecuteReader** method, which returns a pointer to the **OleDbDataReader** object.

2. Retrieves the result set schema information using the **GetSchemaTable** method.

3. Forward-navigates the command result set rows by invoking the **Read** method on the **OleDbDataReader** object until the **Read** method returns **false** indicating that the last data row in the current result set have been read.

4. Retrieves titles, data types, and values of the columns in the current result set row by using the data reader **GetName**, **GetDataTypeName**, and **GetValue** methods.

5. Forward-navigates the result sets (in case the command produces more than one result set), using the **NextResult** method until the **NextResult** method returns **false** indicating that all result sets have been processed.

    NOTE: After calling the **ExecuteReader** method, the data reader points to the first result set returned by the command. However, the current data row is not loaded until the **Read** method is invoked.

```cpp
#using <mscorlib.dll>
#using <system.dll>
#using <system.data.dll>
using namespace System;
using namespace System::Data;
using namespace System::Data::OleDb;

void main()
{
    OleDbConnection* MyConnection;
    try {
        // Create OLE DB connection for MS Access database
        MyConnection = new OleDbConnection(
            "Provider=Microsoft.Jet.OLEDB.4.0;\
            Data Source=UltraMax-Music.mdb");
        MyConnection->Open();
        // Create command
        OleDbCommand* MyCommand = new OleDbCommand("SELECT * FROM Music",
            MyConnection);

        // 1. Execute command and create DataReader
        OleDbDataReader* MyReader = MyCommand->ExecuteReader();

        do {
            // 2. Get schema information
            DataTable* SchemaTable = MyReader->GetSchemaTable();
            // 3. Navigate reader rows
            while ( MyReader->Read() )
            {
                for ( int i = 0; i < MyReader->FieldCount; i++ )
                    // 4. Print column header and value
                    Console::WriteLine("{0} ({1}):\t{2}", MyReader->GetName(i),
                        MyReader->GetDataTypeName(i), MyReader->GetValue(i));
                Console::WriteLine();
            }
        // 5. Navigate result sets
        } while ( MyReader->NextResult() );
    }
    catch(Exception* e) {
        Console::WriteLine(e->Message);
    }
    __finally {
        MyConnection->Close();
    }
}
```

NOTE: OLE DB data provider for Microsoft Jet databases does not support batches of semicolon-separated SQL statements, while OLE DB provider for SQL Server (SQLOLEDB) and ADO.NET SQL Server providers do.

Reading Hierarchal OLE DB Result Sets

The ADO.NET data provider for OLE DB allows you to generate hierarchal result sets using the Microsoft Data Shaping Services for OLE DB. The Data Shaping Services provider supports combining database tables fetched by another OLE DB provider in a hierarchal structure, where individual tables are linked by means of parent/child relations. The Data Shaping Services provider uses special keywords for expressing hierarchal relations between tables in an OLE DB command text:

* SHAPE { *parent table SQL statement* } AS *ParentAlias*: Specifies a parent table.

* APPEND ({ *child table SQL statement* } AS *ChildAlias* RELATE *PK* TO *FK*) AS *ChapterAlias*: Specifies a child table including the relation between the parent and this child table expressed as a parent table column (*PK*) to child table column (*FK*) mapping.

   NOTE: The AS *alias* directive is optional.

When a result set, which is a part of a parent/child relation, is read using an **OleDbDataReader**, the child rows of the current row are returned in another **OleDbDataReader** object called *chapter*, which is stored in the last column of the row. This allows you to navigate the nested rows (chapters) by navigating the nested **OleDbDataReader** reader objects of each row.

The code example shown next illustrates hierarchal OLE DB data navigation:

1. The Data Shaping Services provider is used to join "Music" and "Genre" tables stored in the MS Access database, with "Music" table being a child of the "Genre."

2. The **TraverseReader** function is executed on the top-level reader obtained using the **ExecuteReader** method.

The **TraverseReader** function reads all rows of the current result set using the **Read** method. If any of the columns in the current row correspond to OLE DB chapters (i.e., the column type is **OleDbDataReader**), then the **TraverseReader** function is recursively executed on the nested data reader. The data reader **Depth** property contains the value indicative of the level of nesting, which is used to indent the output of the function.

```
#using <mscorlib.dll>
#using <system.dll>
#using <system.data.dll>
using namespace System;
using namespace System::Data;
using namespace System::Data::OleDb;

// Routine for printing reader rows including child rows
void TraverseReader(OleDbDataReader* Reader)
{
    while ( Reader->Read() )
        for ( int i = 0; i < Reader->FieldCount; i++ )
        {
            Object* Value = Reader->GetValue(i);
            // Check to see if the column corresponds to OLE DB chapter
            if ( Value->GetType() == __typeof(OleDbDataReader) )
                // Recursively print rows
```

```
            TraverseReader(static_cast<OleDbDataReader*>(Value));
         // Indent
         Console::Write(new String(' ', Reader->Depth*2));
         // Print column header and value
         Console::WriteLine("{0} ({1}):\t{2}", Reader->GetName(i),
            Reader->GetDataTypeName(i), Value);
      }
}

void main()
{
   OleDbConnection* MyConnection;
   try {
      // 1. Create OLE DB connection for MS Access database
      MyConnection = new OleDbConnection("Provider=MSDataShape;\
         Data Provider=Microsoft.Jet.OLEDB.4.0;\
         Data Source=UltraMax-Music.mdb");
      MyConnection->Open();


      // 2. Create command for retrieving hierarchal data
      // using OLE DB Data Shaping Service
      OleDbCommand* MyCommand = new OleDbCommand(
         "SHAPE {SELECT Name, Description FROM Genre}\
         APPEND ({SELECT GenreName, Title, Duration FROM Music}\
         AS MusicByGenre\
         RELATE Name TO GenreName)",
         MyConnection);

      // 3. Execute command and navigate reader hierarchy
      TraverseReader(MyCommand->ExecuteReader());
   }
   catch(Exception* e) {
      Console::WriteLine(e->Message);
   }
   __finally {
      MyConnection->Close();
   }
}
```

Using Data Readers with Sequential Access to Read BLOB Data

When you read a command result set using a data reader object, the entire data row is transmitted to the client each time you move to the next row. If a data row contains many columns or the columns contain large values (e.g., large binary objects-BLOBs), your code may consume a noticeable chunk of network bandwidth and client memory for transmission and allocation of row data. You can use the sequential access to the data row data by setting the **CommandBehavior** property to **SequentialAccess** to control exactly how many bytes of each data row to transmit. Then, you can fetch data row columns sequentially using the **GetData** method or you can access the data row data on byte level using the **GetBytes** method, transmitting as much or as little data as necessary.

The code example shown next implements fetching MP3 files from a Microsoft Access database and writing the files to disk. The MP3 data is stored in the "MP3Data" column of the "MP3Storage" table. The code performs the following steps:

1. Creates a SELECT command for the "MP3Storage" by constructing the **OleDbCommand** object. The SELECT statement is written such that the BLOB column is the last column in the result set.

2. Executes the command and creates the **OleDbReader** configured for sequential access (**CommandBehavior::SequentialAccess**).

3. Allocates an I/O buffer for fetching row data.

4. Fetches current row using the **Read** method.

5. Fetches the first column in the data row using the **GetValue** method to obtain an MP3 name.

6. Fetches MP3 data from the second column into the I/O buffer using the **GetBytes** method and writes the buffer to the file until there is no more data left in the current row.

```
#using <mscorlib.dll>
#using <system.dll>
#using <system.data.dll>
using namespace System;
using namespace System::Data;
using namespace System::IO;
using namespace System::Data::OleDb;

void main()
{
    OleDbConnection* MyConnection;
    try {
        // Create OLE DB connection for MS Access database
        MyConnection = new OleDbConnection(
            "Provider=Microsoft.Jet.OLEDB.4.0;\
            Data Source=UltraMax-Music.mdb");
        MyConnection->Open();
        // 1. Create command for reading BLOB data
        OleDbCommand* MyCommand = new OleDbCommand(
            "SELECT FileName, MP3Data FROM MP3Storage", MyConnection);

        // 2. Execute command and create DataReader for sequential access
        OleDbDataReader* MyReader = MyCommand->ExecuteReader(
            CommandBehavior::SequentialAccess);
        // 3. Allocate file I/O buffer
        unsigned char buffer __gc[] = new unsigned char __gc[65536];

        // 4. Read rows and dump them to files
```

```
while ( MyReader->Read() )
{
    // 5. Get file name from the first field
    String* FileName = __try_cast<String*>(MyReader->GetValue(0));
    // 6. Create file
    FileStream* fs = new FileStream(FileName, FileMode::Create);

    __int64 BytesRead, Position = 0;
    // 7. Read data from DataReader and dump it to file
    while ( BytesRead = MyReader->GetBytes(1, Position, buffer,
        0, buffer->Count) )
    {
        fs->Write(buffer, 0, (int)BytesRead);
        // Keep track of total bytes written
        Position += BytesRead;
    }
    // Report bytes written
    Console::WriteLine("{0} bytes written to {1} file",
        __box(Position), FileName);
    // Close file
    fs->Close();
    }
}
catch(Exception* e) {
    Console::WriteLine(e->Message);
}
__finally {
    MyConnection->Close();
}
}
```

NOTE: When reading fields using sequential access, it is a good idea to arrange columns in the result set in the order of importance with the most important columns coming first. In this way, you can examine the bigger columns first and decide whether to transmit subsequent columns, thus saving the bandwidth and improve the code's performance.

Filling Dataset Schemas

Before loading a **DataSet** with database data of unknown structure, you can call the **FillSchema** method to create the necessary structure in the **DataSet**. The **FillSchema** method creates **DataTable**, **DataColumn**, and **DataRelation** objects corresponding to the type of data retrieved by the **FillSchema** method. The **FillSchema** method initializes the following **DataColumn** properties based on the database schema information: **AllowDBNull, AutoIncrement, AutoIncrementStep, AutoIncrementSeed, MaxLength, ReadOnly**, and **Unique**. The schema information is retrieved from a database using the **SelectCommand** of the **DataAdapter** object. Alternatively, you can specify your own SELECT command in the *command* parameter to the **FillSchema** method.

The **Fill/FillSchema** methods assign names to unnamed columns using the following pattern: The first unnamed column remains unnamed, and each subsequent column is assigned a numeric name, e.g., "", "1", "2", and so on. Columns with duplicate names are automatically numbered, e.g., "*column*", "*column*1", "*column*2", and so on.

> **NOTE:** Filling schemas from database data is similar to reading/inferring schemas from XML documents. Unlike with XML documents, you cannot write **DataSet/DataTable** schema to database.

Using Data Adapters to Fill Datasets

You can use the data adapter **File** method to fill an empty **DataSet** with database data. If the data adapter **MissingSchemaAction** is set to **Add** (default) or **AddWithKey**, a new table (or tables representing hierarchal result set) will be added to the **DataSet** and loaded with database data. To replicate only the schema of a database data, you should use the **FillSchema** method, which creates dataset schema based on the database data including constraints and primary keys. The code example shown next demonstrates filling a **DataSet** using the data adapter **Fill** method. The code performs the following actions:

1. Creates an **OleDbDataAdapter** object for reading "Music" table and an empty **DataSet**.

2. Sets the data adapter **MissingSchemaAction** property to **Add** and fills the **DataSet** using the **Fill** method.

3. Creates an **OleDbDataAdapter** object for readingthe "Genre" table.

4. Extends the **DataSet** schema to accommodate the "Genre" table using the **FillSchema** method. (The **FillSchema** method creates a new "Genre" **DataTable** in the **DataSet**.)

5. Fills the "Genre" table in the **DataSet** using the data adapter **Fill** method.

6. Verifies that the "Genre" **DataTable** is populated properly, including primary key values, by conducting a search on the primary key using the **Find** method.

```
#using <mscorlib.dll>
#using <system.dll>
#using <system.data.dll>
#using <system.xml.dll>
using namespace System;
using namespace System::Data;
using namespace System::Data::OleDb;

void main()
{
    OleDbConnection* MyConnection;
    try {
        // Create OLE DB connection for MS Access database
        MyConnection = new OleDbConnection(
            "Provider=Microsoft.Jet.OLEDB.4.0;\
            Data Source=UltraMax-Music.mdb");
        MyConnection->Open();

        // 1. Create DataAdapter and DataSet
        OleDbDataAdapter* DataAdapter = new OleDbDataAdapter(
            "SELECT * FROM Music", MyConnection);
```

```
    // Create DataSet
    DataSet* MyDataSet = new DataSet();

    // 2. Fill Music table (PK and constraints are not filled)
    DataAdapter->MissingSchemaAction = MissingSchemaAction::Add;
    DataAdapter->Fill(MyDataSet, "Music");

    // 3. Set new DataAdapter SELECT command
    DataAdapter->SelectCommand = new OleDbCommand(
        "SELECT * FROM Genre", MyConnection);

    // 4. Fill schema of the Genre table (including PK and constraints)
    DataAdapter->FillSchema(MyDataSet, SchemaType::Source, "Genre");

    // 5. Fill Genre table
    DataAdapter->Fill(MyDataSet, "Genre");

    // 6. Test the primary keys
    DataRow* Row = MyDataSet->Tables->Item["Genre"]->Rows->Find(
        S"Techno/Classical");
    if ( Row )
        Console::WriteLine("{0} = {1}!", Row->Item["Name"],
            Row->Item["Description"]);
    // Will throw an exception
    Row = MyDataSet->Tables->Item["Music"]->Rows->Find(S"Anything");
}
catch(Exception* e) {
    Console::WriteLine(e->Message);
}
__finally {
    MyConnection->Close();
}
}
```

Related solution: Found on page:
Creating Datasets, Adding Tables, and Establishing Relations   Chapter 8

Setting Up Column and Table Mappings

When filling a **DataSet** that already has schema with database data, you may have to specify table and column mappings for the data adapter to establish correspondence between the dataset **DataTable/DataColumn** objects and the database tables/columns. The names of **DataSet** tables/columns do not have to match the names of database tables/columns, but the target data column's data types must be compatible or the **Fill** operation may fail.

The table mappings are specified by adding elements to the **TableMappings** collection of a data adapter object, while column mappings are specified for each **TableMapping** object contained in the **TableMappings** collection by adding elements to the **ColumnMappings** collection. The code example shown next illustrates filling a dataset, which already contains schema, with database data, using the table and column mappings. The code performs the following steps:

1. Creates an **OleDbDataAdapter** object for reading "Music" table.

2. Creates a **DataSet** containing a "New Music" table with "Track Title" and "Track Duration" columns.

3. Creates a table mapping for the data adapter using the **TableMappingsCollection::Add** method, which maps the database "Music" table into the **DataSet** "New Music" **DataTable**.

4. Creates column mappings for the table mapping using the **ColumnMappingsCollection::Add** method: the "Title" database column is mapped into a "Track Title" **DataTable** column, and so on.

5. Fills the **DataSet** using the data adapter table/column mappings and ignores missing schema (**MissingSchemaAction = Ignore**).

6. Displays the content of the **DataSet** "New Music" table to verify the success of the **Fill** operation.

```cpp
#using <mscorlib.dll>
#using <system.dll>
#using <system.data.dll>
#using <system.xml.dll>
using namespace System;
using namespace System::Data;
using namespace System::Data::Common;
using namespace System::Data::OleDb;

void main()
{
    OleDbConnection* MyConnection;
    try {
        // Create OLE DB connection for MS Access database
        MyConnection = new OleDbConnection(
            "Provider=Microsoft.Jet.OLEDB.4.0;
            Data Source=UltraMax-Music.mdb");
        MyConnection->Open();

        // 1. Create DataAdapter
        OleDbDataAdapter* DataAdapter = new OleDbDataAdapter(
            "SELECT * FROM Music", MyConnection);

        // 2. Create DataSet
        DataSet* MyDataSet = new DataSet();
        // Add 'New Music' table to the DataSet
        DataTable* NewMusic = MyDataSet->Tables->Add("New Music");
        NewMusic->Columns->Add("Track Title");
        NewMusic->Columns->Add("Track Duration");

        // 3. Create Table Mappings
        DataTableMapping* MyMapping = DataAdapter->TableMappings->Add(
```

```
                "Music", "New Music");

      // 4. Create Column Mappings
      MyMapping->ColumnMappings->Add("Title", "Track Title");
      MyMapping->ColumnMappings->Add("Duration", "Track Duration");

      // 5. Fill 'New Music' ignoring schema inconsistencies
      DataAdapter->MissingSchemaAction = MissingSchemaAction::Ignore;
      DataAdapter->Fill(MyDataSet, "Music");

      // 6. Display 'New Music' table content
      for ( int i = 0; i < NewMusic->Rows->Count; i++ )
        Console::WriteLine("{0}: {1}",
          NewMusic->Rows->Item[i]->Item["Track Title"],
            NewMusic->Rows->Item[i]->Item["Track Duration"]);
   }
   catch(Exception* e) {
      Console::WriteLine(e->Message);
   }
   __finally {
      MyConnection->Close();
   }
}
```

Building Update, Delete and Insert Commands and Updating a Database with Dataset Changes

Data adapters allow updating database data with changes made to the **DataSet** by means of the **Update** method. The **Update** method executes data adapters **UpdateCommand**, **DeleteCommand**, and **InsertCommand** to reconcile **DataSet** changes with the database data. Thus, to use the **Update** method you either have to create the data reader commands manually or you can generate them automatically using the command builder object.

The code example shown next demonstrates automatic generation of data reader commands and updates database with the dataset changes. The code performs the following steps:

1.   Creates an **OleDbDataAdapter** using the "SELECT * FROM Music" command.
2.   Creates an **OleDbCommandBuilder** for the data adapter object using the constructor.
3.   Sets the data adapter update, delete, and insert commands using the command builder **GetUpdateCommand**, **GetDeleteCommand**, and **GetInsertCommand** methods.
4.   Creates a **DataSet**, fills it with the database data, and changes it by modifying, adding, and deleting rows.
5.   Updates database data with the **DataSet** changes by invoking the data adapter **Update** method.

```
#using <mscorlib.dll>
#using <system.dll>
#using <system.data.dll>
#using <system.xml.dll>
```

```cpp
using namespace System;
using namespace System::Data;
using namespace System::Data::OleDb;

void main()
{
    OleDbConnection* MyConnection;
    try {
        // Create OLE DB connection for MS Access database
        OleDbConnection* MyConnection = new OleDbConnection(
            "Provider=Microsoft.Jet.OLEDB.4.0;\
             Data Source=UltraMax-Music.mdb");
        MyConnection->Open();
        // 1. Create DataAdapter
        OleDbDataAdapter* DataAdapter = new OleDbDataAdapter(
            "SELECT * FROM Music", MyConnection);

        // 2. Create command builder
        OleDbCommandBuilder* CmdBuilder = new OleDbCommandBuilder(DataAdapter);
        // 3. Build commands
        DataAdapter->UpdateCommand = CmdBuilder->GetUpdateCommand();
        DataAdapter->DeleteCommand = CmdBuilder->GetDeleteCommand();
        DataAdapter->InsertCommand = CmdBuilder->GetInsertCommand();

        // 4. Create DataSet and fill it with database data
        DataSet* MyDataSet = new DataSet();
        // Make sure that PK is created
        DataAdapter->MissingSchemaAction = MissingSchemaAction::AddWithKey;
        DataAdapter->Fill(MyDataSet);

        // Modify DataSet data
        DataTable* MyTable = MyDataSet->Tables->Item[0];
        // Delete
        DataRow* Row = MyTable->Rows->Find(S"Consequential2");
        if ( Row ) Row->Delete();
        // Update
        Row = MyTable->Rows->Find(S"Sweet Harp");
        if ( Row ) Row->Item["Title"] = S"Sweet Harp (Classical Mix)";
        // Insert
        Row = MyTable->NewRow();
        Row->Item["Title"] = S"Consequential (Classical Mix)";
        Row->Item["GenreName"] = S"Classical";
        Row->Item["Duration"] = S"4:20";
        MyTable->Rows->Add(Row);
        // 5. Update DataSet
        DataAdapter->Update(MyDataSet);
```

```
   }
   catch(Exception* e) {
      Console::WriteLine(e->Message);
   }
   __finally {
      MyConnection->Close();
   }
}
```

Handling Data Adapter Events

A data adapter object can fire events when an error occurs while filling a **DataSet** (**FillError** event) or before and after a database row is updated (**RowUpdating** and **RowUpdated** events). You can hook up your own event handlers to the data adapter events to specify a custom action for handling **Fill** errors (e.g., whether to continue filling dataset or abort), and to specify custom action for handling **Update** errors (e.g., **SkipCurrentRow**, **SkipAllRemainingRows**, and so on).

The following code example illustrates how to handle data adapter events when filling a **DataSet** with database data and how to update the database with the **DataSet** data. The code performs the following steps:

1.   Attaches event handler delegates to the **FillError** and **RowUpdated** events of an **OleDbDataAdapter** object.

2.   Fills a **DataSet** with the database data. The **FillError** event handler (**MyEventHandler::FillError** method) instructs the data adapter to continue the **Fill** operation when a fill error occurs, by setting the **FillErrorEventArgs::Continue** property to **true**.

3.   Modifies **DataSet** data to violate the database foreign key constraint. Although the **DataSet** does not have the constraints enforced, setting a row "Genre" column value to "Trance" will cause FK constraint violation when attempting to update the row in the database because there is not a "Trance" entry in the "Genre" table in the database. (The "Genre" table is a parent table for the "Music" table loaded into the data adapter.)

The **MyEventHandler::RowUpdated** method attached to the data adapter **RowUpdated** event examines the **Status** property of the **OleDbRowUpdatedEventArgs** to see if an error occurred (**Status = ErrorsOccurred**), reports the primary key value of the row that was not updated due to the error, and instructs the data adapter to continue the **Update** operation by setting the **Status** property to the **SkipCurrentRow** value.

```
#using <mscorlib.dll>
#using <system.dll>
#using <system.data.dll>
#using <system.xml.dll>
using namespace System;
using namespace System::Data;
using namespace System::Data::OleDb;

// Class for handling fill errors
__gc struct MyEventHandler {
   static void FillError(Object* sender, FillErrorEventArgs* e)
```

```
    {
        // Always continue
        e->Continue = true;
    }
    static void RowUpdated(Object* sender, OleDbRowUpdatedEventArgs* e)
    {
        // Skip records that cause update errors
        if ( e->Status == UpdateStatus::ErrorsOccurred )
        {
            e->Status = UpdateStatus::SkipCurrentRow;
            Console::WriteLine("Error occurred in row with PK='{0}'",
                e->Row->Item[e->Row->Table->PrimaryKey[0]->ColumnName]);
        }
    }
};

void main()
{
    OleDbConnection* MyConnection;
    try {
        // Create OLE DB connection for MS Access database
        OleDbConnection* MyConnection = new OleDbConnection(
            "Provider=Microsoft.Jet.OLEDB.4.0;\
            Data Source=UltraMax-Music.mdb");
        MyConnection->Open();
        // Create DataAdapter
        OleDbDataAdapter* DataAdapter = new OleDbDataAdapter(
            "SELECT * FROM Music", MyConnection);
        // Create command builder
        OleDbCommandBuilder* CmdBuilder = new OleDbCommandBuilder(
            DataAdapter);
        DataAdapter->UpdateCommand = CmdBuilder->GetUpdateCommand();

        // 1. Attach FillError and RowUpdated event handlers
        DataAdapter->FillError += new FillErrorEventHandler(0,
            MyEventHandler::FillError);
        DataAdapter->RowUpdated += new OleDbRowUpdatedEventHandler(0,
            MyEventHandler::RowUpdated);

        // 2. Create DataSet and fill it with database data
        DataSet* MyDataSet = new DataSet();
        // Make sure that PK is created
        DataAdapter->MissingSchemaAction = MissingSchemaAction::AddWithKey;
        DataAdapter->Fill(MyDataSet);

        // Modify DataSet data
```

```
        DataTable* MyTable = MyDataSet->Tables->Item[0];
        DataRow* Row = MyTable->Rows->Find(S"EnTrance");
        // Violates FK constraint, the row will not be updated
        if ( Row ) Row->Item["GenreName"] = S"Trance";
        // This row will be updated
        Row = MyTable->Rows->Find(S"Automatic");
        if ( Row ) Row->Item["Title"] = S"Automatic (Dance Mix)";
        // 3. Update DataSet
        DataAdapter->Update(MyDataSet);
    }
    catch(Exception* e) {
        Console::WriteLine(e->Message);
    }
    __finally {
        MyConnection->Close();
    }
}
```

Working with Transactions

Database transactions are essential for enforcing data integrity. Transactions can be used to ensure that all requested updates succeed or not. Also, transactions help you to hide incomplete database changes from other database users until the transaction is complete and provide a means for record locking to avoid unpredictable concurrent modification of the same record by multiple users. To perform database updates in a transaction you must create a transaction object for the connection's **BeginTransaction** method. To finish the transaction and accept its results you can call the transaction **Commit** method. Alternatively, you can call the **Rollback** method to discard data updates made in the transaction.

The code example shown next demonstrates updating a database using a transaction where the transaction is rolled back if an **Update** error occurs. The code performs the following actions:

1. Creates an **OleDbDataAdapter** object for the database "Music" table and attaches a **RowUpdated** event handler, which throws an exception if an update error occurred (**Status == ErrorsOccurred**).

2. Creates a **DataSet** and fills it with the "Music" table data.

3. Begins a database transaction using the **OleDbConnection::BeginTransaction** method.

4. Modifies the **DataSet** data and violates the FK constraint by setting the "Music" table "GenreName" column to "Trance."

5. Invokes the data reader **Update** method to update the database. The **RowUpdated** event handler detects the FK violation and throws the exception. The exception is caught by the **catch** block, and the pending transaction is rolled back using the **Rollback** method. This allows the discarding changes made to the database within the transaction.

```
#using <mscorlib.dll>
#using <system.dll>
#using <system.data.dll>
#using <system.xml.dll>
```

```
using namespace System;
using namespace System::Data;
using namespace System::Data::OleDb;

// Class RowUpdated event errors
__gc struct MyEventHandler {
    static void RowUpdated(Object* sender, OleDbRowUpdatedEventArgs* e)
    {
        if ( e->Status == UpdateStatus::ErrorsOccurred )
          // Throw an exception
          throw new Exception("Row update failed!");
    }
};

void main()
{
    OleDbConnection* MyConnection;
    OleDbTransaction* MyTransaction;
    try {
        // Create OLE DB connection for MS Access database
        MyConnection = new OleDbConnection(
            "Provider=Microsoft.Jet.OLEDB.4.0;\
            Data Source=UltraMax-Music.mdb");
        MyConnection->Open();
        // 1. Create DataAdapter and autogenerate the UpdateCommand
        OleDbDataAdapter* DataAdapter = new OleDbDataAdapter(
            "SELECT * FROM Music", MyConnection);
        OleDbCommandBuilder* CmdBuilder = new OleDbCommandBuilder(
            DataAdapter);
        DataAdapter->UpdateCommand = CmdBuilder->GetUpdateCommand();
        // Attach RowUpdated handler
        DataAdapter->RowUpdated += new OleDbRowUpdatedEventHandler(0,
            MyEventHandler::RowUpdated);

        // 2. Create DataSet and fill it with database data
        DataSet* MyDataSet = new DataSet();
        DataAdapter->MissingSchemaAction = MissingSchemaAction::AddWithKey;
        DataAdapter->Fill(MyDataSet);

        // 3. Begin transaction to make sure that all DataSet changes
        // propagate to the database or none
        MyTransaction = MyConnection->BeginTransaction();

        // 4. Modify DataSet data
        DataTable* MyTable = MyDataSet->Tables->Item[0];
        // OK
```

```
      DataRow* Row = MyTable->Rows->Find(S"Automatic");
      if ( Row ) Row->Item["Title"] = S"Automatic (Dance Mix)";
      Row = MyTable->Rows->Find(S"EnTrance");
      // Violates FK constraint, Update method will throw an exception
      if ( Row ) Row->Item["GenreName"] = S"Trance";

      // 5. Update DataSet
      DataAdapter->Update(MyDataSet);
      // Commit transaction
      MyTransaction->Commit();
   }
   catch(Exception* e) {
      Console::WriteLine(e->Message);
      // Rollback transaction in case of error
      if ( MyTransaction )
      {
         MyTransaction->Rollback();
         Console::WriteLine("Transaction rolled back.");
      }
   }
   __finally {
      MyConnection->Close();
   }
}
```

NOTE: If you close a database connection without committing the transaction, the transaction will be automatically rolled back.

Creating ASP.NET Web Services

QUICK JUMPS

CHAPTER 10

Creating ASP.NET Web Services

In Depth

The .NET Framework supports two methods for creating Web services. You can use ASP.NET or .NET Remoting. While .NET Remoting is closer to more general distributed computing and remote procedure calling (RPC), ASP.NET is the mainstream approach for developing XML web services. In this chapter, I will focus on writing ASP.NET web services using Managed C++ and I'll provide the necessary background information on ASP.NET. You will learn how to create, deploy, configure, and debug ASP.NET web services written in Managed C++. If you are totally unfamiliar with web services and related terminology, I recommend that you read the introduction to web services and the .NET Framework in Chapter 1.

Web Services as Components of Distributed Computing

Ubiquitous networking and the exponential growth of the Internet gave birth to the era of *distributed computing*. Distributed computing is essentially the process of conducting calculations on numerous computers for the purpose of solving a single task. This definition implies that mere web browsing amounts to distributed computing, because multiple machines are involved in producing tasks, such as reading hypertext, displaying images, and managing media streams, whichyou view in your web browser. Thus, you could say that a basic client-server communication is distributed computing, too.

Distributed computing always involves providing and consuming computational *services*. When you connect to a web server, the web server provides a web page retrieval service that your web browser *consumes*. Thus, a computational service amounts to software that can accept *service requests* and can deliver *results* back to the requester. If the software accepts requests but does not deliver results other than request confirmations, such interaction corresponds to *automation*.

Software services communicate with clients by means of various protocols. Software services that rely on HTTP as a means of communication with clients are thought of as *web services*. Finally, an *XML web service* is a web service that uses XML as a means for representing structured data when exchanging information with clients. This definition leaves many degrees of freedom. For that matter, standards such as WSDL and SOAP are emerging to unify web services and to deliver standard means for providing and consuming web services. The .NET Framework provides such standardized (*formally* soon to be standardized, but *de facto* already standard) means for developing XML Web Services using any CLS-compliant language.

The Pros and Cons of Web Services

Prior to diving into a discussion of development of XML web services using .NET and Managed C++, let's focus on the reasons *why* and *when* it is appropriate to use software services. Unfortunately, there has been much misconception about the applicability and usability of software services as compared to local ldesktop software.

To help you form your own judgment, let's examine the advantages and disadvantages of software services from both service consumer and service provider points of view. Software services offer the following advantages for consumers:

* *Access to volatile or voluminous information*: Some information such as news articles, stock quotes, or statistical data changes too frequently or occupies too much space to be distributed on any type of medium. Thus, it is a big advantage for consumers to be able to access the most up-to-date information on demand in smaller, manageable chunks.

* *Access to sensitive information*: Some information such as intellectual property, audio/video recordings, and consumer data is too dear to copyright owners to be given away in its entirety on any type of medium. Thus, the only way for consumers to gain access to such information is to leave the copyright owners in control of the "pipe" and be happy with what is *allowed* to consume.

* *Less software maintenance:* Since the software service is running on a provider's hardware, it is the responsibility of the service provider to maintain the software and to ensure the service is available and usable.

* *Less hardware maintenance*: Since the software service is running on a provider's hardware, the consumer does not need to maintain additional hardware otherwise required for running the software locally.

The disadvantages for consumers include:

* *Leap of faith*: Since the service is not owned by a consumer, there is no guarantee that it will be available tomorrow.

* *Less reliable access*: Unpredictable network problems (such as illiterate excavator operators who can't read "Call this number before digging" label), unanticipated outages on the provider's side (black outs, terrorist acts, hardware failures, and so on), or spontaneous service demand jumps (like everybody reading breaking news on a media web site) make access to the service less reliable then when running locally.

* *Slower access*: Since the service is running on a provider's computer at a remote location, the access time is usually slower than the access time to the data stored locally.

* *Additional expenses*: Unlike most of the traditionally distributed software, software services are generally offered on a subscription basis, and everybody knows that recurring payments mean more out-of-pocket expenses in the long run.

From the developer's point of view, software services offer the following advantages for service providers:

* *Could be the only option for conducting business*: Delivering stock quotes and news is inherently a service.

* *Higher revenues*: Subscription fees mean constant cash flow, less manufacturing expenses (no need to press CD-ROMs or other media), and less sales costs incurred when selling media in stores.

* *Lower customer support expenses*: Less hassle in providing support for customers who can't install or run software because plugging into the service should be easier than installing a standalone software package.

On the downside, software service represents the following challenges for service providers:

* *Maintaining consumer privacy*: Software service providers usually have access to consumer data, which must be closely guarded against unauthorized access.

* *Maintaining more hardware*: Reliable, redundant, constantly backed-up, and closely guarded hardware is required to provide uninterrupted, highly accessible, and secure service to consumers.

Thus, before deciding to develop a web service you should weigh all of the options and make an intelligent decision: Do not write a web service simply because web services are fashionable.

Future of Web Services

Web services are becoming very popular because more applications want to take advantage of programmable web sites. Existing web site interfaces offer little if any convenience for software developers looking for reliable ways to automate information gathering and web content parsing. For instance, numerous webbots exist that scout the Web, performing user searches, price comparisons, news mining, stock quote retrieval, and so on. While such webbots primarily use hyperlink navigation combined with HTML/XML content parsing, they often fail due to unexpected content format changes and are often blocked by the content providers that do not wish to share their content with third parties without explicit prior authorization. Hence, developing a robust and usable webbot or a programmable web application becomes a true challenge.

The new web service architecture makes it easier to develop webbots and programmable web applications. In theory, content providers that are interested in sharing their information with third parties would post web services on their websites to facilitate access to the content such as consumer-goods pricing, weather reports, stock quotes, and so on. By posting a web service, the provider gives developers a chance to tap into their website content using a standard reliable interface, which among other things is easy to program because it is object-oriented, and with the help of .NET, is supposed to be cross platform and cross language.

Besides providing easy and standardized access to the provider website content, web services can (and will) go a step further by providing *computational services* along with content retrieval. Such computational services are likely to be linked to ever-changing business rules, evolving standards, state or government regulations, on-going research or any other activity, which makes the results of a particular computation performed by a web service vary with time. For instance, the Internal Revenue Service (IRS) could post a web service, which would compute the amount of tax due based on supplied income, number of exemptions, and other tax information. Since the IRS will stay in business for years to come and taxation rules vary from year to year, it may be practical to rely on a hypothetical tax computation web service provided by the IRS when developing a consumer tax application.

Why Use Web Services?

The most compelling reason for developing a web service is *when you have no other choice*. For example, a compelling reason to incorporate web services in *your* product is to consume volatile, voluminous, or sensitive *third-party* data. Integrating web services in your software for other reasons creates dangerous dependencies on third party software and hardware infrastructure that may fail without warning. Such failure will make *your* software fail, too. Therefore, I particularly discourage using web services when they offer no compelling advantage when compared with the same code being statically linked (or consumed from a private DLL/assembly).

Minimizing Risk by Implementing a Fall Back Scheme

An alternative for minimizing the risk of web services going off-line involves providing a library version of the service to fall back to. This should be done only if the development of such a library is practical.

Along the same line of thinking, a software packages relying on third-party web services should be designed to cope with unexpected unavailability of a particular web service and provide a limited application functionality when such a failure occurs versus no functionality at all when the fallback scenario was not considered.

XML Web Services and ASP.NET

XML Web Services use HTTP for communication and rely on XML to represent data. HTTP communication requires the ability to accept HTTP requests and to transmit HTTP responses, which is a prime function of any web server. Although it is conceivable to create an XML Web Service that incorporates a web server, it is more practical to use existing web server software. Then, you can rely on the web server to dispatch HTTP requests for your service and focus on developing a web service *component* that you can plug in to an existing HTTP server software (see Figure 10.1).

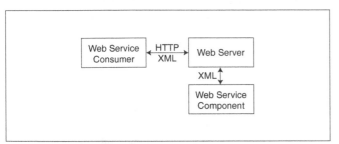

Figure 10.1 XML Web Service using an HTTP server.

Not surprisingly, Microsoft has decided to use its Internet Information Server (IIS) to provide HTTP service for XML Web Services developed using the .NET Framework and Visual C++ .NET. IIS provides two different methods for routing HTTP requests to server components (e.g., web services). The first is through Internet Service API (ISAPI) extensions and the second is through Active Server Pages (ASP). You can use either ISAPI or ASP to connect an XML Web Service to IIS. The technique of using ISAPI in conjunction with web services created with .NET Framework is called *.NET Remoting*. Using ISAPI in conjunction with web services developed using standard C++ refers to ATL Server Web Service programming. Both of these techniques are beyond the scope of this book. Instead, I will focus on developing XML Web Services in conjunction with the new version of Active Server Pages, compatible with the .NET Framework— ASP.NET.

ASP.NET Web Service Overview

Active Server Pages (ASP) technology allows you to write scripts representing a mixture of code and HTML. When an ASP page (.asp-file) is processed, the script is interpreted by the ASP.DLL and the resulting HTML and HTTP responses are sent back to the client. ASP.NET goes one step further by providing smooth integration of ASP with the .NET Framework and allows you to use classes written in any CLS-compliant language, including Managed C++ in scripts embedded in ASP.NET pages (.asmx-files). Consequently, an ASP.NET web service corresponds to a web service class written in some CLS-compliant language embedded in an ASP.NET page.

When an ASP.NET page containing an embedded web service class is requested by a consumer, the web server processes the ASP.NET web page first, determines if the page corresponds to a web service class, and dispatches the request to the associated web service component (see Figure 10.2).

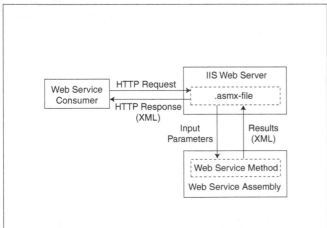

Figure 10.2 XML Web Service using ASP.NET.

Each ASP.NET web service typically resides in a separate virtual directory on a web server and contains a single ASP.NET page (.asmx-file) corresponding to a web service entry point, which usually contains a single line of code declaring that the ASP.NET page is actually a web service. Here's an example of the format:

```
<%@ WebService Class=WebServiceNET.TestService %>
```

This directive declares an ASP.NET web service and the **Class** attribute specifies the name of the .NET class corresponding to the web service component. The class designated by the **Class** attribute must reside in an assembly stored in the bin subdirectory of the virtual directory of the web service. Thus, the only two mandatory files required to implement an ASP.NET web service are the .asmx page containing the **WebService** directive and the web service assembly. The directory structure depicted below corresponds to the simplest case of a web service:

```
WebServiceVirtualRoot
|- WebService.asmx
|- bin
   |- WebService.dll
```

In practice, however, there are three other files that are commonly found in an ASP.NET web service virtual root directory:

*   *Global.asax*: ASP.NET application object file.
*   *Web.config*: Web service configuration file (see the "Web Service Configuration" section in this chapter).
*   *WebService.disco or WebService.vsdisco*: Web service discovery document. (See the "Web Service Discovery" section in this chapter.)

In the case of an ASP.NET web service, the Global.asax file typically contains a single line of code as shown here:

```
<%@ Application Inherits=WebServiceNET.Global %>
```

The **Application** directive declares an ASP.NET HTTP application object, and the **Inherits** attribute specifies the name of the .NET class implementing the ASP.NET application. The class designated by the **Inherits** attribute must reside in an assembly stored in the bin subdirectory of the virtual directory of the web service. Both the web service class and the ASP.NET HTTP application class can reside in the same assembly.

System::Web Namespace

ASP.NET functionality is implemented in the .NET Framework in the System::Web namespace. The System::Web namespace classes are summarized in Table 10.1, and the System::Web namespace class hierarchy is shown in Figure 10.3.

Table 10.1. System::Web namespace classes and exceptions.

Class	Description
HttpApplication	Defines the methods, properties, and events common to all application objects within an ASP.NET application. This class is the base class for applications defined by the user in the global.asax file.
HttpApplicationState	Enables sharing of global information across multiple sessions and requests within an ASP.NET application.
HttpBrowserCapabilities	Enables the server to gather information on the capabilities of the browser that is running on the client.
HttpCachePolicy	Contains methods for setting cache-specific HTTP headers and for controlling the ASP.NET page output cache.
HttpCacheVaryByHeaders	Provides a type-safe way to set the **VaryByHeaders** property that identifies the request headers that ASP.NET adds to the Vary HTTP header sent to the client.
HttpCacheVaryByParams	Provides a type-safe way to set the **VaryByParams** property that identifies the HTTP Get or Post parameters that ASP.NET uses to choose a response from multiple cached responses.
HttpClientCertificate	Provides the client certificate fields issued by the client in response to the server ' s request for the client s identity.
HttpCompileException	The exception that is thrown when a compiler error occurs.
HttpContext	Encapsulates all HTTP-specific information about an individual HTTP request.
HttpCookie	Provides a type-safe way to create and manipulate individual HTTP cookies.
HttpCookieCollection	Provides a type-safe way to manipulate HTTP cookies.
HttpException	Provides a means of generating HTTP exceptions.
HttpFileCollection	Provides access to and organizes files uploaded by a client.
HttpModuleCollection	Provides a means of indexing and retrieving a collection of IHttpModule objects.
HttpParseException	The exception that is thrown when a parse error occurs.
HttpPostedFile	Provides a way to access individual files that have been uploaded by a client.
HttpRequest	Enables ASP.NET to read the HTTP values sent by a client during a Web request.
HttpResponse	Encapsulates HTTP response information from an ASP.NET operation.
HttpRuntime	Provides a set of ASP.NET run-time services for the current application.
HttpServerUtility	Provides helper methods for processing Web requests.

<Continued on Next Page>

<Table 10.1 Continued>

Class	Description
HttpStaticObjectsCollection	Provides a static objects collection for the **StaticObjects** property.
HttpUtility	Provides methods for encoding and decoding URLs when processing Web requests.
HttpWorkerRequest	Provides an abstract class that defines the base worker methods and enumerations used by ASP.NET managed code to process requests.
HttpWriter	Provides a **TextWriter** object that is accessed through the intrinsic **HttpResponse** object.
ProcessInfo	Provides information on processes currently executing.
ProcessModelInfo	Contains methods that return information about worker processes.
TraceContext	Captures and presents execution details about a Web request. This class cannot be inherited.

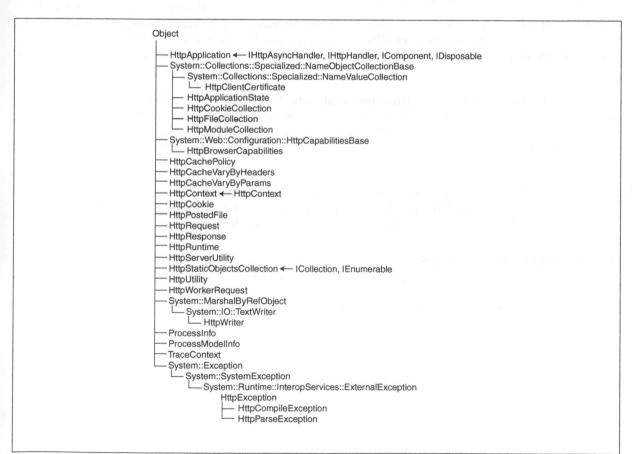

Figure 10.3 System::Web namespace class hierarchy.

ASP.NET Architecture Overview

For the purpose of developing ASP.NET web services using Managed C++, you'll need to understand the basic ASP.NET application architecture as illustrated in Figure 10.4.

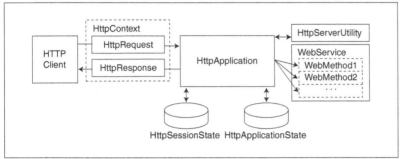

Figure 10.4 ASP.NET application architecture.

The centerpiece of an ASP.NET application is the **HttpApplication** object, which accepts incoming HTTP requests, invokes **WebService** methods, dispatches HTTP responses, and allows handling events associated with beginning and ending of the HTTP request processing. HTTP requests/responses are implemented by means of the **HttpRequest/ HttpResponse** classes that jointly combine an HTTP context of the current operation, which is represented by the **HttpContext** class. An ASP.NET application has access to the **HttpServerUtility** class that corresponds to the **Server** ASP/ASP.NET scripting object. The **HttpServerUtility** performs miscellaneous operations, such as instantiating COM objects, mapping of web server virtual paths to physical ones, and encoding/decoding URLs and HTML text.

Finally, the **HttpSessionState** and the **HttpApplicationState** classes allow you to maintain session and application-level state information. *Session*-level state is maintained for each individual client connection when the client sends the first request to the ASP.NET application and until the client disconnects and the session state expires. Thus, the session state storage can be used for keeping information specific to a particular client to maintain state between requests.

Application-level state is maintained for the entire life time of the ASP.NET application, from the moment the application is accessed for the first time and until removed or until the web server is reset. Thus, the application state storage can be used for keeping global information accessible to all clients all the time.

HttpApplicationState Class

The **HttpApplicationState** class corresponds to the **Application** ASP.NET scripting object that provides support for application-level storage. Application-level storage is shared among all clients accessing the ASP.NET web application. The **HttpApplicationState** class has the following inheritance structure:

```
System::Object
|- System::Collections::Specialized::NameObjectCollectionBase
   |- System::Web::HttpApplicationState
```

```
Attributes: None
Abstract: No
Sealed: Yes
Implements Interfaces: None
```

The **HttpApplicationState** class properties and methods are summarized in Tables 10.2 and 10.3. The **HttpApplicationState** class supplies the **Item** indexer property that allows accessing objects stored in the application-level storage either by name or by index. The **Item** indexer can be used to add, retrieve, and remove objects from the application-level storage.

Table 10.2 **HttpApplicationState** class properties.

Get/Set	Type	Property	Description
Get	HttpApplicationState*	Contents	Contains a pointer to self.
Get	Object*	Item(String* *name*)	Returns an application variable with the specified name.
Get	Object*	Item(int *index*)	Returns an application variable at the specified index.
Get	String*[]	AllKeys	Contains a pointer to the collection of names of all objects stored in the **Application**.
Get	HttpStaticObjectsCollection*	StaticObjects	Contains a pointer to the collection of static objects defined using the <object> tag in Global.asax file.

Table 10.3 **HttpApplicationState** class methods.

Constructor	Description
void Add(String* *name*, Object* *value*)	Adds new application variables with the specified name and value to the collection.
void Clear()	Removes all object application variables from the collection.
Object* Get(String* *name*)	
Object* Get(int *index*)	Returns an application variable with the specified *name* or *index*.
String* GetKey(int *index*)	Returns the name of the application variable at the specified index.
void Lock()	Locks the ASP.NET **Application** object for safe concurrent access.
void Remove(String* *name*)	Removes an application variable with the specified name from the collection.
void RemoveAll()	Removes all application variables from the collection.
void RemoveAt(int *index*)	Removes an application variable at the specified index from the collection.
void Set(String* *name*, Object* *value*)	Sets the application variable with the specified name to the specified value.
void Unlock()	Unlocks the ASP.NET **Application**.

HttpSessionState Class
The **HttpSessionState** class corresponds to the **Session** ASP.NET scripting object that provides support for session-level storage. When a particular client contacts the web server for the first time, a session is created and all subsequent requests by the same client operate within the context of the session created by the first request. The **HttpSessionState** class provides a means for storing state data in between such requests. If the client

remains idle for a long time, the session expires, and all session state data is discarded. If the client transmits a new request after the session had expired, a new session is created.

The **HttpSessionState** class is very similar to the **HttpApplciationState** class and has the following inheritance structure:

```
System::Object
|- System::Web::SessionState::HttpSessionState
```

```
Attributes: None
Abstract: No
Sealed: Yes
Implements Interfaces: ICollection, IEnumerable
```

The **HttpSessionState** class properties and methods are summarized in Tables 10.4 and 10.5. As with the **HttpApplicationState** class, the **HttpSessionState** class supplies the **Item** indexer property that allows accessing objects stored in the session storage by name or by index. Also, the **Item** indexer can be used to add, retrieve, and remove objects from the session storage.

Table 10.4 **HttpSessionState** class properties.

Get/Set	Type	Property	Description
Get/Set	int	CodePage	Gets or sets the session code page ID.
Get	HttpSessionState*	Contents	Contains a pointer to self.
Get	bool	IsCookieless	Contains **true** if the session ID is imbedded in the URL rather than passed as a cookie.
Get	bool	IsNew	Contains **true** if the session was created by the current request.
Get	bool	IsReadOnly	Contains **true** if the session is read-only.
Get	Object*	Item(String* *name*)	Returns a session variable with the specified name.
Get	Object*	Item(int *index*)	Returns a session variable at the specified index.
Get	NameObjectCollectionBase::KeysCollection*	Keys	Contains a pointer to the collection of names of all objects stored in the **Session**.
Get/Set	int	LCID	Gets or sets the locale ID of the session.
Get	SessionStateMode	Mode	Contains the current session-state mode.
Get	String*	SessionID	Session ID.
Get	HttpStaticObjectsCollection*	StaticObjects	Contains a pointer to the collection of objects defined using the <object RunAt= Server scope= Session > tag in the Global.asax file.
Get/Set	int	Timeout	Gets or sets the session timeout in minutes.

Table 10.5 **HttpSessionState** class methods.

Constructor	Description
void Abandon()	Cancels the current session and releases all session variables.
void Add(String* *name*, **Object*** *value*)	Adds a new session variable with the specified name and value to the collection.
__sealed void CopyTo(Array* *array*, **int** *index*)	Copies all session variables to the specified array at the specified index.
void Remove(String* *name*)	Removes a session variable with the specified name from the collection.
void RemoveAll()	Removes all session variables from the collection.
void RemoveAt(int *index*)	Removes a session variable at the specified index from the collection.

HttpServerUtility Class

The **HttpServerUtility** class corresponds to the **Server** ASP.NET scripting object. The **HttpServerUtility** class performs various utility functions such as instantiating COM objects, processing ASP.NET pages, mapping paths and encoding/decoding text and URLs. The **HttpServerUtility** class has the following inheritance structure:

```
System::Object
|- System::Web::SessionState::HttpServerUtility

Attributes: None
Abstract: No
Sealed: Yes
Implements Interfaces: None
```

The **HttpServerUtility** class properties and methods are summarized in Tables 10.6 and 10.7.

Table 10.6 **HttpServerUtility** class properties.

Get/Set	Type	Property	Description
Get	**String***	**MachineName**	Contains the web server's computer name.
Get/Set	**int**	**ScriptTimeout**	Gets or sets the maximum allowable time (in seconds) for processing a request.

Table 10.7 **HttpServerUtility** class methods.

Constructor	Description
void ClearError()	Clears the previous exception.
Object* CreateObject(String* *progID*)	Creates a COM object with a specified class programmatic ID.
Object* CreateObject(Type* *type*)	Creates a COM object of the specified type.
Object* CreateObjectFromClsid(String* *clsID*)	Creates a COM object with a specified class ID.

<Continued on Next Page>

<Table 10.7 Continued>

Constructor	Description
void Execute(String* *path*)	
void Execute(String* *path*, TextWriter* *writer*)	Executes an ASP.NET page at the specified path. Optional *writer* argument allows capturing the page output to the specified text output stream.
Exception* GetLastError()	Returns a pointer to the previous exception.
String* HtmlDecode(String* *str*)	Decodes the specified HTML-encoded string.
void HtmlDecode(String* *str*, TextWriter* *output*)	Decodes the specified HTML-encoded string and places it into the specified output stream.
String* HtmlEncode(String* *str*)	Encodes the specified string.
void HtmlEncode(String* *str*, TextWriter* *output*)	Encodes the specified string and places it into the specified output stream.
String* MapPath(String* *path*)	Maps the specified virtual path to the physical path.
void Transfer(String* *path*)	
void Transfer(String* *path*, bool *preserveForm*)	Transfers the execution to an ASP.NET page at the specified path. Optional *preserveForm* argument indicates whether to preserve the **QueryString** and **Form** collections of the **Request** object.
String* UrlDecode(String* *url*)	URL decodes the specified string.
void UrlDecode(String* *str*, TextWriter* *output*)	URL decodes the specified string and places it into the specified output stream.
String* UrlEncode(String* *str*)	URL encodes the specified string.
void UrlEncode(String* *str*, TextWriter* *output*)	URL encodes the specified string and places it into the specified output stream.
String* UrlPathEncode(String* *urlStr*)	URL encodes the path portion of the specified URL string.

System::Web::Services Namespace

All ASP.NET web service components must inherit from the same base class **WebService**, which is defined in the System::Web::Services namespace. The System::Web::Services namespace classes and attributes are summarized in Tables 10.8 and 10.9.

Table 10.8 System::Web::Services namespace classes.

Class	Description
WebService	Base class for ASP.NET web services.

Table 10.9 System::Web::Services namespace attributes.

Attribute	Description
WebMethodAttribute	Makes a web service method callable across the Internet.
WebServiceAttribute	Specifies additional information about a web service.
WebServiceBindingAttribute	Specifies binding information for a web service method.

WebService Class

The **WebService** class is the base class for all ASP.NET web services and has the following inheritance structure:

```
System::Object
|- System::ComponentModel::MarshalByValueComponent
   |- System::Web::Services::WebService
```

```
Attributes: None
Abstract: No
Sealed: No
Implements Interfaces: None
```

You must derive your own class from the **WebService** and add your own methods to the class when developing a new ASP.NET web service. Then, you can connect the derived web service class to an ASP.NET application by inserting the @**WebService** directive into the main .asmx-file of the ASP.NET application. (See the ASP.NET Overview section presented earlier for details.) It is the responsibility of the ASP.NET application object, which is an instance of the **HttpApplication** class, to map incoming HTTP requests into the web service method calls (see Figure 10.4).

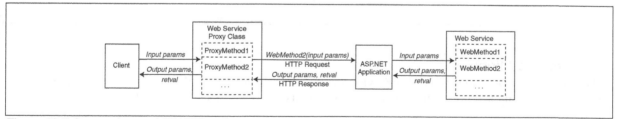

Figure 10.5 Consuming an ASP.NET web service.

A **WebService**-based class should have one or more *web methods* (i.e., methods accessible to the web service consumers). To declare a web method you should declare a "normal" method and apply the **WebMethod** attribute to it. The **WebMethod** attribute informs the ASP.NET application object hosting the web service about the publicly accessible web service entry points. Methods that are not decorated with the **WebMethod** attribute remain private to the web service and can't be accessed directly by the service consumer. A typical scenario for consuming a web service is illustrated on Figure 10.5.

From the point of view of a web service consumer, the web service is represented by a *web service proxy class*, which looks just like any other object. The process of web service consumption involves invoking web service proxy class methods, passing input parameters, and accepting output parameters and the method return value (if any). It is a duty of a proxy class to dispatch requests made to the proxy class methods to the actual web service, receive a response from the web service, and provide the results back to the callee. When a web service consumer invokes a web method of a particular ASP.NET web service, the method name is encoded in the HTTP request. The ASP.NET application object receives the request, extracts the method name, extracts input parameters, invokes the appropriate web method from the web service class, obtains output parameter values and the method return value (if any), packs the data into an HTTP response message, and sends the response back to the consumer.

The **WebService** class has no original methods and its constructors and properties are summarized in Tables 10.10 and 10.11. As you can see from Table 10.11, the **WebService** class properties correspond to the ASP.NET scripting objects such as **Application**, **Server**, and **Session**, and you can freely use these ASP.NET objects in the web service methods (e.g., to access application-level or session level state information).

Table 10.10 **WebService** class constructors.

Constructor	Description
WebService()	Default constructor.

Table 10.11 **WebService** class properties.

Get/Set	Type	Property	Description
Get	**HttpApplicationState***	**Application**	Contains a pointer to the ASP.NET **Application** object.
Get	**HttpContext***	**Context**	Contains a pointer to the HTTP context of the current request.
Get	**HttpServerUtility***	**Server**	Contains a pointer to the ASP.NET **Server** object.
Get	**HttpSessionState***	**Session**	Contains a pointer to the ASP.NET **Session** object.
Get	**IPrincipal***	**User**	Contains a pointer to the ASP.NET **User** object.

WebService Attribute

The .NET Framework supplies the **WebService** attribute implemented by the **WebServiceAttribute** class to allow you to specify additional information about a web service. The attribute has the following syntax:

```
[WebService(Name="WebServiceName", Description="WebServiceDescription",
   Namespace="namespace")]
```

The **WebService** attribute is applicable only to class definitions corresponding to web services. The attribute accepts the following optional parameters:

* **Name**: Specifies the web service name, which is displayed on the web service information page and is contained in the **name** attribute of the **service** element in the web service description, WSDL (see Chapter 11).

* **Description**: Specifies the web service description, which is displayed on the web service information page and is contained in the **documentation** element in the **service** section in the web service, WSDL (see Chapter 11).

* **Namespace**: Specifies the web service namespace, which is used as the target namespace and in the **soap-Action** attributes of **<soap:operation>** elements in the WSDL description of the service (see Chapter 11).

WebMethod Attribute

The .NET Framework supplies the **WebMethod** attribute implemented by the **WebMethodAttribute** class to make a web service method callable from remote clients. The attribute has the following syntax:

```
[WebMethod(BufferResponse=BooleanValue, CacheDuration=NumSeconds,
    Description="MethodDescription", EnableSession=BooleanValue,
    MessageName="MessageName", TransactionOption=option)]
```

The **WebService** attribute is applicable only to web service method definitions. The attribute accepts the following parameters:

* **BufferResponse**: When set to **true**, the framework serializes the response of the web service method into a buffer and transmits the buffer when the response is complete, or when the buffer is full. If **BufferResponse=false**, the method response is sent back to the client as it is being serialized.

* **CacheDuration**: Specifies the number of seconds to keep the method output cached in the server memory (zero indicates no caching).

* **Description**: Specifies the web service method description, which is displayed on the web service information page and is contained in the **documentation** element in **operation** sections in the service WSDL.

* **EnableSession**: When set to **true**, the session state is enabled for the method through the **HttpSessionState** object. If the method does not require session state set the **EnableSession** to **false** for improved performance.

* **MessageName**: Specifies the web service method name, which is displayed on the web service information page and is referenced in the service WSDL (see Chapter 11). The attribute can be used to specify unique names for methods with multiple overloads.

* **TransactionOption**: Specifies transaction behavior of the web method. The **TransactionOption** parameter accepts the following values (defined in the **TransactionOption** enumeration in the System::EnterpriseServices namespace):

    * **Disabled, NotSupported, Supported**: New transaction is not created.

    * **Required, RequiresNew**: New transaction is created: The transaction is automatically committed if the method terminates normally and does not invoke **ContextUtil::SetAbort**; if the method throws an exception the transaction is automatically rolled back.

    NOTE: Due to the stateless nature of HTTP protocol, ASP.NET web services only can be in the root of a transaction. Thus, a web service method can either create a new transaction or do not use transactions at all.

If you prefer positional parameter syntax you can use one of the **WebMethodAttribute** constructors:

```
WebMethodAttribute();
WebMethodAttribute(bool enableSession);
WebMethodAttribute(bool enableSession, TransactionOption transactionOption);
WebMethodAttribute(bool enableSession, TransactionOption transactionOption,
    int cacheDuration);
WebMethodAttribute(bool enableSession, TransactionOption transactionOption,
    int cacheDuration, bool bufferResponse);
```

WebServiceBinding Attribute

Each web service method represents an operation that can be bound to one or more network protocols, such as HTTP-GET, HTTP-POST, or SOAP. By default, all web service methods are members of the default binding. However, you can define a custom method binding using the **WebServiceBinding** attribute implemented by the **WebServiceBindingAttribute** class. You can apply the **WebServiceBinding** attribute to a web service class definition several times to define multiple bindings. Then, you can apply as **SoapDocumentMethod** or **SoapRpcMethod** attributes to a method and specify one of the manually defined bindings to override the default SOAP formatting for the method.

> NOTE: If you define a custom binding using the **WebServiceBinding** attribute and do not use the binding with either **SoapDocumentMethod** or **SoapRpcMethod** attributes, the binding will be unused and thus will not appear in the WSDL definition of the web service.

The **WebServiceBinding** attribute has the following syntax:

```
[WebServiceBinding(Location="location", Name="name",
   Namespace="namespace")]
```

The **WebService** attribute is applicable only to class definitions corresponding to web services. The attribute accepts the following parameters:

* **Location**: Specifies the binding location, e.g., **soapLocation** attribute for a SOAP-bound operation.
* **Name**: Specifies the name of the binding to be used in the WSDL description of the service.
* **Namespace**: Specifies the namespace of the binding to be used in the WSDL description of the service.

If you prefer positional parameter syntax you can use one of the **WebServiceBindingAttribute** constructors:

```
WebServiceBindingAttribute();
WebServiceBindingAttribute(String* name);
WebServiceBindingAttribute(String* name, String* namespace);
WebServiceBindingAttribute(String* name, String* namespace, String* location);
```

Immediate Solutions

Creating ASP.NET Web Services Using ClassWizard

The easiest way to create an ASP.NET web service is to use the Visual C++ ClassWizard:

1. Select the File | New | Project menu item from the Visual C++ .NET Menu to open the New Project dialog. Select "Managed C++ Web Service" in the list of templates, type in the project name, and click the OK button to generate the code. Unlike most class wizard templates, the "Managed C++ Web Service" application template does not ask the user any questions and generates "Hello World" web service code as soon as you type a project name and click the OK button on the New Project dialog.

2. The application wizard generates the following files:

    * *ProjectName.h*: Contains "Hello World" web service declaration. The web service class is given the default name **Class1** and is contained within the *ProjectName* namespace.
    * *ProjectName.cpp*: Contains code behind the "Hello World" web service (i.e., web method implementations).

* *AssemblyInfo.cpp*: Specifies the global assembly-level attributes.

* *stdafx.h and stdafx.cpp*: Precompiled header files.

* *ProjectName.asmx*: Main ASP.NET application page that contains a single @**WebService** directive indicating that the page is in fact a web service.

* *Global.asax.h*: Defines an **HttpApplication**-derived class called **Global**, which can be used for performing custom actions for the following events: **Application_Start, Session_Start, Application_BeginRequest, Application_EndRequest, Session_End**, and **Application_End**.

* *Global.asax*: ASP.NET application object file. Normally this file contains inline C# or VB.NET code for handling the aforementioned application and session-level events. But in our case the file contains a single ASP.NET @**Application** directive declaring that the application object is represented by the **Global-class** defined in Global.asax.h file.

* *Web.config*: ASP.NET web service configuration file.

* *ProjectName.vsdisco*: Web service dynamic discovery document.

TIP: If you do not want to mess with application or session-level events you can safely remove Global.asax.h and Global.asax files from your project.

3. Open the *ProjectName*.h header file and edit the web service class declaration:

* Change the name of the web service class from the default **Class1** to a meaningful name of your choice.

* Insert the **WebService** attribute in front of the web service class definition and specify the web service **Name**, **Description,** and **Namespace** properties.

* Remove the default **HelloWorld** method and add your own web service methods. You declare web methods by marking the web service methods with the **WebMethod** attribute and specify the web method description in the **Description** attribute parameter.

The code example below illustrates definition of a sample **MyWebService** web service class providing a single web method called **Uppercase**:

```
#pragma once
#using <mscorlib.dll>
#using <System.dll>
#using <System.Web.dll>
#using <System.Web.Services.dll>
#using <System.EnterpriseServices.dll>

using namespace System;
using namespace System::Web;
using namespace System::Web::Services;

namespace Test {
    [WebService(Name="MyWebService", Namespace="http://www.Gems3D.com")]
    public __gc class MyWebService: public WebService {
    public:
        [WebMethod(Description="Sample web method")]
        String* Uppercase(String* SomeText);
    };
}
```

4. Open the *ProjectName*.cpp file and edit the web service class implementation:

* Change the name of the web service class from the default **Class1** to the name that you specified in the header file.

* Remove the default **HelloWorld** method and add implementations of the methods that you declared in the header file.

The code example below illustrates implementation of the **Uppercase** web method of the sample **MyWebService** web service class:

```
#include "WebService.h"
#include "Global.asax.h"

namespace Test {
    String* MyWebService:: Uppercase(String* SomeText)
    {
        return SomeText ->ToUpper();
    }
};
```

5. Open the *ProjectName*.asmx file and replace the **Class1** in the **@WebService** directive with the new web service class name, e.g.,

```
<%@ WebService Class=Test.MyWebService %>
```

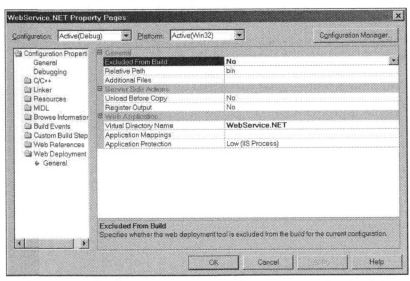

Figure 10.6 Web Deployment folder on the Project Property Pages dialog.

6. Check and optionally modify the web service deployment settings by examining options on the Web Deployment page of the Project Property Pages dialog (see Figure 10.6). You may want to modify the Virtual Root Directory name, which is set to the *ProjectName* by default.

7. Compile and deploy the web service by selecting the Build | Build Solution menu item (same as clicking F7 key). Visual C++ .NET will build the web service and automatically deploy it to the local web server to the new *ProjectName* virtual directory. The actual web service assembly (DLL file) is deployed under the *bin* subdirectory in the web service virtual directory.

8. Test the web service by browsing the http://localhost/*ProjectName*/*ProjectName*.asmx URL in a web browser and make sure that the web service documentation page is displayed. By default, the web service documentation page contains the following information:

   * Instructions on how to customize the web service.

   * "Service Description" link: A reference to the web service description WSDL document, specified by the http://localhost/*ProjectName*/*ProjectName*.asmx?WSDL URL. Follow the link to view the web service WSDL.

   * The list of web service methods. For the sample web service discussed here the list will contain a single Uppercase entry pointing to the http://localhost/*ProjectName*/*ProjectName*.asmx?op=Uppercase URL, which represents the documentation page for the **Uppercase** method.

9. Test the web service methods by following the individual web method's URLs, supplying input parameters and clicking the Invoke button to invoke web methods using the HTTP-GET protocol.

> **NOTE:** You *should* specify your web service namespace in the **WebService** attribute **Namespace** parameter. The default http://tempuri.org namespace is used if you do not specify your own namespace. You should not deploy your web service in production with the web service namespace set to http://tempuri.org. Instead, initialize the namespace with the address of your company or product web page.

Creating ASP.NET Web Services Manually

Although the Visual C++ .NET ClassWizard provides an easy way to generate a "Hello World" ASP.NET web service, in the long run it is beneficial to known how to generate an ASP.NET web service from scratch. Here are the steps to follow to create an ASP.NET web service manually using Managed C++:

1. Create a new Managed C++ Class Library project.

2. Open the *ProjectName*.h file and add a definition of the web service class. Here's an example:

```
// Include references necessary to compile the code
#using <System.dll>
#using <System.Web.dll>
#using <System.Web.Services.dll>
#using <System.EnterpriseServices.dll>
using namespace System;
using namespace System::Web;
using namespace System::Web::Services;

namespace Test {
    [WebService(Name="MyWebService", Description="Test Web Service",
        Namespace="http://www.Gems3D.com")]
    public __gc class MyWebService : public WebService {
    public:
        [WebMethod(Description="Returns the uppercased text")]
        String* Uppercase(String* text);
    };
}
```

It is a good practice to specify **Description** properties of the **WebService** and **WebMethod** attributes so you can understand them later when examining the web service documentation.

WARNING! The web service class should be defined using the **public** assembly-level visibility specifier. If the web service class references other classes in web method parameter types or return values, the referenced classes also must be defined using the **public** assembly-level visibility specifier.

3. Open the *ProjectName*.cpp file and provide implementations of the web service methods.

4. Create and add to the project a new ASP.NET application file *ProjectName*.asmx containing a single line of code:

```
<%@ WebService Class=Test.MyWebService %>
```

NOTE: If you define your web service class in a namespace, you must prefix your class name with the namespace (e.g., *Namespace.ClassName*) in the **WebService** directive.

5. Open the *ProjectName*.asmx file properties window and set the Content property to True to indicate that you wish to deploy the file.

6. Open the Project Property Pages dialog, go to the Web Deployment folder, and set the "Exclude From Build" option to No.

7. Build the solution. The solution will be automatically deployed to the http://localhost/*ProjectName*/ folder, and you can test the web service by viewing the http://localhost/*ProjectName*/*ProjectName*.asmx URL in browser.

NOTE: Do not forget to specify the web service namespace in the **Namespace** parameter of the **WebService** attribute. Also, you can create and add to the project a dynamic discovery file named *ProjectName*.vsdisco containing the following code:

```
<?xml version="1.0" encoding="utf-8"?>
<dynamicDiscovery xmlns="urn:schemas-dynamicdiscovery:disco.2000-03-17">
</dynamicDiscovery>
```

The discovery document is optional.

Adding Web Methods to a Web Service

To add a web method (i.e., a method that can be called by remote clients) to an ASP.NET web service, add a new method to a web service class and decorate the method with a **WebMethod** attribute:

```
#using <System.dll>
#using <System.Web.dll>
#using <System.Web.Services.dll>
#using <System.EnterpriseServices.dll>
using namespace System;
using namespace System::Web;
using namespace System::Web::Services;
```

```
namespace Test {
    [WebService(Name="MyWebService", Namespace="http://www.Gems3D.com")]
    public __gc class MyWebService : public WebService {
    public:
        [WebMethod(EnableSession=false, CacheDuration=60, BufferResponse=true,
            Description="Returns the uppercased text")]
        String* Uppercase(String* text)
        {
            return text->ToUpper();
        }
        [WebMethod(Description="Adds two integers and returns the result")]
        int AddTwo(int a, int b)
        {
            return a + b;
        }
        [WebMethod]
        void DoNothing() {}
    };
}
```

> **TIP:** For improved performance, disable the session state (**EnableSession=false**) when it is not required. You can also cache the method output (**CacheDuration=60**) if you anticipate frequent calls to the method with the same parameters, and use response buffering (**BufferResponse=true**).

In the simplest case it is sufficient to use the **WebMethod** attribute without any parameters, although it is beneficial to provide the method description in the **Description** parameter. If you do not specify any additional web method attributes such as **HttpMethod, SoapDocumentMethod,** or **SoapRpcMethod,** the method will support HTTP-GET, HTTP-POST, and SOAP over HTTP protocols.

> **WARNING!** If a web method uses parameters other than primitive types, the method will support SOAP over HTTP binding exclusively. HTTP-GET and HTTP-POST protocols do not support custom types and can be used only with methods that accept parameters of primitive unstructured types.

Debugging Web Services Locally and Remotely

Follow these steps to debug an ASP.NET web service *locally or remotely*, provided that the web service is *not yet running*:

1. Open your ASP.NET web service project.

2. Set the current project configuration to Debug.

3. Set the **debug** attribute to **true** in the **compilation** section (**<compilation debug="true"/>**) of the web service web.config configuration file.

4. Make sure that on the Debugging page of the Project Property Pages dialog the Connection option is set to Local and the HTTP URL parameter is set to the web service deployment URL, then press F5 to start debugging (Debug | Start menu item). Visual C++ .NET will automatically deploy the web service and attach to the aspnet_wp.exe process.

5.   Set the break points (F9 key) and invoke the web service methods using web browser or a web service client application.

To debug *locally* an ASP.NET web service, which is *already running,* follow these procedures:

1.   Open your ASP.NET web service project.

2.   Open the Processes dialog by selecting Debug | Processes menu item.

3.   Make sure that the "Show System processes" check box is checked, locate the aspnet_wp.exe process in the list of Available Processes, click the Attach button, and then click the OK button to close the dialog window.

4.   Set the break points (F9 key) and invoke the web service methods using web browser or a web service client application.

Finally, to debug an ASP.NET web service running on a *remote system*, follow these steps:

1.   Install Visual Studio .NET on the remote system if it is not already installed.

2.   Make sure that your user ID has administrator privileges on the remote system.

3.   Open your ASP.NET web service project.

4.   Open the Debugging page of the Project Property Pages dialog and specify the following settings:

   *   Set the Connection to "Remote via DCOM."

   *   Specify the Remote Machine UNC name or address.

   *   Specify the web service URL in the HTTP URL field.

5.   Start the debugging process by clicking F5 (or select the Debug | Start menu item).

6.   Set the break points (F9 key) and invoke the web service methods using web browser or a web service client application.

Creating Web Services That Use Database Access

A more interesting (and more practical) web service example involves database access. To learn how to use database access in a web service, consider the implementation of a sample Music Catalog Service given below.

The Music Catalog Service exposes two methods: **GetFiles** for retrieving the list of music files in the catalog and **GetData** for retrieving music file data (MP3) for a specified file. The web service uses MS Access database (UltraMax-Music.mdb) to store the music catalog data. The database contains a single table MP3Storage with two fields – textual FileName and long binary MP3Data. The first field contains an MP3 file name, while the second field contains MP3 file data.

For the Music Catalog Service to operate properly the MS Access database needs to be deployed alongside with the web service. Hence the database must be added to the web service project and its Content deployment property must be set to true.

The Music Catalog Service uses OLE DB to access the MS Access database. Besides traditional web service **#using** and **using namespace** statements, the Music Catalog Service also creates a reference to the System.Data.dll assembly required for database access and includes the **using namespace System::Data::OleDb** statement for getting rid of namespace prefixes when referring to OLE DB database classes.

The **GetFiles** method performs the following actions:

1. Initializes an OLE DB connect string pointing to UltraMax-Music.mdb MS Access database file. Note the **Server->MapPath(".")** statement that maps the virtual database path into the file system path needed for the OLE DB provider to locate the database file.

2. Opens database connection by initializing and opening the **OleDbConnection**.

3. Creates a SELECT command by initializing the **OleDbCommand** object.

4. Executes the command and constructs a simple data reader by calling the **ExecuteReader** method.

5. Initializes a dynamic array for holding the resulting file names.

6. Reads all data reader rows and populates the dynamic array with MP3 file names.

7. Closes the database connection using the **Close** method.

8. Casts the dynamic array to the array of **String** objects using the **ArrayList's ToArray** method.

The **GetData** method is very similar except for steps 7 through 9. Unlike the **GetFiles** method, the **GetData** method constructs a SELECT statement for requesting binary MP3 data for a given file name. Hence the method produces a single row of binary data, which must be read using the **OleDbDataReader::GetBytes** method. In step 7 the **GetBytes** method is called with all parameters set to zero to obtain the binary data size. Then an array is allocated to hold the data and the **GetBytes** method is invoked one more time to retrieve the data into the array.

Once you compile and deploy the Music Catalog Service, you can test it by invoking **GetFiles** and **GetData** method via HTTP-GET from the web service URL. You will see that the XML output of the **GetData** method is not very efficient since each byte in the resulting array is encoded separately. Hence the actual transmitted XML response packet size will be about 10 times larger than the original MP3 file. For a more efficient communication, the **GetData** method should return a UTF-8 encoded **String** instead of a **char** array. Such modification is left for the reader as an exercise.

Here is the Music Catalog Service code:

```
#using <mscorlib.dll>
#using <System.dll>
#using <System.Web.dll>
#using <System.EnterpriseServices.dll>
#using <System.Web.Services.dll>
using namespace System;
using namespace System::Web;
using namespace System::Web::Services;
// For database access
#using <System.Data.dll>
using namespace System::Data::OleDb;
// For ArrayList
using namespace System::Collections;

namespace Test {
[WebService(Name="Music Catalog Service", Namespace="http://www.Gems3D.com")]
public __gc class MyWebService: public WebService {
```

```
public:
[WebMethod]
String* GetFiles() __gc[]
{
    // 1. Initialize connection string
    String* ConnectStr = String::Format(
    "Provider=Microsoft.Jet.OLEDB.4.0; Data Source={0}\\UltraMax-Music.mdb",
        Server->MapPath("."));

    // 2. Open database connection
    OleDbConnection* Conn = new OleDbConnection(ConnectStr);
    Conn->Open();
    // 3. Create SELECT command
    OleDbCommand* Cmd = new OleDbCommand("SELECT FileName FROM MP3Storage",
        Conn);
    // 4. Create simple data reader by executing the command
    OleDbDataReader* Reader = Cmd->ExecuteReader();

    // 5. Initialize empty dynamic array
    ArrayList* Results = new ArrayList();

    // 6. Read all rows, field 0 returned by the command
    while ( Reader->Read() )
        Results->Add(Reader->GetString(0));
    // 7. Close database connection
    Conn->Close();

    // 8. Convert from dynamic to static array
    String* ReturnValue[] = dynamic_cast<String* __gc[]>(
        Results->ToArray(__typeof(String)));
    return ReturnValue;
}


[WebMethod]
char GetData(String* FileName) __gc[]
{
    // 1. Initialize connection string
    String* ConnectStr = String::Format(
    "Provider=Microsoft.Jet.OLEDB.4.0; Data Source={0}\\UltraMax-Music.mdb",
        Server->MapPath("."));

    // 2. Open database connection
    OleDbConnection* Conn = new OleDbConnection(ConnectStr);
    Conn->Open();

    // 3. Initialize command SQL statement
```

```
String* Sql = String::Format(
    "SELECT MP3Data FROM MP3Storage WHERE FileName='{0}'", FileName);
// 4. Create SELECT command
OleDbCommand* Cmd = new OleDbCommand(Sql, Conn);
// 5. Create simple data reader by executing the command
OleDbDataReader* Reader = Cmd->ExecuteReader();

char Result __gc[] = 0;
// 6. Read the binary data
if ( Reader->Read() )
{
    // 7. Determine the data length
    int Size = (int)Reader->GetBytes(0, 0, 0, 0, 0);

    if ( Size )
    {
        // Allocate array
        Result = new char __gc[Size];
        // 8. Read data from the reader
        Reader->GetBytes(0, 0, Result, 0, Size);
    }
}
// 9. Close database connection
Conn->Close();
return Result;
    }
};
}
```

Using Web Services in Place of ISAPI Extensions

Because an ASP.NET web service class is embedded into an ASP.NET web page, the web service has full access to HTTP request/response by means of the ASP.NET **Request** and **Response** objects. Hence, it is possible to read directly from HTTP request and write directly to HTTP response from a web service method. This fact opens a possibility for creating "cheating" ASP.NET web services that return no XML (i.e., expose methods of type **void**) and instead generate HTML code as ISAPI extensions.

Below is a familiar Music Catalog Service from the "Creating Web Services That Use Database Access" immediate solution above. The web service was modified to return no XML (i.e., **GetFiles** and **GetData** web methods are of type **void**) and the **Context->Response** property is used to write the resulting HTML to the HTTP response.

The **GetFiles** method builds an HTML page containing a table of all MP3 files in a database with a download link for each file. The method uses the **Response->Write** method familiar to ASP developers to write HTML tags to HTTP response. To view the page you must type the following URL in your browser (provided that the web service is deployed into the WebServiceISAPI virtual root on the local machine):
http://localhost/WebServiceISAPI/WebService.asmx?GetFiles.

The **GetData** method produces a binary MP3 stream corresponding to the MP3 data of a selected file. Because binary streams are a little different from ordinary HTML pages, the method writes Content-Disposition, Content-Type, and Content-Length HTTP headers to indicate the MP3 file name (useful when saving the stream on disk), "application/mp3" content type and specify the file length. The actual data is written to HTTP response in chunks by means of the **Response->BinaryWrite** method. The **Response->BinaryWrite** method writes a specified byte array to HTTP response. If the response is buffered (which is true by default) the HTTP data is transmitted when the buffer gets full.

```cpp
#using <mscorlib.dll>
#using <System.dll>
#using <System.Web.dll>
#using <System.Web.Services.dll>
#using <System.EnterpriseServices.dll>
using namespace System;
using namespace System::Web;
using namespace System::Web::Services;
// For database access
#using <System.Data.dll>
using namespace System::Data::OleDb;
// For Path
using namespace System::IO;
// For ArrayList
using namespace System::Collections;

// ISAPI-like Web Service example
namespace Test {
[WebService(Name="Music Catalog Service", Namespace="http://www.Gems3D.com")]
public __gc class MyWebService : public WebService {
public:
    [WebMethod]
    // Retrieves the list of MP3 files for download
    void GetFiles()
    {
        // 1. Initialize connection string
        String* ConnectStr = String::Format(
        "Provider=Microsoft.Jet.OLEDB.4.0; Data Source={0}\\UltraMax-Music.mdb",
            Server->MapPath("."));

        // 2. Open database connection
        OleDbConnection* Conn = new OleDbConnection(ConnectStr);
        Conn->Open();
        // 3. Create SELECT command
        OleDbCommand* Cmd = new OleDbCommand(
            "SELECT FileName FROM MP3Storage", Conn);
        // 4. Create simple data reader by executing the command
```

```
        OleDbDataReader* Reader = Cmd->ExecuteReader();

        // 5. Write HTML header
        Context->Response->Write("<html><body><table border='1'><tr><td>File Name</td><td>Download
Link</td></tr>");

        // 6. Read each data row and build an HTML table with each row
        // containing file name and hyperlink for downloading the file
        while ( Reader->Read() )
        {
            String* FileName = Reader->GetString(0);
            Context->Response->Write("<tr><td>");
            Context->Response->Write(FileName);
            Context->Response->Write("</td>");
            Context->Response->Write("<td><a href='GetData?FileName=");
            Context->Response->Write(Server->UrlEncode(FileName));
            Context->Response->Write("'>Download ");
            Context->Response->Write(Path::GetExtension(FileName));
            Context->Response->Write(" file</a></td></tr>");
        }

        // 7. Write HTML footer
        Context->Response->Write("</table></html></body>");
        // 8. Close database connection
        Conn->Close();
}

[WebMethod]
// Retrieves MP3 file data based of MP3 file name
void GetData(String* FileName)
{
    // 1. Initialize connection string
    String* ConnectStr = String::Format(
    "Provider=Microsoft.Jet.OLEDB.4.0; Data Source={0}\\UltraMax-Music.mdb",
        Server->MapPath("."));

    // 2. Open database connection
    OleDbConnection* Conn = new OleDbConnection(ConnectStr);
    Conn->Open();
    // 3. Initialize command SQL statement
    String* Sql = String::Format(
        "SELECT MP3Data FROM MP3Storage WHERE FileName='{0}'", FileName);
    // 4. Create SELECT command
    OleDbCommand* Cmd = new OleDbCommand(Sql, Conn);
    // 5. Create simple data reader by executing the command
    OleDbDataReader* Reader = Cmd->ExecuteReader();
```

```
#define BUFFER_SIZE 16384
      // 6. Allocate I/O buffer
      char Buffer __gc[] = new char __gc[BUFFER_SIZE];
      // 7. Read binary data
      if ( Reader->Read() )
      {
          // Get data size for HTTP header
          __int64 BytesRead = Reader->GetBytes(0, 0, 0, 0, 0);

          // 8. Write HTTP headers
          Context->Response->AddHeader("Content-Disposition",
                String::Format("inline; filename={0}", FileName));
          Context->Response->AddHeader("Content-Type",
                String::Format("application/{0}", Path::GetExtension(FileName)));
          Context->Response->AddHeader("Content-Length", BytesRead.ToString());

          // 9. Using the I/O buffer read binary chunk from database and...
          for ( __int64 Position = 0; (BytesRead = Reader->GetBytes(0, Position,
                Buffer, 0, BUFFER_SIZE)) > 0; Position += BytesRead )
                // ...write the chunk to HTTP Response
                Context->Response->BinaryWrite(Buffer);
      }

      // 10. Close database connection
      Conn->Close();
   }
};
}
```

> **NOTE:** Attentive reader will find a small defect in the **GetData** method. The last **Reader-> GetBytes** method will return less than **BUFFER_SIZE** bytes, yet the entire buffer is transmitted with the **Response->BinaryWrite** method anyway. To trim the last binary packet to the proper length, one must allocate a new byte array to contain **BytesRead** < **BUFFER_SIZE** bytes, copy **BytesRead** from the **Buffer** to the new array, and transmit the new array instead of the **Buffer** array. Do this for an exercise. This extra hassle is caused by the fact that the **HttpResponse::BinaryWrite** method does not allow specifying only a portion of the buffer to transmit.

CHAPTER 11

Consuming Web Services Made with HTTP-GET, HTTP-POST, and SOAP

QUICK JUMPS

CHAPTER 11

Consuming Web Services Made with HTTP-GET, HTTP-POST, and SOAP

In Depth

You have now learned how to create basic ASP.NET Web Services using Managed C++. In this chapter, I will show you how to write Managed C++ code for *consuming* web services. The process of consuming a web service involves declaring the web services proxy class. Web service proxy classes essentially isolate the web service provider from the web service consumer and handle the necessary communication between the client and the web server. This communication is done according to a particular web service communication protocol. When developing ASP.NET Web Services with Visual C++ .NET you can choose a communication protocol—HTTP-GET, HTTP-POST, and SOAP over HTTP. In this chapter, I will examine HTTP-GET, HTTP-POST, and SOAP over HTTP protocols and related web service proxy classes that focus primarily on SOAP. You will learn how to declare web service methods to use a particular protocol, how to declare web service proxy classes in web service consumer applications tailored for communication with web services using a particular protocol, how to call web service methods synchronously and asynchronously, how to throw and catch exceptions thrown from a web service method, and how to use SOAP headers for communicating additional information to and from a web service.

Web Service Protocols

Communication with a web service involves transmitting messages between the service consumer and the service provider. When you invoke a web service method, a request message (which typically contains the method name and the input parameter values) is sent to the web service. The web service receives the requests, processes it, and usually (*but not always*) sends back a response message to the client containing output parameter values, the return method value (if any), or fault/exception information if the method invocation created an error.

Theoretically, a web service can use an arbitrary data format in combination with an arbitrary network protocol to communicate with clients. However, using proprietary protocols complicates integration of web services with other applications and may cause problems when transmitting data across the Internet due to architectural dependencies of proprietary protocols and proprietary data formats. Therefore, it is preferable (*but not required*) to use universally accepted *standard* protocols, which can travel through the Internet and penetrate firewalls. The following three protocols are most commonly used for communication with web services:

*   *HTTP-GET*: Uses the HTTP GET verb for initiating requests and transmitting data.

*   *HTTP-POST*: Uses the HTTP POST verb for initiating requests and transmitting data.

*   *Simple Object Access Protocol (SOAP)*: Defines an XML format for representing request or response messages that can be carried by any transport protocol.

HTTP-GET and HTTP-POST Protocols

HTTP-GET and HTTP-POST protocols provide the simplest way of invoking web service methods. Both protocols represent web service method parameters as URL-encoded (MIME type "application/x-www-form-urlencoded") name/value pairs. In the case of HTTP-POST, these parameters are stored in the HTTP request header, and in the case of HTTP-GET, they are appended to the URL as shown here:

http://*ServerName*/*dir*/*WebServiceName*.asmx/*MethodName*?*ParamName1*=*value1*& *ParamName2*=*value2*&...

When an ASP.NET web service receives and successfully processes an HTTP-GET or HTTP-POST request, it responds by returning an XML document containing the values of web method output parameters and/or the return value (if any). To illustrate invocation of a web service method using HTTP-GET protocol let's pretend that a www.UltraMax-Music.com web site hosts an ASP.NET web service called **DJ**. The **DJ** web service is represented by the DJ.asmx ASP.NET page and exposes a **GetSongCount** method, which accepts the **ArtistName** parameter and returns the number of songs by a specified artist available for download. Then, we must form the following URL to obtain the count of songs by "UltraMax:":

```
http://www.UltraMax-Music.com/DJ/DJ.asmx/GetSongCount?ArtistName=UltraMax
```

And the web service response may look like this:

```
<?xml version="1.0" ?>
<int xmlns="http://www.UltraMax-Music.com/">15</int>
```

In case of a failure, the web service would respond with an HTTP 500 (Internal Server Error) code as shown here:

> **WARNING!** HTTP-GET/HTTP-POST protocols do not support web methods that accept or return parameters other than primitive types. To implement web methods that transmit structured data or managed objects you should use SOAP protocol.

Simple Object Access Protocol (SOAP)

HTTP-GET and HTTP-POST are not the mainstream protocols for communicating with web services although they are very easy to use. Unfortunately, they provide no means for representing structured data. The also do not provide a means for describing parameter data types. Because of this, a new Simple Object Access Protocol (SOAP) was developed. Unlike HTTP-GET and HTTP-POST, SOAP was designed to represent messages that contain structured, typed data. SOAP is a high-level protocol that defines XML syntax and semantics for exchanging information in a distributed environment. SOAP offers much more functionality to developers in comparison with HTTP-GET or HTTP-POST protocols.

Since SOAP is a high-level protocol it must be carried by some *transport* protocol (i.e., TCP, HTTP, SMTP, and so on). SOAP is designed to be independent of any transport protocol. Thus, developers must implement *SOAP bindings* to particular transport protocols. The SOAP specification, however, defines a SOAP binding to a HTTP-POST protocol, which is most commonly used for communication with web services. Communication with a web service using SOAP involves a client sending a *SOAP request* message and the web service responding with a *SOAP response* message. The web service input/output parameter values are encoded as XML inside of the SOAP request/response messages. The process of invoking a web service method using SOAP is illustrated in Figure 11.1.

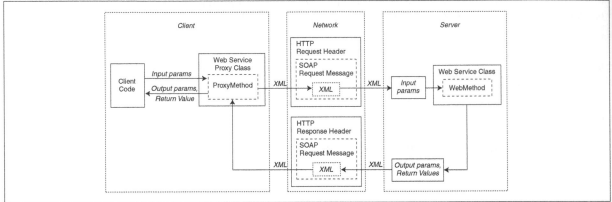

Figure 11.1 Communication with a web service by means of SOAP over HTTP.

To communicate with a web service a client usually constructs a *web service proxy* class, which *looks like* the web service and has local methods corresponding to web service methods. The following is a sequence of events that occur when the client invokes a proxy class method to communicate with the web service using a SOAP protocol bound to HTTP-POST:

1. The proxy class *serializes* the method input parameters to XML.

2. The proxy class constructs a SOAP request message using the target web method name and the XML parameter data.

3. The client framework initiates an HTTP-POST request and injects the SOAP message in the HTTP header.

4. The HTTP request travels across the network and arrives at the web server hosting the target web service.

5. The HTTP server (e.g., ASP.NET application) examines the request and extracts the SOAP request message.

6. The server framework extracts the web method name from the SOAP request and deserializes the data.

7. The server framework invokes the target web service method with the input parameter data extracted from the SOAP request message.

8. The web method finishes running and the framework serializes the values of output parameters and the method return value (if any) to XML.

9. The server framework constructs a SOAP response message, crams the return XML data inside the message, and packs the SOAP response message into the HTTP response header.

10. The web server transmits the HTTP response.

11. The HTTP response travels across the network and arrives back at the client.

12. The client framework examines the HTTP response and extracts the SOAP response message.

13. The client framework deserializes the XML with return data and passes the results to the proxy class.

14. The proxy method returns which concludes the communication. The proxy method output parameters and the return value are initialized with the deserialized XML data received in the SOAP response message.

SOAP Message Architecture

SOAP request/response messages have a similar simple architecture as shown in Figure 11.2.

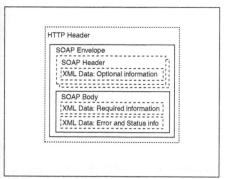

Figure 11.2 SOAP response/request message architecture.

The entire SOAP message is encapsulated inside of a *SOAP envelope* (**Envelope** XML element) and can contain the following elements:

* *SOAP headers (**Header** XML elements)*: Represents optional information.

* *SOAP body (**Body** XML element)*: Represents required information.

* *SOAP fault (**Fault** XML element)*: Represents error and status information.

SOAP request/response messages do not have to have headers but they must have a body. The response messages may contain a **Fault** element in the message **Body** if the message resulted in failure. The following example illustrates a SOAP request message embedded in HTTP header (i.e., SOAP message *bound* to HTTP-POST protocol):

```
POST /GameHost HTTP/1.1
Host: www.Gems3D.com
Content-Type: text/xml; charset="utf-8"
Content-Length: 382
SOAPAction:

<SOAP-ENV:Envelope
    xmlns:SOAP-ENV="http://schemas.xmlsoap.org/soap/envelope/"
    SOAP-ENV:encodingStyle="http://schemas.xmlsoap.org/soap/encoding/">
  <SOAP-ENV:Body>
      <m:RegisterHighScore xmlns:m="http://www.Gems3D.com">
          <firstName>Vlad</firstName>
          <lastName>Fomitchev</lastName>
          <score>998</score>
      </m:RegisterHighScore>
  </SOAP-ENV:Body>
</SOAP-ENV:Envelope>
```

The SOAP request message shown corresponds to a **RegisterHighScore** web service method call, which accepts **firstName**, **lastName**, and **score** input parameters. The successful web service SOAP response message embedded in the HTTP header may look like this:

```
HTTP/1.1 200 OK
Content-Type: text/xml; charset="utf-8"
Content-Length: 346

<SOAP-ENV:Envelope
    xmlns:SOAP-ENV="http://schemas.xmlsoap.org/soap/envelope/"
```

```
    SOAP-ENV:encodingStyle="http://schemas.xmlsoap.org/soap/encoding/"/>
    <SOAP-ENV:Body>
        <m:RegisterHighScoreResponse xmlns:m="http://www.Gems3D.com">
            <highScore>2784</highScore>
        </m:RegisterHighScoreResponse>
    </SOAP-ENV:Body>
</SOAP-ENV:Envelope>
```

The message indicates that **RegisterHighScore** method call succeeded and returned 2764 as the value of the **highScore** output parameter.

SOAP Header

A SOAP **Header** element can be used for extending a SOAP message with custom data, which does not require prior knowledge on behalf of the message recipient. Thus, the SOAP header can be used for passing auxiliary information. A SOAP header can be decorated with the following optional attributes:

* **actor**: Specifies the URI of the recipient in case the message is processed by multiple applications arranged in a chain. By examining the **actor** attribute an application can tell if the header was intended for it or not. "http://schemas.xmlsoap.org/soap/actor/next" actor value indicates the first application in the chain.

* **mustUnderstand**: When set to "1", indicates that the header recipient must be able to parse the header information and indicate in the response message whether it could make sense of the data. Otherwise, the recipient does not have to indicate whether it understood the header or not.

Here is an example of a required SOAP header:

```
<SOAP-ENV:Header>
    <t:GameType xmlns:t="http://www.Gems3D.com" SOAP-ENV:mustUnderstand="1">
        Simple
    </t:GameType>
</SOAP-ENV:Header>
```

SOAP Body

A SOAP **Body** element provides a way for exchanging mandatory information. A SOAP body corresponds to an XML fragment that represents data passed in the message. Data in the SOAP **Body** is encoded using the encoding rules identified in the SOAP specification (see http://www.w3.org/TR/SOAP/ for SOAP encoding details).

> **NOTE:** A SOAP **Body** element must directly follow the SOAP **Header** element in the SOAP **Envelope**. If the **Header** is not present, the **Body** element must be the first element in the SOAP **Envelope**.

SOAP Fault

A SOAP **Fault** element is used to pass error and status information in response messages. The **Fault** element can have the following subelements:

* **faultcode**: Status code, indicating *why* the error occurred:

  * **VersionMismatch**: SOAP **Envelope** element does not have valid namespace.

  * **MustUnderstand**: The application did not understand the header marked with the **mustUnderstand="**1" attribute.

  * **Client**: The fault was caused by the client supplying invalid data in the SOAP **Body.**

  * **Server**: An error occurred on the server for other reasons.

* **faultstring**: Error text.

* **faultactor**: URI of the application that caused the error (applicable for chained SOAP message processing).

* **detail**: Detailed error description.

Here is an example of a SOAP response message indicating an error in the method call caused by the unknown user data (i.e., the client passed bad data to the web service):

```
HTTP/1.1 500 Internal Server Error
Content-Type: text/xml; charset="utf-8"
Content-Length: 346

<SOAP-ENV:Envelope
    xmlns:SOAP-ENV="http://schemas.xmlsoap.org/soap/envelope/"/>
    <SOAP-ENV:Body>
        <SOAP-ENV:Fault>
            <faultcode>SOAP-ENV:Client</faultcode>
            <faultstring>No such user</faultstring>
        </SOAP-ENV:Fault>
    </SOAP-ENV:Body>
</SOAP-ENV:Envelope>
```

SOAP Binding to HTTP

The only SOAP binding defined in the SOAP specification is the HTTP-POST binding. When SOAP messages are transmitted using HTTP-POST, the SOAP envelope is embedded in the HTTP header. The following rules apply when transmitting SOAP messages using HHTP-POST protocol:

1. "text/xml" **content-type** must be used for both SOAP requests and responses.

2. SOAP requests *must* specify **SOAPAction** HTTP header field, which *should* contain the URI of the recipient of the SOAP message. An empty **SOAPAction** field is allowed. The field can be used by firewalls to filter SOAP requests.

3. SOAP responses must respond with a 2*xx* status code indicating a success, or a 500 status code (Internal Server Error) indicating a failure. In case of failure, the embedded SOAP message must contain the **Fault** element in the message **Body** describing the reason why the error occurred.

System::Web::Services::Protocols Namespace

The .NET Framework provides built-in support for communicating with web services using HTTP-GET, HTTP-POST, and SOAP protocols in the System::Web::Services::Protocols namespace. The System::Web::Services::Protocols namespace classes, exceptions, attributes, and enumerations are summarized in Tables 11.1 through 11.4, and the System::Web::Services::Protocols namespace class hierarchy is shown in Figure 11.3.

Table 11.1 System::Web::Services::Protocols namespace classes.

Class	Description
HttpGetClientProtocol	The base class for web service client proxies that use HTTP-GET protocol.
HttpPostClientProtocol	The base class for web service client proxies that use HTTP-POST protocol.
HttpSimpleClientProtocol	Abstract base class for the **HttpWebClientProtocol** class.
HttpWebClientProtocol	Abstract base class for **HttpGetClientProtocol** and **HttpPostClientProtocol** classes.
LogicalMethodInfo	Represents information (including parameter names and types) for a web service method.
SoapClientMessage	Represents a SOAP message sent by a web service client.
SoapExtension	The base class for SOAP extensions used by ASP.NET web services
SoapHeader	Abstract base class for SOAP headers.
SoapHeaderCollection	Implements a collection of **SoapHeader** objects.
SoapHttpClientProtocol	The base class for web service client proxies that use the SOAP protocol over HTTP.
SoapMessage	Represents a SOAP request or SOAP response message.
SoapServerMessage	Represents a SOAP message sent by a web service to a client.
SoapUnknownHeader	Represents SOAP header containing data in arbitrary (i.e., unknown) format.
WebClientAsyncResult	Represents an implementation of the **IAsyncResult** to be used when calling web service methods asynchronously.
WebClientProtocol	Abstract base class for all web service client proxies created using ASP.NET.

Table 11.2 System::Web::Services::Protocols namespace exceptions.

Exception	Description
SoapException	Thrown when a web service method is called using SOAP protocol and an exception occurs (an exception can be thrown by the CLR or by the web service method itself).
SoapHeaderException	Thrown when an XML Web service method is called using SOAP protocol and an exception occurs during the SOAP header processing (e.g., malformed header).

Table 11.3 System::Web::Services::Protocols namespace attributes.

Attribute	Description
HttpMethodAttribute	The attribute used by web service clients to specify input/output parameter formatters for serializing/de-serializing web method parameters transmitted over HTTP-GET or HTTP-POST protocols.
MatchAttribute	The attribute used for text pattern matching when parsing HTML pages.
SoapDocumentMethodAttribute	Specifies that SOAP messages to and from the method to which the attribute is applied use **Document** formatting.
SoapDocumentServiceAttribute	Specifies the default formatting style for SOAP requests and responses sent to/from a web service.
SoapExtensionAttribute	Abstract attribute for specifying that a SOAP extension should run with a web service method.
SoapHeaderAttribute	Specifies a SOAP header the client can process when applied to a web service method or a web service client.
SoapRpcMethodAttribute	Specifies **RPC** formatting for SOAP messages sent by a web service method to which the attribute applies.
SoapRpcServiceAttribute	Specifies the default formatting style for SOAP requests and responses sent to/from a web service.

Table 11.4 System::Web::Services::Protocols namespace enumerations.

Enumeration	Description
LogicalMethodTypes	Defines constants for synchronous or asynchronous web service method invocation: **Sync** and **Async**.
SoapHeaderDirection	Defines constants for specifying if the recipient of a **SoapHeader** is a web service, a web service client, or both: **In**, **InOut**, and **Out**.
SoapMessageStage	Defines constants for specifying the SOAP message processing stage: **AfterDeserialize**, **AfterSerialize**, **BeforeDeserialize**, and **BeforeSerialize**.
SoapParameterStyle	Defines constants for specifying the SOAP message parameter formatting: **Bare**, **Default**, and **Wrapped**.
SoapServiceRoutingStyle	Defines constants for specifying SOAP message routing: **RequestElement** and **SoapAction**.

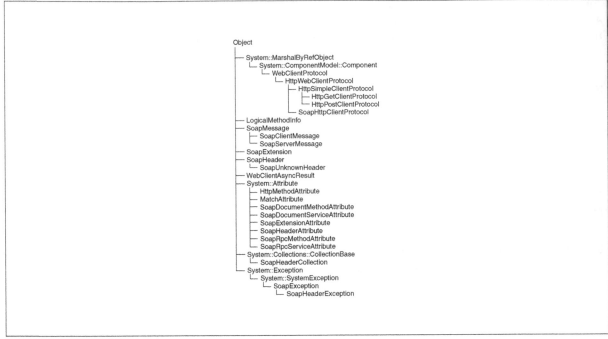

Figure 11.3 System::Web::Services::Protocols namespace class hierarchy.

Consuming Web Services

The .NET Framework encourages web service consumption by means of web service client proxies. A web service client proxy is a class that resides on a client's computer and has the same methods as the web service. When the client wants to call a web service method it calls the method of a web service proxy class. Then, the proxy class must perform necessary parameter serialization and send a request to a web service using a specified protocol. If a web service supports multiple protocols it is possible to create several proxy classes for the same web service, with each proxy class communicating using different protocols.

The System::Web::Services::Protocols supplies the following base proxy classes from which you must derive your own classes for communicating with a web service:

*   *any web protocol*: **HttpWebClientProtocol**

*   *HTTP-GET*: **HttpGetClientProtocol**

*   *HTTP-POST*: **HttpPostClientProtocol**

*   *SOAP over HTTP*: **HttpSoapClientProtocol**

Visual C++ .NET provides a means for automatic generation of web service proxy classes. (See the "Immediate Solutions" section in this chapter.) When manually implementing a web service client proxy class, you should define proxy class methods that match the web service methods and hide the web service communication details from the web service consumer in the proxy class methods.

WebClientProtocol Class

The base class for all XML web service client proxies is the **WebClientProtocol** class:

```
System::Object
|- System::MarshalByRefObject
   |- System::ComponentModel::Component
      |- System::Web::Services::Protocols::WebClientProtocol
```

```
Attributes: None
Abstract: Yes
Sealed: No
Implements Interfaces: None
```

The **WebClientProtocol** class constructors, properties, and methods are summarized in Tables 11.5 through 11.7.

Table 11.5 **WebClientProtocol** class constructors.

Constructor	Description
WebClientProtocol()	Default constructor.

Table 11.6 **WebClientProtocol** class properties.

Get/Set	Type	Property	Description
Get/Set	**String***	**ConnectionGroupName**	Gets or sets the name of the connection group.
Get/Set	**ICredentials***	**Credentials**	Gets or sets the credentials for the web service client authentication.
Get/Set	**bool**	**PreAuthenticate**	Gets or sets a Boolean value indicating whether to transmit a **WWW-authenticate** header in the first request to the web service.
Get/Set	**Encoding***	**RequestEncoding**	Gets or sets the encoding (e.g., UTF-8) used to transmit client requests.
Get/Set	**int**	**Timeout**	Gets or sets the timeout in milliseconds to wait for a synchronous web method request to complete.
Get/Set	**String***	**Url**	Gets or sets the base URL of the target web service.

Table 11.7 **WebClientProtocol** class methods.

Method	Description
virtual void Abort()	Cancels the current web method request.
protected: WebRequest* GetWebRequest(Uri* *uri***)**	Creates a **WebRequest** object for the specified URL.
protected: WebResponse* GetWebResponse(WebRequest* *request***)**	Returns a response of the synchronous web method request indicated by the specified **WebRequest** object.
protected: WebResponse* GetWebResponse(WebRequest* *request***, IAsyncResult*** *result***)**	Returns a response of the asynchronous web method request indicated by the specified **WebRequest** object and the **IAsyncResult**.

The **WebClientProtocol** class supports both synchronous and asynchronous communication with a web service on the level of web requests, which is the lowest level of communication. The proxy class requires the following steps to communicate with a web service:

1. Creates a **WebRequest** for a URL corresponding to the web service method, using the **GetWebRequest** method.

2. Packs the data to transmit to the web service method into the **WebRequest** object directly.

3. Transmits the request to the web server (e.g., using the **WebRequest::GetRequestStream** method).

4. Reads the response returned by the web service method using the **GetWebResponse** method and extracts the output data from the returned **WebResponse**.

HttpWebClientProtocol Class

The base class for XML web service client proxies that rely on HTTP for transport is the **HttpWebClientProtocol** class:

```
System::Object
|- System::MarshalByRefObject
   |- System::ComponentModel::Component
      |- System::Web::Services::Protocols::WebClientProtocol
         |- System::Web::Services::Protocols::HttpWebClientProtocol

Attributes: None
Abstract: Yes
Sealed: No
Implements Interfaces: None
```

The **HttpWebClientProtocol** class constructors, properties, and methods are summarized in Tables 11.8 and 11.9.

Table 11.8 **HttpWebClientProtocol** class constructors.

Constructor	Description
HttpWebClientProtocol()	Default constructor.

Table 11.9 **HttpWebClientProtocol** class properties.

Get/Set	Type	Property	Description
Get/Set	**bool**	**AllowAutoRedirect**	Gets or sets a Boolean value indicating whether to follow web server redirections.
Get	**X509CertificateCollection***	**ClientCertificates**	Contains a pointer to the collection of client certificates.
Get/Set	**CookieContainer***	**CookieContainer**	Gets or sets a pointer to the collection of cookies that can be used to maintain session state.
Get/Set	**IWebProxy***	**Proxy**	Gets or sets a pointer to the local web server proxy/firewall information.
Get/Set	**String***	**UserAgent**	Gets or sets the user application description.

HTTP-GET/HTTP-POST Proxy Classes

To implement HTTP-GET/HTTP-POST proxy classes, the .NET framework supplies **HttpSimpleClientProtocol** abstract base class and two concrete sealed classes: **HttpGetClientProtocol** and **HttpPostClientProtocol**, which are derived from the **HttpSimpleClientProtocol**:

```
System::Object
|- System::MarshalByRefObject
   |- System::ComponentModel::Component
      |- System::Web::Services::Protocols::WebClientProtocol
         |- System::Web::Services::Protocols::HttpWebClientProtocol
            |- System::Web::Services::Protocols::HttpSimpleClientProtocol
               |- System::Web::Services::Protocols::HttpGetClientProtocol
               |- System::Web::Services::Protocols::HttpPostClientProtocol
```

These classes do not have original members except for default public constructors. The **HttpSimpleClientProtocol** class extends the **HttpWebClientProtocol** class by providing the **BeginInvoke/EndEnvoke** and **Invoke** methods for asynchronous and synchronous calling of web service methods (see Table 11.10).

Table 11.10 **HttpWebClientProtocol** class methods.

Method	Description
protected: IAsyncResult* BeginInvoke(String* *methodName*, Object* *parameters* __gc[], AsyncCallback* *callback*, Object* *asyncState*)	Begins asynchronous invocation of the specified web service method using the specified parameters and callback delegates.
protected: Object* EndInvoke(IAsyncResult* *asyncResult*) __gc[]	Ends the asynchronous web service method request specified by the *asyncResult* and returns the array of output and by-reference parameter values including the method return value (if any).
protected: Object* Invoke(String* *methodName*, Object* *parameters* __gc[]) __gc[]	Invokes the specified web service method synchronously using the specified parameters and returns the array of output and by-reference parameter values including the method return value (if any).

SoapHttpClientProtocol Class

To communicate with web services using SOAP over HTTP you should use the **SoapHttpClientProtocol** class, which has the following inheritance structure:

```
System::Object
|- System::MarshalByRefObject
  |- System::ComponentModel::Component
    |- System::Web::Services::Protocols::WebClientProtocol
      |- System::Web::Services::Protocols::HttpWebClientProtocol
        |- System::Web::Services::Protocols::SoapHttpClientProtocol

Attributes: None
Abstract: No
Sealed: No
Implements Interfaces: None
```

The **SoapHttpClientProtocol** class constructors and methods are summarized in Tables 11.11 and 11.12.

Table 11.11 **SoapHttpClientProtocol** class constructors.

Constructor	Description
SoapHttpClientProtocol()	Default constructor.

Table 11.12 **SoapHttpClientProtocol** class methods.

Method	Description
protected: IAsyncResult* BeginInvoke(String* *methodName*, **Object*** *parameters* **__gc[], AsyncCallback*** *callback*, **Object*** *asyncState*)	Begins asynchronous invocation of the specified web service method using the specified parameters and callback delegate.
void Discover()	Binds the **SoapHttpClientProtocol**-derived class to a web service described by the discovery document referenced in the **Url** property of the class.
protected: Object* EndInvoke(IAsyncResult* *asyncResult*) **__gc[]**	Ends the asynchronous web service method request specified by the *asyncResult* and returns the array of output and by-reference parameter values including the method return value (if any).
protected: Object* Invoke(String* *methodName*, **Object*** *parameters* **__gc[]) __gc[]**	Invokes the specified web service method synchronously using the specified parameters and returns the array of output and by-reference parameter values including the method return value (if any).

When implementing web service client proxy classes that uses SOAP to communicate with the web service, you should derive your own class from the **SoapHttpClientProtocol** class. Then, you can define proxy methods corresponding to the web service methods and use the **Invoke** or **BeginInvoke** methods to call the web service methods synchronously or asynchronously.

SoapMessage Class

SOAP request or response messages are represented by the .NET Framework **SoapMessage** abstract base class as shown here:

```
System::Object
|- System::Web::Services::Protocols::SoapMessage

Attributes: None
Abstract: Yes
Sealed: No
Implements Interfaces: None
```

The **SoapMessage** class properties and methods are summarized in Tables 11.13 and 11.14.

Table 11.13 **SoapMessage** class properties.

Get/Set	Type	Property	Virtual	Description
Get	**String***	**Action**	Yes	Contains the value of the **SOAPAction** HTTP header field.
Get/Set	**String***	**ContentType**	No	Gets or sets the value for the HTTP header **content-type** field.
Get	**SoapException***	**Exception**	No	Contains a pointer to the exception that occurred during the web service method call.
Get	**SoapHeaderCollection***	**Headers**	No	Contains a pointer to the collection of SOAP headers contained in the SOAP message.
Get	**LogicalMethodInfo***	**MethodInfo**	Yes	Contains a pointer to the description of the web service method involved with the SOAP message.
Get	**bool**	**OneWay**	Yes	Contains **true** if the message is one-way (i.e., the response message is not expected).
Get	**SoapMessageStage**	**Stage**	No	Contains the current processing stage of the message.
Get	**Stream***	**Stream**	No	Contains a pointer to the stream containing the message data.
Get	**String***	**Url**	Yes	Contains the URL of the web service.

Table 11.14 **SoapMessage** class methods.

Method	Description
protected: virtual void EnsureInStage() = 0	Asserts that the current SOAP message processing stage is when the input message parameters are available.
protected: virtual void EnsureOutStage() = 0	Asserts that the current SOAP message processing stage is when the output message parameters are available.
protected: void EnsureStage(SoapMessageStage *stage*)	Asserts that the current SOAP message processing stage is the same as the specified stage
Object* GetInParameterValue(int *index*)	Returns the value of an input parameter at the specified index.
Object* GetOutParameterValue(int *index*)	Returns the value of an output parameter at the specified index.
Object* GetReturnValue()	Returns the web service method return value.

The most useful methods of the **SoapMessage** class are **GetInParameterValue, GetOutParameterValue**, and **GetReturnValue** methods. They allow you to retrieve values of the message input/output parameters and the return value of the web method.

SoapClientMessage and SoapServerMessage Classes

The implementations of SOAP request and SOAP response methods are provided by the **SoapClientMessage** and **SoapServerMessage** sealed classes, which are inherited from the **SoapMessage** abstract base class. The **SoapClientMessage** and **SoapServerMessage** classes have no original properties or methods and merely implement pure virtual properties and methods of the **SoapMessage** class.

SoapHeader Class

The .NET Framework supplies a **SoapHeader** abstract base class for representing SOAP message headers:

```
System::Object
|- System::Web::Services::Protocols::SoapHeader
   |- System::Web::Services::Protocols::SoapUnknownHeader


Attributes: None
Abstract: Yes
Sealed: No
Implements Interfaces: None
```

This class has no methods and provides properties corresponding to the SOAP **Header** element attributes. Its class constructors and properties are summarized in Tables 11.15 and 11.16.

Table 11.15 **SoapHeader** class constructors.

Constructor	Description
protected: SoapHeader()	Default constructor.

Table 11.16 **SoapHeader** class properties.

Get/Set	Type	Property	Description
Get/Set	**String***	**Actor**	Gets or sets the recipient of the SOAP header.
Get/Set	**bool**	**DidUnderstand**	Gets or sets a Boolean value indicating if the web service processed and understood the header.
Get/Set	**bool Encoded**	**MustUnderstand**	Gets or sets a Boolean value indicating if the message recipient must parse and understand the header data (i.e., **mustUnderstand** header attribute) for the Section 5 encoded SOAP messages.
Get/Set	**bool**	**MustUnderstand**	Gets or sets a Boolean value indicating whether the message recipient must parse and understand the header data (i.e., **mustUnderstand** header attribute).

SoapHeaderCollection Class

The .NET Framework supplies a **SoapHeaderCollection** class, which implements a collection of SOAP headers stored inside of a SOAP request/response message:

```
System::Object
|- System::Collections::CollectionBase
   |- System::Web::Services::Protocols::SoapHeaderCollection
```

```
Attributes: None
Abstract: No
Sealed: No
Implements Interfaces: None
```

The **SoapHeaderCollection** provides a public default constructor and the **Item** indexer property. The **SoapHeaderCollection** class properties and methods are summarized in Tables 11.17 and 11.18.

Table 11.17 **SoapHeaderCollection** class properties.

Get/Set	Type	Property	Description
Get/Set	**SoapHeader***	**Item(int *index*)**	Gets or sets the SOAP header at the specified index.

Table 11.18 **SoapHeaderCollection** class methods.

Method	Description
int Add(SoapHeader* *header*)	Adds the specified SOAP header to the collection.
bool Contains(SoapHeader* *header*)	Returns **true** if the specified SOAP header is found in the collection.
void CopyTo(SoapHeader* *array*[], int *index*)	Copies all SOAP headers from the collection to the specified array at the specified index.
int IndexOf(SoapHeader* *header*)	Returns the index of the specified SOAP header in the collection, or -1 if the header is not in the collection.
void Insert(int *index*, SoapHeader* *header*)	Inserts the specified SOAP header into the collection at the specified index.
void Remove(SoapHeader* *header*)	Removes the specified SOAP header from the collection.

SoapUnknownHeader Class

The .NET Framework supplies a **SoapUnknownHeader** class for representing SOAP headers that can contain arbitrary data in unknown format:

```
System::Object
|- System::Web::Services::Protocols::SoapHeader
   |- System::Web::Services::Protocols::SoapUnknownHeader
```

```
Attributes: None
Abstract: No
Sealed: Yes
Implements Interfaces: None
```

The **SoapUnknownHeader** provides a default constructor and a single original property, **Element**, that allows retrieving XML elements stored in the SOAP message header (see Tables 11.19 and 11.20).

Table 11.19 **SoapUnknownHeader** class constructors.

Constructor	Description
SoapUnknownHeader()	Default constructor.

Table 11.20 **SoapUnknownHeader** class properties.

Get/Set	Type	Property	Description
Get/Set	**XmlElement***	**Element**	Gets or sets the XML element of the SOAP header.

HttpMethod Attribute

HttpMethod attribute can be used to specify custom parameter formatters for a method of a proxy class that uses HTTP-POST/HTTP-GET protocol for communicating with a web service. The **HttpMethod** attribute has the following syntax:

```
[HttpMethod(ParameterFormatter=type1, ReturnFormatter=type2)]
```

The **ParameterFormatter** parameter specifies the formatter to be used to serialize input parameters, while the **ReturnFormatter** specifies the type to be used to deserialize output parameters.

> **NOTE:** When using the **HttpMethod** attribute with HTTP-GET/HTTP-POST proxies, the **ReturnFormatter** parameter must be set to **XmlReturnReader**. The **ParameterFormatter** type must be set to **UrlParameterFormatter** when using the HTTP-GET protocol, and to **HtmlFormParameterWriter** when using HTTP-POST protocol.

If you prefer the positional syntax, you can use the **HttpMethodAttribute** constructor to initialize the attribute as shown here:

```
HttpMethodAttribute();
HttpMethodAttribute(Type* returnFormatter, Type* parameterFormatter);
```

SoapDocumentService and SoapRpcService Attribute

You can use the **SoapDocumentService** and **SoapRpcService** attributes to specify the SOAP message formatting style for all web methods in the web service. The attributes have the following syntax:

```
[SoapDocumentService(ParameterStyle=ParameterStyle, RoutingStyle=RoutingStyle,
    Use=SOAPBindingUse)]

[SoapRpcService(RoutingStyle=RoutingStyle)]
```

Document Formatting

Document formatting requires that the XML data in the **Body** of a SOAP message is formatted according to an XSD schema. When the **Document** formatting is used, the XML data can consist of one ore more message parts following the **Body** element. Each message part is formatted according to the **Use** and **ParameterStyle** properties of the **SoapDocumentMethod** attribute. The **ParameterStyle** specifies whether each parameter should reside in an individual message part.

Rpc Formatting

Rpc formatting (same as Section 7 formatting) requires that all parameters are encapsulated within a single XML element in the SOAP message **Body** named after the web service method (i.e., structured XML representation). Each method parameter is represented as a child XML entity and must be named after the method parameter.

The **SoapDocumentService** and **SoapRpcService** attributes accept the **RoutingStyle** parameter, which specifies how SOAP messages are routed in case there is more than one application/recipient registered for processing SOAP messages:

* **RequestElement**: The message is routed based on the recipient specified in the first element (e.g., **Header** or SOAP message part) found in the SOAP message **Body**.

* **SoapAction**: The message is routed based on the recipient specified in the **SOAPAction** field in the HTTP header.

The following parameters are specific to the **SoapDocumentService** attribute:

* **ParameterStyle**: Specifies how to encode all method parameters:
    * **Bare**: The parameters are encoded as separate XML elements that directly follow the **Body** element of the SOAP message (i.e., SOAP message parts).
    * **Default**: Indicates that the *default* parameter encoding should be used, which was specified at the web service class level using the **SoapDocumentService** attribute.
    * **Wrapped**: The parameters are encoded in a single XML element following the **Body** element of the SOAP message (similar to **Rpc** formatting).
* **Use**: Specifies how to encode individual parameters:
    * **Default**: Indicates that the *default* parameter encoding should be used, which was specified at the web service class level using the **SoapDocumentService** attribute.
    * **Encoded**: The parameters (i.e., the message parts) is encoded using the *Section 5* encoding rules.
    * **Literal**: The parameters (i.e., the message parts) are encoded using the predefined XSD schema.

Section 5 Encoding

Section5 of the SOAP specification describes rules on encoding message parameters, including describing the parameter type information, without resorting to an XSD schema. See SOAP Specification at http://www.w3.org/TR/SOAP/ for details.

If you prefer the positional syntax, you can use the **SoapDocumentService** and **SoapRpcService** constructors to initialize the attributes:

```
SoapDocumentService();
```

```
SoapDocumentService(SoapBindingUse* use);
SoapDocumentService(ParameterStyle* style);
SoapRpcService();
```

> **NOTE:** SOAP message formatting affects only the structure of the SOAP messages sent to/from the web service (i.e., how method input/output parameters are represented). You may want to choose a particular formatting when manually implementing a custom web service proxy class.

SoapDocumentMethod and SoapRpcMethod Attribute

While the **SoapDocumentService** and **SoapRpcService** attributes allow specifying SOAP formatting for all web methods in the web service class, you can use the **SoapDocumentMethod** or **SoapRpcMethod** attributes to specify SOAP formatting for an individual web method. The **SoapDocumentMethod** and **SoapRpcMethod** attributes have the following syntax:

```
[SoapDocumentMethod(Action="Action", Binding="Binding",
    OneWay=BooleanValue, ParameterStyle=style,
    RequestElementName="RequestName", RequestNamespace="RequestNamespace",
    ResponseElementName="ResponseName", ResponseNamespace="ResponseNamespace",
    Use=SOAPBindingUse)]

[SoapRpcMethod(Action="Action", Binding="Binding", OneWay=BooleanValue,
    RequestElementName="RequestName", RequestNamespace="RequestNamespace",
    ResponseElementName="ResponseName", ResponseNamespace="ResponseNamespace")]
```

The **SoapDocumentMethod** and **SoapRpcMethod** attributes accept the following optional parameters:

* **Action**: Specifies **SOAPAction** HTTP header field.

* **Binding**: Specifies the name of the binding to be used in the WSDL description of the service.

* **OneWay**: When set to **true**, indicates that the web service client does not have to wait for the web service to finish processing the request. As soon as the web service receives a request, it responds with HTTP 202 status code, and the web service proxy method returns (no output parameters or return value is set).

* **RequestElementName**: Defines the name of the XML element used to encapsulate the method input parameters in the **Body** element of the SOAP request message.

* **RequestNamespace**: Defines the XML namespace for the SOAP request message.

* **ResponseElementName**: Defines the name of the XML element used to encapsulate the method output parameters in the **Body** element of the SOAP response message.

* **ResponseNamespace**: Defines the XML namespace for the SOAP response message.

If you prefer the positional syntax, you can use the **SoapDocumentMethod** and **SoapRpcMethod** constructors to initialize the attributes:

```
SoapDocumentMethod();
SoapDocumentMethod(String* action);
SoapRpcMethod();
```

```
SoapRpcMethod(String* action);
```

SoapHeader Attribute

To indicate that a particular web service method can process information from the SOAP message **Header**, you should mark the method with the **SoapHeader** attribute, which has the following syntax:

```
[SoapHeader("MemberName", Direction=direction, Required=BooleanValue)]
```

The **SoapHeader** attribute accepts a mandatory parameter, *MemberName*, which specifies the name of the web service class corresponding to the SOAP message Header data. The optional parameters are as follows:

* **Direction**: Specifies the SOAP header direction:

  * **In**: The header is sent to the web service.

  * **Out**: The header is sent to the web service client.

  * **InOut**: The header is sent both ways.

* **Required**: When set to **true** indicates that the header must be understood (e.g., **mustUnderstand Header** attribute set to 1) by the recipient.

If you prefer the positional syntax, you can use the **SoapHeaderAttribute** constructor:

```
SoapHeaderAttribute(String* memberName);
```

Immediate Solutions

Creating Web Service Proxies Using ClassWizard

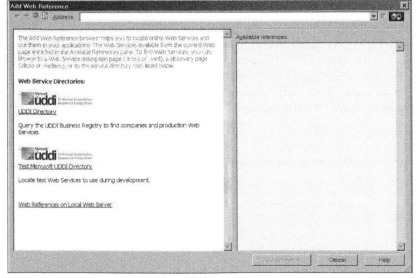

You can generate web service proxy classes either manually or automatically using the Visual C++ .NET wizard. To generate a web service proxy class automatically, right click anywhere in the Visual C++ .NET Solution Explorer and select "Add Web Reference" menu item from the context menu to open a Visual C++ "Add Web Reference" Wizard (see Figure 11.4).

TIP: The wizard supports generating web service proxy classes for both managed and unmanaged code.

Figure 11.4 Add Web Reference dialog.

To generate a web service proxy class you must either type the URL of a web service discovery, documentation, or WSDL document in the dialog's Address field and click the Add Reference button. If you do not know the web service URL, you can use the Microsoft UDDI directory to locate a particular service by following the "UDDI Directory" link. Alternatively, you can locate web services on your local web server by following the "Web References on Local Web Server" link or by typing the http://localhost/default.vsdisco URL in the dialog's Address field. The dialog will display the discovery document in the dialog's left pane and list the web service references in the right pane of the dialog. Select a desired web service by clicking on one of the web service references link on the right pane. The dialog will display the web service discovery document in the left pane and show links to the web service documentation and WSDL description document in the right pane. You can view the web service WSDL and documentation files, or you can conclude the process of adding a web service reference by clicking the Add Reference button. (The Add Reference button is originally disabled and enabled only when you find a valid web service reference.)

As soon as you click the Add Reference button the class wizard will generate three files:

*   *WebServiceName.h*: Web service client proxy class header file:

```
#using <System.DLL>
#using <WebServiceName.dll>
#using <System.Web.Services.DLL>
#using <System.Data.DLL>
```

*   *WebServiceName.cs*: Web service client proxy class C# implementation file.

*   *WebServiceName.dll*: Compiled web service client proxy class.

Where *WebServiceName* corresponds to the name of the added web service.

> **NOTE:** ClassWizard-generated web service proxy classes use SOAP over HTTP binding by default. To use other protocols you must either generate the web service proxy class manually or use the wsdl.exe .NET Framework SDK utility.

It may strike you that the web services client proxy class is generated using C#. The truth is that you would never have to get involved in the details of the web service client proxy class implementation. For that matter, the proxy class comes already compiled in a DLL to which you refer by means of the **#using <*WebServiceName*.dll>** statement. All you need to know about the web service client proxy class is web service method definitions, but you already know this from the web service documentation. Thus, simply instantiate the web service proxy class in your code using the default constructor and call its methods corresponding to the remote web service web methods.

> **TIP:** To obtain information on the web service methods and method parameters, view the web service documentation page. ASP.NET web services automatically generate the documentation page when you navigate to the webs service base URL (e.g., http://*SomeHost*/*SomeDir*/*WebService*.asmx). Alternatively, you can examine the C# source code generated by the ClassWizard (.cs-file) to see what web methods are available and what parameters they accept.

Manually Creating Web Service Proxies That Use SOAP over HTTP

Visual C++ .NET ClassWizard generates web service client proxies already compiled in a standalone DLL with the proxy class code expressed in C#. Thus, to modify the wizard-generated proxy class you have to deal with C#. You also have to distribute one more DLL along with your application.

For greater control over the proxy class and for tighter integration with the rest of the code in your program, you can create a web service proxy class from scratch (or you can manually convert the ClassWizard-generated C# code to Managed C++, which is for the most part a straight-forward process). Follow these steps to create a web service client proxy class that uses SOAP over HTTP from scratch:

1. Discover the web service for consumption and examine the web service documentation or WSDL document to find the supported protocols (e.g., HTTP-GET, HTTP-POST, or SOAP), available methods, and method parameter names and types.

2. Create a web service proxy class by deriving your own class from **SoapHttpClientProtocol**.

3. Decorate the web service proxy class with the **WebServiceBinding** attribute and set the **Namespace** parameter to match the web service namespace. (You do not have to specify the **Name** parameter of the **WebServiceBinding** attribute, but if you do, it must match the name of the SOAP binding, which is listed under the **service** entity, **port** subentity in the web service WSDL file).

4. In the proxy class constructor, initialize the class **Url** property with the web service base URL (e.g. http://*server*/*dir*/*WebSrvice*.aspx).

5. Define proxy class methods for calling web service methods *synchronously*:

   * Decorate the proxy class methods with the **SoapDocumentMethod** attribute. (Use the **SoapRpcMethod** attribute only if the corresponding web service method was defined using **SoapRpcMethod** attribute.)

   * Create an array of type **Object*** and initialize it with the parameters to the method. Here's an example:

     ```
     Object* params[] = {param1, param2, param3};
     ```

     If the web method does not accept any parameters, use an empty array:

     ```
     Object* params[] = new Object*[0];
     ```

   * Use the **Invoke** method to invoke the web method:

     ```
     Object* results[] = Invoke("MethodName", params);
     ```

   * The **results** array will contain the web method return value (if any) and the values of the output parameters. If the web method returns a value, cast the **results[0]** element into the proper return type:

     ```
     return dynamic_cast<String*>(results[0]);
     ```

6. To invoke web methods asynchronously, you must define pairs of **Begin***MethodName*/**End***MethodName* proxy class methods for initiating/completing asynchronous web method calls:

   * Use the **BeginInvoke** method to initiate the request.

   * Use the **EndInvoke** methods to complete the request.

To visualize the process of manual proxy class generation, consider the code example shown next, which demonstrates definition of the **WebServiceSoap** web service client proxy class that uses SOAP to HTTP binding:

```cpp
#using <mscorlib.dll>
#using <system.dll>
#using <system.web.dll>
#using <system.web.services.dll>
using namespace System;
using namespace System::Web::Services;
using namespace System::Web::Services::Protocols;

// Web service client proxy class
[WebServiceBinding(Name="MyWebServiceSoap", Namespace="http://www.Gems3D.com")]
public __gc class WebServiceSoap: public SoapHttpClientProtocol {
public:
    WebServiceSoap()
    {
        // Initialize the web service base URL
        Url = "http://localhost/WebService/WebService.asmx";
    }
    // Uppercase: synchronous
    [SoapDocumentMethod]
    String* Uppercase(String* text)
    {
        Object* params[] = {text};
        Object* results[] = Invoke("Uppercase", params);
        return dynamic_cast<String*>(results[0]);
    }
    // Uppercase: asynchronous
    IAsyncResult* BeginUppercase(String* text, AsyncCallback* callback,
        Object* asyncState)
    {
        Object* params[] = {text};
        return BeginInvoke("Uppercase", params, callback, asyncState);
    }
    String* EndUppercase(IAsyncResult* asyncResult)
    {
        Object* results[] = EndInvoke(asyncResult);
        return dynamic_cast<String*>(results[0]);
    }

    // AddTwo: synchronous
    [SoapDocumentMethod]
    int AddTwo(int a, int b)
    {
```

```
        Object* params[]  = {__box(a), __box(b)};
        Object* results[] = Invoke("AddTwo", params);
        return *dynamic_cast<__box int*>(results[0]);
    }
};
```

> **NOTE:** Web service proxy class methods that accept parameters that are in actuality value types require boxing of value types to form the array of parameters and unboxing of the value types when extracting the values of the output parameters.

You can also use the WSDL.exe .NET Framework SDK utility to automatically generate client proxy classes. When using WSDL.exe, you can specify the desired protocol (SOAP, HttpGet, or HttpPost) for the proxy class and the target language (VB, JS, or CS; C++ is not currently supported). The WSDL.exe utility is usually located in the "C:\Program Files\Microsoft Visual Studio .NET\FrameworkSDK\bin" folder and has the following typical usage syntax:

```
Wsdl.exe /p:protocol /l:language WebService_WSDL_URL.
```

Manually Creating Web Service Proxies That Use HTTP-GET/HTTP-POST

Unfortunately, the Visual C++ .NET Class Wizard does not allow you to generate web service client proxy classes bound to protocols other than SOAP over HTTP. Although the .NET Framework SDK wsdl.exe utility allows you to generate client proxy classes that use a specified protocol, the utility does not support generating client proxy classes in Managed C++ (JScript .NET, VB.NET, and C# are the only supported languages). Thus, if you want to use the HTTP-GET or HTTP-POST protocol in the web service client proxy class, you have no other choice but to write the web service client proxy class from scratch. Here are the steps required:

1. Create a web service proxy class by deriving your own class from **HttpGetClientProtocol** or **HttpPostClientProtocol**.

2. Decorate the web service proxy class with the **WebServiceBinding** attribute and set the **Namespace** parameter to match the web service namespace.

3. In the proxy class constructor initialize the class **Url** property with the web service base URL (e.g., http://*server*/*dir*/*WebSrvice*.aspx).

4. Define proxy class methods for calling web service methods *synchronously*:

    *   Decorate the proxy class methods of the HTTP-GET class with the **[HttpMethod(__typeof(XmlReturnReader), __typeof(UrlParameterWriter))]** attribute, for HTTP-POST proxy use the **[HttpMethod(__typeof(XmlReturnReader), __typeof(HtmlForm-ParameterWriter))]** attribute (these attributes specify method parameter formatting).

    *   If the method returns a value, decorate it with the second attribute **[returnvalue: System::Xml::Serialization::XmlRootAttribute("*ReturnType*", Namespace="http://www.Gems3D.com")]** (this attribute is required to specify the root element-*ReturnType*-of the XML returned as a result of the method execution; the *ReturnType* must match the return type name of the method spelled with lowercased first letter, e.g., **String** should be "string").

    *   Follow the same instructions as in the case of the SOAP over HTTP proxy to initialize the parameters and invoke the web method.

5. To invoke web methods asynchronously you must define pairs of **Begin***MethodName*/**End***MethodName* proxy class methods for initiating/completing asynchronous web method calls (no attributes are required).

```
#using <mscorlib.dll>
#using <system.dll>
#using <system.web.dll>
#using <system.web.services.dll>
using namespace System;
using namespace System::Web::Services;
using namespace System::Web::Services::Protocols;
// For XmlRootAttribute
#using <system.xml.dll>
using namespace System::Xml::Serialization;

[WebServiceBinding(Name="MyWebServiceHttpGet",Namespace="http://www.Gems3D.com")]
public __gc class WebServiceHttpGet: public HttpGetClientProtocol {
//public __gc class WebServiceHttpGet: public HttpPostClientProtocol {
public:
   WebServiceHttpGet()
   {
      Url = "http://localhost/WebService/WebService.asmx";
   }
   // Uppercase: synchronous
   //[HttpMethod(__typeof(XmlReturnReader), __typeof(HtmlFormParameterWriter))]
   [HttpMethod(__typeof(XmlReturnReader), __typeof(UrlParameterWriter))]
   [returnvalue: XmlRootAttribute("string",
      Namespace="http://www.Gems3D.com", IsNullable=true)]
   String* Uppercase(String* text)
   {
      Object* params[] = {text};
      Object* result = Invoke("Uppercase", String::Concat(Url,
         S"/Uppercase"), params);
      return dynamic_cast<String*>(result);
   }
   // Uppercase: asynchronous
   IAsyncResult* BeginUppercase(String* text, AsyncCallback* callback,
      Object* asyncState)
   {
      Object* params[] = {text};
      return BeginInvoke("Uppercase", String::Concat(Url,S"/Uppercase"),
         params, callback, asyncState);
   }
   String* EndUppercase(IAsyncResult* asyncResult)
   {
      Object* result = EndInvoke(asyncResult);
      return dynamic_cast<String*>(result);
   }
};
```

TIP: It may be easier to use the wsdl.exe utility to generate the HTTP-GET (/p:HttpGet option) or HTP-POST (/p:HttpPost option) proxy class in C# and convert the resulting C# code to Managed C++.

Invoking Web Service Methods Synchronously and Asynchronously

To invoke web service methods you must instantiate the web service client proxy class using the default constructor. Then, you can call the web service methods *synchronously* simply by calling methods of the proxy class. To call the web service methods *asynchronously* you must follow these steps:

1. Create a class that provides an **AsyncCallback**-compatible method for handling the notification raised on the asynchronous web method completion.

2. Create an **AsyncCallback**-compatible delegate.

3. Invoke the **Begin***MethodName* proxy class method, which invokes the web service method *MethodName* asynchronously and supply pointers to the **AsyncCallback** delegate and the client proxy class as parameters.

4. In the event-handling method behind the **AsyncCallback** delegate, obtain a pointer to the web service client proxy class by casting the **AsyncState** property of the **IAsyncResult** parameter and invoke the **End***MethodName* method of the web service proxy class to conclude the asynchronous method invocation and obtain the method output parameters and return value.

The code example shown next illustrates both synchronous and asynchronous web method invocation. The code constructs a web service client proxy class **WebServiceProxy**. Then, the **Uppercase** and **AddTwo** web service methods are invoked synchronously. Later, to invoke web methods asynchronously, the **CallbackClass** is constructed, and the **MyCallback** delegate is initialized with a pointer to the **UppercaseCallback** method of the **CallbackClass** class, which is compatible in signature with the **AsyncCallback** delegate. Also, the **CallbackClass** supplies a **SyncObject** synchronization object that is used to block the execution of the main thread until the **UppercaseCallback** method is invoked.

To call the **Uppercase** asynchronously the code invokes the **BeginUppercase** method of the **WebServiceProxy** class and waits until the **SyncObject** of the **CallbackClass** is signaled (**MyCallbackClass->SyncObject->WaitOne()**). When the web service finishes processing the **Uppercase** call, the **UppercaseCallback** is invoked, the **Uppercase** return value is extracted using the **EndUppercase** call, and the **SyncObject** is signaled (**SyncObject->Set()**).

```
#include "WebService.h"
#using <mscorlib.dll>
using namespace System;
using namespace System::Threading;

__gc struct CallbackClass {
   CallbackClass()
   {
      SyncObject = new AutoResetEvent(false);
   }
   void UppercaseCallback(IAsyncResult* result)
   {
      WebServiceSoap* WebServiceProxy = dynamic_cast<WebServiceSoap*>(
         result->AsyncState);
      Console::WriteLine("Uppercase completes asynchronously: {0}",
         WebServiceProxy->EndUppercase(result));
```

```
        SyncObject->Set();
    }
    AutoResetEvent* SyncObject;
};

void main()
{
    // 1. Instantiate a web service client proxy class
    WebServiceSoap* WebServiceProxy = new WebServiceSoap();

    // 2. Call web method synchronously
    String* Result = WebServiceProxy->Uppercase("ultramax music");
    Console::WriteLine(Result);

    int iResult = WebServiceProxy->AddTwo(11, 14);
    Console::WriteLine("11 + 14 = {0}", __box(iResult));

    // 3. Create notification callback
    CallbackClass* MyCallbackClass = new CallbackClass();
    AsyncCallback* MyCallback = new AsyncCallback(MyCallbackClass,
        CallbackClass::UppercaseCallback);
    // 4. Call web method asynchronously
    WebServiceProxy->BeginUppercase("veronica's art", MyCallback, WebServiceProxy);

    // 5. Wait for callback to be invoked
    MyCallbackClass->SyncObject->WaitOne();
}
```

Handling and Throwing Exceptions in Web Services

A web service method can throw an exception. On the web service consumer side the exception thrown by the web service method translates into an exception thrown by the web service client proxy class. Thus, you should handle web service exceptions in the same way you handle exceptions thrown by managed classes in your code. The following code example illustrates a simple web service, which exposes a single method **ThrowException** that throws an exception:

```
#using <mscorlib.dll>
#using <System.dll>
#using <System.Web.dll>
#using <System.Web.Services.dll>
#using <System.EnterpriseServices.dll>
using namespace System;
using namespace System::Web;
using namespace System::Web::Services;

namespace Test {
    [WebService(Name="MyWebService", Description="Test Web Service",
```

```
      Namespace="http://www.Gems3D.com")]
   public __gc class MyWebService : public WebService {
   public:
       [WebMethod(Description="Throws an exception")]
       void ThrowException(String* Text)
       {
           throw new Exception(String::Concat("An exception occurred, Text=",
               Text));
       }
   };
}
```

To practice catching exceptions thrown by web service methods, take a look at the following code example, which defines the web service client proxy class **WebServiceSoap** and calls the **ThrowException** web method inside of a **try-catch** block:

```
#using <mscorlib.dll>
#using <system.dll>
#using <system.web.dll>
#using <system.web.services.dll>
using namespace System;
using namespace System::Web::Services;
using namespace System::Web::Services::Protocols;

// Web service client proxy class
[WebServiceBinding(Name="WebServiceSoap", Namespace="http://www.Gems3D.com")]
public __gc class WebServiceSoap: public SoapHttpClientProtocol {
public:
   WebServiceSoap()
   {
       Url = "http://localhost/WebService7/WebService.asmx";
   }
   [SoapDocumentMethod]
   void ThrowException(String* Text)
   {
       Object* params[] = {Text};
       Object* results[] = Invoke("ThrowException", params);
   }
};
void main()
{
   // 1. Instantiate a web service client proxy class
   WebServiceSoap* WebServiceProxy = new WebServiceSoap();
   try {
       // 2. Invoke the web method that throws an exception
```

```
        WebServiceProxy->ThrowException("test");
    }
    catch(Exception* e) {
        Console::WriteLine("ERROR: {0}", e->Message);
    }
}
```

When you run the program, it outputs the detailed exception description including the custom exception text specified in the web service's **throw new Exception**(…) statement.

Managing Application and Session State

ASP.NET web services gain full access to ASP.NET application and session-state storage by means of the **Application** and the **Session** properties implemented by the **WebService** class. If you recall Chapter 10, application state allows storing data shared by all clients accessing particular ASP.NET application, while session-state allows storing data specific to a particular client session. Application state is always enabled, while session state is enabled by setting the **sessionState** parameter to **Inproc, StateServer,** or **SQLServer** in the web.config ASP.NET configuration file (see Chapter 12). Alternatively, you can enable session state for a particular ASP.NET application by launching Internet Information Services management console, locating the desired ASP.NET application virtual root under the Default Web Site, right-clicking on the virtual root to bring up the Properties dialog, on the Virtual Directory tab clicking the Configuration button to open the Application Configuration dialog, and checking the Enable session state check on the App Options tab of the Application Configuration dialog. You can also specify session timeout in minutes, which corresponds to the amount of time a client can remain idle within a particular session without causing the session state to expire and all session data to be lost.

Furthermore, the session state can be enabled or disabled for individual methods of a web service by specifying the **EnableSession** parameter of the **WebMethod** attribute applied to a particular web service method. (The **EnableSession** parameter is set to **true** by default.)

Once you enable session state, you can rely on the **Session** property of your web service class to store session data. The **Session** property is implemented by means of the **HttpSessionState** class, which corresponds to a simple name/value collection and exposes the **Item** accessor for reading/writing collection data.

The following web service example illustrates the usage of **Application** and **Session** properties of the **WebService** class. The web service provides two methods—**WriteState** and **ReadState** that allow writing/reading application and session state: The **bApplication** parameter discriminates between **Application** and **Session** state access.

```
#using <mscorlib.dll>
#using <System.dll>
#using <System.Web.dll>
#using <System.Web.Services.dll>
#using <System.EnterpriseServices.dll>
using namespace System;
using namespace System::Web;
using namespace System::Web::Services;
```

```
namespace Test {
    [WebService(Name="MyWebService", Namespace="http://www.Gems3D.com")]
    public __gc class MyWebService : public WebService {
    public:
        [WebMethod(Description="Writes application or session state",
            EnableSession=true)]
        void WriteState(String* Name, Object* Value, bool bApplication)
        {
            if ( bApplication )
                Application->Item[Name] = Value;
            else
                Session->Item[Name] = Value;
        }
        [WebMethod(Description="Reads application or session state",
            EnableSession=true)]
        Object* ReadState(String* Name, bool bApplication)
        {
            Object* Value;
            if ( bApplication )
                Value = Application->Item[Name];
            else
                Value = Session->Item[Name];
            return Value;
        }
    };
}
```

When session state is maintained in between HTTP requests, a session ID cookie is usually employed to identify a particular client session. Using cookies for identifying client sessions is most common, although it is possible to pass the session ID as a query string parameter.

To test the web service you can develop a simple client application as show here:

```
#using <mscorlib.dll>
#using <system.dll>
#using <system.web.dll>
#using <system.web.services.dll>
using namespace System;
using namespace System::Web::Services;
using namespace System::Web::Services::Protocols;
using namespace System::Threading;

// Web service client proxy class
[WebServiceBinding(Name="MyWebServiceSoap", Namespace="http://www.Gems3D.com")]
public __gc class WebServiceSoap: public SoapHttpClientProtocol {
```

```
public:
   WebServiceSoap()
   {
      Url = "http://localhost/WebService8/WebService.asmx";
   }
   // WriteState
   [SoapDocumentMethod]
   void WriteState(String* Name, Object* Value, bool bApplication)
   {
      Object* params[] = {Name, Value, __box(bApplication)};
      Object* results[] = Invoke("WriteState", params);
   }
   // ReadState
   [SoapDocumentMethod]
   Object* ReadState(String* Name, bool bApplication)
   {
      Object* params[] = {Name, __box(bApplication)};
      Object* results[] = Invoke("ReadState", params);
      return results[0];
   }
};
void main()
{
   // 1. Instantiate a web service client proxy class
   WebServiceSoap* WebServiceProxy = new WebServiceSoap();
   // 2. Initialize cookie container so that session state could
   // be maintained via session cookie
   WebTestProxy->CookieContainer = new CookieContainer(1);

   // 3. Read session state
   Console::WriteLine("Session(\"UltraMax Music\")={0}",
      WebServiceProxy->ReadState(S"UltraMax Music", false));
   // 4. Read application state
   Console::WriteLine("Application(\"Gems 3D\")={0}",
      WebServiceProxy->ReadState(S"Gems 3D", true));
   // 5. Write session state
   WebServiceProxy->WriteState(S"UltraMax Music", S"Techno/Classical", false);
   // 6. Write application state
   WebServiceProxy->WriteState(S"Gems 3D", S"Puzzle Game", true);
   // 7. Read back session state
   Console::WriteLine("Session(\"UltraMax Music\")={0}",
      WebServiceProxy->ReadState(S"UltraMax Music", false));
   // 8. Read back application state
   Console::WriteLine("Application(\"Gems 3D\")={0}",
      WebTestProxy->ReadState(S"Gems 3D", true));
}
```

Note the **WebTestProxy->CookieContainer = new CookieContainer(1)** statement in the aforementioned code (Step 2). This statement initializes and assigns a cookie container to the web service proxy class. This cookie container is necessary for storing a session ID cookie, which is required for identifying current session in between web method calls. (The **CookieContainer** is not initialized by default.)

The client application reads and writes both application and session state data using the **ReadState** and **WriteState** web methods. When you run the application for the first time both application-state and session-state storage is empty. Once you write data to the session storage in Step 5 you can read it back in Step 7. If you run the application again, the program in Step 4 will output data previously written to the application state. Application-state data is maintained until you reset the IIS Admin Service, or reboot the web server, or unload your ASP.NET application manually (i.e., by clicking the Unload button on the Virtual Directory tab of the Properties dialog of a particular ASP.NET virtual directory in Internet Information Services management console). Session state is reset every time a new client initializes a connection with the web service, or when the session expires

> **TIP:** Resetting ASP.NET application state also resets session state for this application.

Using SOAP Headers for Exchanging Data with a Web Service

SOAP headers can be used to exchange optional information between web service provider and consumer. Also, SOAP headers can be viewed as a mechanism for implementing persistence in web service fields. Since ASP.NET web services do not maintain state information automatically, one of the ways to keep the web service public fields in sync with the web service client proxy class fields is by transmitting persistent field values in each call to the web service methods. SOAP provides a mechanism for synchronizing the web service class fields with the client proxy class fields by transmitting the field data in the SOAP header. (Alternatively you can use ASP.NET session state to store web service persistent fields.)

To use SOAP headers you must modify both the web service server and client proxy code. On the server side, here are the steps required:

1.   Create a public class derived from the **SoapHeader** and define fields that you will transmit in the SOAP header. (You can create as many **SoapHeader**-derived structures as you want and use them in different SOAP headers.)

2.   Add a public web service field that is a pointer to the defined SOAP header class.

3.   Decorate a web service method with the **SoapHeader** attribute supplying the SOAP header field name as a parameter (the **SoapHeader** attribute indicates that the web service method is interested in the SOAP header).

4.   Feel free to modify and access the SOAP header fields in the web method code.

The following web service example defines a custom SOAP header class called **MyHeader**, which contains two **String** fields, **SessionID** and **SessionDesc**. To implement the header, the web service class defines a member variable (i.e., field) **SessionInfo** of type **MyHeader***. Finally, the **SoapHeaderTest** method is decorated with the **[SoapHeader("SessionInfo")]** to indicate that the method requires the **SessionInfo** data to be transmitted in the SOAP header:

```
#using <mscorlib.dll>
#using <System.dll>
#using <System.Web.dll>
#using <System.Web.Services.dll>
#using <System.EnterpriseServices.dll>
using namespace System;
using namespace System::Web;
using namespace System::Web::Services;
using namespace System::Web::Services::Protocols;

namespace Test {
   // SOAP Header
   public __gc struct MyHeader: public SoapHeader {
      String* SessionID;
      String* SessionDesc;
   };

   [WebService(Name="MyWebService", Description="Test Web Service",
      Namespace="http://www.Gems3D.com")]
   public __gc class MyWebService: public WebService {
   public:
      MyHeader* SessionInfo;
      [WebMethod(Description="Accesses required SOAP header")]
      [SoapHeader("SessionInfo")]
      String* SoapHeaderTest()
      {
         return String::Format("Session ID of the '{0}' session is {1}",
               SessionInfo->SessionDesc, SessionInfo->SessionID);
      }
      [WebMethod(Description="Access optional SOAP header ")]
      [SoapHeader("SessionInfo", Required=false)]
      String* SoapHeaderTest2()
      {
         if ( SessionInfo )
            return String::Format("Session ID of the '{0}' session is {1}",
                  SessionInfo->SessionDesc, SessionInfo->SessionID);
         else
            return S"Session information is missing";
      }
   };
}
```

SOAP headers defined with the **SoapHeader** attribute are required by default. To save network bandwidth you may elect to transmit the SOAP header data only when necessary. To indicate that the SOAP header data is optional, you should decorate the web service method with the **SoapHeader** attribute and set the **Required** attribute parameter to **false**. (See the **SoapHeaderTest2** method of the web service class in the example above.) Then, you would have to check whether the pointer to the web service class field implementing the SOAP header is initialized. If the pointer to the field is not initialized, no SOAP header data was supplied during the call to the web service method.

To complete the round of SOAP header communication, you must add the following changes to the web service client proxy class:

1.   Copy the declaration of the SOAP header class to the web service client proxy class.

2.   Add a public web service proxy class field that is a pointer to the defined SOAP header class.

3.   Decorate a web service proxy class method with the **SoapHeader** attribute supplying the SOAP header field name as a parameter. (The **SoapHeader** attribute ensures that the SOAP header data is transmitted when you invoke the web method decorated with the attribute.)

The following code example illustrates the web service client proxy class corresponding to the web service class defined in the previous sample. The proxy class defines the same **MyHeader** SOAP header structure. It also defines the **SessionInfo** field of type **MyHeader***, decorates the **SoapHeaderTest** method with the **[SoapHeader("SessionInfo")]** attribute to indicate required header, and decorates the **SoapHeaderTest2** method with the **[SoapHeader("SessionInfo", Required=false)]** attribute to indicate optional header:

```
#using <mscorlib.dll>
#using <system.dll>
#using <system.web.dll>
#using <system.web.services.dll>
using namespace System;
using namespace System::Web::Services;
using namespace System::Web::Services::Protocols;

// SOAP Header
public __gc struct MyHeader: public SoapHeader {
    String* SessionID;
    String* SessionDesc;
};

// Web service client proxy class
[WebServiceBinding(Name="MyWebServiceSoap", Namespace="http://www.Gems3D.com")]
public __gc class WebServiceSoap: public SoapHttpClientProtocol {
public:
    MyHeader* SessionInfo;
    WebServiceSoap()
    {
        Url = "http://localhost/WebService9/WebService.asmx";
    }
    [SoapHeader("SessionInfo")]
    [SoapDocumentMethod]
    String* SoapHeaderTest()
```

```
   {
      Object* results[] = Invoke("SoapHeaderTest", new Object*[0]);
      return dynamic_cast<String*>(results[0]);
   }
   [SoapHeader("SessionInfo", Required=false)]
   [SoapDocumentMethod]
   String* SoapHeaderTest2()
   {
      Object* results[] = Invoke("SoapHeaderTest2", new Object*[0]);
      return dynamic_cast<String*>(results[0]);
   }
};

void main()
{
   // 1. Instantiate a web service client proxy class
   WebServiceSoap* WebServiceProxy = new WebServiceSoap();

   try {
      // 2. Instantiate SOAP header object
      WebServiceProxy->SessionInfo = new MyHeader;
      // Set header data
      WebServiceProxy->SessionInfo->SessionID = S"ABC";
      WebServiceProxy->SessionInfo->SessionDesc = S"test";

      // 3. Invoke the web methods that use the SOAP header
      Console::WriteLine("SoapHeaderTest: {0}",
         WebServiceProxy->SoapHeaderTest());
      Console::WriteLine("SoapHeaderTest2: {0}",
         WebServiceProxy->SoapHeaderTest2());

      // 4. Remove SOAP header
      WebServiceProxy->SessionInfo = 0;
      // 7. Invoke the web methods that use the SOAP header
      Console::WriteLine("SoapHeaderTest2: {0}",
         WebServiceProxy->SoapHeaderTest2());
      Console::WriteLine("SoapHeaderTest: {0}",
         WebServiceProxy->SoapHeaderTest());
   }
   catch(Exception* e) {
      Console::WriteLine("ERROR: {0}", e->Message);
   }
}
```

The sample program instantiates a web service client proxy class, allocates and initializes the **SessionInfo** header data, and invokes the web service methods. The **SessionInfo** data is transmitted to the web service in the SOAP message header.

In Step 4, the sample program deallocates the SOAP header by setting the **SessionInfo** pointer to Null. Thus, when the **SoapHeaderTest2** and **SoapHeaderTest** methods are invoked no header data is transmitted. Since the **SoapHeaderTest2** does not require the header data, the method call succeeds. But the **SoapHeaderTest** method requires the SOAP header data and throws an exception because the **SessionInfo** pointer is Null.

> **NOTE:** If you generate a web service client proxy class using the ClassWizard and the target web service uses SOAP headers, the SOAP header support is added automatically to the web service client proxy class and the proxy class *HeaderType*Value member variable of type *HeaderType** is defined to hold the header data.

Web Services: Definition Language (WSDL), Discovery, Security, and Configuration

QUICK JUMPS

CHAPTER 12

Web Services: Definition Language (WSDL), Discovery, Security, and Configuration

In Depth

In the previous two chapters you learned how to create and consume a simple ASP.NET web service. Consuming a web service involves locating (*discovering*) a web service, obtaining information about a web service (querying a *web service definition*), and generating a web service proxy class based on the supported communication protocols and available methods acquired about the web service. In this chapter, you will learn about the Web Service Definition Language (WSDL)—a powerful tool used to completely describe web services. I will also discuss the ASP.NET Web Service configuration by means of ASP.NET web.config configuration files and securing web services using Windows integrated authentication, SSL and encrypted SOAP headers.

Web Service Description Language (WSDL)

In order for a client to consume a web service, the client must know which methods the web service has to offer, the parameters these methods accept, and how to invoke the web service methods in general. Although you can describe a web service in a number of ways (e.g., using text files, HTML pages, or other types of electronic or printed documentation), the *standard* way to describe a web service is to use an XML-based *Web Service Description Language* (WSDL). This language defines a web service as a collection of communication end points that can send and receive messages.

The WSDL specification is quite voluminous and somewhat convoluted. You will probably never have to deal with WSDL directly. It is used primarily by the .NET Framework and Visual Studio .NET behind the scenes. Yet it is helpful to understand the basic concepts of WSDL so that you can read and comprehend basic WSDL definitions describing a web service that you are about to consume.

A WSDL document conveys two types of information about a web service:

* Lists the methods available to a web service consumer, including method names and input/output parameter names and types.

* Lists communication protocols supported by the web service (SOAP, HHTP GET, HTTP POST, or MIME) and provides details on invoking the web service methods using a particular protocol.

These two types of information are completely separated in a WSDL document to allow you to reuse elements and separate the abstract web service information from the details of a specific implementation scenario.

In general, a WSDL document contains the following elements:

* **Operation**: Describes a web service method that can be called by a client.

* **Message**: Describes an input/output parameter of a web service method.

* **Types**: Represents type definitions used by **Message** elements.

* **Port Type**: Describes web service communication end points (i.e., web service methods).

* **Binding**: Defines a binding of particular **Port Type** to a concrete protocol.

* **Port**: Represents a communication end point defined as a combination of a particular **Binding** to a network address-URL (i.e., an entry point for a concrete protocol).

* **Service**: A collection of web service communication end points.

NOTE: WSDL relies on XSD to express data type information in **Types** and **Message** definitions.

A structure of a WSDL document is illustrated on Figure 12.1.

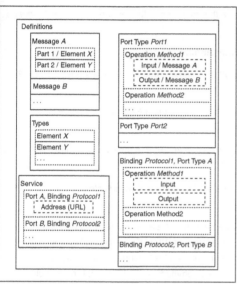

Figure 12.1 WSDL document element hierarchy.

A web service is described as a collection of communication end points or **Port Types**. Each **Port Type** contains a collection of **Operation** entities, where each individual operation corresponds to a method of a web service that can be called by a web service client. An **Operation** is characterized by a set of **Input/Output** parameters, which correspond to **Message** entities. Messages are described in a separate WSDL entity with each **Message** consisting of multiple **Element** entities. Types of all **Element** entities are described using XSD schemas in the **Types** entity.

Binding entities provide the details necessary for implementing a communication channel to a web service using a specific protocol such as HTTP-GET, HTTP-POST, or SOAP. A binding lists web service methods that can be invoked using the specified protocol and specifies how input/output parameters are transmitted and encoded. Finally, **Port** elements grouped under the **Service** entity define a web service entry-point URL to be used by a particular protocol binding (e.g., the web service URL to use for SOAP communication, the service URL for HTTP-GET, the service URL for HTTP-POST, and so on).

For a complete reference on WSDL, visit the W3 Consortium website at http://www.w3.org/TR/wsdl.

System::Web::Services::Description Namespace

A web service description document can be stored in a separate static WSDL file or it can be generated on the fly. ASP.NET web services support generating web service WSDL document dynamically. The web service WSDL is returned when you append "?WSDL" to an ASP.NET web service URL. Here's an example:

```
http://www.UltraMax-Music.com/DJ/DJ.asmx?wsdl
```

To provide developers with means to programmatically access, modify, and generate web service description information using WSDL standard, the .NET Framework supplies the System::Web::Services::Description namespace that defines classes and enumerations corresponding to XML entities of a WSDL document.

System::Web::Services::Description namespace classes and enumerations are summarized in Tables 12.1 and 12.2. The System::Web::Services::Description namespace class hierarchy is presented in Figure 12.2.

Table 12.1 System::Web::Services::Description namespace classes.

Class	Description
Binding	Encapsulates the **binding** WSDL element, which describes operations and message formats supported by a particular protocol.
BindingCollection	Implements a collection of **Binding** objects.
DocumentableItem	An abstract base class for key WSDL elements such as **Binding**, **Message**, and so on.
FaultBinding	Represents an error messages that might be output as a result of a web service operation.
FaultBindingCollection	Implements a collection of **FaultBinding** objects.
HttpAddressBinding	Encapsulates **http::address** WSDL element that specifies the base URI for the **Port**.
HttpBinding	Encapsulates **http::binding** WSDL element that indicates that the **Binding** uses the HTTP protocol.
HttpOperationBinding	Encapsulates **http::operation** WSDL element that specifies a relative URI for the **Operation**.
HttpUrlEncodedBinding	Encapsulates **http::urlEncoded** WSDL element that indicates that all message parts must be URL encoded.
HttpUrlReplacementBinding	Encapsulates **http::urlReplacement** WSDL element that indicates that all message parts must be encoded into an HTTP URL using custom replacement algorithm (e.g., one can derive /name1=value1 /name2=value2 syntax for encoding web method parameters submitted using HTTP-GET instead of standard name1=value1&name2=value2).
Import	Encapsulates the **import** WSDL element that associates an XML namespace with a document URL.
ImportCollection	Implements a collection of **Import** objects.
InputBinding	Encapsulates the **input** WSDL element that specifies information about web service input messages.
Message	Encapsulates the **message** WSDL element that describes a web service method parameter.
MessageBinding	Specifies how abstract content is mapped into a concrete format.
MessageCollection	Implements a collection of **Message** objects.
MessagePart	Encapsulates a **part** WSDL element that represents a part of a **message**.

<Continued on Next Page>

<Table 12.1 Continued>

Class	Description
MessagePartCollection	Implements a collection of **MessagePart** objects.
MimeContentBinding	Encapsulates a **mime:content** WSDL element that specifies the MIME format for the body of a HTTP transmission.
MimeMultipartRelatedBinding	Encapsulates a **mime:multipartRelated** WSDL element that specifies the MIME format for the individual parts of multi-part HTTP transmission.
MimePart	Encapsulates a **mime:part** WSDL element that represents an single part of a multipart HTTP transmission.
MimePartCollection	Implements a collection of **MimePart** objects.
MimeTextBinding	Represents an extensibility element for **InputBinding**, **OutputBinding**, or **MimePart**, specifying HTTP transmission search patterns.
MimeTextMatch	Represents a text pattern to search the HTTP transmission for.
MimeTextMatchCollection	Implements a collection of **MimeTextMatch** objects.
MimeXmlBinding	Encapsulates a **mime:part** WSDL element that specifies non SOAP-compliant XML messages.
Operation	Encapsulates an **operation** WSDL element that represents a web service method.
OperationBinding	Represents a binding of an **operation** to a concrete protocol.
OperationBindingCollection	Implements a collection of **OperationBinding** objects.
OperationCollection	Implements a collection of **Operation** objects.
OperationFault	Encapsulates a **fault** WSDL element that specifies an error message returned by the operation.
OperationFaultCollection	Implements a collection of **OperationFault** objects.
OperationInput	Encapsulates an **input** WSDL element that specifies **operation** input parameters.
OperationMessage	Represents a message type used by an **operation**.
OperationMessageCollection	Implements a collection of **OperationInput** and **OperationOutput** objects.
OperationOutput	Encapsulates an **output** WSDL element that specifies **operation** output parameters.
OutputBinding	Encapsulates the **output** WSDL element that specifies information about web service output messages.
Port	Encapsulates the **port** WSDL element that represents a web service entry point.
PortCollection	Implements a collection of **Port** objects.

<Continued on Next Page>

<Table 12.1 Continued>

Class	Description
PortType	Encapsulates the **portType** WSDL element that represents a collection of web service methods.
PortTypeCollection	Implements a collection of **PortType** elements.
Service	Encapsulates the **service** WSDL element that represents a collection of web service entry points.
ServiceCollection	Implements a collection of **Service** objects.
ServiceDescription	Supports creating, reading, and writing WSDL documents.
ServiceDescriptionBaseCollection	Abstract base class for the **ServiceDescriptionCollection**.
ServiceDescriptionCollection	Implements a collection of **ServiceDescription** objects.
ServiceDescriptionFormatExtension	Represents an extensibility element added to a web service.
ServiceDescriptionFormatExtensionCollection	Implements a collection of **ServiceDescriptionFormatExtension** objects.
ServiceDescriptionImporter	Supports generating client proxy classes for web services.
ServiceDescriptionReflector	Supports dynamic creation and viewing of types defined by a web service.
SoapAddressBinding	Represents an extensibility element added to a Port within an XML Web service. This class cannot be inherited.
SoapBinding	Encapsulates the **soap:binding** WSDL element that specifies binding to SOAP protocol.
SoapBodyBinding	Encapsulates the **soap:body** WSDL element that specifies how input/output messages appear inside the SOAP Body element.
SoapFaultBinding	Encapsulates the **soap:fault** WSDL element that specifies the contents of the SOAP Fault Details element.
SoapHeaderBinding	Encapsulates the **soap:header** WSDL element that specifies information transmitted inside of a SOAP Header element in the SOAP Envelope.
SoapHeaderFaultBinding	Encapsulates the **soap:headerFault** WSDL element that specifies fault information transmitted inside of a SOAP Header element in the SOAP Envelope.
SoapOperationBinding	Encapsulates the **soap:operation** WSDL element that specifies additional information on the SOAP operation.
SoapTransportImporter	Abstract base class for classes importing SOAP transmission protocols into web services.
Types	Encapsulates **types** WSDL element that represents a collection of types used in web service messages.

Table 12.2 System::Web::Services::Description namespace enumerations.

Enumeration	Description
OperationFlow	Defines constants for specifying types of web service operations: **None**, **Notification**, **OneWay**, **RequestResponse**, and **SolicitResponse**.
SoapBindingStyle	Defines constants for specifying procedure-oriented (i.e., parameter/return value messages) or document-oriented SOAP messages: **Default**, **Document**, and **Rpc**.
SoapBindingUse	Defines message part encodings for SOAP: **Default**, **Encoded**, and **Literal**.

Figure 12.2 The System::Web::Services::Description namespace class hierarchy.

ServiceDescription Class

In addition to classes encapsulating WSDL document elements, the System::Web::Services::Description namespace provides a **ServiceDescription** class that provides a means of loading and parsing WSDL documents:

```
System::Object
|- System::Web::Services::Description::DocumentableItem
   |-
System::Web::Services::Description::ServiceDescription

Attributes: None
Abstract: No
Sealed: Yes
Implements Interfaces: None
```

The **ServiceDescription** class constructors, fields, properties. and methods are summarized in Tables 12.3 through 12.6.

Table 12.3 **ServiceDescription** class constructors.

Constructor	Description
ServiceDescription()	Default constructor.

Table 12.4 **ServiceDescription** class fields.

Field	Description
const String* Namespace	The XML namespace in which the **ServiceDescription** is defined.

Table 12.5 **ServiceDescription** class properties.

Get/Set	Type	Property	Description
Get	**BindingCollection***	**Bindings**	Contains a pointer to the collection of WSDL **Binding** elements.
Get	**ServiceDescriptionFormatExtensionCollection***	**Extensions**	Contains a pointer to the collection of WSDL extensibility elements.
Get	**ImportCollection***	**Imports**	Contains a pointer to the collection of WSDL **Import** elements.
Get	**MessageCollection***	**Messages**	Contains a pointer to the collection of WSDL **Message** elements.
Get/Set	**String***	**Name**	Gets or sets the **name** attribute of the **<descriptions>** tag enclosing the WSDL document.
Get	**PortTypeCollection***	**PortTypes**	Contains a pointer to the collection of WSDL **PortType** elements.
Get/Set	**String***	**RetrievalUrl**	Gets or sets a URL from which the WSDL is retrieved.
Get	**ServiceDescriptionCollection***	**ServiceDescriptions**	Contains a pointer to the collection that owns the current **ServiceDescription** object.
Get	**ServiceCollection***	**Services**	Contains a pointer to the collection of WSDL **Service** elements.
Get/Set	**String***	**TargetNamespace**	Gets or sets the **targetNamespace** attribute of the **<descriptions>** tag enclosing the WSDL document.
Get/Set	**Types***	**Types**	Gets or sets the collection of the **Type** elements.

Table 12.6 **ServiceDescription** class methods.

Method	Description
static bool CanRead(XmlReader* *reader*)	Returns **true** if the specified **XmlReader** stream contains a valid WSDL document.
static ServiceDescription* Read(String* *path*)	
static ServiceDescription* Read(Stream* *stream*)	
static ServiceDescription* Read(TextReader* *stream*)	
static ServiceDescription* Read(XmlReader* *stream*)	Reads and parses a WSDL document from the specified file or stream.
void Write(String* *path*)	
void Write(Stream* *stream*)	
void Write(TextWriter* *stream*)	
void Write(XmlWriter* *stream*)	Writes the WSDL document to the specified file or stream.

You can use the **Read** method of the **ServiceDescription** class to read and parse a WSDL document. Then, you can modify the web service description, or manually create a totally new WSDL document and write it to a file or stream using the **Write** method. The .NET Framework supplies an additional class, **ServiceDescriptionCollection,** to provide storage and retrieval means for multiple **ServiceDescription** objects.

Web Service Discovery

Once you develop and deploy a web service you may want to "advertise" the web service so that clients can locate and use the service. Clients, on the other hand, should be able to locate a particular web service for consumption. Both tasks of declaring a web service existence and locating a web service on a particular server can be achieved by means of the *web service discovery*. From the client's perspective, web service discovery encompasses the process of locating a web service and obtaining the web service description. From the server's point of view, the process of discovery involves specifying the crucial information about a web service in a *discovery document*.

There are two types of web service discovery:

* *Static*: Involves examining a static discovery document (.disco file) located at a specified URL.

* *Dynamic*: Involves iterative search of a web server directory tree for static discovery files (.disco), dynamic discovery files (.vsdisco files), or ASP.NET web services (.asmx files).

In the end, both types of discovery yield URLs containing WSDL descriptions of web services found on the webs server.

Static Discovery Files (.disco)

A static discovery file is an XML document, which contains the following information:

* *Discovery References (**discoveryRef** XML element)*: Links to other discovery documents.
* *Contract Reference (**contractRef** XML element)*: A link to the WSDL description of the web service.
* *Schema Reference (**schemaRef** XML element)*: A link to the discovery document XSD schema.

NOTE: A static discovery file must contain the **contractRef** element specifying the URL of a WSDL description of the web service. Discovery and schema reference information is optional.

Here is an example of a static discovery file (.disco):

```
<?xml version="1.0" encoding="utf-8" ?>
<discovery xmlns:xsd="http://www.w3.org/2001/XMLSchema"
    xmlns:xsi="http://www.w3.org/2001/XMLSchema-instance"
    xmlns="http://schemas.xmlsoap.org/disco/">
    <contractRef ref="http://localhost/WebService.NET/WebService.NET.asmx?wsdl"
        docRef="http://localhost/WebService.NET/WebService.NET.asmx"
        xmlns="http://schemas.xmlsoap.org/disco/scl/"/>
</discovery>
```

The body of a static discovery document must be enclosed in the **discovery** element and must contain a single **contractRef** element specifying the URL of the web service WSDL description in the **ref** attribute. In addition, the **contractRef** element can specify a link to the web service documentation in the **docRef** attribute.

Dynamic Discovery Files (.vsdisco)

A dynamic discovery file is an XML document, which contains the list of the web server directories to exclude from the search for discovery documents in the **exclude** XML elements. Here is an example of a dynamic discovery file (.vsdisco):

```
<?xml version="1.0" encoding="utf-8" ?>
<dynamicDiscovery xmlns="urn:schemas-dynamicdiscovery:disco.2000-03-17">
    <exclude path="_vti_cnf" />
    <exclude path="_vti_pvt" />
    <exclude path="_vti_log" />
    <exclude path="_vti_script" />
    <exclude path="_vti_txt" />
    <exclude path="Web References" />
</dynamicDiscovery>
```

NOTE: The body of a dynamic discovery document must be enclosed within the **dynamicDiscovery** element.

On a development server running .NET Framework and ASP.NET, the IIS root folder typically contains a default.vsdisco file, which represents a starting point for web service discovery. When a client (web browser) requests the default .vsdisco file (or any other .vsdisco file corresponding to a dynamic discovery document), the

IIS invokes the aspnet_isapi.dll, which generates and returns a combined discovery document containing references (in the **discoveryRef** elements) to all discovery documents found on the web server. Here's an example:

```
<?xml version="1.0" encoding="utf-8" ?>
<discovery xmlns:xsd="http://www.w3.org/2001/XMLSchema"
    xmlns:xsi="http://www.w3.org/2001/XMLSchema-instance"
    xmlns="http://schemas.xmlsoap.org/disco/">
    <discoveryRef
        ref="http://localhost/WebService.NET/WebService.NET.vsdisco" />
    <discoveryRef
        ref="http://localhost/WebServiceATL/WebService.ATL.disco" />
</discovery>
```

To continue the process of a web service discovery, the client should request one of the discovery documents found by the process of dynamic discovery.

> **NOTE:** When manually constructing discovery files you must specify the following namespaces for the discovery XML elements: **discovery**-http://schemas.xmlsoap.org/disco/; **contractRef**-http://schemas.xmlsoap.org/disco/scl; **schemaRef**-http://schemas.xmlsoap.org/disco/.

System::Web::Services::Discovery Namespace

The .NET Framework supplies the System::Web::Services::Discovery namespace that supports web service discovery and corresponds to static and dynamic discovery documents. The System::Web::Services::Discovery namespace classes are summarized in Table 12.7. The System::Web::Services::Discovery namespace class hierarchy is illustrated in Figure 12.3.

Table 12.7 System::Web::Services::Discovery namespace classes.

Class	Description
ContractReference	Encapsulates the **contractRef** XML document, which specifies the URL of the web service WSDL description.
DiscoveryClientDocumentCollection	Represents a collection of documents obtained during web services discovery.
DiscoveryClientProtocol	Supports programmatic webs service discovery, including reading, downloading, and writing web service discovery documents.
DiscoveryClientResultsFile **DiscoveryClientProtocol::WriteAll**	Represents the root element of an XML document written using the method.
DiscoveryClientReferenceCollection	Implements a collection of the **DiscoveryReference** objects.
DiscoveryClientResult **DiscoveryClientProtocol::WriteAll**	Represents the details of a discovery reference written using the method.
DiscoveryClientResultCollection	Contains a collection of DiscoveryClientResult objects. This class cannot be inherited.

<Continued on Next Page>

<Table 12.7 Continued>

Class	Description
DiscoveryDocument	Represents a discovery document (static or dynamic).
DiscoveryDocumentReference	Encapsulates the **discoveryRef** XML document, which specifies the URL of a web service discovery document.
DiscoveryExceptionDictionary	Implements a collection of exception occurred during the process of web services discovery.
DiscoveryReference **SchemaReference**	Abstract base class for the **ContractReference**, **DiscoveryDocumentReference** and classes.
DiscoveryReferenceCollection	Implements a collection of **DiscoveryReference** objects.
SchemaReference	Encapsulates the **schemaRef** XML document, which specifies the URL of the XSD schema of a web service discovery document.
SoapBinding	Represents a SOAP binding in a discovery document.

Figure 12.3 The System::Web::Services::Discovery namespace class hierarchy.

DiscoveryClientProtocol Class

To programmatically discover web service information, the System::Web::Services::Discovery namespace supplies a **DiscoveryClientProtocol** class:

```
System::Object
|- System::MarshalByRefObject
   |- System::ComponentModel::Component
      |- System::Web::Services::Protocols::WebClientProtocol
         |- System::Web::Services::Protocols::HttpWebClientProtocol
            |- System::Web::Services::Discovery::DiscoveryClientProtocol
```

Attributes: None
Abstract: No
Sealed: No
Implements Interfaces: None

The **DiscoveryClientProtocol** class supports downloading, reading, and writing discovery documents, including all referenced XSD schemas and WSDL documents to and from URLs, files, and streams. The **DiscoveryClient-Protocol** class constructors, properties, and methods are summarized in Tables 12.8 through 12.10.

Table 12.8 **DiscoveryClientProtocol** class constructors.

Constructor	Description
DiscoveryClientProtocol()	Default constructor.

Table 12.9 **DiscoveryClientProtocol** class properties.

Get/Set	Type	Property	Description
Get	**IList***	**AdditionalInformation**	Contains additional information found in the discovery document.
Get	**DiscoveryClientDocumentCollection***	**Document**	Contains a pointer to the collection of the discovery documents found.
Get	**DiscoveryExceptionDictionary***	**Errors**	Contains a pointer to the collection of errors encountered during the web service discovery.
Get	**DiscoveryClientReferenceCollection***	**References**	Contains a pointer to the collection of the discovery document references found.

Table 12.10 **DiscoveryClientProtocol** class methods.

Method	Description
DiscoveryDocument* Discover(String* *url***)**	Returns a discovery document at the specified URL.
DiscoveryDocument* DiscoverAny(String* *url***)**	Returns a discovery, WSDL, or XSD document at the specified URL.
Stream* Download(String** *url***)**	
Stream* Download(String** *url***, String**** *contentType***)**	Downloads the specified discovery document and returns it as a stream. Optional *contentType* argument specifies the MIME encoding of the discovery document.
DiscoveryClientResultCollection* ReadAll(String* *mapFile***)**	Reads a file containing a map of previously saved discovery documents, including XSD schemas and WSDL files.
void ResolveAll()	Resolves all references to discovery documents, XSD schemas, WSDL files, and referenced discovery documents.
void ResolveOneLevel()	Resolves all references to discovery documents, XSD schemas, WSDL files, and referenced discovery documents.
DiscoveryClientResultCollection* WriteAll(String* *directory***, String*** *mapFile***)**	Writes all discovery documents, including XSD schemas, WSDL files and referenced discovery documents to the specified map file directory (all related documents are stored in the specified directory, which is created if necessary).

DiscoveryDocument Class

A discovery document (.disco or .vsdisco file) is represented in the .NET Framework by means of the **DiscoveryDocument** class:

```
System::Object
|- System::Web::Services::Discovery::DiscoveryDocument

Attributes: None
Abstract: No
Sealed: Yes
Implements Interfaces: None
```

The **DiscoveryDocument** class exposes **Read** and **Write** for reading and writing a single discovery document from and to a specified stream. The **DiscoveryDocument** class constructors, fields, properties, and methods are summarized in Tables 12.11 through 12.14.

Table 12.11 **DiscoveryDocument** class constructors.

Constructor	Description
DiscoveryDocument()	Default constructor.

Table 12.12 **DiscoveryDocument** class fields.

Constructor	Description
const String*	**Namespace** XML namespace of the **discovery** XML element.

Table 12.13 **DiscoveryDocument** class properties.

Get/Set	Type	Property	Description
Get	**IList***	**References**	Contains a pointer to the list of references contained in the discovery document.

Table 12.14 **DiscoveryDocument** class methods.

Method	Description
static bool CanRead(XmlReader* reader)	Returns **true** if the specified **XmlReader** stream contains a valid discovery document.
static DiscoveryDocument* Read(Stream* stream)	
static DiscoveryDocument* Read(TextReader* stream)	
static DiscoveryDocument* Read(XmlReader* stream)	Reads and parses a discovery document from the specified stream.
void Write(Stream* stream)	
void Write(TextWriter* stream)	
void Write(XmlWriter* stream)	Writes the discovery document to the specified stream.

The UDDI Service

To locate a particular web service on the Internet or to find out about web services offered by a particular company, developers should use the Universal Description, Discovery, and Integration (UDDI) Service. The UDDI Service provides the means for implementing a searchable directory of web services. To see a UDDI Service in action you can visit Microsoft's UDDI page, http://uddi.microsoft.com/visualstudio. This page allows you to search for web services given the name of a business. (The same page is used by Visual C++ .NET when you are adding a web reference to the project using the Add Web Reference context menu in Solution Explorer.)

The key component of UDDI is the *UDDI business registration*, an XML document describing a business entity and its web services. The information provided in a UDDI business registration consists of three components:

* *Business information*: Address, contact information, and other known identifiers.

* *Service information*: Categorized list of web services based on standard taxonomies.

* *Binding information*: References to WSDL and discovery documents of the web services.

By examining a business registration, XML documents residing in a UDDI Web Service directory it is possible to find all services provided by a particular company, or to find a web service matching a desired description (or a web service with desired function). Once a desired service is located and its WSDL document is obtained, the web service can be integrated into a client application.

Unfortunately, the UDDI Service is not directly supported by .NET Framework. To enable programmatic registration and location of web services using UDDI Service you should use the Microsoft UDDI SDK, which is available as a free download from Microsoft's MSDN site.

Web Service Configuration

To fine-tune web services after deployment, the .NET Framework and ASP.NET provides a configuration system for specifying ASP.NET application and web service runtime settings. ASP.NET application configuration information is stored in the Web.config file, which uses XML syntax to represent configuration data.

The Web.config file can have the following format for configuring web services:

```
<configuration>
    <system.web>
        <authentication>
        <authorization>
        <compilation>
        <customErrors>
        <globalization>
        <httpRuntime>
        <identity>
        <sessionState>
        <trace>
        <trust>
        <webServices>
    </system.web>
<configuration>
```

Hierarchal Configuration Architecture

ASP.NET employs a *hierarchical configuration architecture*. Configuration files residing in parent directories provide default configuration settings for child directories. Configuration files in child directories can be used to override settings specified by the parent configuration file.

The **<system.web>** XML entity identifies configuration information applicable to ASP.NET web applications. The following settings can be used when configuring web services:

*   **authentication**: Specifies ASP.NET authentication settings in the **mode** attribute:

```
<authentication mode="Windows|Forms|Passport|None">
```

*   **authorization**: Allows specifying users that are explicitly granted or denied access to the web service:

```
<authorization>
   <allow users="users" roles="roles" verbs="verbs"/>
   <deny users="users" roles="roles" verbs="verbs"/>
</authorization>
```

The **users** attribute specifies the list of user IDs ("*" indicates all users). The **roles** attribute specifies the comma-separated list of user groups. The **verbs** attribute specifies HTTP verbs (GET, HEAD, POST, and DEBUG) that are allowed or denied access to the web service.

* **compilation**: Specifies code generation settings for dynamically compiled ASP.NET pages. The only useful attribute of the **compilation** XML entity is **debug** because ASP.NET web services built with Visual C++ .NET are already compiled. This attribute specifies whether to include debug symbols into the resulting ASP.NET application:

```
<compilation debug="true|false"/>
```

* **customErrors**: Specifies information about custom errors:

```
<customErrors defaultResirect="url" mode="On|Off|RemoteOnly">
   <error statusCode="code" redirect="url"/>
</customErrors>
```

The **defaultResirect** attribute specifies the default page that is displayed when an HTTP server error occurs. The **mode** attribute specifies whether custom errors are enabled or disabled (**On/Off**), or shown only to remote clients (**RemoteOnly**), while the ASP.NET errors are shown only to the local host. The error tags specify redirect pages associated with particular HTTP error codes.

* **globalization**: Specifies request/response encoding (e.g., UTF-8, ASCII, ISO, and so on):

```
<globalization requestEncoding="encoding" responseEncoding="encoding"
   fileEncoding="encoding" culture="culture"/>
```

The **fileEncoding** attribute specifies ASP.NET file parsing. The **culture** attribute specifies culture information (**System::Globalization::CultureInfo** strings) for processing incoming web requests.

* **httpRuntime**: Specifies ASP.NET application runtime settings:

```
<httpRuntime useFullyQualifiedRedirectUrl="true|false"
   maxRequestLength="kbytes" executionTimeout="seconds"
   minFreeThreads="threads" minFreeLocalRequestFreeThreads="threads"
   appRequestQueueLimit="requests"/>
```

The **useFullyQualifiedRedirectUrl** attribute specifies whether client-side redirects will appear as fully qualified or relative URLs. The **maxRequestLength** attribute specifies the maximum request length in kilobytes. The **executionTimeout** attribute specifies the request execution/web method processing timeout in seconds. The **minFreeThreads** attribute specifies the minimum number of free threads for servicing new requests that require additional threads (e.g., for multithreaded web methods). The **minFreeLocalRequestFreeThreads** attribute specifies the minimum number of free threads for servicing requests originating from the local host. Finally, the **appRequestQueueLimit** attribute specifies the maximum number of requests that the ASP.NET application will queue before issuing the HTTP 503 "Server Too Busy" error.

* **identity**: Specifies the identity, which the web service will impersonate (i.e., the web service will operate as if it was launched from a specified user account given the security restrictions/privileges of the specified user):

```
<identity impersonate="true|false" userName="username"
    password="password"/>
```

* **sessionState**: Configures session state management:

```
<sessionState mode="Off|Inproc|StateServer|SQLServer"
    cookieless="true|false" timeout="minutes"
    stateConnectionString="tcpip=server:port"
    sqlConnectionString="ConnectString"/>
```

The **mode** attribute specifies the session state management mode. The options are:

* **off**: Session state is not maintained.

* **Inproc**: Session state is managed and stored locally.

* **StateServer**: Session state is stored on a remote server.

* **SQLServer**: Session state is stored in the SQL Server database.

TIP: The **Inproc** session-state handler is by far the fastest. However, if you implement a web farm (i.e., multiple web servers connected in parallel for load balancing) you should use the **StateServer** or **SQLServer** option. When using web farms requests pertaining to the same session can be handled by different servers. Thus, in order to maintain session state among web farm servers you must implement an external session storage accessible to all web servers in the farm, e.g., a dedicated state server or a dedicated SQL Server database. **Inproc** storage is private to a particular web server and cannot be accessed by another web server in the web farm.

The **cookieless** attribute indicates if a session cookie is used to identify client sessions. The **timeout** attribute specifies the session timeout in minutes. The **stateConnectionString** attribute specifies the name and port of the remote server for storing the session state if the **mode=StateServer**. The **sqlConnectionString** attribute specifies the SQL Server connect string for storing session information if the **mode=SQLServer**.

* **trace**: Specifies the application-level tracing/logging settings:

```
<trace enabled="true|false" localOnly="true|false"
    pageOutput="true|false" requestLimit="limit"
    traceMode="SortByTime|sortByCategory"/>
```

The **enabled** attribute indicates if the tracing is enabled. The **localOnly** attribute indicates if the trace viewer is available only on the web server hosting the service. The **pageOutput** attribute indicates if the trance information is automatically appended at the end of each page (if **pageOutput=false** you can view the application trance by requesting the trace.axd file from the application root directory). The **requestLimit** attribute specifies the number of trace requests to store on the server. The **traceMode** attribute specifies the sort order for trace information.

* **trust**: Specifies the code access security level associated with a particular requester URL (i.e., different web service clients can be assigned different trust levels):

```
<trust level="Full|High|Low|None" originUrl="url"/>
```

* **webServices**: Specifies ASP.NET web service settings:

```
<webServices>
    <protocols>
        <add name="HttpPost|HttpGet|HttpSoap|Documentation"/>
    </protocols>
    <wsdlHelpGenerator href="HelpPage"/>
</webServices>
```

The **protocols** section defines one ore more protocols supported by the web service. The **wsdlHelpGenerator** section specifies the URL of the web service help page. Typically, an ASP.NET web service automatically generates the help page when you request the web service URL without specifying any parameters. You can, however, specify a different URL for the web service documentation.

Web Service Authentication

Not all web services are meant to be publicly accessible for everybody. In some cases you may want to restrict access to the web service and/or require password authentication. You can use several types of authentication with ASP.NET web services:

* *Basic*: Basic Windows authentication with the password sent as clear text.
    * *Advantages*: Fast, easy, and versatile; you can gain access to various resources provided that you supply the correct user name and password.
    * *Disadvantages*: Dangerously insecure (anybody can sniff network packets and steal the unprotected password).
    WARNING! You should never use basic authentication with passwords sent as clear text when working with secure data such as customer information, credit-card numbers, and so on. A potential theft of such information may doom your business.

* *Basic over SSL*: Basic Windows authentication with the password sent as clear text. Secure Socket Layer (SSL) encryption is used to communicate with the web service.
    * *Advantages*: Easy and versatile.
    * *Disadvantages*: Results in substantially increased CPU load due to computational complexity inherent with the public key encryption.

* *Integrated Windows*: Windows integrated security is used to authenticate web service clients. Passwords are encrypted using Windows encryption services.
    * *Advantages*: Transparent and secure.
    * *Disadvantages*: Web service clients are granted access based on the user ID, under which account the client software is running. With Integrated Window security you cannot supply an alternate user ID and password to acquire different access rights.

*   *Client Certificate*: Web service may require clients to identify themselves by providing digital certificates issued by a mutually trusted authority (such as VeriSign). Certificate information is transmitted via SSL.

> *   *Advantages*: Extremely secure.
>
> *   *Disadvantages*: Increases the CPU load for service providers due to the use of SSL. Increases the need to obtain (purchase) and maintain (protect) digital certificates for the consumer.

*   *Forms*: Web service redirects unauthenticated requests to a specially provided HTML form, which collects user credentials and submits them to the web service. Each subsequent request must contain encrypted user credentials in the request header.

> *   *Advantages*: Visual for user as it provides custom login page.
>
> *   *Disadvantages*: Intended primarily for "normal" web applications and generally not suitable for web services.

*   *Passport*: Web service relies on centralized Microsoft Passport service to authenticate users. The idea behind Passport is to eliminate numerous separate credentials that are required when accessing different web sites or online services: Simply register once with Passport and use your credentials everywhere (or more accurately with sites that honor Passport-authenticated credentials).

> *   *Advantages*: In theory, provides "register once – login anywhere" paradigm.
>
> *   *Disadvantages*: In practice, not enough sites honor Passport authentication, plus web service/content provider needs to register with Passport themselves in order to be able to tap into Passport authentication.

Obviously, each authentication method has its own area of applicability. When developing Internet applications it is customary to use Basic authentication over SSL. Intranet applications, on the other hand, frequently rely on Integrated Windows authentication.

> **WARNING!** Web service authentication options specified in the Web.config configuration file do not override authentication options for the virtual directory specified in the Internet Information Services management console.

Immediate Solutions

Discovering Web Services

To discover web services programmatically, you instantiate a **DiscoveryClientProtocol** object and invoke the **Discover** method on the URL you wish to search for web services. The code example shown next illustrates how to recursively discover web services on a specified path by means of the **Discover** routine. This routine works if the web service discovery document contains references to other discovery documents. The **Discover** routine performs the following steps:

1.   Instantiates the **DiscoveryClientProtocol** object using the default constructor.

2.   Obtains a reference to the **DiscoveryDocument** at a specified path by invoking the **DiscoveryClientProtocol**::**Discover** method.

3.   Iterates through all references contained in the current discovery document using the **DiscoveryDocument**::**References** property.

4.   Determines if the current discovery document contains references to web service description documents by casting each reference to **ContractReference**.

5.   If the web service contract reference is found, the routine writes the contract (WSDL document) to disk using the **ContractReference::WriteDocument** method.

6.   Determines if the current discovery document contains references to other discovery documents by casting each reference to **DiscoveryDocumentReference**.

7.   If a reference to another discovery document is found, the **Discover** routine is invoked recursively on its URL.

```cpp
#using <mscorlib.dll>
#using <system.dll>
#using <system.xml.dll>
#using <system.web.dll>
#using <system.web.services.dll>
using namespace System;
using namespace System::IO;
using namespace System::Web::Services::Discovery;


void Discover(String* Url)
{
  // 1. Instantiate a discovery object
  DiscoveryClientProtocol* Discovery = new DiscoveryClientProtocol();
  // 2. Obtain the discovery document for the localhost
  DiscoveryDocument* Disco = Discovery->Discover(Url);

  // 3. Iterate through the list of references
  for ( int i = 0; i < Disco->References->Count; i++ )
  {
    // 4. Check if reference item is a WSDL document
    ContractReference* ContractRef = dynamic_cast<ContractReference*>(
      Disco->References->Item[i]);
    if ( ContractRef )
    {
      Console::WriteLine("Web Service description found at {0}",
        ContractRef->Url);
      // 5. Write to disk
      ContractRef->WriteDocument(ContractRef->Contract,
        new FileStream(ContractRef->DefaultFilename, FileMode::Create));
    }
    // 6. Check if reference item is a discovery document
    DiscoveryDocumentReference* DiscoRef = dynamic_cast
      <DiscoveryDocumentReference*>(Disco->References->Item[i]);
    if ( DiscoRef )
    {
      Console::WriteLine(DiscoRef->Url);
      // 7. Continue with recursive discovery
      Discover(DiscoRef->Url);
    }
  }
}
```

```
void main()
{
    // Initiate recursive discovery on the specified path
    Discover("http://localhost/default.vsdisco");
}
```

Retrieving Web Service WSDL

To programmatically examine a web service description stored in a WSDL document, you use the **ServiceDescription** class defined in the System::Web::Services::Description namespace. The following code example traverses the WSDL description of a web service and reports **Port**, **Binding**, and **Operation** information for the web service. In other words, the program enumerates protocols supported by the service and lists web service methods implemented for each protocol. The code performs the following steps:

1. Reads a WSDL document from disk using the **ServiceDescription::Read** method. (The WSDL document can be written to disk using the discovery mechanism described in the previous solution in this chapter.)

2. Reports the web service name (**ServiceDescription::Name** property).

3. Iterates through all **Services** defined in the web service description. Although in most cases, there is only one service description per WSDL.

4. Reports **Service** name (**Service::Name** property).

5. Iterates through all **Ports** of each service and reports the name and the **Binding** name (**Port::Binding::Name** property) of each port. Each port/binding combination corresponds to a different protocol supported by the web service.

6. Obtains a pointer to the **OperationBinding** object using the **ServiceDescription::Bindings** collection and the port binding name.

7. Reports the names of all **Operations** supported by the binding by iterating through the **OperationBinding::Operations** collection.

```cpp
#using <mscorlib.dll>
#using <system.dll>
#using <system.xml.dll>
#using <system.web.services.dll>
using namespace System;
using namespace System::Web::Services::Description;

void main()
{
    // 1. Read WSDL from file
    ServiceDescription* Desc = ServiceDescription::Read("WebService.wsdl");
    // 2. Report the web service name
    Console::WriteLine("Web Service: {0}", Desc->Name);

    // 3. Report all services
    for ( int i = 0; i < Desc->Services->Count; i++ )
    {
        Service* Svc = Desc->Services->Item[i];
        // 4. Report service name
        Console::WriteLine(" Service {0}: {1}", __box(i), Svc->Name);
```

```
    // 5. Report all ports of each service
    for ( int j = 0; j < Svc->Ports->Count; j++ )
    {
        Port* Prt = Svc->Ports->Item[j];
        Console::WriteLine(" Port {0}: {1}", __box(j), Prt->Name);
        // Report binding information
        Console::WriteLine(" Binding: {0}", Prt->Binding->Name);
        // 6. Get binding
        Binding* Bnd = Desc->Bindings->Item[Prt->Binding->Name];
        // 7. Report all operations of the binding
        for ( int k = 0; k < Bnd->Operations->Count; k++ )
        {
            OperationBinding* Oper = Bnd->Operations->Item[k];
            Console::WriteLine(" Operation {0}: {1}", __box(k), Oper->Name);
        }
    }
  }
}
```

Securing a Web Service Using Basic and Integrated Windows Authentication

The easiest way to secure a web service is to disable anonymous access to the corresponding ASP.NET application and to require Basic or Integrated Windows authentication. Authenticated access requires user to specify user name or password when connecting to a secured web service. Basic authentication requires explicitly specifying both user name and password and transmits both unencrypted (i.e., sends password as clear text). Integrated authentication on the other hand, employs credentials of the current user who access the web service, and transmits both user name and password in encrypted form.

To require client authentication, you must configure security settings of the web server virtual directory hosting the web service:

1. Launch the Internet Information Service manager console, select the web site root where the web service is installed, locate the web service virtual directory, right-click on it and select Properties from the context menu.

2. On the virtual root Properties dialog go to the Directory Security tab and click on the Edit button in the Anonymous access and authentication control section (see Figure 12.4).

3. Uncheck the Anonymous access check box and check Basic authentication, or Integrated Windows authentication or both.

4. In the ASP.NET web service web.config configuration file set the **authentication mode** to "Windows". If your web service does not have a configuration file yet, you can create one:

```
<?xml version="1.0" encoding="utf-8" ?>
<configuration>
    <system.web>
        <authentication mode="Windows"/>
    </system.web>
</configuration>
```

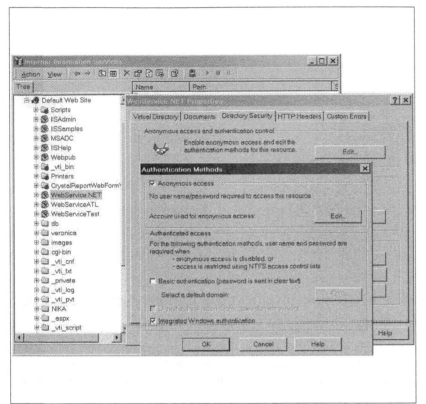

Figure 12.4 IIS Authentication Methods dialog launched from the Internet Service Manager console (Windows 2000 and IIS 5.0).

No modifications are required to the web service code. However, additional code is required on the client side to handle the authentication. Follow these steps to programmatically authenticate the web service client:

1. Instantiate a web service client proxy class.

2. For Basic authentication, you must instantiate a **CredentialCache** object and add a new set of credentials containing the user name and password required for the web service authentication.

3. Initialize the **Credentials** property of the web service client proxy class with the constructed **CredentialCache** object.

4. For Integrated Windows authentication, you must initialize the **Credentials** property of the web service client proxy class with the default set of credentials (**CredentialCache::Default-Credentials**) corresponding to the user account under which the web service client code is running.

You can now call the web service method: Authentication will be performed each time you invoke a web method.

The following code example demonstrates Basic and Integrated Windows authentication. The web service directory security settings must be configured to use *both* Basic and Integrated Windows authentication in order for the sample code to work:

```
#using <mscorlib.dll>
#using <system.dll>
#using <system.web.dll>
#using <system.web.services.dll>
using namespace System;
using namespace System::Net;
using namespace System::Web::Services;
using namespace System::Web::Services::Protocols;

// Web service client proxy class
```

```cpp
[WebServiceBinding(Name="MyWebService", Namespace="http://www.Gems3D.com")]
public __gc class WebServiceSoap: public SoapHttpClientProtocol {
public:
    WebServiceSoap()
    {
        Url = "http://localhost/WebService/WebService.asmx";
    }
    [SoapDocumentMethod]
    String* Uppercase(String* text)
    {
        Object* params[] = {text};
        Object* results[] = Invoke("Uppercase", params);
        return dynamic_cast<String*>(results[0]);
    }
};
void main()
{
    // 1. Instantiate a web service client proxy class
    WebServiceSoap* WebServiceProxy = new WebServiceSoap();

    try {
        // 2. Create credentials for BASIC authentication
        CredentialCache* CredCache = new CredentialCache();
        CredCache->Add(new Uri(WebServiceProxy->Url),
            "Basic", new NetworkCredential("user", "pwd", "domain"));

        // 3. Set the web service proxy credentials
        WebServiceProxy->Credentials = CredCache;

        // 4. Invoke the web method
        Console::WriteLine("Uppercase: {0}",
            WebServiceProxy-> Uppercase("test #1"));

        // 5. Must use default credentials for INTEGRATED WINDOWS authentication
        WebServiceProxy->Credentials = CredentialCache::DefaultCredentials;

        // 6. Invoke the web method
        Console::WriteLine("Uppercase: {0}",
            WebServiceProxy->Uppercase("test #2"));
    }
    catch(Exception* e) {
        Console::WriteLine("ERROR: {0}", e->Message);
    }
}
```

Securing a Web Service Using SSL

When communication with a web service involves transmission of sensitive information you may want to ensure totally private communication with a web server by means of secure HTTP protocol (HTTPS). Although HTTPS offers extreme privacy its drawback is increased load on the server that has to perform additional computations in order to encrypt/decrypt HTTP response and request packets.

A hybrid solution involves using HTTPS only when transmitting sensitive information (e.g., log-in credentials, private user information, credit-card data, etc.) and using HTTP for all other web method calls. In any event, if you want to use HTTPS in conjunction with your web service, your web server must be configured for secure communications – SSL. Follow these steps to configure your web server for SSL:

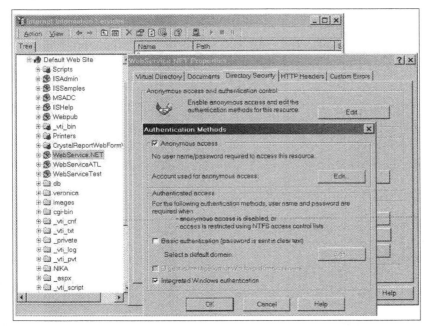

1. Launch the Internet Information Service manager console, select the web site root where the web service is installed, locate the web service virtual directory, right-click on it and select Properties from the context menu.

Figure 12.5 IIS Certificate Wizard screen for processing pending certificate requests.

2. On the virtual root Properties dialog go to the Directory Security tab and click on the Server Certificate button to request a new server certificate if you do not already have one.

3. Follow the IIS Certificate Wizard steps, provide accurate information about your business and finish by saving the certificate request into a text file (e.g., certreq.txt file).

4. Go to a certificate authority site (e.g., wwwVeriSign.com, www.Thawte.com or other) and purchase a server certificate. Certificates are normally issued for 1 or 2 years with one-year certificates costing about $300 to 400. Renewal rates are usually lower. When purchasing a server certificate you would have to paste the contents of the certificate request file generated in Step 3 into the certificate authority certificate request form. Once the transaction is complete the certificate authority will issue you a server certificate file (.cer-file).

5. Once you have a server certificate file you must launch the IIS Certificate Wizard again to install the certificate. On the IIS Certificate Wizard screen select the Process pending request and install the certificate option (see Figure 12.5) and specify the path to the certificate file. Once the certificate is installed you can view it by clicking the View Certificate button on the virtual root Properties dialog.

6. Configure SSL options for the virtual root by clicking the Edit button in the Secure communications section of the Directory Security page on the virtual root Properties dialog to bring the Secure Communications configuration screen (Figure 12.6), which is accessible only when a server certificate is

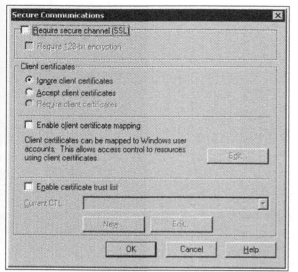

Figure 12.6 IIS virtual root Secure Communications screen.

installed. By default, SSL communication is enabled, but not required. You can forcibly require SSL communication for the virtual root (and for the web service hosted under the virtual root) by checking the Require secure channel (SSL) checkbox. For ultimate security you can also require 128-bit encryption by checking the corresponding checkbox on the Secure Communications screen.

TIP: When pursuing a hybrid solution with the HTTP protocol applied only to selected web method calls, you must leave the Require secure channel (SSL) option unchecked.

Now your web server is ready to process HTTPS requests and you should modify both web service and web service client code to ensure HTTPS encryption when invoking particular web service methods.

Little modification is needed on the web service side: to ensure that a particular web service method is accessed using HTTPS, verify the **Context->Request->IsSecureConnection** property and throw an exception if it is set to **false**. The following web service example illustrates how to implement a web service that provides secure **Login** method and nonsecure **DoSomething** method. The **Login** method verifies **Context->Request->IsSecureConnection** property, then verifies username and password and if everything is OK sets the session-state LoggedIn flag, which is used by nonsecure **DoSomething** method to confirm that the service client is logged in and authenticated OK.

Here is the code:

```
#using <mscorlib.dll>
#using <System.dll>
#using <System.Web.dll>
#using <System.Web.Services.dll>
#using <System.EnterpriseServices.dll>
using namespace System;
using namespace System::Web;
using namespace System::Web::Services;

namespace Test {
// SSL Web Service
[WebService(Name="MyWebService", Description="SSL Authentication Test",
   Namespace="http://www.Gems3D.com")]
public __gc class MyWebService : public WebService {
public:
   [WebMethod(Description="Processes user login", EnableSession=true)]
   void Login(String* UserName, String* Password)
   {
```

```
    // Remove previous login flag (if any)
    Session->Remove("LoggedIn");

    // Indicate that SSL is required
    if ( !Context->Request->IsSecureConnection )
        throw new Exception(S"SSL is required!");

    // Verify user name and password
    if ( UserName == S"UltraMax" && Password == S"Music" )
        // OK
        Session->Item["LoggedIn"] = __box(true);
    else
        // Bad user name/password
        throw new Exception(S"Invalid user name or password!");
}


[WebMethod(Description="Utility method", EnableSession=true)]
String* DoSomething()
{
    // Get login glag
    bool __gc* pbLoggedIn = dynamic_cast<__box bool*>(
        Session->Item["LoggedIn"]);
    // Logged in?
    if ( pbLoggedIn && *pbLoggedIn )
        throw new Exception(S"Not logged in!");

    // Do something...
    return S"DoSomething(), Logged in OK";
}
};
}
```

No other modifications are necessary on behalf of the web service. On the web service client side, you should slightly modify the web service client proxy class (preferred) or use the wizard-generated code, and set the web service client proxy **URL** property to use the HTTPS protocol when invoking secure web methods and modify the to use the HTTP protocol for nonsecure methods.

The web service client code below illustrates the first approach. The **WebServiceSoap** proxy class provides the cust **SetSecure** method that switches the **Url** property from HTTP to HTTPS and vice versa. Thus, before invoking the secure **Login** web method, one must execute **SetSecure(true)** to direct the web method request to use HTTPS. Then, for improved server-side performance one *should* switch back to HTTP by executing **SetSecure(false)** before invoking the nonsecure **DoSomething** web method. The code is as follows:

```
#using <mscorlib.dll>
#using <system.dll>
```

```cpp
#using <system.web.dll>
#using <system.web.services.dll>
using namespace System;
using namespace System::Net;
using namespace System::Web::Services;
using namespace System::Web::Services::Protocols;

// Web service client proxy class
[WebServiceBinding(Name="MyWebServiceSoap", Namespace="http://www.Gems3D.com")]
public __gc class WebServiceSoap: public SoapHttpClientProtocol {
public:
   WebServiceSoap()
   {
      // SSL is off by default
      SetSecure(false);
   }
   // SSL selection method
   void SetSecure(bool bSecure)
   {
      if ( bSecure )
         Url = "https://localhost/WebServiceSSL/WebService.asmx";
      else
         Url = "http://localhost/WebServiceSSL/WebService.asmx";
   }
   // Login
   [SoapDocumentMethod]
   void Login(String* UserName, String* Password)
   {
      Object* params[] = {UserName, Password};
      Object* results[] = Invoke("Login", params);
   }
   // DoSomething
   [SoapDocumentMethod]
   String* DoSomething()
   {
      Object* results[] = Invoke("DoSomething", new Object*[0]);
      return dynamic_cast<String*>(results[0]);
   }
};

void main()
{
   // 1. Instantiate a web service client proxy class
   WebServiceSoap* MyWebService = new WebServiceSoap();
   // 2. Initialize cookie container so that session state could
   // be maintained via session cookie
```

```
MyWebService->CookieContainer = new CookieContainer(1);

try {
    // 3. Attempt logging in without SSL (SSL is off by default)
    MyWebService->Login("UltraMax", "Music");
}
catch(Exception* e) {
    Console::WriteLine("ERROR: {0}", e->Message);
}
try {
    // 4. Attempt logging-in using SSL
    MyWebService->SetSecure(true);
    MyWebService->Login("UltraMax", "Music");


    // 5. Turn off SSL and call web service methods
    // WARNING! You must enable SSL for the web service or login will fail.
    MyWebService->SetSecure(false);
    Console::WriteLine("DoSomething()={0}", MyWebService->DoSomething());
}
catch(Exception* e) {
    Console::WriteLine("ERROR: {0}", e->Message);
}
}
```

The **main()** routine also demonstrates what would happen if you call the secure **Login** method without HTTPS: Because we added a check on the web service side for the secure communication channel, the web service throws an exception when the **Login** is called over regular HTTP. This safety check on the web service side prevents accidental security violation by selectively requiring a secure channel for transmission of sensitive username and password information.

Securing a Web Service Using Encrypted SOAP Header Authentication

If you cannot afford or for some reason cannot use server certificates (and thus cannot use HTTPS/SSL), you can always implement custom authentication for your web service. When implementing custom authentication there is a rule to remember, however: Hackers are patient and smart, never underestimate them. What this means for your code is that you *must* forget those bedroom-bred encryption algorithm unless you have a degree in statistics, number theory, and random signals: However complex security you think you devise, it will be cracked in a matter of hours by an experienced hacker.

To be sure that your encryption presents a considerable challenge, you should use Windows CryptoAPI or an equivalent professional cryptographic service to encode sensitive information. Windows CryptoAPI is encapsulated within the .NET Framework by means of numerous classes located in the System::Security::Cryptography namespace.

To illustrate custom encryption using .NET cryptography consider the following web service provider and consumer code that implements custom login using encrypted SOAP header:

```cpp
#using <mscorlib.dll>
#using <System.dll>
#using <System.Web.dll>
#using <System.Web.Services.dll>
#using <System.Web.Services.dll>
#using <System.EnterpriseServices.dll>
using namespace System;
using namespace System::Web;
using namespace System::Web::Services;
using namespace System::Web::Services::Protocols;
using namespace System::IO;
using namespace System::Security::Cryptography;
// Login credentials (SOAP Header)
public __gc struct MyHeader: public SoapHeader {
    unsigned char Buffer __gc[];
};


namespace Test {
[WebService(Name="MyWebService", Description="SOAP Authentication Test",
    Namespace="http://www.Gems3D.com")]
public __gc class MyWebService : public WebService {
public:
    // Login credentials (SOAP Header)
    MyHeader* LoginInfo;
    [SoapHeader("LoginInfo")]
    [WebMethod(Description="Processes user login", EnableSession=true)]
    void Login()
    {
        // Remove previous login flag (if any)
        Session->Remove("LoggedIn");

        // 1. Create stream for reading encrypted data
        MemoryStream* MemStream = new MemoryStream(LoginInfo->Buffer);
        // 2. Create DES algorithm
        SymmetricAlgorithm* Decoder = SymmetricAlgorithm::Create("DES");
        // 3. Specify decoder key (min decoder key size is 8 bytes)
        unsigned char Key __gc[] = {'s','o','m','e','k','e','y',123};
        Decoder->Key = Key;
        Decoder->Padding = PaddingMode::Zeros;
        // 4. Create stream for reading decrypted data
        CryptoStream* DecryptedStream = new CryptoStream(MemStream,
            Decoder->CreateDecryptor(), CryptoStreamMode::Read);
        // 5. Create StreamReader for reading decrypted data
        StreamReader* Reader = new StreamReader(DecryptedStream);
        // 6. Decrypt and read user name and password
```

```
      String* S = Reader->ReadLine(); // Read 8-byte padding
      String* UserName = Reader->ReadLine();
      String* Password = Reader->ReadLine();
      DecryptedStream->Close();
      MemStream->Close();

      // Verify user name and password
      if ( UserName->CompareTo(S"UltraMax") == 0 &&
         Password->CompareTo(S"Music") == 0 )
         // OK
         Session->Item["LoggedIn"] = __box(true);
      else
         // Bad user name/password
       throw new Exception("Invalid user name or password!");
   }

   [WebMethod(Description="Utility method", EnableSession=true)]
   String* DoSomething()
   {
      // Get login flag
      Object* Obj = Session->Item["LoggedIn"];
      bool __gc* pbLoggedIn = 0;
      if ( Obj ) pbLoggedIn = dynamic_cast<__box bool*>(Obj);
      // Logged in?
      if ( !pbLoggedIn || !(*pbLoggedIn) )
         throw new Exception(S"Not logged in!");
      // Do something...
      return S"DoSomething(), Logged in OK";
   }
};
}


#using <mscorlib.dll>
#using <system.dll>
#using <system.web.dll>
#using <system.web.services.dll>
using namespace System;
using namespace System::Web::Services;
using namespace System::Web::Services::Protocols;
using namespace System::Net;
using namespace System::IO;
using namespace System::Security::Cryptography;
// Login credentials (SOAP Header)
public __gc struct MyHeader: public SoapHeader {
   unsigned char Buffer __gc[];
};
```

```cpp
// Web service client proxy class
[WebServiceBinding(Name="MyWebServiceSoap", Namespace="http://www.Gems3D.com")]
public __gc class WebServiceSoap: public SoapHttpClientProtocol {
public:
    // Login credentials (SOAP Header)
    MyHeader* LoginInfo;
    WebServiceSoap()
    {
        Url = "http://localhost/WebServiceSOAPHeader/WebService.asmx";
    }
    [SoapHeader("LoginInfo")]
    [SoapDocumentMethod]
    void Login()
    {
        Object* results[] = Invoke("Login", new Object*[0]);
    }
    [SoapDocumentMethod]
    String* DoSomething()
    {
        Object* results[] = Invoke("DoSomething", new Object*[0]);
        return dynamic_cast<String*>(results[0]);
    }
};

void main()
{
    WebServiceSoap* MyWebService = new WebServiceSoap();
    MyWebService->CookieContainer = new CookieContainer(1); // For session-state

    try {
        // Instantiate SOAP header object
        MyWebService->LoginInfo = new MyHeader;

        // 1. Create stream for writing unencrypted login credentials
        MemoryStream* MemStream = new MemoryStream(256/*capacity*/);
        // 2. Create DES algorithm
        SymmetricAlgorithm* Encoder = SymmetricAlgorithm::Create("DES");
        // 3. Specify encoder key (min encoder key size is 8 bytes)
        unsigned char Key __gc[] = {'s','o','m','e','k','e','y',123};
        Encoder->Key = Key;
        Encoder->Padding = PaddingMode::Zeros;
        // 4. Create stream for encrypting data
        CryptoStream* EncryptedStream = new CryptoStream(MemStream,
            Encoder->CreateEncryptor(), CryptoStreamMode::Write);
        // 5. Create StreamWriter for writing unencrypted data
```

```
StreamWriter* Writer = new StreamWriter(EncryptedStream);
    // 6. Write unencrypted user name and password
    Writer->WriteLine(S"1234567"); // Write 8-byte padding
    Writer->WriteLine(S"UltraMax");
    Writer->WriteLine(S"Music");
    Writer->Flush();
    EncryptedStream->Close();
    MemStream->Close();

        // 7 .Place encrypted data to SOAP header
        MyWebService->LoginInfo->Buffer = MemStream->ToArray();
        // Login
        MyWebService->Login();

        // Call test webservice method without SOAP header
        MyWebService->LoginInfo = 0;
        Console::WriteLine(MyWebService->DoSomething());
    }
    catch(Exception* e) {
        Console::WriteLine("ERROR: {0}", e->Message);
    }
}
```

The code above is very similar to the code in the "Securing a Web Service Using SSL" solution except that the **Login** method uses an encrypted SOAP header to transmit username and password information instead of SSL. The custom SOAP header defined by the **MyHeader** class corresponds to a simple binary **Buffer**, which is set to the web service by the web service client. This buffer contains encrypted username and password, which is decrypted by the web service and compared against required credentials.

The encryption on the web service client side is executed in the following steps:

1.   Memory buffer represented by the **MemoryStream** class is created to hold resulting encrypted data.

2.   An instance of DES encoder is created using the **SymmetricAlgorithm** class.

3.   DES private key is generated.
      TIP: Most encryption algorithms, including DES, require keys, which length is a multiplicative of 8.

4.   An instance of the **CryptoStream** is created for encrypting data, which will write the encrypted data to the **MemoryStream** buffer.

5.   Conventional **StreamWriter** stream is instantiated for simultaneous writing and encrypting of user output to the **CryptoStream**.

6.   User name and password is written to the **StreamWriter**, transparently encrypted by the **CryptoStream,** and written in binary form to the **MemoryStream** buffer.
      TIP: Most encryption algorithms, including DES, operate on chunks of data whose length must be proportional to the key size. Thus, because in the example above we used a private key of 8 bytes, the size of the resulting encrypted binary block is a multiplicative of 8.

7.   When the streams are closed, the contents of the **MemoryStream** buffer is copied to the buffer provided by the custom SOAP header and transmitted to the web service when the **Login** method is called.

Symmetric and Asymmetric Encryption

There are two basic encryption/decryption schemes: symmetric and asymmetric. The main difference between the two is that symmetric algorithms require one private key, i.e., the same private key is used for encrypting/decrypting the message. Asymmetric encryption/decryption requires two keys: public key and private key. With asymmetric algorithms the message is usually encrypted with public key and decrypted with private key. HTTPS/SSL is the most common example of asymmetric algorithm.

.NET Cryptography Algorithms

The Microsoft .NET Framework class library provides immediate support for the following cryptography algorithms:

*   *Symmetric*: DES, RC2, Rijndael, TripleDES;

*   *Asymmetric*: DSA, RSA.

Decryption steps executed in the web service class **Login** method are very similar to the encryption steps, except that a DES-decryptor instance is created instead of the DES-encryptor instance.

.NET Interoperability with Unmanaged Code and COM

QUICK JUMPS

CHAPTER 13

.NET Interoperability with Unmanaged Code and COM

In Depth

The .NET Framework was designed with interoperability in mind. By interoperability, I don't just mean across different languages (such as C#, VB.NET, Perl.NET, and so on), but also interoperability between managed and unmanaged code. Interoperability with managed code is very important because it provides a means for integrating existing COM components with the new .NET code and vice versa. In this chapter, you will learn how to leverage .NET interoperability to consume COM objects in managed code, how to expose .NET classes to COM components, and how to access unmanaged DLLs in managed code.

Interoperability with Unmanaged Code

The key advantage of the .NET Framework is interoperability. Interoperability across different languages is achieved seamlessly by means of CLS and code compilation into Intermediate Language. Interoperability between managed and unmanaged code, on the other hand, is implemented by means of COM and *platform invoke*. Interoperability between managed and unmanaged code can be viewed as interoperability between *new* (.NET) and *legacy* (COM) code. .NET does not eliminate the need for COM development, and the demand for purely unmanaged components remain in performance-critical projects. Thus, the problem of interoperability between managed and unmanaged code is going to be a lasting issue.

Fortunately, the .NET Framework provides a mechanism for smooth integration of managed and unmanaged code by means of COM interoperability services. On one hand, the framework delivers .NET classes to unmanaged code developers as COM objects. On the other hand, the framework delivers COM components to managed code developers as .NET classes. Theoretically, it should be equally easy to work with COM objects or .NET classes whether you develop managed or unmanaged code.

Besides supporting COM, .NET provides managed developers with a way of hooking into native APIs or any unmanaged functions exported in DLLs by means of the *platform invoke*. But the complimentary mechanism for accessing managed functions from unmanaged code through "reverse platform invoke" is missing. COM unmanaged code interoperability is supported in .NET by means of the System::Runtime::InteropServices namespace, which provides interoperability utility classes and attributes.

Runtime Callable Wrappers and COM Callable Wrappers

At first glance, it may seem impossible to reconcile COM and .NET because both environments are governed by very different programming paradigms. Yet the seamless interoperation between COM and .NET is possible if you trick unmanaged code into believing that .NET classes are actually COM components, and fool managed code into thinking that .NET classes are just COM components. Fortunately, the .NET Framework does just that. The framework employs wrappers to reconcile managed and unmanaged code:

* *runtime callable wrappers (RCW)*: Used to wrap COM components in .NET attire for consumption in managed code (see Figure 13.1).

* *COM callable wrappers (CCW)*: Used to wrap .NET classes in COM outfit for consumption in unmanaged code (see Figure 13.2).

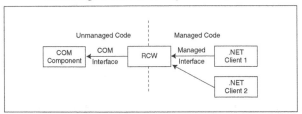

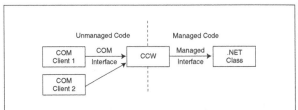

Figure 13.1 Runtime callable wrapper for calling COM classes from .NET.

Figure 13.2 COM callable wrapper for calling .NET classes from COM.

Runtime and COM callable wrappers can be considered proxy classes. The framework on demand generates exactly one wrapper for each referenced COM object or .NET class and internally directs all clients to use the same proxy.

Data Marshalling

Both runtime and COM wrappers are responsible for marshalling data, such as input/output parameters, return values, and exceptions between managed and unmanaged code. COM types are converted to and from .NET types as shown in Table 13.1.

Table 13.1 COM/.NET type conversion table.

COM Type	.NET Type
BSTR	String
BYTE	unsigned char
CHAR	char
CY	Decimal
DATE	DateTime
DOUBLE	double
FLOAT	float
IDispatch	Object*
IUnknown	Object*
LONG	int
LONGLONG	__int64

<Table 13.2 Continued>

COM Type	.NET Type
OLE_HANDLE	int
SCODE	int
SHORT	short
ULONG	unsigned int
ULONGLONG	unsigned __int64
USHORT	unsigned short
VARIANT	Object*
VARIANT_BOOL	bool
SAFE_ARRAY(type)	type[]

NOTE: *Output parameters and return values are converted as passed by reference, e.g.,* **[out] BSTR* [] String* &.**

The type conversions shown in Table 13.1 correspond to default conversions. It is possible to specify alternate marshalling for types that can be converted differently, such as character strings. To support this, the .NET Framework System::Runtime::InteropServices namespace defines the **MarshalAs** attribute for specifying custom data marshalling. Data marshalling can be a costly process in terms of performance. Some types such as numeric types, arrays, and structures of numeric types can be transmitted across the managed/unmanaged code boundary without any transformations. These types are called *blittable*. Other types, such as strings and date/time, require a marshaling process because managed and unmanaged code use different representations for strings and dates.

> **TIP:** For optimal performance you should use blittable data types (which correspond to primitive types in managed code) when developing COM/.NET interoperability classes.

Exception Marshalling

COM and .NET Framework utilize different approaches to error reporting. COM primarily relies on **HRESULT** return values, while .NET almost exclusively relies on exceptions. Thus, when marshalling calls across the managed/unmanaged code boundary, COM and Runtime callable wrappers implement exception/error code marshalling to ensure that the error information is reported in the appropriate way for the environment. RCW automatically converts COM **HRESULT** codes into corresponding managed exceptions. Similarly, CCW automatically converts managed exceptions into COM **HRESULT** codes. Thus, when designing a managed class that you intend to expose to COM, you should initialize the **HResult** property of the custom exceptions when reporting errors. Here's an example:

```
__gc class MyException: public Exception {
  MyException() {
    HResult = E_INVALIDARG;
  }
};
```

Similarly, when a COM interface method returns a failure **HRESULT**, the CLR constructs an exception object and throws the exception in managed code. If the COM class supports the **IErrorInfo** interface, CLR uses it to initialize the fields of the **Exception** class (see Table 13.2).

Table 13.2 **Exception** class properties initialized when the COM method fails.

Exception class property	Description
ErrorCode	**HRESULT** method return value
HelpLink	IErrorInfo->HelpContext
Message	IErrorInfo->GetErrorDescription
Source	IErrorinfo->GetSource
TargetSite	The name of the method that caused the error

> **TIP:** Throwing/catching exceptions is a costly process in terms of performance. When designing COM components for consumption in managed code, you should return failure **HRESULT** codes only when a *critical* failure occurs. Use output parameters to return noncritical failure status codes while setting the **HRESULT** return value to **S_OK**.

Class Interfaces

Unlike .NET, COM always accesses objects by means of an interface. In .NET, on the other hand, you can instantiate an object and call its methods directly without explicitly casting to any of the interfaces implemented by the class. Moreover, some .NET classes do not implement interfaces at all. Does this mean that such classes will be inaccessible to COM? No. When the Common Language Runtime generates a CCW for a managed type, it automatically generates an interface that includes all public members of the managed class. Such an interface is called a *class interface*.

> **NOTE:** When exporting managed class to COM using the Tlbexp.exe utility, the name of the class interface usually matches the name of the managed class prefixed with an underscore (e.g., the class interface for the **MyClass** will be _**MyClass**).

Similarly, when you consume a COM component in managed code, RCW generates a class interface for the co-class. The class interface is a sum of all interfaces implemented by the coclass.

When designing managed classes for consumption in unmanaged code you should explicitly define an interface to be used as the class interface. Should you change the order of members or add new members to the class, dispatch IDs of the class interface members will also change, causing the early-bound unmanaged code to break. If the unmanaged code uses late binding, the problem goes away. However, if you use an explicitly defined class interface you can expect predictable behavior with both managed and unmanaged code.

To control automatic generation of the class interface you can decorate the managed class with the **ClassInterface** attribute defined in the System::Runtime::InteropServices namespace. The attribute has the following syntax:

```
[Classinterface(type)]
```

where the *type* parameter specifies the class interface type. The *type* parameter can accept values defined in the **ClassInterfaceType** enumeration in the System::Runtime::InteropServices namespace:

* ***AutoDispatch***: Generates a dispatch class interface, i.e., the interface that supports late binding only (default).

* ***AutoDual***: Generates dual class interface.

* ***None***: Does not generate a class interface.

Generating Runtime Callable Wrappers

The System::Runtime::InteropServices namespace provides ample resources for manually generating RCWs. The framework, however, discourages developers from doing so manually by requiring the complete knowledge of the COM coclass being imported as well as the nuances type/method conversion. Instead, the framework supplies a command line tool called Type Library Importer (Tlbimp.exe). This tool generates class metadata automatically based on a specified COM type library. The syntax for using this utility is:

```
Tlbimp.exe TlbFile /out:FileName
```

where *TlbFile* is the name of the COM type library, DLL, executable, or OCX-file containing an embedded type library. The **/out** option specifies the name of the resulting .NET assembly, which you should move to your project folder and distribute with the application.

Metadata Conversion

Once you produce an assembly based on the COM type library, you can inspect the assembly metadata using the Intermediate Language Disassembler utility (Ildasm.exe). Simply run the utility and load the generated assembly DLL. Then, you can expand each managed type listed in the metadata and inspect its properties, fields, and methods.

Alternatively, you can use the following heuristic to figure out how type library information is converted into .NET metadata:

* IDL **library** definition is converted into Managed C++ **Namespace**:

```
library UltraMax {
    interface IMusic {};
    coclass TechnoMusic {};
};
```

will be converted to

```
namespace UltraMax {
    __interface IMusic {};
    __gc class TechnoMusic {};
};
```

* IDL **module** definition is converted into Managed C++ **class**:

```
module Genres {
    const short Techno = 0x01;
    const short Classical = 0x02;
};
```

will be converted to

```
public __gc class Genres {
    public: const short Techno = 0x01;
    public: const short Classical = 0x02;
};
```

* IDL **interface** and **coclass** definitions are converted into Managed C++ **__interface** and **class** definitions:

```
[uuid(…)]
interface IMusic: IDispatch {
    [id(1)] HRESULT Play();
}
[uuid(…)]
coclass NewMusic {
    [default] interface IMusic;
}
```

will be converted to

```
[Guid(…)]
public __interface IMusic {
    [DispId(1)] void Play();
};
[Guid(…)]
public __gc class NewMusic: public IMusic {
public:
    [DispId(1)] void Play();
};
```

* IDL enumerations are imported as managed **Enum** declarations.
* Interface methods are imported according to the following rules:

* Method name remains unchanged

* Parameter names remain unchanged

* COM types such as **BSTR, DATE**, and **long** are replaced with the corresponding managed types such a **String, DateTime, Int32**, and so on.

* COM component method parameters designated as **[out, retval]** become the return value of the .NET wrapper class method.

```
HRESULT Play(BSTR Song, [out, retval] DATE Duration);
```

will be converted to

```
DateTime Play(String* Song);
```

* COM events are imported according to the following rules:

  * Delegates are created for each method of the event-source interface. The delegates are named as *SorceInterface_MethodName***EventHandler**.

  * In addition to importing the source interface, COM interoperability service creates a second interface called *SorceInterface_***Event**, which has events as members and contains additional add/remove methods for adding/removing event handlers to/from the events.

  TIP: When using COM interoperability, try to minimize the number of cross-boundary calls. Call marshalling is a costly process that may aversely impact the performance of your interoperability application.

Generating Runtime Callable Wrappers

To expose certain managed types to COM, you must make sure that the types meet the COM interoperability requirements:

* Managed types that you want to expose should implement interfaces explicitly.

* Managed types that you want to expose must be public.

* Methods, properties, and fields that you want to expose must be public.

* Managed types must have public default constructors (or the class can not be instantiated by COM).

* Managed types cannot be abstract.

To convert a managed class into a COM type library, you should use the .NET Framework SDK Type Library Exporter Utility (Tblexp.exe). This utility has the following typical usage syntax:

```
Tlbexp.exe Assembly /out:FileName
```

where *Assembly* is the name of the assembly containing managed classes you want to convert to the COM type library.

Method Signature

When managed type metadata is exported into a COM type library, signatures of managed methods usually change to match the COM standard. Managed data types are replaced with COM data types, the return value is moved to the **[out, retval]** parameter, and the default **HRESULT** return value is applied. You can override the default signature changing behavior, however, by decorating methods of the managed type with the **PreserveSig** attribute. This attribute enforces no method signature changes when the type metadata is exported into a COM type library.

Overloaded Methods

Unlike managed code, COM does not support multiple method overloads that differ only by parameters. Thus, if the exported managed type contains multiple overloaded methods, the methods will be given unique names in the type library. A unique name is generated by appending _X to the method name, where X is a sequence number. For example, the following overloaded methods in a managed type

```
void print(int a);
void print(float a);
```

will be converted to

```
void print(int a);
void print_2(float a);
```

Assembly Registration

Once you convert the assembly into a type library you must register the managed .NET types contained in the assembly with COM. You can do this using the .NET Framework SDK Assembly Registration Utility (Regasm.exe). Once the managed types are registered, you can access them from unmanaged code, including COM components. Also, you can use the Regasm.exe utility to generate a type library based on the managed assembly. You can do this by specifying the /tlb command line switch:

```
Regasm.exe Assembly /tlb:TlbFile
```

Importing Type Libraries

To reference the exported .NET type library in COM, you must import it using the **#import** statement:

```
#import "TlbFile"
```

When you compile the source file that contains the **#import** statement, the compiler automatically generates type library header/implementation (.tlh/.tli) files that are placed in the output file directory (e.g., Debug or Release). The generated .tlh/.tli files correspond to the attributed definitions of the imported COM coclasses and interfaces. You can examine the .tlh header file to see how the managed type was converted to COM and obtain information on the exact syntax of class/interface properties and methods and data types of method/property parameters.

COM Smart Pointers

The generated .tlh-files usually contain one or more COM smart pointer definitions:

```
_COM_SMARTPTR_TYPEDEF(Interface, __uuidof(Interface));
```

The definition above defines the ***Interface*Ptr** smart pointer. Smart COM pointers were created to facilitate COM programming. You can use smart pointers in your code to instantiate interface pointers to the encapsulated COM interfaces using the following constructor syntax:

```
InterfacePtr VarName(__uuidof(CoclassName));
```

where *CoclassName* is the name of the coclass implementing the interface encapsulated by the smart pointer. Once you instantiate a smart pointer you can call methods on the encapsulated COM interface. Also, you do not have to explicitly release the interface by calling the **Release** method. The interface will be released automatically when the smart pointer goes out of scope.

Deploying COM Interoperability Applications

Deployment of COM/.NET interoperability applications involves proper deployment of COM component and managed assemblies:

* COM components must be deployed to the target deployment location (typically, application folder).
* Shared (strong-named) managed assemblies must be deployed to global assembly cache, while private assemblies must be deployed to the application folder.
* COM components must be registered (e.g., using regsvr32.exe utility) before first use.
* Managed types exposed to COM must be registered with COM using the Regasm.exe utility.

   NOTE: When you launch an interoperability application which uses managed types exposed via COM, it first encounters the Mscoree.dll, which in turn locates the assembly (shared or private) containing the managed type.

Consuming Unmanaged DLLs

Besides interoperating with COM, Common Language Runtime supports calling unmanaged DLLs from managed code by means of the *platform invoke* (see Figure 13.3). Such functionality is extremely useful for invoking OS/platform APIs or dynamically linking to third-party libraries.

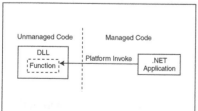

Figure 13.3 Invoking an unmanaged DLL function from managed code.

Platform invoke is similar to CCW in the sense that the framework has to perform data marshalling to convert managed input parameters into unmanaged types, unmanaged output parameters into managed types, and to replace unmanaged **HRESULT** error codes with managed exceptions. Also, the framework converts callback functions into managed delegates.

Function Prototypes

To consume an unmanaged DLL function in managed code, you must define the function prototype and decorate it with the **DllImport** attribute. The attribute has the following syntax:

```
[DllImport("DllName", CallingConvention=convention, CharSet=charSet,
    EntryPoint="name", ExactSpelling=BooleanValue, PreserveSig=BooleanValue,
    SetLastError=BooleanValue)]
extern "C" ReturnType Function(...);
```

The parameters are defined as following:

* **CallingConvention**: Specifies the function calling convention. Possible values are defined in the **CallingConvention** enumeration: **Cdecl**, **FastCall**, **StdCall** (default), **ThisCall**, and **Winapi**.

* **CharSet**: Specifies which character set marshalled strings should use. Possible values are defined in the **CharSet** enumeration: **Ansi** (default), **Auto**, **None**, and **Unicode**.

* **EntryPoint**: Specifies function entry point name. If omitted, the entry point name is assumed to be the same as the name of the prototype function.

* **ExactSpelling**: Indicates whether the name of the exported DLL function should be modified to match the selected **CharSet**.

* **PreserveSig**: Indicates whether to preserve the function signature.

* **SetLastError**: Indicates whether the function calls the Win32 API **SetLastError** function to set the error code before returning from the call.

The challenge is to provide the accurate prototype declaration for the unmanaged function. Unfortunately, the .NET Framework SDK does not provide a tool for automatic generation of DLL function prototypes. Thus, you must conduct the conversion manually.

Passing Structures

When converting parameters, you must pay special attention to parameters corresponding to data structures. Data structures are *blittable* by default. Thus, you must define an unmanaged type corresponding to the structure expected by the DLL and use it when declaring the DLL function prototype. Alternatively, you can use *fixed-layout* managed types to define such structures. Members of managed types can be relocated at run time to optimize memory usage and performance. However, if a managed type is marked as a fixed-layout, CLR will not relocate members, thus ensuring predictable results when using such types for calling unmanaged DLLs.

You can use the **StructLayout** attribute to mark a managed type as fixed layout:

```
[StructLayout(layout)]
```

where the *layout* parameter specifies member layout. The parameter accepts the following values (defined in the **LayoutKind** enumeration):

* **Auto**: Automatic (nonfixed layout).

* **Explicit**: Members are laid out according to the **FieldOffset** attribute.

*   ***Sequential***: Fixed layout where members are laid out sequentially.

If you choose the **Explicit** layout, you must specify the member offset in bytes from the beginning of the structure using the **FieldOffset** attribute. Here's an example:

```
[StructLayout(LayoutKind::Explicit)]
__gc struct POINT {
    [FieldOffset(0)] int x;
    [FieldOffset(4)] int y;
};
```

COM Interoperability Attributes

The System::Runtime::InteropServices namespace provides the following additional attributes that may come in handy when developing interoperability code. The attributes are summarized in Table 13.3.

Table 13.3 COM interoperability attributes.

Attribute	Description
[AutomationProxy(*BooleanValue*)]	Indicates if the class should be marshaled using Automation Marshaller (***BooleanValue*=true**) or proxy stub marshaller (***BooleanValue*=false**).
[ClassInterface(*InterfaceType*)]	Specifies class interface type.
[ComImport]	Indicates If the class was previously defined in a COM type library.
[ComRegisterFunction]	Indicates a class method to be called when the assembly is registered with COM.
[ComSourceInterfaces(*InterfaceName*)]	Specifies a list of COM event source interfaces for the managed class.
[ComUnregisterFunction]	Indicates a class method to be called when the assembly is unregistered with COM.
[ComVisible(*BooleanValue*)]	Indicates if the class should visible be unmanaged code when the assembly metadata is converted to a COM type library.
[DispId(*num*)]	Specifies member dispatch ID.
[FieldOffset(*num*)]	Specifies member offset from the beginning of the structure.
[Guid(*guid*)]	Specifies class, interface, structure, enumeration, or delegate GUID.
[IDispatchImpl(*type*)]	Indicates the **IDispatch** implementation to use when exposing interfaces to COM.
[In]	Indicates an input parameter.
[InterfaceType(*type*)]	Specifies COM interface type (**ComInterfaceType::InterfaceIsDual**, **ComInterfaceType::InterfaceIsIDispatch**, or **ComInterfaceType::InterfaceIsIUnknown**).

<Continued on Next Page>

<Table 13.3 Continued>

Attribute	Description
[LCIDConversion(*lcid*)]	Specifies the locale ID for the method's unmanaged signature.
[MarshalAs(*type*)]	Indicates if the parameter should be marshaled as a specified unmanaged type.
[Optional]	Indicates an optional parameter.
[Out]	Indicates an output parameter.
[PreserveSig(*BooleanValue*)]	Indicates if the method signature should be preserved.
[ProgId(*ProgID*)]	Specifies the class ProgID.
[StructLayout(*layout*)]	Specifies fixed/auto managed structure layout.

Immediate Solutions

Consuming COM Components in .NET Applications

Two typical scenarios exist for consuming COM components in .NET applications: You can either consume an existing COM component or you can create a new COM component to be used with .NET. From the .NET Framework point of view, it does not matter how you arrive at the COM component that you want to consume. The only requirement is that you *must* have the component type library, which can be embedded as a resource in the component code (e.g., DLL, EXE, or OCX-file), or it can be in a stand-along type library .tlb-file. Follow these steps to consume a COM component in a .NET application:

1. Convert the type library of your COM component into a .NET assembly by running the Framework SDK Type Library Importer utility:

```
Tlbimp.exe TypeLib /out:ClassName.DLL
```

   where *TypeLib* is the file name of the component's type library, or the name of the component's DLL in case the type library is embedded in the component.

2. To obtain information on equivalent managed definitions of COM coclasses and interfaces, inspect the generated *ClassName.DLL* assembly metadata by running the Framework SDK Intermediate Language Disassembler utility:

```
Ildasm.exe ClassName.DLL
```

   NOTE: If you create a COM coclass named **Foo** , it will be converted to a managed type named **FooClass**. COM interfaces are converted to the same-named managed interfaces.

3. Copy the *ClassName.DLL* assembly to your Managed C++ application project folder and into Debug and Release directories. To be accessible at compile time, the DLL must be on the same path with the source files. To be accessible at runtime, the DLL must be on the same path with the executable application.

4.   Add the following statements to your code to reference the assembly in your code:

```
#using "ClassName.DLL"
using namespace ClassName;
```

> **NOTE:** Managed types corresponding to COM coclasses and interfaces converted using the Tlbimp.exe utility are always defined in the namespace that matches the name of the generated assembly.

5.   Instantiate types corresponding to converted COM coclasses using the default constructor and invoke their methods as necessary.

Consider the following header file, which defines a COM coclass named **Music**:

```
[object, uuid("C28FD0A3-6B2C-49B5-9C8E-11015448DD25"), dual,
    pointer_default(unique)]
interface IMusic: IDispatch {
    [id(1)] HRESULT Play([in] BSTR SongName, [out,retval] LONG* Duration);
    [propget, id(2)] HRESULT SongTitle([out, retval] BSTR* pVal);
    [propput, id(2)] HRESULT SongTitle([in] BSTR newVal);
};


[coclass, threading("apartment"), vi_progid("ComTest.Music"),
    progid("ComTest.Music.1"), version(1.0),
    uuid("B5102D2C-3317-4D7D-A4FF-F171F7407BEB")]
class ATL_NO_VTABLE Music: public IMusic {
public:
    Music() : SongTitle(0) {}
    STDMETHOD(Play)(BSTR SongName, LONG* Duration);
    STDMETHOD(get_SongTitle)(BSTR* pVal);
    STDMETHOD(put_SongTitle)(BSTR newVal);
protected:
    BSTR SongTitle;
};
```

The **Music** coclass implements a single **IMusic** interface, which defines the **Play** method and the **SongTitle** get/set property. When you import the class using the Tlbimp.exe utility, the **Music** coclass is converted into a **MusicClass** managed type, which you can instantiate in managed code and use just like any other managed type, including invoking methods and getting/setting properties:

```
#using <mscorlib.dll>
#using "ComTestAsm.dll"
using namespace System;
using namespace ComTestAsm;


void main()
```

```
{
    // 1. Create COM object
    MusicClass* Music = new MusicClass();
    // 2. Call methods
    int Duration = Music->Play("EnTrance");
    Console::WriteLine("Duration of EnTrance is {0}", __box(Duration));
    // 3. Set properties
    Music->SongTitle = "Trans-Country Express";
    Console::WriteLine("Song Title = {0}", Music->SongTitle);
}
```

Handling COM Events in Managed Code

.NET/COM interoperability allows managed clients to sink COM events in the same way managed classes sink events raised by other managed classes. Follow these steps to sink COM events in managed code:

1. When developing a COM component, define a separate event interface for your coclass.

2. Indicate that the coclass can source events by marking the coclass definition with the **event_source("com")** attribute.

3. Add the **__event __interface** *EventInterface* statement to the coclass definition to specify the event source interface for the class.

The code example shown next defines the sample **Music** coclass, which implements the **IMusicEvents** event interface containing a single **Stopped** method:

```
[object, uuid("C28FD0A3-6B2C-49B5-9C8E-11015448DD25"), dual,
    pointer_default(unique)]
__interface IMusic : IDispatch
{
    [id(1)] HRESULT Play([in] BSTR SongName, [out,retval] LONG* Duration);
};
// Event source interface
[dispinterface, uuid("23C5ADED-7408-426D-8939-E4652E9C3787")]
__interface IMusicEvents
{
    [id(1)] HRESULT Stopped([in] BSTR SongName, [in] LONG Duration);
};

[coclass, threading("apartment"), event_source("com"),
    vi_progid("ComTest.Music"), progid("ComTest.Music.1"),
    version(1.0), uuid("B5102D2C-3317-4D7D-A4FF-F171F7407BEB")]
class ATL_NO_VTABLE Music : public IMusic
{
public:
    Music() {}
    __event __interface IMusicEvents;
```

```
public:
    STDMETHOD(Play)(BSTR SongName, LONG* Duration)
    {
        *Duration = 123;
        // Raise event
        Stopped(SongName, 456);
        return S_OK;
    }
};
```

When you convert the COM coclass to a managed type using the Tlbimp.exe utility, the event source interface is converted to the ***EventInterface*_Event** managed interface, and delegate classes are created for each event method in the event source interface. The delegates use the following naming convention:

***EventInterface_Methodname*EventHandler**.

Also, add event handler/remove event handler methods to the class implementing the event interface to provide support for hooking/unhooking events using the +=/-= operator syntax. The following code example shows how to hook the **EventClass::Stopped** method to handle the **Stopped** events raised by the **Music** coclass:

```
#using <mscorlib.dll>
#using "ComTestAsm.dll"
using namespace System;
using namespace ComTestAsm;

// Event handler class
__gc struct EventClass {
    static void Stopped(String* SongName, int Duration)
    {
        Console::WriteLine("Song {0} stopped at {1}", SongName, __box(Duration));
    }
};

void main()
{
    // 1. Create COM object
    MusicClass* Music = new MusicClass();
    // 2. Raise event without an event handler
    Music->Play("EnTrance");
    // 3. Add event handler
    Music->Stopped += new IMusicEvents_StoppedEventHandler(0,
        EventClass::Stopped);
    // 4. Raise the event again
    Music->Play("EnTrance");
}
```

To attach to the event, the **IMusicEvents_StoppedEventHandler** delegate is constructed and hooked to the **Stopped** event delegate of the **Music** class.

Consuming .NET Classes in Unmanaged Code

Unless you are exposing an existing managed type to COM, there are only a few rules that you must follow to expose a new managed class to COM:

1. Explicitly define a public interface and make your managed class implement the interface.
2. Add a public default constructor to the class and make sure that the methods and properties that you want to expose to COM are public.

Once you build the new managed type or locate an existing managed type assembly to be consumed by COM, you must perform the following actions:

1. Convert the managed class assembly DLL into a COM type library by running the Tlbexp.exe utility:

```
Tlbexp.exe Managed.DLL
```

2. Copy the resulting *Managed.tlb* type library into the same folder with your unmanaged project files.
3. Copy the original *Managed.DLL* into Debug and Release directories. To be accessible at runtime, the DLL must be on the same path with the executable application.
4. Register the managed class with COM by running the Assembly Registration Utility Regasm.exe:

```
Regasm.exe Managed.DLL
```

5. In your source code, reference the *Managed.tlb* type library using the **#import** statement.
6. Instantiate the managed type and access its properties and methods as you would normally do for a COM type.

The following code example defines a simple managed type called **Music**, which implements the **IMusic** interface. Note the default constructor and **public** assembly-level visibility specifier in front of the **IMusic** interface and **Music** class definitions:

```
#using <mscorlib.dll>
using namespace System;
namespace ManagedClass {
    // 1. Interface for COM
    public __gc __interface IMusic {
        int Play(String* SongName);
        __property String* get_SongTitle();
        __property void set_SongTitle(String* NewTitle);
    };

    // 2. Managed class to be used in COM
    public __gc class Music: public IMusic {
    public:
```

```cpp
        // Default constructor required by COM
        Music()
        {
            pSongTitle = "No song";
        }
        int Play(String* SongName)
        {
            pSongTitle = SongName;
            return 123;
        }
        // SongTitle property
        __property String* get_SongTitle()
        {
            return pSongTitle;
        }
        __property void set_SongTitle(String* NewTitle)
        {
            pSongTitle = NewTitle;
        }
    private:
        String* pSongTitle;
    };
}
```

The managed class in this example is compiled into a ManagedClass.dll assembly.

The following code sample illustrates a simple unmanaged program, which consumes the **Music** managed type contained in the ManagedClass.dll assembly by means of COM interoperability:

```cpp
#include "stdio.h"
#import "ManagedClass.tlb"
using namespace ManagedClass;
void main()
{
HRESULT hr = CoInitialize(NULL);
    {
        // 1. Instantiate .NET class
        IMusicPtr pMusic(__uuidof(Music));
        // 2. Call method
        int Duration = pMusic->Play("EnTrance");
        printf("Duration of EnTrance is %i\n", Duration);
        // 3. Set properties
        pMusic->SongTitle = L"Trans-Country Express";
        printf("Song Title = %S\n", (BSTR)pMusic->SongTitle);
    }
```

```
    CoUninitialize();
}
```

Handling .NET Events in Unmanaged Code

To handle unmanaged code events raised by a managed type you must follow these steps when designing the managed type to ensure compatibility with the COM event model:

1. Declare public delegates for each event that you want to handle in unmanaged code.

2. Declare an event handling interface to be used by COM. The interface definition must be decorated with the **Guid** and **[InterfaceType(ComInterfaceType::InterfaceIsIDispatch)]** attributes.

3. Add event handler delegates to the managed class definition using the **__event** keyword.

4. Decorate the managed class definition with the **[ComSourceInterfaces("***Namespace.EventInterface***")]** attribute, where *Namespace* is the namespace in which the event handler interface *EventInterface is* defined.

The following code example illustrates the **Music** managed class definition. The **Music** class can raise a single **Stopped** event, which is described by means of the **IMusicEvents** interface:

```
#using <mscorlib.dll>
using namespace System::Runtime::InteropServices;
using namespace System;

namespace ManagedClass {
    // 1. Event handler delegate
    public __delegate void Stopped_EventHandler(String* SongTitle, int Time);

    // 2. Interface for handling events in COM
    [Guid("1A585C4D-3371-48dc-AF8A-AFFECC1B0967")]
    [InterfaceType(ComInterfaceType::InterfaceIsIDispatch)]
    public __gc __interface IMusicEvents {
        void Stopped(String* SongTitle, int Time);
    };

    // Interface for COM
    public __gc __interface IMusic {
        int Play(String* SongName);
    };

    // 4. Music class
    [ComSourceInterfaces("ManagedClass.IMusicEvents")]
    public __gc class Music: public IMusic {
    public:
        // Default constructor required by COM
        Music() {}
        int Play(String* SongName)
        {
```

```
        // Raise event
        Stopped(SongName, 456);
        return 123;
    }
    // 3. Event delegate
    __event Stopped_EventHandler* Stopped;
    };
}
```

Once you convert the **Music** managed class into a type library using the Tlbexp.exe utility and reference the resulting type library in your unmanaged code using the **#import** statement, you must add extra code to the unmanaged client to be able to consume events raised by the managed class via COM:

1. Manually define the managed class event handler interface and decorate the definition with the **dispinterface** and **uuid** attributes. (The COM event handler interface definition must match the managed event handler interface definition and both interface definitions must have the same GUID/UUID.)

2. Add the **module** attribute to your code. If you don't use this attribute you can't sink COM events.

3. Define a COM event receiver class and decorate it with the **event_receiver(com)** attribute:

    *   The event receiver class must supply one or more methods with signatures matching the method in the event handler interface.

    *   The event receiver class should supply hook-event and unhook-event methods for hooking and unhooking to and from the class events of a specified event handler interface.

4. Instantiate both the managed types exposed via COM and the event receiver class. Hook up the events raised by the managed class to the event receiver class using the event receiver hook method, supplying the pointer to the main interface of the managed type.

5. Raise the events.

6. When finished using the events, unhook the events raised by the managed class from the event receiver class using the event receiver unhook method, supplying the pointer to the main interface of the managed type.

The code example shown next illustrates how to handle the **Stopped** event raised when the **Play** method of the **Music** managed class is invoked:

```
#include "stdio.h"
#import "ManagedClass.tlb"
using namespace ManagedClass;

[dispinterface, uuid("1a585c4d-3371-48dc-af8a-affecc1b0967")]
__interface _IMusicEvents {
    [id(1)] HRESULT Stopped(BSTR SongTitle, long Duration);
};

[module(name="UnmanagedTest")];
// Event receiver class
[event_receiver(com)]
```

```
class CReceiver {
public:
    HRESULT Stopped(BSTR Song, long Time)
    {
        printf("Song %S stopped at %i", Song, Time);
        return S_OK;
    }
    void HookEvent(IMusicPtr pSource) {
        __hook(&_IMusicEvents::Stopped, pSource, &CReceiver::Stopped);
    }
    void UnhookEvent(IMusicPtr pSource) {
        __unhook(&_IMusicEvents::Stopped, pSource, &CReceiver::Stopped);
    }
};

void main()
{
    HRESULT hr = CoInitialize(NULL);
    {
        // 1. Instantiate .NET class
        IMusicPtr pMusic(__uuidof(Music));
        // 2. Raise event
        pMusic->Play("EnTrance");
        // 3. Add event handler
        CReceiver Receiver;
        Receiver.HookEvent(pMusic);
        // 4. Raise the event again
        pMusic->Play("EnTrance");
        Receiver.UnhookEvent(pMusic);
    }
    CoUninitialize();
}
```

First, the **_IMusicEvents** event handler interface is declared. The **#import "ManagedClass.tlb"** statement generates the **IMusicEvents** structure corresponding to the **IMusicEvents** interface of the managed class. Thus, to declare the event handler interface you must supply an alternative name (e.g., **_IMusicEvents**), although the interface UUID must be the same as the UUID of the **IMusicEvents** structure in the ManagedClass.tlh file generated by the **#import** statement.

The **CReceiver** class represents COM event sink. The class exposes a single **Stopped** method corresponding to the **_IMusicEvents::Stopped** event. Also, the class provides the **HookEvent/UnhookEvent** methods for hooking/unhooking a specified COM event interface from the **CReceiver** event sink class using the **__hook/__unhook** compiler intrinsics. When the **CReceiver ::HookEvent/ CReceiver::UnhookEvent** methods are called in the main program code, a pointer to the **Music** class **IMusic** interface is specified to designate the COM event source.

Consuming Unmanaged DLL Functions in .NET Applications

Follow these steps to consume an unmanaged DLL function in a managed application:

1. Locate a DLL function for consumption and obtain the function declaration in C.

2. Declare a prototype of the unmanaged function using the **extern "C"** keyword.

3. Decorate the function prototype definition with the **[DllImport("*DllName*")]** attribute, where *DllName* specifies the DLL file name which contains the function.

4. If the function accepts parameters corresponding to C++ structures, declare the structures in your code, either as unmanaged types or as managed types with fixed layout (**[StructLayout(LayoutKind::Sequential)]** attribute).

The code example shown next illustrates consumption of two Windows API functions: **GetDC** (defined in user32.dll) and **EnumFonts** (defined in gdi32.dll). The **EnumFonts** function accepts a pointer to the font enumeration callback function as the third parameter. The **EnumFontsProc** callback function accepts two parameters of type **LOGFONT** and **TEXTMETRIC**. The **LOGFONT** and **TEXTMETRIC** structures are defined in the code based of their definition found in the Platform SDK documentation. The **LOGFONT** is implemented as unmanaged structure, while the **TEXTMETRIC** is implemented as a managed type with fixed layout, which is enforced by means of the **[StructLayout(LayoutKind::Sequential)]** attribute.

When the program is executed it enumerates all fonts that belong to the "Arial" family.

```
#using <mscorlib.dll>
using namespace System;
using namespace System::Runtime::InteropServices;

// Unmanaged structure
struct LOGFONT {
  int lfHeight;
  int lfWidth;
  ...
  char lfFaceName[32];
};
// Managed structure with fixed layout
[StructLayout(LayoutKind::Sequential)]
__gc struct TEXTMETRIC {
  int tmHeight;
  int tmAscent;
  ...
  char tmCharSet;
};

// Callback delegate
__delegate int EnumFontsProc(LOGFONT* LogFont, TEXTMETRIC* TextMetric,
    int dwType, int LParam);
// Callback class
__gc struct CallbackClass {
```

```
    static int Callback(LOGFONT* LogFont, TEXTMETRIC* TextMetric,
        int dwType, int LParam)
    {
        Console::WriteLine(L"Font: {0}-{1}", new String(LogFont->lfFaceName),
            __box(LogFont->lfHeight));
        return 1;
    }
};

// Imported DLL functions
[DllImport("user32")]
extern "C" int GetDC(int hWnd);
[DllImport("gdi32")]
extern "C" int EnumFonts(int hDC, String* Face, EnumFontsProc* Callback,
    int LParam);

void main()
{
    // 1. Call DLL function
    int hDC = GetDC(0);
    // 2. Create callback delegate
    EnumFontsProc* MyEnumFontsProc = new EnumFontsProc(0,
        &CallbackClass::Callback);
    // 3. Call DLL function with callback
    EnumFonts(hDC, S"Arial", MyEnumFontsProc, 0);
}
```

Microsoft Extensions to The C++ Language

QUICK JUMPS

CHAPTER 14

Microsoft Extensions to The C++ Language

In Depth

In this chapter, I'll describe Microsoft's extensions to the C++ programming language that add to the language back bone but are not specific to any task. Task-specific extensions, such as Managed Extensions and Attributed Programming, are described in detail in Chapter 3, Chapters 17 and 18, respectively. In this chapter, I'll discuss new C++ 64-bit data types, language keywords, and compiler intrinsic functions including intrinsics representing MMX, 3DNow!, SSE, and SSE2 processor instructions.

Microsoft Extensions

With each new version of Visual C++ Microsoft adds something new to its implementation of the C++ language. Visual C++ .NET is no exception. The new language features introduced include keywords, data types, and compiler intrinsics. They are all intended to simplify C++ programming for the Windows operating system running on x86 family of PCs.

> **NOTE:** Microsoft C++ language extensions are easy to recognize because they all begin with a single-underscore or double-underscore prefix.

Most of the new Visual C++ .NET language extensions relate to "black belt" programming techniques and require a strong understanding of C++, operating systems, compilers, and CPU architecture. The following new features were added by Microsoft in the release of the Visual C++ .NET:

* *Managed Extensions to C++*: This feature provides support for .NET Framework programming (Chapter 2).

* *Attributed Programming*: This feature simplifies .NET, ATL COM, and ATL OLEDB programming (Chapters 2, 17, and 18).

* *Class programming extensions*: A feature that facilitates both managed and native C++ coding including:

    * Support for interfaces

    * Constructs for catching exceptions thrown from the constructor's initialization list

    * Support for covariant return types in virtual functions

    * Explicit function overrides

* *New intrinsic functions*: A feature that allows you to take advantage of the newest CPU, compiler, and linker features:

    * SSE, SSE2, and 3DNow! instruction set intrinsics

    * Compiler and linker support intrinsics

ANSI C and C++ Standard Compliancy

The good news for C programmers is that Microsoft C conforms to the standard for the C language as set forth in the 9899:1990 edition of the ANSI C standard. The bad news is that Visual C++ .NET does not comply with the newest C99 standard defined by the ISO committee, simply because the standard is so new.

With each new version of Visual C++, Microsoft strives to improve ANSI C++ compliance. Unfortunately, despite numerous improvements, the fact remains that *Visual C++ .NET is not fully ANSI C++ compliant*. The deviations from the ANSI C++ standard are listed in Table 14.1.

Table 14.1 Visual C++ .NET language deviations from ANSI C++ standard.

ANSI C++ Standard Section Number	Section Description
n/a	Compiler Limits
2.11	Alternative Keyword Representations
3.4.2	Argument-Dependent Name Lookup
6.4	Scope of a Name Declaration in a Selection Statement
14	**export** Keyword on a Template
13.5.2	Out-of-Class Template Definitions
13.5.4	Class Template Partial Specialization
13.5.5.2	Partial Ordering of Function Templates
15.4	Function Exception Specifiers
18.6.4	The **uncaught_exception** Function

You can consider the incompliant language features "minor and obscure" because they are not part of the main language functionality. But if you need to port your code to another C++ compiler that *is* fully ANSI C++ compliant, you could encounter problems. The chances of this happening, however, are very low.

Support for 64-bit Architecture

As the hype for new 64-bit PC processors such as the Intel Itanium or AMX x86-64 technology increases, the emergence of a 64-bit Windows operating system seems inevitable. But will *your* code benefit from 64-bit? The answer is that *it depends* on how your code will be used. Unless you are working with *huge* amounts of data (e.g., video processing, data mining and warehousing, virtual simulations, 3D animation, and so on) you will not benefit from terabytes of memory promised by the 64-bit address space. Similarly, if you do not perform precise computations (e.g., image/signal processing, statistical analysis, and so on) your code will not benefit from the extended 64-bit integer precision. So why bother with 64-bit code?

It turns out that new CPUs tend to support the new architecture much better than the legacy architecture. For that matter, 16-bit programs work slower on 32-bit processors than native 32-bit programs. The same fate awaits 32-bit programs running on 64-bit CPUs: Intel Itanium can only *emulate* 32-bit applications compiled for x86 architecture. (Itanium uses a totally different instruction set from x86.) AMD x86-64 architecture, on the other hand, *may* allow legacy 32-bit programs to run as well as 64-bit in most cases. To achieve the best performance on a 64-bit CPU you would have to recompile your code. Although, if you do recompile your code without changing 32-bit data types to 64-bit, your programs will likely work *slower*, since CPUs typically require additional instructions to operate on data types, which are narrower than the CPU architecture. At the same time, if you change all 32-bit data types with 64-bit data types you will lose performance when running your programs on a conventional 32-bit CPU. The option of maintaining two versions of your source code is not wise because it could be prohibitively expensive.

Fortunately, Visual C++ .NET provides a solution to the problem. Although you can't compile 64-bit code just yet, Visual C++ already contains features for supporting 64-bit and introduces a new integral data type called **INT_PTR. INT_PTR,** which is a platform-specific integer type. When compiling for a 32-bit platform, **INT_PTR** operates as a 32-bit integer. When compiling for a 64-bit platform, **INT_PTR** serves as a 64-bit integer. Many MFC classes, including collection classes such as **CArray**, **CList**, and so on, already rely on the new **INT_PTR** data type by using it in method parameters, class fields, pointers, and return values.

Microsoft is trying to make it easy for you to port your code to a future 64-bit version of Windows. All new projects generated with Visual C++ .NET are created with the Detect 64-bit Portability Issues compiler option (/Wp64) enabled by default. You can set this option on the Project Property Pages, C/C++ folder, or General page (See Appendix B, Figure B.3). When compiling your code with the Detect 64-bit Portability Issues option enabled, the compiler will produce C4244 warnings corresponding to *potentially* unsafe assignment of **INT_PTR** variables to 32-bit **int** variables. Although the **INT_PTR** data type is currently the same as **int** (i.e., 32-bit), when the next release of Visual C++ supporting compilation to 64-bit code comes out, **INT_PTR** data types may become true 64-bit integers, and all **INT_PTR** to **int** assignments will become unsafe *for real*. Therefore, to avoid the difficulties of porting your code to a 64-bit version of Windows in the *future*, you should do the work now by going through your code and addressing all C4244 warnings by replacing **int** data types with **INT_PTR** wherever possible.

To produce even better code and to ensure smooth code portability to a 64-bit platform you should replace all of your **int** data types with **INT_PTR** wherever possible. In other words, **INT_PTR** should be your default integer type and not **int**.

Data Alignment

Software performance depends heavily on the way your data is allocated in system memory. Most modern CPUs execute data operations faster if the data is properly aligned. Typically, 8-, 16-, or 32-bit data should be aligned on a 32-bit boundary, 64-bit data should be aligned on a 64-bit boundary, and 128-bit data should be aligned on a 128-bit boundary. If your data is not properly aligned, you'll encounter a performance penalty. Because proper data alignment is very critical for achieving optimal software performance, Visual C++ .NET provides ample means for managing data alignment, including:

* **__alignof**(*type*) intrinsic function for obtaining the alignment requirements of a specified data type.

* **__declspec**(**align**(*alignment*)) keyword for forcing data type alignment of a specified boundary.

* **_aligned_malloc, _aligned_free, _aligned_remalloc, _aligned_offset_malloc,** and **_aligned_offset_realloc** CRT functions to dynamically allocate data aligned on a specified boundary.

__alignof Function

The **__alignof** function allows you to obtain the alignment requirements of a specified data type. Table 14.2 contains the alignment requirements of the built-in data types.

Table 14.2 Alignment requirements for built-in data types.

Data Type	Alignment in Bytes
__alignof(char)	1
__alignof(short)	2
__alignof(int)	4
__alignof(__int64)	8
__alignof(float)	4
__alignof(double)	8
__alignof(void*)	4

The **__alignof** function is similar to the **sizeof** function except when applied to structures. The **__alignof** returns the alignment requirements of the largest structure member. Thus, for the following data structure

```
typedef struct {
   int myInt;
   double myDouble;
} MyStruct;
```

the **__alignof(MyStruct)** function will return the value 8.

__declspec(align) Keyword

To enforce a desired alignment of static or stack-allocated data, you can use the **__declspec**(**align**(*alignment*)) keyword in data type declarations. Here's an example:

```
typedef __declspec(align(4)) struct {
      int myInt;
} MyAlignedStruct;
```

This declaration forces the **MyAlignedStruct** data types to be aligned on a 32-bit boundary, regardless if an instance of the type is allocated on the stack or statically.

_aligned_*xyz* Functions

Heap allocated data is managed and aligned differently than statically or stack-allocated data. The **__declspec**(**align**) keyword has no effect on dynamic memory allocation. To ensure that your heap-allocated variables are properly aligned you should use **_aligned_*xyz*** functions, defined in the malloc.h header file:

* **void* _aligned_malloc(size_t** *size***, size_t** *alignment***)**: Allocates data on a specified boundary.
* **void* _aligned_realloc(void*** *alignedPtr***, size_t** *size***, size_t** *alignment***)**: Reallocates a specified aligned memory block using a specified new size and alignment requirements.

*   **void* _aligned_free(void* *alignedPtr*)**: Releases aligned memory block.

*   **void* _aligned_offset_malloc(size_t *size*, size_t *offset*, size_t *alignment*)**: Allocates data and ensures that the specified offset in the data is aligned on a specified boundary.

*   **void* _aligned_offset_realloc(void* *alignedPtr*, size_t *size*, size_t *offset*, size_t *alignment*)**: Reallocates a specified aligned memory block and data to ensure that the specified offset in the data is aligned on a specified boundary.

MMX, 3DNow!, SSE, and SSE2 Intrinsics

Single instruction, multiple data (SIMD) instruction sets such as MMX, SSE/SSE2, and 3DNow! have been around for a while. SIMD instructions allow you to greatly improve the performance of numerical computations by executing the same operation on many data items at once. The only way to use SIMD instructions with Visual C++ 6.0 was to use inline assembler. Programming in assembler is not a picnic. Inline assembler makes it difficult to work with function parameters, pointers, and classes (because you have to do all the work normally done by the compiler by hand).

Visual C++ .NET simplifies SIMD programming by introducing a number of compiler intrinsics corresponding to MMX, 3DNow!, SSE, and SSE2 instructions. Visual C++ .NET also supports four new data types related to SIMD instruction sets and SIMD data. The new SIMD data types are summarized in Table 14.3.

Table 14.3 SIMD data types.

Data Type	Precision	Integer/Floating Point	SIMD Instruction Set	CPU Registers	Description
__m64	64-bit	Both	MMX, 3DNow!	mm0..mm7	8 packed bytes, 4 packed words, 2 packed double-words, single quad-word, or 2 packed 32-bit floats
__m128	128-bit	Floating Point	SSE, SSE2	xmm0..xmm7	4 packed 32-bit floats
__m128i	128-bit	Integer	SSE2	xmm0..xmm7	16 packed bytes, 8 packed words, 8 packed double-words, 2 quad-words
__m128d	128-bit	Floating Point	SSE2	xmm0..xmm7	2 64-bit doubles

NOTE: You can use SIMD data types only on the left side of an assignment, as a return value, or as a parameter. You cannot use SIMD data types with any conventional arithmetic operators such as +, -, *, and so on.

SIMD compiler intrinsics are too numerous to list in this book. In brief, SIMD compiler intrinsics correspond one-to-one with CPU instructions. Each SIMD compiler intrinsic accepts the same parameters as the corresponding SIMD instruction. The advantages of intrinsics versus inline assembler is that they support C style syntax and you can manipulate their arguments with more flexibility than you can with inline assembler.

You don't have to remember the names of all SIMD instrinsics. If you are familiar with the underlying SIMD instruction set (e.g., MMX or 3DNow!), you'll be able to derive SIMD intrinsic function names based on the following conventions:

* *For Intel MMX, SSE, and SSE2 instructions* use the following syntax to derive the intrinsic function name:

  _mm_*op_suffix*(*operand1, operand2*)

  where *op* is the corresponding MMX, SSE, or SSE2 operation (e.g., **add**, **adds**, **sub**, **cmp**, etc.) and *suffix* designates the type of data. Intel intrinsic data type suffixes are summarized in Table 14.4.

* *For AMD 3DNow! instructions* use this syntax:

  _m_*op*(*operand1, operand2*)

  where *op* directly corresponds to a 3DNow! instruction name.

  NOTE: AMD 3DNow! intrinsics operate exclusively on **__m64** data types, except for **__m_from_float(float f)**, **__m_prefetch(void* p)** and **__m_prefetchw(void* p)** intrinsic functions.

Table 14.4 Intel intrinsic data type suffixes.

Suffix	Description
S	Single-precision floating point
D	Double-precision floating point
i128	Signed 128-bit integer
i64	Signed 64-bit integer
u64	Unsigned 64-bit integer
i32	Signed 32-bit integer
u32	Unsigned 32-bit integer
i16	Signed 16-bit integer
u16	Unsigned 16-bit integer
i8	Signed 8-bit integer
u8	Unsigned 8-bit integer

NOTE: *Intel MMX intrinsics operate on* **__m64** *data types, SSE intrinsics — on* **__m128** *data, and SSE2 intrinsics operate on* **__m128**, **__m128i** *and* **__m128d** *data types.*

To use the SIMD compiler intrinsics in your code, you must include proper header files containing the intrinsic function definitions. Header files corresponding to MMX, SSE, SSE2, and 3DNow! intrinsics are listed in Table 14.5. If you forget to include the appropriate header your code will not compile.

Table 14.5 Header files for SIMD intrinsics.

Instruction Set	Header File
Intel MMX	mmintrin.h
Intel SSE	xmmintrin.h
Intel SSE2	emmintrin.h
AMD 3DNow!	mm3dnow.h

> **NOTE:** When working with SIMD instructions or compiler intrinsics, keep in mind that you can achieve maximum performance only if your data is properly aligned. Typically, 32-bit data should be aligned on a 32-bit boundary, 64-bit data on 64-bit boundary, and so on.

For a detailed description of SIMD programming techniques with Visual C++ in general, and AMD 3DNow! and Intel MMX, SSE, and SSE2 instruction sets, in particular, see the following references:

* *MMX*: Max I. Fomitchev, *MMX Technology Code Optimization*, Dr. Dobb's Journal, September 1999.

* *3DNow!*: Max I. Fomitchev, *Optimizing 3DNow! Real-Time Graphics*, Dr. Dobb's Journal, August, 2000.

* *SSE and SSE2*: Shreekant Thakkar, Tom Huff, *Internet Streaming SIMD Extensions*, IEEE Computer, Vol. 32, No. 12, December 1999, pp.26-34.

* *Intel® Architecture Optimization Reference Manual*, Intel Corporation, Order Number: 245127-001.

Immediate Solutions

Writing Portable Code

To minimize the difficulties of porting your code to another platform and/or to another C++ compiler follow these steps:

1. Adhere to ANSI C/C++ standard and refrain from using any Microsoft extensions. You must compile your code with /Za compiler option to disable the Microsoft C++ language extensions. You can disable Microsoft C++ language extensions by setting the Disable Language Extensions option to "no" on the Project Property Pages, C/C++ folder, Language page.

2. Minimize usage of the inline assembler or any hardware or OS-specific functions.

3. Minimize usage of C runtime library (CRT) and Windows API. Use standard C/C++ library functions instead.

4. Separate portable code from OS/platform specific code.

It may not be possible to make your entire project portable, because certain functionality such as GUI or networking is not part of the C++ standard and the implementation details may differ wildly from one platform to another. Some projects will always contain platform-specific code. The free software MP3 player, FreeAmp (http://www.freeamp.org), represents an excellent example of portable software. If you download the FreeAmp source code and examine it, you will notice that the core of the FreeAmp functionality (MP3 decoding and play list management) consists of portable code that is separated from OS-specific code such as Internet communication and GUI support. You should employ the same technique when writing your own portable applications by partitioning source code into application logic, presentation, and communication/data management layers.

Using Interfaces

Functionality shared among multiple and otherwise unrelated C++ classes was traditionally implemented using multiple inheritance. Nowadays multiple inheritance is out of fashion: Old and new "C++ clones" such as Java and managed C++ do not allow multiple inheritance and rely on interfaces instead. Visual C++ .NET supports interfaces by means of the **__interface** keyword, which is discussed in depth in Chapter 2. You can use interfaces both in managed and native C++ applications. Follow these steps to implement functionality shared among several C++ classes by means of an interface:

1. Declare an interface and define common methods.

2. Make derived classes to implement the interface and provide concrete implementations for the common methods.

3. Use a pointer to an interface rather than a pointer to a class to access common functionality specified by the interface.

These techniques are illustrated in the following code example, which shows how to add common "owned by" functionality to otherwise unrelated classes **CFishTank** and **CShovel**:

```
#include <stdio.h>
__interface IOwnedBy {
    char* GetName();
    char* GetOwner();
};

class CFishTank: public IOwnedBy {
    char* GetName(){ return "Fish Tank"; }
    char* GetOwner() { return "Max"; }
};

class CShovel: public IOwnedBy {
    char* GetName(){ return "Shovel"; }
    char* GetOwner() { return "Vlad"; }
};

void InventoryCheck(IOwnedBy* aSubject)
{
    printf("A %s is owned by %s\n", aSubject->GetName(), aSubject->GetOwner());
}

void main()
{
    CFishTank* aFishTank = new CFishTank();
    CShovel* aShovel = new CShovel();
    InventoryCheck(aFishTank);
    InventoryCheck(aShovel);
}
```

Although the **CFishTank** and **CShovel** classes are unrelated they share common functionality specified by means of the **IOwnedBy** interface, which allows you to obtain the name of a subject and the name of a person who owns a subject. The **CheckInventory** method uses a pointer to the **IOwnedBy** interface to obtain information about the subjects.

Resolving Ambiguous Interface Method Names

When defining a class that implements more than one interface you might encounter a situation where several interfaces define methods with the same name. Methods specified in different interfaces are considered different even though they may have the same name and parameter lists. To resolve the ambiguity and to proper reference similarly named methods specified by different interfaces, you should use the following syntax when referring to the interface method:

```
InterfaceName::MethodName
```

The following code example shows how to resolve ambiguous method names in a class that implements two interfaces specifying the same **myFunc** method:

```
#include <stdio.h>
__interface MyInterface1 {
   void myFunc(int);
};
__interface MyInterface2 {
   void myFunc(int);
};

class MyClass: public MyInterface1, public MyInterface2 {
public:
   void MyInterface1::myFunc(int)
   {
      printf("MyInterface1::myFunc");
   }
   void MyInterface2::myFunc(int)
   {
      printf("MyInterface2::myFunc");
   }
};
void main()
{
   MyClass* pClass = new MyClass();
   ((MyInterface2*)pClass)->myFunc(1);
   ((MyInterface2*)pClass)->myFunc(2);
}
```

NOTE: To invoke an ambiguous interface method you must explicitly cast to the desired interface, or you may get a C2668 ambiguous call to overloaded function compiler error.

Catching Exceptions Thrown from Constructor's Initialization List

In earlier versions of Visual C++ you could not catch an exception thrown from a constructor's initialization list within the body of the constructor itself. Visual C++ .NET allows catching exceptions thrown from the constructor's initialization list by supporting *function-try* blocks. A function-try block is applicable only to class constructor and has the following syntax:

```
ClassName::ClassName(parameters)
try
: Initialization_List
{
    // Constructor body
}
catch (...) {
    // Handles exceptions thrown Initialization_List
    // and from the constructor body
}
```

The following code sample illustrates how to use a function-try block to catch an exception thrown from a constructor's initialization list:

```
int myFunc(int N)
{
    throw "exception";
    return N;
}

class MyClass {
public:
    MyClass(int N);
private:
    int m_N;
};

MyClass:: MyClass (int N)
try     // function-try block
: m_N(myFunc(N))
{
    // Constructor body
}
catch (...) {
    // Handle exceptions thrown from the constructor initialization list
    // and from the constructor body
}
void main()
```

```
{
    MyClass *MyC = new MyClass(10);
}
```

Invoking Base Class Members

Visual C++ .NET provides a new keyword named **__super** that can be used in place of a base class name when referring to base class methods, constructors, or fields. The **__super** keyword has the following syntax:

* base class method: **__super**::*MethodName*(*parameters*)

* base class constructor: **__super**(*parameters*)

* base class field: **__super**::*field*

You can use the **__super** keyword to access base class members without knowing the name of the base class. The code example shown next illustrates how to use the **__super** keyword for invoking base class methods:

```
struct MyClass1 {
    void myFunc(int) {
    }
};
struct MyClass2 {
    void myFunc(short) {
    }
    void myFunc(char) {
    }
};
struct MyDerived : MyClass1, MyClass2 {
    void MyFunc(short) {
        __super::myFunc(1);      // Calls MyClass1::MyFunc(int)
        __super::myFunc('a');    // Calls MyClass2::MyFunc(char)
    }
};
```

> **NOTE:** If you use the **__super** keyword to invoke a base class method having multiple overloads, the compiler will pick an overload that provides the best match to the supplied parameters.

The **__super** keyword is intended to simplify programming with ATL attributes (see Chapters 17 and 18). In some cases code injected by ATL attributes involves automatic class inheritance. In this event you may not know the base class name of your class, but you can use the **__super** keyword to access the base class methods anyway.

Overloading Functions with Covariant Return Types

Dealing with covariant return types in virtual class methods has been a hassle for Visual C++ developers. A type A is called *covariant from* type B if A inherits from B. To appreciate the problem of overloading functions with covariant return types, let's consider the following situation. You have a class **myClass** that supports cloning by implementing the **Clone** method that returns a reference to **myClass**. You want to derive your own class **myNewClass** and override the **Clone** method. However, in previous versions of Visual C++, overriding a method involved declaring an overriding method that exactly matched the method being overridden. Thus, **myNewClass::Clone** would have to return a reference to **myClass** rather than the desired reference to **myNewClass** because **myClass::Clone** returns a reference to **myClass**.

Visual C++ .NET solves the problem by allowing you to specify covariant return types when overloading virtual functions. The following example illustrates how to declare methods with covariant return types:

```
#include <stdio.h>
struct C1 {
    virtual C1* myFunc() { printf("C1::myFunc()"); return new C1(); }
};
struct C2 : C1 {
    virtual C2* myFunc(){ printf("C2::myFunc()"); return new C2(); }
};
void main()
{
    C1* pC1 = new C2();
    pC1 ->myFunc(); // Prints "C2::myFunc()"
}
```

> **WARNING!** Visual C++ 6.0 does not allow virtual methods that differ only by covariant return types by generating compilation errors.

Indicating Exceptions Thrown by Functions

Many C++ programming errors arise from the fact that code does not always catch all the exceptions thrown. The problem increases when you use third-party libraries and you simply don't know if the library functions can throw exceptions and what kind of exceptions they throw. Visual C++ .NET provides a solution to the problem by allowing you to specify exceptions that can be thrown by a function using the **throw** keyword in function declarations:

```
Function_Declaration throw(ExceptionType)
```

The following code snippet illustrates the declaration of a function that may throw an exception of type **char***:

```
void myFunc() throw(char*)
{
    throw("Exception");
}
```

The **throw** keyword in a function declaration does not produce any additional code but serves purely informational purposes so you would know right away if a function can throw an exception. If you omit the *ExceptionType* parameter and declare the function like this

```
void myFunc() throw()
{
}
```

you would indicate that the function does not throw exceptions.

Managing Data Alignment

Follow these steps to ensure that a data type is aligned on a particular memory boundary:

1.   If you are working with a custom data type, declare it using the **__declspec(align)** keyword to specify a desired alignment for statically and stack-allocated instances of the type.
2.   If you are working with an unknown data type, determine its alignment requirements using the **__alignof** function.
3.   Dynamically allocate memory using the **_aligned_malloc** function.
4.   Free the dynamically allocated aligned memory using the **_aligned_free** function.

The following code example illustrates declaration, stack allocation, and dynamic allocation of the aligned **AlignedRGB** type:

```
#include <malloc.h>

// Make sure that the RGB structure is aligned on a 32-bit boundary
typedef __declspec(align(32)) struct {
    unsigned char r, g, b;
} AlignedRGB;

void main()
{
    // Stack-allocate the aligned data
    AlignedRGB rgb;

    // Dynamically allocate the RGB data
    AlignedRGB* prgb = (AlignedRGB*)_aligned_malloc(10*sizeof(AlignedRGB),
        __alignof(AlignedRGB));

    // Free the aligned data
    _aligned_free(prgb);
}
```

Using SIMD Instruction Sets

You can dramatically improve the performance of computationally extensive code by rewriting/redesigning critical sections of the original C/C++ code to use the new MMX, SSE, SSE2, or 3DNow! compiler intrinsic functions. Although it is difficult to come up with a general recipe on how to redesign code to take advantage of parallelized processing using SIMD instructions, there are three steps that you must follow when using compiler SIMD intrinsics:

1. Choose the target instruction set: MMX for integer computations, 3DNow! or SSE/SSE2 for floating-point calculations.

2. Include the header file defining the intrinsics for the target instruction set (see Table 14.5).

3. Determine your data alignment requirements: MMX and 3DNow! instruction sets usually operate on 64-bit data and 64-bit data alignment, while SSE/SSE2 instruction sets operate on 128-bit data and require 128-bit alignment.

4. Align static and stack allocated data using the **__declspec(align)** keyword or dynamically allocate aligned data using the **_aligned_malloc** CRT function.

5. Cast integral types to built-in SIMD data types (see Table 14.3) when passing data as parameters to the SIMD intrinsic functions.

    NOTE: Besides using intrinsics you can use SIMD instructions directly with inline assembler. You do not have to include any header files to use SIMD instructions with inline assembler.

The code sample shown next demonstrates how to use the compiler intrinsic functions corresponding to AMD 3DNow! instructions to perform fast addition of two arrays of floating-point values:

```
#include <mm3dnow.h>
void add(float* dest, const float* src, int N)
{
    _m_femms();
    for ( int i = 0; i < N; i += 2 )
        _m_pfadd(*((__m64*)&dest[i]), *((__m64*)&src[i]));
    _m_femms();
}
int main()
{
    __declspec(align(32)) float a[16], b[16];
    add(a, b, sizeof(a)/16);
}
```

The **_m_pfadd** intrinsic function corresponds to the 3DNow! **pfadd** instruction, which allows performing two floating-point additions at the same time. Therefore, the **_m_pfadd** allows speeding up floating-point additions by a factor of two compared with ordinary x87 code.

When working with SIMD instructions or compiler intrinsics, keep in mind that you can achieve maximum performance only if your data is properly aligned. Typically, 32-bit data should be aligned on 32-bit boundary, 64-bit data on 64-bit boundary, and so on. The code example above uses the **__declspec(align(32))** keyword to align stack-allocated arrays of floating-point numbers.

Deprecating Functions

As APIs and class libraries mature, some of the older features become deprecated and get replaced by the new features. The intent of deprecation is to discourage developers from using deprecated features as they may not be supported in future releases. Visual C++ .NET supports deprecation of functions and class methods through the __declspec(deprecated) keyword. The __declspec(deprecated) keyword declares a particular form of function overload as deprecated. Whenever a compiler encounters a call to a deprecated function it generates a C4996 warning, as illustrated in the example here:

```
void myFunc1()
{
    //...
}
__declspec(deprecated) void myFunc1(int)
{
    //...
}
void main()
{
    myFunc1();
    myFunc1(1);    // C4996 warning
}
```

Alternatively, you can use the **#pragma deprecated**(*function*) statement to mark a particular function as deprecated. The **#pragma deprecated** keyword is similar to the __declspec(deprecated) declaration except that it marks *all* overloads of a specified function as deprecated:

```
void myFunc1() {}
void myFunc1(int) {}
#pragma deprecated(myFunc1)

void main()
{
    myFunc1();    // C4995 warning
    myFunc1(1);   // C4995 warning
}
```

Managing Function Inlining

The Visual C++ .NET compiler automatically decides which functions to inline. The decision is made based on the structure of your code. Even if you use the __inline keyword in the function declaration, there is no guarantee that the compiler will actually inline the function. Instead, the compiler will note the function as a *candidate* for inlining. To ensure 100 percent predictable inlining/no inlining behavior, you use the __forceinline keyword to instruct the compiler to always inline a particular function, or use the __declspec(noinline) keyword to instruct the compiler to never inline a particular member function. The following code example illustrates how to use the __forceinline and __declspec(noinline) keywords:

```
#include <stdio.h>
__forceinline void myFunc1()
{
    printf("I'm inlined");
}
__declspec(noinline) void myFunc2()
{
    printf("I'm not inlined");
}
void main()
{
    myFunc1();
    myFunc2();
}
```

> **NOTE:** If a function is declared with C++ **inline** or **__inline** keywords, the function will be inlined only when the compiler determines that such inlining is beneficial for the code's size or performance. To force the inlining regardless of whether it is going to be beneficial or not, use the **__forceinline** keyword.

Resolving Multiple Symbol Definitions

It is a common programming practice to declare global variables and use them in different source files. It is convenient to declare global variables in a header file using the **extern** statement. Then, you must pick a spot in one of the source files and actually *instantiate* the global variables. When there are many global variables it becomes a hassle to instantiate all of them. Also, picking the right source file to instantiate the global variables can be difficult.

Visual C++ .NET provides a neat solution to the problem by introducing the **__declspec(selectany)** keyword. To declare a global variable, use **__declspec(selectany)** in place of **extern**. The compiler will generate multiple definitions of the global variable, but the linker will select and use only one such definition and will discard all the duplicates. Consider the following sample header file myHeader.h:

```
class CMyClass {
public:
    CMyClass(int N) { m_N = N; };
    int m_N;
};
CMyClass MyClass(10);
```

If you include myHeader.h in more than one C++ file in the same project, you will get a "symbol **MyClass** already defined" linker error. To make your code link without errors, declare the **MyClass** as:

```
__declspec(selectany) CMyClass MyClass(10);
```

The linker will pick the first instance of **MyClass** and will use it everywhere **MyClass** is referenced. To eliminate duplicate or unused copies of the **MyClass** variable located in other modules, specify the /OPT:REF linker option. This option (Linker folder, Optimization page, reference item in Project Properties dialog) instructs the linker to remove unreferenced duplicate symbols (functions or variables), thus reducing your code size.

Generating Code Conditional on Symbol Existence

New Visual C++ .NET **__if_exists** and **__if_not_exists** keywords allow generating code that will or will not execute based on whether a particular symbol is defined. The following code example produces output only if the **g_MyGlobal** symbol is defined:

```
#include <stdio.h>
int g_MyGlobal;
void main()
{
    __if_exists(g_MyGlobal)
    {
        printf("g_MyGlobal exists.");
    }
}
```

If you comment out the declaration of **g_MyGlobal** in this code sample, the **printf**() statement will not be executed.

The best application of **__if_exists** and **__if_not_exists** keywords is to generate conditional code that depends on the existence or absence of particular member functions or member variables in derived or template-based classes. The code sample shown next demonstrates how to use a template class derivation where the template code depends on the presence of the **myFunc** member function in the based class:

```
#include <stdio.h>
template<typename T> class MyTest : public T {
public:
    void myFunc()
    {
        __if_exists(T::myFunc)
        {
            T::myFunc();
            printf("T::myFunc() exists;");
        }
        __if_not_exists(T::myFunc)
        {
            printf("T::myFunc() does not exist;");
        }
    }
};
```

```
class A {
public:
   void MyFunc()
   {
        printf("A::myFunc();");
   }
};
class B {
};
int main()
{
   MyTest<A> t1;
   MyTest<B> t2;
   t1.myFunc();      // Prints 'A::myFunc();T::myFunc() exists;'
   t2.myFunc();      // Prints 'T::myFunc() does not exist;'
   return 0;
}
```

Obtaining a Function Return Address

Visual C++ .NET provides two new compiler intrinsics, **_AddressOfReturnAddress** and **_ReturnAddress**, that facilitate function return address manipulation. The intrinsics are defined as:

```
void* _AddressOfReturnAddress();
void* _ReturnAddress();
```

The **_AddressOfReturnAddress** intrinsic function returns the address of the memory location that holds the return address of the current function. To overwrite the return address you must overwrite the value in memory pointed by **_AddressOfReturnAddress**. The **_ReturnAddress** intrinsic returns the return address itself (i.e., the address of the first instruction executed when the function returns). The following code example illustrates how to obtain the return address of the current function call:

```
#include <stdio.h>
extern "C" void* _AddressOfReturnAddress();
extern "C" void* _ReturnAddress();
// Mark the routines as intrinsic
#pragma intrinsic(_AddressOfReturnAddress)
#pragma intrinsic(_ReturnAddress)

// Block inlining so that we would have a return address
__declspec(noinline) void myFunc()
{
   void* pvAddressOfReturnAddress = _AddressOfReturnAddress();
   printf("func() return address: %p\n", *((void**)pvAddressOfReturnAddress));
   printf("func() return address: %p\n", _ReturnAddress());
}
```

```
int main()
{
    myFunc();
    return 0;
}
```

> **NOTE:** You must declare the **_AddressOfReturnAddress** and **_ReturnAddress** intrinsics before you can use them.

Adding Break Points Programmatically

You can add a break point to your code programmatically by using the **__dbgbreak** compiler intrinsic. When the program execution reaches the **__dbgbreak** statement, an alert window is displayed prompting to run a debugger, unless you are already running your program in debug mode within Visual Studio. In order for the **__dbgbreak** intrinsic to work, you must run your program stand alone (e.g., at the command prompt). The following code example illustrates how to use the **__debugbreak** compiler intrinsic:

```
void main()
{
    if ( some condition )
        // Display a prompt for launching a Debugger
        __debugbreak();
}
```

Selectively Eliminating Function Calls

To eliminate a function or a section of code based on a preprocessor definition, C++ programmers traditionally use **#ifdef / #ifndef** precompiler directives. The disadvantage of using these directives is that your code can become cluttered and confusing. Visual C++ .NET provides a cleaner solution by introducing the **__noop** compiler intrinsic. This intrinsic can be used to substitute any function name and can accept any number of function parameters. Unlike any function, **__noop** instructs the compiler to discard the supplied parameters without evaluating them. Thus, **__noop** reduces the function and its parameters to nothing. The following code shows how to use **__noop** for precompiler driven message logging:

```
#include <stdio.h>
#define ERROR_LOGGING
#ifdef ERROR_LOGGING
    #define PRINT    printf
#else
    #define PRINT    __noop
#endif
void main()
{
    PRINT("Sample log message\n");
}
```

If the **ERROR_LOGGING** in the example above is undefined, the code produces no output.

CHAPTER 15

C Runtime Library Enhancements

QUICK JUMPS

CHAPTER 15
C *Runtime Library Enhancements*

In Depth

In this chapter, I'll discuss the C Runtime Library (CRT) enhancements introduced in Visual C++.NET, focusing on the new CRT features such as runtime error checking, buffer overrun detection, aligned memory allocation, throwing **new** operator, new string functions, and routines for manipulating dates beyond year 2038.

C Runtime Library

The C Runtime Library is an essential component of any C++ program. The CRT typically handles system tasks such as error reporting, memory management, and operating-system support. Although it is possible to bypass CRT and write code that does not depend on it, the CRT provides necessary *convenience* for everyday programming needs. The CRT is used in virtually all unmanaged Visual C++ projects. By default, the CRT manages the C++ program lifetime from A to Z. First, the CRT initializes a program and it passes the control to the program entry point such as **main** or **WinMain**. Lastly, the CRT performs the clean up work and terminates the program when the **main/WinMain** function returns.

Although it is possible to write a C++ program that does not rely on the CRT (i.e., by minimizing CRT use in ATL), there are very few scenarios when eliminating the CRT is beneficial. Most programs written in Visual C++ use the CRT and dynamically link to the msvcrt.dll, which typically resides in the Windows system directory (e.g., windows\system on Windows 95/98/ME or winnt\system32 on Windows NT family of operating systems).

Besides using the CRT for housekeeping tasks, you can explicitly call exported CRT functions, which are Microsoft-specific. CRT functions are easy to recognize as they begin with a single underscore prefix ('_'). If you are going to use new CRT features introduced in Visual C++ .NET, you might have to distribute the new version 6.1 msvcrt.dll because most of the existing Windows installations are likely to contain the older version of the library. Distribution of msvcrt.dll usually requires creation of the installer script such as Microsoft Installer (MSI script) or the InstallShield package. In most cases it is impossible to overwrite the existing version of the msvcrt.dll because the library is locked as it is constantly used by other applications and the Windows operating system itself. With the help of the installation script, however, you can replace the library on the next system reboot before the library is loaded for the first time. Alternatively, you can write an installation script in C++ and use the **MoveFileEx** Win32 API function with the **dwFlags** parameter set to **MOVEFILE_DELAY_UNTIL_REBOOT** to overwrite the library.

Runtime Error Checking

There is nothing worse then contemplating your program crash as you stare at a "program has performed an illegal operation" message box. What can you do to make your code more stable? Besides fixing bugs you can employ the CRT runtime error checking (RTC) capabilities to avoid uncontrolled program crashes and recover gracefully when your code performs an illegal operation. As a part of the enhanced robustness of the C++ language, the CRT allows you to perform the following runtime error checking on the code being executed:

*   Stack pointer corruption
*   Overruns of local arrays
*   Stack content corruption
*   Dependencies on uninitialized local variables
*   Loss of data on an assignment to a lower precision variable

To enable runtime error checking, you must compile your program with the /RTC option enabled (C/C++ folder, Code Generation page, Basic Runtime Checks option in Project Property Pages dialog). Then, you can programmatically hook custom error handling routines to perform custom processing when an error occurs.

The new CRT error checking routines are declared in the rtcapi.h header file and summarized in Table 15.1.

Table 15.1 Run-time error checking functions.

Function Name	Description
int _RTC_NumErrors()	Returns the total number of RTC errors that can be detected.
_RTC_GetErrDesc(_RTC_ErrorNumber *ErrNum*)	Returns a brief description of a runtime error specified by the error number ***ErrNum***.
_RTC_error_fn _RTC_SetErrorFunc(_RTC_error_fn *ErrorFunc*)	Specifies a new handler function ***ErrorFunc*** for reporting RTC errors and returns a pointer to the previously defined RTC error handler.
_RTC_SetErrorType(_RTC_ErrorNumber *ErrNum*, int *0ErrType*)	Assigns a level of severity ***ErrType*** to an RTC error specified by the error number ***ErrNum***.

*NOTE: There are three levels of error severity: **_CRT_WARN**, **_CRT_ERROR**, and **_CRT_ASSERT**. By default all RTC errors have **_CRT_ERROR** severity level. Severity level controls the way errors are reported at runtime.*

To handle runtime errors you must supply a custom error handling function with the following signature (defined by the **_RTC_error_fn typedef**):

```
int MyErrorFunc(int errorType, const char* fileName, int lineNumber,
    const char* moduleName, const char* format, ...);
```

The routine accepts the following arguments:

*   **errorType**: Specifies the RTC error type.
*   **fileName**: The source file name where the error occurred.
*   **lineNumber**: The source file line number where the error occurred.
*   **moduleName**: .exe or .dll file name where the error occurred.
*   **format–printf:** Formatted stock error message with formatting parameters following in the optional **va_arg** list. (The first **va_arg** list parameter contains the current runtime error number.)

The custom error reporting function must return 1 if you want to break into the debugger, or 0 of you want to ignore the error.

#pragma runtime_checks

You may have to use the new Visual C++ .NET **#pragma runtime_checks** precompiler directive that disables/restores the /RTC compiler settings when writing custom error handling code for runtime error checking. The **runtime_checks** directive has the following syntax:

```
#pragma runtime_checks("runtime_checks", {restore | off})
```

The *runtime_checks* parameter can be set to any combination of the following values:

*   *s*-stack frame verification

*   *c*-precision loss on assignment to smaller data types reporting

*   *u*-uninitialized variable usage reporting

By using the **runtime_checks** directive, you can designate the sections of your code where a particular type of runtime error checking should be disabled: You simply insert the **#pragma runtime_checks(**"*runtime_checks*", **off)** directive at the beginning of the code to disable error checking and insert the **#pragma runtime_checks(**"*runtime_checks*", **restore)** at the end of the code to reenable error checking.

> **NOTE:** If you do not specify a value for the *runtime_checks* and use the empty string, all runtime error checks will be disabled or restored.

Buffer Overrun Detection

Buffer overruns represents a common security threat. A security hole may appear in your application if you do not programmatically check for possible local array overruns. For example, imagine that you are developing a server-side application that handles HTTP requests. In your request handler routine, you implement a fixed but large local array. An enterprising hacker could then come along and submit a request larger than your maximum buffer size and include a virus or a Trojan horse code as a part of the request. To activate the malicious code, the intruder would have to append to the request another chunk of data with the new return address pointing to the virus code. In a situation like this, the intruder could override the local array so that the new return address pointing to the malicious code contained in the request will overwrite the original return address of the request handler routine. Thus, when the request handler routine returns, the uploaded virus code will be executed.

To protect your code from buffer overruns, you must compile it with the /GS option (C/C++ Folder, Code Generation Page, Buffer Security Check option in Project Property Pages dialog). Once you set the /GS option and recompile your program, your code will throw an exception when a buffer overrun occurs. Also, you can install a custom buffer overrun exception handler by calling the new CRT **_set_security_error_handler** function. This function is declared in the stdlib.h header file:

```
_secerr_handler_func _set_security_error_handler(_secerr_handler_func);
```

The **_secerr_handler_func** function accepts a pointer to the security error handler function and returns a pointer to the previously installed handler. The signature of the security handler function is the following (**_secerr_handler_func typedef**):

```
void __cdecl MyHandler(int code, void* unused);
```

The only defined code for the **code** parameter is **_SECERR_BUFFER_OVERRUN**.

Stack Overflow Recovery

A stack overflow is a typical cause of a program crash. Ideally, an application should be free of stack overflows. If a stack overflow occurs, however, the application should be able to recover gracefully, and perhaps give the user an opportunity to save his or her work. To support recovery from stack overflows, Visual C++ .NET provides the new **_resetstkoflw** function (declared in the malloc.h header file):

```
int _resetstkoflw();
```

When a stack overflow occurs, the **STATUS_STACK_OVERFLOW** exception is thrown. If the code captures the exception, it can attempt to recover from the overflow by calling the **_resetstkoflw** function. The function returns a nonzero value if the stack overflow was successfully reset, or zero if the stack overflow cannot be reset. If the stack overflow was reset successfully, the program may continue normal execution. If the **_resetstkoflw** function fails to reset the stack overflow, the application *must* terminate as soon as possible or the program crash may occur.

Throwing **new** Operator

When allocating memory using the **new** operator, Visual C++ 6.0 developers had to check whether the **new** operator returned a valid memory address or **NULL** indicating that the memory allocation had failed. If the memory is allocated frequently, the code quickly becomes cluttered with countless pointer checking. Visual C++ .NET takes care of the mess by supporting two types of the **new** operator:

*   *CRT **new** operator:* This operator does not throw an exception and returns **NULL** if memory allocation failed. This operator is defined in libc.lib, libcd.lib, libcmt.lib, libcmtd.lib, msvcrt.lib, and msvcrtd.lib.
*   *Standard C++ Library **new** operator:* This operator throws an exception when memory allocation fails. This operator is defined in libcp.lib, libcpd.lib, libcpmt.lib, libcpmtd.lib, msvcprt.lib, and msvcprtd.lib.

You can elect to use the Standard C++ Library **new** operator, which throws an exception when memory allocation fails. This eliminates numerous pointer checking. To change the behavior of the **new** operator from the default CRT to Standard C++ Library, you must add the **#include <new.h>** statement to your source code. The inclusion of the new.h header file will force the linker to link with Standard C++ Libraries rather than with CRT libraries.

Alternatively, or in addition to the **#include <new.h>** statement, you can link your program with the thrownew.obj module to ensure that the linker finds the Standard C++ Library **new** operator that you want to use in your code. The throwing **new** operator has a caveat, however. When developing static libraries for third parties, you cannot be sure that your library will be linked with the CRT or the Standard C++ Library unless your code contains explicit dependencies on either one of the libraries. You must use the **std::nothrow** keyword in conjunction with the **new** operator to ensure predictable non-throwing behavior:

```
char* pText = new (std::nothrow) char[1024];
```

Support for Dates Beyond Year 2038

The CRT **time_t** data type, which is defined in the time.h header file, supports dates only in the range of January 1st, 1970 to January 18th, 2038. Therefore, all CRT date/time management routines that rely on the **time_t** data type are confined to the same date range. To a void the "Year 2038" problem, Microsoft defined a new data type **__time64_t** that supports dates beyond year 2038 and up to December 31st, 3000. Along with the new **__time64_t** data type, the CRT supplies a new set of routines that are equivalent to the old **time_t**-routines except that they operate on the new **__time64_t** data type.

The new CRT functions that support **__time64_t** data type include:

* *General date/time management routines* (declared in the time.h header file):
    * **struct tm* _localtime64(const __time64_t* *pTime*)**: Converts time from **__time64_t** to **tm** format and corrects for the local time zone.
    * **__time64_t _time64(__time64_t* *pTime*)**: Returns system time.
    * **void _time64(__time64_t* *pTime*)**: Retrieves current time.
    * **char* _ctime64(const __time64_t* *pTime*)**: Converts time to ASCII string accounting for local time zones.
    * **wchar_t* _wctime64(const __time64_t* *pTime*)**: Converts time to wide-character string accounting for local time zones.
    * **__time64_t _mktime64(struct tm* *pTime*)**: Converts time from **tm** to **__time64_t** format.
    * **struct tm* _gmtime64(const __time64_t* *timer*)**: Converts time from the **__time64_t** to **tm** format.
* *File date/time modification routines* (declared in the utime.h header file):
    * **int _utime64(const char* *FileName*, struct __utimbuf64* *FileTime*)**: Sets file modification time.
    * **int _wutime64(const wchar_t* *FileName*, struct __utimbuf64* *FileTime*)**: Sets file modification time using wide-character file name.
    * **int _futime64(int *handle*, struct __utimbuf64* *FileTime*)**: Sets file modification time for an open file specified by *handle*.
* *File status retrieval routines* (declared in the sys/stat.h header file):
    * **int _stat64(const char* *path*, struct __stat64* *buffer*)**: Retrieves file status information.
    * **int _stati64(const char* *path*, struct __stati64* *buffer*)**: Retrieves file status information.
    * **int _wstat64(const wchar_t* *path*, struct __stat64* *buffer*)**: Retrieves file status information using wide-character file name.
    * **int _wstati64(const wchar_t* *path*, struct __stati64* *buffer*)**: Retrieves file status information using wide-character file name.

* *File-find routines* (declared in the io.h header file):

    * **intptr_t _findfirst64(const char*** *FileSpec***, struct __finddata64_t*** *FileInfo***)**: Retrieves information about the first file matching the file specification *FileSpec*.

    * **intptr_t _findfirsti64(const char*** *FileSpec***, struct __finddatai64_t*** *FileInfo***)**: Retrieves information about the first file matching the file specification *FileSpec*.

    * **intptr_t _wfindfirst64(const wchar_t*** *FileSpec***, struct __wfinddata64_t*** *FileInfo***)**: Retrieves information about the first file matching the file specification *FileSpec* given in wide characters.

    * **intptr_t _wfindfirsti64(const wchar_t*** *FileSpec***, struct __wfinddatai64_t*** *FileInfo***)**: Retrieves information about the first file matching the file specification *FileSpec* given in wide characters.

    * **intptr_t _findnext64(intptr_t** *handle***, struct __finddata64_t*** *FileInfo***)**: Retrieves information about the next file matching the file specification given by *handle* (*handle* is returned by the previous call to **_findfirst64**).

    * **intptr_t _findnexti64(intptr_t** *handle***, struct __finddatai64_t*** *FileInfo***)**: Retrieves information about the next file matching the file specification given by *handle*.

    * **intptr_t _wfindnext64(intptr_t** *handle***, struct __fwinddata64_t*** *FileInfo***)**: Retrieves wide-character information about the next file matching the file specification given by *handle*.

    * **intptr_t _wfindnexti64(intptr_t** *handle***, struct __wfinddatai64_t*** *FileInfo***)** Retrieves wide-character information about the next file matching the file specification given by *handle*.

File status routines define new a **_stati64** structure that unlike the old **_stat** structure contains date/time fields in **__time64_t** format. Similarly, the new file-find routines require the new **__wfinddata64_t** structure to store information about a file. All new programs should use the **_time64** data type and the new CRT date management routines. If you primarily use MFC, you have nothing to worry about: MFC 7.0 classes such as **CTime** and **CTimeSpan** internally implement the **__time64_t** data type to represent date/time information rather than **time_t** as in previous versions of MFC.

New Math Constants

The standard math.h header file finally defines common math constants such as π, e, and their common variations to facilitate numerical computations. The new constants are defined as double precision floating-point numbers and are summarized in Table 15.2.

Table 15.2 New math constants defined in math.h header file.

Constant	Math Expression	Value
M_E	e	2.71828182845904523536
M_LOG2E	$\log2(e)$	1.44269504088896340736
M_LOG10E	$\log10(e)$	0.434294481903251827651
M_LN2	$\ln(2)$	0.693147180559945309417
M_LN10	$\ln(10)$	2.30258509299404568402
M_PI	π	3.14159265358979323846
M_PI_2	$\pi/2$	1.57079632679489661923

<Continued on Next Page>

<Table 15.2 Continued>

Constant	Math Expression	Value
M_PI_4	$\pi/4$	0.785398163397448309616
M_1_PI	$1/\pi$	0.318309886183790671538
M_2_PI	$2/\pi$	0.636619772367581343076
M_2_SQRTPI	$2/\mathrm{sqrt}(\pi)$	1.12837916709551257390
M_SQRT2	$\mathrm{sqrt}(2)$	1.41421356237309504880
M_SQRT1_2	$1/\mathrm{sqrt}(2)$	0.707106781186547524401

Aligned Memory Allocation

Achieving maximum performance of computation-intensive code requires that your data is properly aligned. Your data should be aligned on 32-bit, 64-bit, or 128-bit boundaries (see the "Using SIMD Instruction Sets" section in Chapter 14) depending on the type of processing and on the data types involved. For instance, efficient MMX or 3DNow! processing requires that your data be aligned on a 64-bit boundary. Unfortunately, traditional memory allocation routines such as the **new** operator or **malloc** function do not guarantee data alignment. To ensure the desired data alignment for dynamically allocated memory, Visual C++ .NET provides three new CRT routines: **_aligned_malloc**, **_aligned_realloc**, and **_aligned_free**. The routines are declared in the malloc.h header file and are defined as follows:

```
void* _aligned_malloc(size_t size, size_t alignment);
void* _aligned_realloc(void* MemBlock, size_t size, size_t alignment);
void _aligned_free(void* MemBlock);
```

When allocating an aligned memory block you can obtain the alignment requirements of the underlying data using the new **__alignof** compiler intrinsic function (see Chapter 14).

Efficient Byte Swapping

Data processing tasks such as image processing frequently rely on a specific order of bytes within integers. A problem arises when an image is acquired on one machine and processed on another machine, and the order of bytes in integers on the two machines do not match. A classical example is the Mac versus the PC: The former uses Big-endian integer format while the latter uses Little-endian integer format. Thus, when you move images from the Mac to the PC you must do byte swapping to restore the representation of integers before you can do any processing on the image data.

Since we all live in the Internet age, and all or almost all computers are connected, and wildly diverse hardware is employed in the acquisition, generation, and processing of data, you almost certainly would encounter the need for byte swapping at some point of time. Efficient byte swapping is a key for fast processing, and a quick-and-dirty byte swapping function quickly thrown together after a cup of coffee may not be the best tool for the job. Visual

C++ .NET addresses the problem by supplying three new CRT routines for fast and efficient byte swapping (declared in the stdlib.h header file):

* **unsigned short _byteswap_ushort(unsigned short *val*)**: Swaps bytes within a 16-bit integer.
* **unsigned long _byteswap_ulong(unsigned long *val*)**: Reverses byte order in a 32-bit integer.
* **unsigned __int64 _byteswap_uint64(unsigned __int64 *val*)**: Reverses byte order in a 64-bit integer.

Accelerating Transcendental Math Functions

Transcendental math functions, such as sine, tangent, or exponent, take a long time to compute. Yet if you look at most math libraries, including Microsoft Visual C++ libraries, you will find that the transcendental math routines are still computed using old x87 instructions. Why not use the new SIMD instruction sets optimized specifically for this kind of operations? Both SSE/SSE2 and 3DNow! instruction sets have built-in instructions that calculate square root or reciprocal square root in just two cycles.

Fortunately, the new Visual C++ .NET CRT library now allows accelerating **atan**, **ceil**, **exp**, **floor**, **log**, **log10**, **modf**, and **pow** math functions by switching to the SSE2 instruction set behind the scene. The switching is not automatic and you must initiate it by calling the new **_set_SSE2_enable** CRT function. This function is declared in the math.h header file:

```
void _set_SSE2_enable(int bEnable);
```

You call the function with the **bEnable** parameter set to 1 to enable the SSE2 instruction set. The function returns 1 if the switching was successful or 0 otherwise (e.g., if the code is running on a AMD Athlon CPU that does not support for SSE2 instructions).

Unfortunately trigonometric functions such as **sin**, **cos**, or **tan** are not accelerated.

> **WARNING!** SSE2-accelerated math functions may produce slightly less precise results than unaccelerated functions. This is due to the fact that SSE2 uses internal 64-bit (C++ **double**) representation of floating-point numbers, while regular x87 instruction set operates on 80-bit (C++ **long double**) extended precision numbers.

Immediate Solutions

Handling Runtime Errors

You must define and install a custom RTC error handler function to handle runtime errors. The code sample shown next demonstrates how you write a simple RTC error handling routine and install it. The code performs the following actions:

1. Defines an RTC-free code block enclosed in the **#pragma runtime_checks("", off)** and **#pragma runtime_checks("", restore)** precompiler directives.
2. Defines the **MyErrorHandler** routine for handling RTC errors inside the RTC-free block. You should disable RTC inside of the RTC error handling routine to avoid possible stack overflow caused by the RTC handler invoking itself recursively.
3. Installs the **MyErrorHandler** RTC error handler using the **_RTC_SetErrorFunc** CRT function and saves a pointer to the original RTC error handler.
4. Restores the original RTC error handler using the **_RTC_SetErrorFunc** function.
   > **NOTE:** You must include the rtcapi.h header file to use RTC functions.

```
#include <windows.h>
#include <stdarg.h>
#include <stdio.h>
#include <rtcapi.h>

#pragma runtime_checks("", off)
// RTC Error Handler
int MyErrorHandler(int errType, const char* file, int line,
    const char* module, const char* format, ...)
{
    // 1. Prevent re-entrance
    static long IsRunning = 0;
    while ( InterlockedExchange(&IsRunning, 1) )
        Sleep(1);

    // 2. Get the RTC error number from the var_arg list
    va_list ArgList;
    va_start(ArgList, format);
    _RTC_ErrorNumber ErrorNumber = va_arg(ArgList, _RTC_ErrorNumber);
    va_end(ArgList);

    char s[1024];
    // 3. Get the error description
    const char* ErrorDesc = _RTC_GetErrDesc(ErrorNumber);
    sprintf(s, "%s occurred.\nLine: %i\nFile: %s\nModule: %s\nClick OK to break into debugger.",
ErrorDesc, line, file ? file : "Unknown", module ? module : "Unknown");
    // 4. Display message box
    MessageBox(NULL, s, "Run-Time Error", MB_OK);
    IsRunning = 0;
    // 5. Go ahead and break into the debugger
    return 1;
}
#pragma runtime_checks("", restore)

int main()
{
    _RTC_error_fn OldHandler;
    // Set new RTC error handler and save the old one
    OldHandler = _RTC_SetErrorFunc(&MyErrorHandler);
    // Do something
    // ...
    // Restore the original error handler
    _RTC_SetErrorFunc(OldHandler);
}
```

The **MyErrorHandler** RTC error handler function displays a message box reporting the error information and prompts the user to break into the debugger. The function executes the following steps:

1. Prevents re-entrancy by constructing a small **while** loop consisting of a single call to the **InterlockedExchange** function. If you do not prevent the re-entrancy, it is possible that the RTC error handler will be called repeatedly several times resulting in multiple message boxes prompting user to run the debugger.

2. Extracts the RTC error number from the function **va_arg** list.

3. Obtains the RTC error description by calling the **_RTC_GetErrDesc** function.

4. Displays a message box reporting the error information and prompting user to run the debugger.

5. Resets the **IsRunning** variable used to control re-entrancy by means of the **InterlockedExchange** loop in Step 1 and returns 1 indicating that the debugger should be launched.

Detecting Buffer Overruns

Follow these steps to enable programmatic detection of security breaches related to buffer overruns:

1. Define a custom security error handler routine.

2. Install the security error handler using the **_set_security_error_handler** function;

3. Compile your code with the /GS option (C/C++ Folder, Code Generation Page, Buffer Security Check option in Project Property Pages dialog).

The following code example illustrates buffer overrun detection by performing the following steps:

1. Defines the **MyHandler** security error handler that prints an error message and terminates the program.

2. Installs the **MyHandler** security error handler using the **_set_security_error_handler** function.

3. Simulates buffer overrun by calling the **SimulateOverrun** function, which overruns local character array.

```c
#include <stdlib.h>
#include <stdio.h>
#include <string.h>

// Security error handler
void __cdecl MyHandler(int code, void* unused)
{
    if ( code == _SECERR_BUFFER_OVERRUN )
    {
        // Buffer overrun detected, report the error and exit
        printf("Darn hackers! Buffer overrun detected.\n");
        exit(1);
    }
}

void SimulateOverrun(char* str)
{
    char buffer[16];
    strcpy(buffer, str);
```

```
}

void main()
{
    // 1. Install security error handler
    _set_security_error_handler(MyHandler);
    // 2. Simulate buffer overrun
    SimulateOverrun("Unexpectedly large input will cause buffer overrun");
}
```

Recovering from Stack Overflows

Follow these steps to enable graceful recovery from stack overflow exceptions:

1. Catch stack overflow exception by complementing your main **try/catch** block with the __except(GetExceptionCode() == STATUS_STACK_OVERFLOW) exception handler.

2. In the __except block, call the _resetstkoflw CRT function to reset the stack overflow, perform necessary clean up, which may include saving user data, and terminate the application.

The following code sample demonstrates graceful stack overflow recovery according to the schema outlined above:

```
#include <windows.h>
#include <malloc.h>

// Infinitely recursive function
void BadFunction()
{
    char s[1024];  // Stack place holder
    BadFunction();
}
int main()
{
    __try {
        // 1. Cause stack overflow
        BadFunction();
    }
    // 2. Catch stack overflow exception
    __except(GetExceptionCode() == STATUS_STACK_OVERFLOW) {
        // 3. Recover from the stack overflow
        if ( !_resetstkoflw() )
            // 4. And exit the program
            return -1;
    }
    return 0;
}
```

Using Throwing **new** Operator

To use the throwing **new** operator as your default **new** operator, you must include the new.h header file in your source code as shown here:

```
#include <stdio.h>
#include <new.h>

int main()
{
    try {
        // 1. Allocate memory using the throwing new operator
        char* pText = new char[1024*1024];
        // 2. Allocate memory using the non-throwing new operator
        pText = new (std::nothrow) char[1024*1024];
        if ( pText == NULL )
        {
            // Report Error
            // ...
        }
    }
    catch(...) {
        printf("Memory allocation error.\n");
    }
}
```

Once you include the new.h header file you can still use the nonthrowing **new** operator that returns a NULL-pointer when memory allocation fails if you explicitly qualify the **new** operator with the **(std::nothrow)** keyword. This is demonstrated in the example above.

Measuring Formatted Strings

When formatting strings, it is often desirable to know the size of the resulting formatted output so we can allocate memory to hold the result. Unfortunately, the standard **printf** function allows neither obtaining formatted string size nor limiting formatted string size. A common work around involves allocating string buffers sufficiently large to hold the largest possible representation of a formatted string. This approach has two drawbacks. Sometimes we guess it wrong and the largest possible buffer size still happens to be too small resulting in a program crash. In other cases, we cannot afford to waste memory for a buffer that is never fully utilized.

The new CRT library provides a solution by introducing two new functions, **_scprintf** and **_scwprintf** that count characters in **printf**-formatted input. These functions are declared in the stdio.h header file:

```
int _scprintf(const char* format,   ...);
int _scwprintf(const wchar_t* format, ...);
```

The following code snippet shows how to measure a formatted string using **_scprintf** and dynamically allocate memory for the formatted result:

```
#include <stdio.h>
void main()
{
    int myVar = 12345;
    int size = _scprintf("%i", myVar);
    char* s = new char[size];
    sprintf(s, "%i", myVar);
}
```

For formatting functions that accept an argument list (**va_list**) parameter, you should use **_vscprintf** or **_vscwprintf** functions. The functions are defined as:

```
int _vscprintf(const char* format, va_list argptr);
int _vscwprintf(const wchar_t *format, va_list argptr);
```

Reading Fixed-Length Formatted Data

The **scanf** routine processes an input string according to the specified format and extracts parameters into a variable list of supplied arguments. Visual C++ .NET adds two new functions, **_snscanf** and **_snwscanf**, that allow you to process only the specified number of characters in the input string. These functions are declared in the stdio.h header file:

```
_snscanf(const char* input, size_t nChar, const char* format, ...);
_snwscanf(const wchar_t* input, size_t nChar, const wchar_t* format, ...);
```

The following code snippet shows how you can use **_snscanf** to process the first 6 characters of **mySrc** string to parse out only the first two parameters:

```
#include <stdio.h>
void main()
{
    char mySrc[] = "1 test 14.0";
    char myText[10];
    int myInt;
    _snscanf(mySrc, 6, "%i %s %g", &myInt, myText);
}
```

Allocating Aligned Memory

To allocate, reallocate, or deallocate aligned memory you should use the **_aligned_malloc**, **_aligned_realloc**, and **_aligned_free** functions declared in the malloc.h header file. The following code example illustrates the usage of the aligned memory management functions by performing the following actions:

1. Allocates a memory block aligned on an 8-byte boundary, corresponding to the alignment requirements of the **__m64** intrinsic MMX data type using the **_aligned_malloc** function.

2. Increases the size of the allocated aligned memory block using the **_aligned_realloc** function.

3. Frees the aligned memory block using the **_aligned_free** function.

```
#include <malloc.h>
#include "mmintrin.h"
void main()
{
    // 1. Allocate aligned memory
    __m64* myData = (__m64*)_aligned_malloc(1024, __alignof(__m64));
    // 2. Resize the allocated aligned memory
    myData = (__m64*)_aligned_realloc(myData, 2048, __alignof(__m64));
    // 3. Free the aligned memory
    _aligned_free(myData);
}
```

> **NOTE:** Data allocated with the **__aligned_malloc** functions must be deallocated using **__aligned_free**.

Accelerating Math Functions with SSE

If your code is running on a hardware system supporting the Intel SSE2 instruction set (e.g., a system that uses an Intel Pentium 4 CPU), you can accelerate math calculations by enabling the SSE2 support. To enable SSE2 acceleration you must call the new **_set_SSE2_enable** CRT function with the **bEnable** parameter set to 1:

```
#include <math.h>
void main()
{
    if ( _set_SSE2_enable(1) )
    {
        // SSE2 enabled
    }
    else
    {
        // Processor does not support SSE
    }
}
```

You should invoke the **_set_SSE2_enable** function with the **bEnable** parameter set to 0 to disable SSE2 support at a later time during the program execution.

Accelerating Math Functions with 3DNow!

If your code is running on a hardware system supporting the AMD 3DNow! instruction set (e.g., a system that uses an AMD Athlon CPU), you can accelerate your math calculations by replacing the calls to the standard math functions declared in the math.h header file with the calls to 3DNow!-accelerated math functions provided as a part of AMD 3DNow! SDK. You can download these functions free of charge from AMD web site at http://cdrom.amd.com/devconn/library.zip. (The http://cdrom.amd.com/devconn/ directory contains few more interesting 3Dnow! downloads, including AMD CodeAnalyst code profiling tool and DirectX 3D Surface Deformation Demo optimized for 3Dnow! Instructions.) The AMD 3DNow! SDK contains amath.h header file that defines 3DNow!-accelerated inline math functions. The names of the 3DNow!-accelerated functions correspond to the names of their unaccelerated counterparts declared in math.h except that they have an underscore prefix in front of the function name: e.g., **cos** -> **_cos**.

Fortunately, AMD accelerated all of the standard math functions including trigonometric functions. But unlike standard math function, 3DNow!-accelerated functions operate on single precision floating point values (i.e., **float** data types). If you are using lots of math in your code, then the advantage of using 3DNow!-accelerated math functions can be very noticeable. The code sample shown next demonstrates how you can compute the value of sine using the accelerated **_sin** function from the AMD 3DNow! SDK:

```
#include "amath.h"
void main()
{
    float v = _sin(1.0f);
}
```

If you decide to use AMD SDK 3DNow! math functions, you must link your program with amdmath.lib (release) or amdmathd.lib (debug) libraries.

> **WARNING!** The 3DNow! instruction set operates only on single-precision floating-point numbers (C++ **float** data type). Thus, if your calculations require double precision numbers (C++ **double** data type) you *must* use CRT math functions declared in the standard math.h header file.

APPENDIX A

Visual C++ .NET Development Environment

In Depth

In this appendix, I will describe the Visual Studio .NET integrated development environment (IDE), focusing on features pertinent to Visual C++ .NET. I will explain not only how to use Solution Explorer, ClassView, and Server Explorer but also how to edit your source code, how to compile it, and how to debug. Although some of the operations in the new development environment are similar to those in Visual C++ 6.0, I will focus on important changes and provide tips for improving productivity.

First Look at the Development Environment

At first glance, Visual Studio .NET IDE looks the same as Visual C++ 6.0, but there are important differences. Instead of traditional Visual C++ workspaces (.dsw files), Visual Studio .NET manages solutions (.sln files) that can contain multiple projects, including projects in Visual C++, Visual Basic, or C#. And Visual C++ 6.0 project files (.dsp) are now replaced with .vcproj files (Although, you can still open old Visual C++ 6.0 projects from Visual Studio .NET., and the projects will be automatically converted by the development environment into the new format).

Also, project wizards are now called "Project Templates" (but the essence remains the same). Visual C++ .NET supports a wider variety of project templates than Visual C++ 6.0 and adds extra functionality to the old wizards. Table 2.1 contains the list of Visual C++ .NET project templates.

Table A.1 Project templates.

Project	Template	Comments New?	New Features
ATL Project	Simple Advanced Template Library (ATL) project	No	Attributes and COM+ Support.
ATL Server Project	ATL Server Component Wizard	Yes	ATL Web Applications, ATL ISAPI Extensions.
ATL Server Web Service	ATL Web Service Wizard	Yes	ATL Web Service.
Custom Wizard	Custom Application Wizard	No	
Extended Stored Procedure DLL	SQL Server stored procedure wizard	No	
Makefile Project	Application project that is built using makefile	No	
Managed C++ Application	Managed console application printing Hello World	Yes	

<Continued on Next Page>

<Table A.1 Continued>

Project	Template	Comments New?	New Features
Managed C++ Class Library	Managed C++ class library exporting an empty sample class, **Class1**	Yes	
Managed C++ Empty Project	Empty project configured for using Managed Extensions to C++ and targeting CLR	Yes	
Managed C++ Web Service Simple	.NET web service with a single method printing Hello World . For a detailed discussion of .NET web services, see Chapters 10 through 12	Yes	
MFC ActiveX Control	MFC ActiveX Control DLL	No	
MFC Application	MDI, SDI, or dialog-based MFC application (.exe file)	No	Windows Explorer style window layout; Multiple top-level documents; Split window support; Browser style toolbar support; Active Accessibility support; Common Control Manifest support.
MFC DLL	MFC Dynamic Link Library	No	
MFC ISAPI Extension DLL	Internet Information Server Extension DLL	No	
Win 32 Project	Embraces all kinds of Visual C++ Win32 projects (Win32 application, Win32 console application, Win32 DLL, Win32 static library)	No	Adds ATL support to console applications.

Changes to existing application wizards are minor, if not cosmetic. Major new chunks of functionality come from Managed Extensions to C++ and Web Services support. For a detailed description of these new features, see Chapters 2 and 10, 11 and 12, respectively.

Visual C++ .NET Installation

Installation of Microsoft Visual Studio .NET starts with the installation of prerequisites. First of all, you must have Windows 2000 installed because Visual Studio .NET will not install on Windows 95, 98, or NT. The Windows Component Update disk, bundled with Visual Studio .NET, provides the required prerequisites, which include:

* Windows 2000 Service Pack 1
* Microsoft Windows Installer 2.0
* Microsoft FrontPage 2000 Web Extensions Client
* Microsoft Data Access Components (MDAC) 2.7
* Microsoft .NET Framework

If you are upgrading from Visual Studio 6.0 or Visual C++ 6.0, I recommend installing Visual Studio .NET into a new location and keeping the old version of Visual C++ around. This with of any unexpected code porting problems and provide a fallback platform in case of unsolvable difficulties.

After a dozen reboots and successful installation of all the prerequisites, Visual Studio .NET can be installed. The default installation folder (C:\Program Files\Microsoft Visual Studio .NET) does not coincide with the Visual C++ 6.0 default installation folder (C:\Program Files\Microsoft Visual Studio) so you do not need to worry about overwriting the existing Visual C++ installation.

Once the installation is complete, launch the Visual Studio .NET integrated development environment (IDE) by clicking on the Visual Studio .NET icon. Unlike Visual Studio 6.0, there are no separate icons for Visual Basic, Visual Interdev, or Visual J++. In Visual Studio .NET, all languages operate from the same unified development environment, providing uniform experience for all Visual Studio developers regardless of the programming language used.

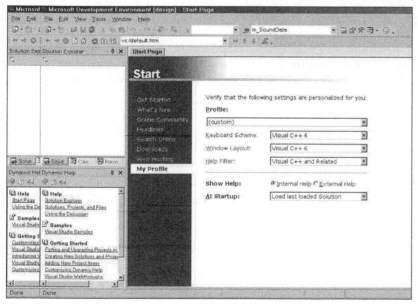

Figure A.1 Visual Studio .NET Start Page.

Setting Visual C++ .NET Preferences

On the first run, you must configure your Visual Studio .NET development environment by indicating your preferences on the Start Page (Figure A.1). When upgrading from Visual C++ 6.0, it makes sense to keep the Visual C++ 6.0 window layout and keyboard scheme and perhaps limit help topics to "Visual C++ and Related" to improve help search relevance.

Should you desire to modify your Visual Studio configuration later, you can display the Start Page by selecting the Help|Show Start Page menu item from the Visual Studio menu.

Checking for Updates

The first thing you should do after installing Visual Studio .NET is check for updates and service releases by selecting the "Check for Updates" item from the Help menu. The development environment will connect to the Microsoft site on the Internet to download and install the most recent service releases and updates if any.

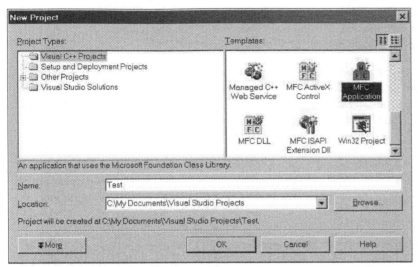

Figure A.2 The New project dialog.

Using Solution Explorer

To get a good starting point, let's begin with an MFC Application Template. Even if you are not very familiar with MFC, I suggest that you go through the steps described below to create a sample project that will help you explore the new Visual Studio .NET development environment features.

NOTE: If you would like to learn about MFC in more detail, I recommend reading *Visual C++ 6 Programming Blue Book*, by Stephen Gilbert and Bill McCarty (The Coriolis Group), for an introduction into Microsoft Foundation Classes programming with Visual C++ 6.0.

To create a new MFC application:

1. Select the New Project menu item from the File menu to open a New project dialog (Figure A.2).

2. Then, select the MFC Application Wizard item from the list of templates located in the Visual C++ Projects folder.

3. Specify the new project name.

4. Click OK.

The MFC Application Wizard screen will appear. You'll notice that the traditional wizard appearance, with "Next" and "Back" buttons, has now been replaced with a tabbed window layout with tab titles listed in the left section of the wizard screen.

5. For the purpose of your introduction to the Visual Studio .NET development environment, it is sufficient to leave all the default wizard settings and click the Finish button to generate the template project source code. (Or you can customize the MFC application settings in the way you want to and click the Finish button when you are done.)

NOTE: For a detailed description of the MFC Application Wizard, see Appendix B.

If you've selected the Visual C++ Developer profile on the Visual Studio .NET Start Page, then the IDE appearance after the successful completion of the MFC Application Wizard will look very familiar. The Visual C++ 6.0 Workspace window is now renamed into "Solution Explorer" and still appears to the left of the screen (Figure A.3).

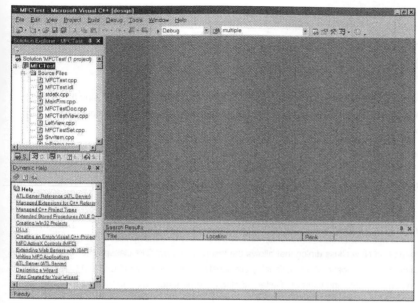

Unlike the Workspace window in Visual C++ 6.0, Solution Explorer can contain a variable number of tabs. You can add additional tabs by dragging other windows into the Solution Explorer. Conversely, you can remove tabs by clicking on the "x" icon at the top right corner of the Solution Explorer.

Figure A.3 Visual Studio .NET Solution Explorer.

NOTE: All user interface windows in Visual Studio .NET support docking and tabbed layout. You can drag and drop entire windows or individual tabs anywhere, arranging them the way you like.

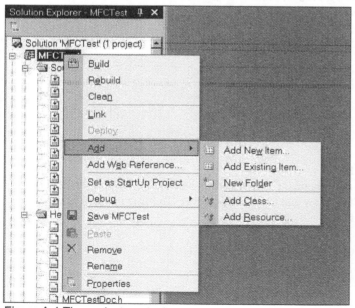

6.   Right-click on the application project in Solution Explorer to open the context menu (Figure A.4).

Figure A.4 The project context menu.

The most useful menu items are summarized in Table A.A.

Table A.2 Project context menu items.

Menu Item	Description
Clean	Deletes temporary build files from project configuration folders. If you are using the default Debug and Release configurations, then all the files in the *ProjectName*\Debug and *ProjectName*\Release folders will be removed.
Add New item	Opens Add New Item dialog that allows adding new files to the project. New files are added in skeleton form with basic markup, commands, or tags already inserted. Visual Studio .NET provides extensive capabilities, including menus and toolbars for editing XML, HTML, ASP, and other files. Appropriate menus and toolbars are loaded automatically when you open a file in Visual Studio .NET. Besides syntax highlighting, Visual Studio .NET allows visual composition of HTML files, HTML frame sets, ASP pages, and database queries.
Add New Class	Opens Add New Class dialog that allows the inserting of new C++ classes into the project. This dialog contains most of the functionality previously found in the Visual C++ 6.0 Class Wizard and Components and Controls Gallery dialogs that no longer exist in Visual Studio .NET.
Add Resource	Opens Add Resource dialog. The Add resource dialog now supports HTML resources.
Add Web Reference	Opens Add Web Reference dialog that facilitates the location and discovery of web services. **NOTE:** *For more information on web services, see Chapters 10, 11, and 12.*
Set As Startup Project	Makes current project active (applies only to multiproject solutions).
Properties	Opens project property pages (Project Settings in Visual C++ 6.0). **NOTE:** *For a detailed reference of the project property pages, see Appendix C.*

Using Class Wizard's Replacement

Unlike Visual C++ 6.0, Visual C++ .NET does not contain a Class Wizard in its original form. Instead, most of the Class Wizard functionality was moved to Class View and to Resource Editor. To bring up the Class View, select menu View|Class View or press Ctrl+Shift+C.

Adding New Class Members

To Add a new member variable/function to the existing class:

1. Simply right-click on the class name.
2. Select Add|Add Variable/Add Function menu item, and the Member Function Wizard window will appear (Figure A.5).

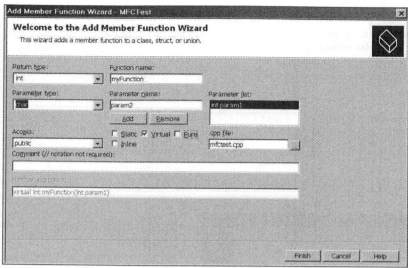

Figure A.5. The Member Function Wizard dialog.

Adding New Classes

To add a new class to your project:

1.   Right-click on your project name in Class View or in Solution Explorer.

2.   Select AddlAdd Class menu item to open the Add Class dialog (Figure A.6).

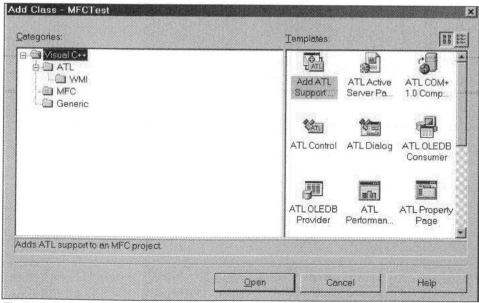

Figure A.6 The Add Class dialog.

3. Then, double-click on the desired type of class to open the appropriate class wizard dialog.

4. Specify additional parameters specific to the selected class (like dialog resource ID for the MFC CDialog class or data source name for the **CRecordset** class).

Adding User Interface Event Handlers
To add a user interface event handler:

1. Go to the Resource Editor (menu View|Resource View or Ctrl+Shift+E) and open a dialog, accelerator, or menu resource you wish to handle events on.

2. Then, right-click on the element you wish to handle event on (e.g., accelerator, menu item, or on dialog control).

3. Select Add Event Handler from the context menu, and the Event Handler Wizard window (Figure A.7) will appear.

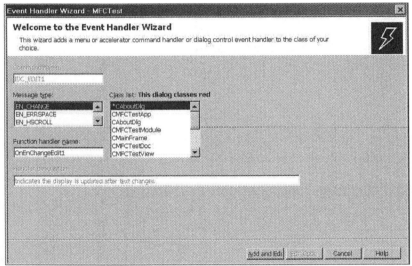

Modifying Class Properties
Adding event handlers, functions, and member variables may not be enough to customize a class. What if you want to add events other than menu command handlers, handle Windows messages, or override virtual functions?

Figure A.7 The Event Handler Wizard dialog.

For additional class customization, you must use the class Properties window. Then, follow these steps:

1. Simply right-click on the class you wish to modify in Class View.

2. Select Properties from context menu. A dockable Properties window will appear. You can "tear off" the Properties window and resize it for convenience.

Using Property Window
The Properties page of the Property window (Figure A.8) contains basic information about the class: header file name, whether the class is abstract, injected (i.e., automatically generated by attribute), managed (i.e., defined with __gc keyword), sealed (i.e., defined with **__sealed** keyword), template, or value (i.e. defined with **__value** keyword). You can not modify any class properties in the class Property window. To change the class properties, you would have to edit source code manually.

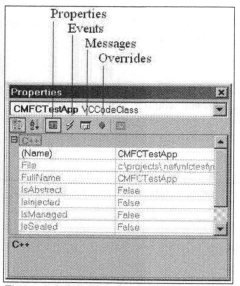

Figure A.8 Class Property window.

Buttons on the Property window toolbar allow for switching between different property pages. Drag your mouse over the Property window toolbar and read the tool tip descriptions to identify buttons that activate Events, Messages, and Overrides pages.

Adding Event Handlers

The Events page lists all the user interface commands, including **COMMAND** and **UPDATE_COMMAND_UI** messages. Events are grouped in two sections: Accelerator Commands and Menu Commands. The Accelerator Commands section is expanded by default.

To handle a specific message, either type your own event handler name in the edit field to the right of the event or select the default event handler name from the drop down list (Figure A.9). Once you specify or select the event handler name, the event handler code will be added to your class. The newly added event handler code will be automatically displayed in the edit window.

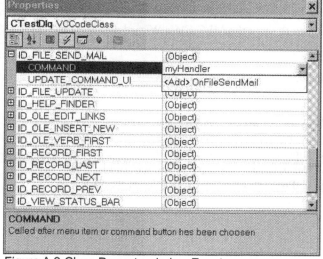

Figure A.9 Class Property window Events page.

Editing and Deleting Event Handlers

If, at a later time, you would want to edit or delete the event handler code, follow these steps:

1. Open the class Properties window and locate the event on the event page.

2. Once again, expand the drop down list to the right from the event.

3. Select <Edit Code> to edit the code or <Delete> to remove the event handler code.

   NOTE: When you delete the event handler code, the code will not be physically removed. The deleted event handler code will be commended out.

Adding Message Handlers

To add a windows message handler, go to the class Properties window Messages page. The procedure for adding, editing, and deleting a windows message handler is absolutely identical to the one for event handlers.

Overriding Functions

To override any existing class members, go to the class Properties window Overrides page. Overrides are logically grouped in two sections: Common and Uncommon (e.g. functions you would normally override, and functions you almost never override, like **DoModal**() of **CDialog** class). Common section is expanded by default. To override a member function, select <Add>*function name* from the drop down list to the right of the function you wish to override.

> **WARNING!** Despite the ability to type in a new function name in the drop-down list, you can not specify a different name for the function you are overriding. Hopefully, this confusing feature will be removed in the final release of Visual C++ .NET.

Adding New Dialog Classes

To create a new dialog class based on a dialog resource:

1.   Open the dialog resource in edit mode by double-clicking on the dialog resource ID in the Resource View window.
2.   Then, right click on the dialog resource.
3.   Select Add Class menu item from the context menu to open the MFC Class Wizard dialog. The Class Wizard dialog will automatically list only compatible base classes, such as **CDhtmlDlg**, **CDialog**, **CFormView** or **CpropertyPage**.
4.   Set the dialog ID to the current dialog resource ID.

Using Resource Templates

Visual Studio .NET adds the notion of resource templates. A *resource template* is a customized resource that you can save as an .rct file. It serves as a starting point for creating other resources. Once you have customized the resource template, you must save your changes in the template folder (or any other location specified in the include path) so that the new resource template will appear under its resource type in the Add Resource dialog box. The Visual Studio .NET default template folder is C:\Program Files\Microsoft Visual Studio .NET\Vc7\VCResourceTemplates\1033.

To add a resource template:

1.   Right-click on your project name in Class View.
2.   Select Add|Add New Item from the context menu to open the Add New Item Dialog.
3.   Then, select the Resource Template File (.rct) from the list of templates.
4.   Specify the file name.
5.   Click OK.

Using Server Explorer

As development strategies shift from developing client-side GUI applications towards server-side middleware, it becomes necessary to manage servers and explore server configuration/properties on a regular basis. When I was using Visual C++ 6.0 to develop server components for Windows NT 4.0 Server, I had to run back and forth between my workstation and the server box, giving my legs quite a work out. Microsoft recognized the need for improvement and added Server Explorer to the Visual Studio .NET development environment. To open the Server Explorer window, select the ViewlServer Explorer menu item or click Ctrl+Shift+S. The Server Explorer window is shown in Figure A.10.

Figure A.10 Server Explorer window.

Setting Up Database Connections

You can add your own data connections and inspect contents of databases by:

1.   Right-clicking on the Data Connections list item in the Server Explorer window, and

2.   Selecting the Add Connection menu item.

If you want to connect to SQL Server databases, it is easier to use another approach. The Servers list item contains all servers to which you can connect, including that of the local system. If the SQL Server database that you want to inspect is located on the local system,

1.   Simply expand the local server list item,

2.   Locate the SQL Servers list item,

3.   Expand it.

The contents of the SQL Servers folder is almost identical to the contents of the SQL Server Enterprise Manager Console and contains the list of database instances that you can further expand to view tables, views, and stored procedures.

To access SQL Server database on a remote machine, you must connect to the remote machine first by right-clicking on the Servers item and selecting the Add Server context menu item. All you have to do is to specify the server network name or IP address, and the new server registration will be added to the list of servers in the Server Explorer. Then, you can inspect and manage the remote server in the same way that you would inspect and manage your local system.

WARNING! Connection to Internet servers is not supported. Any IP address or server name that you specify must be local to your network.

NOTE: To access the server resources, you must have sufficient privileges. If your current user ID does not have administrator privileges on the remote server, then click on Connect using a different user name link in Add Server dialog to specify the administrator user name and password.

Managing Event Logs, Message Queues, Performance Counters, and Services

Besides data connections and SQL Server databases, you can inspect and manage event logs, message queues, performance counters, and services.

To examine the Event Log, expand event log categories (Application, System, or Security) to view the list of events. For extra convenience, events in each category are grouped by the type and application that generated them. Event grouping by application simplifies event navigation, since you don't have to scroll the endless list of all events until you find logs generated by your application.

Perhaps the most useful feature of the Server Explorer is the ability to start and stop services. To start or stop the service:

1. Locate the desired service.

2. Right click on it.

3. Select the Start or Stop context menu items.

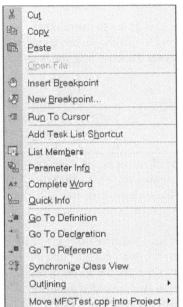

Figure A.11 Edit context menu.

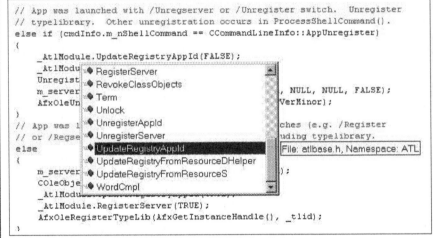

Figure A.12 Class members window.

Editing Source Code

Visual C++ .NET editor provides ample improvements to facilitate manual code editing. The source code editing improvements go far beyond traditional syntax highlighting. The best way to explore these is to right-click somewhere in the edit window to open the context menu (Figure A.11).

Listing Class Members

To view all members of a class (Figure A.12):

1. Position your mouse cursor over a variable or function that you wish to explore.

2. Select the List Members context menu item. Visual C++ .NET editor will automatically select the current member in the Member list window. Also, Visual C++ .NET editor automatically displays the header file name, member comment line, and namespace where the current member of the current class is defined in a tool tip window next to the Member list window.

TIP: To view global functions, variables, and macros, position your mouse cursor over white space before invoking the context menu.

Obtaining Parameter Information

To obtain parameter information:

1. Position your mouse cursor over a function or a function parameter that you wish to explore.

   TIP: Sometimes, functions have parameters that are functions themselves. Thus, if you want to obtain parameter information for which a function is called, you must highlight the entire statement that appears as a parameter to the function call and right click on the selection.

2. Select the Parameter Info context menu item.

The function declaration tool tip will appear with the current parameter shown in bold. If you clicked on the function name rather than on the function parameter, then the function name itself will be bolded.

   TIP: If you just typed in a statement that calls a function, and you do not remember all the parameters, use the Parameter Info rather than context sensitive help. Parameter Info is much faster and provides more accurate results than online help.

Auto-Completing Keywords

We occasionally forget the exact function names. To save yourself the hassle of opening the online help yourself the hassle of opening the online help and conducting an index search:

1. Type as much as you remember for sure.
2. Right-click on the word.
3. Select the Complete Word context menu item.

A list of matching functions and definitions will pop up with the best match highlighted and less exact matches listed in the order of relevance.

Using Quick Info

If you're memory is in impaired, you are definitely going to love the Quick Info feature. Also accessible from the edit context menu, the Quick Info tool tips pop up automatically as you drag your mouse over functions, constants, variables, and classes.

Drag your mouse over a variable, and you will see its type. Drag your mouse over a function, and you will see its parameter information. Wait, it gets better. Drag your mouse over a constant, and you will see the constant value or the entire preprocessor definition!

Using Task List

Visual Studio .NET provides a new Task List window that summarizes errors and warnings encountered during compilation and linking (Figure A.13). There is a row in the Task List window for each user-defined task, build error, or warning. The task list window contains columns with a brief task/error/warning description, source file name, and line number where an error or warning had occurred.

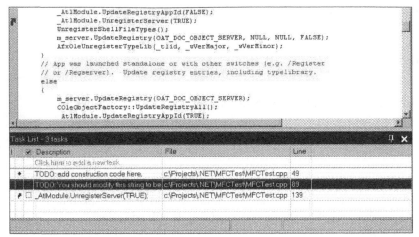

To open the Task List window, select other Windows|Task List from the View menu or click (Ctrl+Alt+K).

Thinking of Visual Studio short-cuts makes me remember Dilbert comics ridiculing software complexity. Soon, you will have to use all your fingers for another "easy-to-remember" shortcut key combination.

Figure A.13 Visual Studio .NET Task List.

Adding
Task List Short Cuts
Besides listing warnings and errors, you can add your own tasks to the task list. Or, if you have sections of codes that you are unsure of or want to modify after launch, right-click on the statement in question and select "Add Task List Short Cut" to add a reference to the statement to the Task List. A small blue arrow will appear to the extreme left of the edit window to indicate the marked statement.

Removing Task List Short Cuts
To remove the task from the task list:

1. Highlight the task in the Task List window.
2. Press the "Delete" key.

When you delete a marked statement, the blue arrow marker is removed accordingly.

> **NOTE:** C++ comments that begin with TODO text are automatically added to the task list. You can not delete TODO tasks unless you modify the comment line by removing the TODO text.

Also, you can remove the marked statement by:

1. Right-clicking on it and,
2. Selecting the Remove Task List Short Cut from the edit context menu.
   > **TIP:** To quickly navigate to a task list item, double-click on the task in the task list.

Browsing Source Code
Visual C++ .NET provides three functions for the quick and easy browsing of source code. These functions are: Go To Definition, Go To Declaration, and Go To Reference.

To quickly jump to the definition of, declaration of, or reference to a particular source code symbol (i.e., function, constant, class, or variable):

1. Right-click on the symbol.
2. Select the Go To Definition, Go To Declaration, or Go To Reference items from the context menu.

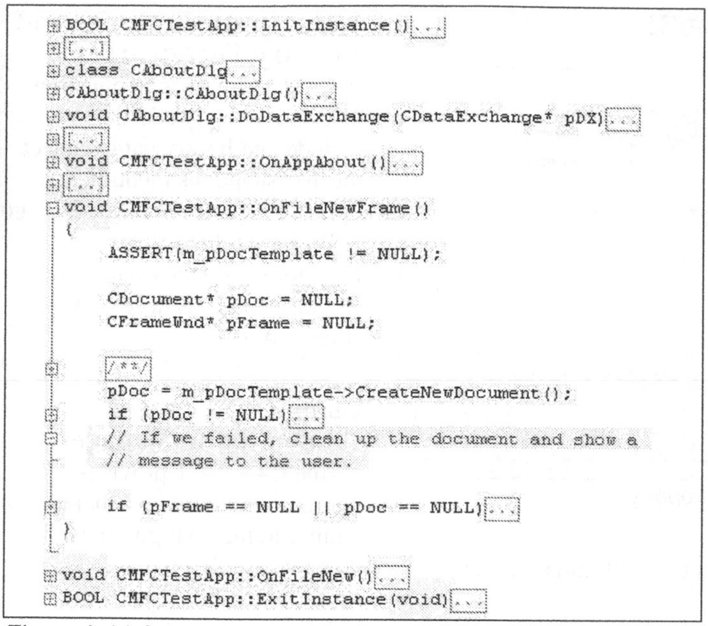

```
BOOL CMFCTestApp::InitInstance()...
[...]
class CAboutDlg...
CAboutDlg::CAboutDlg()...
void CAboutDlg::DoDataExchange(CDataExchange* pDX)...
[...]
void CMFCTestApp::OnAppAbout()...
[...]
void CMFCTestApp::OnFileNewFrame()
{
      ASSERT(m_pDocTemplate != NULL);

      CDocument* pDoc = NULL;
      CFrameWnd* pFrame = NULL;

      /**/
      pDoc = m_pDocTemplate->CreateNewDocument();
      if (pDoc != NULL)...
      // If we failed, clean up the document and show a
      // message to the user.

      if (pFrame == NULL || pDoc == NULL)...
}
void CMFCTestApp::OnFileNew()...
BOOL CMFCTestApp::ExitInstance(void)...
```

Figure A.14 Source code outlining.

You will be redirected to the source or header file where the symbol is defined, declared, or referenced.

Synchronizing Class View

Use the Synchronize Class View context menu item to synchronize the source code in the edit view with the Class View. Visual Studio .NET will automatically locate and highlight the member function you invoked the class view synchronization from. If you were editing a header file and your cursor was inside a class declaration, then the appropriate class would be located and highlighted in the Class View.

Outlining Source Code

Outlining is an exciting new feature of the Visual C++ .NET source code editor. Outlining provides visual aid for managing source code size and complexity.

To do this, select the Outlining|Collapse to Definitions menu item from the edit context menu; your source code will look something like what's in Figure A.14. All function and class definitions will be collapsed and hidden within dotted boxes.

Expand individual sections like you expand tree elements in tree views by clicking on the "plus" icon to the left of the collapsed section. Alternatively, you can double-click on the dotted box that represents the collapsed contents to expand their contents. If you drag your mouse over such a dotted box, a large tool tip window will pop up, displaying some of the collapsed content.

Outlines are hierarchical, and it may take a while for you to expand all of the source code manually. To revert back to the normal (expanded) code view quickly, use the Outlining|Stop Outlining context menu item.

Also, you can collapse only a selected portion of your code. Simply highlight the desired section to collapse, right-click on it, and select Outlining|Hide Selection from the context menu.

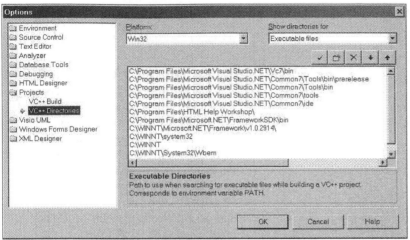

Figure A.15 Options dialog, VC++ directories property page.

Specifying Include and Library Directories

Prior to building an application, you must specify additional include and library paths. Select the Tools|Options menu item to open the Options dialog. Then, go to Projects folder, VC++ Directories property page, and add directories as necessary (Figure A.15).

Using Configuration Manager

Visual C++ .NET provides a configuration manager that is similar to the configuration manager in Visual C++ 6.0 (Figure A.16). Open the configuration manager window by selecting the Build|Configuration Manager menu item.

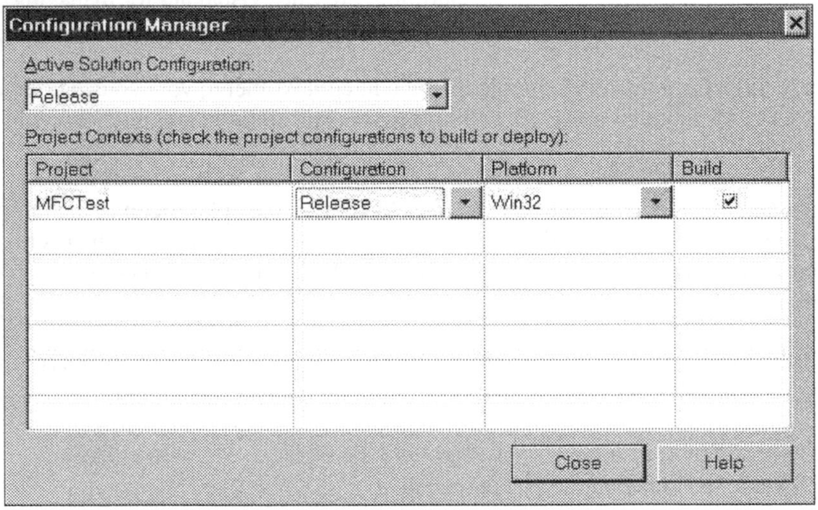

Define your own configurations (i.e., debug build, or release build; optimized build or default build, etc.) and customize their settings by selecting a configuration name from the Configuration drop down list in the project Property Pages dialog.

Figure A.16 Configuration Manager dialog.

Building Projects

To build the application, press the F7 key or select the Build|Build menu item. If you have multiple projects in the solution, the build command will build all of them. To build projects individually, you must right-click on the project name in the Solution Explorer and select the Build menu item from the context menu.

If there are any build errors or warnings, they will be automatically added to the Task List window.

When developing server-side components, such as ATL Server components, ISAPI DLLs, or COM components, the process of solution building may involve deployment of your application components, e.g., copying them to the server and performing component registration. Specify your deployment settings on the Web Deployment property page in the project Property Pages dialog. For a complete reference of project settings, see Appendix C.

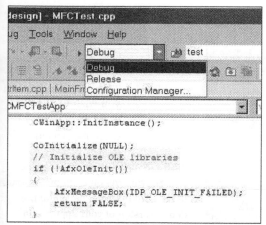

Figure A.17 Configuration drop down list in Visual C++ .NET toolbar.

Setting Active Project Configuration

To debug your application, you must successfully build it in debug mode first. To change the active configuration to Debug (or whatever the name of your custom debug configuration is), select the debug configuration name in the Visual C++ .NET tool bar (Figure A.17).

Debugging Locally

To start debugging:

1. Press the F5 key or select the Debug|Start menu item. Visual C++ .NET will launch your application locally or remotely based on the settings specified on the Debug property page in the project Property Pages.

2. On the Debug property page, you must specify a Command to be executed by the Visual C++ .NET debugger. The most common scenario is when you are debugging your executable locally. In this case, the command should be set to the ($TargetPath) macro.

3. Specify optional command line parameters in the Command Arguments edit box.

    NOTE: If your project output is a DLL, you must specify an application executable that will launch your DLL in the Command edit box. DLLs can not be launched or debugged stand-alone without an application that references them.

Also, take a look at the following:

TIP: If you are debugging an ActiveX component, select ActiveX Control Test Container from the Command drop down list. As soon as you start your debug session, ActiveX Control Container will be loaded. To test your control, insert it into the container and call a method that you wish to debug.

Attaching to a Process

When debugging certain application types, such as ISAPI DLLs, COM components, or ATL Server components, you must attach to a process that invokes your application DLL. For ISAPI DLLs and Internet Information Server (IIS) components, the process is going to be inetinfo.exe.

The reason that you have to attach to a process rather than launch an application is that the application you attach to is already running.

To start debugging by attaching to a process, select the Debug|Processes menu item to open Processes dialog (Figure A.18). You can attach to processes running locally or to processes running on remote machines. To attach to a process running on a remote machine, specify your Transport (default = DCOM or TCP/IP) and provide the machine Name. To attach to a process on the local system, make sure that the Name edit box contains your local computer name.

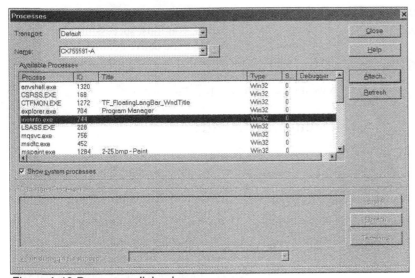

Figure A.18 Processes dialog box.

To see all processes running on the system:

1. Check the Show system processes box.

2. Then, locate a process you wish to attach to (e.g., inetinfo.exe)

3. Click the Attach button.

WARNING! If you are attaching to a process running on a remote system, make sure that you distribute the debug version of your application and all necessary dependencies to the remote system.

Once you attach to a process, Visual C++ .NET will switch into a debugging mode. The rest of the discussion is the same for both local and remote debugging.

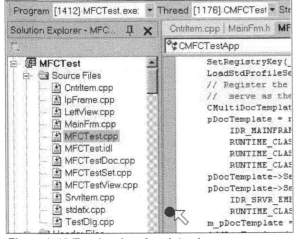

Figure A.19 Toggle a break point using a mouse.

Setting Break Points

To set a break point in your code:

1. Move your edit cursor to the desired line.

2. Press the F9 key (or select Insert Breakpoint from the context menu).

A red circle corresponding to a breakpoint will appear to the left of the current statement.

Alternatively, you can left-click in the edit window on the gray area to the left of your code to toggle break points (Figure A.19).

NOTE: Don t be alarmed if your break point mark appears on a different line than the line you intended. Visual C++ .NET can insert breakpoints only at statement boundaries. Some statements can span multiple lines, and Visual C++ puts a break point mark where the statement *ends*.

It's also important to know the following:

> **WARNING!** When you have attached to a process, your break points marks may contain question marks inside. A question mark indicates an inactive break point. Your breakpoints will remain inactive until your DLL is actually loaded by the process you have attached to. To make the process load your DLL, provoke it to do so by opening web pages that reference your COM components, or by opening a browser with the address URL pointing to your ISAPI extension DLL or ATL Server component. If, after "provoking" the process, the execution still does not stop at one of your break points and the question marks remain, make sure that you've deployed your DLLs correctly and that you've attached to the right process on the right machine.

Breaking on Exceptions

When developing a C++ application, it may be desirable to break the code execution whenever a specific type of exception occurs. Traditionally, developers used to put break points in **catch** blocks. However, exceptions are often caught very far away from where they were thrown. Thus, it may become a challenge to track down the actual place where the exceptions were thrown.

To overcome this difficulty:

1. Use the Exceptions dialog to specify the exception that you want to break on.

2. Select the Debug|Exception menu item to open the Exceptions dialog (Figure A.20).

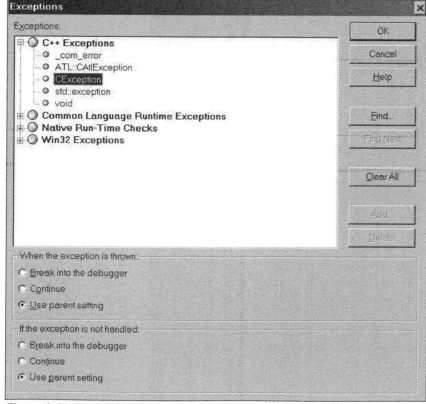

3. Expand one of four exception classes and locate the exceptions you are interested in.

4. Specify the desired debugger behavior in the "When the exception is thrown" and "When the exception is not handled" sections.

Watching Variables

To watch a variable, simply drag your mouse over it, and its value will pop up in a yellow tool tip window. Alternatively, you can add a variable to a Watch window by right-clicking on it and selecting Add Watch from the context menu.

The Quick Watch context menu item opens a pop-up window that displays the variable's value without adding it to the Watch window.

Figure A.20 Exceptions dialog.

> **TIP:** Visual C++ .NET debugger automatically detects constants associated with variables, such as error codes, and displays them next to the actual variable value. It means that you no longer have to browse through endless header files looking for error code definitions.

Using Other Debug Windows

Additional debug windows, such as Call Stack, Registers, and Disassembly, can be found under the Debug|Window submenu.

It is worth noting that Visual C++ .NET debugger provides up to four new Memory windows for watching memory locations directly (menu Debug|Windows|Memory|Memory 1/2/3/4). Press Ctrl+Alt+M,1 through Ctrl+Alt+M,4 to activate one of the four memory watch windows. Now you've got to use four fingers to activate a shortcut!

Stepping Through Code and Stopping Debugging

Fortunately, such common debug commands as stepping through the code and stopping the debugging session have truly easy shortcuts:

* Press Shift-F5 to stop debugging.

* Press F10 to step through the code without going into functions and subroutines (i.e., stepping *over* subroutines).

* Press F11 to step into subroutines when possible.

* Press Shift+F11 to step out of a subroutine that you no longer wish to step through. The next step position will be on the statement following the call to the subroutine you were stepping through. The Step Out function is very useful for unwinding deeply nested calls.

APPENDIX B

MFC Application Wizard Reference

The traditional wizard appearance, with "Next" and "Back" buttons, has now been replaced with tabbed window layout and tab titles listed in the left section of the wizard screen. The MFC Application Wizard tabs/pages include the eight features described in this appendix. The features consist of:

* The overview

* The application type page

* The compound document support page

* The document template strings page

* The database support page

* The user interface page

* The advanced features page

* The generated class page

The Overview
The overview provides brief textual description of current wizard settings.

The Application Type Page

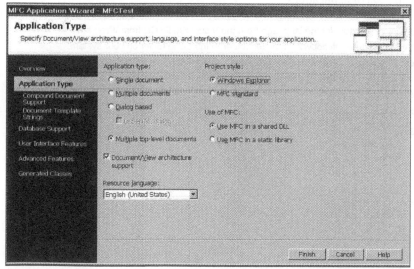

Figure B.1 MFC Application Wizard Application Type page.HTTP.

The application type page (as shown in Figure B.1) is a page that contains the following sections:

* The application type, which consists of:

* *Single document*–this creates a single document interface (SDI) application. The SDI application main window contains only one document view (the child window). The main application window is derived from **CFrameWnd**. WordPad is an example of SDI application.

* *Multiple Document*–this creates a multiple document interface (MDI) application

that can contain multiple document views (the child windows). Main window is derived from **CMDIFrame**. Microsoft Word 97 is an example of MDI application.

* *Dialog based*–the main application window is dialog based and does not contain any document views. If you check "Use HTML dialog", the main dialog window will be derived from **CDhtmlDialog** class rather than from **CDialog**. **CDhtmlDialog** allows the using of HTML resources to define your dialog appearance, whence **CDialog** uses standard Win32 dialog resources. For more information on **CDhtmlDialog,** see Chapter 16. Windows Calculator is an example of a dialog based application.

* *Multiple top-level documents*–the main application window is SDI, yet the application can handle multiple documents by opening each additional document in its own top-level window. Each top-level window is operated by a separate instance of the application. Microsoft Word XP is an example of multiple top-level document application.

* The Document/View architecture support check box controls whether generated the MFC application supports the document/view paradigm. If this option is checked, child windows are derived from **CView** class. Also, **CDocument**-based class is created to provide support for standard document handling operations, such as opening/saving (serializing) and creating new documents. If this option is unchecked, child windows are derived from **CWnd** class. It is a good idea to uncheck this option when creating simple applications that do not work with "documents." Such document-less applications could be database client applications, graphic apps, or games.

* The Project Style radio buttons allow for selecting between the MFC Standard and Windows Explorer windows layouts. If the Windows Explorer option is selected, the child window of an SDI application or child windows of an MDI application are split on two panes with a list view (**CListView**) automatically assigned to the left pane and a "normal" document view assigned to the right pane.

* The use of MFC radio buttons, just like in Visual C++ 6.0, specifies static or dynamic linking to MFC libraries.

* The resource language drop down list allows the specifying of language for project resources (i.e., dialogs and string tables). This list is one of many Visual C++.NET enhancements geared towards simplifying globalization and internationalization of applications.

TIP: If you want to create an MFC application in another language that is not listed in the Resource language drop down list, then you must copy the template directory for the language from the Visual Studio CD from \Program Files\Microsoft Visual Studio.NET\Vc7\VCWizards\mfcappwiz\templates folder to the same folder on your system.

Once you have copied the folder, the language will appear in the Resource language list on the Application Type page of the MFC Application Wizard. Each language is assigned a code that corresponds to a template folder name. Language codes are listed in Table B.1.

Table B.1 Language template codes.

Language	Template
Chinese (Taiwan)	1028
Chinese (Simplified)	2052
English	1033
French	1036
German	1031
Italian	1040
Japanese	1041
Korean	1042
Spanish	1034

TIP: To edit the created project resources, you must set your system locale to the locale of the selected language.

The Compound Document Support Page

The Compound Document Support page (Figure B.2) allows for specifying OLE document support and active document container/server settings.

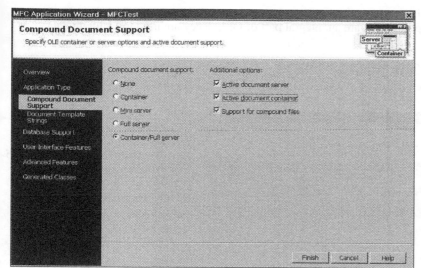

Figure B.2 MFC Application Wizard Compound Document Support page.

An active document container allows you to work with several documents of different application types within a single application window frame (instead of forcing you to create and use multiple application window frames for each document type).

OLE compound documents allow users to insert other documents into your application document and enable your application documents to be inserted in other OLE compound documents. Microsoft Word is both an OLE document container (because you can drop and embed other documents, like Excel spreadsheets, into your Word document) and server (because you can drop and embed your Word documents in other applications, like PowerPoint or Outlook).

Compound document support radio buttons include:

* *None*—an application does not support embedded or linked documents. This option is default for most applications.

* *Container*—an application's document can contain embedded or linked documents. In other words, you can drag and drop documents in your application's document.

* *Mini server*—you can drag and drop your application's documents into other applications that support compound documents (i.e., MS Word or MS Excel). Mini server can not run standalone and only supports embedded documents (linked documents are not supported).

* *Full server*—you can both link and embed your application's documents into other applications' compound documents.

* *Container/Full server*—your application is going to be both OLE container and full server. Microsoft Word is both container and full server since you can drop other documents in Word files and drop word documents in other applications, such as Excel or Outlook.

* *The additional options check box group*—this specifies active document features. Unlike OLE embedded objects that are simply displayed within the page of another document, active documents provide complete functionality of the applications that create them by merging their menus with File and Help menus of the container, occupying the entire editing area of the container, and controlling page layout when printing. The additional options include:

* The active document server check box specifies whether the application is going to be an active document server.

* The active document container check box specifies if the application is going to allow active document behavior for embedded active documents.

* The support for compound files check box specifies whether the application document is serialized in compound-file format. Compound files are an integral part of OLE. They are used to facilitate data transfer and OLE document storage.

The Document Template Strings Page

The Document Template Strings page (Figure B.3) collects additional information needed to manage applications' documents. It consists of the following:

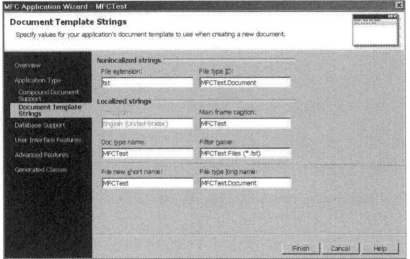

Figure B.3 MFC Application Wizard Document Template Strings page.

* *File extension*—file association for application documents (i.e., "doc" for MS Word documents or "xls" for MS Excel files).

NOTE: If you ve selected Mini server, Full server, or Container/Full server options on the Compound Document Support page, then you MUST provide a file extension.

* *File type ID*—sets the label for your document type in the system registry under HKEY_CLASSES_ROOT and other places.

* *Main frame caption*—caption that appears in your application main frame window title.

* *Doc type name*—textual description of the document.

* *Filter name*—application document filter name that appears in standard Windows Open and Save As dialogs (i.e., "Word Document [*.doc]").

* *File new short name*—specifies the name that appears in the standard Windows New dialog box when you have more than one document template (**CDocTemplate**) associated with your application. You typically use the MFC **CWinApp::AddDocTemplate**() method to add doc templates to your application in your application **OnInitInstance**() handler. If your application is an Automation server, this name is used as the short name of your Automation object.

* *File type long name*—specifies the file type name in the system registry. If your application is an Automation server, this name is used as the long name of your Automation object.

NOTE: Compound Document Support and Document Template Strings pages are applicable only when the Document/View architecture support check box is checked.

The Database Support Page

The Database Support page (Figure B.4) allows for the specifying of database connectivity options, if any. Database support options include:

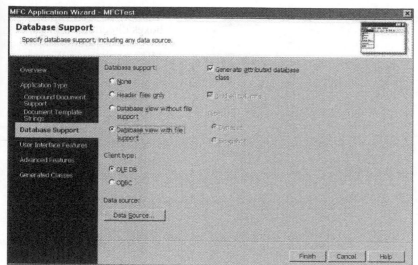

Figure B.4 MFC Application Wizard Database Support page.

* *None*—no database support.

* *Header files only*—just like in Visual C++ 6.0, when this option is selected, an additional **#include** <afxdb.h> line is added to the application's stdafx.h file. The afxdb.h header file contains MFC database class declarations (e.g., **CDatabase**, **CRecordset**).

* *Database view without file support option*—eliminates from the application menu standard File menu items, such as Open, Save, and Save As and removes document serialization support. The application view automatically derived from **CRecordView** or from **COleDBRecordView**, depending on which database client option you selected (ODBC or OLE DB).

* *Database view with file support option*—provides record viewing in addition to document serialization. The application view is derived from **CRecordView** or from **COleDBRecordView** depending on which database client you selected (ODBC or OLE DB).

    NOTE: If you selected any of Database view options you MUST specify a data source (database table, data file, etc.) by clicking of Data Source button.

* *Client type radio buttons*—allow selecting between ODBC and OLE DB providers. OLE DB provides wider data access than ODBC and encompasses database access, data mining, OLAP, mail box access, and more. When ODBC client type is selected, user recordset class is automatically derived from MFC **CRecordset**. Alternatively, when you select OLE DB client type ATL **CCommand**-based and **CAccessor**-based OLE DB, consumer classes are created.

* *Generate attributed database class option*—applies only when the OLE DB client type is selected. This option effectively enables attribute support in a Visual C++ project. Attributes are introduced by Microsoft to simplify common programming tasks and COM programming specifically. For a detailed overview of ATL COM attributes, see Chapter 17.

* *Bind all columns, Dynaset, and Snapshot options*—are applicable only when the ODBC client type is selected and specifies the type of recordset (**CRecordset::dynaset** or **CRecordset::snapshot**) and whether you want to bind all data columns returned by the recordset by default.

The User Interface Features Page

The User Interface Features page (Figure B.5) allows the specifying of main application frame styles, child window styles (for MDI applications), and toolbar style.

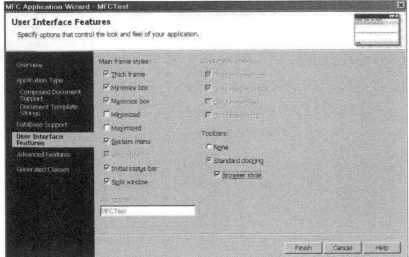

Figure B.5 MFC Application Wizard User Interface Features page.

* Main frame styles check boxes directly translate into **WS_xxx** attributes that the MFC Application Wizard adds to your application main frame style in **PreCreateWindow()** handler:

* Thick Frame— **WS_THICKFRAME**.

* Minimize box— **WS_MINIMIZEBOX**.

* Maximize box— **WS_MAXIMIZEBOX**.

* System menu— **WS_SYSMENU**.

* The About box option adds an About dialog to your application and inserts an About menu item into the Help menu in the MDI/SDI application or into the system menu in a dialog-based application.

* The split window option allows for inserting a splitter (**CSplitWnd**) MDI application child windows or SDI application main window. The Split window option is not applicable for dialog based applications.

* The toolbars radio button controls style and appearance of the application toolbar (**CToolBar**). Select "None" if you do not want the MFC Application Wizard to create a standard toolbar for your application, or select the Standard docking option if you want a toolbar.

* The Browser style check box alters the toolbar style and creates an advanced toolbar that provides layout, persistence, and state information. Your toolbar class will be derived from **CReBar**. Unlike standard toolbars, browser-style rebars can contain various controls, like dialog buttons and list boxes. **IDR_MAINFRAME** dialog resource is automatically generated when the browser-style toolbars option is selected so you can add your controls to the toolbar.

The Advanced Features Page

The Advanced Features page (Figure B.6) provides further customizations for the MFC application project.

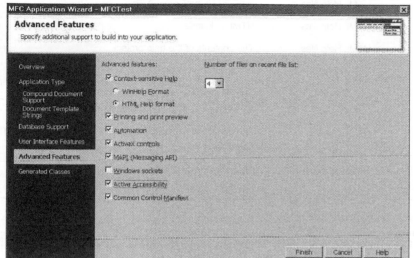

* The Context-sensitive Help option adds on-line help support to your application. When this option is selected, prototype help file is automatically generated and an extra help button is added to the application toolbar.

* The WinHelp Format radio button allows for the selecting of traditional Windows help file format. WinHelp files are compiled into .HLP-files. Table B.2 contains the list of files that will be automatically generated and added to your project when you select the WinHelp Format option.

Figure B.6 MFC Application Wizard Advanced Features page.

Table B.2 List of automatically generated help files in WinHelp format.

File Name	File Location	Solution Explorer	Description
ProjectName.hpj	Project folder \hlp	Source Files	Main WinHelp help project file.
ProjectName.rtf	Project folder \hlp	Help Files	Sample topics and information on customizing your .hpj file.
ProjectName.cnt	Project folder \hlp	Help Files	WinHelp table of contents.
Makehelp.bat	Project folder	Source Files	Batch file used to build the help project.
Print.rtf	Project folder \hlp	Help Files	The file contains prefabricated help topics for the printing commands.
*.bmp	Project folder \hlp	Resource Files	Images embedded in help pages.

* HTML Help format radio button allows for selecting the compressed HTML (.chm-files) help file format. Most new applications use compressed HTML help files. Table B.3 contains the list of files that are automatically generated and added to your project when you select the HTML Help format option.

Table B.3 List of automatically generated help files HTML Help format.

File name	File location	Solution Explorer	Description
ProjectName.hhp	Project folder\hlp	HTML Help files	Main HTML help project file.
ProjectName.hhk	Project folder \hlp	HTML Help files	HTML help index.
ProjectName.hhc	Project folder \hlp	HTML Help files	The contents of the help project.
Makehtmlhelp.bat	Project folder	Source Files	Batch file used to build the help project.
Afxcore.htm	Project folder \hlp	HTML Help	The file contains prefabricated help topics covering standard MFC commands and screen objects.
Afxprint.htm	Project folder \hlp	HTML Help	The file contains prefabricated help topics for the printing commands.
*.jpg; *.gif	Project folder \hlp\Images	Resource Files	Images embedded in help pages.

* Printing and print preview option generates code for document printing and previewing. The generated code relies on **CView** and **CDocument** class members. Therefore, this option is available only when the Document/view architecture support option is selected.

* The automation option specifies whether your application can be an OLE automation client or an automation server. OLE automation allows your application to control other applications and, at the same time, allows other applications to control yours.

* ActiveX controls are an option you should check if you are going to use ActiveX controls in your application. When this option is selected, a call to **AfxEnableControlContainer**() function is inserted into application's **InitInstance**() member function.

* MAPI (Messaging API) is an option you should check if you want to be able to email application documents from your application. When this option is selected, Send menu item is added to the application's File menu.

* Windows sockets is an option you should check if you are going to use MFC Windows Socket classes (**CSocket**, **CAsyncSocket**, etc.). When Windows sockets option is selected, a **#include** <afxsocket.h> line is added to the application's stdafx.h header file. The afxsocket.h header file contains MFC Windows Socket classes' definitions.

* The Active accessibility option adds implementation **IAccessible** interface to all application classes derived from **CWnd**. **IAccessible** interface propagates user-defined Accessibility Options (i.e., Accessibility Options specified in the Windows Control panel) to window classes that implement **IAccessible**.

* The Common control manifest option represents a new feature added with Windows XP support in mind. When this option is selected, your application will use the new version 6 Common Control DLL that gives old common controls a cool new look and enables support for Windows XP themes.

* The Number of files on recent file list is an option available to you if your application supports document/view architecture. This option defines the maximum number of the most recently used document files to include in the application File menu.

The Generated Classes Page

Finally, the Generated Classes page allows for customization of the MFC Application Wizard-generated class/file names.

APPENDIX C

Visual C++ .NET Project Property Pages Reference

Project property pages (Figure C.1) allow you to control almost every aspect of code generation, object module linking, and application deployment. In general, it is best to use the default project configuration options because incorrectly specified settings may result in compilation or link errors or even worse—bad code. Modify project options only when you are certain that you understand the consequences.

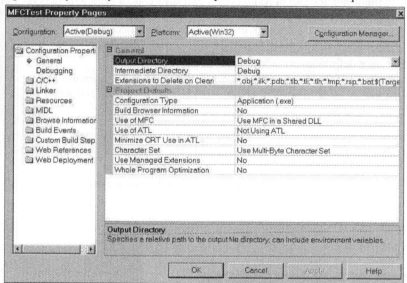

Figure C.1 Project Property Pages General page.

General Page

The general page consists of the following:

* *Output Directory* specifies a relative path to the output file (e.g., executable, DLL, etc.) folder.

  NOTE: All directory paths can contain environment variables or macros. Macros begin with a dollar sign followed by the macro name in parenthesis, e.g. $(TargetPath). To insert macros, you can type them directly or select <Edit > from the drop down list, selecting macros from the dialog that lists all the macros along with their values.

* *Intermediate Directory* specifies a relative path to the intermediate file folder. The intermediate folder contains object files (.obj), precompiled headers (.pch), program database (.pdb), browser information files (.sbr), and others.

* *Configuration Type* specifies application (.exe), dynamic library (.dll), static library (.lib), or utility. Contents of the project property pages depend on the selected configuration type. Utility configuration type displays MIDL, custom build, prebuild, postbuild events.

* *Build Browser Information* specifies whether to build browser (.sbr) files. Browser information may come handy during debugging by letting you examine information about all the symbols in any source file, relationships between base classes and derived classes, relationships between calling functions and called functions, etc.

* *Use of MFC* specifies whether to link with MFC libraries statically or dynamically. While static linking results in bigger program size, you do not have to worry about distributing appropriate MFC DLLs, (e.g. mfc70.dll). As a rule of thumb, use static linking all the time unless you developing a whole bunch of ActiveX controls, COM objects, and server-side components that will run simultaneously. Then, it makes sense to save system memory by linking dynamically to MFC and having only one instance of the library loaded in memory (vs. multiple instances of MFC library loaded statically as a part of each individual component).

* *Use of ATL*is similar argument applies to ATL library and ATL.dll.

* *Minimize CRT Use in ATL* is an ATL-specific option. Since the whole idea behind ATL is to reduce memory footprint, checking the "Minimize CRT Use in ATL" option will save you an extra 25K of code. On the downside, you can not use any CRT functions (such as **memmove**(), **memcpy**(), etc.) in your code. If you can not eliminate all CRT references, you must uncheck this option or your project would not link.

* *Character Set option*—allows selecting between ASCII, Unicode, and multibyte character (MBCS) sets. **_UNICODE** or **_MBCS** preprocessor definitions are added accordingly.

   NOTE: **_UNICODE** or **_MBCS** preprocessor definitions affect generic text data type **_TCHAR** mapping. If you use **_tc**-prefixed string routines in your code, the routines will be automatically substituted by their ASCII, Unicode, or multibyte character equivalents based on the Character Set option settings.

* *Use Managed Extensions* instructs the compiler to target CLR and compile your source code in MSIL, rather than in native x86 instruction set. For more information on CLR and Managed Extensions to C++, see Chapter 2.

* *Whole Program Optimization - /GL compiler option* enables program optimization across object file/module (.obj) boundaries.

Debug Page

The debug page (Figure C.2) contains the following:

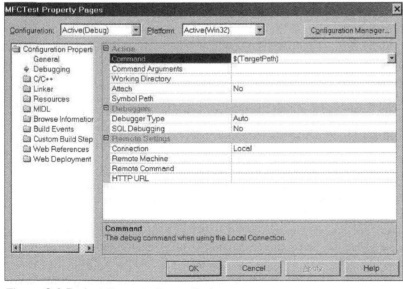

Figure C.2 Project Property Pages Debug page.

* *Command*is the executable name for debugging session.

* *Command arguments* are optional arguments to pass to the executable specified in Command.

* *Working directory* is a directory for the debugging session.

* *Attach*, here you select "yes" if you are going to attach to a process running on local or remote machine (e.g., when debugging COM components, ISAPI extensions, or other applications that do not run standalone or can not be launched directly).

* *Symbol path* specifies additional folders that contain symbols for DLLs that your application references.

* *Debugger type* specifies whether you are going to debug native code, CLR, or both. "Auto" is the best choice.

* *SQL Debugging,* you select this option if you are going to debug SQL Server stored procedures from within Visual C++.NET.

* *Connection* must be set to "local" if you are going to debug an application running on the same computer as Visual Studio.NET (i.e. debugging locally). "Local" is the most common option. Otherwise, specify "Remote via DCOM" or "Remote via TCP/IP". DCOM protocol is usually the preferred choice for remote debugging. However, if you can not or do not wish to install DCOM on the remote machine, you can use Remote Debug Monitor (msvcmon.exe) to debug using TCP/IP protocol.

* *Remote command*is a remote executable with any command line parameters for the remote debugging session.

* *HTTP URL* applies only when debugging ATL Server components or C++ Web Services. Debugging Web Services or ATL Server components requires access to a specific URL that invokes components or services being debugged.

C/C++ Folder
The C/C++ folder consists of several pages:

* General Page

* Optimization Page

* Preprocessor Page

* Code Generation Page

* Language Page

* Precompiled Headers Page

* Output Files Page

* Browse Information Page

* Advanced Page

General Page
The general page contains the following:

* *Additional Include Directories (/Ipath compiler option)*—were a major source of frustration in Visual C++ 6.0 where you could specify C++ header file folders only in one place–in IDE Options. Fortunately, in Visual C++ .NET, you can specify additional include folders on a per-project basis.

* *Resolve #using References (/AIpath compiler option)*—applies only for Managed Extensions to C++. It specifies additional search path for the **#using** preprocessor directive. The **#using** preprocessor directive is similar to the Java **import** command. For more information on the **#using** preprocessor directive and managed extensions, see Chapter 2.

* *Debug Information Format*—specify "disabled" for faster compilation albeit no debug information. If you want to save space and reduce debug executable size, choose Line numbers only (/Zd) option. The Line numbers only option will let you step through the code, but you would not be able to watch variables in the Watch window. The C7 Compatible (/Z7) option produced all symbolic information necessary for comprehensive debugging. The Program Database (/Zi) option is very similar to C7 Compatible, except that the debugging information is stored in program database files (.pdb). If you compile a library using the Program Database option, you must distribute both the library (.lib) file and the program database (.pdb file), or debugging of the library will not be possible. Finally, if you are going to use the Edit and Continue

debugger feature (i.e., when you can change and re-compile your program on the fly without stopping the debugging session), you should choose the Program Database Edit and Continue (/ZI) option.

* *Compile as Managed option*—pertains to Managed Extensions to C++. "Not using managed extensions" is the default setting and it should be kept for all non-managed (i.e., Win32, MFC or ATL) applications. Assembly Support (/clr) forces compilation into MSIL, and Meta Data Only (/clr:noAssembly) forces assembly manifest not to be inserted into output file. For more information on assemblies and assembly manifests, see Chapter 1.

* *Detect 64-bit Portability Issues (/Wp64)*—if this option is turned on, then the code is checked for **long**, **int**, and **pointer** variables as if they were 64-bits. Visual C++.NET provides integer type definitions, such as **INT_PTR**, whose representation (i.e. 32-bit or 64-bit) depends on the selected platform. If you use platform-dependent integer types everywhere, your could would port to a 64-bit operating system without a problem. The Detect 64-bit Portability Issues option detects unsafe integer type conversions resulting from the improper mixing of standard types, such as **long** and **int** with platform-specific types, such as **INT_PTR**.

* *Treat Warnings As Errors (/WX)*—set this option to "yes" to prohibit your project from building if the compiler or linker warnings are encountered. For the best quality code, you should resolve all warnings.

Optimization Page
The optimization page contains the following:

* *Optimization*—specify Disabled (/Od) to turn the optimization off, "Minimize Size" (/O1) to generate the smallest possible code, "Maximize Speed" (/O2) to produce the fastest code, or "Full Optimization" (/Ox) to optimize the application for both size and performance.

* *Global Optimizations (/Og)*—select "yes" to enable automatic common subexpression elimination, loop optimization, and register variable allocation.

* *Inline Function Expansion*—select "Disable" (/Ob0) to disable function inlining, "Only __inline" (/Ob1) to inline functions defined using **inline** or **__inline** keywords, or "Any Suitable" (/Ob2) to rely on the compiler's judgment for finding suitable functions for inlining in addition to function defines with **inline** or **__inline** keywords.

* *Enable Intrinsic Functions*—select "yes" (/Oi) to automatically inline such common string and utility functions as **strcpy()**, **abs()**, etc.

* *Floating-Point Consistency*—select "Improve Consistency" to improve the consistency of floating-point tests for equality and inequality by disabling optimizations that could change the precision of floating-point calculations. It is a well-known problem in numerical computing that tests for floating-point zero value may not always be predictable due to rounding errors. Compiler optimization may adversely affect rounding, resulting in 0.0f equality or inequality tests passing or failing sporadically. Use the "Improve Consistency" option to ensure the same behavior in all such tests.

* *Favor Size or Speed*—select "Favor Fast Code" (/Ot) to produce the fastest possible code, "Favor Small Code" (/Os) to generate smallest possible code, or "Neither" to bypass the optimization. The "Favor Size or Speed" options are applicable only when Global Optimization (/Og) is turned on.

* *Omit Frame Pointers (/Oy)*—this rather complicated option comes in handy when using a lot of inline assembler or optimizing for performance. When the Omit Frame Pointers option is set to "yes," the x86 processor EBP register is no longer used by the compiler for local variable addressing. Typically, when you call a function, a stack frame is constructed to accommodate the function local variables. The stack frame is destroyed whenever the function returns. You can improve your code performance by omitting the frame pointer and eliminating the extra code that manages frame pointer construction and destruction.

* *Enable Fiber-safe Optimizations (/GT)*—this option relates to multithreaded programming. In some cases, it may be desirable to maintain static variables in thread-local storage (TLS). Such variables are declared

with **__declspec(thread)** keyword. When an application manipulates more than one thread, it becomes unsafe to optimize TLS references across function calls (e.g. using Global Optimization option). To reconcile Global Optimization with threads, set the "Enable Fiber-safe Optimizations" option to "yes."

* *Optimize For Processor*—select "Pentium" (/G5) to enable Pentium-specific code optimization techniques, or select "Pentium Pro and Above" (/G6) to optimize for later CPU models. The default "Blended" choice favors neither CPU architecture.

* *Optimize for Windows Application (/GA) option*—generates faster code for accessing TLS variables. For more information on Thread Local Storage, see the "Platform SDK, DLLs Processes and Threads" section.

    WARNING! The "Optimize for Windows Application" option should be used only when compiling an executable (.exe). When used with DLLs, this option may result in malfunctioning code generation.

Preprocessor Page
The preprocessor page consists of:

* *Preprocessor Definitions*—list your preprocessor definitions here.

* *Ignore Standard Include Path (/X)*—when set to "yes", directories specified in PATH and INCLUDE environment variables are not automatically searched for header files. This option may help switch between different versions of the same header file without modifying environment variables.

* *Generate Preprocessed File (/P)*—option results in all precompiler definitions being processed and the resulting "clean" C/C++ file written to disk with the same name as the original .cpp file but with extension .I.

* *Keep Comments (/C)*—if you specify both the /P and /C options, then comments from the source .cpp file will propagate to the resulting preprocessed .I file.

Code Generation Page
The code generation page consists of the following:

* *Enable String Pooling (/Gf or /GF)*—use this option to save memory by consolidating equivalent string expressions into a single read-only variable. For example, if you have string "foo" repeated 100 times in your code, the memory for the string will be allocated 100 times unless you enable string pooling.

* *Enable Minimal Rebuild (/Gm)*—compiler analyzes which source file depends on which class definition on the first compile and writes this information into .idb file. Enabling minimal rebuild results in faster compilation because only those files are recompiled that were affected by definition changes. The caveat of the minimal rebuild is incorrectly generated code resulting from equivalent (redundant) definitions located in multiple source files.

* *Enable C++ Exceptions (/EH)*—select "yes" (/EHc) to enable an automatic object (i.e., an object that was created on a stack) destructor calling during stack unwind caused by the exception thrown. This option is incompatible with the "Managed Extensions to C++" because CLR exceptions are handled differently. For more information, see Chapter 2.

* *Smaller Type Check (/RTCc)*—generates a warning when a value is assigned to a smaller data type that results in data loss.

* *Basic Runtime Checks*—select this option if you want the compiler to check for uninitialized local variables (/RTCu) and stack frame integrity (/RTCs). Common stack frame error checking includes detection of stack variable overruns/underruns and stack pointer verification.

* *Runtime Library*—select static or dynamic, debug or release, multithreaded or single-threaded runtime library linkage. It is important to keep this setting consistent with the static libraries (.lib files) that you

link with your application. If you have a library that is compiled with the Multi-threaded Debug DLL option and you link your application with the Single-threaded Debug DLL option, you will get link errors.

*   *Struct Member Alignment*—specify whether you want to align structure members on byte, word, double-word, quad-word, or 16-byte boundaries. Quad-word alignment is more efficient because most CPUs load quad-word aligned data from memory much faster than misaligned. On the second hand, you may have structures that map into file formats. In this event, padding for better alignment is unacceptable.

*   *Buffer Security Check (/GS)*—this option inserts additional code that detects when buffer overrunning overwrites the function return address.

*   *Enable Function-Level Linking (/Gy)*—generates smaller executables by linking only referenced subroutine rather than the entire libraries.

Language Page
The language page consists of:

*   *Disable Language Extensions (/Za)*—disable language extensions if you want your C/C++ code to adhere to ANSI C/C++ standard. You must definitely disable language extensions if you intend on porting your code to another compiler and/or another operating system (e.g., Linux).

*   *Default Char Unsigned (/J)*—use this option to make the compiler interpret **char** type as **unsigned char**. The Default Char Unsigned option simplifies managed and unmanaged code interoperability because **char** is unsigned by default when using Managed Extensions to C++.

*   *Treat wchar_t as Built-in type (/Zc:wchar_t)*—if you select this option, the compiler will automatically recognize **wchar_t** as a built-in type. Alternatively, you can include wchar.h header file to define **wchar_t** manually.

*   *Force Conformance for For Loop Scope (/Zc:forScope)*—this option controls the scope of variables defined as part of the For loop control statement. Traditionally, Microsoft extended the scope of loop control variables defined in the loop control statement beyond the scope of the loop. Such behavior violates the ANSI C/C++ standard and may cause compiler errors when compiling ANSI C/C++ code with Microsoft C++. Below is an example of a potential problem:

```
for ( int i = 0; i < 10; i++ )
{
...
}
int i = 100; // In ANSI C++ previous definition of variable i
             // is already out of scope. Yet unless the loop
             // conformance is enforced Visual C++ will produce
             // a duplicate definition compiler error.
```

*   *Enable Runtime Type Info (/GR)*—this option adds additional code that allows for checking and examining pointer and reference type information at runtime by using **dynamic_cast**, **typeid** operators and **type_info** class.

Precompiled Headers Page

The Precompiled Headers Page did not undergo any changes from Visual C++ 6.0. As usual, use precompiled headers to speed up compilation. This page consists of the following:

* *Create/Use Precompiled Header option*—allows speeding up C/C++ source code compilation by precompiling header files, storing, and reusing the precompiled header information for successive builds. Precompiled headers are stored in the ProjectName.pch file. The following choices are available for the Create/Use Precompiled Header option:

  * *Not Using Precompiled Headers*—headers will be processed every time you compile your source code.

  * *Create Precompiled Header (/Yc)*—recreate a precompiled header file every time you compile your project.

  * *Use Precompiled Header (/Yu)*—use existing precompiled header file. If the precompiled header file is not found, the program will not compile.

  * *Automatic (/YX)*—this option instructs the compiler to use the existing precompiled header file if one exists or creates a new one otherwise.

* *Create/Use PCH Through File*—specify an include file name that limits the precompiled header processing. When the compiler is processing your source code, it will look for the specified include file name in your source file. The compiler will not process include files that appear prior to inclusion of the PCH include file assuming that the files already processed in PCH. If you do not specify a PCH include file, then the compiler will not process any include files in your source code unless you use **#pragma hdrstop** preprocessor directives to limit the precompiled header processing.

  WARNING! **If you specified a PCH header file name and some of your source files do not #include the specified PCH header file, those source files will not compile.**

The following tip may help you as well:

  TIP: For the most efficient compilation, group your **#include** statements this way: first, **#include** all the static include files that would not change as you work on your source code, i.e., header files for standard libraries, ATL headers, MFC headers, etc.; then, **#Include** your PCH header file or insert the **#pragma hdrstop** preprocessor directive. Then, **#include** your own header files. Alternatively, you can move all your static includes into the PCH header file, select the Use Precompiled Header option, and create a dummy source file that does nothing but includes your PCH header file. The dummy source file is needed to initiate the precompiled header generation; therefore, you must specify the Create Precompiled Header option for the dummy file and Use Precompiled Header for all other files in the project. Files that do not include your PCH header file (e.g., third party source files) should be marked as Not Using Precompiled Headers .

* *Precompiled Header File (/FpFileName)*—specify the precompiled header file name and path. The default is $(IntDir)/$(TargetName).pch.

Output Files Page

The output files page consists of:

* *Expand Attributed Source (/Fx)*—when using attributes, you may want to inspect the merged source code that results from the replacement of all the attributes with injected code. The merged code for file *MyFile*.cpp will be written to *MyFile*.mrg.cpp.

* *Assembler Output (/FA)*—specify assembler output listing options. The fedault "No Listing" setting prevents the generation of assembler output files (.asm). If you are curious to know how your C/C++ code

was translated into machine instructions, select the "Assembly, Machine Code and Source" option (/FAcs) to generate the most complete assembler output file.

* *ASM List Location (/FAFileName)*—specify the file name and path for the assembler output file. The default assembler output file name is the same as the name of the source file being compiled with extension .asm.

* *Object File Name (/FoFileName)*—specify an object file name (.obj) and path for the source file being compiled. The default assembler object file name is the same as the source file name with extension .obj.

* *Program Database File Name (/FdFileName)*—specify program database file name. The default program database file name is $(IntDir)/vc70.pdb.

Browse Information Page

The browse information page contains the following:

* *Enable Browse Information (/FR)*—specify "yes" if you want to generate browse information. Browse information allows you browse debug symbols, including class definitions. If this option is set to "yes", the compiler will produce .sbr files for each source file compiled. Later Browse Information File Maintenance Utility (BSCMAKE) will convert these files into .bsc files, which are used to display browse information

* *Browse File*—specify your own browse file name. You must keep .sbr extension in the file name.

Advanced Page

The advanced page consists of:

* *Calling Convention*—modify default calling convention from **__cdecl** (/Gd) to **__stdcall** (/Gz) or **__fastcall** (/Gr). Calling convention matters when importing or exporting functions and when working with assembler routines.

  WARNING! An incorrectly specified calling convention may result in messed up function parameters and/or link errors. It is preferable to modify the calling convention of individual functions by specifying __cdecl, __stdcall, or __fastcall keywords in function declaration.

  TIP: When developing performance-critical applications you can achieve a performance boost by declaring the most frequently called functions with __**fastcall**. When a function is defined using __**fastcall** the compiler attempts to pass function parameters using CPU registers rather than the processor stack.

* *Compile As*—specify if you want to compiler your source as C-code (/TC) or C++ code (/TP).

* *Disable Specific Warnings*—list compiler warnings you want to disable.

* *Force Includes (/FIfilename)*—specify a file name that you want to implicitly include in each C/C++ source file compiled. This option is equivalent to inserting **#include** "*filename*" statement as the first line of each source file.

* *Force #using (/FUfilename)*—this option applies only to projects that support Managed Extensions to C++. The option forces automatic referencing of the specified metadata file in every Managed C++ source file. Force #using option is equivalent to including **#using** *filename* statement as the first line of each source file.

* *Show Includes (/showIncludes) option*—forces compiler to output to the Output Window names of all the header files included in the source file being compiled. This option may help to uncover all the references hidden in multi-level includes or include files masked by complex preprocessor definitions.

* *Undefine Preprocessor Definitions (/Uname)*—list preprocessor definitions you wish to **#undef**.

* *Undefine All Preprocessor Definitions (/U)*—self explanatory.

Linker Folder

The linker folder consists of the following:

*   General Page
*   Input Page
*   Debug Page
*   System Page
*   Optimization Page
*   Embedded IDL Page
*   Advanced Page
*   Resources Folder
*   MIDL Folder
*   Browse Information
*   Build Events Folder
*   Custom Build Steps
*   Web References Folder
*   Web Deployment Folder

General Page

The general page contains the following:

*   *Output File*—specify output file name (e.g., *ProjectName*.exe).
*   *Version (/VERSION:major.minor)*—specify version number to appear in the executable file header. This version information is independent of VERSION resource.
*   *Enable Incremental Linking (/INCREMENTAL)*—use this option to speed up linking and turn it off for final release. Incrementally linked files are larger because individual modules are padded and may contain jump thunks to handle function relocation to new addresses.
*   *Ignore Import Library*—if your project contains child projects that produce resource-only or COM DLLs (e.g., DLLs that do not contain any exports), then you must set this option to "yes" to avoid linker errors. Visual C++ .NET will attempt to automatically link any export libraries generated by child DLL projects to your main application. Since resource-only DLLs and COM DLLs do not produce export libraries, if the "Ignore Import Library" is not turned on, you will get linker errors.
*   *Register output*—Run regsvr32.exe /s $(TargetPath) to register your COM component or ActiveX DLL. This option is applicable only to DLL projects.
*   *Additional Library Directories (/LIBPATH:path)*—comma separated list of additional directories to search for libraries. Linker will search the specified directories before searching the directories specified in LIB environment variable.

Input Page

The input page contains:

*   *Additional Dependencies*—list any additional static libraries (.lib files) here.
*   *Ignore All Default Libraries (/NODEFAULTLIB)*—use this option to exclude default libraries (e.g., libc.lib,

libcmt.lib, or msvcrt.lib for release build; libcd.lib, libcmtd.lib, or msvcrtd.lib for debug build) from the list of libraries implicitly linked to your project. You can use Ignore All Default Libraries option to avoid duplicate symbol definition link errors when linking with other modules or libraries that already have symbols from the default libraries statically linked.

WARNING! **If you exclude all default libraries when linking an executable or a DLL, you may get unresolved external symbols.**

Also, consider the following note:

NOTE: If you use /NODEFAULTLIB option to exclude the C run-time library (msvcrt.lib or msvcrtd.lib), then you must specify the program entry point using the /ENTRY linker option.

* *Ignore Specific Library (/NODEFAULTLIB:library)*—use this option to exclude a specific default library.

* *Module Definition File (/DEF:filename)*—module definition files (.def) are generally considered archaic. Instead, use the **__declspec(dllexport)** statement to explicitly specify exported functions in your source code.

* *Add Module to Assembly (/ASSEMBLYMODULE:filename)*—this option will add the specified .NET Framework modules to the application assembly (for more information on Assemblies, see Chapter 1). When you compile the assembly DLL, you should list here all .NET Framework modules (.netmodule files) that you want to add to your assembly.

* *Embed Managed Resource File (/ASSEMBLYRESOURCE:filename)*—embed .NET framework resource (.resources) files in the resulting assembly. .NET framework resources must be generated with the Resource File Generator utility (ResGen.exe).

* *Force Symbol References (/INCLUDE:symbol)*—specify additional symbols to link to your project. If a symbol is not directly referenced, it will not be linked.

* *Delay Loaded DLLs (/DELAYLOAD:filename)*—is a helpful option that may improve your application performance. If your application references a lot of DLLs and, depending on the program execution flow, some of them may never be called or will be called late in the program execution. In this case, it makes sense to delay-load such DLLs to conserve system memory and reduce program loading time. Simply list the DLLs that you wish to delay-load here.

NOTE: You must link your program with Delayimp.lib if you are delay-loading any DLLs.

Debug Page
The debug page consists of:

* *Generate Debug Info (/DEBUG)*—use this option to create debugging information for your executable or DLL.

* *Generate Program Database File (/PDF:filename)*—specify .pdb file name.

* *Strip Private Symbols (/PDFSTRIPPED:pdb_file)*—specify .pdb file name that will not contain private symbols, such as type information and line number information. If you want to better protect your intellectual property, you may choose to distribute stripped PDBs along with your static library rather than full PDBs.

* *Generate Map File (/MAP:FileName)*—select "yes" to direct linker to generate map (.map) file. Map file is a text file containing a list of public symbols including symbol name, address, and object file where the symbol is defined.

* *Map File Name*—specify a map file name. The default map file name is *ProjectName*.map.

* *Map Exports (/MAPINFO:EXPORTS)*—directs linker to include exported symbol information in the map file.

* *Map Lines (/MAPINFO:LINES)*—directs linker to include line number information in the map file.

System Page

The system page contains:

* *Subsystem*—specify your application subsystem:

    * *Windows (/SUBSYSTEM:WINDOWS)* for a regular Win32 application.

    * *Console (/SUBSYSTEM:CONSOLE)* for a regular console application.

    * *Native (/SUBSYSTEM:NATIVE)* when building Windows NT device drivers.

    * *Posix (/SUBSYSTEM:POSIX)* when targeting Windows NT POSIX subsystem.

    * *Windows CE (/SUBSYSTEM:WINDOWSCE)* when building an application that is going to run on a Windows CE device.

* *Heap Reserve Size (/HEAP:reserve,commit)*—specify the amount of additional heap memory allocated for your executable at startup. The default value is 1 MB.

* *Heap Commit Size*—specify the heap increment size to allocate for your application when the application needs more heap space.

* *Stack Reserve and Stack Commit Size (/STACK:reserve,commit) options*—are similar to Heap options except that they control stack memory allocation rather than heap memory allocation.

* *Enable Large Addresses (/LARGEADDRESSAWARE)*—indicates that your application can handle addresses larger than 2 GB.

* *Terminal Server (/TSAWARE)*—if you anticipate that your application is going to be used a lot with the Microsoft Terminal Server (TS), you can improve application performance by setting the Terminal Server option to "yes".

    NOTE: TS-aware applications should not rely on INI files nor write to HKEY_CURRENT_USER registry. Since, during the Terminal Server session, multiple instances of the application can be run simultaneously by multiple users, such data may be overwritten. If you do not wish to deal with the difficulties that arise from this situation, disable the Terminal Server option, and the Terminal Server will handle the situation automatically without any side effects (but at the expense of extra processing and slightly increased application load time).

* *Swap Run From Network (/SWARRUN:NET) and Swap Run From CD (/SWARRUN:CD) options*—also improve application performance by speeding up swapping. If you application is going to be run from network or CD, it may take a very long time to swap the program due to higher access time when loading data from the network or from the CD-ROM drive. Thus, for improved performance, set the Swap Run From Network or Swap Run From CD options to "yes," and the operating system will copy the application image to the local swap file/page file and swap from there. Swap Run From Network/CD options take effect only under Windows NT 4.0, Windows 2000 or later.

Optimization Page

The optimization page consists of:

* *References (/OPT:REF)*—set this option to "Eliminate Unreferenced Data" to produce smaller output files by eliminating references to functions and data that are never used.

* *Enable COMDAT Folding (/OPT:ICF)*—set this option to "Remove Redundant COMDATs" to produce smaller output files by eliminating duplicate package functions and duplicate static data.

* *Optimize for Windows 98 (/OPR:WIN98)*—set this option to "yes" if you would like to reduce application load time under Windows 98. Windows 98 memory manager works best with executable images aligned on a 4K boundary. If you want to minimize your executable size, set this option to "no."

* *Function Order (/ORDER:@filename)*—allows for the rearranging of order of functions in your package by specifying a text file that contains a list of decorated function names in the desired order. Each function name must be on a separate line.

  TIP: Since decorated names are hard to devise manually, use Dumpbin.exe tool to extract decorated names from the .OBJ file.

  Also,

  NOTE: Optimization Page options are applicable only when Function-Level linking (/Gy) is enabled.

Embedded IDL Page

The Embedded IDL Page pertains to Attributed Programming using ATL attributes (see Chapters 17 and 18). It contains the following:

* *Ignore Embedded IDL (/IGNOREIDL)*—indicates that IDL attributes embedded in your source code will not be processed into an .idl file.

* *Merged IDL Base File Name (/IDLOUT:filename)*—specifies merged output file name for IDL file compilation. When an IDL file is compiled, the following files will be automatically generated: *filename*.tlb, *filename*_c.c, *filename*_p.c, *filename*.h.

* *Type Library (/TLBOUT:filename)*—manually specify .tlb file name.

* *TypeLib Resource ID (/TLBID:id)*—resource ID of an embedded type library. Default value is 1. Specify a different value if you already have a resource with ID=1.

Advanced Page

The advanced page consists of:

* *Entry Point (/ENTRY:functionName)*—specify an alternative entry point to your executable or DLL. The program entry point must be defined in a way similar to **WinMain**() function for .exe or **DllEntryPoint**() function for .dll, as specified in Win32 API. The default program entry point is located in C runtime library (CRT).

  NOTE: If you are not linking with C runtime library (e.g., you removed all references to CRT and specified the /NODEFAULTLIB linker option), then you MUST explicitly define an entry point.

* *Resource Only DLL (/NOETNRY)*—select this option if you are building a DLL that does not export anything and contains only resources, e.g., bitmaps, dialog templates, string tables, etc.

* *Set Checksum (/RELEASE)*—you must set this option if you are building a device driver. Operating systems typically require a valid checksums in driver headers.

* *Base Address (/BASE:address or /BASE:@filename,key)*—if your application references a lot of DLLs, you can reduce paging and improve performance of your program by assigning base address to each referenced DLL so that DLLs do not overlap in the address space. You can create a simple text file that contains module addresses and sizes, as in the following example:

```
; key    base         size
app      0x00010000   0x08000000   ; for MyApp.exe
dll1     0x28000000   0x00100000   ; for MyDll1.DLL
dll2     0x28100000   0x00300000   ; for MyDll2.DLL
```

Then you can use the key value from the first column (app, dll1, or dll2 in this example) to indicate which line from the file to use when specifying the base address of your project's executable or DLL in /BASE:*@filename,key* command.

The drawback of the manual base address assignment, though, is that should your DLL sizes change in the future, your application may once again suffer from excessive paging due to DLL overlapping. Alternatively, you can specify larger than the actual module sizes to accommodate for future DLL size growth.

* *Turn Off Assembly Generation (/NOASSEMBLY) option*—applies to CLR executable and effectively prevents assembly generation. Use this option if you intend to include the module in another assembly.

* *Delay Loaded DLL*—select "Support Unload" (/DELAY:UNLOAD) option if you are going to manually unload delay-loaded DLLs in your code.

* *Import Library (/IMPLIB:filename)*—manually specify an import library file name for your DLL.

* *Merge Sections (/MERGE:from=to)*—indicate that you want to merge code or data section named *from* into a new section called *to*. This option is useful when compiling VXDs to override compiler-generated section names.

* *Target Machine (/MACHINE:xx)*—select a machine identifier for which you are generating code. Currently, there is only one choice—MachineX86.

* *Command Line*—summary of all linker options in command line format.

Resources Folder

The resources folder contains:

* *Preprocessor Definitions*—specify resource compiler (rc.exe) precompiler definitions.

* *Culture option*—allows selecting resource language (e.g., English, French, etc.).

* *Additional Include Directories*—specify a semi-colon separated list of directories to search for resource include files.

* *Ignore Standard Include Path*—use this option to ignore standard include path specified in Visual C++.NET Options dialog.

* *Resource File Name*—specify the compiled resource (.res) file name. The default compiled resource file name is $(IntDir)/$(InputName).res.

MIDL Folder

MIDL Folder contains options for Interface Definition Language (.idl) files compilation.

Browse Information

The browse information folder contains anoutput file, which specifies a browse information file name for your project.

Build Events Folder

The Build Events folder allows for the specifying of commands that will be executed prior to compilation (Pre-Build Event), right before linking (Pre-Link Event), and after linking (Post-Build Event). When developing COM components or ActiveX controls, the Post-Build Event page typically contains a component registration command, i.e., "$(TargetPath)" /RegServer.

Custom Build Step Folder
The Custom Build Step folder provides yet another way of specifying additional build commands.

* *Command Line*—specify your custom build command.
* *Description*—optional custom build command description.
* *Outputs*—list files produced as a result of the custom build command.
* *Additional Dependencies*—specify the list of additional input files to use for the custom build step.

Web References Folder
The Web References folder controls the generation of web service proxy classes. If your project contains any web service references, then a web service proxy class (.h and .cpp files) will be automatically generated for each web reference included in the project.

* *Output file*—specify a header file name for the generated web service proxy class. Default settings is $(InputName).h.
* *Generated Proxy Language*—use this option to specify Native C++ or in Managed C++ language to use for the proxy code generation.

Web Deployment Folder
The Web Deployment folder enables automatic deployment of server components to Internet Information Server (IIS) web.

* *Exclude from Build*—set this option to "yes" to disable deployment or when your project does not contain any deployable components, such as ISAPI DLLs, or ATL Server COM components.
* *Relative Path*—is the path relative to the virtual directory to which the primary project output will be copied.
* *Additional Files*—semicolon-separated list of additional files to be deployed.
* *Unload Before Copy option*—facilitates deployment of ISAPI extensions by resetting the World Wide Web publishing service. After the first use, an ISAPI extension DLL remains locked by the IIS process. Therefore, the web service must be reset in order to release lock on the DLL.
* *Register output option*—is applicable to server-side COM components that need registering before first use. When this option is set to "yes," the **regsvr32** *OutputName* command will be executed right after the component deployment.
* *Virtual Directory Name*—specifies IIS virtual directory that will hosts the deployed application files.
* *Application Mappings option*—applies to ISAPI filters and a specified semicolon-separated list of file extensions to be associated with the deployed ISAPI DLL.
* *Application Protection option*—specifies the level of IIS process isolation (Low, Medium, or High) for ISAPI extensions and other server-side components.

APPENDIX D

.NET Framework System Namespace Hierarchy

```
Object
│
├── Activator
├── AppDomainSetup <-- IAppDomainSetup
├── Array - ICloneable, Collections.IList, Collections.ICollection, Collections.IEnumerable
├── Attribute
│   ├── AttributeUsageAttribute
│   ├── CLSCompliantAttribute
│   ├── ContextStaticAttribute
│   ├── FlagsAttribute
│   ├── LoaderOptimizationAttribute
│   ├── MTAThreadAttribute
│   ├── NonSerializedAttribute
│   ├── ObsoleteAttribute
│   ├── ParamArrayAttribute
│   ├── SerializableAttribute
│   ├── STAThreadAttribute
│   └── ThreadStaticAttribute
├── BitConverter
├── Buffer
├── CharEnumerator <-- Collections.IEnumerator, ICloneable
├── Console
├── Convert
├── DBNull <-- Runtime.Serialization.ISerializable, IConvertible
├── Delegate
│   └── MulticastDelegate
│       ├── AssemblyLoadEventHandler
│       ├── AsyncCallback
│       ├── CrossAppDomainDelegate
│       ├── EventHandler
│       ├── ResolveEventHandler
│       └── UnhandledExceptionEventHandler
├── Environment
├── EventArgs
│   ├── AssemblyLoadEventArgs
│   ├── ResolveEventArgs
│   └── UnhandledExceptionEventArgs
├── Exception
│   ├── ApplicationException
│   └── SystemException
│       ├── AppDomainUnloadedException
│       ├── ArgumentException
│       │   ├── ArgumentNullException
│       │   ├── ArgumentOutOfRangeException
│       │   └── DuplicateWaitObjectException
│       ├── ArithmeticException
```

```
                ├─ DivideByZeroException
                ├─ NotFiniteNumberException
                └─ OverflowException
            ├─ ArrayTypeMismatchException
            ├─ BadImageFormatException
            ├─ CannotUnloadAppDomainException
            ├─ ContextMarshalException
            ├─ ExecutionEngineException
            ├─ FormatException
            │    └─ UriFormatException
            ├─ IndexOutOfRangeException
            ├─ InvalidCastException
            ├─ InvalidOperationException
            │    └─ ObjectDisposedException
            ├─ InvalidProgramException
            ├─ MemberAccessException
            │    ├─ FieldAccessException
            │    ├─ MethodAccessException
            │    └─ MissingMemberException
            │         ├─ MissingFieldException
            │         └─ MissingMethodException
            ├─ MulticastNotSupportedException
            ├─ NotImplementedException
            ├─ NotSupportedException
            │    └─ PlatformNotSupportedException
            ├─ NullReferenceException
            ├─ OutOfMemoryException
            ├─ RankException
            ├─ StackOverflowException
            ├─ TypeInitializationException
            ├─ TypeLoadException
            │    ├─ DllNotFoundException
            │    └─ EntryPointNotFoundException
            ├─ TypeUnloadedException
            └─ UnauthorizedAccessException
    ├─ GC
    ├─ LocalDataStoreSlot
    ├─ MarshalByRefObject
    │    ├─ AppDomain <-- _AppDomain, Security.IEvidenceFactory
    │    ├─ ContextBoundObject
    │    └─ Uri <-- Runtime.Serialization.ISerializable
    ├─ Math
    ├─ OperatingSystem <-- ICloneable
    ├─ Random
    ├─ Reflection.MemberInfo
    │    └─ Type <-- Reflection.IReflect
```

```
─── String <-- IComparable, ICloneable, IConvertible, Collections.IEnumerable
─── TimeZone
─── UriBuilder
─── ValueType
     ─── ArgIterator
     ─── Boolean <-- IComparable, IConvertible
     ─── Byte <-- IComparable, IFormattable, IConvertible
     ─── Char <-- IComparable, IConvertible
     ─── DateTime <-- IComparable, IFormattable, IConvertible
     ─── Decimal <-- IFormattable, IComparable, IConvertible
     ─── Double <-- IComparable, IFormattable, IConvertible
     ─── Enum
          ─── AttributeTargets
          ─── DayOfWeek
          ─── Environment.SpecialFolder
          ─── LoaderOptimization
          ─── PlatformID
          ─── TypeCode
          ─── UriHostNameType
          ─── UriPartial
     ─── Guid <-- IFormattable, IComparable
     ─── Int16 <-- IComparable, IFormattable, IConvertible
     ─── Int32 <-- IComparable, IFormattable, IConvertible
     ─── Int64 <-- IComparable, IFormattable, IConvertible
     ─── IntPtr <-- Runtime.Serialization.ISerializable
     ─── RuntimeArgumentHandle
     ─── RuntimeFieldHandle <-- Runtime.Serialization.ISerializable
     ─── RuntimeMethodHandle <-- Runtime.Serialization.ISerializable
     ─── RuntimeTypeHandle <-- Runtime.Serialization.ISerializable
     ─── SByte <-- IComparable, IFormattable, IConvertible
     ─── Single <-- IComparable, IFormattable, IConvertible
     ─── TimeSpan <-- IComparable
     ─── TypedReference
     ─── UInt16 <-- IComparable, IFormattable, IConvertible
     ─── UInt32 <-- IComparable, IFormattable, IConvertible
     ─── UInt64 <-- IComparable, IFormattable, IConvertible
     ─── UIntPtr <-- Runtime.Serialization.ISerializable
     ─── Void
─── Version <-- ICloneable, IComparable
─── WeakReference <-- Runtime.Serialization.ISerializable
```

.NET Framework System Data Namespace Hierarchy

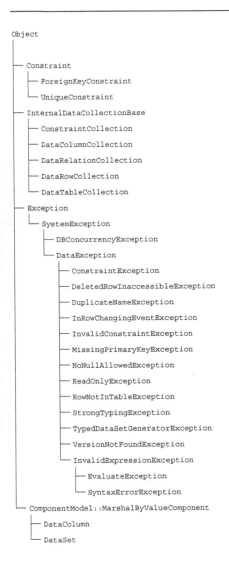

```
Object
│
├── Constraint
│     ├── ForeignKeyConstraint
│     └── UniqueConstraint
├── InternalDataCollectionBase
│     ├── ConstraintCollection
│     ├── DataColumnCollection
│     ├── DataRelationCollection
│     ├── DataRowCollection
│     └── DataTableCollection
├── Exception
│     └── SystemException
│           ├── DBConcurrencyException
│           └── DataException
│                 ├── ConstraintException
│                 ├── DeletedRowInaccessibleException
│                 ├── DuplicateNameException
│                 ├── InRowChangingEventException
│                 ├── InvalidConstraintException
│                 ├── MissingPrimaryKeyException
│                 ├── NoNullAllowedException
│                 ├── ReadOnlyException
│                 ├── RowNotInTableException
│                 ├── StrongTypingException
│                 ├── TypedDataSetGeneratorException
│                 ├── VersionNotFoundException
│                 └── InvalidExpressionException
│                       ├── EvaluateException
│                       └── SyntaxErrorException
└── ComponentModel::MarshalByValueComponent
      ├── DataColumn
      └── DataSet
```

APPENDIX F

.NET Framework System: Data Common, System Data OleDb and System Data SqlClient Namespace Hierarchy

```
Object
│
├── System::MarshalByRefObject
│    ├── DataColumnMapping <-- IColumnMapping, ICloneable
│    ├── DataColumnMappingCollection <-- IColumnMappingCollection, IList, ICollection, IEnumerable
│    ├── DataTableMapping <-- ITableMapping, ICloneable
│    ├── DataTableMappingCollection <-- ITableMappingCollection, IList, ICollection, IEnumerable
│    ├── OleDbTransaction <-- IDbTransaction, IDisposable
│    ├── SqlTransaction <-- IDbTransaction, IDisposable
│    ├── OleDbParameter <-- IDbDataParameter, IDataParameter, ICloneable
│    ├── SqlParameter <-- IDbDataParameter, IDataParameter, ICloneable
│    ├── OleDbParameterCollection <-- IDataParameterCollection, IList, ICollection, IEnumerable
│    ├── SqlParameterCollection <-- IDataParameterCollection, IList, ICollection, IEnumerable
│    └── System::ComponentModel::Component
│         ├── DataAdapter <-- IDataAdapter
│         │    └── DbDataAdapter <-- ICloneable
│         │         ├── OleDbDataAdapter <-- IDataAdapter
│         │         └── SqlDataAdapter <-- IDataAdapter
│         ├── OleDbCommandBuilder
│         ├── SqlCommandBuilder
│         ├── OleDbCommand <-- ICloneable, IDbCommand
│         ├── SqlCommand <-- ICloneable, IDbCommand
│         ├── OleDbConnection <-- ICloneable, IDbConnection
│         ├── SqlConnection <-- ICloneable, IDbConnection
│         ├── OleDbDataReader <-- IDataReader, IDisposable, IDataRecord, IEnumerable
│         └── SqlDataReader <-- IDataReader, IDisposable, IDataRecord, IEnumerable
├── OleDbError
├── SqlError
├── OleDbErrorCollection <-- ICollection, IEnumerable
├── SqlErrorCollection <-- ICollection, IEnumerable
├── OleDbSchemaGuid
├── System::Security::CodeAccessPermission
│    └── DBDataPermission <-- IUnrestrictedPermission
│         ├── OleDbPermission
│         └── SqlClientPermission
├── System::Attribute
│    └── System::Security::Permissions::SecurityAttribute
│         └── System::Security::Permissions::CodeAccessSecurityAttribute
│              └── DBDataPermissionAttribute
│                   ├── OleDbPermissionAttribute
│                   └── SqlClientPermissionAttribute
├── System::EventArgs
│    ├── OleDbInfoMessageEventArgs
│    ├── SqlInfoMessageEventArgs
│    ├── RowUpdatedEventArgs
│    │    └── OleDbRowUpdatedEventArgs
```

```
        └─ SqlRowUpdatedEventArgs
 ─ RowUpdatingEventArgs
    ├─ OleDbRowUpdatingEventArgs
    └─ SqlRowUpdatingEventArgs
 └─ System::Exception
    └─ System::SystemException
       └─ System::Runtime::InteropServices::ExternalException
          ├─ OleDbException
          └─ SqlException
```

Index

Printed and bound by CPI Group (UK) Ltd, Croydon, CR0 4YY

23/10/2024

01777685-0003